Oracle® 10g RAC
Grid, Services & Clustering

Oracle Database Related Book Titles:

Oracle 9iR2 Data Warehousing, Hobbs, et al,
ISBN: 1-55558-287-7, 2004

Oracle 10g Data Warehousing, Hobbs, et al,
ISBN 1-55558-322-9, 2004

Oracle High Performance Tuning for 9i and 10g, Gavin Powell,
ISBN: 1-55558-305-9, 2004

Oracle SQL Jumpstart with Examples, Gavin Powell,
ISBN: 1-55558-323-7, 2005

Oracle Database Programming using Java and Web Services, Kuassi Mensah,
ISBN 1-55558-329-6, 2006

Implementing Database Security and Auditing, Ben Natan,
ISBN 1-55558-334-2, 2005

Oracle Real Applications Clusters, Murali Vallath,
ISBN: 1-55558-288-5, 2004

For more information or to order these and other Digital Press
titles, please visit our website at www.books.elsevier.com/digitalpress!
At www.books.elsevier.com/digitalpress you can:
•Join the Digital Press Email Service and have news about
our books delivered right to your desktop
•Read the latest news on titles
•Sample chapters on featured titles for free
•Question our expert authors and editors
•Download free software to accompany select texts

Oracle® 10ᵍ RAC
Grid, Services & Clustering

Murali Vallath

ELSEVIER
DIGITAL
PRESS

AMSTERDAM • BOSTON • HEIDELBERG • LONDON
NEW YORK • OXFORD • PARIS • SAN DIEGO
SAN FRANCISCO • SINGAPORE • SYDNEY • TOKYO

Elsevier Digital Press
30 Corporate Drive, Suite 400, Burlington, MA 01803, USA
Linacre House, Jordan Hill, Oxford OX2 8DP, UK

∞ Recognizing the importance of preserving what has been written, Elsevier prints its books on acid-free paper whenever possible.

Library of Congress Cataloging-in-Publication Data
Application Submitted.

ISBN 13: 978-1-55558-321-7
ISBN 10: 1-55558-321-0

British Library Cataloguing-in-Publication Data
A catalogue record for this book is available from the British Library.

For information on all Elsevier Digital Press publications
visit our Web site at www.books.elsevier.com

06 07 08 09 10 9 8 7 6 5 4 3 2 1

Printed in the United States of America

To my elders for all your guidance and blessings.

To Jaya, Grishma, and Nabhas:
you are my dearest
and everything to me.

Table of Contents

About the Author

Murali Vallath has more than 18 years of IT experience, with more than 13 years using Oracle products. His work spans industries such as broadcasting, manufacturing, telephony, transportation logistics, and most recently tools development. Vallath is no stranger to the software development life cycle; his solid understanding of IT covers requirement analysis, architecture, database design, application development, performance tuning, and implementation. His clustering experience dates back to working with DEC products on VMS and Tru64 platforms, and his clustered database experience dates back to DEC Rdb, Oracle Parallel Server, and Real Application Clusters. Vallath is an Oracle Certified Database Administrator who has worked on a variety of database platforms for small to very large implementations, designing databases for high-volume, machine-critical, real-time OLTP systems.

As president of the Oracle RAC Special Interest Group (www.oracleracsig.org), president of the Charlotte Oracle Users Group (www.cltoug.org), and a contributing editor to the *IOUG SELECT* journal, Vallath is known for his dedication and leadership. He has been an active participant in the Oracle Database 10g Release 1 and Oracle Database 10g Release 2 Beta programs, including participating in the invitation-only IOUC Beta migration tests at Oracle headquarters in Redwood Shores, California.

Vallath is a regular speaker at industry conferences, including the Oracle Open World, UKOUG, AUSOUG, and IOUG on Oracle RAC and Oracle RDMS performance and tuning related topics.

Vallath provides independent consulting services in the areas of capacity planning, high-availability solutions, and performance tuning of Oracle environments through Summersky Enterprises LLC (www.summersky.biz). He has successfully completed more than 60 small, medium, and terabyte-sized RAC implementations (Oracle 9i and Oracle 10g) for reputed corporate firms.

Vallath is a native of India and resides in Charlotte, North Carolina, with his wife Jaya and children, Grishma and Nabhas. When Vallath is not working on complex databases or writing books, his hobbies include photography and playing on the *tabla*, an Indian instrument.

About the Technical Contributors

Chapter 11: Best Practices

Kirk McGowan is a Technical Director (RAC Pack) of Cluster and Parallel Storage Technology, Server Technologies Development with Oracle Corporation (www.oracle.com). Kirk has more than 25 years of IT industry experience, covering the spectrum of applications development, systems administration (OS, DB, network), database administration, network administration, systems analysis and design, technical architecture, and IT management. The focus throughout his career has been on high-availability and scalable systems design and implementation. For the past seven years, Kirk has specialized in Oracle's clustering and HA technologies and has been Technical Director of Oracle's RAC Pack since its inception and the first GA release of RAC. The RAC Pack team has been a key stakeholder in hundreds of successful customer RAC deployments.

Chapter 5 and Chapter 6: Java Code Support

Sudhir Movva is a Sun Certified Java Developer. He completed his masters degree in computer engineering, and he is currently working as a Senior Software Consultant. He loves programming, and when he is not working, he likes to ski, ride horses, and play his violin.

Sridhar Movva received his masters in computer engineering from the University of South Carolina. He is currently working as a Technical Team Lead. For the past few years, he has been architecting enterprise-level applications using Java. His areas of interest are clustering and distributed systems. He also worked as a technical consultant, setting up clustered servers for high-availability systems.

About the Technical Reviewers

Guy Harrison is the Chief Architect for Quest Software's database solutions. A recognized expert with more than 15 years of experience, Harrison has specialized in application and database administration, development, performance tuning, and project management. Harrison frequently speaks at trade shows and events and is the author of *Oracle SQL High Performance*

Tuning (Prentice Hall, 2000), *Oracle Desk Reference* (Prentice Hall, 2000), and numerous articles in technical journals.

Kirtikumar (Kirti) Deshpande is a Senior Oracle DBA with Verizon Information Services (www.superpage.com). He has more than 25 years of experience in the IT field, including more than 12 years as an Oracle DBA. He holds bachelor of science (physics) and bachelor of engineering (biomedical) degrees. He co-authored *Oracle Wait Interface: A Practical Guide to Performance Diagnostics & Tuning* (Oracle Press, 2004) and *Oracle Performance Tuning 101* (Oracle Press, 2001). He has presented papers in a number of Oracle User Group meetings and Conferences within the United States and abroad.

Ramesh Ramaswamy has worked in the IT industry since 1987. He has been an application developer and DBA in various industries such as heavy engineering, manufacturing, and banking, developing applications using Oracle relational databases starting from version 5.0. Currently, Ramesh works as an Oracle domain expert at Quest Software, specializing in performance monitoring and diagnostic products, including Foglight, Spotlight on Oracle, and Quest Central. He is an active member of the Australian Oracle User Groups and has published many papers for the Australia, New Zealand, and Thailand user groups.

Zafar Mahmood is a senior consultant in the database and applications team of the Dell Product Group. Zafar has master of science and bachelor of science degrees in electrical engineering from the City University of New York. Zafar has more than nine years of experience with Oracle databases and has been involved with Oracle Real Applications Clusters administration, tuning, and optimization for the last four years. Zafar also worked for Oracle Corporation as an RDBMS Support Analyst prior to joining Dell.

Anthony Fernandez is a senior analyst with the Dell Database and Applications Team of Enterprise Solutions Engineering, Dell Product Group. His focus is on database optimization and performance. He has a bachelor's degree in computer science from Florida International University.

Erik Peterson has worked on high-end database architectures since 1993, including more than 11 years at Oracle. His focus in on environments of extreme scalability and availability. He is currently a member of Oracle's RAC Development team and is a board member and one of the founding members of the Oracle RAC Special Interest Group.

Nitin Vengurlekar has worked in the database software industry for almost 20 years. He has worked for Oracle for more than 10 years. He is currently working in the RAC-ASM development group at Oracle, concentrating on

ASM integration as well as customer deployments. Nitin has authored several papers, including most recently the ASM Technical Best Practices and ASM-EMC Best Practices papers.

Acknowledgments

Per Indian mythology, the hierarchy of gratitude for life is in the order of mother (Matha), father (Pita), teacher (Guru), and god (Deivam). The Mother gives birth to the child, takes care of it, and shows the child its father. The Father provides for the child and takes the child to a Guru for education. The Guru then guides the child through spirituality and leads the child ultimately to God.

If you think of it, it is more than a mythology considering the sacrifices parents have to undergo during the process of bringing up their children from birth until they are successful in life. Any other type of sacrifice is really unmatchable on this earth. Thank you, Achha and Amma, you have provided the true light and directions; you just don't know how much you have helped me.

When I completed my first book on RAC, I had a brief plan on writing another book, so my family was aware of this. However, they never knew it was going to be this soon and long. This was really hard on every one of them. I am beyond words again in expressing my thanks to Jaya and my two children, Grishma (10 years) and Nabhas (9 years), for the days we have missed each other either because I was away on some assignment or working on my book at home. During this process they have helped me many times with my book either directly or indirectly. When working with the reference section, I remember Grishma criticizing me for not following the conventions and volunteering to help. She deserves all the credit for researching and placing the right information in the right format (MLA) for items in the reference section (Appendix A). My son Nabhas, with his sister, occasionally looked over my shoulder and pointed out some grammar issues. Thanks, to all of you once again, for I am blessed with such a wonderful family.

When the book writing process started, I needed some good reviewers who would be honest in reading through the material and finding flaws or mistakes, including my English and the technical details, and honestly providing feedback. I had great help in this process. I would like to thank Ramesh for agreeing to review my book and, besides being very detailed with his review, he was very punctual in providing the feedback.

While visiting Australia to present at the AUSOUG conference in Sydney, I told Kirti (Kirtikumar Deshpande) about my second venture and asked him to help by reviewing the book. Kirti, while immediately agreeing, remarked about his lack of knowledge or experience using RAC. I felt there was a positive side to this. With his extensive knowledge of the Oracle technology and his minimum knowledge of RAC, Kirti would help provide that blend to the review team by correcting me on foundation. Because, after all, RAC is a composition of many instances of Oracle, and if the foundation is bad, it does not matter how big the book was because it would be a total waste.

Thanks to the folks at Dell, Zafar Mahmood and Anthony (Tony) Fernandez, for reviewing the book and catching those errors that I had missed even after repeated reads. I had the opportunity to understand their in-depth knowledge while working on a benchmarking assignment at Dell scaling their hardware platforms seamlessly from two through ten nodes.

Thanks to Guy Harrison, whose Oracle knowledge goes back to that first SQL tuning book that several of us have used for years again and again, wearing it out and patiently waiting for the next edition with updates to the latest version of Oracle. Guy, where is your next edition of the book? We are waiting and we miss that great help the book always gave us. Guy's IT knowledge is just remarkable. Every time I have met him, it brought a feeling that I am just in elementary school. Thanks for reviewing the book.

It would be the biggest mistake not to thank my friends inside Oracle. I had the great experience of meeting some of the best technical minds from Oracle, while I was invited to the onsite 10g beta testing[1] program at Redwood Shores. I would like to thank the entire RAC Pack Development Team, including Sar Maoz, Su Tang, Duane Smith, Krishnadev Telikicherla, Mike Pettigrew, Nitin Vengurlekar, Erik Peterson, Kirk McGowan and Sohan DeMel, as well as the beta testing staff, especially Debbie Migliore and Sheila Cepero. The one week I spent at headquarters was such a great experience. Hats off to you all!

Erik Peterson, Patricia McElroy, and Nitin Vengurlekar, thanks a million for the internal reviews in your areas of expertise. From these reviews I had

---

1.   www.oracle.com/technology/pub/articles/betaweek_r2.html.

several rewrites to make this book gratifying. Not to mention that more than 40 percent of the storage management chapter comes from Nitin's contributions. Thanks once again. Special thanks to Kirk McGowan for the best practice chapter and Sudhir Movva and his brother Sridhar Movva for the Java examples contained in this book.

Thanks to my technical editor Mike Simmons, who fixed several of my English grammar issues; the folks at Multiscience Press, especially Alan Rose and his team for managing and coordinating the efforts of editing, typesetting, and proofreading the final product; and freelance copyeditor Ginjer L. Clarke for her excellent final touches to the technical editing process. The book would not have been published without help from the friendly folks at Elsevier (Digital Press); thanks for all of your support and patience when I slipped my manuscript dates several times, making the book behind schedule by almost a year. I am sure this delayed delivery has definitely added better quality to the material in the book.

I would also like to thank the customers of Summersky Enterprises for providing sustenance to my family and for making learning and solving issues an everyday challenge. Thank you all for your business.

I am proud to have been involved in such an incredible project, and I hope my readers benefit from the efforts of so many, to bring this book to life. Enjoy!

—Murali Vallath

Preface

In 2004, with the takeover of Compaq by HP, Oracle acquired Compaq's cluster management architecture; it was clear that Oracle's direction into the clustering world was moving from a flux to a more solid environment. After all, Compaq had acquired Digital Equipment Corporation (DEC, the original pioneers of clustering) and inherited this clustering technology.

While Oracle had released its first version of RAC in Oracle 9*i*, it was in Oracle Database 10*g* that the original impact of the purchase was seen. Apart from having the core clustering pieces, from its original version, Oracle enhanced this software and added several areas of functionality, providing a more robust, proactive method of systems management. A stepping stone toward Grid strategy, Oracle also introduced its own storage management solution called Automatic Storage Management (ASM).

All of these enhancements have brought some robust functionality to the database in particular, and Oracle's grid strategy and direction in general identified several areas that could be taken advantage of. Meanwhile, the Oracle 10*g* RAC uptake was also good, but several of the new features were seldom being implemented. The combined effect of the technology and slow uptake of the new features of this technology prompted me to write this second book on RAC.

About This Book

Similar to the core database functionality enhancements between the various versions of Oracle, functionalities and features around RAC have also increased several fold. This book tries to exploit these new features with examples by analyzing why and how these features work. Besides discussing commands and implementation steps, the book discusses how these features work by stepping to its internals. As the title describes, *Oracle 10g RAC: Grid, Services, and Clustering*, the book discusses the core functionality of grid, services, and clustering features supported focusing primarily on Oracle Database 10*g* Release 2.

Throughout the book, examples are provided with dump outputs followed by discussions and analysis into problem solving. The book also provides discussions on migrating from older versions of Oracle to the newer versions using the newer features.

How to Use This Book

The chapters are written to follow one another logically by introducing topics in the earlier chapters and building on the technology. Thus, it is advised that you read the chapters in order. Even if you have worked with clustered databases, you will certainly find a nugget or two that may be new to you. For the experienced reader, the book also highlights wherever applicable the new features introduced in Oracle 10*g*. The book contains the following chapters:

Chapter 1 provides an overview of Oracle Grid strategy and directions. It looks at the basic Grid principles and highlights the various grid-related features introduced in Oracle Database 10*g*.

Chapter 2 takes an in-depth look into the RAC architecture. Starting with the discussion on the architecture of the new Clusterware, it also discusses the RAC database architecture. Then the various additional background and foreground processes required by RAC, their functions, and how they work together in clustered database architecture are discussed. The roles of the GCS, GES, and GRD are given in great detail. This chapter discusses scenarios using the architecture behind this configuration, how data sharing occurs between nodes, and data sharing when the cluster has more than two nodes.

Through examples, this chapter will explain how cache fusion is handled based on requests received from processes on various nodes participating in the cluster. It details the discussions around the cache fusion behavior in a transaction, and provides various scenarios of clustered transaction management, including the various states of GCS operation, such as the PI and XI states of a block.

Chapter 3 focuses on storage management. While starting with the fundamentals of storage management principles and the technologies that have existed for several years, the chapter takes a deeper look into the new storage management solution from Oracle called Automatic Storage Management (ASM), covering its internal functioning and administrative options.

Chapter 4 covers the installation and configuration steps required for RAC implementation. The chapter also covers installation of the Clusterware and Oracle RDBMS using the DBCA utility.

Chapter 5 covers the services and distributed workload management features introduced in Oracle Database 10*g*. This chapter provides an extensive discussion on the service features and, through a workshop, explains the steps required to implement one such scenario. Furthermore, the chapter discusses the fast application notification (FAN) technology and how the events sent by the Oracle Clusterware event manager captured by the middle tier can be traced and diagnosed.

Chapter 6 describes the availability and load-balancing features of RAC, including transparent application failover (TAF) and fast connection failover (FCF). Discussions include using these features with the tnsnames file and making OCI-based calls directly from a Java application. Later, this chapter discusses the various load-balancing functions, including how to implement the new proactive load-balancing features introduced in Oracle Database 10*g* Release 2.

Chapter 7 covers the various new utilities available with Oracle Clusterware. The chapter provides a quick reference guide to the Clusterware utilities, including the framework and other utilities such as `ocrconfig`, `srvctl`, `crs_start`, and `crs_register`.

Chapter 8 covers the backup features available, including implementation and configuration of RMAN in a RAC environment, with special focus on some of the new features.

Chapter 9 starts with a single instance and discusses performance tuning. Starting with a tuning methodology, the chapter approaches tuning from the top down, tuning the application, followed by the instance, and then the database. In this chapter the various wait interface views are drilled down and analyzed to solve specific performance issues. The chapter also discusses capturing session-level statistics for a through analysis of the problem and tuning the cluster interconnect, the shared storage subsystems, and other global cache management areas, including cache transfer and inter-instance lock management.

Chapter 10 discusses the maximum availability solutions from Oracle. Acts of nature are beyond human control, but tools such as Data Guard and Oracle Streams provide opportunities to protect data from such disasters with minimal interference to users. This chapter discusses implementing a Data Guard solution by incorporating the new features such as fast-start failover through workshops. Similarly, with Oracle Streams, a workshop helps understand how to implement this feature in a RAC environment while understanding some of the failover and administrative functions.

Chapter 11 is the RAC best practices chapter. Kirk McGowan has provided the best practices to be followed while implementing a RAC solution. This chapter discusses all tiers of a RAC configuration and what one should and should not do while implementing RAC.

Appendices

The following appendices are included at the end of the book for your information:

Appendix A: References

Appendix B: Scripts and Procedures

Appendix C: Oracle Clustered File System

Appendix D: TAF and FAN

Appendix E: Step-by-Step Migration

Appendix F: Add a Node to the Cluster

Graphics

Icon	Name	Description
	Note	Notes provide additional information related to the subject area. Important information is marked with a note icon.
	Caution	Warnings and cautions appear next to some commands that could result in data loss if not properly used.
	Reference	For more information on a topic, the book icon will provide the names of other manuals or books.
	Best Practice	Best practice tips used for command shortcuts and to provide pointers on a topic.
	Windows	A note or information applies only to the Windows operating system.

Oracle Grid

Information Technology (IT) infrastructure is scattered throughout an organization. Hardware and software resources available in organizations are either underutilized or unable to be put into efficient use due to lack of resources. Many times IT resources are not used to their full potential. In some cases, IT resources are overused; therefore, there may not be sufficient resources to complete tasks on time. When one part of IT resources fails, other resources may not be available to fill the void, meaning there is not a balanced utilization of resources within an already existing pool. Due to these limitations, systems are expensive to maintain.

This imbalance of resource utilization within an organization exists because the application and the underlying infrastructure to support shared utilization of resources are not in place. For example, when the application is not able to obtain enough resources, it is then unable to utilize the resources available on other machines because the applications can only connect to one database server or set of servers. The primary reason for this is, the independence vested within each business unit in an organization as it tries to deliver the required functionality and quality of service to its users, it inadvertently creates silos of applications and IT systems infrastructure. This in turn creates groups of IT infrastructure within the same enterprise isolated from each other. These groups of computers are not configured to communicate with each other; hence, the larger infrastructure is not aware of the level of resources in them. The infrastructure consists of several components, including hardware, software, business applications, databases, and other home-grown systems. Apart from being isolated from each other, the computers are also managed and maintained by an independent set of system administrators. Looking at these components reveals the existing complexities:

Storage. Most enterprises have multiple storage units, units that contain direct-attached storage, network-attached storage (NAS), and storage-area networks (SANs). Such storage is acquired over a period of time based on the organization's needs at any given point. The variations in the type of storages used are based on diverse requirements for performance, high availability, security, and management of the various business units. Since these storage units exist in isolation from one another, they do not share the storage resources, resulting in overall underutilization of storage. For example, there could be an abundance of storage capacity available in the data warehousing segment; however, because of its isolation and decentralized management, it cannot be reassigned to other applications that are running short of storage capacity.

Servers. Enterprises traditionally have servers from multiple vendors ranging from low-cost desktop computers to large symmetric-multiprocessor systems (SMPs) and mainframes. These computers exist in isolation from each other and are typically overprovisioned to the applications based on estimated peak load, and in the case of critical applications, additional headroom capacity is allocated to handle unexpected surges in demand. Thus, servers end up highly underutilized.

Operating systems. In order to support the various permutations and combinations of hardware and software owned by the various business units, IT departments manage a heterogeneous array of operating system environments. They typically consist of Unix, Linux, and Windows operating systems. Because each of these systems is managed individually, this results in high-cost management for the systems and the applications running on them. This is because, despite having identical operating systems, patch-level differences prevent applications from running on them.

Databases. Each application managed by each business unit in an enterprise is deployed on one database. This is because the database is designed and tuned to fit the application behavior, and such behavior may cause unfavorable results when other applications are run against them. Above this, for machine-critical applications, the databases are configured on independent hardware platforms, isolating them from other databases within the enterprise. These multiple databases for each type of application managed and maintained by the various business units in isolation from other business units cause islands of data and databases. Such configurations results in several problems, such as

- Underutilization of database resources
- High cost of database management
- High cost of information management
- Limited scalability and flexibility

In other words, there are no options to distribute workload based on availability of resources. Thus emerges the concept of grid computing.

So, what is a grid? Does it indicate street signs found in Australia (Figure 1.1), or is it the method by which electricity is transmitted to an outlet in a house or office? It is probably both and much more. Each one has its respective concepts of "grid" embedded in it. Grid computing derives its concept from the greatest wonder since the invention of electricity, and that is the electric power grid.

Figure 1.1
GRID Ahead

1.1   Electric power grid

The electric power grid is a single entity that provides power to billions of devices in a relatively efficient, low-cost, and reliable fashion. For example, the North American grid alone links more than 10,000 generators with billions of outlets via a complex web of physical connections and trading mechanisms. When a device is plugged into the electric outlet of a home or office, the outlet passes electricity to the device that makes it function. How

Figure 1.2
Electric Power Grid

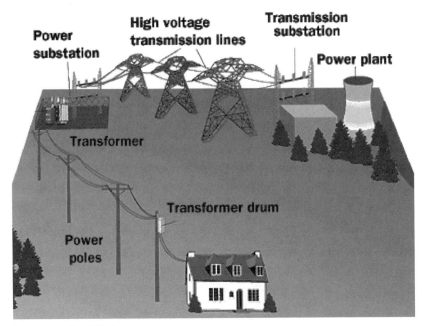

Source: www.HowitWorks.com

did this electricity reach this outlet? As illustrated in Figure 1.2, the power plant generates electricity, which travels through the transmission lines and the power substations before it reaches the transformer outside a house or office. From this transformer, connections are made to the office or house, which then provide power to the outlets. In the United States, several such power plants generate electricity that is fed to several power substations, and these substations transmit electricity through generators. The point is that when power is required to run a device, it is available from the outlet regardless of where the electricity is being generated. This is the power of the amazing electric power grid, amazing because, before the power grid, electricity was generated at isolated levels. Consumers who could afford it generated electricity to meet their personal needs (e.g., the Henry Ford estate in Michigan, generated all the electricity that the estate needed), while others went without any electricity. The power grid allowed electricity to be funneled so it could reach end users, like you and me.

1.2   Computational grids

While the electric power grid provides the foundation for the concept, grids in the technology arena are not new either. The term "grid" was coined in the mid-1990s to denote a proposed distributed computing infrastructure for advanced science and engineering. In the United States alone, several grid projects are being funded by the National Science Foundation (NSF), Department of Defense (DoD), and National Aeronautics and Space Administration (NASA). Similar to a power grid, the technology or computational grid involves the use of resources from computers. There are two types of resource utilization. The first type is where the resources within a controlled environment, such as a cluster of computers or data center, are utilized when required. The other is where the resources on any computer within the organization can be utilized when required (scavenging). A perfect example of the second type of resource utilization is desktop computers that are idle during the day. By managing the resource availability on these desktops, applications can be deployed or scheduled when needed.

Computational grids have been used and implemented in different projects. *A computational grid is a hardware and software infrastructure that provides dependable, consistent, pervasive, and inexpensive access to high-end computational capabilities* [12].

1.3   Evolution

A scientific implementation of a computational grid could be found at NASA, where data is collected by the Goddard Space Flight Center in Maryland, and this raw data is then sent to the Ames computer facility in California for analysis. These large data results are then sent back to the flight center in Maryland. With more and more raw data being collected from satellites, this data will then be used for general circulation model (GCM) weather simulation. This large processing of data requires dynamic provisioning of resources and efficient management of workloads.

The earliest examples of a scientific grid are SETI@home (SETI, Search for Extraterrestrial Intelligence), a distributed data mining project for identifying patterns of extraterrestrial intelligence. Signals from telescopes, radio receivers, and other sources monitoring deep space are distributed to personal computers (PCs) via the Internet. These small computers are used for number crunching to identify patterns that could suggest signs of intelligent life. SETI@home provided directions to enterprise grid concept. This is a very computing-intensive application; hence, no single source of computer resources could satisfy the resources requirements. This project attempts to utilize existing resources available on household PCs and desktop systems to help the high-end number-crunching needs. Participating users downloaded a small program onto their desktops. When the machine is found to be idle, the downloaded program detects this and starts using the idle machine cycles and uploads the results back to the central site during the next Internet connection.

CERN (European Organization for Nuclear Research), a research organization involved in the development of the Web, is also among the scientific users of the grid. They are building a Large Hardron Collider (LHC) computing grid to manage data generated by LHC experiments. Data generated in one experiment can exceed one petabyte of data per year. Data generated from these experiments is used by over 2,000 users and 150 institutes all over the world.

1.4   Enterprise grid computing

As discussed earlier, there are resources on several computers and systems that are not being utilized to their full potential. These resources need to be pulled together within an enterprise data center and utilized. Enterprise grid computing involves balancing resources and distributing workload across small-networked computers. In other words, at the highest level, the central idea of grid computing is computing as a utility. The user of the grid should not care where the data resides or which computer processes the requests. Instead, the user should be able to request information or computations and have them delivered according to his or her needs and in a timely fashion. This is analogous to the way electric utilities work, in that irrespective of where the generator is or how the electric grid is wired, when the equipment is plugged into the electric outlet, there is power. Enterprise grid computing provides the following characteristics:

- *Implement one from many.* Many computers are networked together to function as a single entity by using clustering concepts. Clustered configuration allows for distribution of work across many servers, providing availability, scalability, and performance using low-cost components.

- *Manage many as one.* This concept allows managing these groups of computers from one central location. While enterprise grid computing defines the above characteristics, it is driven by five fundamental attributes: virtualization, dynamic provisioning, resource pooling, self-adaptive systems, and unified management.

1.4.1 Virtualization

Virtualization is the abstraction into a service of every physical and logical entity in a grid. This decouples the various components of a system, such as storage, processors, databases, application servers, and applications. This allows replacement of underlying resources with comparable resources without affecting the consumer.

1.4.2 Dynamic provisioning

Dynamic provisioning is the allocation of resources to consumers, making them available where needed. In today's enterprise computing, resources are preallocated based on statistics collected over trial runs and expected peak demand of the application. Provisioning also involves pooling of all available resources together from all sources so they can be dynamically provisioned when called into service.

1.4.3 Unified management

Finally, unified (central) management enables treating virtualized components as a single logical entity. One fundamental requirement for a true grid environment is that it be a cross section of heterogeneous environments. This includes different applications, such as operating systems and databases, enabling to coexist and communicate with each other. This indicates that a sharing relationship exists, including interoperability among any potential participants in the grid. The grid architecture has standards for interoperability protocols. Protocols define basic mechanisms for resource negotiation, management, and resource sharing between entities in the grid. Such protocols may be defining application programming interfaces (APIs) that will provide application abstraction as services and help in handshaking between heterogonous environments. This is the vision of an enterprise grid computing environment. However, in order for this type of grid to work, some stringent standards need to be implemented. Until a set of standards is available (currently being defined by the Global GridForum, www.gridforum.org, and the Enterprise Grid Alliance, www.gridalliance.org) to provide easy transparent, handshaking between heterogeneous environments, this grid architecture may not be possible.

1.5   Globus Toolkit

In the arena of grid standards, the Globus Toolkit is of primary importance. This toolkit is an open-source enabling technology for the grid, letting computer users share computing power, databases, and other tools securely online across corporate, institutional, and geographic boundaries without sacrificing local autonomy.

The toolkit includes software for security, information infrastructure, resource management, data management, communication, fault detection, and portability. It is packaged as a set of components that can be used either independently or together to develop applications. Every organization has unique modes of operation, and collaboration between multiple organizations is hindered by incompatibility of resources, such as data archives, computers, and networks. The Globus Toolkit was conceived to remove obstacles that prevent seamless collaboration. Its core services, interfaces, and protocols allow users to access remote resources as if they were located within their own machine room, while simultaneously preserving local control over who can use resources and when [13].

While standards are being defined and accepted by the industry, grids in homogenous environments are taking shape. Oracle is not far behind in this arena.

1.6   Oracle grid

Starting with the release of Oracle 10*g*, Oracle provides the integrated software infrastructure supporting the five attributes discussed earlier and is moving toward its strategy of supporting an enterprise grid solution. The software infrastructure includes the three primary tiers of any enterprise solution:

- Oracle Database Clustering
- Oracle Application Server
- Enterprise Manager

 Note: Oracle application server also supports features of clustering, including high availability and resource management. Discussions regarding the various features of this tier are beyond the scope of this book.

1.6.1 **Oracle Database Clustering**

The clustering feature in Oracle Database 10*g* is provided by the Real Application Cluster (RAC) feature. RAC is a composition of multiple (two or more) Oracle instances communicating with a single shared copy of the physical database. Clients connecting to the various instances in the cluster access and share the data between instances via the cluster interconnect. Low-end commodity hardware servers can be grouped together, connecting to shared storage containing low-cost disks to form a clustered solution. In such a configuration, nodes can be added or removed based on the need for resources. Similarly, using the Automatic Storage Management (ASM) feature, disks can be added or removed from the storage array, allowing dynamic provisioning of disks as required by the system. Once these disks are provisioned to Oracle, they are transparently put to use by resizing and reorganizing the contents of the disks. Figure 1.3 illustrates a deployment study performed using Oracle Database 10*g* Release 1 using 63 nodes from the 187 nodes in the cluster. These studies illustrated that Oracle clustered databases can scale and maintain data integrity across 63 instances configured on small commodity hardware. While the primary reasons for these scalability numbers is that data block lookup by an instance is limited to fewer than three instances, irrespective of the number of instances in the cluster, RAC supports the grid attributes providing a cohesive environment.

Figure 1.3
AC3 187 Node Cluster

> **Short overview of the cluster illustrated in Figure 1.3[*]:**
>
> - ac3 Dell Linux Beowulf Cluster (Barossa) is a 187-node Linux cluster consisting of 374 Pentium IV Xeon CPUs running at 3.06 GHz.
>
> - The theoretical peak performance of the cluster is 2.20 teraflops (flops, floating point operations per second), and a measured performance reached approximately 1.1 teraflops; this was measured on the initial 155-node configuration, which was later extended to 187 nodes.
>
> - On ac3 Dell Linux Beowulf Cluster (Barossa), universities from New South Wales, Australia, are running many different projects, including a variety of applications, for example,
>   - Abaqus (mechanical engineering software package)
>   - Fluent (software for fluid mechanics)
>   - NWChem (computational chemistry)
>   - LAM MPI, MPICH, pvm (parallel computing libraries)

[*] Insert on AC3 and Figure 1.3 provided by Vladas Leonas, AC3, Australia.

 Note: In Oracle Database 10*g* Release 2, Oracle supports 100 nodes in a cluster.

RAC supports several of the attributes required by an enterprise grid infrastructure:

1. Oracle supports the Service-Oriented Architecture (SOA) by allowing multiple services. Services help bring a level of abstraction to the application into components for easy manageability, monitoring, and resource allocation based on demand and importance of the service.

2. By provisioning resources to database users, applications or services within an Oracle database allow for controlling the number of resources that are allocated to the various levels of users. This ensures that each user, application, or service gets a fair share of the available computing resources, based on the priority and importance of the service. This balance is achieved by defining resource policies for resource allocation to services based on resource usage criteria such as CPU utilization or the number of active sessions.

3. As part of resource provisioning, Oracle can automatically bring up additional instances in the cluster. When these additional

resources are no longer needed, Oracle will automatically migrate active sessions to other active instances of the database and shut down an instance.

4.   Transparently connecting sessions to instances that have higher resources provides a proactive load-balanced environment. Stepping toward a grid solution, when the resource availability on any server is high and other servers are not as utilized or have resources available, the database server can proactively notify the client machines regarding the status of the instances, and the clients can assign all future connections to servers that have additional resources.

5.   With integrated clusterware for identical platforms, applications can cross platforms and share data between different hardware platforms supporting the same operating system. Oracle clusterware in Oracle Database 10*g* eliminates the need to purchase, install, configure, and support third-party clusterware. Oracle clusterware also eliminates any vendor-imposed limits on the size of a cluster by increasing the limit on the number of nodes to 100 in Oracle Database 10*g* Release 2. Servers can be easily added and dropped into an Oracle cluster with no downtime. Features such as "addnode" will allow the adding of extra nodes to the cluster to be much easier. Apart from these features, Oracle clusterware also provides an API interface allowing non-Oracle applications to be configured for high availability and failover.

6.   The new industry-standard Sockets Direct Protocol (SDP) network helps provide high-speed data movement between applications residing on various computers, the database servers, and the storage subsystems.

7.   Support for Java Database Connectivity (JDBC) implicit connection caching helps reuse prepared statements, which in turn eliminates the overhead of repeated cursor creation and prevents repeated statement parsing and creation. The statement cache is associated with a physical connection. Oracle JDBC associates the cache with either an `OracleConnection` object for a simple connection or an `OraclePooledConnection` or `PooledConnection` object for a pooled connection. An implicit statement is enabled by invoking `setImplicitCachingEnabled(true)`.

8.   ASM automates and simplifies the optimal layout of datafiles, control files, and log files by distributing them across all available

disks. ASM enables dynamic adding and removal of disks from a disk group in a storage array, providing the plug-and-play feature. When the storage configuration changes, database storage is transparently rebalanced between the allocated disks. Oracle also controls the placement of files based on the usage statistics gathered from the activity on the various areas of the disk. A disk group is a set of disk devices that Oracle manages as a single logical unit.

9. ASM allows the traditional benefits of storage technologies such as Redundant Array of Independent Disks (RAID) or Logical Volume Manager (LVM). ASM will strip and mirror disks (optional) to improve input/output I/O performance and data reliability. Because it is tightly integrated with the Oracle database, ASM can balance I/O from multiple databases across all devices in a disk group.

10. By pooling individual disks into storage arrays and individual servers into blade farms, the grid runtime processes dynamically couple service consumers to service providers, providing flexibility to optimize the available resources.

11. Tablespaces can be transported across different platforms; while this is not a true RAC-only feature, it plays an important role in the overall availability of the enterprise configuration. Tablespaces can be transported across nonidentical platforms providing help during migration from one operating system to another.

12. The scheduler feature helps group jobs that share common characteristics and behavior into larger entities called job classes. These job classes can then be prioritized by controlling the resources allocated to each class and by specifying the service where the job should run. The prioritization can be changed from within the scheduler.

1.6.2 Enterprise Manager

As discussed earlier, one primary characteristic of enterprise grid computing is that it allows monitoring of all tiers of the enterprise system from one central location. This level of monitoring is provided and supported by Enterprise Manager (EM) Grid Control (GC). GC monitors and manages the various tiers of the enterprise solution (e.g., the Web interfaces, application server, database server, and storage subsystem). Starting with Oracle

Database 10*g* Release 2, GC supports third-party application servers such as Weblogic and JBoss.

GC provides a simplified, centralized management framework for managing enterprise resources and analyzing a grid's performance. Administrators can manage the complete grid environment through a web browser through the whole system's software life cycle, front-to-back from any location on the network.

GC views the availability and performance of the grid infrastructure as a unified whole rather than as isolated storage units, databases, and application servers. Database Administrators (DBAs) can group databases and servers into single logical entities and manage a group of targets as one unit.

1.7   Conclusion

In this section, we briefly looked at the "G" (grid) in Oracle 10*g*. The chapter discussed the various grid technologies, their origin, and how Oracle is integrated to utilize grid environments. Several grid-based projects, both at the research level and in the commercial sectors, are under way. Oracle's mega-grid project is a notable area in this regard. The Oracle database grid, which includes RAC, ASM, and GC, are all indications of Oracle support for the "G" in Oracle Database 10*g*.

2

Real Application Cluster Architecture

Real Application Cluster (RAC) can be considered an extension of the regular single-instance configuration. As a concept, this is true because RAC is a composition of several instances of Oracle. However, there are quite a few differences in the management of these components, the additional background process, the additional files, and the sharing of resources between instances, not to mention the additional layered components present at the operating system level to support a clustered hardware environment. All of these additional components in a RAC system make it different from a single-instance configuration. The real difference between a database and an instance is also noticed in a RAC configuration. While this difference does exist in a regular single-instance configuration, this is seldom noticed because the database and an instance are not distinguished from each other as they are in a RAC configuration (e.g., in a single-instance configuration, the instance and the database are identified by the same name).

If you are not familiar with the single-instance version of an Oracle database, it is advised that you gain familiarity by reading the *Concepts Guide* available at Oracle Technology Network (OTN, http://otn.oracle.com).

2.1   RAC components

RAC is a clustered database solution that requires a two or more node hardware configuration capable of working together under a clustered operating system. A clustered hardware solution is managed by cluster management software that maintains cluster coherence between the various nodes in the cluster and manages common components, such as the shared disk subsystem. Several vendors provide cluster management software to manage their respective hardware platforms. For example, Hewlett Packard Tru64 manages HP platforms, Sun Cluster manages Sun platforms, and others such as Veritas Cluster Manager have cluster management software that supports more than one hardware vendor. In Oracle Database 10*g*, cluster management is provided using Oracle's Clusterware.[1]

Figure 2.1 illustrates the various components of a clustered configuration. In the figure, the nodes are identified by a node name `oradb1`, `oradb2`, `oradb3`, and `oradb4`, and the database instances are identified by an instance name `SSKY1`, `SSKY2`, `SSKY3`, and `SSKY4`. The cluster components are

- Operating system
- Communication software layer
- Interprocess communication protocol (IPC)
- Oracle Clusterware, or cluster manager (CM)

The communication software layer manages the communication between the nodes. It is also responsible for configuring and passing messages across the interconnect to the other nodes in the cluster. While Oracle Clusterware uses the messages returned by the heartbeat mechanism, the communication layer ensures the transmission of the message to the Oracle Clusterware.

The network layer, which consists of both the Interprocess communication (IPC) and Transmission Control Protocol (TPC) in a clustered configuration, is responsible for packaging the messages and passing them to and from the communication layer for the interconnect access.

Various monitoring processes consistently verify different areas of the system. The heartbeat monitor continually verifies the functioning of the heartbeat mechanism. The listener monitor verifies the listener process, and the instance monitor verifies the functioning of the instance.

Oracle Clusterware, or CM is an additional software that resides on top of a regular operating system that is responsible for providing cluster integrity. A high-speed interconnect is used to provide communication between nodes in the cluster. Oracle Clusterware uses the interconnect to process heartbeat messages between nodes. The function of the heartbeat messaging system is to determine which nodes are logical members of the cluster and to update the membership information. The heartbeat messaging system

---

1.   Oracle Clusterware was called cluster-ready services (CRS) in Oracle Database 10g Release 1.

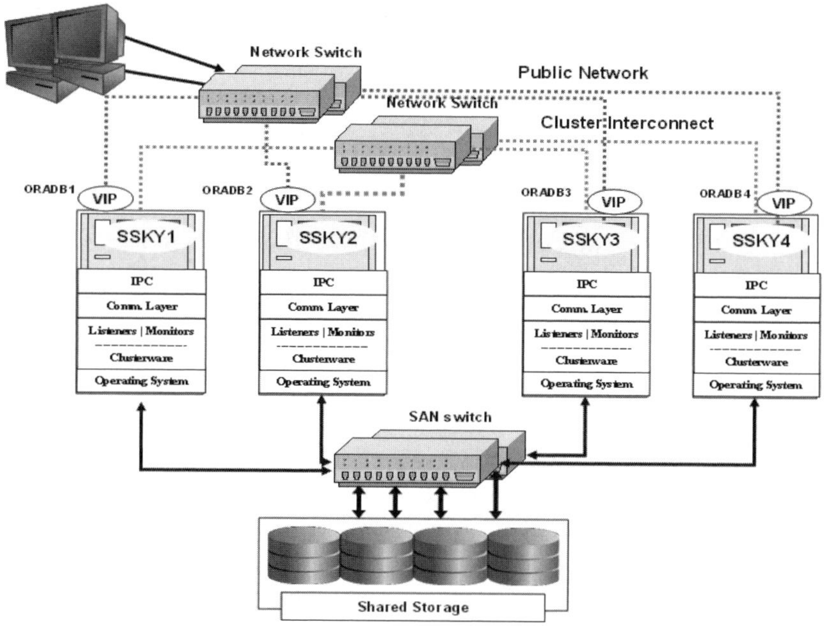

Figure 2.1
Cluster Components

enables Oracle Clusterware to understand how many members are in the cluster at any given time.

The CM does the following:

- Acts as a distributed kernel component that monitors whether cluster members can communicate with each other
- Enforces rules of cluster membership
- Initializes a cluster, adds members to a cluster, and removes members from a cluster
- Tracks which members in a cluster are active
- Maintains a cluster membership list that is consistent on all cluster members
- Provides timely notification of membership changes
- Detects and handles possible cluster partitions

Oracle Clusterware in Oracle Database 10*g* comprises additional processes, such as the cluster synchronization services (CSS) and the event manager (EVM).

2.1.1   Oracle Clusterware

Oracle Clusterwarem Oracle's CM is a new feature in Oracle Database 10*g* RAC that provides a standard cluster interface on all platforms and performs high-availability operations that are not available under the previous versions.

Oracle Clusterware architecture

Besides the various components that make up the cluster and hardware infrastructure in a RAC environment, the nodes are placed into communication and unity through a kernel component called the cluster manager. Cluster manager are available from several vendors supporting a clustered hardware solution (e.g., HP, SUN, Veritas). Oracle Clusterware is a primary component in the configuration and implementation of RAC. Oracle's Clusterware can be the only clusterware (platform independent) in the clustered configuration. It can also work in conjunction with preinstalled third-party clusterware. When third-party clusterware is already present, Oracle Clusterware will integrate with it to provide a single point of clustered solution.

When integrated with the third-party clusterware, Oracle Clusterware relies on the vendor clusterware for node membership information and self-manages the high-availability features. However, Oracle Clusterware is the only cluster management application that manages the entire stack (from the operating system layer through the database layer) and performs node monitoring and all RAC-related functions.

Oracle Cluster Registry

Oracle Cluster Registry (OCR) is a cluster registry used to maintain application resources and their availability within the RAC environment. The registry is a file created on the shared storage subsystem during the Oracle Clusterware installation process (illustrated in Figure 4.12).

OCR, which contains information about the high-availability components of the RAC cluster, is maintained and updated by several client applications: server control utility (`srvctl`), cluster-ready services utility[2] Enterprise Manager (EM), database configuration assistant (DBCA), data-

---

2.   The CRS utility provides several command-line functions such as register, unregister, start, and stop.

base upgrade assistant (DBUA), network configuration assistant (NetCA), and Virtual IP configuration assistant (VIPCA).

OCR also maintains application resources defined within Oracle Clusterware, specifically, database, instances, services, and node applications[3] information. Oracle Clusterware reads the `ocr.loc` file (located in the `/etc/` directory on Linux and Unix systems; on Windows systems the pointer is located in the Windows Registry) for the location of the registry and to determine which applications resources need to be started and the nodes on which to start them.

Oracle uses a distributed shared cache architecture during cluster management to optimize queries against the cluster repository. Each node maintains a copy of the OCR in memory. Oracle Clusterware uses a background process to access the OCR cache. As illustrated in Figure 2.2, only one OCR process (designated as the master) in the cluster performs any disk read/write activity. Once any new information is read by the master OCR process, it performs a refresh of the local OCR cache and the OCR cache on other nodes in the cluster. Since the OCR cache is distributed across all nodes in the cluster, OCR clients communicate directly with the local OCR process on the node to obtain required information. While reading from the registry is coordinated through a master process across the cluster, any write (update) to disk/registry activity is not centralized. It is performed by the local OCR process where the client is attached.

Figure 2.2 illustrates the OCR architecture. The OCR process on node `ORADB2` is acting as the master, retrieving information from the repository and updating the OCR cache processes on all nodes in the cluster. Also in the figure, the client processes such as the EM Agent, the `srvctl` utility, and the Oracle universal installer (OUI), which is attached to the local OCR process, perform update operations.

The OCR file contains information pertaining to all tiers of the clustered database. A dissection of the OCR file would reveal various parameters stored as name-value pairs used and maintained at different levels of the architecture. At a high level, the OCR file contains the tiers listed in Table 2.1.

Each tier is managed and administrated by daemon processes with appropriate privileges to manage them. For example, all `SYSTEM` level resource or application definitions would require `root`, or superuser, privileges to start, stop, and execute resources defined at this level. However, those defined at the `DATABASE` level will require `dba` privileges to execute.

---

3. The various processes, such as the VIP, ONS, GSD, and listener, are called node applications. Node applications are discussed later in this chapter.

Figure 2.2
OCR Architecture

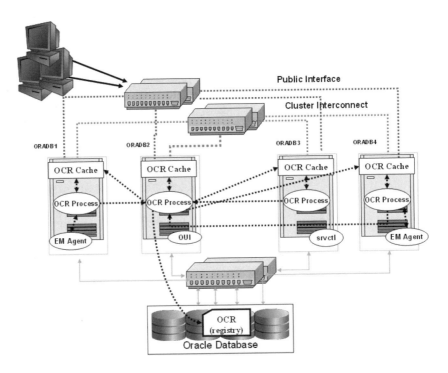

Table 2.1   *OCR Dissection*

	Level	Resource Name
1	System	CSS
		EVM
		CRS
		LANGUAGE
		VERSION
		ORA_CRS_HOME
		OCR
2	Database	DATABASES
		ASM
		NODEAPPS
		VIP_RANGE
		LOG

Table 2.1   *OCR Dissection (continued)*

		ONS_HOSTS
3	CRS	CUR (current)
		HIS (history)
		SEC (security)

Cluster Synchronization Services (CSS)

CSS is a subcomponent of Oracle Clusterware. It maintains membership in the cluster through a special file called a voting disk (also referred to as a quorum disk), which is also on a shared storage subsystem visible to all nodes participating in the cluster. The CSS voting disk is configured during the Oracle Clusterware installation process (illustrated in Figure 4.13). This is the first process that is started in the Oracle Clusterware stack. During the system boot process, CSS performs the following 14 steps in configuring the various members in the cluster:

1. CSS identifies a clustered configuration. (CSS is also used in a single-instance configuration when ASM is used for storage management.)

2. Oracle Clusterware determines the location of the OCR from the `ocr.loc` file (located in the `/etc/` directory in Linux and Unix systems and in the Windows Registry on Windows system) during system startup. It reads the OCR file to determine the location of the voting disk. (This is the only time CSS needs to read the OCR file.)

3. Subsequently, the vote disk is read to determine the number and names of members in the cluster.

4. Using a vacuous monitoring over the voting disk locations, CSS performs state changes to bring the voting disk online. This is to determine if CSS has a registered MASTER node already active. The various states of the voting disk are

    - 1 - Not configured and no thread has been spawned
    - 2 - Threads are spawned
    - 3 - Thread started and disk is offline
    - 4 - The voting disk is online

5.   CSS tries to establish connection to all nodes in the cluster using the private interconnect. There are three listeners on each node in the cluster that use different communication protocols (TCP or IPC) depending on the type of message. The listeners perform the following functions:

    a.   CSS local listener listens for messages and requests on the cluster. The listener uses IPC to send and receive messages.

    b.   CSS local listener listens for messages and requests at the node level; as before, the listener uses IPC to send and receive messages.

    c.   CSS local listener listens across the private interconnect for messages and requests from other members in the cluster. Oracle Clusterware uses the TCP protocol to send and receive messages between other nodes in the cluster.

 Note: These are listeners used by Oracle Clusterware and should not be confused with the database listener.

6.   Once connection is established between the various listeners, the node moves to an `ALIVE` state.

7.   Now, to determine if the voting disk continues to be available, CSS performs a verification check. After an acknowledgement message is received from the vote disk, the node status moves to an `ACTIVE` state.

8.   CSS verifies the number of nodes already registered as part of the cluster by performing an active count function.

9.   After verification, if no `MASTER` node has been established, CSS authorizes the verifying node to be the `MASTER` node. This is the first node that attains the `ACTIVE` state.

10. Then Oracle Clusterware performs synchronization of group/locks for the node. At this stage, the incarnation of the cluster is complete.

11. Once the local node is confirmed as a member of the cluster, the other nodes that went through similar steps (with the exception of step 8, which is only performed by one node), the CSS brings other members to `ALIVE` state.

12. Following this, all nodes are made ACTIVE.

13. Cluster synchronization begins when the MASTER node synchronizes with the other nodes in the cluster and all nodes that are ALIVE are made ACTIVE members of the cluster.

14. These ACTIVE nodes register with the MASTER node.

This completes the reconfiguration, and a new incarnation of the cluster is established.

Oracle Clusterware stack

At the cluster level, the main processes of the Oracle Clusterware provide a standard cluster interface on all platforms and perform high-availability operations on each node in the cluster. Figure 2.3 illustrates the various processes that compose the Oracle Clusterware stack.

Initiated by the CSS process after the start of the nodes (described in previous earlier section), the Oracle Cluster Synchronization Service Daemon (CSSD) performs the basic synchronization services between the various resources in the cluster. With the help of the voting disk (created as part of the Oracle Clusterware installation illustrated in Figure 4.13), it arbitrates ownership of the cluster among cluster nodes in the event of a complete private network failure. CSSD is a critical daemon process, and a failure of this process causes the node (server) to reboot. These services are performed by the Node Membership (NM) and the Group Membership (GM) services.

The NM checks the heartbeat across the various nodes in the cluster every second. It also alternates to check the heartbeat of the disk by performing a read/write operation every second. If the heartbeat/node members do not respond within 60 seconds, the node (among the surviving nodes) that was started first (master) will start evicting the other node(s) in the cluster.

NM also checks the voting disk to determine if there is a failure on any other nodes in the cluster. During this operation, NM will make an entry in the voting disk to inform its vote on availability. Similar operations are performed by other instances in the cluster. The three voting disks configured also provide a method to determine who in the cluster should survive. For example, if eviction of one of the nodes is necessitated by an unresponsive action, then the node that has two voting disks will start evicting the other node. NM alternates its action between the heartbeat and the voting disk to determine the availability of other nodes in the cluster.

The GM provides group membership services. All clients that perform I/O operations register with the GM (e.g., the LMON, DBWR). Reconfiguration of instances (when an instance joins or leaves the cluster) happens through the GM. When a node fails, the GM sends out messages to other instances regarding the status.

The Event Manager Daemon (EVMD) is an event-forwarding daemon process that propagates events through the Oracle Notification Service (ONS). It also scans the node callout directory and invokes callouts in reaction to detected events (e.g., node up and node down events). While this daemon is started subsequent to the CSSD, EVMD is the communication bridge between the Cluster-Ready Service Daemon (CRSD) and CSSD. All communications between the CRS and CSS happen via the EVMD.

The CRSD, or Oracle Clusterware daemon, function is to define and manage resources. A resource is a named entity whose availability is managed by Clusterware. Resources have profiles that define metadata about them. This metadata is stored in the OCR. The CRS reads the OCR. The daemon manages the application resources: starts, stops, and manages failover of application resources; generates events during cluster state changes; and maintains configuration profiles in the OCR. If the daemon fails, it automatically restarts. The OCR information (described in the OCR section above) is cached inside the CRS. Beyond performing all these functions, CRS also starts and communicates with the RACGIMON daemon process.

Resources that are managed by the CRS include the Global Service Daemon (GSD), ONS Daemon, Virtual Internet Protocol (VIP), listeners, databases, instances, and services, as listed in Table 2.1. Resources are grouped based on the level at which they apply to the environment. For example, some of these resources are referred to as node applications (nodeapps), and they pertain to individual nodes in the cluster. Nodeapps are needed on a per-node basis, independent of the number of databases on the node. GSD, ONS, VIPs, and listeners are the list of nodeapps. Nodeapps are created and registered with the OCR during installation of the Oracle Clusterware. Listener, database, and service resources are created during the database creation process.

RACGIMON is a database health check monitor and performs the tasks of starting, stopping, and failover services. It monitors the instances by reading a memory-mapped location in the SGA that is updated by the PMON process on all nodes. There is only one instance of the RACGIMON process for the

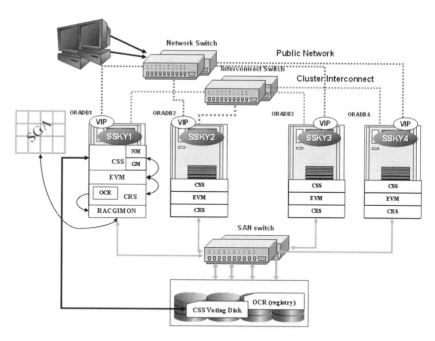

Figure 2.3
Oracle Clusterware
Stack

entire cluster, and when the node that houses it fails, the RAGIMON process is started on the MASTER node of the surviving nodes by the CRS process.

PROCD is a process monitor that runs on hardware platforms supporting other third-party cluster managers and is present only on hardware platforms other than Linux. Its function is to create threads for the various processors on the system and to check if the processors are hanging. Every second, the PROCD thread wakes up and checks the processors on the system, and then goes to sleep for about 500 ms and tries again. If it does not receive any response after *n* seconds, it reboots the node. On Linux environments, the hangcheck timer module performs the same work that PROCD does on other hardware platforms.

Cluster interconnect

As the word "interconnect" implies, the cluster interconnect connects all the computers together. How is this different from any other sort of network relationship? Normal networking between computers is used for user access, in other words, for public access, hence the name public network. The interconnect, on the other hand, is only used by computers to communicate between each other; it's not available for public access, at least not directly. Hence, it is also called a private network.

The cluster interconnect is a high-bandwidth, low-latency communication facility that connects each node to other nodes in the cluster and routes messages among the nodes. Several types of interconnects are available from various vendors today (e.g., Hyper Messaging Protocol [HMP] from HP, Low Latency Transport [LLT] from Veritas). However, one common traditional type is the Gigabit Ethernet, and the one gaining popularity now is the InfiniBand™.

Gigabit Ethernet

Gigabit Ethernet evolved out of the original 10 Mbps Ethernet standard, 10 BASE-T, and the 100 Mbps Fast Ethernet standards, 100BASE-TX and 100BASE-FX. The Institute of Electrical and Electronics Engineers (IEEE) and the 10-Gigabit Ethernet Alliance support a 10-Gigabit Ethernet standard. Gigabit Ethernet is the latest evolution of networking options providing excellent high-speed communication between devices.

Benefits of using Gigabit Ethernet over its predecessors or over fiber optics include the following:

- Gigabit Ethernet is 100 times faster than regular 10 Mbps Ethernet and 10 times faster than 100 Mbps Fast Ethernet.
- Increased bandwidth yields higher performance and eliminates bottlenecks.
- Full-duplex capacity, allows for the virtual doubling of the effective bandwidth.
- It provides full compatibility with the large installed base of Ethernet and Fast Ethernet nodes.
- Large amounts of data can be transferred quickly across networks.

Oracle supports and recommends the use of User Datagram Protocol (UDP) for Linux/Unix environments and TCP for Windows environments as the communication layer for the interconnect.

This UDP is defined to make available a datagram mode of packet-switched computer communication in the environment of an interconnected set of computer networks. The protocol is transaction oriented, and delivery and duplicate protection are not guaranteed [6]. This protocol assumes that the Internet Protocol (IP) [5] is used as the underlying protocol.

TCP is a set of rules used along with IP to send data in the form of message units between computers over the Internet. While IP handles the actual delivery of the data, TCP keeps track of the individual units of data (called packets) that a message is divided into for efficient routing through the Internet.

Infiniband technology

The demands of the Internet and distributed computing are challenging the scalability, reliability, availability, and performance of servers. InfiniBand architecture represents a new approach to I/O technology and is based on the collective research, knowledge, and experience of the industry's leaders and computer vendors.

InfiniBand architecture specifies channels that are created by attaching host channel adapters (HCAs) within a server chassis to host channel adapters in other server chassis. This is done for high-performance IPC and to target channel adapters connecting Infiniband-enabled servers to remote storage and communication networks through InfiniBand switches. InfiniBand links transfer data at 2.5 Gbps, utilizing both copper wire and fiber optics for transmission. It can carry any combination of I/O, network, and IPC messages.

InfiniBand architecture has the following communication characteristics:

- User-level access to message passing
- Remote Direct Memory Access (RDMA) in read/write mode
- Up to a maximum of 2-Gb message in a single transfer

The memory protection mechanism defined by the InfiniBand architecture allows an InfiniBand HCA to transfer data directly into or out of an application buffer. To protect these buffers from unauthorized access, a process called memory registration is employed. Memory registration allows data transfers to be initiated directly from user mode, eliminating costly context switches to the kernel. Another benefit of allowing the InfiniBand HCA to transfer data directly into or out of application buffers is that it can remove the need for system buffering. This eliminates the context switches to the kernel and the need to copy data to or from system buffers on a send or receive operation, respectively.

InfiniBand architecture also has another unique feature called a memory window. The memory window provides a way for the application to grant remote read and/or write access to a specified buffer at byte-level granularity to another application. Memory windows are used in conjunction with RDMA read or RDMA write to control remote access to the application buffers. Data could be transferred by either the push or pull method (i.e., either the sending node would send [push] the data over to the requester, or the requester could get to the holder and get [pull] the data).

While InfiniBand is a fairly new technology, it promises tremendous potential and benefits in a clustered configuration where high-speed data transfer is required via the cluster interconnect. While RAC has been tested to work under InfiniBand, as the popularity of this technology evolves, more and more implementations using this technology will become commonplace.

Table 2.2 lists the throughput differences between the two types of interconnect protocols.

Table 2.2   *Interconnect Throughput*

Interconnect Type	Throughput (Mbps)
Gigabit Ethernet	80
Infiniband	160

Virtual Interface or Virtual IP

The Virtual Interface (VI) architecture is a user-level memory-mapped communication architecture that is designed to achieve low-latency, high-bandwidth network communication. The VI architecture attempts to reduce the amount of software overhead imposed by traditional communication models by avoiding the kernel involvement in each communication operation. In traditional models, the operating system multiplexes access to the hardware between communication endpoints; therefore, all communication operations require a trap into the kernel.

A Virtual IP (VIP) definition in Oracle Clusterware 10*g* is a logical, public IP address assigned to a node. It is not physically assigned to the network card. This logical nature allows the CRS to manage easily its start, stop, and migration features.

Two types of VIP implementations are supported by Oracle Clusterware:

1. *Database VIP.* Oracle Clusterware 10*g* configuration requires the use of VIP as the common interface between each node in the database server and the client machines; this interface is called the database VIP. The advantage of using VIP when making connections to the database compared to the traditional TCP method is that it overcomes the delay in receiving a failure signal that is encountered by the user connection when a node is not reachable. These delays sometimes exceed 10 minutes. VIP configured by Oracle Clusterware provides a good, high-availability network interface. This is done by migrating the VIP address from the failed node to another node; when a user session attempts to connect to this failed VIP address, it returns a negative acknowledgement (NAK), causing the client to try another VIP from an available address list.

    A NAK is received by the client because the listener on the node the VIP fails over to is not listening on this new IP address; it is never meant to. So, when the VIP fails over and the client tries to connect to, say, port 1521, it gets an immediate failure rather than having to wait for a TCP timeout. It gets the immediate failure (or NAK) because the IP is active, but nothing behind that IP has opened the port the client is trying to connect to. The IP address the listener opens the port on is restricted using the lines (`IP = FIRST`) in the `listener.ora` file.

    Under this new architecture, Transparent Network Substrate (TNS) connect descriptors and listeners reference the VIP in their definitions. Besides returning an immediate failure signal when the VIP is migrated, it helps the database administrators (DBAs) change the definitions to the `tnsnames.ora` and `listener.ora` files for users to connect to the surviving instances.

2. *Application VIP.* In Oracle Database 10*g* Release 2, Oracle introduced application VIPs, which are like database VIPs, the one difference being that they can be used to access the application irrespective of the node the application is running on. Database VIPs can only be used to access the application (the listener) on the home node for the VIP. This means that when a node fails and the VIP gets migrated to one of the surviving nodes, it is usable by the application, and the VIP will provide a positive acknowledgement. For example, when an application is bound to a VIP and when the application fails over, the VIP fails over with

it. The clients continue to make network requests to the VIP and continue to operate as normal.

 Note: Examples for binding applications to VIPs can be found in Chapter 7.

2.2   Real Application Cluster

RAC supports all standard Oracle features, such as fast commits, group commits, and deferred writes. It supports standard row-level locking across instances. Blocks can be shared by multiple transactions, accessing the data from any instance participating in the clustered configuration (see Figure 2.4).

Figure 2.4
Real Application
Cluster (RAC)

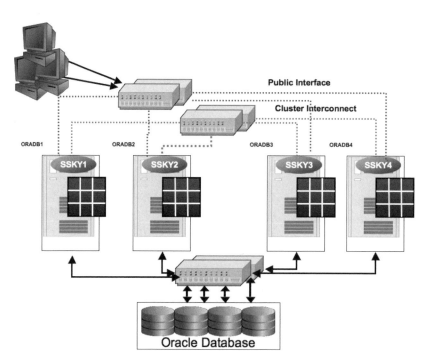

The following characteristics are unique to a RAC implementation as opposed to a single-instance configuration:

- Many instances of Oracle running on many nodes
- Many instances sharing a single physical database
- All instances having common data and control files
- Each instance having individual log files and undo segments
- All instances being able to execute simultaneously transactions against the single physical database
- Instances participating in the clustered configuration communicate via the cluster interconnect using cache fusion technology
- Oracle's maintaining cache synchronization between instances across the cluster interconnect

RAC provides additional performance benefits by enabling the following features:

- *Cache fusion.* Cache fusion is the technology that allows requests for specific blocks to be satisfied through the cluster interconnect.
- *Sequence generators.* All objects, including sequence numbers in the shared database, are accessible from one or more instances simultaneously.
- *System change number (SCN).* The SCN generated on one instance is communicated via the cluster interconnect to the other instances, providing a single view of the transaction status across all instances. This communication of SCN across the interconnect takes place without any additional overhead by piggybacking against any message that is passed across the cluster interconnect.
- *Failover.* A clustered configuration consists of two or more nodes participating in a collective configuration. In a clustered database, this type of configuration provides application failover by allowing reconnection to the database using another active instance in case the connection to the original instance is broken.
- *Distributed workload management.* By distributing workload across the various instances, based on the application functionality and the requirement for system resources, RAC componentizes applications across instances.

■ *Scalability.* By allowing members in a cluster to leave (in case of node failures or for maintenance) or join the cluster (when new nodes are added to the cluster), RAC provides scalability. Scalability helps to add additional configurations based on increased user workload.

■ *Load balancing.* A clustered database solution that consists of two or more instances helps achieve load balancing, allowing balanced utilization of resources across all instances in the cluster. Load balancing also helps increase scalability.

2.3   Background processes in RAC

A RAC implementation comprises two or more nodes (instances) accessing a common shared database (i.e., one database is mounted and opened by multiple instances concurrently). In this case, each instance will have all the background process used in a stand-alone configuration, plus the additional background processes required specifically for RAC. Each instance has its own SGA, as well as several background processes, and runs on a separate node having its own CPU and physical memory. Keeping the configurations in all the nodes identical is beneficial for easy maintenance.

Best Practice: RAC does not require all nodes to be of identical configuration. However, to help with easy maintenance and load balancing, it is advisable to have all nodes be of identical configuration.

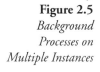

Figure 2.5
Background Processes on Multiple Instances

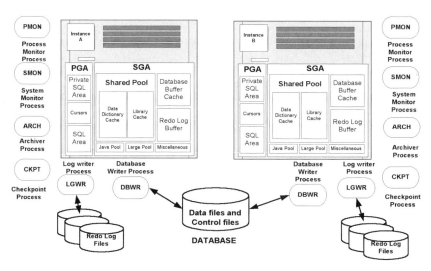

Figure 2.5 shows multiple instances of Oracle accessing a common shared database. Each instance has its own SGA, PGA, and various background processes. The background processes illustrated in Figure 2.5 are found in a single-instance configuration and in a RAC configuration. Each instance will have its own set of these background processes. RAC does have unique background processes that do not play any role in a single-instance configuration.

Figure 2.6
*Background
Processes in RAC*

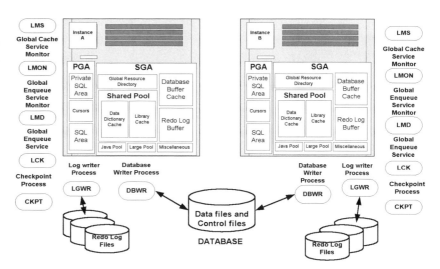

Figure 2.6 defines the additional background processes and their role in a RAC implementation. The functionality of these background processes is described as follows.

LMS

Global cache services (LMSn) are processes that, when spawned by Oracle, copy blocks directly from the holding instance's buffer cache and send a read-consistent copy of the block to the foreground process on the requesting instance. LMS also performs a rollback on any uncommitted transactions for any blocks that are being requested for consistent read by the remote instance.

The number of LMS processes running is driven by the parameter GCS_SERVER_PROCESSES. Oracle supports up to 36 LMS processes (0–9 and a–z). If the parameter is not defined, Oracle will start two LMS processes, which is the default value of GCS_SERVER_PROCESSES.

LMON

The Global Enqueue Service Monitor (LMON) is a background process that monitors the entire cluster to manage global resources. By constantly probing the other instances, it checks and manages instance deaths and the associated recovery for Global Cache Services (GCS). When a node joins or leaves the cluster, it handles the reconfiguration of locks and resources. In particular, LMON handles the part of recovery associated with global resources. LMON-provided services are also known as cluster group services (CGS).

LMD

The Global Enqueue Service Daemon (LMD) is a background agent process that manages requests for resources and controls access to blocks and global enqueues. It manages lock manager service requests for GCS resources and sends the requests to a service queue to be handled by the LMSn process. The LMD process also handles global deadlock detection and remote resource requests (remote resource requests are requests originating from another instance).

LCK

The Lock process (LCK) manages noncache fusion resource requests such as library, row cache, and lock requests that are local to the server. LCK manages instance resource requests and cross-instance call operations for shared resources. It builds a list of invalid lock elements and validates lock elements during recovery. Because the LMS process handles the primary function of lock management, only a single LCK process exists in each instance.

DIAG

The Diagnostic Daemon (DIAG) background process monitors the health of the instance and captures diagnostic data regarding process failures within instances. The operation of this daemon is automated and updates the alert log file to record the activity it performs.

The following is an extract from the alert log file, showing the various background processes started by Oracle during instance startup.

Cluster communication is configured to use the following interface(s) for this instance:

```
10.1.2.168
Sun Apr 17 14:38:28 2005
```

```
cluster interconnect IPC version:Oracle UDP/IP
IPC Vendor 1 proto 2 Version 1.0
PMON started with pid=2, OS id=22367
DIAG started with pid=3, OS id=22369
LMON started with pid=4, OS id=22371
* allocate domain 0, invalid = TRUE
LMD0 started with pid=5, OS id=22374
LMS0 started with pid=6, OS id=22376
LMS1 started with pid=7, OS id=22378
MMAN started with pid=8, OS id=22380
DBW0 started with pid=9, OS id=22382
LGWR started with pid=10, OS id=22384
CKPT started with pid=11, OS id=22386
SMON started with pid=12, OS id=22388
RECO started with pid=13, OS id=22390
Sun Apr 17 14:38:29 2005
starting up 1 dispatcher(s) for network address
'(ADDRESS=(PARTIAL=YES)(PROTOCOL=TCP))'...
CJQ0 started with pid=14, OS id=22392
Sun Apr 17 14:38:29 2005
starting up 1 shared server(s) ...
Sun Apr 17 14:38:29 2005
lmon registered with NM - instance id 1 (internal mem no 0)
Sun Apr 17 14:38:31 2005
Reconfiguration started (old inc 0, new inc 8)
```

2.4   Database files in RAC

In a RAC environment, most of the database-related files are shared between the various instances. However, certain files, such as the redo log files, archive log files, and so on, are not shared. In the following sections, the various files and their behaviors in a RAC implementation are explored.

2.4.1   Server parameter file

The server parameter (SP) file contains parameter definitions required for the functioning of an instance. While these parameters are instance specific, certain parameter values have identical values on all the instances. SP files have a new definition syntax that allows storing of all parameters that are unique and common to all instances in one file. This file can then be stored in the shared disk subsystem with soft links to the $ORACLE_HOME/dbs directory, allowing visibility to a single file from all instances. By qualifying the parameter with the instance name, the parameter is instance specific. On the other hand, if the parameter is not qualified with an instance name, it then applies to all instances participating in the cluster.

```
*.CONTROL_FILE =
SSKY1.UNDO_TABLESPACE = UNDO_TBS1
SSKY2.UNDO_TABLESPACE = UNDO_TBS2
SSKY3.UNDO_TABLESPACE = UNDO_TBS3
SSKY4.UNDO_TABLESPACE = UNDO_TBS4
*.DB_BLOCK_SIZE = 16K
```

Figure 2.7
Database Files in a
RAC Configuration

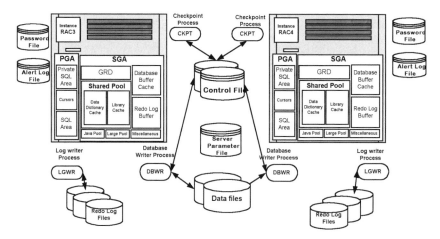

Figure 2.7 illustrates the files used in a RAC configuration. Certain files, such as the control files and datafiles, are shared, whereas the alert log files, redo log file, and so on, are specific to every instance.

2.4.2   Datafiles

Datafiles contain data shared by all instances participating in the cluster, such as those that reside on a shared disk subsystem. During instance startup, Oracle verifies if all the files are visible and accessible.

2.4.3   Control files

Control files store the status of the physical structure of the database and are crucial to its operation. Control files are shared across all instances participating in the cluster. For example, instance-specific information pertaining to redo log files, the redo log thread details, log file history information, archived log records information, Recovery Manager (RMAN) backup information, and so on could be viewed by querying the data dictionary views.

2.4.4   **Online redo log files**

The redo logs contain information relating to an instance and reside in the shared storage. This helps in recovery operations during an instance failure. When users on an instance make changes to data, these changes are stored in a rollback segment or in an undo tablespace. Periodically, or in response to a COMMIT request, the Log Writer (LGWR) process writes the information to the log files.

As in a single-instance configuration of Oracle, each instance contains at least two groups of the redo log files. To identify one set of redo logs created by an instance from another, the redo log files are organized into threads. While group numbers are unique to an instance, assignment of threads is arbitrary. For example, in a two-node RAC configuration, the following query illustrates the usage of the thread and group numbers:

```
SQL> SELECT LG.INST_ID,LG.GROUP#,LG.THREAD#, LF.MEMBER
  2 FROM GV$LOG LG, GV$LOGFILE LF
  3 WHERE LG.INST_ID= LF.INST_ID AND LG.GROUP# = LF.GROUP#
  4 ORDER BY INST_ID,GROUP#,THREAD#;


INST_ID GROUP#  THREAD#  MEMBER
------- ------- -------- -----------------------------------------------
   1       1       1     +ASMGRP1/sskydb/onlinelog/group_1.272.568082379
   1       2       1     +ASMGRP1/sskydb/onlinelog/group_2.273.568082393
   1       3       2     +ASMGRP1/sskydb/onlinelog/group_3.278.568083209
   1       4       2     +ASMGRP1/sskydb/onlinelog/group_4.279.568083225
   1       5       1     +ASMGRP1/sskydb/onlinelog/group_5.274.568082407
   1       6       2     +ASMGRP1/sskydb/onlinelog/group_6.280.568083241
   2       1       1     +ASMGRP1/sskydb/onlinelog/group_1.272.568082379
   2       2       1     +ASMGRP1/sskydb/onlinelog/group_2.273.568082393
   2       3       2     +ASMGRP1/sskydb/onlinelog/group_3.278.568083209
   2       4       2     +ASMGRP1/sskydb/onlinelog/group_4.279.568083225
   2       5       1     +ASMGRP1/sskydb/onlinelog/group_5.274.568082407
   2       6       2     +ASMGRP1/sskydb/onlinelog/group_6.280.568083241
```

In a single-instance configuration, there are no restrictions on the number of members in a group; however, it is advisable to create groups that contain the same number of members. Similarly, in a RAC implementation, each instance must have at least two groups of redo log files. When one group fills up, a log switch happens and the instances start writing to the next group. At each log switch, Oracle updates the control files. Each log is identified by its thread number, sequence number (within a thread), and the range of SCNs spanned by its redo records. The thread number, sequence number, low SCN, and next SCN are found in the log file header.

The redo records in a log are ordered by SCN, and redo records containing change vectors for a given block occur in increasing SCN order across threads. Only some records have SCNs in their header; however, every record is applied after the allocation of an SCN appearing with or before it in the log. The header of the log contains the low SCN and the next SCN. The low SCN is the SCN associated with the first redo record. The next SCN is the low SCN of the log with the next higher sequence number for the same thread.

For each log file, Oracle writes a control file record that describes it. The index of a log's control file record is referred to its log number. These log numbers are equivalent to log group numbers and are globally unique across all threads.

2.4.5   Archived redo log files

As redo log files store information pertaining to a specific instance, archive files, which are copies of redo log files, also contain information pertaining to that specific instance. As in the case of redo log files, write activities to the archived redo log happen from only one instance. Archive log files can be on shared or local storage. However, for easy recovery and backup operations, these files should be visible from all instances.

 Note: On hardware platforms that require usage of raw partitions for implementation of RAC, it is required that the archived redo log files be stored on "cooked" file systems. On a raw partition, writing multiple files to the same destination overwrites the previously written files.

2.4.6   Other files

Files that contain instance-specific information, such as the alert logs or trace files generated by the various background and foreground processes, are maintained at the instance level.

2.5   Maintaining read consistency in RAC

In order to provide users with a consistent image of the rows while other users are modifying the rows and have not completed their operation, Oracle maintains read-consistent images of data. A consistent image of the row provides all users with a view of the data that is self-consistent, regardless of whatever transactions might be in progress at the time (e.g., uncommitted changes will not be seen in another session).

Undo management

When a user makes changes to the data in a database, Oracle stores the original data (before changes are made) relating to a transaction in an undo segment until the user has issued a commit or rollback statement. At which time, the modified data is saved permanently in the database (commit statement) or the changes are undone and the original data is restored (rollback statement).

The undo management feature is enabled by setting the following parameters:

```
*.UNDO_MANAGEMENT = AUTO
SSKY1.UNDO_TABLESPACE = (undo tablespace name)
```

The undo tablespaces need to be built with the UNDO TABLESPACE clause. This clause creates the tablespace as a locally managed tablespace, and its space-extent is managed via bitmaps that reside in the file header. The advantage of locally managed tablespaces is that space transaction and management are performed using bitmaps versus expensive recursive calls to maintain these values in the data dictionary.

In a RAC environment, each instance participating in the cluster will have its own copy of an undo tablespace. During instance startup, an instance binds an undo tablespace to itself. At instance startup, each undo tablespace will contain 10 undo segments. The number of additional segments brought online during instance startup is based on the SESSIONS parameter. Oracle allocates approximately one undo segment for every transaction. These are sized according to the autoallocate algorithm for locally managed tablespaces. The basic algorithm is that the first 16 extents are 64 KB in size. During subsequent allocation, the next 63 extents are 1 MB, the next 120 extents are 8 MB, and all additional extents are 64 MB [7].

This method of undo management provides quite a few new features or options. One such feature is to go back into history to reconstruct a transaction. This feature is enabled by setting the UNDO_RETENTION parameter to an appropriate value. Setting this parameter allows the DBAs to go back in history to retrieve any specific data as it appeared at that point using the "flashback query" feature. The parameter is set in seconds and defaults to 900 seconds. For example, if data is to be retained for a 24-hour period, the parameter is set to a value of 86,400.

All rules that apply to single instance undo management apply to a RAC configuration, except that in the case of a redo log file, the undo tablespace should also be located on a shared storage.

2.6   Cache fusion

Cache fusion is a new technology that uses high-speed interprocess communication to provide cache-to-cache transfer of data blocks between instances in a cluster. This technology for transferring data across nodes through the interconnect became a viable option as the bandwidth for interconnects increased and the transport mechanism improved. Cache fusion architecture is revolutionary in an industry sense because it treats the entire physical distinct RAM for each cluster node logically as one large database SGA, with the interconnect providing the physical transport among them.

The GCS and Global Enqueue Service (GES) processes on each node manage the cache synchronization by using the cluster interconnect. Cache fusion addresses transaction concurrency between instances. The different scenarios of block sharing are broadly stated as follows:

- *Concurrent reads on multiple nodes.* This occurs when two or more instances participating in the clustered configuration are required to read the same data block. The block is shared between instances via the cluster interconnect. The first instance that reads the block would be the owning instance, and the subsequent instances that require access to the same block will request it via the cluster interconnect.

- *Concurrent reads and writes on different nodes.* This is a mixture of read/write operations against a single data block. A block available on any of the participating instances could be modified by a different instance while maintaining a copy/image that is different from the database. Such transactions use the interconnect. A block can be read as is (i.e., in current version), or a read-consistent version could be built by applying the required undo.

■ *Concurrent writes on different nodes.* This is a situation where multiple instances request modification of the same data block frequently.

During these block transfer requests between instances using the interconnect, the GCS process plays a significant role as the master/keeper of all requests between instances. The GCS tracks the location and status of data blocks as well as the access privileges of various instances. Oracle uses the GCS for cache coherency when the current version of a data block is on one instance's buffer cache and another instance requests that block for modification.

When multiple instances require access to a block, and a different instance masters the block, the GCS resources track the movement of blocks through the master instance. Because of block transfer between instances, copies of the same block could be on different instances. The number of instances a block can exist on is determined by the parameter _FAIRNESS_THRESHOLD and defaults to four, meaning only four images of the same block of a particular DBA can exist in a RAC cluster (irrespective of the number of instances) at any given point in time.

Once the holder reaches the threshold defined by the parameter _FAIRNESS_THRESHOLD, it stops making more copies, flushes the redo to the disk, and downgrades the locks. [9]

When blocks are required by more than one process on the same instance, Oracle will clone the block. The number of times a block can be cloned is defined by the parameter _DB_BLOCK_MAX_CR_DBA and defaults to six, meaning only six cloned copies of the same block of the same DBA (data block address) can exist in the local buffer of an instance (SSKY1 in Figure 9.10) at any given point in time. These blocks in different instances have different resource characteristics. These characteristics are identified by the following factors:

■ Resource mode

■ Resource role

Resource mode

Resource mode is determined by various factors, such as who is the original holder of the block, what operation is the block acquired to perform, what

operation is the requesting holder intending to perform, what will the outcome of the operation be, and so on. Table 2.2 lists the resource modes and
their identifiers and describes each.

Table 2.3   *Resource Modes*

Resource Mode	Identifier	Description
Null	N	Nodes holding blocks at this level convey no access rights
Shared	S	This level indicates that the block is being held in protected read mode, that is, multiple instances have access to read this block but cannot modify it
Exclusive	X	Thus indicates that the resource is held in Exclusive mode, while consistent versions of the older blocks are available, other processes or nodes cannot write to the resource

Resource role

Role indicates if the mode is maintained local to the instance or if it's maintained across multiple instances, hence, at a global level. Table 2.3 lists the
different roles and their descriptions.

Table 2.4   *Resource Roles*

Role	Description
Local	When the block, for the first time, is read into an instance's cache, and no other instance in the cluster has read the same block or is holding a copy of the block, then the block has a local role
Global	If the block that was originally acquired has been modified by the holding instance and, based on a request from another instance, has copied the block, the block that was originally on one node is now present on multiple nodes and therefore has a global role

2.7   Global Resource Directory

The Global Resource Directory (GRD) contains information about the
current status of all shared resources. It is maintained by the GCS and GES
to record information about resources and enqueues held on these
resources. The GRD resides in memory and is used by the GCS and GES

to manage the global resource activity. It is distributed throughout the cluster to all nodes. Each node participates in managing global resources and manages a portion of the GRD.

When an instance reads data blocks for the first time, its existence is local; that is, no other instance in the cluster has a copy of that block. The block in this state is called a current state (XI). The behavior of this block in memory is similar to any single-instance configuration, with the exception that GCS keeps track of the block even in a local mode. Multiple transactions within the instance have access to these data blocks. Once another instance has requested the same block, then the GCS process will update the GRD, changing the role of the data block from local to global.

Figure 2.8
A Dissection of the Global Resource Directory

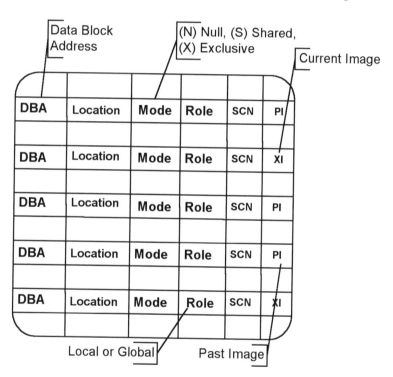

Figure 2.8 shows the contents of the GRD. The structure and function of the GRD is similar to a redo log buffer. The redo log buffer contains the current and past images of the rows being modified; the GRD contains information at a higher level, specifically the current and past image of the blocks being modified by the various instances in the cluster. As illustrated in Figure 2.8, the GRD consists of the following.

Database block address (DBA)

This is the basic address of the block. An example would be block 500. This indicates that block 500 is accessed by a user on its current instance, and based on other values like mode (null, shared, and exclusive) and role (local or global), it is then determined if the current instance is the original holder or a requester of the block.

Location

This indicates the instance where the current version of the data block is located.

Mode

This indicates the resource mode in which the data block is held by the instance. The various resource modes are described in Table 2.3.

Role

This indicates the resource role in which the data block is held by the instance. The various resource roles are described in Table 2.4.

System change number

The SCN is required in a single-instance configuration to serialize activities such as block changes, redo entries, and replay of redo logs during a recovery operation. It has a more robust role in a RAC environment.

In a RAC configuration, more than one instance can make updates to the data blocks. These data blocks are transferred via the cluster interconnect between the instances. To track these successive generations of data blocks across instances, Oracle assigns (uses) to each data block that is generated a unique logical timestamp, or SCN. The SCN is used by Oracle to order the data block change events within each instance and across all instances.

In a RAC environment, separate SCNs are generated by each instance. However, in an effort to keep the transactions in a serial order, these instances have to resynchronize their SCNs to the highest SCN known in the cluster.

Oracle uses two methods to synchronize its SCN to the highest SCN in the cluster:

1.   *Lamport generation.* Under this scheme, SCNs are generated in parallel on all instances, and Oracle piggybacks an instance's current SCN onto any message being sent via the cluster interconnect to another instance. This allows the SCN to be propagated between instances without incurring any additional message overhead. Once propagated, the GCS process will manage the SCN synchronization process. The default interval is based on the platform-specific message threshold value of seven seconds.

     The Lamport SCN generation scheme is used when the value of the `MAX_COMMIT_PROPAGATION_DELAY` parameter is greater than 100. In Oracle Database 10*g* Release 1, this parameter defaults to 700 hundredths of a second, or seven seconds.

2.   *Broadcast on commit.* Under this method, SCNs are propagated to other instances when data is committed on an instance, meaning Oracle does not wait to piggyback the SCN change onto another message. Broadcast on commit is implemented by reducing the default value defined by the parameter `MAX_COMMIT_PROPAGATION_DELAY`. Reducing the value to less than 100 hundredths of a second increases the SCN propagation between instances.

     In Oracle Database 10*g* Release 2, `MAX_COMMIT_PROPAGATION_DELAY` defaults to 0, meaning the broadcast on commit method is used for SCN propagation.

Past image

The past image (PI) is a copy of a globally dirty block image maintained in the cache. It is saved when a modified block is served to another instance after setting the resource role to global. A PI must be maintained by an instance until it or a later version of the block is written to disk. The GCS is responsible for informing an instance that its PI is no longer needed when a recent version of the block is written to disk. PI can be discarded when an instance writes a current block image to disk.

Current image

The current image (XI) is a copy of a block held by the last (current) instance in the chain of instances that requested and transferred an image of the block. The GRD tracks consistent read block images with a local resource in NULL mode. Once tracked, GRD does not have to retain any information about a resource being held in NULL mode by an instance. However, once it has some kind of global allocation, global block resource information is stored in the GRD to manage the history of block transfers, even if the resource mode is NULL. With local resources, the GCS discards resource allocation information for instances that downgrade a resource to NULL mode.

2.8   **Mastering of resources**

Based on the demand for resources on a specific file, the resource is maintained on the instance that uses it the most. For example, if instance SSKY1 were accessing an object A1 and data from object were being processed for about 1,500 user requests, all connected to instance SSKY1, and say instance SSKY2 also required access to the object A1 for 100 users, obviously SSKY1 would have more users accessing this object A1. Hence, instance SSKY1 would be allocated as the resource master for this object, and the GRD for this object would be maintained on instance SSKY1. When instance SSKY2 required information from this object, it would have to coordinate with the GCS and the GRD on instance SSKY1 to retrieve/transfer data across the cluster interconnect.

If the usage pattern changed, for example, the number of users on instance SSKY2 increased to 2,000 and on SSKY1 it dropped to 500, the GCS and GES processes, in combination, would evaluate the current usage pattern and transfer the mastering of the resource via the interconnect to instance SSKY2. This entire process of remastering of resources is called resource affinity. In other words, *resource affinity is the use of dynamic resource remastering to move the location of the resource masters for a database file to the instance where block operations are most frequently occurring.*

Resource affinity optimizes the system in situations where update transactions are being executed on one instance. If activity is not localized, the resource ownership is distributed to the instances equitably.

Figure 2.9 illustrates resource distribution in a four-node cluster. That is, instances SSKY1, SSKY2, SSKY3, and SSKY4 are mastering resources R1, R2, R3, R4, R5, R6, and R7, respectively.

Mastering resources on the instance where the user activity is the highest enables optimization across the cluster and helps achieve workload distribution and quicker startup time. On a busy system, system performance can be affected if there is a constant change of workload on the instance, causing resource utilization to change and, in turn, causing frequent remastering activity.

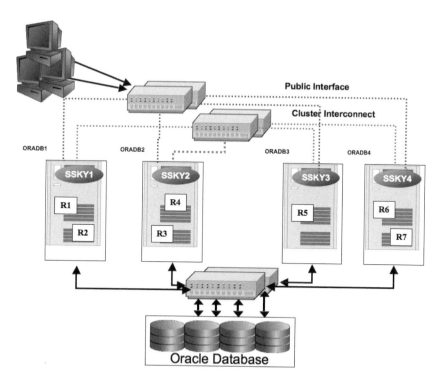

Figure 2.9
Resource Mastering

Remastering also happens when an instance joins or leaves the cluster. However, instead of remastering all locks/resources across all nodes, Oracle uses an algorithm called "lazy remastering." Basically, under this method, instead of load balancing resources by removing all resources and remastering them evenly across instances, Oracle only remasters the resources owned by instances that have crashed.

Figure 2.10 illustrates the remastering of resources from instance SSKY4 to instances SSKY2, and SSKY3; respectively.

If instance SSKY4 crashes, instance SSKY1 and instance SSKY2 will continue to master their resources, namely R1, R2, R3, and R4. As part of the recovery process, the resources mastered on the failed instance will now have to be mastered by one of the surviving instances. Oracle uses the lazy remastering concept and dynamically places the resource master on one of the surviving instances. Consequently, per Figure 2.10, R6 is inherited by instance SSKY2 and R7 is inherited by instance SSKY3, instance SSKY1 is not affected.

At a later time, when the user workload has stabilized (i.e., recovery is completed, and users have failed over), the GCS and GES will reassess the

Figure 2.10
Resource
Remastering

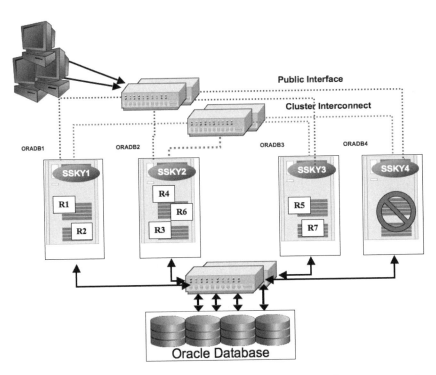

situation and perform a remastering operation to place the master on the instance where the demand is high. A similar operation happens when an instance joins the cluster. Basically, a resource is removed from each of the available instances and moved to the instance that joined the cluster.

Remastering also happens when a master is located on an instance that is not active. Oracle requires additional resources to manage another resource master. Under these circumstances, Oracle will move the resource master that is not being accessed to a less active instance.

 Note: Resource mastering was first introduced in Oracle Database 9*i*, but since then Oracle has been improving the level at which these masters are maintained. In Oracle Database 10*g* Release 1, Oracle mastered resources at the tablespace level, where if a single instance is identified as the sole user of a tablespace, the block resource masters for files of that tablespace are lazily and dynamically moved to that instance. In Oracle Database 10*g* Release 2, resource mastering has undergone further changes, with resource mastering occurring at the object level.

For dynamic remastering to happen, the number of sessions touching an object should be 50 times more than the other instances over a period of 10 minutes.

2.9   Lock management

In the case of an Oracle implementation, be it a single stand-alone configuration or a multi-instance configuration, there is a considerable amount of sharing of resources among sessions. These resources can be a table definition, a transaction, or any type of structure that is shareable among sessions. To ensure that the right sessions get access to these resources based on their need and the type of activity being performed, some type of lock must be placed on them.

For example, a session trying to perform a SQL query, SELECT * FROM PRODUCT, will require a shared lock on the PRODUCT table. When a number of sessions try to access the same resource, Oracle will serialize the processing by placing a number of these sessions in a wait mode until the work of the blocking sessions has completed.

Every session requiring access to these resources acquires a lock, and when it has completed the function or operation, it releases the lock. Releasing of locks is performed by the sessions when the user issues a commit or executes a DDL statement or by the SMON process if the session was killed.

Throughout its operation, Oracle automatically acquires different types of locks at different levels of restrictiveness depending on the resource being locked and the operation being performed.

A RAC implementation is a composition of two or more instances that talk to a common shared database. Hence, all transactional behaviors that apply to a single-instance configuration will apply to a RAC implementation.

Apart from the lock management of DML, DDL, latches, and internal locks apply to a single-instance configuration, the lock management in a multi-instance configuration involves management of locks across instances and across the cluster interconnects. A major difference between single-instance configuration and a multi-instance configuration is that while row-level locks continue to be maintained and managed at the instance level, when it comes to inter-instance locking, the locking is at a much higher level and the locks are held at the block level. A block contains multiple rows or records of data.

2.10   **Multi-instance transaction behavior**

An instance reads a block from disk when either a user session or a process from another instance places a request. While all instances participating in the cluster could access the block directly from disk (as in the previous versions of Oracle),[4] such an access would be expensive, especially when another instance in the cluster was already holding a copy of the block in its buffer, and the same block could be accessed via the cluster interconnect. This operation may be as simple as transferring the block via the cluster interconnect to the requesting instance. However, other factors are involved during this process; for example, the block held by the original holder may have been modified, and the copy may not be placed on disk. It could very well be that the instance is holding only a copy of the block, while the block was initially modified by another instance, and the block may have already undergone considerable changes. Yet, in another scenario, one of the instances requesting the block could be intending to delete a row from the block, while yet another instance is intending to update the block.

How are these changes by multiple instances coordinated? How does Oracle ensure that these blocks are modified and tracked? DBAs familiar with a single-instance configuration would know that Oracle is required to provide read consistency and ensure that multiple sessions do not see the in-flight transactions or rows that are being modified but not saved. RAC is no different; read consistency is provided at the cluster level across all instances. In a RAC configuration, while the data movement is at the block level, a single row from the block behaves similarly to how it would in a regular single-instance configuration.

To cover all possible scenarios of cache fusion and sharing of blocks among the instances, the block behavior could be broadly classified into the following categories:

- Read/read behavior

- Read/write behavior

- Write/write behavior

---

4.   By enabling the `gc_files_to_lock` parameter, Oracle will disable the cache fusion functionality and instead use the disks for sharing blocks. In other words, it will use the Oracle Parallel Server (OPS) behavior.

While these are just the high-level behaviors, there are quite a few possibilities that will be discussed.

Read/read behavior

Under this behavior, there are basically two possibilities:

1.   The instance that first requested the block is the only instance holding the block for read purposes (read/read behavior with no transfer).

2.   The first instance is holding the block for read purposes; however, other instances also require access to the same block for read only purposes (read/read behavior with transfer).

Read/read behavior with no transfer

Figure 2.11 illustrates the steps involved when an instance acquires the block from disk, and no other instance currently holds a copy of the same block. Instance SSKY3 will have to request a shared resource on the block for read-only purposes. (*For the purpose of this discussion, let us assume that SSKY3 is the first instance that requested this block, and it is not present in the shared areas of any other instances [SSKY1, SSKY2, and SSKY4].*)

Figure 2.11
*Read/Read
Behavior with No
Transfer*

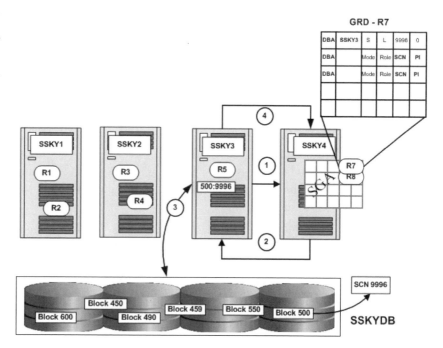

The following steps are undertaken by SSKY3 to acquire the block from disk:

1.   A user session or process attached to instance SSKY3 makes a request for a specific row of data. SSKY3 determines that the master for this specific resource is SSKY4. The request is directed to instance SSKY4, where the GRD for the object is maintained. *Oracle allocates a node to be the resource master based on the demand for the resource on a specific instance. If the object access increases on another node, Oracle performs a remastering operation to move the resource master for the object to the node.*

2.   The GCS, on verifying the GRD, determines that no other instance in the cluster has a copy of the block. The GCS sends a message to SSKY3 requesting that it read the block from disk.

3.   Instance SSKY3 initiates the I/O request to read the row from disk. The row is contained in block 500 and has an SCN 9996. Since Oracle reads a block of data at a time, other rows are also retrieved as part of this read operation. The block is read into the buffer of instance SSKY3. Instance SSKY3 holds the block with SCN 9996 using a shared local mode and, because the block is requested for read-only purposes, will have an XI status.

4.   SSKY3 now informs the GCS that the operation is successful. The GCS makes an entry in the GRD on instance SSKY4.

Read/read behavior with transfer

Let us continue with the previous illustration. The Oracle process accessed the disk to retrieve a row contained in block 500 via instance SSKY3. The block is held in local shared mode (i.e., no other instance has a copy of the block). Let's assume another user requires access to another row that is part of the same data block 500. This request is made by a user connected to instance SSKY2.

Figure 2.12 illustrates the steps involved when an instance SSKY2 requires a block that is currently held by instance SSKY3. (*To maintain clarity of the figure, steps 1 to 4 are not repeated. Readers are advised to see Figure 2.11 in conjunction with Figure 2.12.*)

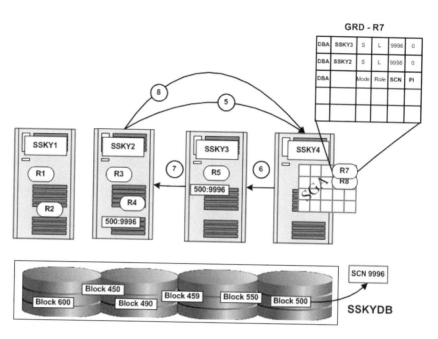

Figure 2.12
*Read/Read
Behavior with
Transfer*

5.   Instance SSKY2 sends a request for a read resource on the block to the GCS. Since the GRD for this resource is maintained on instance SSKY4, SSKY2 requests access to SSKY4.

6.   Instance SSKY4 checks against its GRD regarding the whereabouts of this block and determines that the block is currently held in instance SSKY3. GCS as the global cache manager for this resource sends a request to instance SSKY3, requesting that it transfer the block for shared access to instance SSKY2.

7.   Instance SSKY3 ships a copy of the block to the requesting instance SSKY2. During this copy operation, SSKY3 indicates in the header of the message that instance SSKY3 is only sharing the block (which means SSKY3 is going to retain a copy of the block). It also informs SSKY2 that it is supposed to maintain the block at the same resource level.

8.   Instance SSKY2 receives the block along with the shared resource level transferred via the message header from instance SSKY3. To complete the communication cycle, instance SSKY2 sends a message to the GCS that it has received a copy of the block. The GCS now updates the GRD.

This discussion is making an optimistic assumption, namely, that everything is available as expected. Now, what if this were not the case, and instance SSKY3 did not have the block? In such a situation, instance SSKY3 would continue with the instruction received from the GCS. However, in the transfer operation, instance SSKY3 would send a message indicating that it no longer had a copy of the block and instance SSKY2 was free to get the block from disk. On receipt of this message, instance SSKY2 would, after confirming and informing the GCS, retrieve the block directly from disk.

What happens if there is a third instance, or for that matter a fourth, fifth, or sixth instance, that is requesting access to read this block? In all these situations, the behavior and order of operation is similar. In Figure 2.12, instance SSKY3 will copy the block to the respective requesting instances, and Oracle will control these copies by maintaining the information in the GRD.

Read/write behavior

A block that was read by instance SSKY3 and now copied to instance SSKY2 is requested by instance SSKY1 for a write operation. A write operation on a block would require instance SSKY1 to have an exclusive lock on this block. Let us go through the steps involved in this behavior.

9.   Instance SSKY1 sends a request for an exclusive resource on the block to the GCS on the mastering instance SSKY4.

10.   The GCS, after referring to the GRD on instance SSKY4, ascertains that the block is being held by two instances, SSKY3 and SSKY2. The GCS sends a message to all (instance SSKY2 in our example) but one instance (instance SSKY3), requesting that the block be moved to a NULL location. (Moving the block to a NULL location or status changes the resource from shared mode to local mode.) This effectively tells the instances to release the buffers holding the block. Once this is done, the only remaining instance holding the block in a shared mode would be instance SSKY3.

11.   The GCS requests that instance SSKY3 transfer the block for exclusive access to instance SSKY1.

Figure 2.13 illustrates the steps involved when instance SSKY1 requires a copy of the block that is currently held by instances SSKY2 and SSKY3 for a write operation.

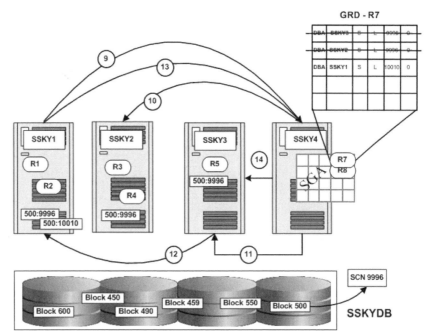

Figure 2.13
Read/Write
Behavior

12.   Instance SSKY3, based on the request received from the GCS, will

   a.   Send the block to instance SSKY1 along with an indicator that it is closing its own resource and giving an exclusive resource for use to instance SSKY1

   b.   Close its own resource, marking the buffer holding the block image as copy for consistent read (CR) and informing itself that the buffer area is available for reuse

13.   Instance SSKY1 converts its resource, makes the required updates to the block, and assigns it a new SCN. SSKY1 then sends a message to the GCS indicating and confirming that it has an exclusive resource on the block. The message also piggybacks the message received from instance SSKY3 indicating that it has closed its own resource on this block. The GCS now updates the GRD regarding the status of the block, and instance SSKY1 can now modify the block.

   Please note that at this stage, the copies of blocks on other instances will also be removed from the GRD.

As illustrated in Figure 2.13, instance SSKY1 has now modified the block, and the new SCN is 10010.

14.   The GCS confirms with instance SSKY3 that it has received notification regarding status of the block in its buffer.

Write/write behavior

Previous discussions centered on shareable scenarios like multiple instances
having read copies of the same block. Now let us look at how cache fusion
operates when multiple instances require write access to the same block.
Please note from our previous scenario in Figure 2.13 that the block has
been modified by instance SSKY1 (new SCN value is 10010); the SCN for
the block on disk remains at 9996.

In a continuous operation, where multiple requests are made between
instances for different blocks, the GCS is busy with the specific resource
documenting all the block activities among the various instances. The GCS
activity is sequential; unless it has recorded the information pertaining to
previous requests, it does not accept or work on another request. If such a
situation occurs, the new request is queued and has to wait for the GCS to
complete its current operation before it is accepted.

Figure 2.14
Write/Write
Behavior

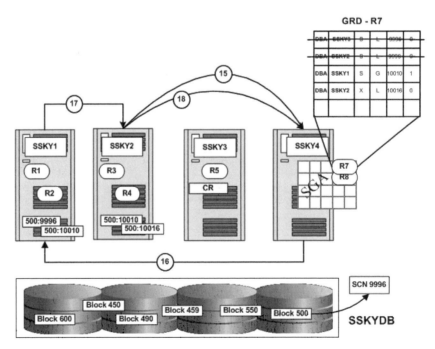

Figure 2.14 illustrates the steps involved when an instance has acquired a block for write activity and another instance requires access to the same block for a similar write operation.

15.   Instance SSKY2, which originally had a read copy of the block and, based on the write request from instance SSKY1, received instructions from the GCS to clear the block buffer (marked as CR), now requires a copy of the block to make updates. Instance SSKY2 requests an exclusive resource on the block from the GCS.

16.   If the GCS has completed all previous activities pertaining to other requests, the GCS requests instance SSKY1 (the current holder of the block) give exclusive resource on the block and that transfer the current image of the block to instance SSKY2.

17.   Instance SSKY1 transfers the block to the requesting instance (SSKY2) after ensuring that the following activities against this block have been completed:

   a.   Logging any changes to the block and forcing a log flush if this has not already occurred.

   b.   Converting its resource to NULL with a PI status of 1, indicating that the buffer now contains a PI copy of the block.

   c.   Sending an exclusive-keep copy of the block buffer to instance SSKY2, which indicates that the block image has an SCN 10010, with an exclusive resource in global mode. SSKY1 also piggybacks a message indicating that the instance SSKY1 is holding a PI of the block.

   GCS resource conversions and cache fusion block transfers occur completely outside the transaction boundaries. That is, an instance does not have to wait for a pending transaction to be completed before releasing an exclusive block resource.

18.   After receipt of the message from instance SSKY1, instance SSKY2 will update the row in the block, assign it a new SCN number 10016, and send a message to the GCS. This message informs the GCS that instance SSKY2 now has the resource with an exclusive global status and that the previous holder instance SSKY1 now holds a PI version of the block with SCN 10010. The GCS will update the GRD with the latest status of the block.

Instance SSKY1 no longer has an exclusive resource on this block and, hence, cannot modify the block.

Write/read behavior

We have looked at read/write behavior before. What would be the difference in the opposite situation; that is, when a block is held by an instance after modification and another instance requires the latest copy of the block for a read operation? Unlike the previous read/write scenario, the block has undergone considerable modification, and the SCN held by the current holder of the block is different from what is found on disk.

In a single-instance configuration, a query looks for a read-consistent image of the row, and the behavior in a clustered configuration is no different; Oracle has to provide a consistent read version of the block. In this example, the latest copy of the block is held by instance SSKY2 (based on our previous scenario as illustrated in Figure 2.14).

Figure 2.15
Write/Read
Behavior

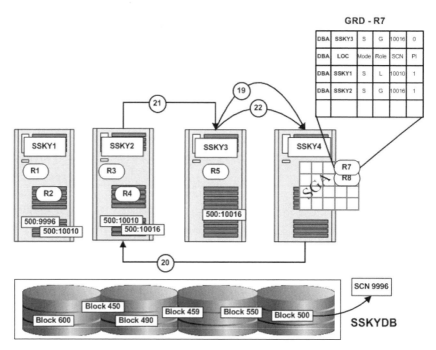

Figure 2.15 illustrates the steps involved when instance SSKY3 requires a block for read purposes. From our previous scenario, it is understood that the latest version of the block is currently held by instance SSKY2 in exclusive mode.

19.   Instance SSKY3 once had a read copy of the block; however, based on a request from the GCS, it had converted it into a NULL resource (step 10, Figure 2.13). Based on a new query request from a user, it now requires a read access to the block. To satisfy this request, instance SSKY3 requests the necessary shared resource from the GCS.

20.   Instance SSKY2 is the current holder of the block. To satisfy the request from instance SSKY3, the GCS requests that instance SSKY2 transfer the block.

21.   Instance SSKY2, on receipt of the message request, completes all required work on the block and sends a copy of the block image to instance SSKY3. The block is to be transferred in a shared status with no exclusive rights, hence, instance SSKY2 has to downgrade its resources to shared mode before transferring the block across to instance SSKY3. While the transfer happens, instance SSKY2 retains the block's PI.

        Instance SSKY1 and instance SSKY2 have a PI of the block at their respective SCNs.

22.   Instance SSKY3 now acknowledges receipt of the requested block by sending a message to the GCS. This includes the SCN of the PI currently retained by instance SSKY2. The GCS makes the required updates to the GRD.

        Instance SSKY3 now has the most recent copy of the block and is now in a global shared mode.

Write-to-disk behavior

What happens when a block needs to be written to disk? Before we step into the mechanics of this, let us recap the current state of the environment:

- Instance SSKY4 continues to be the master of the resource and holds the GRD for the block.

- Instance SSKY1 had once modified the block and currently holds the block with SCN 10010, having a global null resource and a PI.

- Instance SSKY2 also contains a modified copy of the block with SCN 10016. The current status of the block held by instance SSKY2 is in exclusive resource mode. This instance also holds a PI.

- Instance SSKY3 holds the latest consistent read image version of the block (in shared global mode) received from instance SSKY2, which means it is a copy of a block held by instance SSKY2.

- The disk contains the original block SCN 9996.

What could cause a write activity in a RAC environment? Transactional behavior in a RAC environment is no different when compared to a single-instance configuration. All normal rules of single instance, also apply in this situation. For example, writing to disk could happen under the following circumstances:

- *The number of dirty buffers reaches a threshold value.* This value is reached when there is insufficient room in the database buffer cache for more data. In this situation, Oracle writes the dirty buffers to disk, freeing up space for new data.

- *A process is unable to find free buffers in the database buffer cache while scanning for blocks.* When a process reads data from the disk and does not find any free space in the buffer, it triggers the least recently used data in the buffer cache (dirty buffer) to be pushed down the stack and finally written to disk.

- *A timeout occurs.* Timeout is configured by setting the required timeout interval (LOG_CHECKPOINT_TIMEOUT) through a parameter defined in the parameter file. On every preset interval, the timeout is triggered to cause the DBWR process to write the dirty buffers to disk. In an ideal system, where the data is modified but not immediately written to disk (because it does not have sufficient activity to cause other mechanisms to trigger the write operation), this parameter is helpful.

- *The checkpoint process is triggered.* During a predefined interval defined by the LOG_CHECKPOINT_INTERVAL or FAST_START_MTTR_TARGET parameters, when the CKPT process is triggered, it causes the DBWR and LGWR processes to write the data from their respective buffer caches to disk. If neither of these parameters is defined, the automatic check pointing is enabled.

In a RAC environment, any participating instance could trigger a write request.

Figure 2.16
Write-to-Disk Behavior

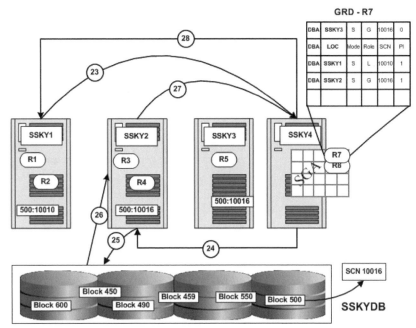

Figure 2.16 illustrates the various steps involved during a write-to-disk activity. In the current scenario, instances SSKY1 and SSKY2 both have a modified version of the block and are different from the version on disk.

Let us assume that in our scenario instance SSKY1, due to a checkpoint request, is required to write the block to disk. The following steps are taken to accomplish this activity:

23. Instance SSKY1 sends a write request to the GCS with the necessary SCN. The GCS, after determining from the GRD the list of instances that currently contain PI copies, marks them as requiring modification.

24. The GCS initiates the write operation by requesting instance SSKY2, which holds the latest modified block, to perform this operation. *During this process, while a write operation is outstanding, the GCS will not allow another write to be initiated until the current operation is completed.*

Note: The GCS, as the controller of resources, determines which instance will actually perform the write operation; when an instance needs to write a block to disk upon a checkpoint request, the instance checks the role of the resource covering the block. If the role is global, the instance must inform the GCS of the write requirement. The GCS is responsible for finding the most current block image and informing the instance holding the image to perform the block write. In the scenario discussed, instance SSKY1 made the request, and SSKY2 is holding a more recent version of the block.

25.   Instance SSKY2 initiates the I/O with a write-to-disk request.

26.   Once the I/O operation is complete, instance SSKY2 logs the fact that such an operation has completed, and a block written record (BWR) is placed in the redo log buffer. This activity advances the checkpoint, which in turn forces a log write.

Note: During a database recovery operation, the recovery process uses the BWR to validate whether the redo information for the block prior to this point is needed.

27.   Instance SSKY2 informs the GCS of the successful completion of the write operation. This notification also informs the GCS of the current resource status of the block that the resource is going to a local role because the DBWR has written the current image to disk.

28.   On receipt of the write notification, the GCS sends a message to all instances holding a PI, instructing them to flush the PI. After completion of this process or if no PI remains, the instance holding the current exclusive resource is asked to switch to the local role. In the scenarios discussed above, SSKY1 and SSKY2 are the two instances holding a PI. When instance SSKY2 receives a flush request from the GCS, it writes a BWR without flushing the log buffer. Once this completes, instance SSKY2 will hold the block with an exclusive local resource with no PIs, and all other PIs to this block held across various instances are purged.

After the dirty block has been written to disk, any subsequent operation will follow similar steps to complete any requests from users. For example, if an instance requires read access to a block after the block has been written to disk, the instance will check with the GCS and, based on the instruction received from the GCS, retrieve the block from disk or from another instance that currently has a copy of the block. The write/write behavior and write-to-disk behavior are possible during a DML operation.

In all these scenarios it should be noted that, unless necessary, no write activity to the disk happens. Every activity or state of the block is maintained as a resource in the instance where it was utilized last and reused many times from this location. It should also be noted, while the illustrations above have discussed block sharing from various instances in the cluster, in a real-world situation there can only be two possibilities:

1. *Block request involving two instances.* As discussed in the remastering section and subsequently in step 1 (Figure 2.13), the resource master is maintained on the instance where the demand for the object is the highest, meaning usually that the requested block should be on the instance that contains the resource master and the GRD for the resource.

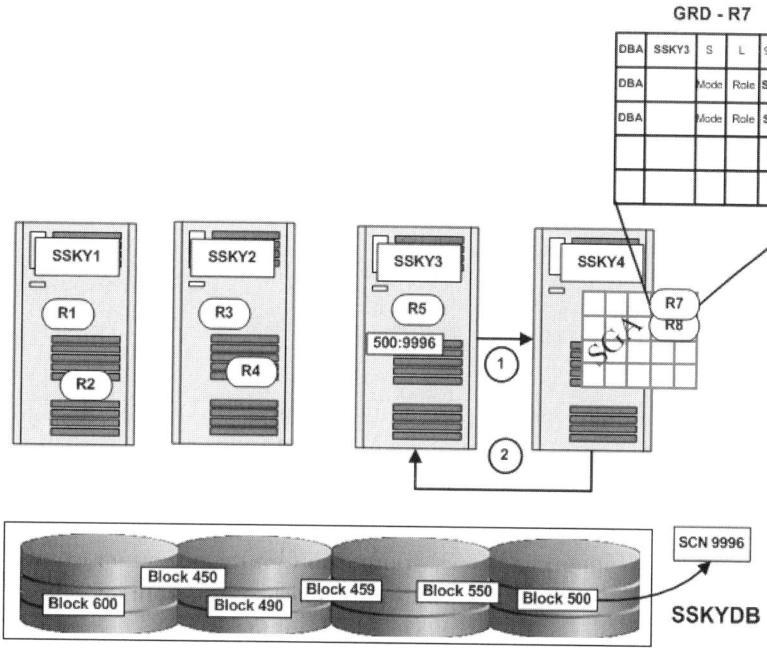

Figure 2.17
Two-Way Block Transfer (two hop)

- In Figure 2.17, the instance SSKY3 requires a row from a block 500 and sends a request to the GCS of the resource.

- The block is found on instance SSKY4, and the GCS sends the block to instance SSKY3.

2.   *Block request involving three instances.* In scenarios where the block requested by another instance is not found on the instance that contains the master, the GCS will request that the block be retrieved from the disk, or if the block is found on another instance, it will send a message to the holding instance to send a copy of the block to the requesting instance.

Figure 2.18
Three-Way Block Transfer (three hop)

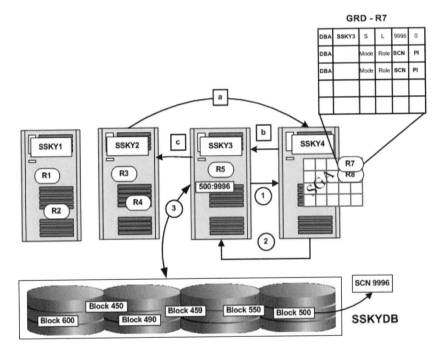

As illustrated in Figure 2.18, there are two possibilities when the block is not found on the instance that is the master of the object (resource):

1.   Read the block from the disk.

a.   Instance SSKY1 requests block 500 from the GCS located on instance SSKY4.

b.   Instance SSKY4, after checking against the GRD, determines that neither instance SSKY4 nor any other instance in the cluster has a copy of the block requested. Hence, it sends a message to the requesting instance to read the block from disk.

    c.   Instance SSKY3 reads the block from disk.

2.   Request that another instance transfer the block.

    a.   Instance SSKY2 requests block 500 from the GCS located on instance SSKY4.

    b.   Instance SSKY4 verifies against its GRD and determines that the block is currently held by instance SSKY3. It sends a message to instance SSKY3 requesting that it send a copy of the block to instance SSKY2.

    c.   Instance SSKY3 accepts the request and sends the block to instance SSKY2.

Note: That is why the RAC architecture scales irrespective of the number of instances in the cluster: no matter how many instances might be associated with the cluster, the number of hops will never exceed three.

2.11 Recovery

Oracle performs recovery operations through a two-phased approach. Under this method of recovery, Oracle reads through the required redo log file twice to complete the recovery operation. This feature speeds up the recovery process while making the system available to users as recovery completes through each phase.

After detection and during the remastering of the GCS of the failed instance and cache recovery, most work in the surviving instance is paused, and while transaction recovery takes place, work occurs at a slower pace. This point is considered full database availability because now all data is accessible, including that which resided on the failed instance. The SELECT statements from applications using transparent application failover (TAF) will fail over; however, for DML operations, applications are responsible for reconnecting users and repeating any uncommitted work they have done. TAF is discussed in detail in Chapter 6.

As part of the failover process when an instance crashes, the processes fail over to the other surviving nodes, and the GCS resources that were previously mastered at the failed instance are redistributed across the surviving instances through the process of resource remastering. Once this is completed, the resources are reconstructed at their new master instances. While resources from the failed instance are distributed among the surviving nodes, not all other resources previously mastered at surviving instances are affected. On completion of the remastering of the resources from the failed instance to the surviving instances, Oracle performs a cleanup operation to remove in-progress transactions from the failed instance.

The active instance that first identified a member in the cluster not responding and deduced its failure is responsible for the recovery operation. The active instance that deduced the failure through its LMON process controls the recovery operation by taking over the redo logs files (in a shared disk subsystem, the redo logs are visible by all instances participating in the cluster) of the failed instance.

Based on the new method of recovery in two passes, the recovery operation is divided into cache recovery and transaction recovery. Apart from these two modes of recovery, another method is unique to a RAC implementation, and it is called online block recovery.

2.11.1   Cache recovery

Cache recovery is the first pass of reading the redo logs by SMON on the active instance. The redo logs files are read and applied to the active instance performing the recovery operation through a parallel execution.

During this process, SMON will merge the redo thread ordered by the SCN to ensure that changes are applied in an orderly manner. It will also find the BWR in the redo stream and remove entries that are no longer needed for recovery because they were PIs of blocks already written to disk. SMON recovers blocks found during this first pass and acquires the locks needed for this operation. The final product of the first-pass log read is a recovery set that only contains blocks modified by the failed instance, with no subsequent BWR to indicate that the blocks were later written. The recovering SMON process will then inform each lock element's master node for each block in the recovery list that it will be taking ownership of the block and lock for recovery. Other instances will not be able to acquire these locks until the recovery operation is completed. At this point, full access to the database is available.

2.11.2   Transaction recovery

Compared to the cache recovery scenario, where the recovery is of a forward nature (i.e., rolling forward of the transactions from the redo logs), the transaction recovery scenario handles uncommitted transactions; hence, operation is to roll back uncommitted transactions. In addition, during this pass, the redo threads for the failed instances are merged by SCN, and the redo is applied to the datafiles.

During this process of rolling back uncommitted transactions, Oracle uses a technology called *fast-start recovery,* where it performs the transaction recovery as a deferred process, hence, as a background activity. Under this feature, Oracle uses a multiversion and consistency method to provide on-demand rollback of only those rows blocked by expired transactions. This feature helps new transactions by not requiring them to wait for the roll-back activity to complete. Fast-start recovery can be of two kinds: fast-start on demand and fast-start parallel rollback.

Fast-start on demand

Under this option, users are allowed to perform regular business and are not interfered with by the uncommitted or expired transactions from the other instance.

Fast-start parallel rollback

Fast-start parallel rollback is performed by SMON, which acts as a coordinator and rolls back transactions using parallel processing across multiple server processes. The parallel execution option is useful where transactions run for a longer duration before committing. When using this feature, each node spawns a recovery coordinator and recovery process to assist with parallel rollback operations.

Fast-start parallel rollback features are enabled by setting the parameter FAST_START_PARALLEL_ROLLBACK. This setting indicates the number of processes to be involved in the rollback operation. The valid values are FALSE, LOW, and HIGH. The default value is LOW, which is twice the CPU_COUNT parameter.

2.11.3 Online block recovery

Online block recovery is unique to the RAC implementation. Online block recovery occurs when a data buffer becomes corrupt in an instance's cache. Block recovery will occur if either a foreground process dies while applying changes or an error is generated during redo application. If the block recovery is to be performed because of the foreground process's dying, then PMON initiates online block recovery. However, if this is not the case, then the foreground process attempts to make an online recovery of the block.

Under normal circumstances, this involves finding the block's predecessor and applying redo records to this predecessor from the online logs of the local instance. However, under the cache fusion architecture, copies of blocks are available in the cache of other instances; therefore, the predecessor is the most recent PI for that buffer that exists in the cache of another instance. If, under certain circumstances, there is no PI for the corrupted buffer, the block image from the disk data is used as the predecessor image.

2.12 Conclusion

In this chapter, the architecture of RAC was explored, as was the new Oracle Clusterware architecture. Then we looked at the clustered database by answering a few questions on cache fusion technology: how cache fusion operates, how blocks are shared across instances, and how they are managed in a such way that only one instance modifies the block at any moment. Also discussed were provision to cache memory between the various instances by the GCS, how resources are mastered on an instance with a new concept of the GRD, and how the GCS and GES communicate with the GRD. The additional background and foreground processes available only in a RAC implementation were also investigated.

We looked at the transaction management principles of cache fusion. We also looked at the various scenarios or behavioral patterns that are encountered in a normal day-to-day operation in an enterprise, with extensive details including process flows and a systematic description of each behavior.

In a RAC configuration, most of the activities are done within the SGA or across the cluster interconnect, and a copy is maintained within an instance. We discussed how when one instance requires a block that is held by another instance, the holding instance will transfer the block to the requesting instance after making updates to the required GRD on the resource master node.

3

Storage Management

Storage has probably been a critical component of any computer system since the invention of the computer. Several of us have seen the transition from card readers to tape devices and removable disks to small and portable disks with storage capacities literally millions of times greater.

Storage systems comprise one or more disks. Since the earliest versions of Oracle, the database administrator (DBA) has always favored several disks of smaller capacity because the limit on I/O operations is determined by the number of disks, not the overall storage capacity of those disks. More disks mean more read/write heads, which in turn means greater I/O operations, and this helps in the overall performance of the database. Despite the I/O advantages obtained by basing a system on many disks of small capacity, it is unfortunate that manufacturers these days only make large-capacity disks. Over the years, disk capacity has gotten larger and larger. This increase has been linear. While the capacity has increased in a linear fashion, the prices of these disks have dropped several fold. For the price of a small-capacity disk about ten years ago, today one can get a much-larger-capacity disk for a fraction of that cost.

The linear growth in disk capacity has led to a corresponding growth in the amount of information stored in the Oracle database. At the same time, the number of users accessing data on these databases has also grown. The requirement to support applications accessing the data from a wider area, such as the Internet, and the requirement for immediate availability (response time) of data from these databases have also increased. This has meant that the throughput (measured in input/output per second [2][1]) to retrieve and return the requested data has increased as well.

3.1   Disk fundamentals

A disk drive comprises several cylindrical platters coated with magnetic material encompassed in a box (steel casing) to keep them away from an unclean environment, which would otherwise ruin the disk and the data it contains. The steel casing also contains arms similar to the arms of a gramophone system, which hold the read/write heads. The time taken to retrieve data from a disk drive is determined by the following factors:

- *Write rate.* the amount of data that can be transferred per second

- *Rotation speed.* the actual speed at which the disk or platters rotate, allowing the read/write heads to retrieve or store the data

- *Seek time.* the average time it takes to find the data on the platters; usually the most significant component in overall disk service time, that is, for the head to move between sectors to locate the data

Figure 3.1
Disk Layout

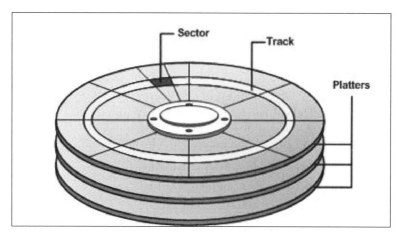

Hard disks are organized as a stack of platters. These platter surfaces contain concentric circles known as tracks, and sections of each track are called sectors. A sector is the basic unit of data storage on a hard disk. The term *sector* emanates from a mathematical term referring to that pie-shaped, angular section of a circle, bounded on two sides by radii and on the third by the perimeter of the circle (see Figure 3.1). Explained most simply, a hard disk comprises a group of predefined sectors that are circular, with smaller sectors on the inside and larger sectors on the outside, as illustrated in Figure 3.2. The circle of predefined sectors is defined as a single track. A group of concentric circles (tracks) defines a single surface of a disk's platter. In earlier days, hard disks had just a single one-sided platter, while today's hard disks comprise several platters with tracks on both sides, all of which make up the hard disk's capacity.

Figure 3.2
Disk Dissections

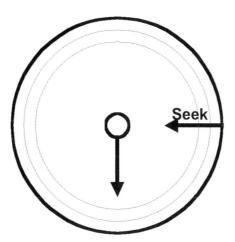

Because the sectors are smaller toward the center and larger toward the outside of the disk, the amount of data stored on these sectors varies, depending on where the actual sector is located on the disk. Sectors on the outside of the disk are larger (in diameter) and will hold more data, while sectors toward the center are smaller and, hence, hold a smaller volume of data.

The inner circles have a limitation on how many sectors can be packed into the tracks, and the outer circles use the same algorithm or constant to create sectors with the same linear bit density as the inner circles. This wastes space on the outer sectors, decreasing the total storage capacity of these disks. To increase capacity and to eliminate this wasted space, a technique called zone bit recording (ZBR) is employed. With this technique, tracks are grouped into zones based on their distance from the center of the disk, and each zone is assigned a number of sectors per track. This means that each outer track has one additional sector compared to the one before it. This type of sector organization allowes for more efficient use of the larger tracks on the outside of the disk.

The read/write head that locates and reads the data can read more blocks of data at a time when reading from the outer sectors. In addition, the read/write head (sector seek) moves from outer to inner circles, which means the probability of getting to the data quicker will be higher if the actual data is located on the outer sectors. Thus, from among the various factors discussed above, the one of primary importance is the seek time because it determines how fast the data can be located before being retrieved. While the newer drives have gotten faster, the seek time has not improved significantly; thus, the goal is to keep frequently accessed data in the outer sectors.

A typical disk drive today has a minimum seek time of approximately 1 ms for seeking the next track and a maximum seek time of approximately 11 ms for seeking the entire width of the disk [3]. Thus, in order to read a block of data from disk, the read/write head should locate the track within a sector that contains the block and allow the disk to rotate to the exact location to read its contents. This means seek and rotational speeds go hand in hand with the overall performance of the disks.

The read and write instructions are received by the disk controller from the operating system. The operating system in turn receives instructions from the application based on user activity or data feeds. The data received is placed on the disk in a more random order. Taking into consideration the seek time and the disk rotation times, in an ideal world, it would be beneficial if data could be placed on the inner or outer sectors based on its importance. However, since the operating systems and the layered applications have no direct control of each other's functions, this is not possible, unless the layered system that controls the placement of data understands the application behavior.

Faster seek times are just one part of the requirement. What happens when a disk that contains important information fails? The solution to this problem is to make a backup of the data. Backing up critical data to alternate storage and restoring it during failures is possible, but in large systems where data is continuously read and written to disks and where the uptime of systems is important, the mean time between failures (MTBF) and mean time to failures (MTTF) should be kept as low as possible. Therefore, the option is to have pairs of disks so that disk images can be duplicated (mirrored) and made available when the primary disk fails.

Having mirrored disks or disk images will not directly solve the issues with I/O contention. The I/O contention can still exist, and performance issues on the system with large numbers of users can remain significantly high. The solution involves spreading the data across multiple disks evenly so as to balance I/O.

Several technologies, such as Redundant Array of Inexpensive Disks (RAID), have evolved over the years, providing redundancy and improved performance by grouping several disks together. However, in today's computing-intensive environments, this growth in performance has not been sufficient.

RAID is the technology for expanding the capacity of the I/O system while providing the capability for data redundancy. RAID is the use of two or more physical disks to create one logical disk, where the physical disks operate in tandem to provide greater size and more bandwidth. RAID provides scalability and high availability in the context of I/O and system performance.

RAID levels ranging from simple striping to mirroring have provided benchmarks for the various types of data suited for their respective technologies. Several types of RAID configurations are available today; let's briefly discuss some commonly used types of RAID for Oracle RDBMS.

3.1.1   RAID 0

RAID 0 provides striping, where a single data partition is physically spread across all disks in the stripe bank, effectively giving that partition the aggregate performance of all the disks combined. The unit of granularity for spreading the data across the drives is called the stripe size or chunk size. Typical settings for the stripe size are 32K, 64K, and 128K.

In Figure 3.3, eight disks are all striped across in different stripes or partitions.

Figure 3.3
RAID 0

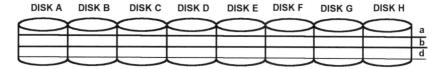

3.1.2   RAID 1

RAID 1 is known as mirroring and is where all the writes issued to a given disk are duplicated to another disk. This provides a high-availability solution; if there is a failure of the first disk, the second disk, or mirror, can take over without any data loss. Apart from providing redundancy for data on the disks, mirroring also helps reduce read contention by directing reads to disk volumes that are less busy.

3.1.3   **RAID 0+1**

RAID 0+1, or RAID 01, is a combination of levels 0 and 1. RAID 01 does exactly what its name implies: stripes and mirrors disks (i.e., stripes first, then mirrors what was just striped). RAID 01 incorporates the advantages of both RAID 0 and RAID 1. RAID 01 is illustrated in Figure 3.4.

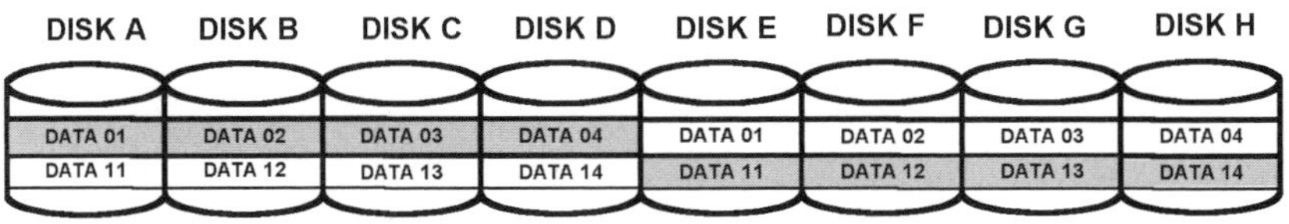

Figure 3.4
RAID 01

Figure 3.4 illustrates a four-way striped mirrored volume with eight disks (A–H). A given set of data in a file is split/striped across the disks (A–D, with the stripe first and then mirrored across disks E–H). Due to the method by which these disks are grouped and striped, if one of the pieces becomes unavailable due to a disk failure, the entire mirror member becomes unavailable. This means loss of an entire mirror reduces the I/O servicing capacity of the storage device by 50% [8].

3.1.4   **RAID 1+0**

RAID 1+0, or RAID 10, is also a combination of RAID 0 and RAID 1. In RAID 10, the disks are mirrored and then striped (i.e., mirrored first, then stripe what was mirrored).

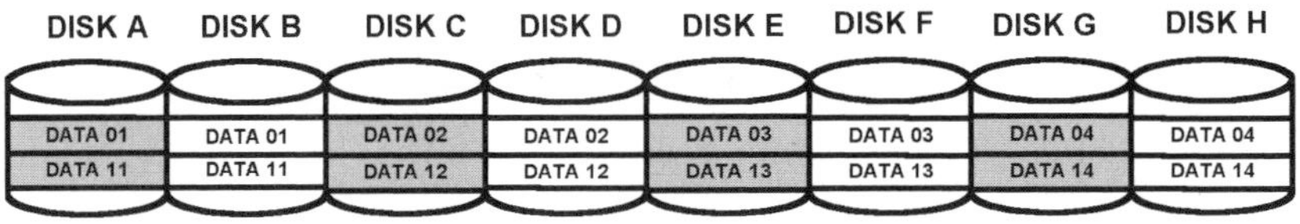

Figure 3.5
RAID 10

In Figure 3.5, DATA 01 is mirrored on the adjoining disks (DISK A and DISK B), and DATA 02 is mirrored on the subsequent two disks (DISK C and DISK D). This illustration contains eight mirrored and striped disks. Unlike RAID 01 (see Figure 3.4), loss of one disk in a mirror member does not disable the entire mirrored volume, which means it does not reduce the I/O servicing capacity of the volume by 50%.

> **Note:** RAID 10 is the most common type of RAID solution deployed for Oracle databases. Hardware RAID is only available with RAID 10.

3.1.5   RAID 5

Under RAID 5, parity calculations provide data redundancy, and the parity is stored with the data. This means that the parity is distributed across the number of drives configured in the volume. (*Parity* is a term for error checking.) Parity algorithms contain Error Correction Code (ECC) capabilities, which calculates parity for a given stripe or chunk of data within a RAID volume. If a single drive fails, the RAID 5 array can reconstruct that data from the parity information held on other disks.

Figure 3.6 illustrates the physical placement of stripes (DATA 01 through DATA 04), with their corresponding parities distributed across the five disks in the volume.

Figure 3.6
RAID 5

DISK A	DISK B	DISK C	DISK D	DISK E
DATA 01	DATA 02	DATA 03	DATA 04	Parity 01
DATA 11	DATA 12	DATA 13	Parity 02	DATA 14
DATA 21	DATA 22	Parity 03	DATA 23	DATA 24
DATA 31	Parity 04	DATA 32	DATA 33	DATA 34

Figure 3.6 is a four-way striped RAID 5 illustration where data and parity are distributed.

RAID 5 is not recommended for OLTP because of the extremely poor performance of small writes at high concurrency levels. This is because the continuous processes of reading a stripe, calculating the new parity, and writing the stripe back to the disk (with new parity) will make the disk write significantly more slowly.

All of these RAID technologies have their pros and cons, but Oracle Corporation has developed a methodology based on the RAID 01 technology for best placement of data among all the allocated group of disks, called Stripe and Mirror Everything (SAME). Before we discuss this methodology at length, let's briefly discuss Oracle data operations, which will help us better understand why Oracle Corporation chose to develop such a methodology.

3.2   Data operations

Oracle RDBMS has several datafiles to store various types of data elements, such as table data, index data, redo data, and so on, and several types of operations, such as INSERT, UPDATE, DELETE, and SELECT, to manipulate this data. Depending on the nature of the application, these operations can affect a very small or a very large amount of data. For example, in an OLTP application, normal operations are singleton SELECT's; queries that return only a single row and are efficiently satisfied by an index lookup. However, in a data warehouse application, the operations are normally range retrievals, and the data is normally retrieved through much more expensive scan operations. In both cases, based on the configuration, the data may be retrieved using Oracle's parallel query technology. In certain cases, this could be a complex operation where multiple tables are joined, and in other cases, this could take place after sorting the data in a specific order. When data is retrieved, it is possible that an appropriate index will be available and Oracle will perform index retrieval, but if the optimizer decides that a scan operation is more efficient, the process steps through all the rows in the table to retrieve the appropriate data.

Now, besides the DML operations and SELECT statements, Oracle's method of operation when managing redo and undo is also different. For example, redo is an open-ended write call, whereas undo is actually an INSERT operation. There is also an INSERT into the advanced queue tables, which is retrieved by Oracle Streams using SELECT queries.

Oracle databases have to support a wide range of data access operations, some of which are relatively simple, whereas others are tremendously complicated. The challenge for Oracle Corporation and Oracle DBAs is to establish a storage subsystem that is easy to manage and yet capable of handling a wide range of data access requests.

3.3   SAME

The goal of the SAME configuration is to make the configuration and management of disks as simple as possible. There are four basic rules followed in the SAME methodology [3]:

1.   Stripe all files across all disks using a 1-MB stripe width.

2.   Provide redundancy to the disks by mirroring them.

3.   Place frequently accessed data on the outside half of the disk drives.

4.   Subset data by partition, not disks.

Let's elaborate a bit more on each of these rules :

1.   *Stripe all files across all disks using a 1-MB stripe width.* Apart from the administrative benefits obtained from not having to constantly move files around in order to compensate for long disk queues caused by overutilized disks, striping files across all disks equalizes load across disk drives, eliminating (or minimizing) hot spots and providing the full bandwidth of all the disk drives for any kind of operation. Removing hot spots improves response time by shortening disk queues. A 1-MB stripe width is good for sequential access. A smaller size could cause seek time to increase and to become a large fraction of the total I/O time [3].

2.   *Provide redundancy to the disks by mirroring them.* Keeping a mirror image of the data provides redundancy to avoid system outages caused by disk failures. The only way to lose data that is mirrored is to have multiple, simultaneous disk failures. With today's advanced disk technologies, the probability of multiple failures is relatively low.

3.   *Place frequently accessed data on the outside half of the disk drives.* As shown in Figure 3.2 and the discussions in the previous sections, files located toward the outer portion of the disks are easily accessible, reducing the access (seek) times to get actual data. We also discussed that since the outer sectors have a larger diameter, more data can be stored as compared to the inner sectors. With larger-capacity high-speed disks available at a much reduced price, it is worthwhile to store frequently used data on the outer sectors, even if the inner sectors have to be left empty or must contain less frequently used data such as backups, archive log files, or other least reused data.

4.   *Subset data by partition, not disks.* The RAID configuration results in files being spread across multiple disks. As illustrated in Figure 3.4, partitions or stripes are created across all disks, providing an opportunity to logically separate datafiles while physically locating them on the same set of disks.

Apart from performance and availability factors, one drawback that all system administrators and DBAs face today is restrictions to adding disks to the existing disk volume groups with the existing technology. Even if the SAME methodology is followed, adding disks to an existing volume group is not easily achievable unless the volume group is redone. Redoing existing volume groups would require the database or tablespace to be taken offline, data copied to secondary storage, disks added and formatted, and data restored back to this location. With the volume of data and the downtime requirements, this is seldom done.

3.4   Oracle Managed Files

In the previous sections, we discussed that one of the key features defined in the SAME methodology is the placement of files on disks. This piece of functionality was originally introduced in Oracle Database Version 9*i* called Oracle Managed Files (OMF). Under this feature, a specific disk is assigned to Oracle, and Oracle creates the required tablespaces and datafiles. The file location is identified by the `DB_CREATE_FILE_DEST` and `DB_RECOVERY_FILE_DEST` parameters. The value is normally a disk or stripe path that contains megabytes or gigabytes of storage space. Using this location, Oracle creates and manages the required files automatically.

Bridging the gaps and deficiencies between the various disk management technologies and those defined in the SAME methodology, Oracle Corporation has introduced a new disk management feature in Oracle Database 10*g* called Automatic Storage Management (ASM). ASM is based on the SAME methodology, but Oracle manages the placement of datafiles on the striped disks. Since Oracle knows how its data is being stored and retrieved, it is able to manage these disks to achieve optimal performance. In essence, ASM leverages both SAME and OMF.

3.5   Storage options for RAC

3.5.1   RAW devices

Raw devices are a contiguous region of a disk accessed by a UNIX character-device interface. This interface provides raw access to the underlying device, arranging for direct I/O between a process and the logical disk. Therefore, the issuance of a write command by a process to the I/O system directly moves the data to the device.

3.5.2 Clustered file system

A traditional file system is a hierarchical tree of directories and files implemented on a raw device partition through the file system of the kernel. The file system uses the concept of a buffering cache, which optimizes the number of times the operating system must access the disk. The file system releases a process that is executing a write to disk by taking control of the operation, thus freeing the process to continue other functions. The file system then attempts to cache or retain the data to be written until multiple data writes can be done at the same time. This can enhance system performance.

System failures before writing the data from the cache can result in the loss of file system integrity. Additionally, the file system adds overhead to any operation that reads or writes data in direct accordance with its physical layout. Clustered file systems allow access from multiple hosts to the same file system data. This reduces the number of multiple copies of the same data, while distributing the load across those hosts going to the same data.

A Clustered File System (CFS) bridges the gap between the raw device and its administrative drawbacks, providing an easier-to-manage storage management solution. Oracle supports several types of clustered file systems (e.g., Oracle Clustered File System [OCFS], Veritas Clustered File System (VCFS), IBM GPFS, Tru64 file system). These file systems have been popularly used on their respective supported platforms. VCFS is used on Sun clusters and more recently on AIX platforms, and Tru64 file system has been used on HP-Tru64 environments. OCFS was developed by Oracle Corporation and supports both the Windows and Linux environments.

 Note: Installation and configuration of OCFS 1.0 and OCFS 2.0 are discussed in Appendix C.

3.6 Automatic storage management (ASM)

One could argue that ASM is not a new or unique technology. Several vendors today, such as Veritas, EMC, IBM, HP, and others, provide storage management solutions. Veritas volume manager software provides options where disks can be added to the existing volume groups. However, ASM is different because it leverages knowledge regarding datafile usage held within the Oracle RDBMS. ASM provides the capabilities of both file system and volume manager, and additionally, using the OMF hierarchical structure, it distributes I/O load across all available resources, optimizing performance.

ASM is implemented as an additional Oracle instance, which is present on each node that hosts an Oracle instance and uses the ASM facilities. ASM virtualizes the underlying disk storage: it acts as an interface between the Oracle instance and the storage devices that contain the actual data.

Here are some of the key benefits of ASM [26]:

- I/O is spread evenly across all available disk drives to prevent hot spots and maximize performance.

- ASM eliminates the need for overprovisioning and maximizes storage resource utilization, facilitating database consolidation.

- ASM provides inherent large file support.

- Supports Oracle single-instance Database 10*g*, as well as RAC.

- ASM reduces Oracle Database 10*g* cost and complexity without compromising performance or availability.

- ASM supports mirroring of data onto different disks, providing for fault tolerance, and can be built on top of vendor-supplied reliable storage mechanisms.

- Files are created (using a standard file-naming convention) on these logical units by spreading them evenly across all disks that belong to the group.

- Disks can be added to existing disk groups dynamically without interrupting the database.

- Extents are automatically rebalanced by moving them among disks when disks are added or removed from the configuration.

- ASM integrates the OMF hierarchical structure and removes the need for file manageability.

- ASM can provide a storage management solution on single or cluster Symmetric Multiprocessor (SMP) machines.

3.6.1   ASM installation

The Oracle software required to manage and maintain the ASM components is installed as part of the regular Oracle software installation. That is, ORACLE_HOME will contain all the binaries required to support an ASM instance. However, Oracle also supports having a separate home for ASM (e.g., `ASM_HOME`). Basically, Oracle binaries are installed twice, once into a new home called `ASM_HOME` and again into the standard `ORACLE_HOME`. Furthermore, these homes can be managed by different users; for example, `ORACLE_HOME` can be owned by the traditional `oracle` user, and `ASM_HOME` can be owned by another user.

While maintaining two separate homes and owners is not a requirement, keeping them separate provides several advantages and should be considered a best practice:

1. *Allowing ASM to support multiple versions of Oracle.* When a single ASM instance supports several databases, there can be situations where one or more of these databases are not at the same release level. Maintaining separate homes will allow support for these situations.

2. *Protecting the ASM instance and its binaries from regular DBAs.* ASM instance and storage configuration can be controlled by a different administrative user.

3. *Allowing disks and storage configurations to be protected by the system administrators.* The `ASM_HOME` will be created using a different administrative operating system user with different privileges and will be managed by the system administrators for security reasons.

 Note:

1. When managing ASM in a separate home managed by a different administrator, it is important that each of the owners be members of the DBA group, and the disks must provide read/write permission to the DBA group.

2. Installation and configuration of Oracle software is discussed in Chapter 4.

On operating systems such as Linux, before the disks are assigned to ASM, they have to be prepared using one of the following options:

- Set up raw disks that will be used by ASM.

- Install and set up disks using Oracle-provided ASM libraries. Libraries required for platforms such as Linux can be downloaded

from Oracle Technology Network (OTN), http://www.oracle.com/
technology/tech/linux/asmlib/index.html).

 Note: Versions of the libraries to be installed depend on the version of
Linux configured on the servers. Linux kernel version 2.4 requires ASM
library version 1.0, and kernel version 2.6 requires ASM library version 2.0.

ASM Library (ASMLIB)

ASMLIB is an add-on (optional) module that simplifies the management
and discovery of ASM disks. It provides an alternative interface for ASM to
identify and access block devices. ASMLIB consists of two components:
API layer and device layer.

The API provides four major enhancements over the standard interfaces:

- *Disk discovery.* Providing more information about the storage
  attributes to the database and the DBA. Device discovery provides
  persistent identification and naming of storage devices and solves
  manageability issues on operating system platforms such as Linux
  and Windows. The discovery process removes the challenges of having disks added to one node and other nodes in the cluster not knowing about the addition. Meaning, once a disk is configured to be an
  ASM disk it will appear on all nodes without a need for a per node
  configuration.

  Standard disk names are typically determined by discovery order
  and can change between system boots. The out of order device discovery and permission problem is resolved by ASMLIB. On systems
  that have smaller number of disks the out of order issue may not be
  of significant issue, however on systems with greater than 100 disks
  this would be a serious manageability issue.

- *I/O processing.* To enable more efficient I/O and optimization. Traditionally every Oracle process on all instances has to open all ASM
  disks. On large systems this could translate to over several millions of
  file descriptors. Certain operating system such as Linux do not allow
  this many descriptors. ASMLIB helps resolve this limitation, by
  allowing one portal device to access all the disks creating one file
  descriptor per process. This reduces the number of calls to the O/S
  when performing I/O.

- *Usage hints.* It is a mechanism for Oracle kernel to pass suggestive metadata information such as I/O priority and caching hints when process an I/O request. This helps the storage device to predict I/O behavior and choose caching policies to optimize performance. For example, hints indicating writes to the online redo log files or writing to a regular data file versus initializing a new online log file. Such hints help determine caching policies.

- *Write Validation.* By creating tags ASMLIB protects administrators from accidentally overwriting a disk that is in use. By associating partition tags with disk partitions can assign a portion of a disk to a particular application and have the disk verify if writes are from the correct application.

The device layer provides the functionality of disk stamping by creating a unique identifier (ASM header) on each disk medium, and it provides access to these identifiers.

Windows: The disk stamping functionality is performed using the Oracle-provided ASMTOOLG utility located in $ORACLE_HOME\BIN if only one home is used or $ASM_HOME/BIN if a separate ASM home is configured (see Figure 3.7). This utility stamps each partition with an ASM label so that Oracle can recognize these partitions as candidate disks for the ASM instance.

ASMLIB installation

Connect to the node as user root to install the various packages:

```
# su root
[root@oradb1 downloads]# rpm -Uvh oracleasm-support-1.0.2-1.i386.rpm \
                oracleasmlib-1.0.0-1.i386.rpm\
                oracleasm-2.4.21-EL-1.0.0-1.i686.rpm
Preparing... ################################### [100%]
```

This operation will install the ASM required library files on Linux.

Figure 3.7
asmtool

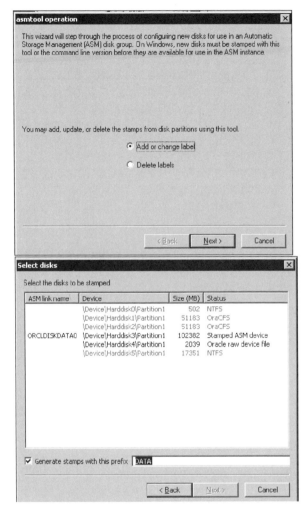

3.6.2 Configuring ASMLIB

The installation of the library packages places a utility in the /etc/init.d/ directory called oracleasm. This utility is used to configure and initialize the various disks for ASM. The next step is to configure ASM:

```
[root@oradb1 root]# /etc/init.d/oracleasm configure
Configuring the Oracle ASM library driver.

This will configure the on-boot properties of the Oracle ASM library
driver.  The following questions will determine whether the driver is
```

```
loaded on boot and what permissions it will have.  The current values
will be shown in brackets ('[]').  Hitting without typing an
answer will keep that current value.  Ctrl-C will abort.

Default user to own the driver interface []: oracle
Default group to own the driver interface []: dba
Start Oracle ASM library driver on boot (y/n) [n]: y
Fix permissions of Oracle ASM disks on boot (y/n) [y]: y
Writing Oracle ASM library driver configuration          [  OK  ]
Creating /dev/oracleasm mount point                      [  OK  ]
Loading module "oracleasm"                               [  OK  ]
Mounting ASMlib driver filesystem                        [  OK  ]
Scanning system for ASM disks                            [  OK  ]
```

 Note: If libraries are used to set up the disks for ASM, the above libraries should be installed and configured on all nodes participating in the cluster.

Once the configuration is complete, the required ASM libraries for Linux are installed and enabled during system boot time. The installation and loading of the library files after system reboot can be verified using the following:

```
[root@oradb1 root]# lsmod
Module                   Size  Used by     Tainted: GF
parport_pc              18724   2  (autoclean)
lp                       8932   0  (autoclean)
parport                 36800   2  (autoclean) [parport_pc lp]
autofs                  13204   0  (autoclean) (unused)
oracleasm               14224   1
ocfs                   297856   7
audit                   89592   1
.......
```

The library configuration creates an ASM parameter file located in the /etc/sysconfig/ directory called oracleasm. This parameter file contains parameters and definitions used during automatic loading of the Oracle ASM library kernel driver. The parameters contained in this file are listed in Table 3.1.

Table 3.1　*ASMLib Configuration Parameters*

Parameter	Value	Description
ORACLEASM_ENABLED	TRUE	This parameter defines if the ASM library kernel driver should be loaded automatically during system startup
ORACLEASM_UID	oracle	This parameter defines the owner of ASM mount points
ORACLEASM_GID	<o/s group>	This defines the operating system group that owns the ASM mount points
ORACLEASM_SCANBOOT	TRUE	This defines if disks are to be fixed to ASM during system startup, identified through a disk scan operation
ORACLEASM_SCANEXCLUDE	<disk pattern>	This identifies matching patterns of disks to be excluded during disk scan operation at system startup or ASM library startup
ORACLEASM_SCANORDER	<disk pattern>	This identifies matching patterns of disks that provide the scan order during disk scanning

 Note: ASMLib can be used with multipath[1] disks; however, it is not recommended with Linux kernel version 2.4.

What is multipathing?

An I/O path generally consists of an initiator port, fabric port, target port, and Logical Unit Number (LUN). Each permutation of this I/O path is considered an independent path. Dynamic multipathing/failover tools aggregate these independent paths into a single logical path. This path abstraction provides I/O load-balancing across the host bus adapters (HBAs), as well as nondisruptive failovers on I/O path failures. Examples of multipathing software include EMC PowerPath, Hitachi HDLM, IBM SDDPCM, and Sun Traffic Manager. While Oracle does not certify these multipathing tools, ASM[2] does leverage multipathing tools, provided the

1.　The reader is advised to read Metalink Note 309815.1 regarding the use of ASMLib with multipath disks.

path or device produced by the multipathing tool returns a successful return code.

3.6.3   Architecture

The ASM database comprises the following components:

- ASM instance
- Disks
- Disk groups
- Failure groups
- ASM templates
- Background processes
- Cluster synchronization services
- ASM allocation units

ASM instance

An ASM instance is an Oracle instance that includes many of the usual background processes and the memory structure of any Oracle instance. However, if you compare this against a normal Oracle RDBMS instance, this new instance is not a complete instance but a smaller subset of a regular RDBMS instance. This means that while most of the background processes are present in an ASM instance and administrators can make a connection to the ASM instance, no queries or dynamic views (with the exception of a few views required by ASM) are available. ASM architecture is vastly different from an RDBMS instance and contains no physical files, such as log files, control files, or datafiles.

The primary function of the ASM instance is to manage the storage system. Apart from being the owner of the disks, the ASM instance acts as a bridge between the Oracle database and the physical storage. To differentiate between a regular database instance and an ASM instance, Oracle has introduced a new parameter called INSTANCE_TYPE. The parameter INSTANCE_TYPE has two possible values, ASM and RDBMS, which represent ASM and a regular database instance, respectively.

---

2.   The reader is advised to read Metalink Note 294869.1 for additional details regarding ASM and multipathing.

```
SQL> show parameter instance_type

NAME                               TYPE          VALUE
---------------------------    -----------   ----------------
instance_type                      string        asm
```

3.6.4 Disks

In Sections 3.1.1 to 3.1.5 we discussed how disks are striped and mirrored. We also discussed how each stripe can be considered a partition that can store one or several files, depending on the method of storage configuration selected (i.e., RAW devices or a file system). ASM is no different. It also requires disks, but disks are allocated to ASM before they are striped and mirrored. ASM will perform its own striping by default and optional mirroring. In other words, ASM has inherent automatic file-level striping and mirroring capabilities.

A disk can be a partition of a physical spindle, the entire spindle, or a RAID group set, depending on how the storage array presents the LUN to the operating system. Each operating system will have its own unique representation of SCSI disk naming. For example, on Solaris systems, the disks will generally have the following SCSI name format: *CwTxDySz*, where "C" is the controller number, "T" is the target, "D" is the LUN/disk number, and "S" is the partition. Again, on Solaris systems, it is a best practice to create a partition on the disk, whereas on certain others it is not.

In SAN environments, the disks are appropriately zoned or LUN masked within the SAN fabric and are visible to the operating system. Once disks have been identified, they need to be discovered by ASM. On Linux-based systems, disks can be configured as direct raw devices or can be ASM aware using the ASMLIB utility discussed earlier. When configuring ASM disks using basic raw devices (as listed in Table 3.2), no additional configuration is required. However, if the ASMLIB utility is used, then ASM disks are created using the oracleasm script as follows:

```
/etc/init.d/oracleasm createdisk <volume name> <physical disk name>

[root@oradb1 root]# /etc/init.d/oracleasm createdisk AVOL1 /dev/sdg
  Creating Oracle ASM disk "AVOL1"                            [  OK  ]
```

When ASM scans for disks, it will use that string (listed in Table 3.2) and find any devices it has permission to open. Upon successful discovery, the V$ASM_DISK view on the ASM instance will list these disks.

On successful completion of making the disks ASM aware, the next step is to group these disks into disk groups. Disk group configuration can be done in one of three ways:

1.   Interactively from the ASM instance (command line)

2.   During the database configuration process using the Database Configuration Assistant (DBCA)

3.   Using Enterprise Manager (EM)

Disk groups are similar in concept to volume groups on traditional storage systems.

Best Practice: Ensure that the disks allocated to ASM have appropriate access rights (read/write) to all the databases and ASM instances.

3.6.5 Disk groups

After disks have been discovered by ASM, they can be grouped together for easy management and for Oracle to apply the SAME methodology (i.e., to stripe and mirror the disks). The disk group is the highest-level data structure in ASM and is analogous to the Logical Volume Manager (LVM) provided by several vendors, such as Veritas. However, unlike the LVM volume groups, the ASM disk groups are not visible to the user. ASM disk groups are only visible to ASM and ASM clients, which include RDBMS instances, RMAN, the ASM command-line interface (asmcmd), and so on. Hence, all access to the Oracle files and other related data must be performed using an Oracle instance and using an Oracle-provided tool such as RMAN or SQL scripts.

How is the ASM instance aware of the disks that have been made ASM aware? Under all operating systems (using Oracle-provided ASM libraries or not), disks to be used by ASM should be made ASM aware. When using tools such as DBCA, disks are automatically discovered by the tool. However, when an ASM instance is manually created, this is achieved by assigning a search string to the `ASM_DISKSTRING` parameter that is part of the ASM instance.

For example, `ASM_DISKSTRING= 'ORCL:AVOL*'` indicates that all disk volumes with the `AVOL` suffix created using the Linux ASMLIB routines are candidates used to create disk groups.

```
SQL> show parameter asm_diskstring

NAME                            TYPE          VALUE
------------------------------  -----------   --------------------------
asm_diskstring                  string        ORCL:AVOL*
```

 Note: Ensure that the ASM instance has been created and started before attempting to create disk groups. ASM instances can be created manually using scripts or using DBCA.

Table 3.2 lists the default ASM disk strings for the various operating systems. The default search string is `NULL`; however, DBCA will search and replace the `NULL` values with the strings presented in Table 3.2.

Table 3.2   *Default ASM Disk Strings*

Operating System	Default Search String
Solaris	/dev/rdsk/*
Windows	\\.orcl:disk*
Linux (ASMLIB)	ORCL:disk*
HPUX	/dev/rdsk/*
HP Tru64	/dev/rdisk/*
AIX	/dev/rhdisk/*

 Best Practice: When configuring raw disks for ASM, make sure they are partitioned using utilities such as `fdisk` on Linux or `idisk` on HP-UX. The goal is to create one partition that comprises the entire disk.

3.6.6   **Using the command line to create disk groups**

Disk groups are created from the command line after connecting to the ASM instance on one node. The following syntax is the simplest form and will create an ASM disk group:

```
SQL> CREATE DISKGROUP asmgrp2 DISK 'ORCL:AVOL10',
'ORCL:AVOL11';


Diskgroup created.
```

After the disk group is created, the metadata information, including the disk group name, redundancy type, and other creation details such as the creation date, is loaded into the SGA of the ASM instance and written to the appropriate disk headers within each disk group. Creating a new disk group also updates the parameter ASM_DISKGROUPS in the ASM instance.

```
SQL> show parameter asm_diskgroup

NAME                             TYPE          VALUE
-------------------------------- ----------- --------------------------------
asm_diskgroups                   string        ASMGRP1, ASMGRP2
```

The disk group is created, and the disks that are allocated to it can be verified using the following query from an ASM instance:

```
COL DiskGroup format a10
COL Disks format a10
SELECT G.NAME DiskGroup,
 G.STATE GroupState,
       D.NAME Disks,
       D.STATE DiskState,
       G.TYPE Type,
       D.TOTAL_MB DSize
FROM   V$ASM_DISKGROUP G,
       V$ASM_DISK D
WHERE D.GROUP_NUMBER=G.GROUP_NUMBER
AND    G.NAME='ASMGRP2'
/
```

DISKGROUP	GROUPSTATE	DISKS	DISKSTATE	TYPE	DSIZE
ASMGRP2	**MOUNTED**	**AVOL10**	NORMAL	**NORMAL**	19085
ASMGRP2	**MOUNTED**	**AVOL11**	NORMAL	**NORMAL**	19085

From this output, it is verified that ASMGRP2 has two disks AVOL10 and AVOL11 that are created with redundancy type NORMAL (listed under the TYPE column) and of equal size, and the group is in a MOUNTED state. While a disk can only be allocated to one disk group at a time, a disk group can contain datafiles from many different Oracle databases. Alternatively, a database can store datafiles in multiple disk groups of the same ASM instance.

 Note: The column DISKS in the output above shows the name assigned to the disk; the physical path of the original disk can be obtained from the PATH column in the V$ASM_DISK view.

Based on the disks that have been configured and allocated to a disk group, the header status of the disk changes. For example, the following query indicates the header status is MEMBER:

```
SQL> SELECT INST_ID,NAME,PATH,STATE,HEADER_STATUS FROM GV$ASM_DISK;
```

INST_ID	NAME	PATH	STATE	HEADER_STATU
3	AVOL1	ORCL:AVOL1	NORMAL	MEMBER
3	AVOL2	ORCL:AVOL2	NORMAL	MEMBER
1	AVOL1	ORCL:AVOL1	NORMAL	MEMBER
1	AVOL2	ORCL:AVOL2	NORMAL	MEMBER

Disks have various header statuses that reflect their membership state with a disk group. Disks can have the following header statuses:

FORMER	This state declares that the disk was formerly part of a disk group.
CANDIDATE	When a disk is in this state, it is available to be added to a disk group.

| MEMBER | This state indicates that a disk is already part of a disk group. |
| PROVISIONED | This state is similar to candidate in that the disk is available to disk groups. However, the provisioned state indicates that this disk has been configured or made available using ASMLIB. |

Best Practice: To take complete advantage of the characteristics of ASM, all of the disks in a disk group should have similar performance characteristics.

Best Practice: Assign the entire disk to a disk group. Assigning multiple slices of the same disk to a disk group can cause significant performance issues.

Note: Check the "How ASM allocates extents?" section later in this chapter for more details on assignment of disks to a disk group.

Best Practice: To avoid polynomial errors, it is good to have an even number of disks of the same size in a disk group.

3.6.7 Failure groups

In non-ASM disk configuration, depending on the criticality of the data stored on the storage devices and the business requirements, the system administrators will select an appropriate RAID implementation (e.g., RAID 10, RAID 01). In such an implementation, the mirrored disks will act as a backup in case the primary storage system fails. This mirrored disks concept is called a failure group in ASM, the only difference being that mirroring is done at the file extent level and not at the disk level. As a result of this, ASM only uses the spare capacity of space available in existing disk groups instead of the traditional mirroring methods that required an additional hot spare disk. Under this method, when ASM allocates a primary extent of a file to one disk in a disk group, it allocates a mirror copy of that extent to another disk in the disk group. Basically, the primary extents on a given disk will have their respective mirror extents on one of several partner disks in the disk group. ASM ensures that the primary extent and its mirror copy never reside in the same failure group.

The failure group is directly related to the type of redundancy used in the configuration of a disk group. ASM supports three types of redundancies:

1.   Normal or two-way mirroring redundancy

2.   High or three-way mirroring redundancy

3.   External redundancy

3.6.8   Normal redundancy

This is the default redundancy level; under this category, Oracle creates a two-way mirror. That is, for every file that is written to this group, Oracle maintains a copy of the information in another set of disks designated by the FAILGROUP command while creating a disk group. If no FAILGROUP is specified and only the DISKGROUP is mentioned, then Oracle will randomly pick disks from the disk group to place files for redundancy.

 Note: Actual placement of files to obtain redundancy is internal to the functioning of ASM and currently[3] there is no external visibility.

The following is the syntax to create normal redundancy with explicit placement of mirror images. If no FAILGROUP is mentioned, Oracle stores the mirrored data within the same disk group.

```
CREATE DISKGROUP ASMGRP3 NORMAL REDUNDANCY
FAILGROUP FLGRP31 DISK 'ORCL:AVOL10','ORCL:AVOL11'
FAILGROUP FLGRP32 DISK 'ORCL:AVOL12','ORCL:AVOL13';

COL DiskGroup format a10
COL Disks format a10
SELECT G.NAME DiskGroup,
  G.STATE GroupState,
        D.NAME Disks,
        D.FAILGROUP FAILGROUP,
```

```
        D.STATE DiskState,
        G.TYPE Type,
        D.TOTAL_MB DSize
FROM   V$ASM_DISKGROUP G,
       V$ASM_DISK D
WHERE D.GROUP_NUMBER=G.GROUP_NUMBER
  AND G.NAME='ASMGRP4';
/
```

DISKGROUP	GROUPSTATE	DISKS	FAILGROUP	DISKSTAT	TYPE	DSIZE
ASMGRP3	MOUNTED	AVOL10	**FLGRP31**	NORMAL	**NORMAL**	19085
ASMGRP3	MOUNTED	AVOL11	**FLGRP31**	NORMAL	**NORMAL**	19085
ASMGRP3	MOUNTED	AVOL12	**FLGRP32**	NORMAL	**NORMAL**	19085
ASMGRP3	MOUNTED	AVOL13	**FLGRP32**	NORMAL	**NORMAL**	19085

 Best Practice: To obtain the true value of redundancy, it is advisable to create failure groups on separate disks that are part of different failure groups

3.6.9 High redundancy

This level of redundancy provides the highest protection of data using three-way mirroring, where Oracle maintains three copies of all data stored on the disks. While creating disk groups with this redundancy level, ASM requires that three failure groups be created.

This syntax is the definition of a three FAILGROUP high-redundancy disk group:

```
CREATE DISKGROUP ASMGRP4 HIGH REDUNDANCY
  FAILGROUP FLGRP41 DISK 'ORCL:AVOL10'
  FAILGROUP FLGRP42 DISK 'ORCL:AVOL11'
  FAILGROUP FLGRP43 DISK 'ORCL:AVOL12';
```

A high-redundancy disk group creation can be verified using the query from the section "Normal redundancy."

DISKGROUP	GROUPSTATE	DISKS	FAILGROUP	DISKSTAT	TYPE	SIZE
ASMGRP4	MOUNTED	AVOL10	**FLGRP41**	NORMAL	**HIGH**	19085
ASMGRP4	MOUNTED	AVOL11	**FLGRP42**	NORMAL	**HIGH**	19085
ASMGRP4	MOUNTED	AVOL12	**FLGRP43**	NORMAL	**HIGH**	19085

 Note: In the previous output, it should be noted that there are three failure groups, each containing only one physical disk.

The following example illustrates that a disk can only be assigned to one disk group. Allocation of disks (AVOL12, AVOL13) to multiple disk groups returns an ORA–15072 error.

```
CREATE DISKGROUP ASMGRP4 HIGH REDUNDANCY
FAILGROUP FLGRP41 DISK 'ORCL:AVOL10','ORCL:AVOL11'
FAILGROUP FLGRP42 DISK 'ORCL:AVOL12','ORCL:AVOL13'
FAILGROUP FLGRP43 DISK 'ORCL:AVOL12','ORCL:AVOL13';

SQL> CREATE DISKGROUP ASMGRP4 HIGH REDUNDANCY
  2  *
  3  ERROR at line 1:
  4  ORA-15018: diskgroup cannot be created
ORA-15072: command requires at least 3 failure groups,
specified only 2
```

Similarly, a disk can be allocated and mounted by only one disk group. In the following example, an attempt was made to assign an already mounted disk to another disk group. This resulted in an ORA–15029 error.

```
SQL> CREATE DISKGROUP ASMGRP6 DISK 'ORCL:AVOL10';
CREATE DISKGROUP ASMGRP6 DISK 'ORCL:AVOL10'
*
ERROR at line 1:
ORA-15018: diskgroup cannot be created
ORA-15029: disk 'ORCL:AVOL10' is already mounted by this
instance
```

Note: On successful creation of a disk group, the disk headers are updated. Disks with preexisting ASM headers cannot be used as part of a disk group. The disks have to be reformatted before they are reused.

3.6.10 External redundancy

The third type of redundancy is where Oracle does not mirror data or files but lets the administrator utilize the redundancy available at the operating system level or that was provided by the storage system vendors. System administrators can set up disk mirroring for the disks allocated to ASM.

```
CREATE DISKGROUP ASMGRP5 EXTERNAL REDUNDANCY
    DISK 'ORCL:AVOL10';
```

DISKGROUP	GROUPSTATE	DISKS	DISKSTAT	TYPE	DSIZE
ASMGRP5	MOUNTED	AVOL10	NORMAL	**EXTERN**	19085

From the previous output, the `TYPE` column indicates that the disk group has been created with the external redundancy type.

Best Practice: External redundancy should be used in the case of high-end storage solutions where an external RAID solution is available. Using external redundancy will result in offloading from the host performance mirroring operations and utilize less CPU. Also, storage-based RAID solutions might perform better since they are more intimate with the disks and have their own cache.

Best Practice: `FAILGROUPS` should be created based on the type of failure and the type of component being protected, meaning that different components of the storage array have different needs and criticality to the storage array varies from one to another. For example, controller failure requires that each `FAILGROUP` be placed on different controllers.

Once a disk group is defined with a specific redundancy type, if this needs to be changed subsequently, another disk group needs to be created with the appropriate redundancy type, and data must be moved from the existing disk group to the new disk group using RMAN or the supplied PL/SQL package `DBMS_FILE_TRANSFER`.

Best Practice: Oracle tablespaces that contain multiple datafiles can span multiple disk groups with each datafile in a separate diskgroup; to get the best benefits of ASM, it would be ideal to place them all on one disk group. If multiple disk groups are required, care should be taken to place them on disk groups of the same redundancy type.

Disk groups can also be created using DBCA at the time of database creation. Apart from defining or creating disk groups, DBCA will also create and start the ASM instance (if it is not already present and available).

Creation of disk groups using DBCA

After allocating disks for ASM using the `oracleasm` utility provided for Linux platforms, disk groups can be created using DBCA during the database configuration process.

Step 7 (Figure 3.8[a]) of the database configuration process is the storage options selection screen. This step provides the option to select ASM as the method of storage for the database that is being created.

Note: When installing ASM on a single-instance configuration, ensure that the cluster synchronization services (CSS) module is installed. When installing ASM on a RAC cluster or when installing ASM on multiple nodes to share single disk groups, ensure that the Oracle Clusterware is installed.

Select the "Automatic Storage Management (ASM)" option in Step 7 (from DBCA) as shown in Figure 3.8(a), if the ASM instance is created for the first time, or the "Configure Automatic Storage Management" option on the initial DBCA screen shown in Figure 3.8(b), if the database was initially created using a file system or raw devices. ASM can be added later using DBCA and selecting the option.

The next few screens are all related to the configuration of the ASM instance. Step 8 (Figure 3.9) identifies the default password for user `SYS`. The Oracle RDBMS instance will use this information to connect to the ASM instance.

Figure 3.8(a)
Storage Options

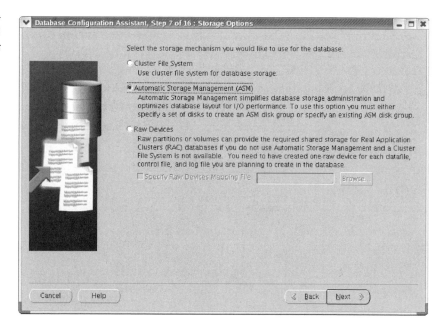

Figure 3.8(b)
Operations

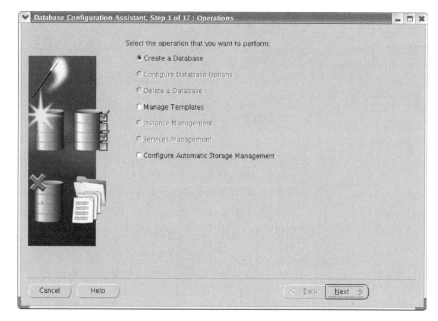

Also part of Step 8 (Figure 3.9) is the parameter file selection screen. Unlike in the standard database configuration process for ASM, Oracle provides the option to create the initialization parameter file (ASCII) or the server parameter file, `SPFILE` (binary). Based on the user's comfort level, the user can select from one of the available options.

Best Practice: To avoid making changes to multiple pfiles when making any ASM parameter modifications, `SPFILE` should be used. `SPFILE` should be located in shared storage either on a clustered file system or raw device.

Figure 3.9
Create ASM Instance

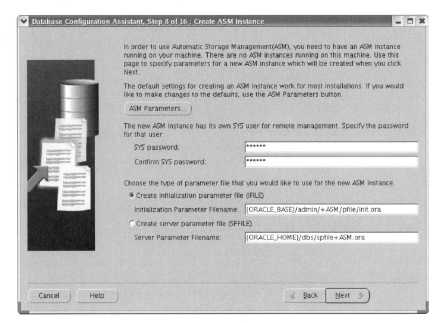

Another option available in Step 8 (Figure 3.9) is to set or change some of the ASM required parameters. This can be accomplished by selecting the ASM parameters button on this screen. If no parameters are to be modified, click "Next."

DBCA will start creating the ASM instances on all nodes in the cluster. Click "OK" to confirm creation of ASM instances (Figure 3.10).

However, in order for ASM to communicate with the Oracle Universal Installer (OUI), the listener should also be present. OUI verifies if the listener is running and prompts the user with a message if it is not (not shown). Click "OK" to start the listener.

The next screen will list all available diskgroups already created for that ASM instance. Selecting a diskgroup from the list will invoke DBCA to create a database within ASM. If no disk groups exist or a new disk group is

Figure 3.10
*ASM Instance
Creation and
Startup*

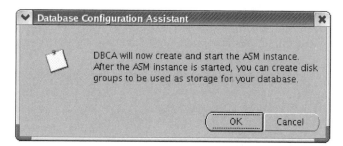

Figure 3.10
*ASM Instance
Creation and
Startup*

desired, then DBCA offers the opportunity to create a new disk group. To create a new disk group, select "Create New" from this screen (not shown).

This will display the "Create Disk Group" screen (Figure 3.11). A list of ASM-ready volumes is listed. Enter a valid ASM disk group name (`ASMRAC_DATA1`) and select the volumes to be part of this group (`ORCL:ASMVOL1` and `ORCL:ASMVOL2`). Click "OK" when selection is complete. This will create the disk group `ASMRAC_DATA1` and mount the disk group on all ASM instances.

Figure 3.11
Create Disk Group

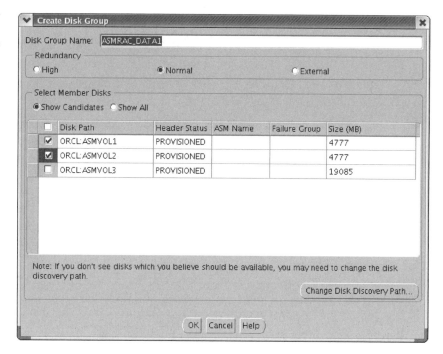

The next screen illustrated in Figure 3.12 (the final screen of step 8) displays all of the ASM disk groups and provides the option to select the appropriate disk groups that will be used for database storage.

Figure 3.12
ASM Disk Groups

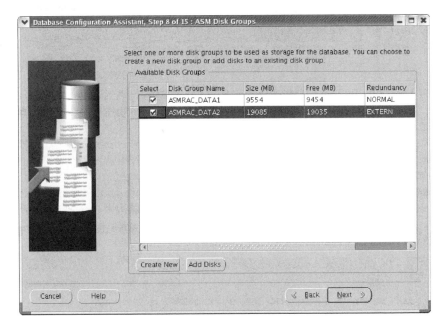

Once selected, click "Next"; this completes the creation of ASM disk groups using the DBCA.

Note: While the ASM instance creation and configuration process is part of DBCA and is invoked during database configuration, this section has been included in this chapter for completeness.

Create disk groups using EM

A third method for creating disk groups is using EM, which provides visibility to an ASM instance and its administration, maintenance, and performance aspects.

The screen illustrated in Figure 3.13 is the main (home) page of the +ASM instance from EM. From this page, other ASM-related pages can be accessed.

Figure 3.13
*EM ASM Home
Page*

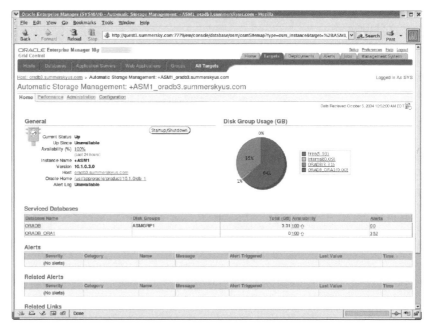

Selecting the "Administration" option from the ASM home page (Figure 3.13) will display any currently present disk groups, as illustrated in Figure 3.14.

From this screen (Figure 3.14), select the "Create" button to start the creation of a new disk group. The screen illustrated in Figure 3.15 is displayed containing all disks that are ASM aware. From this list of disks, a set of disks can be selected to create the disk group. Give the disk group a unique name in the appropriate column.

On this screen, there is also an option to automatically mount the disk group on all participating instances. Click "OK" when all selections are complete. This will start the disk group definition process. When the creation process has completed, EM displays a confirmation message (Figure 3.16), along with a list of disk groups present.

3.6.11 ASM templates

Under the traditional methods of tablespace definition, certain characteristics (e.g., type of file, size, type of organization) are specified during tablespace creation. While these characteristics are also required when creating tablespaces on ASM, such characteristics are predefined in the form of templates.

Figure 3.14
*EM ASM
Administration*

Figure 3.14
*EM ASM
Administration*

Figure 3.15
*EM Disk Group
Creation*

Oracle provides several predefined templates that are included in the characteristics of a disk group during its creation. Depending on the type of

Figure 3.16
*EM Disk Group
Creation
Confirmation*

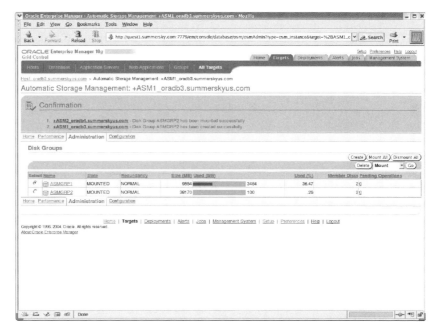

file (e.g., datafile, control file) used during tablespace creation, the appropriate templates are assigned to it. These templates have predefined attributes. Oracle also permits the creation of custom templates or modification of existing templates, based on the specific needs of users.

Table 3.3 provides a list of templates provided by Oracle and their default attributes.

Table 3.3 *Oracle-Provided ASM Templates*

Template	File Type	Redundancy Level	Stripe Type
PARAMETERFILE	Server parameter file (Spfile)	Mirrored	Coarse
DUMPSET	Data pump dumpset	Mirrored	Coarse
CONTROLFILE	Control file	Mirrored	Fine
ARCHIVELOG	Archive logs	Mirrored	Coarse
ONLINELOG	Online logs	Mirrored	Fine
DATAFILE	Datafiles and copies	Mirrored	Coarse

Table 3.3   *Oracle-Provided ASM Templates (continued)*

Template	File Type	Redundancy Level	Stripe Type
TEMPFILE	Temp (temporary) files	Mirrored	Coarse
BACKUPSET	All RMAN-related backup pieces	Mirrored	Coarse
AUTOBACKUP	Automatic backup files	Mirrored	Coarse
XTRANSPORT	Cross-platform converted datafiles	Mirrored	Coarse
CHANGETRACKING	Block change tracking data	Mirrored	Coarse
FLASHBACK	Flashback logs	Mirrored	Fine
DATAGUARDCONFIG	Disaster recovery configuration used by the standby database	Mirrored	Coarse

Since templates are maintained at the disk group level, if a new custom or modified template needs to be created, it has to be defined along with the disk group and applied to a datafile. Existing datafiles cannot be modified to use a different Oracle-provided template. If the datafile attributes need to be changed, a new template should be created with the new attributes and assigned to the disk group. Once this is assigned, it can be applied to the datafile.

The following shows how the template can be created:

```
SQL> ALTER DISKGROUP ASMGRP1 ADD TEMPLATE SSKYDATA ATTRIBUTES
(MIRROR FINE);

Diskgroup altered.
```

In this example, a new template called SSKYDATA, having the attributes MIRRORED with a FINE stripe, was added to the disk group ASMGRP1. Other operations permitted on a template are ALTER and DROP.

Note: System (Oracle-provided) templates are assigned by default to all disk groups when the disk group is created. User-defined templates can only be created for a specific disk group, meaning, once created and assigned to one disk group, they cannot be applied to other disk groups.

The templates contained in a disk group can be determined using the following query:

```
COL DISKGRP FORMAT A15
COL TEMPLATE FORMAT A15

SELECT G.NAME DISKGRP,
       T.NAME TEMPLATE,
       T.REDUNDANCY,
       T.STRIPE
FROM   V$ASM_DISKGROUP G,
       V$ASM_TEMPLATE T
ORDER BY DISKGRP


DISKGRP          TEMPLATE         REDUND STRIPE
---------------  ---------------  ------ ------
ASMGRP1          PARAMETERFILE    MIRROR COARSE
ASMGRP1          DUMPSET          MIRROR COARSE
ASMGRP1          ARCHIVELOG       MIRROR COARSE
ASMGRP1          DATAFILE         MIRROR COARSE
ASMGRP1          BACKUPSET        MIRROR COARSE
ASMGRP1          XTRANSPORT       MIRROR COARSE
ASMGRP1          FLASHBACK        MIRROR FINE
ASMGRP1          SSKYDATA         MIRROR FINE
ASMGRP1          DUMPSET          MIRROR COARSE
ASMGRP1          CHANGETRACKING   MIRROR COARSE
ASMGRP1          XTRANSPORT       MIRROR COARSE
    . . .
```

3.6.12 Stripe types

By default, a database created under ASM will be striped and optionally mirrored as specified in the SAME methodology. Oracle provides two different stripe types while creating disk groups: FINE and COARSE.

1. *FINE stripe type*. When this stripe type is specified, interleaves of 128K chunks across groups of eight allocation units are used. Such a small allocation unit helps in the distribution of I/O operations into multiple smaller-sized I/O operations that can then be executed in parallel.

2. *COARSE stripe type*. When this stripe type is specified, files are spread in one-allocation-unit chunks (with each allocation unit containing at least one file extent) across all of the disks in a disk group. Under this method, ASM evenly spreads files in 1-MB-allocation-unit chunks across all of the disks in a disk group.

Best Practice: Disks in a disk group should have similar size and performance characteristics to obtain optimal I/O.

3.6.13   Disk group in a RAC environment

When using the PFILE option, disk groups created using the command line in a RAC environment are only mounted on the instance where the disk group was initially created. On all other instances, the disk group will have to be manually mounted using the ALTER command.

For example, when a disk group ASMGRP2 is created on instance SSKY1, the disk group is mounted automatically for this instance; however, it remains in a dismounted state on the second instance, SSKY2. This is no different from mounting a disk volume at the operating system level using traditional volume managers. Each disk volume has to be mounted on every node that requires access to it. In an ASM environment, all disk groups created on one instance will have to be manually mounted on all other instances. Once mounted, the disk group will be registered and will automatically be mounted on subsequent restarts of the instances.

```
SQL> CREATE DISKGROUP ASMGRP2 DISK
'ORCL:AVOL10','ORCL:AVOL11';

Diskgroup created.

SQL> SELECT INST_ID,
GROUP_NUMBER,
NAME,
STATE
```

```
FROM GV$ASM_DISKGROUP;

    INST_ID GROUP_NUMBER NAME       STATE
---------- ------------ ---------- -----------
         1            1 ASMGRP1    MOUNTED
         1            2 ASMGRP2    MOUNTED
         2            1 ASMGRP1    MOUNTED
         2            0 ASMGRP2    DISMOUNTED
```

Note: In a RAC configuration, data from multiple ASM instances could be viewed using the GV$ views in place of V$ views (e.g., GV$ASM_DISKGROUP).

The following statement on +ASM2 will mount the newly created disk group:

```
ALTER DISKGROUP ASMGRP2 MOUNT;
```

Note: Only mounted disk groups can be accessed from a database instance.

3.6.14 ASM files

Oracle defines templates for 12 different file types, such as datafile, control file, and so on. Each file type is given a different storage structure and directory layout. Files stored on ASM devices are no different from those stored on regular file systems. However, unlike the files on non-ASM devices, files stored on ASM devices can only be viewed at the operating system level using the ASM command-line utility (asmcmd) or EM.

Another difference is in the naming of a file created on ASM. File names in ASM leverage the file names created under OMF. ASM file names can appear cryptic at first, but the file names actually include information about the file itself.

ASM file names are of the following format:

```
+diskgroup_name/database_name/database file type/
tag_name.file_number.incarnation
```

For example, querying the V$DATAFILE on the database instance shows the following output:

```
SQL> SELECT NAME FROM V$DATAFILE;

NAME
--------------------------------------------------------
+ASMGRP1/sskydb/datafile/example.264.571954419
```

While file naming and the placement of files in specific directories and locations on the device are automatic, Oracle has followed the OFA directory structure. In the output above, +ASMGRP1 is the disk group name, sskydb is the database name, datafile is the file type, "example," which corresponds to the tablespace name, is the tag name, 258 is the file number (that could be mapped to file number in the V$ASM_FILE view), and 1 is the incarnation. The *incarnation* is a system-generated number, which is a timestamp plus a machine number.

Oracle calls this file name structure a fully qualified file name. Isn't this file name long and difficult to view and manage? To make this effort easy, a user can define aliases that map to specific file names. Thus, while you can have cryptic file names that are controlled by Oracle, you can define user-specific aliases (aliases are similar in concept to synonyms) that are more user friendly.

The syntax to define an alias is as follows:

```
ALTER DISKGROUP asmgrp2 ADD ALIAS <alias name> FOR <datafile
name>
```

3.6.15   ASM-related V$ Views

ASM views are visible to both the ASM instance and the database instance. However, when rows are selected from the respective instances, the contents displayed by these views are different (see Table 3.4).

3.6.16   Background process

In a Linux or UNIX environment, the following command lists the background processes in an ASM instance:

Table 3.4   *V$ Views in ASM[29]*

ASM View	ASM Instance	Database Instance
V$ASM_DISKGROUP	Displays one row for every disk group discovered by the instance	Displays one row for every ASM disk group mounted by the local database instance
V$ASM_DISK	Displays one row for every disk discovered across all disk groups as well as disks that do not belong to any disk groups	Displays one row for every ASM instance across all disk groups used by the local database instance
V$ASM_CLIENT	Displays one row for every client connected to the ASM instance	Displays one row for the ASM instance if the data-base has open ASM files
V$ASM_ALIAS	Displays one row for every alias present in every disk group mounted by the ASM instance	Has no meaning and contains no rows
V$ASM_OPERATION	Displays one row for every active ASM operation exe-cuting in the ASM instance	Is not relevant in the database instance and contains no rows
V$ASM_TEMPLATE	Displays one row for every template present in every disk group mounted by the ASM instance	Displays one row for every template present in every disk group mounted by the ASM instance with which the database instance com-municates
V$ASM_FILE	Displays one row for every file allocated across all cli-ent instances and disk groups	Is not relevant in the database instance and contains no rows

```
[oracle@oradb1 oracle]$ ps -ef | grep asm_
oracle     4035    1  0 00:35 ?        00:00:00 asm_pmon_+ASM1
oracle     4040    1  0 00:35 ?        00:00:00 asm_diag_+ASM1
oracle     4042    1  0 00:35 ?        00:00:00 asm_lmon_+ASM1
oracle     4044    1  0 00:35 ?        00:00:00 asm_lmd0_+ASM1
oracle     4048    1  0 00:35 ?        00:00:00 asm_lms0_+ASM1
oracle     4050    1  0 00:35 ?        00:00:00 asm_mman_+ASM1
```

```
oracle    4052    1   0 00:35 ?          00:00:00 asm_dbw0_+ASM1
oracle    4054    1   0 00:35 ?          00:00:00 asm_lgwr_+ASM1
oracle    4057    1   0 00:35 ?          00:00:00 asm_ckpt_+ASM1
oracle    4061    1   0 00:35 ?          00:00:00 asm_smon_+ASM1
oracle    4064    1   0 00:35 ?          00:00:00 asm_rbal_+ASM1
oracle    4109    1   0 00:35 ?          00:00:00 asm_lck0_+ASM1
```

The two distinct details from this output are the process name prefix and the new additional background processes. The ASM processes are identified by "asm_"as opposed to "ora_" in regular Oracle RDBMS instances. Secondly, as indicated in this output, there are two new background processes specific to an ASM instance: RBAL and ARBn.

1. *Rebalance (RBAL).* The primary function of this background process is to open all disks listed under each disk group and to make them available to the various clients. Apart from this, the RBAL background process also creates a rebalance plan to move extents between the disks when a disk is added to the disk group or removed from an existing disk group. The actual rebalancing act is performed by the ARBn background process.

2. *ARBn.* This is a messaging and extent management background process invoked only when disk rebalance or extent relocation (redistribution) activity is required. Such activity happens when a disk is added to the existing disk group or a disk is dropped from an existing disk group. After the RBAL background process creates the rebalancing plan, it sends messages to the ARB process to execute the plan.

There can exist at any given time a maximum of 11 ARB background processes. The number of ARB processes invoked is based on the parameter ASM_POWER_LIMIT default value 1. ASM_POWER_LIMIT is the driving factor for how quickly the data from the existing group should be rebalanced on the newly added disk. Setting the ASM_POWER_LIMIT parameter to a value of zero halts the rebalance operation.

 Note: The rebalance operation uses the resources (CPU and I/O) of the node on which the disk structure changes are being made.

Any change in the storage configuration will trigger a rebalance. The main objective of the rebalance operation is always to provide an even distribution of file extents and space usage across all disks in the disk group. Each file extent map is examined, and the new extents are replotted onto the new storage configuration. Rebalancing is performed on all database files on a per-file basis; however, some files may not require a rebalancing. Thus, only a minimal number of files have to be managed and rebalanced.

For example, in a disk group that consists of 8 disks, with a datafile with 40 extents (each disk will house 5 extents), when 2 new drives of the same size are added, that datafile is rebalanced and spread across 10 drives, with each drive containing 4 extents. Only 8 extents are to be moved to complete the rebalance (i.e., only a minimum number of extents are moved to reach equal distribution).

The following is a typical process flow for ASM rebalancing:

1. On the ASM instance, a DBA adds (drops) a disk to (from) a disk group.

2. This invokes the RBAL process to create the rebalance plan and then begin coordination of the redistribution.

3. RBAL will estimate time and work required to perform the task and then message the ARBn processes to handle the request. The number of ARBn processes started is directly determined by the ASM_POWER_LIMIT parameter setting. For example, the output below indicates the number of ARB background process started when a new disk was added to the ASMGRP1 group and the ASM_POWER_LIMIT parameter was increased to a value of 4:

```
oracle   13486   1  0 15:37 ?        00:00:00 asm_pz99_+ASM2
oracle   13643   1  3 15:41 ?        00:00:00 asm_arb0_+ASM2
oracle   13645   1  2 15:41 ?        00:00:00 asm_arb1_+ASM2
oracle   13647   1  2 15:41 ?        00:00:00 asm_arb2_+ASM2
oracle   13649   1  2 15:41 ?        00:00:00 asm_arb3_+ASM2
```

The rebalance activity is an asynchronous operation, meaning that the control is returned immediately to the DBA after the operation is sent to the background.

4. The metadata will be updated to reflect a rebalance activity.

5. Each extent to be relocated is assigned an ARBn process.

6.   ARBn performs rebalance on these extents. Each extent is locked, relocated, and unlocked. This is shown as operation REBAL value in the V$ASM_OPERATION view.

The following query against the V$ASM_OPERATION view indicates the progress of disk rebalancing activity:

```
SQL> SELECT * FROM V$ASM_OPERATION;

GN OPERA STAT POWER ACTUAL  SOFAR  EST_WORK  EST_RATE  EST_MINUTES
-- ----- ---- ----- ------ ------- --------- --------- -----------
 1 REBAL RUN     4      4     676      2202       486           3
```

In this output, the columns of primary importance (from a performance point of view) are ACTUAL and EST_MINUTES. If the ACTUAL column has a value less than the value in the POWER column, this would indicate that the rebalance operation was unable to keep up with the request due to other resource limitations (e.g., lack of CPU cycles or I/O contention). The EST_MINUTES column indicates the estimated completion time for the rebalance operation. An other column that could be of interest is SOFAR, which indicates the current progress of the rebalance operation.

 Note: The POWER column directly reflects the value in the parameter ASM_POWER_LIMIT or the power level of the ALTER DISKGROUP command. Setting the value to a very high number completes the operation quickly, but this could affect the overall performance of the database. A lower value reduces resource consumption, such as of CPU and I/O resources.

 Best Practice: To reduce the number of rebalance operations needed for storage changes, addition or removal of several disks should be performed all at once.

ASM-related RDBMS background processes

ASMB. This process contacts CSS using the disk group name and acquires the associated ASM connect string. This connect string is then used by the RDBMS instance to connect to the ASM instance. Using this persistent connection, periodic messages are exchanged to update statistics and provide a heartbeat mechanism. During operations that require ASM intervention, such as file creation by a database foreground, the database foreground connects directly to the ASM instance to perform the operation. Upon successful completion of file creation, database file extent maps are sent by ASM to ASMB. Additionally, ASMB also sends database I/O statistics to the ASM instance.[29]

O00n. A group of slave processes establishes connections to the ASM instance, where *n* is the number from 1 to 10. Through this connection pool, database processes can send messages to the ASM instance. For example, opening a file sends the open request to the ASM instance via a slave. However, slaves are not used for long-running operations such as creating a file. The slave (pool) connections eliminate the overhead of logging into the ASM instance for short requests. These slaves are shut down when not in use. [26]

Cluster synchronization services (CSS)

The CSS is a cluster layer that is part of Oracle Clusterware in a RAC configuration. While CSS is automatically installed when Oracle Clusterware is installed in a RAC environment, CSS is also required on single-instance configuration when the node has an ASM instance.

CSS provides cluster management and node monitoring. It inherently monitors ASM and its shared storage, such as disks and disk groups. When the ASM instance is started, it updates the CSS with status information regarding the disk groups, along with any connection information. CSS also helps keep all ASM instances in the cluster to keep the metadata information in sync.

3.6.17 How do they all work?

To understand how all the various components related to ASM work together, let us examine Figure 3.17.

1. When the disk group is created, the ASM instance loads this information into the SGA and is stored on each disk header within the disk group.

2. On instance start, the RBAL background process will discover and open all ASM disk groups on the respective nodes and mount them on the respective ASM instances. When a disk group is mounted (on instance startup), ASM registers the disk group

Figure 3.17
High-level
ASM/RDBMS
Interaction

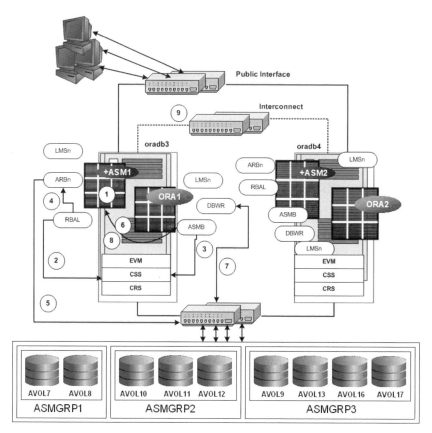

name, the instance name, and the corresponding Oracle home path with CSS.

3. The ASMB background process on the RDBMS instance will verify with the CSS if any disk groups are assigned to it and obtain the connect string to the ASM instance. During the RDBMS instance startup process, this information is used by the RDBMS instance to retrieve all disk group information from the ASM instance.

4. When a user adds a new disk to an existing disk group, the RBAL background process will create a plan to reorganize the extents in the disk group. The RBAL process will then send a message to the ARBn background process to execute the plan. The number of ARBn background processes started is based on the parameter ASM_POWER_LIMIT.

5. The ARBn background process will perform datafile reorganization. The time taken to complete the reorganization is directly dependent on the number of ARBn processes started and, as discussed earlier, on the value of the parameter ASM_POWER_LIMIT.

6. When the RDBMS instance opens a file, or when a new file is created by the DBA, the RDBMS instance interacts with the ASM instance as a client to obtain the file layout from the ASM instance.

7. Based on user activity on the database instance, any updates to the data on the ASM devices are performed by the DBWR process on the RDBMS instance. Such activity is performed using the layout obtained by the RDBMS instance from the ASM instance (illustrated in step 6).

8. Using a persistent connection established with the information obtained in step 3, the ASMB background process will connect to the ASM instance as its foreground process and update the ASM instance with all performance metrics and statistics, including database I/O statistics related to the ASM disks and disk groups. This connection and periodic messages will also provide the function of a heartbeat mechanism between the RDBMS instance and the ASM instance. This is performed by the O00n slave processes.

9. In a clustered configuration such as RAC, the various ASM instances on their respective nodes use the interprocess communication mechanisms to keep the ASM metadata information in sync.

Note: While the ASMB process itself is not transient, the connection between the RDBMS instance and the ASM instance is transient in nature, and the RDBMS instance uses a bequeath connection and, hence, does not require any TNS names configuration.

3.6.18   **ASM allocation units**

As discussed earlier, ASM is based on the SAME methodology. That is, it will stripe all disks assigned to it in 128K strip sizes using a strip width of 8 MB for normal redundancy. So how does Oracle allocate extents or units of space when required for the database? ASM uses a round-robin mechanism to create allocation units across the stripes allocated to it from the various disks in a given disk group. For example, in Figure 3.18, the disk group ASMGRP1 has six disks AVOL1 through AVOL6. When ASM allocates 1-MB units or extents, ASM follows a round-robin mechanism while allocating them. That is, the first 1-MB is allocated on AVOL1, the next on AVOL2, AVOL3, and so on to AVOL6, after which the allocation starts back at the beginning (AVOL1).

Table 3.4 lists all the values used by ASM during disk group configuration.

Figure 3.18
ASM Extent
Allocation

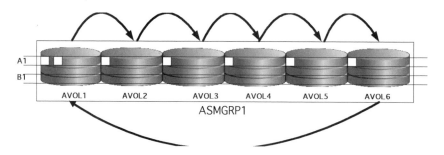

Figure 3.18 is a simple configuration where disks are directly allocated to Oracle, and ASM will stripe, mirror, and allocate extents from each of these disks.

Organizations that have already invested in a RAID technology and would like to utilize this technology can implement it on a group of disks before allocating these groups to ASM. Such a configuration is illustrated in Figure 3.19.

In Figure 3.19, 16 disks are grouped into 4 hardware groups HG1 through HG4. When allocated to ASM to form a disk group, HG1 through HG4 are treated by ASM as individual disks and could all be allocated to form one disk group ASMGRP1. ASM will allocate extents using the same round-robin process illustrated earlier. However, allocation will be across all 4 hardware disk groups and the 16 disks before starting again from AVOL1 on HG1. In other words, 16 MB will be allocated from 16 distinct disks. Such a configuration is ideal for bringing the total distribution of extents across all disks in the storage array.

Best Practice: To obtain maximum spindle count, double striping or plaiding should be implemented. As illustrated in Figure 3.19, logical units with hardware-based stripe and mirror (RAID 0+1) should be created before allocation to ASM.

Figure 3.19
*Hardware and
ASM Grouping*

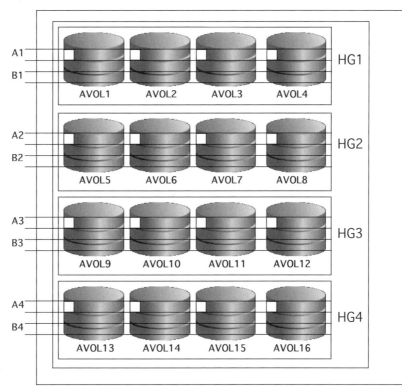

3.6.19 ASM component relationship

ASM has several components, all of which are related to one another in some form. The various ASM components represented through a relationship model are illustrated in Figure 3.20.

Figure 3.20
*ASM File
Relationship*

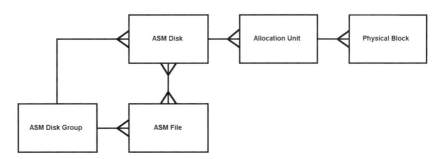

Reading this model indicates that a disk group can consist of one or more ASM disks and also one or more ASM files. Similarly, an ASM file can be spread over many ASM disks, and an ASM disk can contain one or more ASM files. An ASM disk can have one or more extents allocated from it, and, finally, depending on the physical block size of the operating system, an allocation unit can contain one or more physical blocks.

3.6.20   New command-line interface

In Oracle Database 10g Release 2, Oracle has introduced a command-line interface to look at the underlying storage layout of ASM. This interface provides visibility to the disk layout and file layout structure that ASM has implemented when creating the disk groups and files stored on these disk groups. The command-line interface utility is called asmcmd.

The environment variables ORACLE_HOME and ORACLE_SID determine the instance to which the program connects, and asmcmd establishes a bequeath connection to it, in the same manner as a sqlplus / as sysdba. The user must be a member of the SYSDBA group.

```
[oracle@oradb1 bin]$ export ORACLE_SID=+ASM1
[oracle@oradb1 bin]$ asmcmd
ASMCMD>
```

The commands provided using the asmcmd utility are similar to the Linux and UNIX commands. For example, to look at the contents of the storage disks, the ls command should be used from the asmcmd command prompt.

```
ASMCMD> ls -ltr
State    Type    Rebal  Unbal  Name
MOUNTED  NORMAL  N      N      ASMGRP2/
MOUNTED  NORMAL  N      N      ASMGRP1/
```

You can change the directory to any of the groups using the cd command from the asmcmd command prompt; for example:

```
ASMCMD> cd RAC10GDB/DATAFILE
ASMCMD> pwd
+ASMGRP1/RAC10GDB/DATAFILE
ASMCMD> ls -ltr
Type      Redund  Striped  Time           Sys  Name
```

```
DATAFILE   MIRROR   COARSE     JAN 25 13:00:00   Y     BMF_DATA.273.572018897
DATAFILE   MIRROR   COARSE     JAN 25 13:00:00   Y     EXAMPLE.264.571954419
DATAFILE   MIRROR   COARSE     JAN 25 13:00:00   Y     SORAC_DATA.272.572018797
DATAFILE   MIRROR   COARSE     JAN 25 13:00:00   Y     SYSAUX.257.571954317
DATAFILE   MIRROR   COARSE     JAN 25 13:00:00   Y     SYSTEM.256.571954317
DATAFILE   MIRROR   COARSE     JAN 25 13:00:00   Y     UNDOTBS1.258.571954317
DATAFILE   MIRROR   COARSE     JAN 25 13:00:00   Y     UNDOTBS2.265.571954545
DATAFILE   MIRROR   COARSE     JAN 25 13:00:00   Y     UNDOTBS3.266.571954547
DATAFILE   MIRROR   COARSE     JAN 25 13:00:00   Y     USERS.259.571954319
ASMCMD>
```

3.7   Migration to ASM

Databases that are already created using RAW devices or using file systems or databases that were migrated from Oracle Database 9i to Oracle Database 10*g* may not be using ASM for storage. In these situations, it may be desirable to convert the datafiles to use ASM. Conversion can be performed using one of two available methods: either the complete database can be converted or specific tablespaces can be converted to use ASM. Converting the entire database to ASM storage is performed using RMAN. However, there are several methods to convert individual datafiles to ASM.

3.7.1   Converting non-ASM database to ASM using RMAN

The following steps are to be followed when migrating an existing database to ASM:

1.   Perform a SHUTDOWN IMMEDIATE on all instances participating in the cluster.

2.   Modify the following initialization parameters of the target database:

    a.   DB_CREATE_FILE_DEST

    b.   DB_CREATE_ONLINE_LOG_DEST[1,2,3,4]

    c.   CONTROL_FILES

    d.   DB_CREATE_*

5.   Using RMAN, connect to the target database and start up the target database in NOMOUNT mode.

6. Restore the control file from its original location to the new location specified in step 2.

7. Once the control file is restored to the new location, the database is ready to be mounted.

8. Using the RMAN copy operation, copy the database to the new location assigned in the ASM disk group.

9. Once the copy operation has completed, the database is ready for recovery. Using RMAN, perform the database recovery operation.

10. Open the database.

11. During the entire process, the temporary tablespace was not copied over; this has to be created manually.

12. The next step is to move the online redo logs into ASM. This step can be accomplished using Oracle-provided PL/SQL scripts found in the Oracle Database 10*g* documentation.

13. The old datafiles can be deleted from the operating system.

14. If the database had enabled block change tracking, this can be reenabled at this stage.

3.7.2   Converting non-ASM datafile to ASM using RMAN

The following steps are to be followed in migrating a single non-ASM datafile to ASM-based volume management:

1. Using RMAN, connect to the target database as follows:

```
[oracle@oradb1 oracle]$ rman
Recovery Manager: Release 10.1.0.3.0 - Production

Copyright (c) 1995, 2004, Oracle.  All rights reserved.
RMAN> connect target
connected to target database: SSKYDB (DBID=2290365532)
```

2. Using SQL, offline the tablespace that will be the migration candidate:

```
RMAN> SQL "ALTER TABLESPACE EXAMPLE OFFLINE";
```

3.   Using the "backup as copy" operation, perform the following
      operation:

```
RMAN> BACKUP AS COPY TABLESPACE EXAMPLE FORMAT '+ASMGRP1';

Starting backup at 01-OCT-04
allocated channel: ORA_DISK_1
channel ORA_DISK_1: sid=252 devtype=DISK
channel ORA_DISK_1: starting datafile copy
input datafile fno=00005 name=/u14/oradata/SSKYDB/example01.dbf
output filename=+ASMGRP1/sskydb/datafile/example.258.1
tag=TAG20041001T221236 recid=2 stamp=538438446
channel ORA_DISK_1: datafile copy complete, elapsed time: 00:01:36
Finished backup at 01-OCT-04
RMAN>
```

4.   Once the "copy complete" message is received, indicating a suc-
      cessful copy, switch the tablespace to use the copied datafile:

```
RMAN> SWITCH TABLESPACE EXAMPLE TO COPY;

datafile 5 switched to datafile copy "+ASMGRP1/sskydb/
datafile/example.258.1"

RMAN>
```

5.   The final step is to ONLINE the tablespace using SQL:

```
RMAN> SQL "ALTER TABLESPACE EXAMPLE ONLINE";
```

6.   Verify the operation by connecting to the target database and
      checking the V$ views.

3.7.3 Converting non-ASM datafile to ASM using DBMS_FILE_TRANSFER stored procedure

The DBMS_FILE_TRANSFER package provides a means to copy files between
two locations. In Oracle Database 10*g*, this procedure is used to move or
copy files between ASM disk groups and is the primary utility used to

instantiate an ASM Data Guard database. Using this procedure, the following transfer scenarios are possible:

1. Copy files from one ASM disk group to another ASM disk group.

2. Copy files from an ASM disk group to an external storage media such as a file system at the operating system level.

3. Copy files from a file system at the operating system level to an ASM-configured disk group.

4. Copy files from a file system at the operating system level to another location or raw device at the operating system level.

Steps to be performed to move datafiles from one location to another using the DBMS_FILE_TRANSFER procedure are as follows:

1. Identify the datafile to be moved or copied from one location to another:

```
SQL>  SELECT FILE_NAME FROM DBA_DATA_FILES;

FILE_NAME
---------------------------------------------------------------------
+ASMGRP1/sskydb/datafile/users.259.571954319
+ASMGRP1/sskydb/datafile/sysaux.257.571954317
+ASMGRP1/sskydb/datafile/undotbs1.258.571954317
+ASMGRP1/sskydb/datafile/system.256.571954317
+ASMGRP1/sskydb/datafile/example.264.571954419
+ASMGRP1/sskydb/datafile/undotbs2.265.571954545
+ASMGRP1/sskydb/datafile/undotbs3.266.571954547
+ASMGRP1/sskydb/datafile/sorac_data.272.572018797
+ASMGRP1/sskydb/datafile/bmf_data.273.572018897
```

2. Identify the destination (ASM or non-ASM) where the file will be copied.

3. The datafile is copied to an external OCFS-based file system location.

4. Take the datafile offline:

```
SQL> ALTER DATABASE DATAFILE '+ASMGRP1/SSKYDB/DATAFILE/
BMF_DATA.273.572018897' OFFLINE;
```

5.   Copy the file to the new location by first creating a `DIRECTORY_NAME` for the source and target locations and using the following procedure:

```
SQL> CREATE DIRECTORY ASMSRC AS '+ASMGRP1/SSKYDB/
DATAFILE';

Directory created.

SQL> CREATE DIRECTORY OSDEST AS '/ocfs9/oradata';

Directory created.

SQL> BEGIN
   DBMS_FILE_TRANSFER.COPY_FILE('ASMRC',
                           'BMF_DATA.273.572018897',
                           'OSDEST',
                           'BMF.dbf');
END;
/
```

6.   Bring the datafile online:

```
ALTER DATABASE DATAFILE '+ASMGRP1/SSKYDB/DATAFILE/
BMF_DATA.273.572018897' ONLINE;
```

7.   Verify the copied file:

```
[oracle@oradb1 oradata]$ ls -ltr /ocfs9/oradata
```

3.7.4   Transferring non-ASM datafile to ASM using FTP

Adding to the other methods of file transfer from and to ASM disk groups, using the virtual folder feature in XML DB ASM files and folders can be manipulated via XML DB protocols such as FTP, HTTP/DAV, and programmatic APIs. Under this method, the ASM virtual folder is mounted as /sys/asm within the XML DB hierarchy. The folder is virtual, meaning that the ASM folders and files are not physically stored within XML DB. However, any operation on the ASM virtual folder is transparently handled by the underlying ASM component. In order to use this method of file transfer, it is important that XML DB be installed and configured in the database using ASM to facilitate this operation.

Note: If XML DB is not already installed, the base objects can be created using the `scatqm.sql` script located in the `$ORACLE_HOME/rdbms/admin` directory on all supported platforms.

3.8   ASM performance monitoring using EM

From the ASM instance home page, selecting the performance tab will display the overall performance of all disk groups defined (see in Figure 3.21). The charts on this page give the average performance characteristics of all disk groups combined that are currently being used or part of the ASM instance. The charts display the disk group I/O response time, the I/O operation, and the throughput.

Figure 3.21
ASM Performance

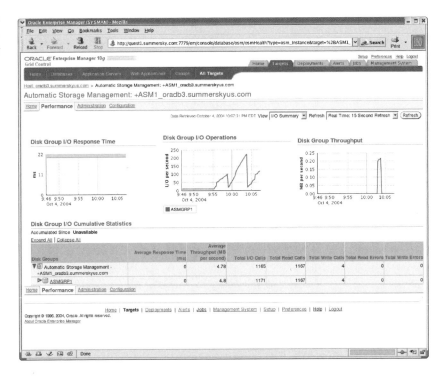

Selecting a specific disk group from the list provided at the bottom of this screen in Figure 3.21, EM provides its performance matrix. The performance chart showing the disk group I/O activity is illustrated in Figure 3.22.

Figure 3.22
ASM Disk Group
Performance

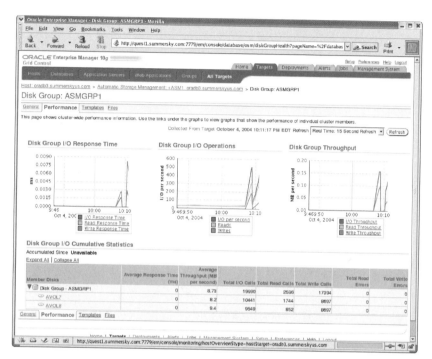

In Figure 3.22, similar to Figure 3.21, the bottom of the screen contains the list of disks that belong to this disk group. When users click on these names (e.g., AVOL7), EM also provides the performance characteristics of the individual disks that belong to the disk group. Selecting a specific disk from the list of disks will provide further charts (Figure 3.23) containing performance characteristics related to the specific disk selected.

Note: While all charts displayed at various drill-down stages have identical titles, the data in them gets more specific to the specific selection.

3.9   ASM implementations

ASM can be implemented in the following three configurations:

1.   Using ASM from a single node

Figure 3.23
*ASM Member
Disk (AVOL7)
Performance*

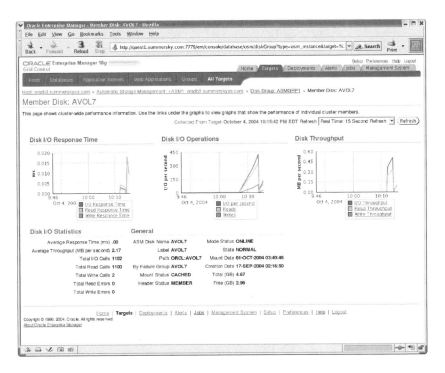

2.   Using ASM from multiple nodes

3.   Using ASM on a RAC environment

3.9.1 Using ASM from a single node

ASM supports both a single-node multiple-database configuration or a clustered configuration such as on a RAC. One instance of ASM is required on a node regardless of the number of databases contained on the node. Besides ASM, as discussed earlier, CSS should also be configured. In a single node that supports multiple databases, disk groups (a composition of multiple disks) can be shared between multiple databases.

As illustrated in Figure 3.24, `oradb1` supports the `DEV` database and stores data in two disk groups, `ASMGRP1` and `ASMGRP2`. If, subsequently, another database `DEV1` is added to the same node, `DEV1` can share the disk groups with the `DEV` database.

Note: ASM instances are identified with "+" prefixed to the name of the instance (e.g., +ASM1, +ASM2).

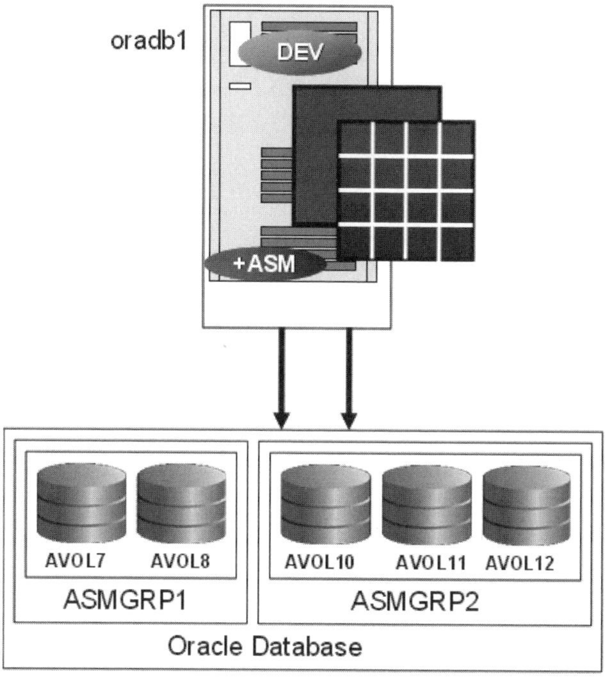

Figure 3.24
Single-Node ASM Configuration

3.9.2 **Using ASM from multiple nodes**

Multiple nodes can contain ASM instances supporting their respective databases and having disk groups located on the same disk farm. For example, in Figure 3.25, instance +ASM1 on node oradb1 and +ASM2 on oradb2 can support their respective databases DEV and TST, mapping to their own disk groups ASMGRP1, ASMGRP2, and ASMGRP3, where +ASM1 contains ASMGRP1, ASMGRP2, and +ASM2 contains ASMGRP3. As in similar to the previous discussion, ASM on the respective nodes can support any number of databases located on that node.

While no specific criterion exists for single-instance databases, the situation changes when ASM instances share disk groups. For example, if the +ASM2 instance needs additional disk space, the DBA has two choices:

1.   Add an additional disk to the storage array and either assign the disk to the existing disk group ASMGRP3 or create a new disk group and create a new datafile for the same tablespace in this group.

2.   Assign from an existing disk group currently owned by instance +ASM1 located on oradb1. However, by default, this would not be possible in certain cases due to configuration limitations. Both +ASM1 and +ASM2 on oradb1 and oradb2, respectively, are single-instance versions of ASM. If multiple instances of ASM located on different nodes require access to the same set of disk groups, the nodes should be clustered together using Oracle Clusterware in Oracle Database 10*g* Release 2 because Oracle has to maintain the metadata information in sync between the various ASM instances.

Note: Starting with Oracle Database 10*g* Release 2, this type of configuration does not require a RAC license.

Figure 3.25
ASM on Multiple Nodes Sharing the Same Disk Group

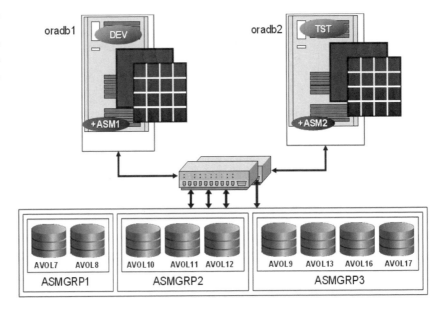

Figure 3.25 is an illustration of multiple nodes having different ASM instances, sharing disk groups on the same storage array. One of the primary benefits of this configuration is server consolidation, where multiple databases residing on different nodes can share one disk group.

3.9.3 **Using ASM in a RAC environment**

RAC is a configuration where two or more instances of Oracle share one common physical copy of the database. This means that all storage systems and disks, including disk groups, are shared between all instances participating in the cluster. Support of ASM on a RAC configuration requires that Oracle Clusterware and the RAC option be installed on all nodes participating in the cluster. In such a configuration, all disk groups created on any node can be used by any other instance participating in the cluster.

Figure 3.26
ASM Configuration in a RAC Implementation

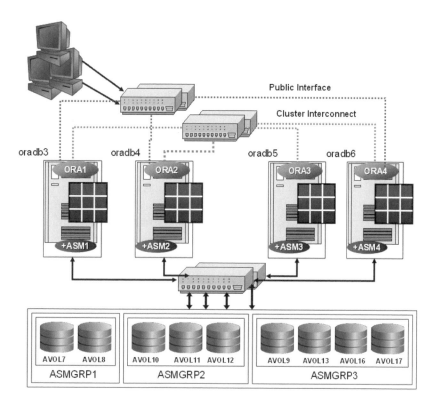

Figure 3.26 is a RAC configuration where multiple instances of Oracle on multiple nodes have multiple ASM instances that manage the same set of disk groups. In this configuration, all of the instances can write to or read from any of the available disk groups in the storage array.

3.10   ASM instance crash

Like any Oracle database, an ASM instance is also prone to failures. Failures can occur under the following situations:

- When a node crashes
- When the underlying cluster components crash
- When an ASM instance crashes
- When the I/O subsystem or storage is taken offline

Like the regular RDBMS instance, the ASM instance is also prone to failures; however, in this configuration, there is a tight dependency between the underlying cluster components (e.g., CSS), the ASM instance, and the RDBMS. Hence, in a configuration (RAC or non-RAC), when there is a failure of the node, the underlying cluster components on the node, or the ASM instance, the RDBMS instance(s) on this node will fail.

When an ASM instance is started after a failure, it will read the disk group logs and perform recovery just like any other RDBMS instance. However, in a RAC configuration, when one of the ASM instances fails, another ASM instance residing on another node will detect the failure and perform instance recovery. During this process, any metadata changes will also be recovered.

3.11   ASM disk administration

Backing up data from an ASM disk

RMAN is the only method currently available to back up data from an ASM disk to external media, such as an external disk volume, or into tape media for archiving. Backup files generated using RMAN can be located on ASM disk volumes. These backed-up files can then be moved to external media using Oracle Secured Backup (OSB), or, as an alternative, the backup files can be written to a non-ASM storage location and then subsequently written to tape media.

Reusing ASM diskgroups

When ASM disk groups are created and datafiles are added, Oracle places header (metadata) information on these disk groups. If the disks in these disk groups are to be reused for either another disk group or by another database, the disk groups should be dropped from the ASM instance, and the metadata must be cleared before attempting to recreate ASM disk-groups:

```
SQL> DROP DISKGROUP ASMGRP1 INCLUDING CONTENTS;
SQL> exit
```

Once the disk group has been dropped, the next step is to clear the metadata information. This is done using the following dd command:

```
dd if=/dev/zero of=/dev/rdsk/sdb bs=8192 count=12800
```

As an alternative, the disk can be assigned to another diskgroup using the diskgroup CREATE or ALTER commands by qualifying it with the FORCE operation. For example:

```
CREATE DISKGROUP asmgrp2 DISK 'OCL:AVOL10', 'ORCL:AVOL11'
FORCE;
```

```
ALTER DISKGROUP ASMGRP1 ADD DISK 'ORCL:AVOL13' FORCE;
```

3.12 Client connection to an ASM instance

As discussed, an ASM instance is not a complete instance; it's a smaller version of a regular database instance. Since an ASM instance remains in a MOUNT state and cannot be opened, the data dictionary views and other Oracle metadata information are not available. Therefore, the only Oracle user present on this instance is sys. All connections to this instance will be using sys (as SYSDBA or SYSOPER).

Another variation from the traditional RDBMS instance is with the registration of the ASM service with the listener. During automatic detection of all services available on the node, the listener determines that the ASM instance is not in an OPEN state. It registers the ASM instance but leaves it in a BLOCKED state (as illustrated in the following output). This prevents normal connections to this instance that involve the listener:

```
[oracle@oradb1 oracle]$ lsnrctl status LISTENER_ORADB1
```

```
LSNRCTL for Linux: Version 10.2.0.1.0 - Production on 01-NOV-2005 18:29:52

Copyright (c) 1991, 2005, Oracle.  All rights reserved.

Connecting to (DESCRIPTION=(ADDRESS=(PROTOCOL=TCP)(HOST=oradb1.sumsky.net)(POR
T=1521)(IP=FIRST)))
STATUS of the LISTENER
------------------------
Alias                     LISTENER_ORADB1
Version                   TNSLSNR for Linux: Version 10.2.0.1.0 - Production
Start Date                20-OCT-2005 18:26:56
Uptime                    12 days 1 hr. 2 min. 56 sec
Trace Level               off
Security                  ON: Local OS Authentication
SNMP                      OFF
Listener Parameter File   /usr/app/oracle/product/10.2.0/db_1/network/admin/
listener.ora
Listener Log File         /usr/app/oracle/product/10.2.0/db_1/network/log/
listener_oradb1.log
Listening Endpoints Summary...
  (DESCRIPTION=(ADDRESS=(PROTOCOL=tcp)(HOST=192.168.2.110)(PORT=1521)))
  (DESCRIPTION=(ADDRESS=(PROTOCOL=tcp)(HOST=192.168.2.10)(PORT=1521)))
  (DESCRIPTION=(ADDRESS=(PROTOCOL=ipc)(KEY=EXTPROC)))
Services Summary...
Service "+ASM" has 1 instance(s).
  Instance "+ASM1", status BLOCKED, has 1 handler(s) for this service...
Service "+ASM_XPT" has 1 instance(s).
  Instance "+ASM1", status BLOCKED, has 1 handler(s) for this service...
Service "SSKY1" has 1 instance(s).
  Instance "SSKY1", status READY, has 2 handler(s) for this service...
. . .
. . .
```

ASM connections are BLOCKED to disallow any kind of normal database connection. This is to ensure that all communications are routed via the ASMB background process and to avoid clogging of the connections, which will restrict normal ASM activity.

3.13 Conclusion

ASM is a new storage management solution from Oracle Corporation that has made the storage management layer more suitable and flexible. In this chapter, we discussed this new technology, and through these discussions, we have learned how the ASM storage management solution is different from other solutions available on the market and how ASM complements RAC. This chapter covered all aspects of ASM, starting with the basic installation and configuration through maintenance administration and performance monitoring. During this process, we also looked at the functioning of an ASM instance in conjunction with the RDBMS instance.

4

Installation and Configuration

The overall goal of the business application can only be achieved by carefully planning the installation, configuration, and administration of the underlying database. Apart from basic manageability and administrative aspects, it helps improve the performance of the environment. But, no matter how well the system has been planned, structured, designed, and developed, the desired results will not become a reality unless the system, including the operating system; the layered products, like the cluster services; the database; and the network are all installed, configured, and managed efficiently.

In this chapter, the steps taken for installing and configuring the RAC environment will be discussed. While planning and creating a work plan are important first steps in the configuration process, it is also important to follow a standard procedure that provides a consistent way to define disks and directory structures. One such standard developed and recommended by Oracle Corporation is the Optimal Flexible Architecture (OFA).[1] This architecture is widely followed by many organizations using Oracle RDBMS.

4.1   Optimal Flexible Architecture

OFA is a standard configuration recommended by Oracle Corporation for its customers. It is a way to promote a consistent standard disk configuration or directory structure. OFA standards are included in many relevant books and in the documentation available from Oracle Corporation. Even though some organizations may not have used OFA to configure their directory structures, it is a good practice to follow some standard so there

---

1.   A white paper describing the OFA standards can be found on the Oracle technology network at www.oracle.com/technology/index.html.

will be consistency among the various installations within an organization. Such standards not only help streamline the process but also allow for easy manageability in the various environments of the organization and provide an easy path of familiarization when new associates are hired. Implementing the OFA is not a requirement for installing and configuring an Oracle database, but its rather a good general guideline.

4.1.1 Installation

Software and applications require that certain basic configuration details be followed before installation. An example of this is the installation of a personal accounting system on a PC at home. The accounting package has certain prerequisites, two of which are, for example, the version of the operating system and minimum memory and storage space. Oracle RDBMS is a software, and it's no different when it comes to prerequisites.

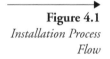

Figure 4.1
Installation Process
Flow

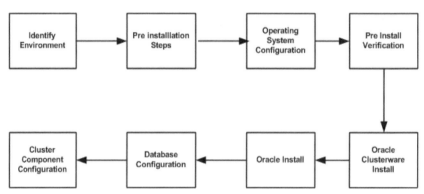

Figure 4.1 illustrates the various steps in the RAC installation and configuration process. For example, at the beginning of a new project, once the business requirements have been compiled and analyzed, identifying the environment may be a prerequisite to the actual implementation and might be done by asking such questions as

- What application will these servers need to support?

- If the application is a preexisting application that is being migrated from a single-instance version of Oracle to the proposed RAC cluster, does it currently scale on an symmetric multiprocessor (SMP) server?

- How many users will this database need to support?

- What should be the platform and its physical configuration (e.g., Linux, Sun, HP, AIX , or Windows server)?

- How much memory and CPU should it have (e.g., 4-GB memory and four-way Xeon processors)?

- What layered products will it have when taking into consideration the basic business requirements of scalability and availability (e.g., Oracle Clusterware, OCFS, and ASM)?

Questions like these will need to be asked until a complete understanding of the proposed configuration is understood and documented. Once this selection has been completed, the next step is to complete the preinstallation steps.

4.1.2 Preinstallation steps

You will need to ensure that

1. Appropriate support service has been obtained from Oracle support services, including the customer service identification (CSI) number. This is the first and most critical step in the installation process.

2. The various products selected for installation are all certified. The certification matrix for all versions of Oracle can be found on Metalink at www.metalink.oracle.com.

3. The release notes are reviewed for any last-minute changes that did not make it into the installation guides.

4. From the time of installing and configuring the software and going into production, are checked for bugs or other patch releases published by Oracle Corporation. This is necessary because no matter how much the applications are tested or tuned, there is always the possibility that some bugs were not handled during the testing phases. Information pertaining to this process is available on Metalink at www.metalink.oracle.com.

5. All required patches for the installation (operating system and Oracle) have been downloaded, verified, and applied successfully.

6. Based on the architecture of the application and database, all tools and utilities installed from the CD have been preselected

(e.g., third-party clusterware [if any], Oracle Clusterware, ASM, and partitioning). This is required because certain products or features could require additional licensing.

7.   A backup is made of the operating system. This is a precautionary measure in case there are any installation issues; the backup can be restored and the system returned to its original state.

8.   There is enough disk space and memory as required in the system requirement section of the installation guide.

9.   Sufficient disk space has been allocated for the Oracle product directory, including the required swap space. Oracle requires a swap space of about one or two times the RAM. This space is released after the installation but is essential to complete the installation. While allocating space, consideration should be given to future releases of Oracle as they become available and require installation or upgrade.

10.   The required directories, including the base directory (`ORACLE_BASE`) for Oracle-related files, have been defined per OFA specifications.

11.   All nodes in the proposed cluster have been set to the same system date and timestamp. It is advised that a network time synchronization utility be used to keep them synchronized.

12.   The terminal or workstation where the installation will occur is X-windows compliant. Since the installers have a Java-based user interface, it is required that the workstation or terminal be xterm compatible.

For a systematic approach and to create an audit trail of the steps during the installation process, it would be advisable for the database administrators (DBAs) to create a detailed implementation work plan containing all the steps that will need to be completed. In order to ensure correctness and to fill in the missing steps, it would also be advisable to review such a plan with other members of the DBA team.

4.2   Selecting the clusterware

Depending on the operating system, Oracle supports one or more clusterware options. For example, Table 4.1 lists the various clusterwares supported by Oracle on the respective platforms. In Oracle Database 10g, irrespective of the third-party clusterware selected for the hardware, Oracle Clusterware must also be installed, in which case, as discussed in Chapter 2, Oracle clusterware communicates with the third-party Clusterware using the PROCD process.

Table 4.1   *Clusterware Options*

Operating System	Clusterware Options
Linux	Oracle Clusterware
Windows	Oracle Clusterware
Solaris	1. Oracle Clusterware 2. Veritas SFOR 3. Sun Cluster 4. Fujitsu-Siemens Prime Cluster
HP-UX	1. Oracle Clusterware 2. ServiceGuard
AIX	1. Oracle Clusterware 2. HACMP 3. Veritas SFOR

Best Practice: Considering that Oracle Clusterware provides additional features above a traditional third-party clusterware and it supports all hardware platforms irrespective of the operating system, third-party clusterware in a RAC environment is an additional overhead and should be avoided in the configuration.

The next step is to configure the hardware, starting with the configuration of a common shared disk subsystem.

Note: Storage methods, including configuration and administration of ASM, are discussed in Chapter 3. Installation and configuration of the Oracle Clustered File System (OCFS) is included in Appendix C.

Once the storage method has been selected and configured, the next step in the prerequisite process is to create the required operating system users.

4.3   Operating system configuration

On most operating systems, Oracle has taken all efforts to ensure that the installation and configuration of the various RAC components are identical with respect to their directory structure, processes, utilities, and so on. On certain operating systems, such as Windows, there are some variations, and all efforts have been made to highlight these differences in the respective sections of this chapter.

The primary focus of this chapter is the installation and configuration of Oracle Database 10*g* Release 2, unless otherwise specified.

4.3.1   Creation of an `oracle` user account

Every installation of Oracle software requires an administrative user account. For example, in most Oracle software installations, an `oracle` user is created who will be the owner of the Oracle software and the database. While creating this user, it is important that the UID and the GID of user `oracle` be the same across all RAC nodes.

Connect to all nodes (Linux or Unix-based environment) in the RAC environment as user `root` and create the following operating system groups:

```
groupadd -g 500 dba
groupadd -g 501 oinstall
groupadd -g 502 oper
```

Once the groups have been created, create the `oracle` user account as a member of the dba group using the following commands, and subsequently reset the user password using the `passwd` command:

```
useradd -u 500 -g dba -G dba, oper oracle

passwd oracle
Changing password for user oracle.
New password:
Retype new password:
passwd: all authentication tokens updated successfully.
```

Once the groups and the user have been created, they should be verified on all nodes to ensure that the output of the following command is identical:

```
[oracle@oradb3 oracle]$ id oracle
uid=500(oracle) gid=500(dba) groups=500(dba),501(oinstall),
502(oper)
```

Windows: User is configured using the Windows administrative tools options, and the appropriate privileges are assigned to the account.

4.4 Network configuration

RAC configuration consists of two or more nodes clustered together that access a shared storage subsystem (see Figure 4.2). Nodes communicate between each other via a dedicated private interconnect or a private network adapter. Interconnects are network adapters connected in a peer-to-peer configuration or through a switch that allows nodes to communicate with one another.

At a minimum, a node needs at least one network adapter that provides the interface (e.g., an Ethernet adapter) to the local area network (LAN) that allows users and applications to connect to and query data from the database. This is normally considered to be the public network interface. Public network adapters are visible to users external to the node participating in the cluster. Network adapters are identified by an Internet static IP address, which is assigned during operating system configuration.

Note: An IP address is a four-part number, with each part represented by a number between 0 and 255. Part of that IP address represents the network the computer exists on, whereas the remainder identifies the specific host on that network. The four-part number is selected based on the size of the network in the organization. Network sizes are classified into three classes based on the size. Class A has a number between 0 and 127, Class B has a number between 128 and 191, and Class C has a number between 192 and 223. An example of an IP address is 192.168.200.60.

Figure 4.2
RAC Configuration

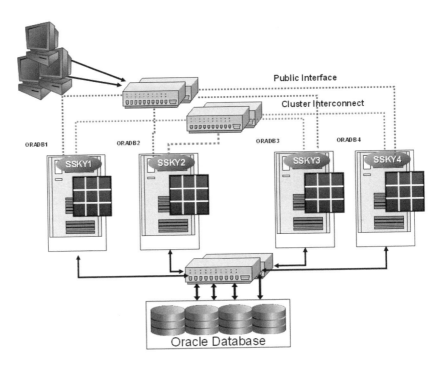

In a RAC environment, where data is transferred between Oracle instances, it is a requirement to dedicate a separate private network (Gigabit Ethernet or InfiniBand) to service such communications. In a private network, IP addresses are only visible between the participating nodes in the cluster. Its backbone is a high-speed interconnect, used exclusively for cluster and RAC-related messaging, such as node monitoring and cache fusion network traffic.

Best Practice: It is recommended that Gigabit Ethernet or InfiniBand connections over user datagram protocol (UDP) be used for interconnect communications.

UDP is defined to make available a datagram mode of packet-switched computer communication in the environment of an interconnected set of computer networks. The protocol is transaction oriented, and delivery and duplicate protection are not guaranteed [6]. This protocol assumes that IP [5] is used as the underlying protocol.

Oracle uses interconnect for both cache fusion traffic and Oracle Clusterware messaging. While UDP is the protocol of choice on non-Windows-based implementations for cache fusion traffic, Oracle uses TCP for cluster-ware messaging on all hardware platforms. On Windows-based implementations, TCP is the protocol used for cache fusion traffic.

To convert from one type of protocol to another (after the Oracle software has been installed), the following commands can be used:

```
cd $ORACLE_HOME/rdbms/lib
```

- To convert to UDP:

```
make -f ins_rdbms.mk ipc_udp
```
- To convert to TCP/IP:

```
make -f ins_rdbms.mk ipc_tcp
```
- To convert to Infiniband (uDAPL):

```
make -f ins_rdbms.mk ipc_ib
```

The only difference in the environment is the interconnect library `libskgxp10.so`. The makefile only removes the current `libskgxp10.so` and copies the desired library into `libskgxp10.so`.

Table 4.2   *IP Library Files*

Library Name	Interconnect Protocol
`libskgxp10.so`	The one being linked in by Oracle
`libskgxpd.so`	Dummy; no interconnect protocol (for single instance)
`libskgxpu.so`	UDP
`libskgxpt.so`	TCP

Based on the number of nodes in the configuration, either the interconnect can be a crossover cable when only two nodes are participating in the cluster or it can be connected via a switch (as illustrated in Figure 4.2).

Caution: Starting with Oracle Database 10*g*, crossover cable is not supported in a RAC configuration.

The network adapters are normally configured by the system administrators and can be identified by using the `ifconfig` command:

```
[oracle@oradb3 oracle]$ ifconfig
eth0      Link encap:Ethernet  HWaddr 00:40:F4:60:34:43
          inet addr:192.168.2.130  Bcast:192.168.2.255  Mask:255.255.255.0
          UP BROADCAST RUNNING MULTICAST  MTU:1500  Metric:1
          RX packets:63 errors:0 dropped:0 overruns:0 frame:0
          TX packets:43 errors:0 dropped:0 overruns:0 carrier:0
          collisions:0 txqueuelen:1000
          RX bytes:5238 (5.1 Kb)  TX bytes:3339 (3.2 Kb)
          Interrupt:11 Base address:0xb000

eth1      Link encap:Ethernet  HWaddr 00:D0:B7:6A:39:85
          inet addr:10.168.2.130  Bcast:10.168.2.255  Mask:255.255.255.0
          UP BROADCAST RUNNING MULTICAST  MTU:1500  Metric:1
          RX packets:4 errors:0 dropped:0 overruns:0 frame:0
          TX packets:4 errors:0 dropped:0 overruns:0 carrier:0
          collisions:0 txqueuelen:1000
          RX bytes:184 (184.0 b)  TX bytes:168 (168.0 b)
          Interrupt:11 Base address:0x2400 Memory:41300000-41300038

lo        Link encap:Local Loopback
          inet addr:127.0.0.1  Mask:255.0.0.0
          UP LOOPBACK RUNNING  MTU:16436  Metric:1
          RX packets:412 errors:0 dropped:0 overruns:0 frame:0
          TX packets:412 errors:0 dropped:0 overruns:0 carrier:0
          collisions:0 txqueuelen:0
          RX bytes:37638 (36.7 Kb)  TX bytes:37638 (36.7 Kb)
```

In the output presented above, `eth0` is the public network interface with IP address 192.168.2.130, and `eth1` is the private (cluster) interconnect with IP address 10.168.2.130.

Networks (as configured and illustrated above), both public and private, can be single points of failure. Such failures can disrupt the operation of the cluster and reduce availability. To avoid such failures, redundant networks should be configured. This means that dual network adapters should be configured for both public and private networks. When dual networks are configured, by default, the additional network adapters are only used when the primary network fails. However, to enable dual network connections and to load-balance network traffic across the dual network adapters, features such as network interface card (NIC) bonding or NIC pairing should be used whenever possible (see Figure 4.4).

Windows: The private and public network configuration is defined using the "Network places" option from startup (see Figure 4.3).

Figure 4.3
Configuring Network for RAC on Windows

4.5 NIC bonding

NIC bonding, or pairing, is a method of pairing multiple physical network connections into a single logical interface. This logical interface will be used to establish a connection with the database server. By allowing all network connections that are part of the logical interface to be used during communication, this provides load-balancing capabilities that would not otherwise be available. In addition, when one of the network connections fails, the other connection will continue to receive and transmit data, making it fault tolerant.

In a RAC configuration, there is a requirement to have a minimum of two network connections. One connection is for the private interface between the nodes in the cluster, and the other connection, called the public interface, is for users or application servers to connect and transmit data to the database server.

Best Practice: To avoid single points of failures on network layers, it is advisable that dual NICs be configured for both the public and private interface.

A node in a RAC implementation should contain at least four network devices (two for the public interface and two for the private interface). As illustrated in Figure 4.4, the two physical public interfaces will be bonded together to make one logical public interface, and the two physical private interfaces will be bonded together to make one logical private interface.

Figure 4.4
Bonding of the Public and Private Interfaces

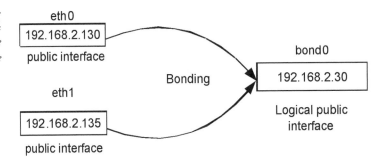

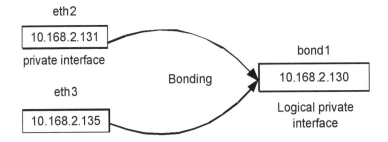

The first step in implementing the bonding functionality is to configure the bonding drivers. For example, in a Linux environment this is done by adding the following to the /etc/modules.conf file:

```
alias bond0 bonding
options bond0 miimon=100 mode=0
alias bond1 bonding
options bond1 miimon=100 mode=0
```

The configuration consists of two lines for each logical interface, where miimon (the media independent interface monitor) is configured in milliseconds and represents the link monitoring frequency. Mode indicates the type of configuration that will be deployed between the interfaces that are bonded or paired together. Mode indicates how the physical interfaces that are part of the logical interface will be used. Mode 0 indicates that a round-robin policy will be used, and all interfaces will take turns in transmitting; mode 1 indicates that one of the interfaces will be configured as a backup device; and mode 2 indicates either of them can be used [4].

The next step is to configure the logical interfaces. The first step in configuring the logical interfaces is to create two files, ifcfg-bond0 and ifcfg-bond1, for the public and private logical interfaces in the /etc/sysconfig/network-scripts directory.

 Note: The /etc/sysconfig/network-scripts directory contains, by default, one configuration file per network interface and all the interface assigned credentials, such as IP address, subnet details, and so on. Users should have superuser or root privileges to complete this operation.

```
[root@oradb3 network-scripts]# more ifcfg-bond0
# Linux NIC bonding between eth0 and eth1
# Murali Vallath
# APRIL-29-2005
#
DEVICE=bond0
BOOTPROTO=none
BROADCAST=192.168.2.255
IPADDR=192.168.2.30
NETMASK=255.255.255.0
NETWORK=192.168.2.0
ONBOOT=yes
USERCTL=no

[root@oradb3 network-scripts]# more ifcfg-bond1
# Linux NIC bonding between eth2 and eth3
# Murali Vallath
# APRIL-29-2005
#
DEVICE=bond1
```

```
BOOTPROTO=none
BROADCAST=192.168.2.255
IPADDR=10.168.2.130
NETMASK=255.255.255.0
NETWORK=10.168.2.0
ONBOOT=yes
USERCTL=no
```

The third step is to modify the individual network interface configuration files to reflect the bonding details:

```
[root@oradb3 network-scripts]# more ifcfg-eth0
# Linux NIC bonding between eth0 and eth1
# Murali Vallath
# APRIL-29-2005
#
DEVICE=eth0
BOOTPROTO=none
ONBOOT=yes
USERCTL=no
MASTER=bond0
SLAVE=yes
```

In this file, the MASTER clause indicates which logical interface this specific NIC belongs to, and the SLAVE clause indicates that it's one among other NICs that are bonded to the master and is only a slave to its master.

 Note: Similar changes should be made to all network configuration files on node oradb3 for both bond0 and bond1 logical interfaces described in this example configuration.

The next step is to restart the network interfaces, and this can be done using the following commands:

```
[root@oradb3 root]# service network stop
Shutting down interface eth0:                              [  OK  ]
Shutting down interface eth1:                              [  OK  ]
Shutting down interface eth2:                              [  OK  ]
Shutting down interface eth3:                              [  OK  ]
```

```
Shutting down loopback interface:                          [  OK  ]
[root@oradb3 root]#


[root@oradb3 root]# service network start
Setting network parameters:                                [  OK  ]
Bringing up loopback interface:                            [  OK  ]
Bringing up interface bond0:                               [  OK  ]
Bringing up interface bond1:                               [  OK  ]
[root@oradb3 root]#
```

The next step in the configuration process is to verify if the new logical interfaces are active. The following two options will help verify the configuration:

1.   Verify from the messages generated during interface startup. This is found in the operating system–specific log files.

```
[root@oradb3 root]# tail -15 /var/log/messages
network: Setting network parameters:  succeeded
kernel: ip_tables: (C) 2000-2002 Netfilter core team
network: Bringing up loopback interface:  succeeded
kernel: ip_tables: (C) 2000-2002 Netfilter core team
ifup: Enslaving eth0 to bond0
kernel: bonding: bond0: enslaving eth0 as an active interface
with a down link.
ifup: Enslaving eth1 to bond0
kernel: eth1: link up.
kernel: eth1: Setting full-duplex based on negotiated link
capability.
kernel: bonding: bond0: enslaving eth1 as an active interface
with an up link.
network: Bringing up interface bond0:  succeeded
kernel: ip_tables: (C) 2000-2002 Netfilter core team
kernel: e100: eth0 NIC Link is Up 100 Mbps Full duplex
kernel: bonding: bond0: link status definitely up for
interface eth0.
network: Bringing up interface eth2:  succeeded
sshd(pam_unix)[5066]: session opened for user root by (uid=0)
[root@oradb3 root]#
```

2.   Verify the new active networks using the `ifconfig` command.

```
[root@oradb3 root]# ifconfig -a
bond0      Link encap:Ethernet  HWaddr 00:D0:B7:6A:39:85
           inet addr:192.168.2.30  Bcast:192.168.2.255  Mask:255.255.255.0
           UP BROADCAST RUNNING MASTER MULTICAST  MTU:1500  Metric:1
           RX packets:3162 errors:0 dropped:0 overruns:0 frame:0
           TX packets:1312 errors:0 dropped:0 overruns:0 carrier:0
           collisions:0 txqueuelen:0
           RX bytes:275327 (268.8 Kb)  TX bytes:142369 (139.0 Kb)


eth0       Link encap:Ethernet  HWaddr 00:D0:B7:6A:39:85
           inet addr:192.168.2.30  Bcast:192.168.2.255  Mask:255.255.255.0
           UP BROADCAST RUNNING SLAVE MULTICAST  MTU:1500  Metric:1
           RX packets:804 errors:0 dropped:0 overruns:0 frame:0
           TX packets:1156 errors:0 dropped:0 overruns:0 carrier:0
           collisions:0 txqueuelen:1000
           RX bytes:83807 (81.8 Kb)  TX bytes:120774 (117.9 Kb)
           Interrupt:11 Base address:0x2800 Memory:41500000-41500038


eth1       Link encap:Ethernet  HWaddr 00:D0:B7:6A:39:85
           inet addr:192.168.2.30  Bcast:192.168.2.255  Mask:255.255.255.0
           UP BROADCAST RUNNING SLAVE MULTICAST  MTU:1500  Metric:1
           RX packets:2358 errors:0 dropped:0 overruns:0 frame:0
           TX packets:156 errors:0 dropped:0 overruns:0 carrier:0
           collisions:0 txqueuelen:1000
           RX bytes:191520 (187.0 Kb)  TX bytes:21933 (21.4 Kb)
           Interrupt:11 Base address:0x9000


bond1      Link encap:Ethernet  HWaddr 00:09:5B:E0:45:94
           inet addr:10.168.2.130  Bcast:10.168.2.255  Mask:255.255.255.0
           UP BROADCAST RUNNING MULTICAST  MTU:1500  Metric:1
           RX packets:31 errors:0 dropped:0 overruns:0 frame:0
           TX packets:31 errors:0 dropped:0 overruns:0 carrier:0
           collisions:0 txqueuelen:1000
           RX bytes:2922 (2.8 Kb)  TX bytes:2914 (2.8 Kb)
           Interrupt:11 Base address:0xa000


eth2       Link encap:Ethernet  HWaddr 00:09:5B:E0:45:94
. . .
eth3       Link encap:Ethernet  HWaddr 00:09:5B:E0:45:94
. . .
```

Note: The `ifconfig` output displays all interfaces available on the node; however, once bonding has been configured, only the new logical IP address assigned to `bond0` and `bond1` will be accessible.

Windows: Use the following steps to configure NIC pairing:

1. On the Windows desktop, click "Start" and select Programs -> appropriate Network Adapters -> ... for wired connections.

2. Click "Action," select "Add to Team" and then select "Create New Team."

3. In the "Select the type of team you want to create" window, select "Adaptive Load Balancing" and click "Next."

4. In the "Select the adapters for this team" window, select the network adapters you identified for NIC teaming and click "Next."

5. In the "Team Configuration" window, ensure that you selected the correct network adapters and click "Finish."

6. In the "Message" window, click "OK."

7. In the "File" menu, select "Exit."

8. Click "Yes" to save your settings.

How many times have we remembered people by their phone numbers instead of their names? Not many would be my guess. This is because phone numbers are difficult to remember. Instead, we recall people's names and then look them up in a telephone directory for their numbers. Similarly, in the Internet space, the Internet Engineering Task Force (IETF), with some help from the University of California, Berkeley, introduced the domain name concept. Like phone numbers, IP addresses are difficult to remember, so instead we remember their domain names. When a domain name is entered by a user, the message is routed to a domain name server (DNS), which helps map the domain name to the appropriate IP address.

In the case of a LAN or a WAN configuration inside an organization, domain names are grouped with the node name, and this helps to form a complete address that maps to an IP address. Such addresses are called hostnames. Hostnames comprise node names and domain names; for example, `oradb3.sumsky.net` is a hostname, where `oradb3` is the node name and `sumsky.net` is the domain name.

In this particular case, to ensure that Oracle is aware of these IP addresses, they have to be defined and mapped in the `hosts` file located in the `/etc` directory in Unix- and Linux-based systems. Apart from making the Oracle kernel aware of them, this definition prevents making DNS a single point of failure for the database cluster. The following output (generated by user `oracle`) shows the contents of the `/etc/hosts` file, illustrating the various IP address mappings for a cluster that consists of four nodes (`oradb1`, `oradb2`, `oradb3`, and `oradb4`). All interface entries should be added to the `/etc/hosts` file on all nodes in the cluster.

```
[oracle@oradb3 oracle]$ more /etc/hosts
127.0.0.1         localhost.localdomain localhost
192.168.2.10      oradb1.sumsky.net oradb1
192.168.2.20      oradb2.sumsky.net oradb2
192.168.2.30      oradb3.sumsky.net oradb3
192.168.2.40      oradb4.sumsky.net oradb4
10.168.2.110      oradb1-priv.sumsky.net oradb1-priv
10.168.2.120      oradb2-priv.sumsky.net oradb2-priv
10.168.2.130      oradb3-priv.sumsky.net oradb3-priv
10.168.2.140      oradb4-priv.sumsky.net oradb4-priv
```

Note: All IP addresses listed in the `/etc/hosts` file are the IP addresses assigned to their respective logical interfaces.

Windows: The various public and private IP addresses are added to `%SystemRoot%\system32\drivers\etc\hosts` file.

Apart from the public and private network address, an Oracle Database 10*g* RAC implementation also requires a public databaseVIP.[2] Oracle uses VIPs to achieve faster failover when a node in the cluster fails. For every logical public IP address defined in the system (where bonding has been implemented or to the one physical public IP address), a VIP address is required, and a definition should be added to the `/etc/hosts` file on Unix and Linux-based systems and `\windows\systems32\drivers\etc\hosts` file on windows-based systems. The VIPs added to the hosts file will be

---

2.   Database VIP is used by the instance versus application VIP used by applications. Refer to Chapter 2 regarding more about these.

used during the VIP configuration process as part of the Oracle Cluster-ware installation, at which time the VIP will be added to the network configuration. The following output shows the VIP definitions that will be added to the /etc/hosts file for the logical public IP addresses 192.168.2.10, 192.168.2.20, 192.168.2.30, and 192.168.2.40, respectively:

```
192.168.2.15    oradb1-vip.sumsky.net oradb1-vip
192.168.2.25    oradb2-vip.sumsky.net oradb2-vip
192.168.2.35    oradb3-vip.sumsky.net oradb3-vip
192.168.2.45    oradb4-vip.sumsky.net oradb4-vip
```

Best Practice: Ensure that UDP checksums is enabled. It helps track any transmission errors. On certain operating systems, such as Red Hat Linux and Sun Solaris, checksum is installed by default.

Checks to ensure if UDP checksum is enabled can be made using the ethtool utility:

```
[root@oradb3 root]$ ethtool -k eth2
Offload parameters for eth1:
rx-checksumming: on
tx-checksumming: on
scatter-gather: on
tcp segmentation offload: on
```

4.6   Verify interprocess communication buffer sizes

The interprocess communication (IPC) buffer sizes are operating system and version specific. Table 4.2 provides the various kernel parameters that define the buffer sizes on their respective platforms. Using the echo command on Unix and Linux systems, verify the current value of these parameters, and with the help of the system and network administrators, ensure that they have been appropriately sized.

Table 4.3   *UDP Parameters*

Solaris	udp_xmit_hiwat
(UDP Protocol)	udp_recv_hiwat
Linux	rmem_default
	rmem_max
	wmem_default
	wmem_max
Tru64 and AIX	udp_recvspace
(UDP Protocol)	udp_sendspace
HP-UX	tcp_xmit_hiwater_def
(UDP Protocol)	tcp_recv_hiwater_deff
Tru64	max_objs
(RDG Protocol)	msg_size
	max_async_req
	max_sessions
HP-UX	clic_attr_appl_max_procs
(HMP Protocol)	clic_attr_appl_max_nqs
	clic_attr_appl_max_mem_epts
	clic_attr_appl_max_recv_epts
	clic_attr_appl_deflt_proc_sends
	clic_attr_appl_deflt_nq_recvs

Best Practice: The network UDP buffer sizes should be set to the maximum allowed by the operating system. Setting the buffer size to a large value helps reduce interconnect contention during peak loads.

In the case of UDP over Infiniband, it is recommended to add the following operating system parameters in the /etc/modules.conf file to tune UDP traffic:

```
ipoib IpoibXmitBuffers=100
IpoibRecvBuffers=2000
```

4.7   **Jumbo frames**

Ethernet traffic moves in units called *frames*. The maximum size of frames is called the Maximum Transmission Unit (MTU) and is the largest packet a network device transmits. When a network device gets a frame larger than its MTU, the data is fragmented (broken into smaller frames) or dropped. As illustrated in the following `ifconfig` output, historically, Ethernet has a maximum frame size of 1,500 bytes,[3] so most devices use 1,500 as their default MTU. To maintain backward compatibility, the standard Gigabit Ethernet also uses 1,500-byte frames. This is maintained so a packet to and from any combination of 10-/100-/1,000-Mbps Ethernet devices can be handled without any layer 2 fragmentation or reassembly. An Ethernet packet larger than 1,500 bytes is called a *jumbo frame*.

```
bond0     Link encap:Ethernet  HWaddr 00:D0:B7:6A:39:85
          inet addr:192.168.2.30  Bcast:192.168.2.255  Mask:255.255.255.0
          UP BROADCAST RUNNING MASTER MULTICAST  MTU:1500  Metric:1
          RX packets:3162 errors:0 dropped:0 overruns:0 frame:0
          TX packets:1312 errors:0 dropped:0 overruns:0 carrier:0
          collisions:0 txqueuelen:0
          RX bytes:275327 (268.8 Kb)  TX bytes:142369 (139.0 Kb)
```

Jumbo frame support is designed to enhance Ethernet networking throughput and reduce significantly the CPU utilization of large file transfers like large multimedia files or large datafiles by enabling more efficient larger payloads per packet. By sending larger payloads per packet, fewer packets need to be routed, reducing the CPU overhead and potentially improving networking throughput. By using jumbo frames, the transfer frame sizes for Ethernet can be increased to 9,000 bytes.

 Note: To obtain the complete benefit of the jumbo frames, all components of the hardware configuration should support jumbo frames (NICs, switches, and storage).

Configuration to enable jumbo frames is different based on the environments. When configuring the private network, the NIC cards and the switches used for the Interconnect should have jumbo frames enabled.

---

3.   Ethernet packet consists of a 1,500-byte payload + 14 bytes for header + VLAN tag 4 bytes + CRC 4 bytes.

4.7.1 Linux kernel version 2.4 and 2.6

In Linux kernel version 2.4 (e.g., Red Hat 3.0) and kernel version 2.6 (e.g., Red Hat 4.0, SuSE 9.0), adding the MTU value to the /etc/sysconfig/network-scripts/ifcfg-eth<n> file (illustrated below) will enable jumbo frames:

```
[root@oradb3 network-scripts]# more ifcfg-eth0
# Linux NIC bonding between eth0 and eth1
# Murali Vallath
# APRIL-29-2005
#
DEVICE=eth0
BOOTPROTO=none
ONBOOT=yes
USERCTL=no
MASTER=bond0
MTU=9000
SLAVE=yes
```

The output of the NIC should resemble the following after the network interfaces have been restarted:

```
bond0     Link encap:Ethernet  HWaddr 00:D0:B7:6A:39:85
          inet addr:192.168.2.30  Bcast:192.168.2.255  Mask:255.255.255.0
          UP BROADCAST RUNNING MASTER MULTICAST  MTU:9000  Metric:1
          RX packets:3162 errors:0 dropped:0 overruns:0 frame:0
          TX packets:1312 errors:0 dropped:0 overruns:0 carrier:0
          collisions:0 txqueuelen:0
          RX bytes:275327 (268.8 Kb)  TX bytes:142369 (139.0 Kb)
```

4.7.2 AIX

Using ifconfig and chdev:

```
chdev -P -l <interface> -a media_speed=Auto_Negotiation
ifconfig <interface> down detach
chdev -l <interface> -a jumbo_frames=yes
chdev -l <interface> -a mtu=9000
chdev -l <interface> -a state=up
```

4.7.3 Solaris

Bring the interface down (`unplumb`) and set the instance to accept jumbo frames:

```
# ifconfig <interface> down unplumb
# ndd -set /dev/<interface> instance 1
# ndd -set /dev/<interface> accept-jumbo 1
# ifconfig <interface> plumb <address> up
```

Best Practice: Jumbo frames provide overall performance improvements in a RAC environment and should be used.

Note: Jumbo frames only help LAN performance; traffic leaving the LAN to the Internet is limited to packets of 1,500 bytes. Since access to and from a RAC environment is mostly limited to the application server and local clients, setting up jumbo frames should provide positive benefits.

4.8   Remote access setup

Depending on the node from which the Oracle installation will be performed using the Oracle Universal Installer (OUI), Oracle copies files from the node where the installation is performed to all the other remaining nodes in the cluster. Such a copy process is performed either by using Secured Shell Protocol (`ssh`) where available or by using the remote copy (`rcp`). In order for the copy operation to be successful, the `oracle` user on all the RAC nodes must be able to log in to other RAC nodes without having to provide a password or passphrase.

For security reasons, most organizations prefer using `ssh`-based operations to remote copy (`rcp`) operations. To configure the `oracle` account to use `ssh` logins without using any passwords, the following tasks should be performed:

1.   Create the authentication key for user `oracle`. In order to create this key, change the current directory to the default login directory of the `oracle` user and perform the following operation:

```
[oracle@oradb4 oracle]$ ssh-keygen -t dsa -b 1024
Generating public/private dsa key pair.
Enter file in which to save the key (/home/oracle/.ssh/id_dsa):
Created directory '/home/oracle/.ssh'.
Enter passphrase (empty for no passphrase):
Enter same passphrase again:
Your identification has been saved in /home/oracle/.ssh/id_dsa.
Your public key has been saved in /home/oracle/.ssh/id_dsa.pub.
The key fingerprint is:
b6:07:42:ae:47:56:0a:a3:a5:bf:75:3e:21:85:8d:30 oracle@oradb4.sumsky.net
[oracle@oradb4 oracle]$
```

This step is to be performed on all nodes participating in the cluster.

2.   Keys generated from each of the nodes in the cluster should be appended to the `authorized_keys` file on all nodes, meaning that each node should contain the keys from all other nodes in the cluster.

```
[oracle@oradb4 oracle]$ cd .ssh
[oracle@oradb3 .ssh]$ cat id_dsa.pub > authorized_keys
```

Once the keys have been created and copied to all nodes, oracle user accounts can connect from one node to another oracle account on another node without using a password. This allows for the OUI to copy files from the installing node to the other nodes in the cluster. The following output is the verification showing the ssh command from node oradb3 to other nodes in the cluster worked:

```
[oracle@oradb3 oracle]$ ssh oradb3 hostname
oradb3.sumsky.net
[oracle@oradb3 oracle]$ ssh oradb4 hostname
oradb4.sumsky.net
```

```
[oracle@oradb3 oracle]$ ssh oradb3-priv hostname
oradb3.sumsky.net
[oracle@oradb3 oracle]$ ssh oradb4-priv hostname
oradb4.sumsky.net
```

 Note: When performing these tests for the first time, the operating system will display a key and request the user to accept or decline. Enter `Yes` to accept and register the key. Tests should be performed on all other nodes across all interfaces (with the exception of the VIP) in the cluster.

4.9   Configuring the kernel

Kernel configuration of operating systems like Unix and Linux involves sizing the semaphores and the shared memory (Table 4.3). Oracle uses the shared memory segments for its SGA.

Table 4.4   *Kernel Parameters*

Kernel Parameter	Purpose
SHMMAX	Maximum allowable size of a single shared memory segment. Normally this parameter is set to half the size of the physical memory.
SHMMIN	Minimum allowable size of a single shared memory segment.
SEMMNI	The number of semaphore set identifiers in the system. It determines the number of semaphore sets that can be created at any one time.
SEMMSL	The maximum number of semaphores that can be in one semaphore set. This should be set to the sum of the **PROCESSES** parameter for each Oracle instance. While setting this value, add the largest one twice, then add an additional 10 for each additional instance.

Table 4.4 shows the recommended semaphore and shared-memory settings for the various operating system. The values for these shared-memory and semaphore parameters are set in the kernel configuration file of the respective operating system. On Linux systems, they are set in the /etc/ sysctl.conf file.

Table 4.5   *Semaphore and Shared Memory Settings*

Parameters/Operating System	Linux	HP-UX	Solaris
Shared Memory Parameters			
SHMALL	3279547		
SHMMAX	4294967296	1073741824	429467295
SHMMESG	4096	120	10
SHMMNI	4096	512	100
Semaphore Parameters			
SEMMNS	32000	(semmni*2)	1024
SEMMSL	256		256
SEMMNI	142	4096	100
SEMOPM	100		
SEMVMX		32767	32767
SEMMAP		(semmni+2)	
SEMMNU		4092	

The following additional parameters should be set in the /etc/
sysctl.conf file on Linux systems:

```
kernel.core_uses_pid = 1
kernel.hostname = oradb3.sumsky.net
kernel.domainname = sumsky.net
kernel.msgmnl = 2878
kernel.msgmnb = 65535
fs.file-max = 65536
net.ipv4.ip_local_port_range = 1024 65000
net.core.rmem_default=262144
net.core.wmem_default=262144
net.core.rmem_max=262144
net.core.wmem_max=262144
```

 Note: Semaphore and shared-memory setting are operating system and version dependent. For example, AIX does not require such settings, and the upcoming release of Solaris 10 also does not require these semaphore definitions.

4.10   Configuring the hangcheck timer on Linux systems

This module monitors the Linux kernel for long operating system hangs that could affect the reliability of a RAC node and cause database corruption. When such a hang occurs, this module reboots the node (after waiting for 240 seconds).

- **hangcheck_tick**. The hangcheck_tick is an interval indicating how often, in seconds, the hangcheck timer checks on the health of the system. The default value is 60 seconds.

- **hangcheck_margin**. Certain kernel activities may randomly introduce delays in the operation of the hangcheck timer. The hangcheck_margin defines how long the timer waits, in seconds, for a response from the kernel. The default value is 180 seconds.

The node reset occurs when the system hang time is greater than hangcheck_tick plus hangcheck_margin.

The hangcheck module should be loaded during system startup. To accomplish this, the following lines are added to the /etc/rc.local file:

```
[root@oradb3 root]$ more /etc/rc.local
#!/bin/sh

touch /var/lock/subsys/local
/sbin/insmod hangcheck-timer hangcheck_tick=30
hangcheck_margin=180
```

 Note: On SuSE 9 Linux, the above entry is added to /etc/init.d/ boot.local.

4.11 Configuring and synchronizing the system clock

In a clustered configuration, it is important that all nodes participating in the cluster maintain the same system date and time. This is because when records are inserted into the database, user sessions attached to different instances will return different SYSDATE values. This can cause records to be stamped with different or out-of-sequence times in DML operations, causing data-resolution issues during instance recovery and when data is replicated to remote destinations.

Best Practice: It is advised that date and time synchronization software such as Network Time Protocol (NTP), be used to keep the time values on all nodes in the cluster in sync.

Once the kernel parameters have been defined and all preinstallation steps have been verified, then you are ready to install various Oracle software components.

4.12 Installing Oracle

Unlike previous versions of Oracle, the installation process has been streamlined considerably in Oracle Database 10*g*. The installation process has been modularized. Based on the options to be configured, the appropriate DVD will have to be used for the installation. Like in the previous versions, the user has the option of installing the standard edition (SE) or the enterprise edition (EE). However, unlike in previous releases, RAC is now also available (with certain conditions[4]) as part of the SE. The following software packages that are part of the Oracle RDBMS product are now contained on one DVD:

- Oracle Clusterware (called cluster-ready services, or CRS, in Oracle Database 10*g* Release 1)

- Oracle Database 10*g* Release 2

- Oracle Database 10*g* companion software

---

4.   These conditions are highlighted later in this application the appropriate section on the installation process.

Depending on what options will be configured, Oracle Database 10*g* can potentially have the following different home directories:

ORACLE_HOME, which contains the Oracle binaries

ORA_CRS_HOME, which contains the binaries for CRS

AGENT_HOME, which contains OEM Management Agent binaries

ASM_HOME (Optional), which contains the Oracle binaries required for ASM

Once all of the preinstallation steps, including the creation of all required directories for the product, have been completed, the next step is to install the RAC product.

As a first step in this process, verify if the nodes are ready for the installation of the required Oracle components. Oracle Corporation has provided a cluster verification utility (CVU) that is part of Oracle Clusterware to verify the cluster status through various stages of the installation. The verification utility allows the administrator to verify the availability and integrity of a wide range of cluster elements before each stage of the installation. While OUI executes several of these verifications automatically, it's in the best interest of the administrator to verify manually at various stages of the installation and configuration process.

Getting the CVU is a simple process and involves the following steps:

1. Execute the Oracle-provided shell script `runcluvfy.sh` provided with the DVD:

   ```
   [root@oradb1 cluvfy]# ls
   cvupack.zip  jrepack.zip  runcluvfy.sh
   ```

2. All required Java binaries are unzipped and the required environment variables are automatically setup into the /tmp folder.

3. Once this is complete, the following two areas should be verified:

   a. System verification: Verify the hardware and operating system configuration using:

   ```
   cluvfy stage -post hwos -n
   oradb1,oradb2,oradb3,oradb4 -v
   ```

b. Clusterware preinstallation verification: Verify if the nodes are ready for Oracle Clusterware installation:

```
cluvfy stage -pre crsinst -n
oradb1,oradb2,oradb3,oradb4
```

Once the verification is complete and the results have been analyzed, the next step is to begin the Oracle installation process. The Oracle Database 10*g* RAC installation process is divided into four phases:

Phase I: Oracle Clusterware installation

Phase II: Oracle Software installation

Phase III: Database configuration

Phase IV: Cluster components

4.12.1 Phase I: Oracle Clusterware installation

The first step in the installation process is to install Oracle Clusterware. To accomplish this task, the DBA connects to one of the nodes participating in the cluster as user `oracle`. Once connected, the DBA inserts the installation DVD into the DVD drive and mounts the DVD if it is not automounted. Next, the DBA changes directories to the Clusterware directory.

To allow the installer to create the required directories, it is advisable that the environment variables be unset (if they are already set). This will allow the OUI to assign default directory structures.

```
unset ORACLE_HOME
unset ORA_CRS_HOME
```

 Note: On platforms (non-Linux and non-Windows) where third-party vendors have already provided the clusterware, the customer has the choice of either installing the Oracle-provided clusterware as a layer above the vendor-provided clusterware or installing it after removing the vendor clusterware.

Using the OUI requires that the terminal from which this installer is run should be X-windows compatible. If it is not, an appropriate X-windows emulator should be installed, and the emulator should be invoked using the `DISPLAY` command using the following syntax:

```
export DISPLAY=<client IP address>:0.0
```

For example:

```
[oracle@oradb3 oracle]$export DISPLAY=192.168.2.101:0.0
```

Next, from the command line, execute the following command:

```
oracle$ /<cdrom_mount_point>/runinstaller
```

For example:

```
[oracle@oradb3 oracle]$ /mnt/cdrom/runInstaller
```

This command invokes the OUI screen. The OUI is self-started when the DVD is inserted into the DVD drive as long as the installation is on a Windows platform.

 Caution: A word of caution is necessary at this stage of the process. The OUI software is written using Java and requires a large amount of memory to load. The DBA should ensure that sufficient memory is available when using this tool, especially on a Windows platform.

Figure 4.5
Welcome Screen

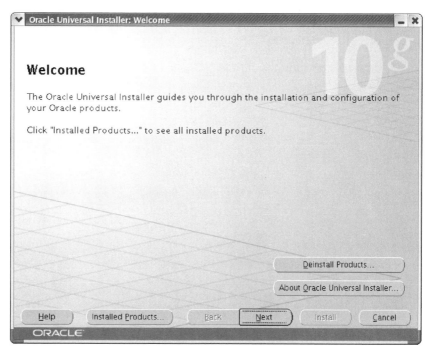

The first screen is the welcome screen (Figure 4.5). Select "Next" if the intention is to install new software. If this is the first time the OUI has been run on this system, the OUI prompts (not shown) for the inventory location. By default, OUI selects $ORACLE_BASE as the primary path for the inventory location and creates the oraInventory directory below it. At this stage, the DBA should provide the default operating system group (identified by the GID when the user was created). Once this is entered, the OUI will generate a script orainstRoot.sh in the inventory directory and prompt the DBA to execute this script as user root. The DBA runs the script as user root, and when it is completed successfully, clicks on OK.

Once the inventory directory and credentials have been specified, the next step is to install the product. The OUI will generate a default directory to install the product. Since the ORACLE_HOME and ORA_CRS_HOME environment variables have been unset, it is advisable to verify if it is pointing to the intended product path. For example, as illustrated in Figure 4.6, to /usr/app/oracle/product/10.2.0/crs.

Figure 4.6
File Location and
*ORA_CRS_*
HOME
Identification
Screens

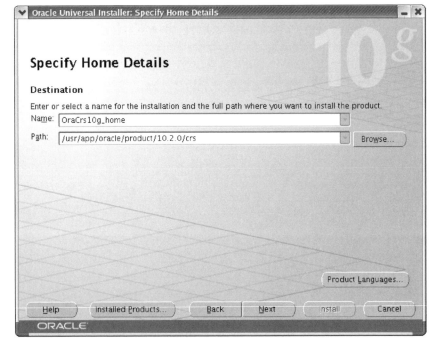

Note: `crs` is the default directory generated by the OUI; it is advisable that the default values be selected for easy installation and subsequent version-management purposes.

The next screen configures the cluster, which includes the interconnect and the VIP, as illustrated in Figure 4.7.

Figure 4.7
Cluster Configuration Screen

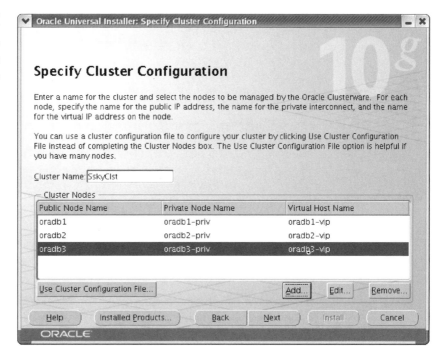

In this screen, the various public node names, the private node names, and the VIP hostnames should be mapped. Oracle uses this mapping for cluster management. The cluster name added in this screen is used to identify the cluster for management and administration purposes. EM will also use this cluster name to identify the cluster.

Depending on the operation to be performed, the appropriate keys can be selected. For example, to add another node, select the Add key, and another window will pop up, as illustrated in Figure 4.8, where the appropriate information can be entered.

Note: While adding new nodes to the cluster, the DBA should ensure that the node does not contain any components of previous versions of Oracle clusterware .

Figure 4.8
Adding a New
Node to the Cluster

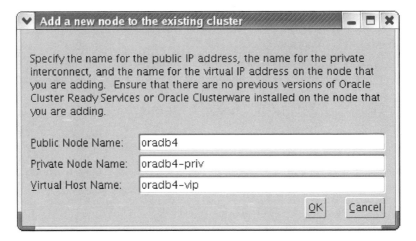

The Oracle cluster has been given a name, and the public node names, private node names, and VIP hostnames have been mapped; now, the next screen is the network interface usage definition screen (Figure 4.9), where the subnets are mapped to the public, private, or logical interfaces.

Note: When the bonding functionality is implemented, all physical network interfaces (e.g., eth0, eth1) should be configured under the "Do not use" category. This can be done by selecting the appropriate interface and using the "Edit" key, which will show another pop-up window, as illustrated in Figure 4.10, where the changes can be applied.

As part of the cluster services, Oracle requires a location on the shared storage where the cluster configuration and cluster database information is stored. One such cluster configuration component is the OCR. The OCR file location can be on either a clustered file system or a raw device. Oracle requires approximately 100 MB of disk space.

Irrespective of whether a cluster file system or a raw device is used, at the time of the installation, the directory or file location should be owned by oracle and should belong to the dba group. For example, in Figure 4.11,

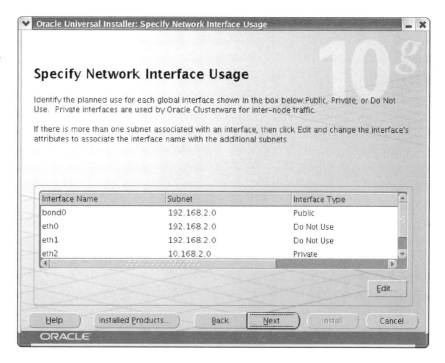

Figure 4.9
Public, Private, and Logical Interface Enforcement Screen

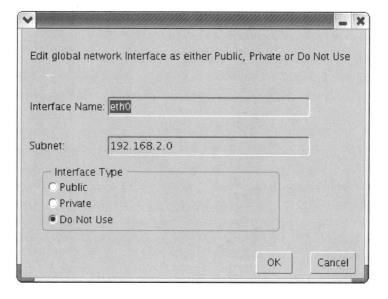

Figure 4.10
Public, Private, and Logical Interface Edit Screen

the file is created at location /u01/oradata on a clustered file system. The DBA should ensure that the directory and parent directories have write permission for the `oracle` user. This can be achieved by performing the following operation as user `root`:

```
chown oracle:dba /u01/oradata
```

```
chmod 640 /u01/oradata
```

The DBCA also maps the location of the OCR file into the `ocr.loc` file located in the `/etc` directory on Linux and Unix systems. In a Windows environment, this file is called `ocrconfig` and is located in the registry (Figure 4.11). This file is read by Oracle Clusterware during system startup to identify application resources that need to be started.

Figure 4.11
*ocrconfig Entry
in the Windows
Registry*

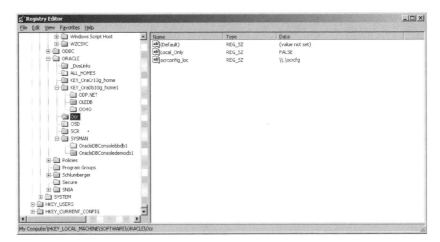

Due to the critical nature of the repository file being configured, it is advisable that some kind of redundancy be provided. If no storage-level redundancy (e.g., hardware-level disk mirroring) is available, then a mirrored physical location needs to be specified for multiplexing the OCR configuration file to more than one disk location (Figure 4.11).

Note: OCR is also used by the ASM instance for storage-layer verification and synchronization between the ASM instance and Oracle instances. ASM configuration and management were discussed in detail in Chapter 3.

Once the cluster definition file has been assigned, Oracle creates the file in the specified location. The next screen (Figure 4.12) prompts the

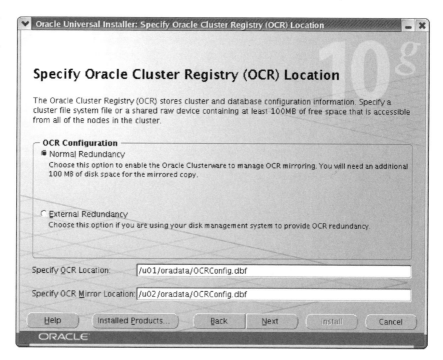

Figure 4.12
*Oracle Cluster
Registry Definition
Screen*

user for the location of the file where other cluster-related information can be stored. This disk or location on the shared storage will be used to store a special file called the voting disk (also called the quorum disk). This is the CSS screen. The CSS uses this file to maintain node membership in the cluster.

Similar to the OCR file, the CSS voting disk can also be configured on a clustered file system or a raw device. The directory or file location should also be owned by `oracle` and belong to the `dba` group. For example, in Figure 4.13, the file is created at location `/u02/oradata`, which is in a clustered file system. The DBA should ensure that the directory and parent directories have write permission for the `oracle` user. This can be achieved by performing the following operation as user `root`:

```
chown oracle:dba /u02/oradata
```

```
chmod 660 /u01/oradata
```

Similar to the OCR configuration file defined using the screen in Figure 4.11, the CSS voting disk is also critical, and Oracle recommends multi-

Figure 4.13
*Voting Disk
or CSS
Definition
Screen*

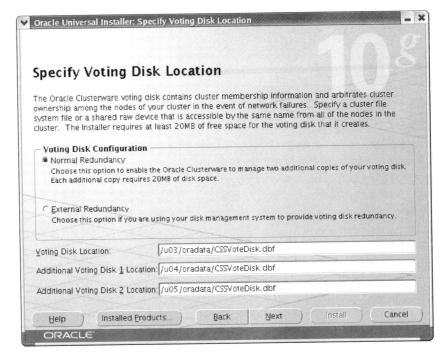

plexing this file to a minimum of three different locations, as illustrated in Figure 4.13.

The next screen (Figure 4.14) is the summary screen of the various Oracle Clusterware components that will be installed. At this stage, it is important to verify if all the required components have been selected by browsing through the list on the summary screen. It is also important to verify if the components have been targeted for all nodes in the cluster. This information is also listed in the summary screen.

Once the "Install" button is depressed, the OUI starts the installation of CRS on the primary node and then copies all the files to all other (remote) nodes. The next screen (not shown) is the installation progress screen, which illustrates the progress through the various stages. Once the install has been completed and files have been copied to all other nodes in the cluster, the OUI prompts the DBA (Figure 4.15) to execute two scripts, `orainstRoot.sh` and `root.sh`, created by the OUI in their appropriate directories listed on the screen.

Once the scripts have been executed on all nodes in the cluster, click the "OK" button. This completes the Oracle Clusterware installation process.

Figure 4.14
*CRS Install
Summary Screen*

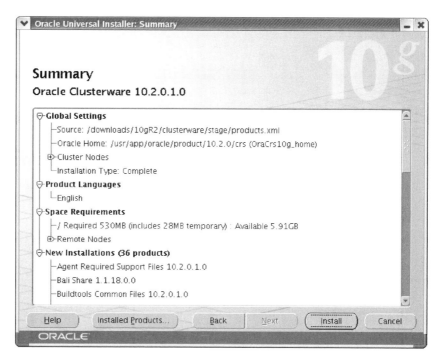

The following output shows the execution steps performed by the root.sh script on node oradb4. Please note that prior to executing script on oradb4, the root.sh script has already been executed on oradb3, oradb2, oradb1 and the cluster have been services started on the respective nodes.

```
[root@oradb4 crs]# ./root.sh
WARNING: directory '/usr/app/oracle/product/10.2.0' is not owned by root
WARNING: directory '/usr/app/oracle/product' is not owned by root
WARNING: directory '/usr/app/oracle' is not owned by root
Checking to see if Oracle CRS stack is already configured
/etc/oracle does not exist. Creating it now.
Setting the permissions on OCR backup directory
Oracle Cluster Registry configuration upgraded successfully
WARNING: directory '/usr/app/oracle/product/10.2.0' is not owned by root
WARNING: directory '/usr/app/oracle/product' is not owned by root
WARNING: directory '/usr/app/oracle' is not owned by root
clscfg: EXISTING configuration version 3 detected.
clscfg: version 3 is 10G Release 2.
assigning default hostname oradb3 for node 1.
```

Figure 4.15
Setup Privileges

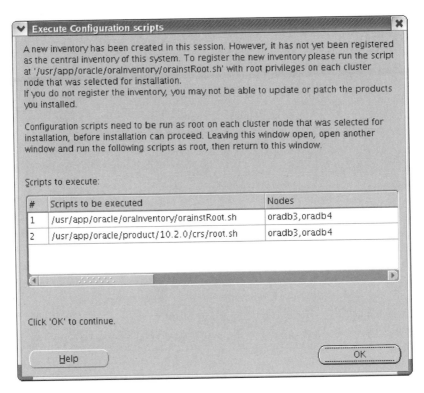

assigning default hostname oradb2 for node 2.

assigning default hostname oradb1 for node 3.

assigning default hostname oradb4 for node 4.

Successfully accumulated necessary OCR keys.

Using ports: CSS=49895 CRS=49896 EVMC=49898 and EVMR=49897.

node <nodenumber>: <nodename> <private interconnect name> <hostname>

node 1: oradb3 oradb3-priv oradb3

node 2: oradb2 oradb2-priv oradb2

node 3: oradb1 oradb1-priv oradb1

node 4: oradb4 oradb4-priv oradb4

clscfg: Arguments check out successfully.

NO KEYS WERE WRITTEN. Supply -force parameter to override.

-force is destructive and will destroy any previous cluster
configuration.

Oracle Cluster Registry for cluster has already been initialized

Startup will be queued to init within 30+60 seconds.

Adding daemons to inittab

Expecting the CRS daemons to be up within 600 seconds.

CSS is active on these nodes.

    oradb3

    oradb2

    oradb1

    oradb4

```
CSS is active on all nodes.
Waiting for the Oracle CRSD and EVMD to start
Waiting for the Oracle CRSD and EVMD to start
Waiting for the Oracle CRSD and EVMD to start
Waiting for the Oracle CRSD and EVMD to start
Oracle CRS stack installed and running under init(1M)
```

Running vipca(silent) for configuring nodeapps

```
Creating VIP application resource on (4) nodes...
Creating GSD application resource on (4) nodes...
Creating ONS application resource on (4) nodes...
Starting VIP application resource on (4) nodes...
Starting GSD application resource on (4) nodes...
Starting ONS application resource on (4) nodes...
Done
```

Note: The **NO KEYS WERE WRITTEN** message while executing the root.sh file on subsequent nodes is normal. All required keys for the cluster configuration are generated when the root.sh file is executed on the first node of the cluster.

The following output illustrates key generation and the initialization of the voting disk from running the root.sh script from oradb3, or the first node where root.sh is executed.

```
. . .
assigning default hostname oradb3 for node 1.
assigning default hostname oradb2 for node 2.
assigning default hostname oradb1 for node 3.
assigning default hostname oradb4 for node 4.
Successfully accumulated necessary OCR keys.
Using ports: CSS=49895 CRS=49896 EVMC=49898 and EVMR=49897.
node <nodenumber>: <nodename> <private interconnect name> <hostname>
node 1: oradb3 oradb3-priv oradb3
```

```
node 2: oradb2 oradb2-priv oradb2
node 3: oradb1 oradb1-priv oradb1
node 4: oradb4 oradb4-priv oradb4
Creating OCR keys for user 'root', privgrp 'root'..
Operation successful.
Now formatting voting device: /u03/oradata/CSSVoteDisk.dbf
Read -1 bytes of 512 at offset 1476395008 in voting device
(CSSVoteDisk.dbf)
Now formatting voting device: /u04/oradata/CSSVoteDisk.dbf
Read -1 bytes of 512 at offset 1476395008 in voting device
(CSSVoteDisk.dbf)
Now formatting voting device: /u05/oradata/CSSVoteDisk.dbf
Read -1 bytes of 512 at offset 1476395008 in voting device
(CSSVoteDisk.dbf)
Format of 3 voting devices complete.
Startup will be queued to init within 30+60 seconds.
Adding daemons to inittab
Expecting the CRS daemons to be up within 600 seconds.
CSS is active on these nodes.
        oradb3
CSS is inactive on these nodes.
        oradb1
        oradb2
        oradb4
Local node checking complete.
Run root.sh on remaining nodes to start CRS daemons.
. . .
```

As shown in the output from oradb4, the root.sh script starts the following three daemon processes on their respective nodes:

1.   *CRSD.* This is the primary daemon process and the primary engine that provides the high-availability features. CRSD manages the application resources; starts, stops, and fails application resources over; generates events when things happen; and maintains configuration profiles in the OCR. If the daemon fails, it automatically starts.

2.   *OCSSD.* This daemon process presents various nodes participating in the cluster as members of the cluster, coordinates and integrates with the vendor clusterware if present, and provides group

services. OCSSD enables synchronization between an ASM instance and the database instances that rely on it for database file storage. In a RAC setup there has to be a process that ensures the health of the cluster so a split brain will not occur. If the process that does the synchronization dies, rebooting the system will be necessary to ensure that a split brain has not occurred.

 Note: A split brain occurs when the nodes in a cluster lose communication with each other and become confused about which nodes are members of the cluster and which nodes are not (this occurs when nodes hang or the interconnects fail).

3.   *EVMD.* This daemon process has the primary function of sending and receiving messages between nodes.

 Note: In a Windows environment, these three functionalities are performed by `OracleCRService`, `OracleCSService`, and `OracleEMService`, respectively.

The **Oracle CRS stack installed and running under init(1M)** message at the end of the execution indicates that all the relevant information required for cluster management was successfully generated and stored in the OCR file and the CSS voting disk. At this stage, verifying the size (to ensure it's not zero) of the two files is also an indication of this completion.

```
[oracle@oradb3 oracle]# ls -ltr /u01/oradata
total 5244
-rw-r-----   1 root     dba       5369856 May  4 22:19 OCRConfig.dbf
[oracle@oradb3 oracle]#
```

```
[oracle@oradb3 oracle]# ls -ltr /u03/oradata
total 10000
-rw-r--r--   1 oracle   dba      10240000 May  4 14:21 CSSVoteDisk.dbf
[oracle@oradb3 oracle]#
```

Note: The ownership on the directory that contains the file `OCRConfig.dbf` is changed by the `root.sh` script to user `root`; however, it continues to belong to group `dba`.

OCR configuration should be verified using the Oracle-provided utility called `ocrcheck`. This utility will perform an integrity check of the OCR file and provide a status output as shown:

```
[root@oradb3 bin]# ocrcheck
Status of Oracle Cluster Registry is as follows :
        Version                  :         2
        Total space (kbytes)     :    262144
        Used space (kbytes)      :      4472
        Available space (kbytes) :    257672
        ID                       : 134017875
        Device/File Name         : /u01/oradata/OCRConfig.dbf
                                   Device/File integrity check succeeded
        Device/File Name         : /u02/oradata/OCRConfig.dbf
                                   Device/File integrity check succeeded

        Cluster registry integrity check succeeded
```

Installation of CRS could be verified using the `olsnodes` command. This lists all the nodes participating in the cluster.

```
[oracle@oradb3 oracle]$ olsnodes
oradb1
oradb2
oradb3
oradb4
[oracle@oradb3 oracle]$
```

VIP: The VIP address is configured and added to the operating system network configuration, and the network services are started. The VIP configuration can be verified using the `ifconfig` command at the operating system level.

```
[oracle@oradb3 oracle]$ ifconfig -a
bond0      Link encap:Ethernet  HWaddr 00:D0:B7:6A:39:85
           inet addr:192.168.2.30  Bcast:192.168.2.255  Mask:255.255.255.0
           UP BROADCAST RUNNING MASTER MULTICAST  MTU:1500  Metric:1
           RX packets:123 errors:0 dropped:0 overruns:0 frame:0
           TX packets:67 errors:0 dropped:0 overruns:0 carrier:0
           collisions:0 txqueuelen:0
           RX bytes:11935 (11.6 Kb)  TX bytes:5051 (4.9 Kb)

bond0:1    Link encap:Ethernet  HWaddr 00:D0:B7:6A:39:85
           inet addr:192.168.2.35  Bcast:192.168.3.255  Mask:255.255.252.0
           UP BROADCAST RUNNING MASTER MULTICAST  MTU:1500  Metric:1
           RX packets:14631 errors:0 dropped:0 overruns:0 frame:0
           TX packets:21377 errors:0 dropped:0 overruns:0 carrier:0
           collisions:0 txqueuelen:0
           RX bytes:6950046 (6.6 Mb)  TX bytes:19706526 (18.7 Mb)
```

In the previous illustration, bond0:1 is the VIP for bond0. Please note that VIP has a distinct IP address (192.168.2.35) from the logical public IP address. It is also relevant at this stage to take note of the notation in which the VIP is listed as a subset of the primary network interface (bond0:1).

- *GSD*. The Global Service Daemon (GSD). The GSD process is created and started as a service. Please note that unlike in Oracle Database 9i, GSD is treated as a service and is automatically started once the CRS daemon is started. GSD has no significant role in Oracle Database 10*g*; however, it is started so that it can monitor any Oracle 8*i* or Oracle 9*i* databases on the node and to provide backward compatibility.

- *ONS*. Oracle Notification Services (ONS). ONS is configured and started. ONS is an Oracle service that allows users to send SMS messages, e-mails, voice notifications, and fax messages in an easily accessible manner. CRS uses the resource application to send notifications about the state of the database instances to mid-tier applications that use this information for load-balancing and for fast failure detection.

Verify if CRS has been installed by checking the /etc/inittab file. The three lines listed as follows are added by the root.sh script file:

```
tail -4 /etc/inittab

x:5:respawn:/etc/X11/prefdm -nodaemon
h1:35:respawn:/etc/init.d/init.evmd run >/dev/null 2>&1 </dev/null
h2:35:respawn:/etc/init.d/init.cssd fatal >/dev/null 2>&1 </dev/null
h3:35:respawn:/etc/init.d/init.crsd run >/dev/null 2>&1 </dev/null
```

Since the CRS manages all the RAC components running on their respective nodes as services, they can be verified and managed using utilities provided by Oracle. For example, to verify if the system services such as GSD, ONS, and VIP have been started and are online, the following command can be used:

```
[root@oradb3 SskyClst]# crs_stat -t -c oradb3
Name              Type          Target    State     Host
-------------------------------------------------------------
ora.oradb3.gsd application    ONLINE    ONLINE    oradb3
ora.oradb3.ons application    ONLINE    ONLINE    oradb3
ora.oradb3.vip application    ONLINE    ONLINE    oradb3
```

Note: Services are discussed in detail in Chapter 6.

Windows: All command-line utilities available on a Linux or Unix environment are also available in a Windows environment.

On successful completion of executing the `root.sh` script and verifying that the installation is successful, click "OK."

The next screen (Figure 4.16) is the configuration of the ONS, Private Interconnect Configuration, and cluster verification. This is an automatic process. As illustrated on the screen, the configuration of these components is optional; however, in order to take advantage of the various high-availability features of RAC, it is advisable to make sure the configuration has completed successfully.

This completes phase I of the installation process. It's good to verify if the installation has completed successfully using CVU.

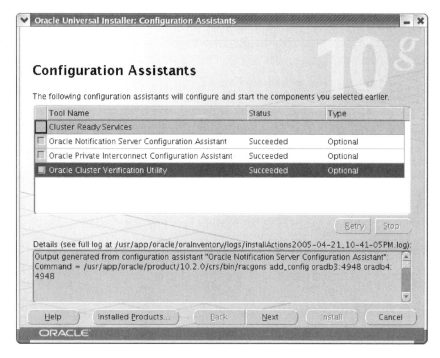

Figure 4.16
*Cluster Component
Configuration*

Cluster verification: At this point using CVU, the installation and configuration of Oracle Clusterware is to be verified using

```
cluvfy stage -post crsinst -n oradb1,oradb2,oradb3,oradb4 -v
```

Once Oracle Clusterware has been verified, the next phase of the installation process is to install the Oracle software.

4.12.2 Phase II: Oracle Software Installation

Before attempting to install the Oracle software, verify that the required cluster-related daemon processes are running on all nodes in the cluster. This can be verified using the following commands:

- *Cluster-Ready Services Daemon*

```
[oracle@oradb4 oracle]$ ps -ef | grep crsd
root      3515     1  0 23:35 ?        00:00:07 /usr/app/
oracle/product/10.2.0/crs/bin/crsd.bin
```

```
root      3804  3515  0 23:36 ?          00:00:00 [crsd.bin
<defunct>]
[oracle@oradb4 oracle]$
```

- *Cluster Synchronization Services Daemon*

```
[oracle@oradb4 oracle]$ ps -ef | grep ocssd
oracle    3905  3865  0 23:36 ?          00:00:00 /usr/app/
oracle/product/10.2.0/crs/bin/ocssd.bin
oracle    3922  3905  0 23:36 ?          00:00:00 /usr/app/
oracle/product/10.2.0/crs/bin/ocssd.bin
oracle    3923  3922  0 23:36 ?          00:00:00 /usr/app/
oracle/product/10.2.0/crs/bin/ocssd.bin
. . .
```

- Event notification services daemon

```
[oracle@oradb4 oracle]$ ps -ef | grep evmd
root      3513     1  0 23:35 ?          00:00:00 /bin/su -l
oracle -c exec /usr/app/oracle/product/10.2.0/crs/bin/evmd
oracle    3767  3513  0 23:36 ?          00:00:00 /usr/app/
oracle/product/10.2.0/crs/bin/evmd.bin
oracle    3837  3767  0 23:36 ?          00:00:00 /usr/app/
oracle/product/10.2.0/crs/bin/evmd.bin
. . .
```

If these commands do not give any output, then the missing daemon processes must be started before proceeding any further. The daemon processes can be started by executing the following command as user root on all the nodes in the cluster:

```
[root@oradb3 root]$ /etc/init.d/init.crs start
```

Change the directory to the Oracle software directory available on the same DVD.

Using the OUI requires that the terminal from where this installer is run, be X-windows compatible. If it is not, an appropriate X-windows emulator should be installed, and the emulator should be invoked using the DISPLAY command using the following syntax:

```
export DISPLAY=<client IP address>:0.0
```

For example:

```
export DISPLAY=192.168.2.101:0.0
```

Once set, execute the following command to invoke the OUI:

```
[oracle@oradb3 oracle]$ /mnt/crdom/runInstaller
```

This command invokes the OUI, which displays a welcome screen; if no uninstall steps are to be performed, click on "Next." The next screen is the installation-type selection screen. The OUI loads all high-level product information that the DVD contains. Figure 4.17 shows the various installation types: Enterprise Edition (EE), Standard Edition (SE), and Custom Install.

Unlike the previous versions of Oracle, RAC is available with the SE option. However, it should be noted that selecting the SE option imposes certain limitations and conditions that are required to meet the licensing requirements. They are as follows:

1.   Such an implementation should be limited to four CPU configurations (i.e., the number of CPUs of all nodes participating in the cluster should not exceed four). For example, the configuration can contain either two two-way systems or four one-way systems.

2.   Such an implementation should use Oracle's ASM for storage management.

3.   Such an implementation should also use Oracle Clusterware and no third-party clusterware.

While this offering from Oracle is an excellent opportunity for small to medium-sized implementations, for serious, high-volume, mission-critical applications, this implementation may not be sufficient; therefore, the EE option will be required. Also, installing the SE option deprives the user of certain scalability features, such as data partitioning.

Figure 4.17
*Select Installation
Type*

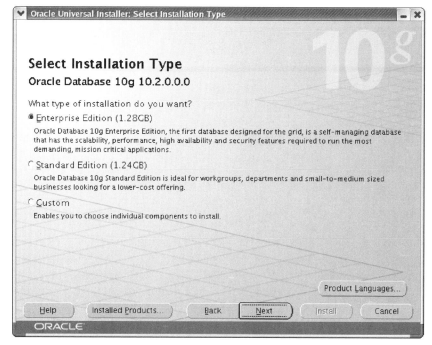

The EE option has been selected, which will install all the advanced options, such as partitioning and advanced replication including RAC.

The next screen (not shown) provides the default location of the Oracle binaries. As with installing Oracle Clusterware, it is advisable that the default location be selected. However, it should be verified that the path matches the proposed $ORACLE_BASE and complies with the OFA standards. For example, the directory path for the Oracle binaries should be /usr/app/oracle/ product/10.2.0/db_1.

Once the location has been identified, the user can proceed with the installation. The next screen in the installation process selects nodes where the Oracle binaries will be installed. The OUI lists all the nodes in the cluster, and the DBA decides if this installation will be a local (single node) installation or if the binaries are to be copied and installed on all nodes (cluster installation) in the cluster. Since the installer is capable of installing the required binaries on all nodes, it is advisable that all nodes listed be selected.

Note: The screen providing a list of nodes in the cluster is another validation that ensures that all cluster service components have been installed and configured and are running correctly. If the list is not complete, please verify and start all the components before proceeding.

Figure 4.18 helps specify the installation mode, that is, if the installation will be a local installation or a cluster installation. All nodes are listed and have been selected for the installation.

Figure 4.18
Hardware Cluster
Installation Mode

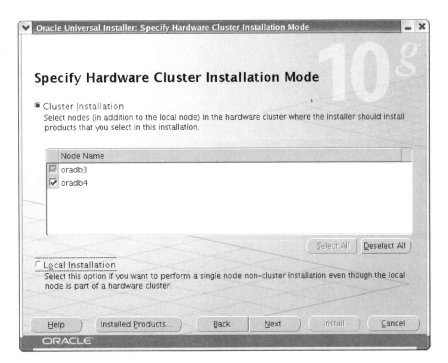

The next screen (not shown) is the verification screen that the OUI performs as part of the installation to ensure that the system meets all the minimum requirements (which includes kernel and operating system patch updates) for installing and configuring the EE option. The following is the output of the verification process:

```
Checking operating system requirements...
Expected result: One of redhat-3,suse-9
Actual Result: redhat-3
Check complete. The overall result of this check is:        Passed
```

```
==========================================================================

Checking operating system package requirements...
Checking for make-3.79; found make-1:3.79.1-17.               Passed
Checking for binutils-2.14; found binutils-2.14.90.0.4-35.   Passed
Checking for gcc-3.2; found gcc-3.2.3-34.                     Passed
Checking for openmotif-2.2.3;
        found openmotif-2.2.3-6.RHEL4.2.                      Passed
Check complete. The overall result of this check is:         Passed
==========================================================================

Checking kernel parameters
Checking for semmsl=250; found semmsl=250.                    Passed
Checking for semmns=32000; found semmns=32000.               Passed
Checking for semopm=100; found semopm=100.                   Passed
Checking for semmni=128; found semmni=150.                   Passed
Checking for shmmax=2147483648; found shmmax=2147483648.     Passed
Checking for shmmni=4096; found shmmni=4096.                 Passed
Checking for shmall=2097152; found shmall=2097152.          Passed
Checking for shmmin=1; found shmmin=1.                       Passed
Checking for shmseg=10; found shmseg=4096.                   Passed
Checking for file-max=65536; found file-max=65536.          Passed
Checking for VERSION=2.4.21; found VERSION=2.4.21-15.       Passed
Checking for ip_local_port_range=1024 - 65000; found ip_local_port_range=1024 -
65000.                                                       Passed
Checking for rmem_default=262144;
found rmem_default=262144.                                   Passed
Checking for rmem_max=262144; found rmem_max=262144.        Passed
Checking for wmem_default=262144; found wmem_default=262144.
                                                             Passed
Checking for wmem_max=262144; found wmem_max=262144.        Passed
Check complete. The overall result of this check is:        Passed
==========================================================================

Checking Shell Limits ...
Actual Result: Detected the following existing settings...
Passed >>   Hard Limit on maximum number of processes for a single user: 16384
Passed >>   Hard Limit on maximum number of open file descriptors: 65536
Passed >>   Soft Limit on maximum number of processes for a single user: 3392
Passed >>   Soft Limit on maximum number of open file descriptors: 1024
Check complete. The overall result of this check is:         Passed
==========================================================================

Checking Recommended glibc version
Expected result: ATLEAST=2.3.2-95.27
Actual Result: 2.3.4-2
Check complete. The overall result of this check is:         Passed
==========================================================================
```

Note: Verify and ensure that all verification steps have passed before proceeding to the next step.

The next screen, illustrated in Figure 4.19, is the database configuration selection screen. At this stage, the DBA can decide if a database should be created as part of the installation. In this specific case, "Install database Software only" has been selected. This gives the option to configure the database later either using the DBCA or manually using a custom-generated script.

Figure 4.19
Configuration Option

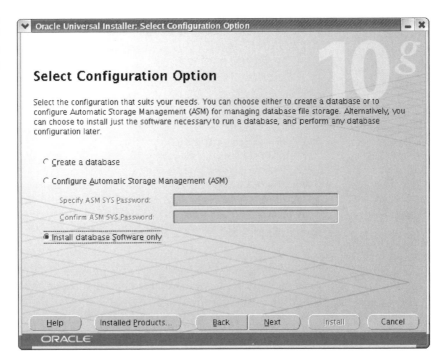

After selecting the "Install database Software only" option, click "Next." The next screen is a listing of all the software components that will be installed. The summary screen is illustrated in Figure 4.20, which shows a list of components that will be installed. It should be verified that all required components are selected by browsing through the screen. If the installation is to be performed on all nodes in the cluster, it should be verified that the nodes are also listed in the summary page. If all options have been verified, selecting the "Install" key will start the installation process.

The next screen (not shown) gives the DBA the current progress of the installation process. Once complete, the OUI creates a script `root.sh` in the `$ORACLE_HOME` directory and prompts the DBA to execute it (as shown in Figure 4.21).

Figure 4.20
Software Selection
Summary Screen

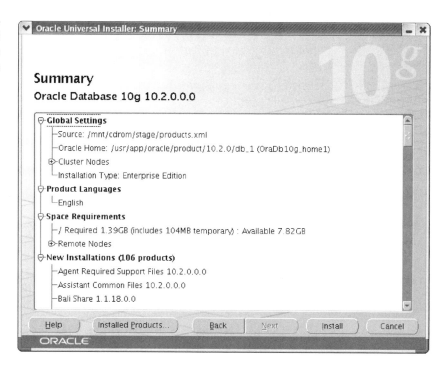

This completes the installation of the Oracle binaries and phase II of the configuration. It's a good practice to verify if the installation has been completed successfully using CVU.

Cluster verification: At this point using CVU, the installation and configuration of the Oracle software is to be verified using:

```
cluvfy stage —pre dbinst -n oradb1,oradb2,oradb3,oradb4 —v
```

Once the verification is complete, the next section is Phase III, in which the database creation process is discussed.

4.12.3 Phase III: database configuration

Database creation can be done in one of two ways, either by using the DBCA, which is a GUI-based interface provided with the product (recom-

Figure 4.21

Script Execution

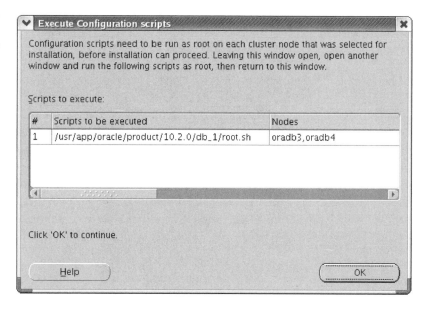

mended), or manually using a script file. In the case of a RAC database, creation of the database is different from the regular stand-alone configuration because in the case of RAC, we have one database and two or more instances.

An advantage of using the GUI interface over using the script file method is that there are fewer steps to remember. This is because, when using the DBCA, the steps are already predefined, and based on the selected template, the type of database is automatically created, sized, and configured. However, the script file approach has an advantage over the GUI interface approach in the sense that the creator is able to see what is happening during the creation process and can physically monitor the process. Another advantage of this option is that the script can be created based on the needs of the enterprise.

Database Configuration Assistant

The DBCA helps in the creation of the database. It follows the standard naming and placement convention defined in the OFA standards. As mentioned earlier, in Figure 4.18, the DBCA can be launched automatically as part of the Oracle installation process (discussed in phase II) or manually (recommended) by directly executing the dbca command from the $ORACLE_HOME/bin directory. Figure 4.22 is the DBCA selection screen. From this screen, the type of database to be created is selected. The screen provides two choices: Oracle Real Application Clusters database or Oracle

Figure 4.22
DBCA Database
Selection Screen

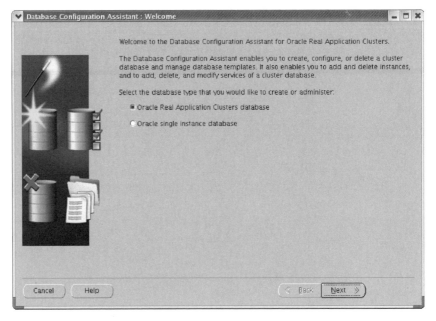

single-instance database. Select the "Oracle Real Application Clusters database" option, and click "Next."

Note: The "Oracle Real Application Clusters database" option is only visible if the clusterware is configured. If this option is not visible in this screen, the DBA should cancel the configuration process and verify that the clusterware has been started and is running before proceeding.

The next screen is the operations window (Figure 4.23). If this is the first database being configured, DBCA provides three options: (1) create a new database, (2) manage database creation templates provided by Oracle, or (3) configure ASM. From this screen, select the "Create a Database" option and click "Next."

The next screen (not shown) is the node selection window. On this screen, the appropriate node where RAC needs to be configured is selected. Since the OUI will copy the required files to all nodes participating in the cluster, it is advisable to select all nodes listed and click "Next."

Following the node selection screen is the template selection screen. Figure 4.24 shows the Oracle templates that can be selected according to the functionality that the database will support.

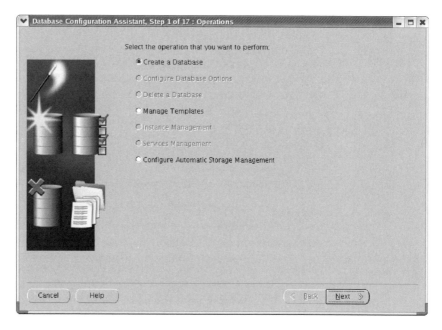

Figure 4.23
DBCA Operation Selection

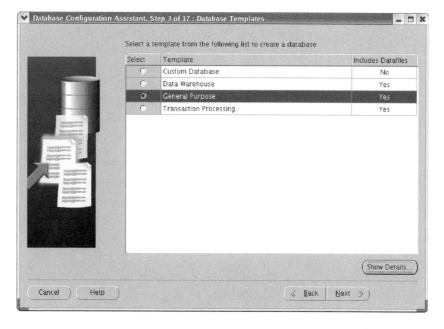

Figure 4.24
Selecting the Template

Once the appropriate database template has been selected, the next screen (not shown) is the database identification screen. In this screen, the proposed database name (e.g., SSKYDB) and the SID (SSKY) should be provided. DBCA will automatically generate an instance number, which will be suffixed to the SID defined. When subsequently the DBCA creates the database and starts the instances, depending on the number of instances being created, the instances will have the following naming convention: SID1, SID2, etc. (e.g., SSKY1, SSKY2, SSKY3, etc.).

Once the database and the instance names have been identified, click "Next." The next screen, illustrated in Figure 4.25, is the database control definition screen. In this screen, the DBA will define the various monitoring and notification methods that will be used.

On this screen, there are two options:

1.   The *default option*, where the EM console is installed by the DBCA process. Under this option, no repository or data collection process is involved. The basic console monitoring and administration functions are only available.

2.   An *advanced option* that would require the EM grid functionality. Under this option, the EM repository is created, and the management agents installed on all nodes are required to be monitored.

As Figure 4.25 shows, the management agent has already been installed on the node; hence, the OUI automatically detects and fills in the appropriate management agent information. Please note that, under this option, since the EM will control e-mail and other administrative functions, only one of the following two options can be selected: (1) "Use Grid Control for Database Management" or (2) "Use Database Control for Database Management."

Once the monitoring control options have been selected, the next step is to assign a name to the database being created. Following that, the next step is to define the default passwords for the SYS and SYSTEM user accounts. This screen (not shown) illustrates the password definition process. Oracle provides two options on this screen:

1.   Create a default password for all accounts created by Oracle.

2.   Define individual passwords specific to each account (e.g., SYS, SYSTEM, and DBSNMP).

Figure 4.25
*Management
Option Selection*

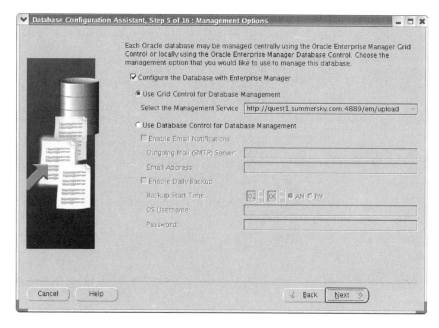

Based on the user requirements and security policies of the organization, either option can be used. Once the password has been assigned and verified, click "Next."

The next screen (Figure 4.26) is the storage mechanism selection option. Oracle Database 10*g* provides three options to choose from:

1. Cluster file system

2. ASM

3. Raw devices

Based on the desired storage mechanism for the database files, the required subcomponents will be installed. In Figure 4.26, the ASM option has been selected.

Figure 4.26
Storage Mechanism
Selection

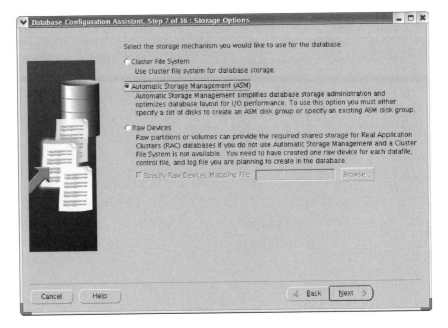

Note:

1. Installation and configuration of ASM, including administration and monitoring functions, is discussed in Chapter 3.

2. If ASM is the storage management method, DBCA will verify, and if not found, will start ASM instances on all nodes participating in the cluster.

3. If cluster file system is the storage method, on platforms such as Linux, it is required that OCFS be installed and the appropriate directory structures defined. OCFS implementation and configuration details can be found in Appendix C.

4. Oracle Database 10*g* RAC supports a combination of storage options (not possible from this screen); that is, some data files can be created on raw devices, some on OCFS, and the others on ASM.

5. If ASM is the primary storage management solution, the DBA will need one other type of file storage (raw or cluster file system) to store the cluster configuration files (illustrated in Figures 4.11 and 4.12) discussed in phase II.

Best practice: For easy management of datafiles, it is advisable that a single type of storage management be selected for all database file types.

Oracle differentiates a regular Oracle database instance from an ASM instance in the following two ways:

1.   The background processes of an ASM instance carry a prefix of `asm_` compared to the Oracle database instance, which carries a prefix of `ora_`.

2.   Oracle introduced a new initialization parameter called `INSTANCE_TYPE`. The ASM instance will have a value of `ASM` for instance type compared to the other Oracle database instance, which is identified by `RDBMS`.

Figure 4.27
ASM Instance
Creation

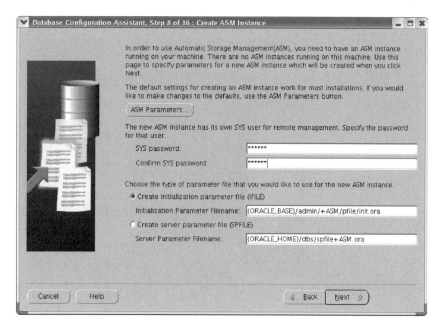

The next screen (Figure 4.27) in the configuration process is the creation of the ASM instance. In this screen, the DBA provides the password for the ASM instance and the type of parameter file to be used for the ASM instance. Once the screen has been completed, click on "Next."

At this point, OUI has all the information required to create the ASM instances on the respective nodes in the cluster. When the new window pops up (Figure 4.28) asking for confirmation, when ready, click "OK."

Figure 4.28
ASM Instance Creation

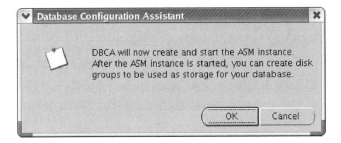

The next screen (not shown) is related to the ASM disk group definition process. Disk groups are used by ASM to store database files. Configuration management and administration of ASM instances, disks, and disk groups are covered in detail in Chapter 3.

Figure 4.29
Database File Management Selection

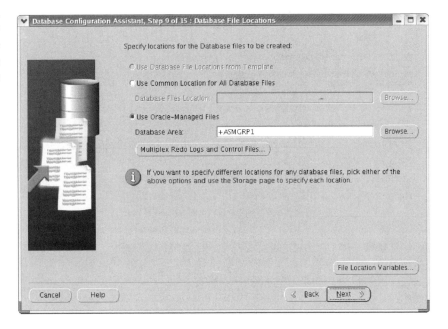

The next screen (Figure 4.29) in the configuration process selects the location for the various database files. In this screen, the DBA chooses between user-managed and Oracle-managed files. It should be noted that if the storage mechanism is ASM, then to take advantage of the ASM architecture, OMF should be the preferred file management method. With OMF, the DBA has further options to multiplex redo logs and control files. Once the screen has been completed click on "Next."

Best Practice: To obtain the maximum benefits from ASM storage management, it is advisable that the OMF mode be selected.

The next screen (Figure 4.30) is the database recovery configuration screen. In this screen, the DBA has the option to create a flashback recovery area and enable archiving. For easy sharing of recovery data between the various nodes participating in the cluster, these areas must be located on a shared storage. OUI has options to select the appropriate location by browsing through a list.

While both of these can be configured on the same type of storage, in Figure 4.30, the flash recovery area is located in an ASM disk group; however, the archive destination is on an external cluster file system (illustrated in Figure 4.31).

Figure 4.30
Database Recovery
Configuration
Screen

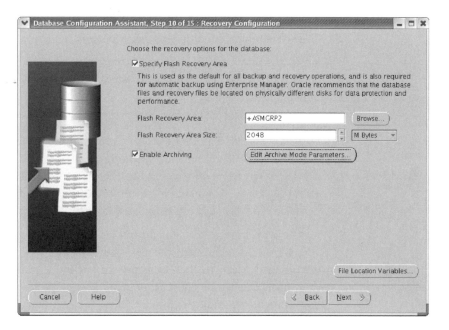

The next screen (step 11 in the DBCA process and not shown) is the option to create sample schemas when the database is configured. After making the appropriate selections, click "Next."

Figure 4.31
*Archiving Mode
Parameter Defini-
tion Screen*

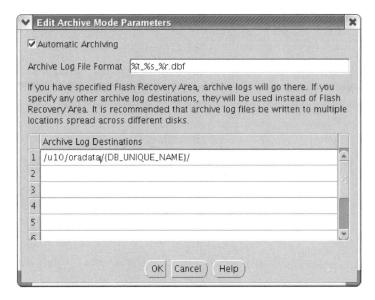

The next screen (Figure 4.32) is the service definition screen. In Oracle Database 10*g*, services play a strategic role and are used in implementing distributed workload management. The next set of screens relate to the service and workload distribution setup process.

Note: Installation, configuration, and management of services are discussed in detail in Chapter 5.

Please note that as a part of the service definition, the transparent application failover (TAF) policies for the respective services can also be defined using this screen. Service names can be verified by checking the parameter SERVICE_NAMES or by querying the V$SERVICES view after the database configuration process has been completed and the instances are started.

Once the storage mechanism is selected and the appropriate services (if any) have been identified, the next few screens are related to the instance definition process. In these screens, the various instance-specific information, such as memory allocation (e.g., shared pool, buffer cache), sizing (e.g., processes), character modes (e.g., UTF8), and connection methods (e.g., dedicated), are selected. These definitions are chosen by selecting the respective tabs from the screen in Figure 4.33.

For example, on selecting the "Connection Mode" tab, DBCA displays the client connection selection screen (Figure 4.34). This screen provides

Figure 4.32
Database Service Configuration Screen

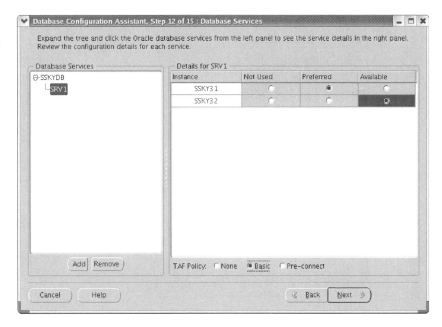

Figure 4.33
Parameter Initialization

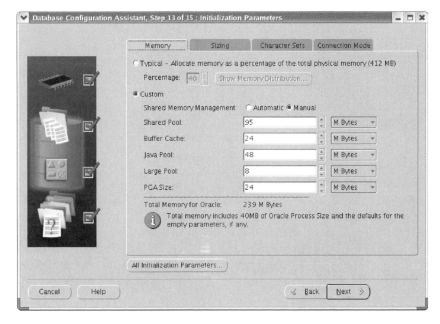

the option to select the type of connection that is intended, such as shared server or dedicated server. After selecting the connection mode, click "Next."

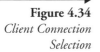

Figure 4.34
*Client Connection
Selection*

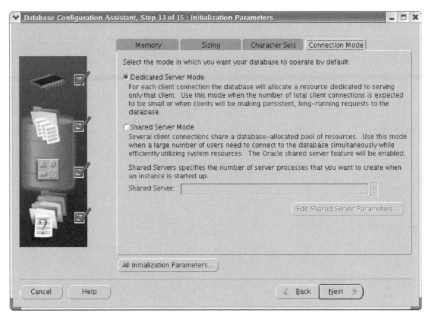

The DBCA now displays (not shown) the database storage window. This window allows the entry of a file name for each type of file, such as the storage definition for the control file, the various tablespaces, rollback segments, and so on. Once all of the storage for the various files has been defined, click "Next."

The next screen (Figure 4.35) shows the database creation options. Ensure that the "Create Database" checkbox is selected, and click "Finish." In this screen, the DBCA also provides the option to generate the database creation scripts. The DBA can select both options, in which case OUI will generate the scripts and subsequently create the database automatically, or users can allow the DBCA to generate the scripts and execute them manually.

Figure 4.35 is the final screen, in which the actual "Create Database" option is selected. On selecting the "Finish" option, the DBCA begins creating the database. Once the process has finished, a new database and the required database instances are created, which can be accessed using SQL*Plus or other applications designed to work on a RAC database.

Based on the database configuration specified, the next screen in Figure 4.36 illustrates the various stages of the installation process.

After all of the installation stages are complete, the DBCA will start the instances on the respective nodes.

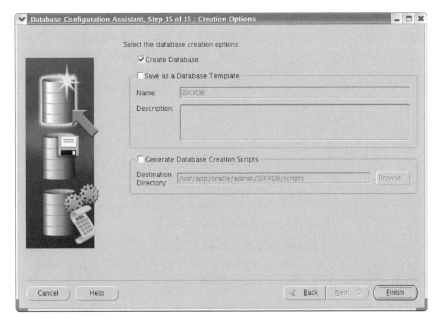

Figure 4.35
*Database Creation
Screen*

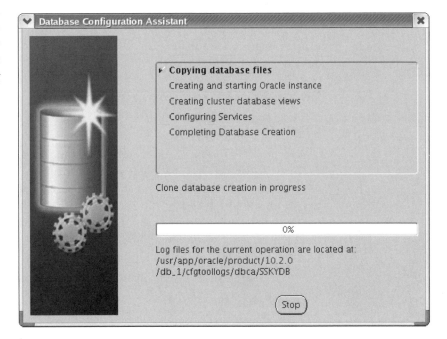

Figure 4.36
*Database
Configuration
Progress Dialog*

Manual database configuration

In the previous section, we looked at how, using the DBCA, the RAC database and the required instances can be created from a GUI interface. Another method, which is a more traditional way of creating the RAC database, is through the script file or manual method.

> **Note:** For the interest of the reader, the database creation script can be downloaded using directions found in Appendix B.

This completes phase III of the installation and configuration process. At this stage, it's a good practice to verify if the installation has been completed successfully using CVU.

Cluster verification: At this point, using CVU, the installation and configuration of the Oracle software is to be verified using

```
cluvfy stage -pre dbcfg -n oradb1,oradb2,oradb3,oradb4 -d
$ORACLE_HOME -verbose
```

In the next and final phase (phase IV), the cluster and database components, which are required for day-to-day administration, will be set up and discussed.

4.12.4   Phase IV: cluster components

Oracle Cluster Registry

Those who have installed, configured, or administered an Oracle Database 9i RAC environment will be able to recollect the use of the `srvConfig.loc` file and the configuration (`srvconfig`) and server control (`srvctl`) utilities. In Oracle Database 10*g*, the `srvConfig.loc` file has taken the form of the OCR. The information contained and the functionalities supported by this OCR have increased several fold. The criticality of the data is so intense that if this file is not readable, the clusterware will not start. In this section, we will discuss the administration and maintenance of this registry.

Several steps that were once performed manually in the previous versions of Oracle are now automated in Oracle Database 10*g*. For example, the registry is automatically created, formatted, and initialized during the installation of Oracle Clusterware. The location of the OCR is stored in a system parameter file `ocr.loc` located in the `/etc/oracle` directory in a Linux environment and in the registry in a Windows environment.

The initial contents of the OCR file are visible, after CRS configuration, using the `crs_stat` utility. This utility lists all of the services and their respective instances on which the services are configured to operate.

```
[root@oradb4 oracle]# crs_stat -t
Name            Type         Target    State     Host

ora....KY1.srv  application  ONLINE    ONLINE    oradb3
ora....KY2.srv  application  ONLINE    ONLINE    oradb4
ora....SRV1.cs  application  ONLINE    ONLINE    oradb4
ora....Y1.inst  application  ONLINE    ONLINE    oradb3
ora....Y2.inst  application  ONLINE    ONLINE    oradb4
ora.SSKYDB.db   application  ONLINE    ONLINE    oradb4
ora....SM1.asm  application  ONLINE    ONLINE    oradb3
ora....B3.lsnr  application  ONLINE    ONLINE    oradb3
ora.oradb3.gsd  application  ONLINE    ONLINE    oradb3
ora.oradb3.ons  application  ONLINE    ONLINE    oradb3
ora.oradb3.vip  application  ONLINE    ONLINE    oradb3
ora....SM2.asm  application  ONLINE    ONLINE    oradb4
ora....B4.lsnr  application  ONLINE    ONLINE    oradb4
ora.oradb4.gsd  application  ONLINE    ONLINE    oradb4
ora.oradb4.ons  application  ONLINE    ONLINE    oradb4
ora.oradb4.vip  application  ONLINE    ONLINE    oradb4
```

Windows: The clusterware services can be viewed using the "Administrative Tools" option and selecting "Services." The output is displayed in Figure 4.37.

Due to its shared location, one of the primary administrative features of the OCR is that, from a single location, all the components running on all nodes and instances of Oracle can be administrated, irrespective of the node on which the registry was created.

4.12.5 OCR backup and restore

The OCR file, created during the CRS installation and configuration process, is critical for its contents and for its requirement to start Oracle Clusterware. During the installation and configuration process, OUI has set up, by default, a backup mechanism where the contents of the OCR file are backed up once every four hours. Oracle retains one backup per day and

Figure 4.37
RAC Services on
Windows

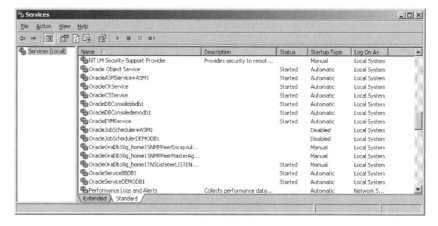

one per week and purges the remaining backups automatically. While currently there are no direct methods to modify the schedule or frequency of these backups, Oracle has provided a tool called `ocrconfig`, which is used to restore the OCR from a backup or to perform other administrative functions (e.g., importing, exporting, mirroring, repairing).

Currently, the default location of the OCR backup files is the location identified by the cluster name (e.g., the directory `$ORA_CRS_HOME/cdata/` `SskyClst` on each node). This creates a single point of failure because if the node that has the latest backup is not available, the OCR cannot be restored. It is advisable to move the OCR backup to the shared storage using the following commands:

```
[root@oradb3 oradata]# ocrconfig -backuploc /u14/oradata/
SskyClst/
```

4.12.6   Setting paths and environment variables

The last, but not least, important step in the configuration process is to ensure that all tools and utilities provided by the operating system vendor and other software vendors are easily accessible without having to change locations to specific directories where they are located. This can be accomplished by defining default search paths as part of the user account login process.

Similarly, in the Oracle environment, certain commands or groups of commands can be redefined by using environment variables. For example, `ORACLE_HOME` is an environment variable that points to the Oracle home directory. Similarly, if the node has multiple instances, before accessing any specific instance via SQL*Plus, it is required that the SID environment variable point to the SID that is of interest or that the SID be specified as part of the connect command.

The following command will set the environment variable for the SID in a Korn/Bash shell environment:

```
[oracle@oradb3 oracle]$ ORACLE_SID=SSKY1
[oracle@oradb3 oracle]$ export ORACLE_SID
```

In a Unix or Linux environment, such definitions are added to the default login scripts located in the home directories of the respective user accounts. For example, for the oracle user, on a Linux operating system system using the bash shell, the login file could be .bash_profile. The contents of the file are as follows:

```
[oracle@oradb3 oracle]$ more .bash_profile
# .bash_profile

# Get the aliases and functions
if [ -f ~/.bashrc ]; then
        . ~/.bashrc
fi
# User specific environment and startup programs
export ORACLE_BASE=/usr/app/oracle
export ORACLE_HOME=$ORACLE_BASE/product/10.2.0/db_1
export ORA_CRS_HOME=$ORACLE_BASE/product/10.2.0/crs
export ASM_HOME=$ORACLE_BASE/product/10.2.0/asm
export AGENT_HOME=/usr/app/oracle/product/10.2.0/EMAgent

export PATH=.:${PATH}:$HOME/bin:$ORACLE_HOME/bin
export PATH=${PATH}:$ORA_CRS_HOME/bin
export PATH=${PATH}:/usr/bin:/bin:/usr/bin/X11:/usr/local/
bin:/sbin
export ORACLE_ADMIN=$ORACLE_BASE/admin
export TNS_ADMIN=$ORACLE_HOME/network/admin

export LD_ASSUME_KERNEL=2.4.19
export LD_LIBRARY=$ORACLE_HOME/lib
export LD_LIBRARY=${LD_LIBRARY}:/lib:/usr/lib:/usr/local/bin
export LD_LIBRARY=${LD_LIBRARY}:$ORA_CRS_HOME/lib
```

```
export CLASSPATH=$ORACLE_HOME/JRE
export CLASSPATH=${CLASSPATH}:$ORACLE_HOME/jlib
export CLASSPATH=${CLASSPATH}:$ORACLE_HOME/rdbms/jlib
export CLASSPATH=${CLASSPATH}:$ORACLE_HOME/network/jlib
export THREADS_FLAG=native
export ORACLE_SID=ORA1
unset USERNAME
```

4.13   Additional information

The following details are found in the areas mentioned later in this book:

Adding additional nodes to to a 10g R2 cluster	Appendix F
Migrating from Oracle 9*i* Release 2 to Oracle 10*g* Release 2	Appendix E
Migration from OCFS to ASM	Appendix E

4.14   Conclusion

In this chapter we discussed various steps to be completed to install and configure an Oracle Database 10g Release 2 RAC. During this process, we also discussed the prerequisites, operating system configuration, network configuration, and the database creation process.

Services and Distributed Workload Management

Business systems infrastructure has increased in complexity, which makes it insecure, fragile, and difficult to maintain. The complexity of compounded functionality changes implemented over the years has made it more difficult and less productive to implement any further changes. The business rules and functionalities that have been built into the application have made organizations rethink the idea of rewriting these systems to make them more manageable. Undoing years of research and development of business systems has been and will be an investment that businesses are seldom interested in making.

The move toward a more loosely coupled composite solution has brought a new wave in the technology architecture that focuses on functionality in the enterprise system as a service. For example, the dot-com and Internet-based solutions brought Web services into existence. While Web services provided loose coupling at the interface level, the business systems did not propagate this architecture to the middle and database tier of the enterprise systems. The new wave is to take this service-oriented approach across the entire stack of the business or enterprise system.

Thus, services are geared toward integrating systems from a business-value perspective rather than an enterprise perspective. This is done by looking at a business transaction and grouping components that belong to its transaction boundaries. Thus, a service-oriented architecture (SOA) should design and build business services that can easily and effectively plug into real business processes to deliver a composite business application.

5.1   Service framework

The concept of services is not new in Oracle. Oracle introduced services in Oracle Database 8*i*, in which services were used by the listener to perform client load-balancing between nodes and instances in the cluster. While client load-balancing continues to be supported in Oracle Database 10*g*, the concept of services has taken a more intensive implementation. Besides the database being a single service that applies to all instances in the cluster, several different types of services can now be created that will help make workload management across nodes much easier and simpler. A service is an abstraction layer of a single system image executed against the same database with common functionality, quality expectations, and priority relative to other services. Examples of services are payroll, accounts payable, order entry, and so on. In Oracle Database 10*g*, a database is considered and treated as an application service. Some of the advantages of using services are the following:

- *Manageability.* The complexity in the management and administration of legacy systems came about because one large application provided all of the business functions for an organization implemented as a single system image. This also brought about issues in troubleshooting and performance diagnosis. However, services enable each workload to be managed in isolation and as a unit. This is made possible because services can span one or more instances of a RAC environment. Load-balancing and other features available to the service can be implemented at a more controlled and functional level.

- *Availability.* Failure of a smaller component or subcomponent is acceptable in most cases compared to the failure of an entire enterprise system. Also, when a service fails, recovery of resources is much faster and independent and does not require restarting the entire application stack. Recovery can also happen in parallel when several services fail. This provides better availability of the enterprise system. When the failed instances are later brought online, the services that are not running (services that are not configured for failover) start immediately, and the services that failed over can be restored/relocated back to their original instances.

- *Performance.* Prior to Oracle Database 10*g*, performance tuning was based on the statistics collected either at the system level or at the session level, meaning that no matter how many applications were running against a given database, there was no instrumentation to provide any performance metric at the application or component level. With services and the enhancements to the database, performance metrics can now be collected at the service level, across instances, enabling a more finite component-level troubleshooting. Performance tuning is covered in Chapter 9.

5.1.1 Types of services

Services can be broadly classified, based on their usage and ownership into two main categories:

1. *Application service.* Application services are normally business related, and they describe business applications, business functions, and database tasks. These services can be either data dependent or function dependent.

    ■ Data-dependent services are based on database or data-related key values. Applications are routed to these services based on keys. Such services are normally implemented on databases that are shared by multiple applications and are associated with data partitioning, meaning, based on the key values, the application will attach itself to a specific partition in the database server. This can be either a set of instances or a section of the database within an instance. Data-dependent services are normally supported by transaction monitors such as Tuxedo from BEA Systems. This type of service is called data-dependent routing.

    ■ Function-dependent services are based on business functions, such as Oracle applications, Accounts Receivable (AR), Accounts Payable (AP), General Ledger (GL), and Bill of Materials (BOM). Here the services create a functional division of work within the database. Such services are also termed function-dependent routing.

    ■ The third type of service used with the earlier versions of Oracle is the PRECONNECT option, where a service spans a set of instances in the cluster. Such a service will preestablish a connection to more than one instance in the Oracle database and support failover when the primary instance that the user session was originally established to fails. Discussions and configuration of preconnect services can be found in Chapter 6.

2. *Internal service.* Internal services are required and administered by Oracle for managing its resources. Internal services are primarily SYS$BACKGROUND, used by the Oracle background processes, and SYS$USERS, used by user sessions that are not associated with any service. Internal services are created by default and cannot be removed or modified.

Characteristics of a service

- Services must be location independent, and the RAC high-availability (HA) framework is used to implement this.

- Services are made available continuously with load shared across one or more instances in the cluster. Any instance can offer services in response to runtime demands, failures, and planned maintenance. Services are always available somewhere in the cluster.

- To implement the workload balancing and continuous availability features of services, CRS stores the HA configuration for each service in the OCR. The HA configuration defines a set of preferred and available instances that support the service.

- A preferred instance set defines the number of instances (cardinality) that support the corresponding service. It also identifies every instance in the cluster that the service will run on when the system first starts up.

- An available instance does not initially support a service. However, it begins accepting connections for the service when a preferred instance cannot support the service. If a preferred instance fails, then the service is transparently restored to an available instance defined for the service.

5.1.2   Service creation

The DBA can create services using the following three basic methods:

1. DBCA

Using the DBCA, application services can be created either

- During the database configuration process (illustrated in Figure 4.32)

- After the database has been created (using the DBCA), selecting the service management option illustrated in Figure 5.1

DBCA has been enhanced severalfold to provide more administrative functionality. Unlike the previous versions of Oracle, in Oracle Database 10*g*, the DBCA can be put to a more repetitive use. With functionalities such as instance management, ASM management, and database administration, DBCA is now usable beyond basic database creation.

The service management option is selected for an already existing database, which means this option can be used after a new database has been created or after the user has migrated or upgraded an existing database to Oracle Database 10*g*.

Services for all instances can be defined from any one node in the cluster. Once the service management option is selected, the next screen (not shown) is the list of all available databases in the cluster or node. Select the database where the services are to be created.

Figure 5.1
*Service
Management
Operations
Selection*

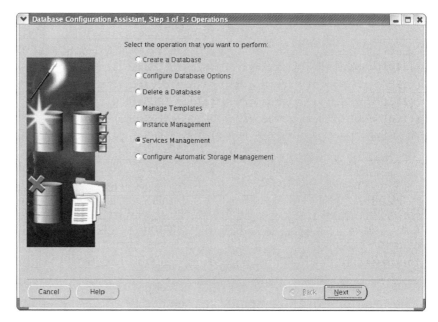

Once the database has been selected, the next screen is the service definition screen (illustrated in Figure 5.2). This is the primary screen where most of the service definition is entered, for example, add or remove a service.

To add a service, click on the "Add" button, which pops up a window to add a new service, as illustrated in Figure 5.3. Once the service name has been identified and entered, click "OK."

Once this is completed, the user is returned to the main service definition screen illustrated in Figure 5.2. The next step is to add service credentials for the service entered, for example, what instances the service will run under, what the preferred instances are, and which instance(s) will be the standby instances (indicated by "available").

Oracle provides an option where one or more of the available instances can be configured as referred instances for the service. When the instance starts, Oracle starts the service on the selected set of "Preferred" instances.

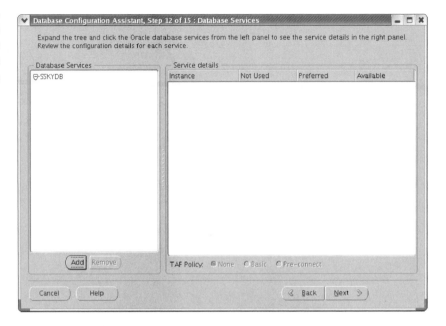

Figure 5.2
Service
Configuration
Screen

Figure 5.3
Add Service
Window

Based on the business rules and the type of application supported by the service, all instances can be configured as "Preferred" instances for the service. Alternatively, instances can be configured as preferred or available instances for the service. If services are divided between preferred and available instances, then when a service cannot run on a preferred instance because it is down when the node or instance has crashed, then Oracle will start the service on one or more of the available instances. The third option is to select "Not used" when Oracle will never start the service on the instance. For example, in Figure 5.4, for service SRV8, instance SSKY2 has been configured as a preferred instance, and SSKY1 is the available instance.

Note: User-defined application services are called HA services.

Figure 5.4
*Service
Configuration and
Instance Preferences*

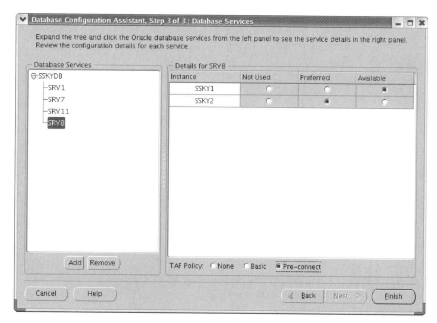

Once the service configuration and instance preferences are complete, the next option on the same screen is to define if the service will be bound by any transparent application failover (TAF) policy. Oracle provides three different policies: NONE, BASIC, and PRECONNECT. Select the appropriate failover policies for each service individually. For example, Figure 5.4 illustrates that SRV8 is configured with a preconnect TAF policy.

Once the TAF policy is defined, click "Finish"; this will start the service configuration. When all services have been configured successfully, the completion status window illustrated in Figure 5.5 is displayed.

Figure 5.5
*Service
Configuration
Completion Status*

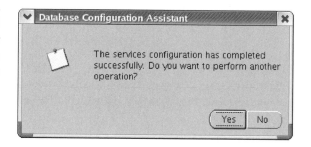

TAF policies are discussed in detail in Chapter 6.

Services added to the database using the DBCA are automatically added to the OCR; entries are made to the `tnsnames.ora` file on the server, and the services are started automatically.

Services can be viewed (apart from adding) using the server control (`srvctl`) and the cluster state utilities (`crs_stat`).

2. Server control (srvctl) utility

Services can be added to the database with the `srvctl` using the following syntax:

```
srvctl add service -d <name> -s <service_name> -r
<preferred_list> [-a "<available_list>"]
```

For example:

```
[oracle@oradb4 oracle]$ srvctl add service -d SSKYDB -s SRV1
-r SSKY1 -a SSKY2
```

Services added through the `srvctl` utility will add the definition to the OCR but will not start these services automatically the first time. This is done using the following command:

```
srvctl start service -d <name> [-s "<service_name_list>" [-i
<inst_name>]]
```

For example:

```
[oracle@oradb4 oracle]$ srvctl start service -d SSKYDB -s
SRV1 -i SSKY1
```

Similarly, other services can be added to the OCR from any node participating in the cluster.

The `srvctl` utility can also be used to check the configuration or status of these services and the instances on which they are currently active or online.

The status can be checked using the following syntax:

```
srvctl status database -d <database name>
```

For example:

```
[oracle@oradb4 oracle]$ srvctl status database -d SSKYDB -f -v
Instance SSKY1 is running on node oradb4 with online services SRV2
SRV1
Instance SSKY2 is not running on node oradb3
```

This command gives a list of services configured on the instances and their current state. For example, in the previous output, instance SSKY2 and the services configured on it are not running. However, instance SSKY1 has two online services, SRV2 and SRV1.

Both the DBCA and srvctl only provide options for a basic configuration of services. If options such as threshold definition, monitoring, tracing, or load-balancing are to be implemented at a service level, DBAs can use other features, such as PL/SQL procedures and/or EM in addition to using the DBCA or srvctl utility. This is discussed later in the chapter. Besides srvctl and the DBCA, PL/SQL procedures and EM also support basic create service functionality

3. PL/SQL procedures

Oracle provides a PL/SQL package (DBMS_SERVICE) to create and maintain application services. Similar to the other methods discussed earlier, services need to be created and started to gain visibility to the administrators. Table 5.1 provides a list of subprograms under the DBMS_SERVICE package.

Table 5.1   *PL/SQL Service Maintenance Procedures*

CREATE_SERVICE	Creates the service. The required parameters are the service name and network name. While both values can be identical, the service name is a user-defined name that can be up to 64 characters long. The network name is the name used for all SQL*Net-related connection descriptions and collection of data.
DELETE_SERVICE	Deletes a service already present.
DISCONNECT_SESSION	Disconnects an already active session for a service.
MODIFY_SERVICE	Provides options to modify existing service definitions.
START_SERVICE	Starts a service. Once a service is created using CREATE_SERVICE, it should be started using START_SERVICE to gain visibility to external users.
STOP_SERVICE	Stops a started service.

To create services, use the DBMS_SERVICE.CREATE_SERVICE procedure, connecting to the database as user SYS. The two required parameters for this package are SERVICE_NAME and NETWORK_NAME. Other parameters are optional.

```
SQL> EXEC DBMS_SERVICE.CREATE_SERVICE(SERVICE_NAME=>'SRV5',
                                      NETWORK_NAME=>'SRV5');


PL/SQL procedure successfully completed.
```

In the previous example, a service named SRV5 is created and will have the identical connection description as defined in the NETWORK_NAME parameter.

```
SQL> EXEC DBMS_SERVICE.START_SERVICE(SERVICE_NAME=>'SRV5',
     INSTANCE_NAME=>'SSKY2');


PL/SQL procedure successfully completed.
```

In this definition, the service SRV5 that was created earlier is started on instance SSKY2.

Execution of DBMS_SERVICE.START_SERVICE also performs an ALTER SYSTEM operation on the database instance to change the current definition of the SERVICE parameter. This operation invokes the service and registers the service with the listener.

```
ALTER SYSTEM SET SERVICE_NAMES='SRV1','SRV8','SSKYDB','SRV5'
SCOPE=MEMORY SID='SSKY2';
```

This operation updates the value of the SERVICE parameter, and it can be verified using the following:

```
SQL> show parameter service

NAME             TYPE         VALUE
---------------- ------------ ------------------------------
service_names    string       SRV1, SRV11_PRECONNECT, SRV7_P
                              RECONNECT, SRV8, SSKYDB, SRV5
```

Once services have been created and started, they can be verified using the following query:

```
SQL> SELECT NAME,NETWORK_NAME FROM V$ACTIVE_SERVICES;

NAME                           NETWORK_NAME
------------------------       --------------------
SRV5                           SRV5
SRV1                           SRV1
SRV8                           SRV8
SSKYXDB                        SSKYXDB
SSKYDB                         SSKYDB
SYS$BACKGROUND
SYS$USERS

7 rows selected.
```

Note: Services created using PL/SQL or EM are not added to the OCR. They will have to be added manually using the `srvctl` utility discussed in this section.

4. EM

EM has an interface to create, administer, and manage application services, besides its myriad of other features. The service administration feature is available in both the Database Control version and the EM Grid Control version of EM. Figure 5.6 provides a list of services already defined for the database and provides the option to create additional services.

In Figure 5.6, of the four services defined for RACDB, all services, except SRV8, are currently running on their configured instances. SRV8 is currently not running on instance RACDB2.

Services that are configured for failover automatically move to the alternate instance. However, they do not fail back when the failed node is brought back online. Under these circumstances, a DBA intervention is required to relocate the service back to its original instance. This can be done by using either the `srvctl` utility or EM, as illustrated in this section.

Figure 5.6
EM Services

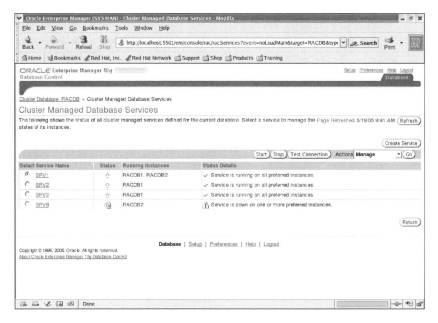

EM provides interfaces to relocate a service from one instance to another (this is also possible using other methods). For example, if SRV8 needs to be relocated to instance RACDB2, the following steps are performed:

1. From the screen illustrated in Figure 5.6, click on the service to be relocated.

2. A screen (illustrated in Figure 5.7) containing all instances currently configured to run the service is displayed.

3. Select the instance (RACDB2) to which this service will be relocated, and click "Relocate."

Note: The relocation feature also helps the DBA during maintenance windows (e.g., when the service from the preferred instance needs to be moved to another instance to facilitate shutdown of the instance).

Once the operation is complete, the status screen (Figure 5.8) is displayed.

Figure 5.7
Instances to Service Mapping Screen

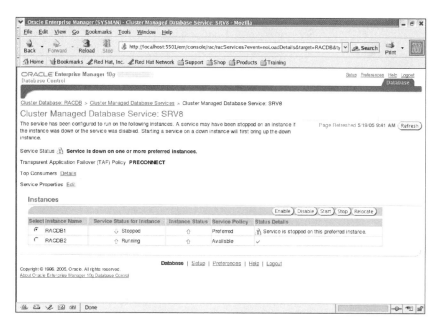

Figure 5.8
Instances Relocation Status

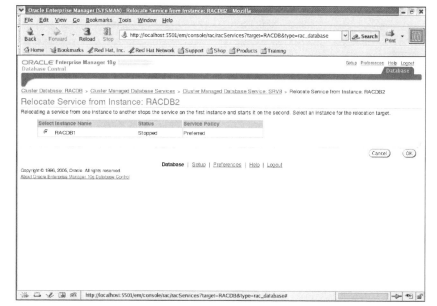

Service structure

One of the new features added to Clusterware is the management and migration of services from one node to another when the current node fails or the services need to be started on other nodes. During the process of service migration or state change, events are automatically generated for notification by the ONS. (ONS is discussed in detail later in this chapter.)

In order for Clusterware to manage services and notify clients of state changes, all service definitions should be added to the OCR. In the various methods discussed above, with the exception of services created using PL/SQL procedures and EM, services are automatically added to the OCR. When other methods are used, the DBA should ensure that they are added to the OCR using the `srvctl` utility discussed previously. The OCR maintains and tracks information pertaining to the definition, availability, and current state of the services.

Services can be viewed using the cluster state (`crsstat`)[1] utility shown as follows:

```
[oracle@oradb4 oracle]$ crsstat
HA Resource                     Target       State
-----------                     ------       -----
ora.SSKYDB.SRV1.SSKY1.srv       ONLINE       ONLINE on oradb4
ora.SSKYDB.SRV1.cs              ONLINE       ONLINE on oradb4
ora.SSKYDB.SRV2.SSKY1.srv       ONLINE       ONLINE on oradb4
ora.SSKYDB.SRV2.cs              ONLINE       ONLINE on oradb4
ora.SSKYDB.SRV3.SSKY2.srv       ONLINE       ONLINE on oradb4
ora.SSKYDB.SRV3.cs              ONLINE       ONLINE on oradb3
ora.SSKYDB.SRV6.SSKY1.srv       ONLINE       ONLINE on oradb4
ora.SSKYDB.SRV6.SSKY2.srv       ONLINE       ONLINE on oradb3
ora.SSKYDB.SRV6.cs              ONLINE       ONLINE on oradb4
```

In the previous output, it should be noted that an HA service definition has a minimum of two entries in the OCR. For example, `SRV1` is configured on `SSKY1` as its preferred instance and is identified by the entry `ora.SSKYDB.SRV1.SSKY1.srv`. This is the application HA service defined by the DBA. The entry `ora.SSKYDB.SRV1.cs` is a header or composite resource that manages the dependent resources, in this case `SSKY1`.

Apart from the functional aspects of services, creation of services also provides another benefit: allocation of resources based on business criteria, the demand (number of users) for the service, and its critical nature to the overall enterprise. For example, while BOM, AR, and so on, are applica-

---

1.   crsstat is a modified version of the crs_stat utility that comes with Oracle Clusterware and provides a formatted output. crststat can be download from metalink note # 259301.1.

tions that are used constantly every day, applications such as payroll or order processing are more seasonal, meaning payroll has a more critical nature before the pay period or order processing has high usage during a holiday season such as Christmas in the United States or Diwali in India.

To accommodate these business needs, Oracle has introduced in Oracle Database 10*g*, distributed workload management (DWM), where workload is distributed between the various instances in the cluster based on various predefined business criteria.

5.2 Distributed workload management

As discussed earlier, the usage of an order-processing application is higher during a holiday season depending on the region of the world from which it's being accessed. Hence, an organization would like to ensure that all resources are available to the order-processing modules, while not limiting the resources required for the nonseasonal applications. Similarly, the payroll application will require more resources during payroll processing, which might take place weekly, biweekly, or monthly. All of these varying seasonal demands for resources, without limiting the resources required by the regular applications (e.g., those that are not seasonal), have been a challenge for many organizations.

Oracle has enhanced and integrated some of its existing features, such as Database Resource Manager and the Scheduler, to support the RAC architecture. This has provided efficient workload management options by controlling the allocation of resources required by the various processes and by efficiently managing allocation based on the priority and importance. Two main areas of incorporation include the Oracle Database Resource Manager (ODRM) and the Oracle Scheduler.

5.2.1 Oracle Database Resource Manager

Provisioning resources to database users, applications, and services within an Oracle database allows DBAs to control the allocation of available resources between the various users, applications, or services. This ensures that each user, application, or service gets a fair share of the available computing resources. This is achieved by creating predefined resource plans that allocate resources to various consumer groups based on resource usage criteria such as CPU utilization or number of active sessions.

The various components of the ODRM are as follows:

■ *Resource Consumer Groups.* A resource consumer group is basically a collection of users or services with similar resource requirements. A user or service can be assigned to more than one resource consumer group; however, at execution time, a specific user session should have only one group mapped. Once a specific resource consumer group is defined (e.g., HIGH_P as illustrated in Figure 5.9), it is subsequently mapped to one or more users or services.

Figure 5.9
OEM Create
Resource Consumer
Group

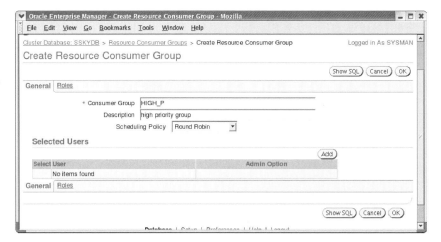

■ *Resource plans.* A resource plan is the allocation of one or more resource consumer groups to services. The rules or directives are used to define how the ODRM will allocate resources to a resource consumer group. A resource plan can encompass numerous consumer groups and subplans:

■ *General.* This is the basic resource allocation. At this level, the percentage of CPU resources is allocated to a group. In Figure 5.10, the consumer group has two levels: level 1 will be allocated 60% of the CPU, and level 2 will be allocated 40%.

■ *Parallelism.* This specifies the maximum number of parallel execution servers associated with a single operation for each resource consumer group.

■ *Session Pool.* This specifies the maximum number of concurrently active sessions allowed within a consumer group.

■ *Undo Pool.* This specifies the maximum bytes on the total amount of undo generated by a consumer group.

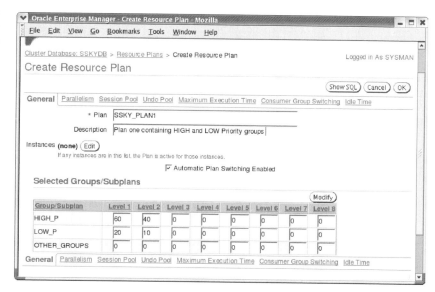

Figure 5.10
*EM Create
Resource Plan*

- *Maximum Execution Time.* This is the allocation of a maximum time in seconds allowed for this consumer group to complete an operation.

- *Consumer Group Switching.* This helps define a criterion that causes the automatic switching of sessions to another consumer group. Once the defined criteria are met, the group will switch to the alternate group specified.

5.2.2   Oracle Scheduler

Oracle replaces its existing DBMS_JOB package, which was used to submit and schedule database jobs, with the new Oracle Scheduler (DBMS_SCHEDULER). The Oracle Scheduler provides scheduling functionality that enables DBAs to manage database maintenance and other routine tasks. It helps group jobs that share common characteristics and behavior into larger entities called *job classes*. These job classes can then be prioritized by controlling the resources allocated to each class and by mapping a service to the class.

Some of the advantages of the Oracle Scheduler are the following:

- Scheduler jobs are modular and can be shared with other users, reducing development time when creating new jobs.

- Because this is a database functionality, Oracle scheduler can take advantage of the standard maintenance functions such as export/ import to move jobs from one system to another.

- It supports grouping of jobs, to enable a chained dependency of scheduled events.

- It allows activities to be logged, providing an audit trail of all scheduler activities.

- It supports time zones, which makes it easy to manage jobs in different time zones.

- It supports job prioritization by controlling the number of jobs that can run at a given time and optimizes system resources effectively to ensure that high-priority jobs finish before low-priority jobs.

- Its can be integrated with ODRM by using resource plans. This allows the administrator to control the resource allocation among the job classes by creating policies to manage resource consumption.

- It supports RAC-specific features such as load-balancing and resource pooling. As illustrated in Figure 5.11, since there is only one job queue and the job coordinator residing on each instance allows effective load-balancing options, the scheduler can pool resources from other instances as and when required.

Oracle Scheduler architecture

Figure 5.11 illustrates the architecture of the Oracle Scheduler in a RAC environment. The components of a job scheduler are as follows:

- *Job queue.* Every scheduler environment has one job queue that stores the scheduler object information, such as object definition, state change, and historical information related to the job. Job queues are created either using EM or the Oracle-provided PL/SQL package DBMS_SCHEDULER. For example, the following procedure creates a job called SRV3 under the BATCH_USER schema. Table 5.2 provides descriptions of the various parameters in the PL/SQL definition.

```
BEGIN
    SYS.DBMS_SCHEDULER.CREATE_JOB (
        JOB_NAME        => 'BATCH_USER.SRV3',
        JOB_TYPE        => 'EXECUTABLE',
        JOB_ACTION      => '/u22/app/oracle/batch/batch_srv3.sh',
```

```
START_DATE        => TO_TIMESTAMP_TZ
    ('2005-06-28 America/New_York','YYYY-MM-DD TZR'),
JOB_CLASS         => 'SRV3',
AUTO_DROP         => FALSE,
ENABLED           => TRUE);


SYS.DBMS_SCHEDULER.SET_ATTRIBUTE (
NAME              => 'BATCH_USER.SRV',
ATTRIBUTE         => 'restartable',
VALUE             => TRUE);
END;
```

Figure 5.11
*Oracle Scheduler
Architecture in a
RAC Environment*

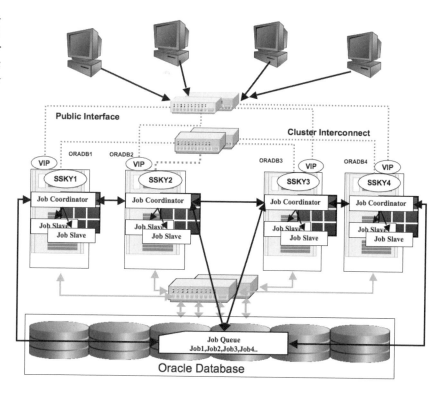

- *Job coordinator.* As the name indicates, it is a coordinator between the job queue and the job slave processes. Depending on the number of jobs scheduled for execution on any given instance, the job coordinator spawns the required job slave processes. It dynamically controls the slave pool, increasing and reducing its size depending on the number of jobs that need to be executed.

- *Job slave*. This executes the job and updates the job information in the job queue.

Table 5.2 *DBMS_SCHEDULER.CREATE_JOB Parameters*

Parameter	Description/Options
JOB_NAME	User-defined name for the job
JOB_TYPE	The type of job that will be handled by the scheduler. The supported types are EXECUTABLE: Application executables can be directly executed using the scheduler. In the previoius example, batch_srv3.sh is a shell script that will be executed. PL/SQL blocks: Jobs can be PL/SQL blocks. PL/SQL and Java Stored Procedures: Jobs can directly execute stored procedures from the database or any user schema depending on the privileges assigned to the job.
JOB_ACTION	The physical task that the job is to perform. In this example, the job is to execute a user-defined UNIX shell script.
START_DATE	The date when the job is scheduled to start; for example, in the definition above, the job is scheduled to start July 28 in the time zone identified by America/New York, which is EST.
JOB_CLASS	If a job class has been defined with additional parameters, this could be referenced in this section. Job class permits contain relations to ODRM definition and will be assigned a specific database service.
AUTO_DROP	Indicates if the job definition is to be dropped after its initial execution.
ENABLED	Indicates if the job is enabled for execution at the time indicated by the **START_DATE** parameter.
ATTRIBUTES	RESTARTABLE If set to **TRUE**, when a failure occurs, either due to an application error or a database/system crash, the job will automatically be restarted.

As illustrated in Figure 5.9, each instance in the cluster consists of a job coordinator and several job slaves. The job coordinators will communicate with each other to exchange information to ensure that they are in sync with Scheduler activities. In a RAC configuration, all coordinators and slaves share one job queue for the entire cluster. The job queue is defined in the Oracle database.

The ODRM and Oracle Scheduler enhancements are integrated with each other and with Oracle's new cluster management features to provide a consolidated and integrated workload management solution.

5.2.3   DWM workshop

To understand how such a distribution can be implemented, let's discuss a typical workload configuration and management scenario using an example. A global operational organization has five applications that it would like to configure on a four-node RAC. Defined by the business needs, the applications must meet the following requirements:

- SRV1. This application is used by the client services to record customer interactions that happen throughout the day. It's an OLTP application and requires 24/7 uptime.

- SRV2. This is a homegrown application used by various members of the organization. Considering the various time zones, except for a few hours between 3 a.m. and 7 a.m. EST, this application is also required to be functional most of the time.

- SRV3. This is another reporting batch application that runs two or three times a week and during weekends.

- SRV4. This online reporting system is a subcomponent of both SRV1 and SRV2. These reports are triggered subprocesses and should support both applications. The load or usage of this application is not very high, and an infrastructure to queue all reporting requests is in place; hence, small outage of this system is acceptable.

- SRV6. This is a critical seasonal application that runs twice a month. The application's criticality is so high that during these two periods of execution, it should complete on time and have a very minimal to zero failure rate.

All of these applications are to be configured over a four-node RAC cluster as illustrated in Figure 5.12. Each node in the cluster has a public IP address, private IP address, and VIP address. Table 5.3 details the various characteristics of the application configuration across the available instances in the cluster.

Figure 5.12
Four-Node RAC
Cluster with ASM

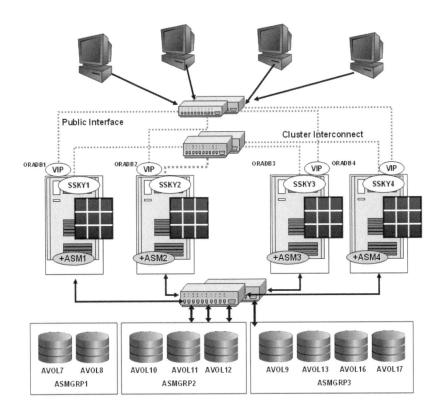

Table 5.3   *Application to Instance Mapping*

Applications	Services	Type of Service	Preferred Instances	Available Instances	Priority/ Criticality
SRV1	SRV1	Client application	SSKY1, SSKY2, SSKY3	SSKY4	High
SRV2	SRV2	Client application	SSKY4	SSKY2, SSKY3	Standard
SRV3	SRV3	Scheduled job	SSKY4	SSKY3, SSKY1	Standard
SRV4	SRV4	Client application	SSKY1, SSKY2, SSKY3	NONE	Low
SRV6	SRV6	Seasonal application	SSKY3, SSKY4	SSKY2, SSKY1	High

Using the services concept discussed in the previous sections, all applications in Table 5.3 are services in the clustered database SSKYDB (i.e., all applications will have a different service definition in the database).

- In Table 5.3, it should be noted that SRV1 is a high-priority service application and is set up to start on the SSKY1, SSKY2, and SSKY3 instances. If any of these instances fail, the service from that instance will migrate to instance SSKY4. If all three preferred instances become unavailable, the service is available on instance SSKY4. When all three instances or nodes are not available, SSKY4 will be busy with all services executing off this one instance. However, since the priority of SRV1 is HIGH, it will get a higher percentage of the resources compared to other services running on the same node, except when SRV6 is running (SRV6 is discussed below). SSKY4 will be shared by both SRV1 and SRV2.

- SRV2 is a standard service and is set up to run on instance SSKY4; if SSKY4 fails, it will run on either SSKY2 or SSKY3, based on the current workload conditions. After failover, this service will not affect the existing services, especially service SRV1 because it runs at a higher priority.

- SRV3 is a standard scheduled job (batch) that runs during the nights and weekends. Since this is not a continuously running application, it is configured to run on SSKY4. From the previous step, SRV2 is also configured on instance SSKY4. Like SRV2, when instance SSKY4 fails, SRV3 will failover to either SSKY3 or SSKY1, depending on the current workload conditions. As an alternative solution, SRV2 can be set to failover to SSKY2, and SRV3 can be set to failover to SSKY1.

- SRV4 is a low-priority, triggered reporting job spawned from both the SRV1 and SRV2 services. Because of this architecture, it is set up to run across all instances, SSKY1, SSKY2, and SSKY3. If any of the nodes or instances fail, the surviving nodes will continue to execute the service; in other words, no failover has been configured.

- SRV6 is a high-priority seasonal application; it's executed twice a month. SRV6 is configured to run on SSKY3 and SSKY4. If there are not sufficient resources to allow SRV6 to complete on time or if one of the preferred instances fails, it has two other spare instances, SSKY2 and SSKY1.

Once the configuration and layout architecture have been defined, the RAC environment is updated to reflect these settings. While most of the network interface definition and mapping them to their respective nodes are completed during the Oracle Clusterware configuration, the service to instance mapping is done using one of three methods listed in the service framework section earlier.

1. The first step in configuring the applications defined in Table 5.3 is to map them to their respective instances and implement the preferred/available rules. For our example, let's define these services to database mapping using the SRVCTL utility:

```
srvctl add service -d SSKYDB -s SRV1 -r SSKY1,SSKY2,SSKY3 -a SSKY4
srvctl add service -d SSKYDB -s SRV2 -r SSKY4 -a SSKY2,SSKY3
srvctl add service -d SSKYDB -s SRV3 -r SSKY4 -a SSKY3,SSKY1
srvctl add service -d SSKYDB -s SRV4 -r SSKY1,SSKY2,SSKY3
srvctl add service -d SSKYDB -s SRV6 -r SSKY3,SSKY4 -a SSKY2,SSKY1
```

2. At this point, the user has to decide if the applications will use the Fast Application Notification (FAN) feature called Fast Connection Failover (FCF) or the standard TAF feature, or both. If the application will use the TAF feature to enable failover, then based on the criticality of the application, the appropriate TAF policies should be added to the service definition using the SRVCTL utility. In our example, SRV1 and SRV6 are highly critical and should be configured with a PRECONNECT option to minimize the connection time during failover. The remainder of the applications will be configured to have the BASIC policy.

```
srvctl modify service -d SSKYDB -s SRV1 -P PRECONNECT
srvctl modify service -d SSKYDB -s SRV2 -P BASIC
srvctl modify service -d SSKYDB -s SRV3 -P BASIC
srvctl modify service -d SSKYDB -s SRV4 -P NONE
srvctl modify service -d SSKYDB -s SRV6 -P PRECONNECT
```

 Note: A complete description and discussion with TAF and FCF is given in Chapter 6.

3.   Service definitions and failover policies defined using SRVCTL can also be verified using SRVCTL; For example;

```
[oracle@oradb4 oracle]$ srvctl config service -d SSKYDB -a
SRV1 PREF: SSKY1 SSKY2 SSKY3 AVAIL: SSKY4 TAF: PRECONNECT
SRV2 PREF: SSKY4 AVAIL: SSKY2 SSKY3 TAF: BASIC
SRV3 PREF: SSKY4 AVAIL: SSKY1 SSKY3 TAF: BASIC
SRV4 PREF: SSKY1 SSKY2 SSKY3 AVAIL: TAF: NONE
SRV5 PREF: SSKY3 SSKY4 AVAIL: SSKY1 SSKY2 TAF: PRECONNECT
```

 Note: While the connection descriptions used by FAN can contain the TAF definitions, they are ignored by the default FAN operation; however, they can be programmatically used as a backup option. When the application service does not receive any event indicating a service failure, the application connection can use TAF.

4.   For service failover and load-balancing, the client-side TNS connection description has to be updated with the appropriate entries, either with or without the TAF feature. Applications connect to an HA service using the TNS connect descriptor. The service names used in the TNS names configuration should match the service names defined in step 1 using the SRVCTL utility.

   a.   TNS connection for the SRV1 service (non-TAF)

   This definition can be used if the architecture of the application will allow connection pooling on the client side and will be implementing the FAN feature:

```
SRV1 =
  (DESCRIPTION =
    (ADDRESS=(PROTOCOL=TCP)(HOST=oradb1-vip.sumsky.net)(PORT=1521))
    (ADDRESS=(PROTOCOL=TCP)(HOST=oradb2-vip.sumsky.net)(PORT=1521))
    (ADDRESS=(PROTOCOL=TCP)(HOST=oradb3-vip.sumsky.net)(PORT=1521))
    (CONNECT_DATA =
      (SERVER = DEDICATED)
      (SERVICE_NAME = SRV1)
    )
  )
```

b. TNS connection for the SRV1 service (TAF)

Due to the critical nature of the application and since
the application is slated as a high-priority application,
the PRECONNECT TAF policy has been implemented as
follows:

```
SRV1 =
  (DESCRIPTION =
    (ADDRESS=(PROTOCOL=TCP)(HOST=oradb1-vip.sumsky.net)(PORT=1521))
    (ADDRESS=(PROTOCOL=TCP)(HOST=oradb2-vip.sumsky.net)(PORT=1521))
    (ADDRESS=(PROTOCOL=TCP)(HOST=oradb3-vip.sumsky.net)(PORT=1521))
    (ADDRESS=(PROTOCOL=TCP)(HOST=oradb4-vip.sumsky.net)(PORT=1521))
    (LOAD_BALANCE=yes)
    (CONNECT_DATA =
      (SERVER = DEDICATED)
      (SERVICE_NAME = SRV1)
      (FAILOVER_MODE = (BACKUP = SRV1_PRECONNECT)
        (TYPE = SELECT)
        (METHOD = PRECONNECT)(RETRIES = 180)(DELAY = 5)
      )
    )
  )


SRV1_PRECONNECT =
  (DESCRIPTION =
    (ADDRESS=(PROTOCOL=TCP)(HOST=oradb1-vip.sumsky.net)(PORT=1521))
    (ADDRESS=(PROTOCOL=TCP)(HOST=oradb2-vip.sumsky.net)(PORT=1521))
    (ADDRESS=(PROTOCOL=TCP)(HOST=oradb3-vip.sumsky.net)(PORT=1521))
    (ADDRESS=(PROTOCOL=TCP)(HOST=oradb4-vip.sumsky.net)(PORT=1521))
  (LOAD_BALANCE = yes)
  (CONNECT_DATA =
    (SERVER = DEDICATED)
    (SERVICE_NAME = SRV1_PRECONNECT)
    (FAILOVER_MODE =
      (BACKUP = SRV1)
      (TYPE = SELECT)(METHOD = BASIC)(RETRIES = 180)(DELAY = 5)
    )
  )
)
```

With the PRECONNECT policy, there are two connection descriptors for every definition. For example, in the previous TNS definition, we have SRV1 and SRV1_PRECONNECT. SQL*Net will use SRV1 to make a primary connection and will connect to another instance defined under the SRV1_PRECONNECT definition.

Note: SQL*Net only preconnects to the instance that is not used for the primary connection.

5.   Listeners should be cross-registered using the REMOTE_LISTENER parameter; this is to ensure that all listeners are aware of all services. As in the TNS names configuration, the listener should use VIP addresses instead of physical hostnames.

Note: Load-balancing is discussed extensively in Chapter 6.

6.   Based on the previous definitions, several applications are sharing instances; each application is to be configured to run at a specific priority level. Priorities should be defined for the service to enable workload management to set up when the scheduler should start the job and for configuration of resources.

6.1   Service priorities

The first step in setting up priorities is the creation of the various consumer groups. In our example, we would require three different consumer groups: (1) HIGH_P, which will support all applications defined in Table 5.3 as having HIGH priority, (2) STANDARD_P, which will support all applications defined in Table 5.3 as having STANDARD priority, and (3) LOW_P for LOW priority. These consumer groups map to the database resource plan. This is done with the Oracle-provided PL/SQL packages using the following steps:

6.1.1   Create a pending work area.

While defining ODRM policies, irrespective of the type of policy being defined, it's required that an initial workspace or working area be defined. This allows for validation and testing of the policies before committing or saving them for actual usage. The pending work area is created using

```
EXEC DBMS_RESOURCE_MANAGER.CREATE_PENDING_AREA();
```

6.1.2   Define the consumer group.

Once a working area has been created, the next step is to create all the different levels of priority. This is done using the CREATE_CONSUMER_GROUP procedure:

```
EXECUTE
DBMS_RESOURCE_MANAGER.CREATE_CONSUMER_GROUP
                (CONSUMER_GROUP=>'HIGH_P',
                 COMMENT=>'High Priority group');
```

6.1.3   Map consumer groups to services

Once the consumer groups are defined, the next step is to map the consumer group to its respective services (e.g., consumer group HIGH_P will be used by both SRV1 and SRV5):

```
EXECUTE
DBMS_RESOURCE_MANAGER.SET_CONSUMER_GROUP_MAPPING

(ATTRIBUTE=>DBMS_RESOURCE_MANAGER.SERVICE_NAME,
                 VALUE=> 'SRV1',
                 CONSUMER_GROUP=>'HIGH_P');
```

In this output, service SRV1 is mapped to HIGH_P, indicating that it's governed by the resource criteria defined for consumer group HIGH_P.

6.1.4   Verify the consumer group and priority definitions by querying against the DBA_RSRC_GROUP_MAPPINGS view:

```
SELECT ATTRIBUTE,
       VALUE,
   CONSUMER_GROUP
   FROM   DBA_RSRC_GROUP_MAPPINGS
   WHERE  ATTRIBUTE LIKE '%SERVICE%';
```

```
ATTRIBUTE        VALUE          CONSUMER_GROUP
--------------   -------------  --------------------
SERVICE_NAME     SRV1           HIGH_P
SERVICE_NAME     SRV2           STANDARD_P
SERVICE_NAME     SRV3           STANDARD_P
SERVICE_NAME     SRV4           LOW_P
SERVICE_NAME     SRV6           HIGH_P
```

6.1.5   Once the consumer group definitions have been verified, save
         and enable these definitions using the following procedure:

```
EXEC DBMS_RESOURCE_MANAGER.SUBMIT_PENDING_AREA();
```

This will save all ODRM definitions created in the workspace
area to disk.

6.2   Job class definition

One application listed in Table 5.3 is a batch job (reporting) that
is triggered by other applications on other services in the cluster.
Batch jobs are normally scheduled to run at predefined intervals
and at a predefined frequency. The DBMS_SCHEDULER can schedule a batch job. One prerequisite to define a batch job using the
DBMS_SCHEDULER is to define a job class using the
CREATE_JOB_CLASS procedure:

```
EXECUTE DBMS_SCHEDULER.CREATE_JOB_CLASS -
             (JOB_CLASS_NAME => 'SRV3', -
              RESOURCE_CONSUMER_GROUP => NULL, -
              SERVICE=> 'SRV3', -
              LOGGING_LEVEL=>
    DBMS_SCHEDULER.LOGGING_RUNS,-
              LOG_HISTORY => 30);
```

This definition will create a job class called SRV3. The parameters for the
CREATE_JOB_CLASS procedure include the name identified by
JOB_CLASS_NAME, the consumer group that the job class belongs to, and the
service name (SERVICE) that is being mapped to the job class. The defini-
tion also contains a logging level (LOGGING_LEVEL) and a log history period
(LOG_HISTORY).

The RESOURCE_CONSUMER_GROUP is NULL because the service was mapped to a resource consumer group in the previous step. Oracle supports three different levels of logging:

1. No logging using DBMS_SCHEDULER.LOGGING_OFF

2. Detailed logging using DBMS_SCHEDULER.LOGGING_RUNS

3. Complete logging that records all operations performed by all jobs in the job class using DBMS_SCHEDULER.LOGGING_FULL

The job definitions can be verified using the following query DBA_SCHEDULER_JOB_CLASSES view:

```
SELECT JOB_CLASS_NAME,
       SERVICE
FROM DBA_SCHEDULER_JOB_CLASSES
WHERE SERVICE LIKE '%SRV%';


JOB_CLASS_NAME     SERVICE
------------------ ------------------------------
SRV3               SRV3
```

6.3   Job definition

Once the job class has been defined, the next step is to add the batch job to the scheduler, from which the job can be executed by the application by submitting it in the background. The job is scheduled using the following command:

```
EXEC DBMS_SCHEDULER.CREATE_JOB-
    (JOB_NAME=>'SRV3_REPORTING_JOB', -
    JOB_TYPE=>'EXECUTABLE', -
    JOB_ACTION=>'/usr/apps/batch/SSKYnightlybatch;', -
    JOB_CLASS=>'SRV3',-
    ENABLED=>TRUE, -
    AUTO_DROP=>FALSE, -
    COMMENTS=>'Batch Reporting');
```

6.4 Resource plans

To ensure that critical applications such as SRV1 and SRV6 can obtain sufficient resources from the Oracle resource pool, the ODRM functionality supports definition of resource plans, where an application can be assigned resource limits such as percentage of CPU available. The resource plan is created using the following PL/SQL definition (or through EM):

```
BEGIN
    DBMS_RESOURCE_MANAGER.CREATE_PLAN (high_p_plan, ' ');
    DBMS_RESOURCE_MANAGER.CREATE_PLAN_DIRECTIVE
        (PLAN                        => 'SSKY_PLAN1',
        GROUP_OR_SUBPLAN             => 'OTHER_GROUPS',
        COMMENT                      => ' ',
        CPU_P1                       => 0,
        CPU_P2                       => 0,
        CPU_P3                       => 0,
        CPU_P4                       => 0,
        CPU_P5                       => NULL,
        CPU_P6                       => NULL,
        CPU_P7                       => NULL,
        CPU_P8                       => NULL,
        PARALLEL_DEGREE_LIMIT_P1     => 40,
        ACTIVE_SESS_POOL_P1          => 100,
        QUEUEING_P1                  => 30,
        SWITCH_GROUP                 => 'LOW_GROUP',
        SWITCH_TIME                  => NULL,
        SWITCH_ESTIMATE              => TRUE,
        MAX_EST_EXEC_TIME            => 15,
        UNDO_POOL                    => NULL,
        MAX_IDLE_TIME                => 40,
        MAX_IDLE_BLOCKER_TIME        => 5,
        SWITCH_TIME_IN_CALL          => 60
        );

    DBMS_RESOURCE_MANAGER.CREATE_PLAN_DIRECTIVE
        (PLAN                        => 'SSKY_PLAN1',
        GROUP_OR_SUBPLAN             => 'HIGH_P',
        COMMENT                      => ' ',
        CPU_P1                       => 60,
        CPU_P2                       => 20,
```

```
          CPU_P3                        => 10,
          CPU_P4                        => 5,
          CPU_P5                        => NULL,
          CPU_P6                        => NULL,
          CPU_P7                        => NULL,
          CPU_P8                        => NULL,
          PARALLEL_DEGREE_LIMIT_P1      => NULL,
          ACTIVE_SESS_POOL_P1           => 100,
          QUEUEING_P1                   => 30,
          SWITCH_GROUP                  => 'LOW_GROUP',
          SWITCH_TIME                   => NULL,
          SWITCH_ESTIMATE               => TRUE,
          MAX_EST_EXEC_TIME             => 15,
          UNDO_POOL                     => NULL,
          MAX_IDLE_TIME                 => 40,
          MAX_IDLE_BLOCKER_TIME         => 5,
          SWITCH_TIME_IN_CALL           => 60
        );

  DBMS_RESOURCE_MANAGER.CREATE_PLAN_DIRECTIVE
        (PLAN                          => 'SSKY_PLAN1',
          GROUP_OR_SUBPLAN              => 'LOW_P',
          COMMENT                       => ' ',
          CPU_P1                        => 20,
          CPU_P2                        => 5,
          CPU_P3                        => NULL,
          CPU_P4                        => NULL,
          CPU_P5                        => NULL,
          CPU_P6                        => NULL,
          CPU_P7                        => NULL,
          CPU_P8                        => NULL,
          PARALLEL_DEGREE_LIMIT_P1      => NULL,
          ACTIVE_SESS_POOL_P1           => 100,
          QUEUEING_P1                   => 30,
          SWITCH_GROUP                  => 'LOW_GROUP',
          SWITCH_TIME                   => NULL,
          SWITCH_ESTIMATE               => TRUE,
          MAX_EST_EXEC_TIME             => 15,
          UNDO_POOL                     => NULL,
          MAX_IDLE_TIME                 => 40,
          MAX_IDLE_BLOCKER_TIME         => 5,
```

```
         SWITCH_TIME_IN_CALL              => 60
         );


    DBMS_RESOURCE_MANAGER.SUBMIT_PENDING_AREA ();


    EXECUTE IMMEDIATE 'ALTER SYSTEM SET resource_manager_plan
=''HIGH_P_PLAN'' SID=''SSKY2''';


    EXECUTE IMMEDIATE 'ALTER SYSTEM SET resource_manager_plan
=''HIGH_P_PLAN'' SID=''SSKY1''';
END;
```

In this definition, we have three groups for which plans are defined. Group OTHER_GROUP is an Oracle-provided default group for every resource plan definition. The HIGH_P and LOW_P groups are created based on Table 5.3 in step 6.1.2. Based on the application distribution in Table 5.3, SRV4 is defined under resource group LOW_P (running under low priority) on instances SSKY1, SSKY2, and SSKY3. Applications SRV1 and SRV6 are defined under resource group HIGH_P and share instances with application SRV4. Based on the requirements, the resource plan shares the resources between the two resource groups HIGH_P and LOW_P, giving resource group HIGH_P more resources.

The default group, OTHER_GROUP, should not be ignored. At times when there are runaway processes and both resource groups consume all of the resources, it would be in the DBA's best interest to allocate some resources under the OTHER_GROUP category so the DBA can interview and perform any administrative operation.

6.5   Performance thresholds definition

Performance thresholds may be defined for each instance participating in this cluster using the following PL/SQL package:

```
EXECUTE
DBMS_SERVER_ALERT.SET_THRESHOLD -

(DBMS_SERVER_ALERT.ELAPSED_TIME_PER_CALL, -
DBMS_SERVER_ALERT.OPERATOR_GE, -
WARNING_VALUE => '500',-
    DBMS_SERVER_ALERT.OPERATOR_GE,-
```

```
                              CRITICAL_VALUE => '7500', -
                              OBSERVATION_PERIOD =>1,-
                              CONSECUTIVE_OCCURRENCES => 5,-
                              INSTANCE_NAME => 'SSKY1',-

           DBMS_SERVER_ALERT.OBJECT_TYPE_SERVICE,-
                              OBJECT_NAME =>'SRV1');
```

6.6   Enabling service, module, and action monitoring

Oracle has provided additional packages and views for monitoring this functionality. Monitoring is set up using the following PL/SQL package. Once set up, the configuration information can be verified using the DBA_ENABLED_AGGREGATIONS view:

```
      EXECUTE
        DBMS_MONITOR.SERV_MOD_ACT_STAT_ENABLE -
                          (SERVICE_NAME=> 'SRV1', -
                          MODULE_NAME => 'CRM', -
                          ACTION_NAME =>'EXCEPTION');
```

 Note: Depending on the type of application, steps 6.1 through 6.5 should be performed for all applications defined in Table 5.3. Monitoring and tracing of services is covered in detail in Chapter 9.

5.3   **Fast Application Notification**

Traditionally, applications connect to the database based on user requests to perform an operation such as retrieve or update information. During the process of connecting to a database that is not accepting any connection requests—because a node, instance, database, service, or listener is down—the connection manager will have to return an error back to the application, which in turn will determine the next action to be taken. In the case of a RAC implementation, the next step (if the node, instance, or listener is down) would be to attempt connecting to the next available address, defined in the address list of the TNS connection descriptor. The time it takes to react to such connection failures and for the application to retry the connection to another node, instance, or listener is often long.

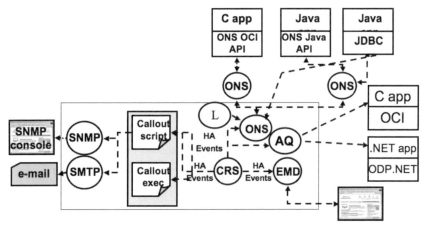

Figure 5.13
FAN Event
Notification
Overview

Source: Oracle Corporation

FAN is a new feature introduced in Oracle Database 10*g* RAC to proactively notify applications regarding the status of the cluster and any configuration changes that take place. FAN uses the Oracle Notification Services (ONS) for the actual notification of the event to its other ONS clients. As illustrated in Figure 5.13, ONS provides and supports several callable interfaces that can be used by different applications to take advantage of the HA solutions offered in Oracle Database 10*g* RAC.

5.3.1   Oracle Notification Services

ONS allows users to send SMS messages, e-mails, voice notifications, and fax messages in an easy-to-access manner. Oracle Clusterware uses ONS to send notifications about the state of the database instances to midtier applications that use this information for load-balancing and for fast failure detection.

ONS is a daemon process that communicates with other ONS daemons on other nodes which inform each other of the current state of the database components on the database server. For example, if a listener, node, or service is down, a down event is triggered by the EVMD process, which is then sent by the local ONS daemon to the ONS daemon process on other nodes, including all clients and application servers participating in the network. Only nodes or client machines that have the ONS daemon running and have registered with each other will receive such notification. Once the ONS on the client machines receives this notification, the application (if using an Oracle-provided API) will determine, based on the notification, which nodes and instances have had a state change and will appropriately handle a new connection request. ONS informs the application of state changes, allowing the application to respond proactively instead of in the traditional reactive method.

ONS configuration

ONS is installed and configured as part of the Oracle Clusterware installation. Execution of the `root.sh` file on Unix and Linux-based systems, during the Oracle Clusterware installation will create and start the ONS on all nodes participating in the cluster. This can be verified using the `crs_stat` utility provided by Oracle.

```
[oracle@oradb3 oracle]# crs_stat -t -c oradb3
Name             Type        Target    State     Host
-------------------------------------------------------------
ora.oradb3.gsd application   ONLINE    ONLINE    oradb3
ora.oradb3.ons application   ONLINE    ONLINE    oradb3
ora.oradb3.vip application   ONLINE    ONLINE    oradb3
```

Configuration of ONS involves registering all nodes and servers that will communicate with the ONS daemon on the database server. During Oracle Clusterware installation, all nodes participating in the cluster are automatically registered with the ONS. Subsequently, during restart of the clusterware, ONS will register all nodes with the respective ONS processes on other nodes in the cluster.

To add additional members or nodes that should receive notifications, the hostname or IP address of the node should be added to the `ons.config` file. The configuration file is located in the `$ORACLE_HOME/opmn/conf` directory and has the following format:

```
[oracle@oradb4 oracle]$ more $ORACLE_HOME/opmn/conf/ons.config
localport=6101
remoteport=6201
loglevel=3
useocr=on
nodes=oradb4.sumsky.net:6101,oradb2.sumsky.net:6201,
oradb1.sumsky.net:6201,oradb3.sumsky.net:6201,
onsclient1.sumsky.net:6200,onsclient2.sumsky.net:6200
```

The `localport` is the port that ONS binds to on the local host interface to talk to local clients. The `remoteport` is the port that ONS binds to on all interfaces to talk to other ONS daemons. The loglevel indicates the amount of logging that should be generated. Oracle supports logging levels from 1 through 9. ONS logs are generated in the $ORACLE_HOME/opmn/ logs directory on the respective instances. The loglevel is described in detail in Chapter 7. The useocr parameter (valid values are on/off) indicates whether ONS should use the OCR to determine which instances and nodes are participating in the cluster. The nodes listed in the nodes line are all nodes in the network that will need to receive or send event notifications. This includes client machines where ONS is also running to receive FAN events for applications.

Note: The nodes listed in the nodes line are public node addresses and not VIP addresses.

A similar configuration is also to be performed on all client machines. All node addresses should be cross-registered in the ons.config file on the respective machines. Just to recap, ONS has the following features:

- It has simple publish/subscribe method to deliver event messages

- It allows both local and remote consumption

- It is required by FAN

- It is installed and configured during Oracle Clusterware installation (Oracle Database 10*g* Release 2)

- It must be installed on all clients using FAN with Oracle Database 10*g* Release 1

ONS communication

As mentioned earlier, ONS communicates all events generated by the EVMD processes to all nodes registered with the ONS. Figure 5.14 illustrates the notification channels that ONS will follow when an Oracle-related state change occurs on any of the nodes participating in the clustered configuration.

As illustrated in Figure 5.14, FAN uses ONS for server-to-server and server-to-client notification of state changes, which includes, up, down, and restart events for all components of the RAC cluster. For example, in Figure 5.14, the ONS daemon on node oradb2 notifies all other nodes in the cluster and all client machines running ONS of any state changes with respect to components on that node. All events, except for the node failure event, are sent by the node on which the event is generated. In the case of a node failure, one of the surviving nodes will send the notification.

Based on the notification received, the FAN calls within the application will proactively react to the situation, which includes failover of connections to another instance where the service is supported.

Figure 5.14
FAN ONS
Communication

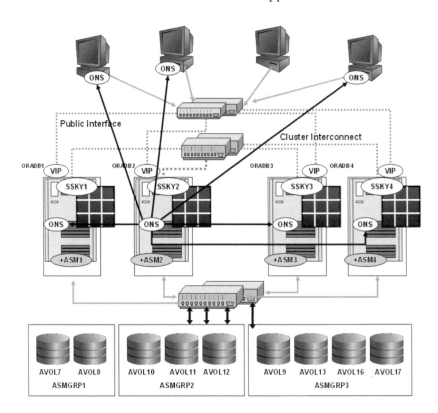

Oracle uses the advanced queuing technology for event notifications between various servers and clients.

 Note: ONS must be started only on client machines not using Oracle Database 10*g* Release 2 SQL*Net client software.

5.3.2   **FAN events**

When state changes occur on a cluster, node, or instance in a RAC environment, an event is triggered by the Event Manager and propagated by the ONS to the client machines. Such events that communicate state changes are termed FAN events and have a predefined structure. Every FAN event consists of header and payload information sent in name-value pairs from the origination to the respective targets participating in the framework. The name-value pair describes the actual name, type, and nature of the event. On receipt of this information, based on the type of notification received, the recipient or the target application will take appropriate steps, such as routing the connection to another instance.

Oracle supports two types of events:

1.   *Service events.* Service events are application events and contain state changes that will only affect clients that use the service. Normally, such events only indicate database, instance level, and application service failures.

2.   *System events.* System events are more global and represent events such as node and communication failures. Such events affect all services supported on the specific system (e.g., cluster membership changes, such as a node leaving or joining the cluster).

Both of these types of events contain the following structure:

```
<Event_Type> VERSION=<n.n>
service=<serviceName.dbDomainName>
[database=<db_unique_name> [instance=<instance_name>]]
[host=<hostname>] status=<Event_Status>
reason=<Event_Reason>[card=<n>] timestamp=<eventDate>
<eventTime>
```

The various attributes used in the event and the descriptions can be found in Table 5.4.

The following example is an event structure when an instance is started on system reboot:

```
INSTANCE VERSION=1.0 service=SSKYDB database=SSKYDB
instance=SSKY2 host=oradb2 status=up reason=boot
timestamp=17-Jun-2005 00:02:49
```

Chapter 5

Table 5.4 *ONS Event Descriptions*

Event Identifier	Description
Event_Type	Several types of events belong to either the service type or system type of event: **SERVICE:** Indicates it is a primary application service event (e.g., database service). **SRV_PRECONNECT:** Preconnect application service event. This event applies to services using primary- and secondary-type of instance configuration. **SERVICEMEMBER:** Application service on a specific instance event. **DATABASE:** Indicates an Oracle database event. **INSTANCE:** Indicates an Oracle instance event. **ASM:** Indicates an Oracle ASM instance event. **NODE:** Belongs to the system-type event and indicates an Oracle cluster node event.
VERSION	Event payload version. Normally reflects the version of the database or clusterware. When an environment supports several databases that have different clusterware versions, the payload version will help determine what actions to take depending on the features supported by the version.
service	Name of the application HA service (e.g., the services listed and defined in Table 5.3).
database	Name of the RAC database for which the event is being raised.
instance	Name of the RAC instance for which the event is being raised.
host	Name of the cluster node from where such an event was raised.

Table 5.4 *ONS Event Descriptions (continued)*

Event Identifier	Description
status	Indicates what has occurred for the event type. The valid status values are
	up: Managed resource is now up and available.
	down: Managed resource is now down and is currently not available for access.
	preconn_up: The preconnect application services are now up and available.
	preconn_down: The preconnect application service has failed or is down and is not currently available.
	nodedown: The Oracle RAC cluster node indicated by the host identifier is down and is not reachable.
	not_restarting: Indicates that one of the managed resources that failed will not restart either on the failed node or on another node after failover. For example, VIP should failover to another and restart when a node fails.
	unknown: Status is unknown and no description is available.
reason	Indicates the reason for the event being raised and is normally related to the status. The following are possible reasons
	user: This indicates that the down or up event raised is use initiated. Operations performed using srvctl or from sqlplus belong to this category. This is a planned type of event.
	failure: During constant polling of the health of the various resources, when a resource is not reachable, a failure event is triggered. This is an unplanned type of event.

Table 5.4 *ONS Event Descriptions (continued)*

Event Identifier	Description
reason	dependency: Availability of certain resources depends on other resources in the cluster being up. For example, the Oracle instance on a specific node depends on the database application being available. This is also an unplanned event. unknown: The state of the application was not known during the failure to determine the actual cause of failure. This is also an unplanned event. system: There has been change in system state (e.g., when a node is started). This reason is normally associated with only system events. For other event types, the reason boot. boot: This indicates the initial startup of the resource after the node was started (e.g., once all system-related resources are started, such as VIP, ONS). All user-defined database service events have a reason code of boot.
card	This represents the service membership cardinality. It is the number of members that are running the service. It can be used by client applications to perform software-based load-balancing.
timestamp	Server-side date and time when the event was detected

When this event is received by an ONS client machine, the application will use this information to reroute any future connections to this instance, until the load profile defined for the service has been met.

Oracle defines services for all components within the RAC environment to monitor its state and to notify the application or client nodes of that state. Figure 5.15 illustrates the relationship between the various components that affect the application servers directly and that are all monitored by ONS for state change notifications.

The number of components or subcomponents affected by a down event depends on the component or service that has failed. For example, if a node fails or is taken out of the cluster membership, then the NODE event is sent to all clients registered with the ONS of the failed node. All components that have a direct or indirect dependency on the NODE are all affected.

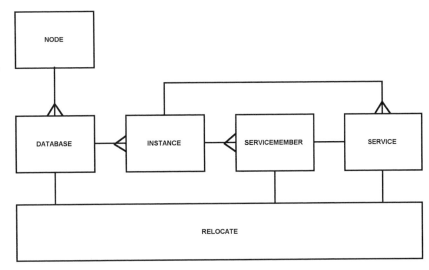

Figure 5.15
ERD and Dependency Relationship of Application Services

In Figure 5.15, all entities—database, instance, and the services that the instance supports—are all affected. While a node or an instance cannot failover to another node in the cluster, certain services, including the database, can failover or relocate to another node in the cluster. The types of service that can failover or relocate depend on the type of service or the service characteristics defined by the administrator. Similarly, if the database service is down or has relocated itself to another node, then all services that depend on the database service will also fail, and ONS will send those notifications to all participating nodes. The following output lists the database service located on the oradb1 node:

```
[oracle@oradb4 oracle]$ crsstat
HA Resource                    Target      State
-----------                    ------      -----
ora.SSKYDB.SRV1.SSKY1.srv      ONLINE      ONLINE on oradb1
ora.SSKYDB.SRV1.cs             ONLINE      ONLINE on oradb1
ora.SSKYDB.SRV2.SSKY1.srv      ONLINE      ONLINE on oradb2
ora.SSKYDB.SRV2.cs             ONLINE      ONLINE on oradb2
-----------
ora. SSKYDB.db                 ONLINE       ONLINE on oradb1
```

As illustrated in Figure 5.15, all components depend on the NODE service. For the DATABASE application, the instances and all services created on the instance are affected. For an INSTANCE, all SERVICEMEMBERs and services are affected, and if a SERVICEMEMBER fails, all services that the SER-VICEMEMBER supports on the failed instance are affected.

How do you monitor and track when these events are fired? Oracle has provided options where a script or utility or application (called server-side callouts), if placed in the $ORA_CRS_HOME/racg/usrco directory, will be executed automatically. For example, the following shell script, when placed in this directory will write out events generated by the Event Manager to the file defined by the symbol FAN_LOGFILE in the script:

```
[oracle@oradb4 oracle]$ more callout.sh
#! /bin/ksh
FAN_LOGFILE=/usr/app/oracle/product/10.2.0/crs/evm/admin/log/
oradb4_FANuptime.log
echo >> $FAN_LOGFILE &
[oracle@oradb4 oracle]$
```

Similarly, any script or executable that can be invoked automatically when an ONS event condition occurs can be put into this directory and will be executed. A few example events (formatted for clarity) generated by the previous script include the following:

ASM instance DOWN event

```
ASM VERSION=1.0 service= database= instance=ASM2 host=oradb2
status=down reason=failure timestamp=17-Jun-2005 00:00:15
```

RDBMS instance DOWN event

```
INSTANCE VERSION=1.0 service=SSKYDB database=SSKYDB
instance=SSKY2 host=oradb2 status=down reason=failure
timestamp=17-Jun-2005 00:00:23
```

ASM instance UP event

```
ASM VERSION=1.0 service= database= instance=ASM2 host=oradb4
status=up reason=boot timestamp=17-Jun-2005 00:01:26
```

RDBMS instance UP event

```
INSTANCE VERSION=1.0 service=SSKYDB database=SSKYDB
instance=SSKY2 host=oradb2 status=up reason=boot
timestamp=17-Jun-2005 00:02:49
```

Application service SRV1 UP event

```
SERVICE VERSION=1.0 service=SRV1 database=SSKYDB instance=
host=oradb2 status=up reason=unknown timestamp=17-Jun-2005
00:14:52
```

DATABASE service UP event

```
DATABASE VERSION=1.0 service=SSKYDB database=SSKYDB instance=
host=oradb2 status=up reason=unknown timestamp=17-Jun-2005
00:14:53
```

SERVICEMEMBER UP event

```
SERVICEMEMBER VERSION=1.0 service=SRV4 database=SSKYDB
instance=SSKY2 host=oradb2 status=up reason=user card=1
timestamp=17-Jun-2005 00:29:16
```

Application SERVICE SRV4 UP event

```
SERVICE VERSION=1.0 service=SRV4 database=SSKYDB instance=
host=oradb2 status=up reason=user timestamp=17-Jun-2005
00:29:17
```

Apart from writing server-side callouts, these events can be tracked on the application server or on the client machines in one of two ways:

1.   ONS logging

2.   By generating logs from the application when such events are received by the FAN APIs

Example of callout usage:

- Log-in status info

- Paging a DBA or opening a support ticket when a resource is in a not-restarting status

- Automatically starting up dependent components collocated with a service

- Ensuring that services have been started after a database has been restarted

- Changing resource plans or shutting down services when the number of available instances decreases (as may occur if nodes fail)

- Automating the fail back of a service to preferred instances, should this be desired

ONS logging

ONS events can be tracked via logs on both the server side and the client side. ONS logs are written to the $ORACLE_HOME/opmn/logs directory. The default logging level is set to three. Depending on the level of tracking desired, this can be changed by modifying the ons.config file located in the `$ORACLE_HOME/opmn/conf` directory discussed earlier. Logging at level eight provides event information received by the ONS on the client machines.

The following extract from the ONS log file illustrates the various stages of the SRV1 HA service as it transitions from a DOWN state to an UP state:

```
05/06/18 17:41:11 [7] Connection 25,192.168.2.30,6200 Message content
length is 94
05/06/18 17:41:11 [7] Connection 25,192.168.2.30,6200 Body using 94
of 94 reUse
05/06/18 17:41:11 [8] Connection 25,192.168.2.30,6200 body:
```
VERSION=1.0 service=SRV1 instance=SSKY1 database=SSKYDB host=oradb1
status=down reason=failure
```
05/06/18 17:41:11 [8] Worker Thread 120 checking receive queue
05/06/18 17:41:11 [8] Worker Thread 120 sending event 115 to servers
05/06/18 17:41:11 [8] Event 115 route:
3232236062,6200;3232236072,6200;3232236135,6200


05/06/18 17:41:20 [7] Connection 25,192.168.2.30,6200 Message content
length is 104
05/06/18 17:41:20 [7] Connection 25,192.168.2.30,6200 Body using 104
of 104 reUse
05/06/18 17:41:20 [8] Connection 25,192.168.2.30,6200 body:
```
VERSION=1.0 service=SRV1 instance=SSKY1 database=SSKYDB host=oradb1
status=not_restarting reason=UNKNOWN
```
05/06/18 17:41:20 [8] Worker Thread 120 checking receive queue
05/06/18 17:41:20 [8] Worker Thread 120 sending event 125 to servers
05/06/18 17:41:20 [8] Event 125 route:
3232236062,6200;3232236072,6200;3232236135,6200

05/06/18 18:22:30 [9] Worker Thread 2 sending body [135:128]:
connection 6,10.1.2.168,6200
```
VERSION=1.0 service=SRV1 instance=SSKY2 database=SSKYDB host=oradb2
status=up card=2 reason=user
```
05/06/18 18:22:30 [7] Worker Thread 128 checking client send queues
05/06/18 18:22:30 [8] Worker queuing event 135 (at head): connection
10,10.1.2.177,6200
05/06/18 18:22:30 [8] Worker Thread 124 checking receive queue
05/06/18 18:22:30 [7] Worker Thread 124 checking server send queues
05/06/18 18:22:30 [8] Worker Thread 124 processing send queue:
connection 10,10.1.2.177,6200
```

```
05/06/18 18:22:30 [9] Worker Thread 124 sending header [2:135]:
connection 10,10.1.2.177,6200
```

This extract from the ONS log file illustrates three notifications received from the ONS server node oradb1 containing instance SSKY1 and application service SRV1. The three notifications received at different times indicate various stages of the service SRV1. The first message indicates a notification regarding the failure of SRV1 on instance SSKY1. The second message indicates a notification regarding a restart attempt of service SRV1 on the same node oradb1. This restart notification also indicates that the instance and node are healthy, or else it would not attempt to restart on the same node. The third message is an UP event notification from the server to the client indicating that the service has started on node oradb2 (instead of its original node). Once this message is received, the application can resume connections using the service SRV1. This illustrates that the service SRV1 has relocated from node oradb1 to oradb2.

FAN API logging

Details or events received can also be tracked at the application tier using the Oracle-provided FAN APIs. For example, the following output illustrates receipt of an UP event by the application server. Based on this event, new connections will be routed to this service on node oradb4.

```
19 Jun 2005 11:25:32 - ONS Notification Received:
19 Jun 2005 11:25:32 - **Message Start**
19 Jun 2005 11:25:32 -   Body:VERSION=1.0 service=SRV1 instance=SSKY2
database=SSKYDB host=oradb4 status=up card=2 reason=user
19 Jun 2005 11:25:32 -   Effected components: null
19 Jun 2005 11:25:32 -   Effected nodes: null
19 Jun 2005 11:25:32 -   Cluster IddatabaseClusterId
19 Jun 2005 11:25:32 -   Cluster NamedatabaseClusterName
19 Jun 2005 11:25:32 -   Creation Time1119194661
19 Jun 2005 11:25:32 -   Delivery Time1119194732398
19 Jun 2005 11:25:32 -   Generating Component: database/rac/service
19 Jun 2005 11:25:32 -   Generating Node: oradb4.sumsky.net
19 Jun 2005 11:25:32 -   Generating Process: oradb4.sumsky.net:4689
19 Jun 2005 11:25:32 -   Is Cluster Only: false
19 Jun 2005 11:25:32 -   Is Local Only: false
19 Jun 2005 11:25:32 -   ID: oradb4.sumsky.net:4689061
19 Jun 2005 11:25:32 -   Instance ID: databaseInstanceId
19 Jun 2005 11:25:32 -   Instance Name: databaseInstanceName
```

```
19 Jun 2005 11:25:32 -  Type: database/event/service
19 Jun 2005 11:25:32 -  **Message Ended**
```

Applying these event rules to the distributed application configuration in Table 5.3, SRV6, which is a seasonal application, will be notified under the following circumstances: Load on nodes SSKY3 and SSKY4 is high and is not able to process all requests received from application SRV6. Application SRV6 requires additional resources; however, the current instances do not have the capacity to provide these resources. In this case, based on the threshold values defined, the Event Manager will notify the monitoring station. Once this notification is received, through a manual operation, an additional instance can be added to process requests from application SRV6 or scripts can be written to handle such notifications and automatically start them on other available instances.

When the node supporting the application service SRV6 fails, an event is sent to the application client from node oradb4, at which time Oracle performs two operations in parallel:

1.   It migrates the service or fails over the service to another instance allocated during service definition.

2.   It sends a node down event to the application server.

On receipt of the event, the application will start directing all connections allocated to the failed node to the new instance. Since the service is already established by the listener on the new node, the application server or client running this specific service will be able to establish connections and complete the required operations.

When either instance SSKY3 or SSKY4 fails, the following two operations are executed in parallel:

1.   SRV6 service is migrated from the failed instance to another backup or available instance.

2.   ONS sends a notification to all clients known to ONS regarding the service down event. When such an event is received by the application, all connections are directed to the new instance.

Such configurations provide a distributed workload across the available nodes, taking advantage of the available resources while balancing workload across them. Such an implementation is a step toward an Oracle grid strategy.

5.4   Conclusion

This chapter discussed, Oracle's new features of service-based architecture with DWM in detail. Other new components that have been integrated with RAC to provide a higher availability, such as ODRM and Oracle Scheduler, were also discussed. To understand how a DWM environment can be configured, a workshop example was used to show the various steps that are performed while configuring the RAC cluster to distribute workload.

6

Failover and Load-Balancing

Since the emergence of the Internet boom, including the era of the dot-com, the common buzzwords have been "availability" and "uptime" of computer systems. Businesses today have applications that are accessed via the Internet from around the world from countries located in varying time zones. When it's 10:30 a.m. in Bangalore, India, or 3:30 p.m. in Melbourne, Australia, it's 9:30 p.m. in North Carolina, United States. If a business establishment, such as an Internet bookstore located in Charlotte, North Carolina, wants to trade a book to a customer in either Bangalore or Melbourne, the bookstore should be up and functional. Keeping the Internet book site up and functional at that time indicates an uptime at non-normal business hours for an organization located in the United States. To support these business needs, applications and enterprise systems should be available for access 24 hours a day, 7 days a week.

Availability is measured by the amount of time the system has been up and is available for operation. In defining availability of the system, the word "system" does not apply to just the database tier or the application tier, because it is not the database tier or the application tier that is prone to failure. All tiers of the application stack that either directly or indirectly play a part in providing information to the user are prone to failures. This includes the application tier, firewalls, interconnects, networks, storage subsystems, and controllers to these storage subsystems. When an availability requirement of 99.999% is specified, it should apply to the entire enterprise system. The availability of the enterprise system is obtained by providing a redundant architecture at the primary location and other methods to protect data during disaster situations by storing data at remote locations. This means that every subsystem or component should have redundant hardware so that if one piece of hardware fails, the other redundant piece is available to provide the required functionality so business may continue.

Providing this type of availability is based on the business requirements. If the business requirement is to support customers on a 24-hour schedule, 365 days per year, such as the Internet bookstore described above, redundant architecture will be necessary. However, if there is no such business requirement and bringing down the system does not affect the entire business, then all of this redundancy might not be required. Consequently, availability can also be measured by the amount of downtime allowed per year.

The primary factor of any organization is to keep the mean time between failures (MTBF) high. (*MTBF is the average time, usually expressed in hours, that a component works without failure. It is calculated by dividing the total number of failures into the total number of operating hours observed. The term can also mean the length of time a user can reasonably expect a device or system to work before a failure occurs.*) Keeping the MTBF high and meeting this 99.999% availability requirement in a single-instance Oracle configuration is no different. Every database, including Oracle, is prone to failures, and when the database or the system composing it fails, the users will have to reconnect to another database at another location (probably a disaster location, if one exists) to continue activity. Using database features such as TAF and FCF in a clustered database environment such as RAC will migrate users, when a node or instance in a cluster fails, to another node transparently as if no such failure has happened.

As illustrated in Figure 6.1, RAC allows multiple Oracle instances residing on different nodes to access the same physical database. GCS and GES maintain consistency across the caches of the different nodes. RAC protects against either a node failure or communication failure. Apart from the availability and failover aspects with a RAC implementation, RAC also brings load-balancing and scalability features by distributing workload across various instances participating in the cluster. This allows the application to take advantage of the available resources on other nodes and instances in the cluster. The load-balancing feature of RAC will be discussed later in this chapter.

In a RAC environment, all nodes in the cluster are in an active state. This means that all instances in the cluster are active, and users can connect to any one or all instances based on their service configuration. If one or more of the instances or nodes fail, only users and sessions from the failed instance are failed over to one of the surviving instances.

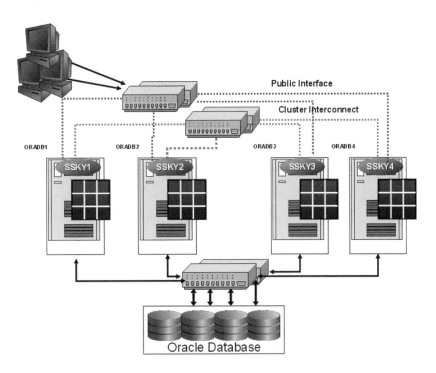

Figure 6.1
*Oracle Real
Application
Clusters*

 Note: In a DWM configuration (discussed in Chapter 5), one or more nodes can be configured as spare nodes to help workload distribution when one or more of the active nodes fail.

6.1   **Failover**

Failover is the mechanism where, when one or more nodes or instances in the cluster fail, the users or sessions that were originally connected to this instance will failover to one of the other nodes in the cluster.

6.1.1   **How does the failover mechanism work?**

RAC relies on the cluster services for failure detection. The cluster services are a distributed kernel component that monitors whether cluster members (nodes) can communicate with each other and, through this process, enforces the rules of cluster membership. In Oracle Database 10*g*, this function is performed by CSS, through the CSSD process. The functions performed by CSS can be broadly listed as follows:

- Forms a cluster, adds members to a cluster, and removes members from a cluster
- Tracks which members in a cluster are active
- Maintains a cluster membership list that is consistent on all member nodes
- Provides timely notification of membership changes
- Detects and handles possible cluster partitions
- Monitors group membership

The cluster services ensure data integrity between communication failures by using a polling mechanism (i.e., processing and I/O activity is allowed only when the cluster has a quorum). A quorum depends on several factors, such as expected votes over a specified period from the participating members in the cluster (node votes) and quorum disk votes.

- *Node votes* are the fixed number of votes that a given member contributes toward quorum. Cluster members can have either 1 or 0 node votes. Each member with a vote 1 is considered a voting member of the cluster, and a member with 0 is considered a nonvoting member.
- *Quorum/voting disk votes* are a fixed number of votes that a quorum/ voting disk contributes toward a quorum. Similar to the node vote, a quorum disk can also have either 1 or 0 votes.

The CSS determines the availability of a member in a cluster using a polling [1] method. Using this method, the CSS allows the nodes to communicate with the other nodes to determine availability on a continuous basis at preset intervals. CSS performs this operation every one to two seconds. This time interval is based on the hardware platform and the operating system.

---

1.   Third-party clusterware, such as Veritas, Tru64, and Sun Cluster, uses the heartbeat mechanism to verify if the other node in the cluster is alive or not.

When a node polls another node (target) in the cluster, and the target has not responded successfully after repeated attempts, a timeout occurs after approximately 60 seconds. Among the responding nodes, the node that was started first and that is alive declares that the other node is not responding and has failed. This node becomes the new MASTER and starts evicting the nonresponding node from the cluster. Once eviction is complete, cluster reformation begins. The reorganization process regroups accessible nodes and removes the failed ones. For example, in a four-node cluster, if one node fails, the cluster services will regroup the cluster membership among the remaining three nodes.

```
2005-03-11 16:36:17.907 [196620]²
>WARNING: clssnmPollingThread: node(3) missed(4) checkin(s)
>WARNING: clssnmPollingThread: node(3) missed(5) checkin(s)
>WARNING: clssnmPollingThread: node(3) missed(6) checkin(s)
>WARNING: clssnmPollingThread: node(3) missed(7) checkin(s)
>WARNING: clssnmPollingThread: node(3) missed(8) checkin(s)
>WARNING: clssnmPollingThread: node(3) missed(9) checkin(s)
>WARNING: clssnmPollingThread: node(3) missed(10) checkin(s)

. . .

>WARNING: clssnmPollingThread: node(3) missed(58) checkin(s)
>WARNING: clssnmPollingThread: node(3) missed(59) checkin(s)
WARNING: clssnmPollingThread: Eviction started for node 3, flags
0x000d, state 3, wt4c 0
>TRACE:   clssnmDoSyncUpdate: Initiating sync 4
>TRACE:   clssnmHandleSync: Acknowledging sync: src[1] seq[1440]
sync[4]
>USER:    NMEVENT_SUSPEND [00][00][00][06]
>WARNING: clssnmHandleSync: received second sync pkt from self
>TRACE:   clssnmWaitForAcks: ceding ownership of reconfig tonode 1,
syncNo 4.
>USER:    clssnmHandleUpdate: SYNC(4) from node(1) completed
>USER:    clssnmHandleUpdate: NODE(1) IS ACTIVE MEMBER OF CLUSTER
>USER:    clssnmHandleUpdate: NODE(2) IS ACTIVE MEMBER OF CLUSTER
>USER:    NMEVENT_RECONFIG [00][00][00][06]
CLSS-3000: reconfiguration successful, incarnation 4 with 2 nodes
CLSS-3001: local node number 2, master node number 2
```

---

2.   The output has been formatted for clarity.

Note: When a new node is added to the cluster or a node joins the cluster after recovery, the cluster services perform similar steps to reform the cluster. The information regarding a node joining the cluster or leaving the cluster is exposed to the respective Oracle instances by the LMON process running on each cluster node.

As discussed previously in Chapter 2, *LMON* is a background process that monitors the entire cluster to manage global resources. By constantly probing the other instances, it checks and manages instance deaths and the associated recovery for GCS. When a node joins or leaves the cluster, it handles reconfiguration of locks and resources. In particular, LMON handles the part of recovery associated with global resources. LMON-provided services are also known as Cluster Group Services (CGS). Failover of a service is also triggered by the EVMD process by firing a DOWN event.

Once the reconfiguration of the nodes is complete, Oracle, in coordination with the EVMD and CRSD, performs several tasks in an asynchronous mode and includes

1. Database/instance recovery

2. Failover of VIP system service

3. Failover of the user/database services to another instance (discussed in Chapter 5)

6.1.2 Database/instance recovery

After a node in the cluster fails, it goes through several steps of recovery to complete changes at both the instance (cache) level and database level:

1. During the first phase of recovery, GES remasters the enqueues, and GCS remasters its resources from the failed instance among the surviving instances.

2. The first step in the GCS remastering process is for Oracle to assign a new incarnation number.

3. Oracle determines how many more nodes are remaining in the cluster. (Nodes are identified by a numeric number starting with

zero and incremented by one for every additional node in the cluster.) In our example, three nodes remain in the cluster.

4.   Subsequently, in an attempt to recreate the resource master of the failed instance, all GCS resource requests and write requests are temporarily suspended (GRD is frozen).

5.   All the dead shadow processes related to the GCS are cleaned from the failed instance.

6.   After enqueues are reconfigured, one of the surviving instances can grab the instance recovery enqueue.

7.   At the same time as GCS resources are remastered, SMON determines the set of blocks that need recovery. This set is called the recovery set. As discussed in Chapter 2, with cache fusion, an instance ships the contents of its block to the requesting instance without writing the block to the disk (i.e., the on-disk version of the blocks may not contain the changes that are made by either instance). Because of this behavior, SMON needs to merge the content of all the online redo logs of each failed instance to determine the recovery set and the order of recovery.

8.   At this stage, buffer space for recovery is allocated, and the resources that were identified in the previous reading of the redo logs are claimed as recovery resources. This is done to avoid other instances from accessing those resources.

9.   A new master node for the cluster is created (a new master node is only assigned if the failed node was the previous master node in the cluster). All GCS shadow processes are now traversed, GCS is removed from a frozen state, and this completes the reconfiguration process.

The following extract is from the alert log file of the recovering instance; it displays the steps that Oracle has to perform during instance recovery:

```
Fri Mar 11 16:37:24 2005
Reconfiguration started (old inc 3, new inc 4)
List of nodes:
 0 1 4
 Global Resource Directory frozen
 * dead instance detected - domain 0 invalid = TRUE
 Update rdomain variables
```

```
Communication channels reestablished
* domain 0 valid = 0 according to instance 0
Fri Mar 11 16:37:25 2005
 Master broadcasted resource hash value bitmaps
 Non-local Process blocks cleaned out
Fri Mar 11 16:37:25 2005
 LMS 0: 0 GCS shadows cancelled, 0 closed
Fri Mar 11 16:37:25 2005
 LMS 1: 0 GCS shadows cancelled, 0 closed
 Set master node info
 Submitted all remote-enqueue requests
 Dwn-cvts replayed, VALBLKs dubious
 All grantable enqueues granted
Fri Mar 11 16:37:25 2005
 LMS 0: 1801 GCS shadows traversed, 329 replayed
Fri Mar 11 16:37:25 2005
 LMS 1: 1778 GCS shadows traversed, 302 replayed
Fri Mar 11 16:37:25 2005
 Submitted all GCS remote-cache requests
 Fix write in gcs resources
Reconfiguration complete
```

10. During the remastering of GCS from the failed instance (during cache recovery), most work on the instance performing recovery is paused, and while transaction recovery takes place, work occurs at a slower pace. Once this stage of the recovery operation is complete, it is considered full database availability, now that all data is accessible, including that which resided on the failed instance.

11. Subsequently, Oracle starts the database recovery process and begins the cache recovery process (i.e., rolling forward committed transactions). This is made possible by reading the redo log files of the failed instance. Because of the shared storage subsystem, redo log files of all instances participating in the cluster are visible to other instances. This makes any one instance (nodes remaining in the cluster and started first) that detected the failure read the redo log files of the failed instance and start the recovery process.

12. After completion of the cache recovery process, Oracle starts the transaction recovery operation (i.e., rolling back of all uncommitted transactions).

This output is from the SMON trace file. The output indicates how SMON traverses the undo segments and recovers the data of the failed instance during instance recovery:

```
*** 2005-03-11 16:37:26.444
SMON: about to recover undo segment 21
SMON: mark undo segment 21 as available
SMON: about to recover undo segment 22
SMON: mark undo segment 22 as available
SMON: about to recover undo segment 23
SMON: mark undo segment 23 as available
SMON: about to recover undo segment 24
SMON: mark undo segment 24 as available
SMON: about to recover undo segment 25
SMON: mark undo segment 25 as available
SMON: about to recover undo segment 26
SMON: mark undo segment 26 as available
SMON: about to recover undo segment 27
SMON: mark undo segment 27 as available
SMON: about to recover undo segment 28
SMON: mark undo segment 28 as available
SMON: about to recover undo segment 29
SMON: mark undo segment 29 as available
SMON: about to recover undo segment 30
SMON: mark undo segment 30 as available
```

6.1.3   Failover of VIP system service

In Oracle Database 10*g*, a new system service (VIP) is also failed over as part of the node failover process. This failover process helps future connections to the environment without any TCP-related timeout delays.

Traditionally, Oracle allowed connections to the database using the regular hostname or host IP address. The network communication protocol used in this case was TCP/IP. When a node that connected using an IP or host address was not available, the application, unaware of the failure, attempted to establish a connection until it received an acknowledgment (success or failure) from the server. This caused a delay for an application or user trying to establish a connection to the database. In a RAC environment, when multiple nodes have been configured, as illustrated in the TNS definition below, and if the user is connected to ORADB3 and ORADB3 is not available, unless an acknowledgment has been received, SQL*Net will not attempt to connect to ORADB4 or any of the other instances in the list until it receives a TCP/IP timeout (i.e., when the client receives a TCP reset). This delay is avoided when the new system service called VIP is used.

```
SSKYDB =
 (DESCRIPTION=
  (ADDRESS_LIST=
   (ADDRESS=(PROTOCOL=TCP)(HOST=ORADB1.SUMSKY.NET)(PORT=1521))
   (ADDRESS=(PROTOCOL=TCP)(HOST=ORADB2.SUMSKY.NET)(PORT=1521))
   (ADDRESS=(PROTOCOL=TCP)(HOST=ORADB3.SUMSKY.NET)(PORT=1521))
   (ADDRESS=(PROTOCOL=TCP)(HOST=ORADB4.SUMSKY.NET)(PORT=1521))
  )
  (CONNECT_DATA=
   (SERVICE_NAME=SSKYDB)
   (FAILOVER_MODE=(TYPE=SELECT)(METHOD=BASIC)(RETRIES=20)(DELAY=15))
  )
 )
```

Under this method, the client uses VIP or a virtual hostname to establish a connection to the instance. When a node fails, the VIP associated with it automatically fails over to some other node in the cluster. When this happens, the machine address associated with the VIP changes, causing the existing connections to see errors (ORA-3113) on their connections to the old address on the failed-over node. Network packets sent to the failed-over VIP go to the new node, which will rapidly return a NAK. This results in the client getting errors immediately that would otherwise be as long as 10 minutes when TCP/IP is used. Once errors are received, subsequent SQL*Net connections will use the next address.

 Note: When connection pooling is used, the Oracle's new event-based notification method will proactively inform the connection manager regarding any node or instance failure by raising a DOWN event. This method will further reduce connections to failed addresses.

How does the VIP failover?

When a node crashes or is no longer available, the VIP system service is automatically moved to an OFFLINE state. The CRS process will determine which node in the cluster can accommodate a new system service recovery operation. Normally, in a three or more node configuration, to accelerate the recovery process, CRS will move the VIP system service to a node that is not performing the database/instance recovery. In the following example output, node ORADB3 has failed, and CRS moves the service to ORADB4 by attempting to start the service and bringing it to an ONLINE state:

```
"11-Mar-2005 08:42:20 CRS ora.oradb3.vip is transitioning from state
OFFLINE to state ONLINE on member oradb4"
"11-Mar-2005 08:42:27 RAC: ora.oradb3.vip: up: "
"11-Mar-2005 08:42:27 CRS ora.oradb3.vip started on member oradb4"
"11-Mar-2005 08:42:27 CRS completed recovery for member oradb3"
```

If the failed node was subsequently fixed and brought online, as part of the system service startup, CRS will determine which node is currently holding its VIP system service and fail the service back to its original node.

The first step in this process of bringing the VIP to its original node and original state is when the EVMD will issue a "node ORADB3 is up" event and start listening for notifications from other services and nodes in the cluster. Once the CRS receives the UP event from the EVMD, the CRS will determine which node is currently holding its VIP system service and request that it be taken OFFLINE. At this point, a VIP service DOWN event is issued on the holding node (ORADB4), followed by stopping the service and transitioning it back to its original node and bringing it to an ONLINE state. A new UP event is issued on node ORADB3, and CRS broadcasts to all other agents in the cluster that it is ready to accept connections on this address.

```
"11-Mar-2005 08:43:26 EVM daemon: Node oradb3 (cluster member 1)
listening"
"11-Mar-2005 08:43:33 CRS ora.oradb3.vip is transitioning from state
ONLINE to state OFFLINE on member oradb4"
"11-Mar-2005 08:45:53 RAC: ora.oradb3.vip: down: "
"11-Mar-2005 08:43:34 CRS ora.oradb3.vip stopped"
"11-Mar-2005 08:43:34 CRS ora.oradb3.vip is transitioning from state
OFFLINE to state ONLINE on member oradb3"
"11-Mar-2005 08:43:41 RAC: ora.oradb3.vip: up: "
"11-Mar-2005 08:43:41 CRS ora.oradb3.vip started on member oradb3"
```

Note: The VIP system service is automatically failed over only when the node crashes or is taken offline. If only the Oracle instance has failed, the VIP system service does not failover.

Although in a clustered configuration the feature to failover is available, the best failover is the one that no one notices. Unfortunately, even though Oracle has been structured to recover very quickly, failures can severely disrupt users by dropping connections from the database. Work in progress at the time of failure is lost. For example, if the user queried 1,000 rows from the database and a failure of one of the nodes occurred midstream while the user was scrolling through these rows on the terminal, the failure would cause the user to reexecute the query and browse through these rows again. This disruption could be eliminated for most situations by masking the failure with the TAF option.

6.1.4 Transparent application failover

TAF allows client applications to continue working after the application loses its connection to the database. While users may experience a brief pause during the time the database server fails over to a surviving cluster node, the session context is preserved. If configured using TAF, after the instance failover and database recovery completes, the application can automatically reconnect to one of the surviving instances and continue operations as if no failure had occurred. Implementation of this feature is grouped under two categories:

1.   Operations that retrieve data, such as SELECT statements

2.   Operations that require transactional integrity, such as DML operations

If the user's connection to instance SSKY1 dies, the transaction is rolled back; however, under TAF, the user can continue working without having to reconnect manually to the other instance, establish another transaction programmatically, and then execute the request again.

To get a good understanding of how the TAF architecture works, it is helpful to walk through a failover scenario using the earlier example, where a user is querying the database to retrieve 1,000 rows. For this illustration,

Figure 6.2
Oracle Transparent
Application
Failover

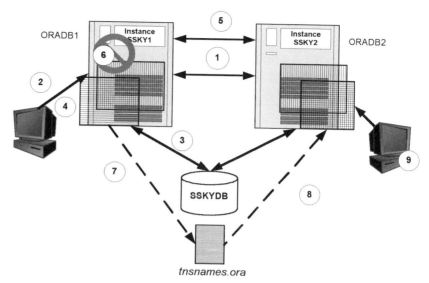

tnsnames.ora

let us assume the user is connected to node ORADB1 instance SSKY1. By following the steps identified in Figure 6.2

1. The polling mechanism between the various nodes in the cluster checks to see if another node in the cluster is available and is participating in the clustered configuration. As discussed earlier, this verification process happens continuously.

2. The user is connected to the database via instance SSKY1 and executes a query to retrieve 1,000 rows.

3. The initial 500 rows are retrieved from the SSKYDB database via instance SSKY1 and returned to the user for browsing via the user's graphical interface.

4. While the user is browsing through the first 500 rows, node ORADB1 fails (crashes).

5. Node ORADB2 polls ORADB1 and deduces that node ORADB1 is not responding to the poll request; it times out after several attempts and declares that the node ORADB1 has failed, evicting it from the cluster membership. It then reforms the cluster membership with the remaining nodes in the cluster. Based on the signal from the LMON process, the EVMD gives a DOWN event to the connection manager, which triggers the following asynchronous tasks.

Instance recovery

System service (VIP) failover to one of the surviving nodes.

6.   In the meantime, the user is unaware of the failure and scrolls pass the initial 500 rows. To retrieve and display the remaining 500 rows, the process tries to connect to instance SSKY1 using its original VIP.

Note: If the application is using connection pooling and has configured FAN features, then ONS will notify the connection manager based on a DOWN event being raised by the event manager.

7.   While attempting to connect using the original VIP for node ORADB1, receives a NAK from node ORADB2 returned by the the failed over VIP. Based on the entries present in the tnsnames.ora file, the application now establishes a connection to instance SSKY2 on node ORADB2 using the VIP assigned to node ORADB2.

      The users and user sessions migrate from the failed node to one of the other surviving node.

8.   Oracle reexecutes the query using the connection on instance SSKY2 and displays the remaining rows to the user. If the data was available in the buffer cache, the rows are returned to the user instantaneously. However, if the rows are not available, Oracle has to perform an I/O operation. This will be delayed until the recovery process has completed.

In Figure 6.2, when node ORADB1 fails, any SELECT statements that have partially executed on instance SSKY1 are migrated as part of the failover process and are displayed through instance SSKY2, when the user process fails over to node ORADB2. All this happens transparently without any interruption to the user. Along with the SELECT statement, the following are also failed over

■ Client/server connection

■ User session state

■ Prepared statements

■ Active cursors that have begun to return results to the user

Using the basic TAF configuration (`tnsnames.ora`), only `SELECT` statements are failed over from one node to another; transactional statements are not failed over. Transactional or DML statements can programmatically be transferred from node `ORADB1` to node `ORADB2` by proper validation of Oracle-returned error messages and taking appropriate actions. (An example of handling failover of DML statements appears later in this chapter.) Some of the common Oracle error codes that should be handled by the application to track and transfer transactional statements include:

`ORA-01012`: not logged on to Oracle

`ORA-01033`: Oracle initialization or shutdown in progress

`ORA-01034`: Oracle not available

`ORA-01089`: immediate shutdown in progress---no operations are permitted

`ORA-03113`: end-of-file on communication channel

`ORA-03114`: not connected to Oracle

`ORA-12203`: TNS—unable to connect to destination

`ORA-12500`: TNS—listener failed to start a dedicated server process

`ORA-12571`: TNS—packet writer failure

`ORA-25408:` cannot safely replay call

Among the transactional statements, the following do not automatically failover when a node fails:

- PL/SQL server-side package variables
- Global temporary tables
- Effect of any `ALTER SESSION` statements
- Applications not using OCI8 and above
- In-flight or in-progress transactional statements (i.e., statements that include `INSERT`, `UPDATE`, and `DELETE` operations must be rolled back)

TAF configuration

TAF can be configured using one of two methods:

- TNSNAMES-based configuration
- OCI API requests

TNSNAMES-based configuration

Under this method, configuring the TAF option involves adding SQL*Net parameters to the tnsnames.ora file, and when one of the participating nodes encounters a failure, the parameter values (listed in Table 6.1) are used to ascertain the next step in the failover process. The parameter that drives the TAF option is the FAILOVER_MODE under the CONNECT_DATA section of a connect descriptor.

Table 6.1   *TAF Subparameters*

Parameter	Description
BACKUP	Specifies a different net service name to establish the backup connection. **BACKUP** should be specified when using **PRECONNECT** to pre-establish connections. Specifying a **BACKUP** is strongly recommended for **BASIC** methods; otherwise, reconnection may first attempt the instance that has just failed, adding delay until the client reconnects.
TYPE	Specifies the type of failover. Two types of Net failover functionality are available by default: *SESSION*: Fails over the session. With this option only connection is established; no work in progress is transferred from the failed instance to the available instance. *SELECT*: Enables a user with open cursors to continue fetching on them after failure. SQL*Net keeps track of any **SELECT** statements issued in the current transaction. It also keeps track of how many rows have been fetched by the client for each cursor associated with a **SELECT** statement. If connection to the instance is lost, SQL*Net establishes a connection to another instance and reexecutes the **SELECT** statement from the point of failure.
METHOD	Determines the speed of the failover from the primary to the secondary or backup node. *BASIC*: Connections are only established to the failed-over instance when the failure happens. *PRECONNECT*: This parameter preestablishes connections. If it is used, connection to the backup instance is made at the same time as the connection to the primary instance.
RETRIES	Specifies the number of times to attempt to connect to the backup node after a failure before giving up.
DELAY	Specifies the amount of time in seconds to wait between attempts to connect to the backup node after a failure before giving up.

Note: Another important parameter or value that should not be configured manually is the GLOBAL_DBNAME parameter in the SID_LIST_listener_name section of the listener.ora. Configuring this parameter in listener.ora disables TAF. If the GLOBAL_DBNAME parameter has been defined, the parameter should be deleted, and the database should be allowed to dynamically register the service names automatically.

TAF implementation

The TAF option using the tnsnames.ora file can be implemented in one of two ways:

1.   Connect-time failover and client load-balancing

2.   Preestablishing a connection

The two implementation options are explained in the following examples.

Connect-time failover and client load-balancing

The connect time failover example listed is the basic method of tnsnames-based failover implementation. When the user session tries to connect to the instance on the first node (ORADB1) and determines that the instance or node is not currently available, the session will immediately try the next virtual hostname defined in the list (namely ORADB2-VIP) to establish a connection. The failover from one instance to another is true for the connections that are made for the first time or for connection retries that occur during an instance crash when a transaction is in progress.

```
SSKYDB =
 (DESCRIPTION=
  (ADDRESS_LIST=
   (ADDRESS=(PROTOCOL=TCP)(HOST=ORADB1-vip.SUMSKY.NET)(PORT=1521))
   (ADDRESS=(PROTOCOL=TCP)(HOST=ORADB2-vip.SUMSKY.NET)(PORT=1521))
   (ADDRESS=(PROTOCOL=TCP)(HOST=ORADB3-vip.SUMSKY.NET)(PORT=1521))
   (ADDRESS=(PROTOCOL=TCP)(HOST=ORADB4-vip.SUMSKY.NET)(PORT=1521))
   (LOAD_BALANCE=YES)
   (FAILOVER=ON)
  )
  (CONNECT_DATA=
```

```
(SERVER=DEDICATED)
(SERVICE_NAME=SSKYDB)
(FAILOVER_MODE=(TYPE=SELECT)(METHOD=BASIC)(RETRIES=20)(DELAY=15))
)
)
```

With the `RETRIES` and `DELAY` parameters as part of the failover mode subparameter, the connections to the instances are automatically retried by the number of times specified by the parameter and the amount of time to wait before each retry. In this scenario, the connection is retried 20 times with a delay of 15 seconds between every retry.

The `RETRIES` and `DELAY` parameters are useful when thousands of users are connected to the instance of the failed node and all these users have to establish connections to the recovering node. In the case of a dedicated connection, there is only a single thread to establish connections, and simultaneous connection requests from a large number of users can cause connection timeouts. The `RETRIES` and `DELAY` parameters help to retry the connection with a delay between retries while trying to establish connections to the failover node. This is less of an issue when the shared server is configured, in which case Oracle establishes a pool of connections to the instance, and each user uses of one of them to establish a connection to the database. Because users are placed in a queue, when a connection becomes available, the user establishes connection.

Preestablishing a connection

Another implementation option available under the TAF configuration is to set up a preestablished connection to a backup or secondary instance. One of the potential performance issues during a failover is the time required to reestablish a connection after the primary instance has failed, which depends on the time taken to establish a connection to the backup or secondary instance. This can be resolved by preestablishing connections, which means that the initial and backup connections are explicitly specified, and when the user session establishes a connection to the primary instance, it establishes another connection to the secondary or backup instance.

 Note: Preestablishing a connection is not without drawbacks because preestablished connections consume resources. During some controlled failover testing, additional resource usage was noticed when using preestablished connections because the process always validates the connection throughout its activity.

In the following example, the SQL*Net connects to the listener on
ORADB1 and simultaneously connects to the other instance on ORADB2.
While the process has to make two connections at the beginning of a transaction, the time required to establish a connection during the failover is
reduced. If ORADB1 fails after the connection, SQL*Net fails over to
ORADB2, preserving any SELECT statements in progress. Having the backup
connection already in place can reduce the time needed for a failover.

Preestablishing a connection implies that the backup node is predefined
or hard coded. This reduces the scope of availability because the connection
to the other nodes or instances is not dynamic.

```
SRV8 =
 (DESCRIPTION =
 (ADDRESS=
   (PROTOCOL=TCP)(HOST=ORADB1-VIP.SUMSKY.NET)(PORT=1521))
   (PROTOCOL=TCP)(HOST=ORADB2-VIP.SUMSKY.NET)(PORT=1521))
   (PROTOCOL=TCP)(HOST=ORADB3-VIP.SUMSKY.NET)(PORT=1521))
   (PROTOCOL=TCP)(HOST=ORADB4-VIP.SUMSKY.NET)(PORT=1521))
 (CONNECT_DATA =
   (SERVER = DEDICATED)
   (SERVICE_NAME=SSKYDB)
   (FAILOVER_MODE=
     (BACKUP=SRV8_PRECONNECT)
     (TYPE=SELECT)
      (METHOD=PRECONNECT)(RETRIES=180)(DELAY=5)))

SRV8_PRECONNECT=
 (DESCRIPTION=
 (ADDRESS=
   (PROTOCOL=TCP)(HOST=ORADB1-VIP.SUMSKY.NET)(PORT=1521))
   (PROTOCOL=TCP)(HOST=ORADB2-VIP.SUMSKY.NET)(PORT=1521))
   (PROTOCOL=TCP)(HOST=ORADB3-VIP.SUMSKY.NET)(PORT=1521))
   (PROTOCOL=TCP)(HOST=ORADB4-VIP.SUMSKY.NET)(PORT=1521))
 (CONNECT_DATA=
   (SERVER = DEDICATED)
   (SERVICE_NAME=SRV8_PRECONNECT)
   (FAILOVER_MODE=
     (BACKUP=SRV8)
      (TYPE=SELECT)
       (METHOD=BASIC)(RETRIES=180)(DELAY=5)))
```

In these TNS entries, the SRV8 connect descriptor establishes a dedicated connection to service SSKYDB and is configured with a backup connection using connect descriptor SRV8_PRECONNECT. SRV8_PRECONNECT is also a connect descriptor that contains the SERVICE_NAME. SRV8_PRECONNECT is configured with a backup connection using connect descriptor SRV8. These TNS entries illustrate how the preconnect method of connection is established and how the connection descriptors are set up, where one is the backup of the other.

Defining TAF rules in the database

In Oracle Database 10*g* Release 2, the TAF definitions can be done on the physical database. This is available with the implementation of the FAN features on the client application (FAN is discussed in Chapter 5). In this case, using the PL/SQL package DBMS_SERVICE, the appropriate TAF rules can be implemented on the database as illustrated. Using its ONS communication mechanism, Oracle will communicate the state and failover rules to the client, and the client will handle the failover.

```
execute DBMS_SERVICE.MODIFY_SERVICE(SERVICE_NAME =>'SRV6',-
       AQ_HA_NOTIFICATIONS => TRUE, -
       FAILOVER_METHOD => DBMS_SERVICE.FAILOVER_METHOD_BASIC,-
       FAILOVER_TYPE => DBMS_SERVICE.FAILOVER_TYPE_SESSION,-
       FAILOVER_RETRIES => 180,
       FAILOVER_DELAY => 5);
```

 Note: Please note that the AQ_HA_NOTIFICATIONS parameter should be set to TRUE for TAF implementation on the database server to work.

OCI API requests

Under this method, implementing TAF involves using Oracle-provided APIs to accomplish what is normally performed through the tnsnames.ora file. Under the OCI-based method, the application servers have a better control of what these APIs accomplish and provide appropriate actions based on the results from these calls.

OCI-based TAF configuration is made possible by using the various failover-type events provided through APIs. The failover events shown in Table 6.2 are part of the OracleOCIFailover interface.

Table 6.2 *OCI API Failover Events*

Failover Event	Description
FO_SESSION	The user session is reauthenticated on the server side while open cursors in the OCI application need to be reexecuted. This call is equivalent to FAILOVER_MODE=SESSION defined in the tnsnames.ora file.
FO_SELECT	The user session is reauthenticated on the server side; however, open cursors in the OCI can continue fetching. This implies that the client-side logic maintains the fetch state of each open cursor. This call is equivalent to FAILOVER_MODE=SELECT defined in the tnsnames.ora file.
FO_NONE	This is the default mode and implies that no failover functionality is used. This call is equivalent to FAILOVER_MODE=NONE defined in the tnsnames.ora file.
FO_BEGIN	This indicates that failover has detected a lost connection, and failover is starting.
FO_END	This indicates successful completion of failover.
FO_ABORT	This indicates that failover was unsuccessful, and there is no option of retrying.
FO_REAUTH	This indicates that a user handle has been reauthenticated.
FO_ERROR	This indicates that failover was temporarily unsuccessful. This gives the application the opportunity to handle the error and retry failover. In the case of an error while failing over to a new connection, the JDBC application is able to retry failover. Typically, the application sleeps for a while and then retries, either indefinitely or for a limited time, by having the callback return FO_RETRY. The retry functionality is accomplished using the FAILOVER_MODE=RETRIES=<>, DELAY=<> defined in the tnsnames.ora file.
FO_EVENT_ UNKOWN	This indicates a bad failover event.

TAF callbacks

TAF callbacks are used to track and trace failures. They are called during the failover to notify the JDBC application regarding events that are generated. In this case, unlike the TNS names-based TAF configuration, the application has some control over the failover operation. To address the issue of failure while establishing a connection of the failover process, the callback function is invoked programmatically several times during the course of reestablishing the user's session.

The first call to the callback function occurs when Oracle first detects an instance connection loss. At this time the client may wish to replay ALTER SESSION commands and inform the user that failover has happened. If failover is unsuccessful, then the callback is called to inform the application that failover will not take place.

This example demonstrates the advantages of utilizing the interface provided by Oracle, OracleOCIFailover:

```
public interface OracleOCIFailover{

// Possible Failover Types
public static final int FO_SESSION = 1;
public static final int FO_SELECT = 2;
public static final int FO_NONE   = 3;
public static final int;

// Possible Failover events registered with callback
public static final int FO_BEGIN  = 1;
public static final int FO_END    = 2;
public static final int FO_ABORT  = 3;
public static final int FO_REAUTH = 4;
public static final int FO_ERROR  = 5;
public static final int FO_RETRY  = 6;
public static final int FO_EVENT_UNKNOWN = 7;

public int callbackFn (Connection conn,
                Object ctxt, // ANy thing the user wants to save
                int type, // One of the above possible Failover
Types
                int event );// One of the above possible Failover
Events
}
```

In the case of a failure of one of the instances, Oracle tries to restore the connections of the failed instance onto the active instance. Depending on the number of sessions or complication of the operation being failed over, there can be potential delays. It is a good practice to notify the user of such delays.

Note: Appendix D contains an example that illustrates the usage and implementation of TAF using a Java application.

In the example, the Oracle JDBC driver is registered, and the connection is obtained from the `DriverManager`.

```
DriverManager.registerDriver(new oracle.jdbc.driver.OracleDriver());
con=OracleConnection)DriverManager.getConnection("jdbc:oracle:oci:@SS
KYDB","user", "pwd");
```

Here, `SSKYDB` represents an entry in the `tnsnames.ora` file that has the connection strings. In this file, failover has been enabled (`FAILOVER=ON`), and the type of failover indicates that all `SELECT` queries will be failed over (`TYPE=SELECT`):

```
SSKYDB =
  (DESCRIPTION=
    (ADDRESS_LIST=
      (FAILOVER=ON)
      (LOAD_BALANCE=ON)
      (ADDRESS=(PROTOCOL=TCP)(HOST=ORADB1-VIP.SUMSKY.NET)(PORT=1521))
      (ADDRESS=(PROTOCOL=TCP)(HOST=ORADB2-VIP.SUMSKY.NET)(PORT=1521))
      (ADDRESS=(PROTOCOL=TCP)(HOST=ORADB3-VIP.SUMSKY.NET)(PORT=1521))
      (ADDRESS=(PROTOCOL=TCP)(HOST=ORADB4-VIP.SUMSKY.NET)(PORT=1521))
    )
(CONNECT_DATA=
  (SERVER=DEDICATED)
    (SERVICE_NAME=SSKYDB)
    (FAILOVER_MODE=(TYPE=SELECT)(METHOD=BASIC)(RETRIES=20)
                  (DELAY=15))
  )
  )
```

This example illustrates the TAF implementation using the JDBC thick driver. Oracle does not support TAF using the thin driver and only supports a basic failover as illustrated in the following thin driver example:

```
con=DriverManager.getConnection("jdbc:oracle:thin:@(DESCRIPTION
=(ADDRESS_LIST=(ADDRESS=(PROTOCOL=TCP)(HOST=oradb1-
vip.sumsky.net)(PORT=1521))(ADDRESS=(PROTOCOL=TCP)(HOST=oradb2-
vip.sumsky.net)(PORT=1521))(ADDRESS=(PROTOCOL=TCP)(HOST=oradb3-
vip.sumsky.net)(PORT=1521))(ADDRESS=(PROTOCOL=TCP)(HOST=oradb4-
vip.sumsky.net)(PORT=1521)))(CONNECT_DATA=(SERVICE_NAME=SSKYDB)))","u
sr","pswd");
```

After a connection is established, the class implementing the Oracle interface should be registered with Oracle:

```
clbFn = new TAFCallbackFn();
strFailover = new String("Register Failover");
((OracleConnection)con).registerTAFCallback(clbFn, strFailover);
```

This notifies Oracle that in the case of a failure, the callback function, which is implemented in the class TAFCallbackFn, is to be called. Oracle also provides the failover type (SESSION, SELECT, or NONE) and the present failover event.

```
package rac.chapter6.taf;

//java imports
import java.sql.Connection;
import java.sql.Statement;
import java.sql.ResultSet;
import java.sql.SQLException;
import java.sql.DriverManager;

//Oracle imports
import oracle.jdbc.OracleConnection;
//log4j imports.
import org.apache.log4j.Category;
```

When the failover starts, Oracle sends the FO_BEGIN event, thus notifying the application that the failover has begun, and tries to restore the connection behind the scenes. As explained earlier, if the failover type is SELECT, the query is reexecuted, and the cursor is positioned to the row where the failure occurred. Additionally, the session on the initial instance may have received session-specific commands (ALTER SESSION), which need to be reexecuted before the failover process is activated and the user session is established to continue. As discussed earlier, session-specific commands will not be replayed automatically on the failed-over instance. In addition, the callback is called each time a user handle besides the primary handle is reauthenticated on the new connection. Since each user handle represents a server-side session, the client program will need to replay the ALTER SESSION commands for that session.

These limitations need to be handled so that the failure is transparent to the user. The possible errors that can occur with Oracle in such a case are handled, the connection is reestablished, and the query is reexecuted.

```
    if ((e.getErrorCode() == 1012) ||         // not logged on to Oracle
        (e.getErrorCode() == 1033) || // Oracle initialization
                                      // or shutdown in progress
        (e.getErrorCode() == 1034) || // Oracle not available
        (e.getErrorCode() == 1089) || // immediate shutdown in
  // progress, no operations are
  // permitted
        (e.getErrorCode() == 3113) ||   // end-of-file on communication
  //  channel
        (e.getErrorCode() == 3114) ||   // not connected to Oracle
        (e.getErrorCode() == 12203) || // TNS---unable to connect
  // to destination
        (e.getErrorCode() == 12500) || // TNS---listener failed to
  //start a dedicated server process
        (e.getErrorCode() == 12571))    // TNS---packet writer failure
      (e.getErrorCode() == 25408))   // cannot safely replay call
    {
        cat.debug("Node failed while executing" +
                         " TRANSACTIONAL Statements");
            // Get another connection
          handleDBConnections();
          // re execute the query.
          runQuery();
    }
```

When the connection is established and the failover has ended, the FO_END event is sent back to the application, indicating that the failover has been completed.

Transitions may not always be smooth. If an error is encountered while restoring a connection to the failed-over instance, the FO_ERROR event is sent to the application, indicating the error and requesting that the application handle this error appropriately. Under these circumstances, the application can provide a retry functionality where the application will rest or sleep for a predefined interval and send back a FO_RETRY event. If during a subsequent attempt a similar error occurs, the application will retry again until the number of retry attempts specified by the property RETRIES in the tnsnames.ora file has been reached. The sleep or rest time is defined by the property DELAY also defined in the tnsnames.ora file.

```
case FO_ERROR:
        cat.info("Error Occurred while failing over. Retrying
to restore connection.");
    try {
            Thread.sleep(2000);
        } catch (InterruptedException e) {  // Trap errors
            cat.error("Error while causing the currently
executing thread to sleep");
        }
        return FO_RETRY;
```

An extract from a debug log shows a scenario in which a failure has, occurred and the query that executed on the primary instance in 47 ms has failed over and reexecuted the query in about 3,026 ms (this includes the time for the session to failover, establish a new connection, and reexecute the query). The entire failover operation is transparent to the user.

```
20:55:54,041 runQuery TAFDetailsExample.java 91 DEBUG: Execution Time
for the query is 47 ms.
20:55:54,041 runQuery TAFDetailsExample.java 91 DEBUG: Execution Time
for the query is 47 ms.
20:55:54,041 runQuery TAFDetailsExample.java 91 DEBUG: Execution Time
for the query is 32 ms.
20:55:54,056 callbackFn TAFCallbackFn.java 45  DEBUG: The Connection
for which the failover Occurred is
:oracle.jdbc.driver.OracleDatabaseMetaData@6b13c7
20:55:54,056 callbackFn TAFCallbackFn.java 49  DEBUG: FAILOVER TYPE
is : SELECT
20:55:54,056 callbackFn TAFCallbackFn.java 50  DEBUG: FAILOVER EVENT
is : BEGIN
20:55:54,072 callbackFn TAFCallbackFn.java 57  INFO: Failover event
is begin
```

```
20:55:54,072 callbackFn TAFCallbackFn.java 89  DEBUG: Before
returning from the callBack Function.
20:55:56,121 callbackFn TAFCallbackFn.java 49  DEBUG: FAILOVER TYPE
is : SELECT
20:55:56,121 callbackFn TAFCallbackFn.java 50  DEBUG: FAILOVER EVENT
is : END
20:55:56,137 callbackFn TAFCallbackFn.java 61  INFO: Failover event
is end
20:55:56,138 callbackFn TAFCallbackFn.java 89  DEBUG: Before
returning from the callBack Function.
20:55:57,018 runQuery TAFDetailsExample.java 91 DEBUG: Execution Time
for the query is 3026 ms.
```

 Note: Please refer to Appendix D for an example of using TAF for DML operations in Java.

TAF verification

Implementation of TAF can be verified by querying the Oracle-provided data dictionary views. V$SESSION has three columns, FAILOVER_MODE, FAILOVER_TYPE, and FAILED_OVER, that provide information pertaining to TAF implementation, and verification of results when the node in the cluster crashes and the session fails over to one of the available nodes.

```
SELECT SID,
       USERNAME,
       FAILOVER_TYPE,
       FAILOVER_METHOD,
       FAILED_OVER
FROM V$SESSION
/
```

SID	USERNAME	FAILOVER_TYPE	FAILOVER_M	FAILED_OVER
316	OLTP_USER	SELECT	BASIC	YES
317	OLTP_USER	SELECT	BASIC	NO
320	OLTP_USER	SELECT	BASIC	NO
326	OLTP_USER	SELECT	BASIC	NO
1257	SRV10	NONE	NONE	NO
328	OLTP_USER	SELECT	BASIC	YES

```
330 OLTP_USER                SELECT        BASIC        YES
332 OLTP_USER                SELECT        BASIC        YES
337 OLTP_USER                SELECT        BASIC        NO
338 OLTP_USER                SELECT        BASIC        NO
341 OLTP_USER                SELECT        BASIC        YES
```

This query provides the details and status of the failover operation. The output of the query indicates that five users' sessions have failed over (FAILED_OVER = YES) from the instance that crashed. The user SCHEMA_OWNER (USERNAME = SRV10) has a connection to the database but has not been set up to use the failover option and has the default FAILOVER_TYPE of NONE.

On systems where there are many sessions or several different database services are configured, it is better to look at the details by grouping the results. The following query gives a consolidated count on another operation:

```
SELECT INST_ID,
       USERNAME,
       SERVICE_NAME,
       FAILOVER_METHOD,
       FAILOVER_TYPE,
       FAILED_OVER,
       COUNT (*)
FROM GV$SESSION
WHERE USERNAME = 'SOE'
GROUP BY INST_ID,
         USERNAME,
         SERVICE_NAME,
         FAILOVER_METHOD,
         FAILOVER_TYPE,
         FAILED_OVER
```

```
INST_ID  USERNAME   Service             FAILOVER_M  FAILOVER_TYPE  FAI  COUNT(*)
-------- ---------- -------------------- ---------- -------------- --- --------
      1  SOE        SRV11               PRECONNECT  SELECT         NO         4
      2  SOE        SRV11_PRECONNECT    NONE        NONE           NO        26
      3  SOE        SRV11               PRECONNECT  SELECT         NO        22
```

When configuring TAF to have the TYPE=SELECT option,

■ The ordering of rows retrieved by a SELECT statement is not fixed. For this reason, queries that might be replayed should contain an ORDER BY clause. However, even without an ORDER BY clause, rows returned by the reissued query are nearly always returned in the initial order; known exceptions are queries that execute using the HASH

JOIN or PARALLEL query features. If an ORDER BY clause is not used, OCI will check to see that the set of discarded rows matches those previously retrieved to ensure that the application does not generate incorrect results.

- Recovery time after a failover can be significantly longer when using TYPE=SELECT. For example, if a query that retrieves 100,000 rows is interrupted by a failure after 99,989 rows have been fetched, then the client application will not be available for new work after a failover until 99.989 rows have been refetched, discarded, and the last 11 rows of the query have been retrieved.

Other benefits of TAF

The main functionality of the TAF features is to failover user sessions from the failed instance to another active instance. However, there are other useful scenarios where TAF improves system availability. Some of these functions are

- Transactional shutdown
- Quiescing the database

Transactional shutdown

In maintenance windows, when an instance needs to be freed from user or client activity (e.g., when applying a database patch to an instance without interrupting any service to the clients), TAF can come in handy. By using transactional shutdown, that is, shutting down selected instances rather than an entire database, users can be migrated from one instance to another. This is done by using the TRANSACTIONAL clause of the SHUTDOWN statement, which removes an instance from the service so that the shutdown event is deferred until all existing transactions are completed. This routes newly submitted transactions to an alternate node.

For example, the following output indicates a SHUTDOWN TRANSACTIONAL operation:

```
SQL> SHUTDOWN TRANSACTIONAL
Database closed.
Database dismounted
ORACLE instance shut down
SQL>
```

Quiescing the database

Certain database administrative activities require isolation from concurrent user transactions or queries. To accomplish such a function, the quiesce database feature can be used. Quiescing the database prevents users' having to shut down the database and reopen it in restricted mode to perform these administrative tasks.

Quiescing of the database is accomplished by issuing the following command:

```
ALTER SYSTEM QUIESCE RESTRICTED
```

The QUIESCE RESTRICTED clause allows administrative tasks to be performed in isolation from concurrent user transactions or queries. In a RAC implementation, this affects all instances, not just the one that issues the statement.

After completion of DBA activities, the database can be unquiesced by issuing the following statement:

```
SQL>ALTER SYSTEM UNQUIESCE;
```

Once the database has been unquiesced, non-DBA activities are allowed to proceed.

6.1.5   Fast Connect Failover

When using connection pooling, failover can also be implemented using a new feature available in Oracle Database 10*g* called Fast Connect Failover (FCF). While FAN is the technology and ONS is the physical notification mechanism, FCF is an implementation of FAN at the connection pool level.

We discussed FAN in Chapter 5. Just to recap, FAN uses the ONS for server-to-server and server-to-client notification of state changes, which includes, up, down, restart, and failover of all application/service state changes that affect the client or application. As illustrated in Figure 5.14, the ONS Daemon on node oradb2 sends notification of any state changes regarding applications or services on that node to all other nodes in the cluster and to all client machines running ONS. All events except for a node failure event are sent by the node where the event is generated; in the case of a node failure, the surviving node sends the notification.

Based on the notification received, the FCF calls inside the application will proactively react to the situation, which includes failover connections to another instance or node where the services are supported. Under this architecture, failover is detected by listening to the UP or DOWN failover events generated by the database and of which the client is notified by the ONS Daemon on the server to the ONS daemon on the client machine.

The basic building blocks of using FCF in JDBC are Implicit Connection Cache (ICC) and ONS.

Implicit Connection Cache

ICC is an improved JDBC 3.0–compliant connection cache implementation for `DataSource`, which can point to different underlying databases. The cache is enabled by invoking `setConnectionCacheEnabled(true)` on `OracleDataSource`. Cache is created when the first connection is requested from the `OracleDataSource`.

ICC creates and maintains physical connections to the database and wraps them with logical connection. One cache is sufficient to service all connection requests, and any number of caches can be created. Ideally, more than one cache is created when there is a need to access more than one `DataSource`. While the ICC creates and maintains physical connections to the database, the Connection Cache Manager creates the cache and manages the connection requests to the cache. ICC provides a number of benefits:

- It can be used with both thin and OCI drivers.
  - OCI clients can register to receive notifications about RAC high-availability events and respond when events occur.
  - During DOWN event processing, OCI
    - Terminates affected connections at the client.
    - Removes connections from the OCI connection pool and the OCI session pool—the session pool maps each session to a physical connection in the connection pool, and there can be multiple sessions per connection.
    - Fails over the connection if TAF has been configured. If TAF is not configured, then the client only receives an error.
  - OCI does not currently manage UP events.

- There is a one-to-one mapping between the `OracleDataSource` instance and the cache. When the application invokes the `close()`method to close the connection, all connections obtained through the datasource are returned to the cache for reuse. The cache either returns an existing connection or creates a new connection.

- The connection cache supports all properties specified by the JDBC 3.0 connection pool specification. The support for these properties allows the application to fine-tune the cache to maximize the performance for each application.

- It also supports a mechanism to recycle and refresh stale connections. This helps refresh old physical connections.

- Only one cache manager is present per virtual machine (VM) to manage all the caches. The `OracleConnectionCacheManager` provides a rich set of APIs to manage the connection cache.

- It provides a connection cache callback mechanism. The callback feature provides a mechanism for users to define cache behavior when a connection is returned to the cache, when handling abandoned connections, and when a connection is requested but none is available in the cache.

  - `public boolean handleAbandonedConnection(OracleConnection oracleConnection, Object 0)`: This function is called when a connection is abandoned.
  - `public void releaseConnection(OracleConnection oracleConnection, Object o`: This function is called when releasing a connection.

  This mechanism provides the ability for the application to define the cache behavior when the events occur.

- It supports user-defined connection attributes that determine which connections are retrieved from the cache. The user attributes are a name-value pair and are not validated by the implicit connection cache. Two methods can retrieve connections based on these properties:

```
getConnection(java.util.Properties
cachedConnectionAttributes)
getConnection(java.lang.String user, java.lang.String passwd,
java.util.Properties cachedConnectionAttributes)
```

Oracle Notification Service

What does notification service have to do with JDBC? The new architecture that Oracle uses to send events about the state change of each node to interested listeners is the ONS. This has been interweaved into ICC, which is required for using FCF. ONS Daemons reside on all the nodes. Whenever the state changes, the server sends asynchronous notifications to all other ONS Daemons (servers and clients) and the Java VM (JVM) where the JDBC application is running. ONS behavior and implementation details are discussed in detail in Chapter 5.

How does the JDBC application get these notifications?

To understand the behavior of all components of FAN and FCF, let's discuss this through a scenario:

1.   When the `setFastConnectionFailoverEnabled` method is used to enable FCF, the datasource checks to see if the ICC is enabled.

2.   The connection cache manager starts the failover event-handler thread. This happens every time a connection cache is created.

3.   The event-handler thread subscribes to ONS events of type "database/event."

4.   When an event or state change occurs on any of the nodes on the database server, the ONS Daemon sends a notification of the following structure to all clients registered with the daemon:

```
<Event_Type>      VERSION=<n.n>      service=<service-
Name.dbDomainName>         [database=<db_unique_name>
[instance=<instance_name>]]  [host=<hostname>]  sta-
tus=<Event_Status>    reason=<Event_Reason>[card=<n>]
timestamp=<eventDate> <eventTime>
```

      The various attributes used in the event and the descriptions can be found in Table 5.4.

5.   The ONS Daemon on the client server receives this notification.

6.   The instance name indicates whether a specific instance is down or if the entire service is down. If the instance value is null, it indicates that the entire service is down. If a specific instance is down, it is identified by the instance name. Applications that have connections to the instance that failed will roll back all open transactions.

7.   The application will receive a connection closed exception `ORA-17008`. The application is responsible for handling the errors.

8.   When the last of the connection caches is closed, the event-handler thread is terminated by the Connection Cache Manager by calling the connection `close()` method to release the connection

back to the cache. Upon receiving the node DOWN event, all connections in a connection cache that are on the node that went down are removed.

9.   The cache is refreshed with new connections to the stable/backup node. When the cache is refreshed, the initial properties used to create the cache are used.

10.   When the failed node is brought back online, the subscriber receives notification, and the cache distributes the connections to load-balance the connections.

Note: Dynamic cleaning of the connections to the failed node eliminates the delay time to realize that the connections are stale and establish the connections to the stable/backup node, thus improving the failover time dramatically.

What is required to use FCF for JDBC applications?

- Oracle Database 10*g* Release 1 or higher must be used.

- ONS should be properly set up on the client where the JDBC application is running. Setup and configuration of ONS is discussed in Chapter 5.

- The `oracle.ons.oraclehome` property should be set to point to ORACLE_HOME.

- An implicit connection cache should be enabled.

- `OracleDataSource` must be used. `OracleConnectionPoolDataSource` will not work with fast connect failover.

The following application illustrates the implementation of JDBC FCF:

```
import oracle.jdbc.pool.OracleDataSource;

import java.sql.SQLException;
import java.sql.Connection;

public class FANEnabledConnectionManagerExample {

    public static Connection getConnection() {
        if (ods == null) {
```

```
                            initializeDataSource();
                    }
                Connection conn = null;
                try {
                    conn = ods.getConnection();
                } catch (SQLException e) {
                    e.printStackTrace();
                } finally {
                }
                return conn;
            }

        public static void main(String[] args) {
            initializeDataSource();
            Connection conn = getConnection();
            /**
             * use the connection.
             */
            try {
                if(conn != null)
                conn.close();//This returns the connection to the cache.
            } catch (SQLException e) {
                e.printStackTrace();
            }
        }


        public static void initializeDataSource() {
            if (ods == null) {
                try {
                    ods = new OracleDataSource();
                    ods.setUser("user");
                    ods.setPassword("password");

/**
 * FCF Supports both thin driver and OCI driver.
 * For OCI driver, just mention the service name in the tnsnames.ora
file
 * For thin driver specify the connection string.
 */

                    ods.setURL("ConnectionURL");
```

```
              java.util.Properties cacheProperties = new
java.util.Properties();

              cacheProperties.setProperty("MinLimit", "5");
              cacheProperties.setProperty("MaxLimit", "20");
              cacheProperties.setProperty("InitialLimit", "3");
              cacheProperties.setProperty("InactivityTimeout",
"1800");

cacheProperties.setProperty("AbandonedConnectionTimeout", "900");
              cacheProperties.setProperty("MaxStatementsLimit",
"10");
              cacheProperties.setProperty("PropertyCheckInterval",
"60");

              ods.setConnectionCacheName("FanConnectionCache01");//
Name of the connection Cache. This has to be unique
              ods.setConnectionCachingEnabled(true);
              ods.setConnectionCacheProperties(cacheProperties); //
set the cache properties.
              /**
               *
               */
              ods.setFastConnectionFailoverEnabled(true);//Enable
the Fast connection Failover.
          } catch (SQLException e) {
              e.printStackTrace();
          } finally {
          }
      }
  }

  /**
   * The DataSource which is used to get connections.
   */
  private static OracleDataSource ods = null;
}
```

As discussed earlier, FCF supports either a thin driver or an OCI (thick) driver. The implementation of both driver types in the above application is indicated below:

Thin Driver:

```
jdbc:oracle:thin:@(DESCRIPTION =
 (ADDRESS=(PROTOCOL = TCP)(HOST = oradb1-vip.sumsky.net)(PORT = 1521))
 (ADDRESS=(PROTOCOL = TCP)(HOST = oradb2-vip.sumsky.net)(PORT = 1521))
 (ADDRESS=(PROTOCOL = TCP)(HOST = oradb3-vip.sumsky.net)(PORT = 1521))
 (ADDRESS=(PROTOCOL = TCP)(HOST = oradb2-vip.sumsky.net)(PORT = 1521))
 (CONNECT_DATA = (SERVER = DEDICATED)
 (SERVICE_NAME = SRV10)) )
```

OCI Driver:

```
jdbc:oracle:oci:@SRVFAN
```

```
In TNSNames.ora file
SRVFAN =
(DESCRIPTION =
 (ADDRESS=(PROTOCOL = TCP)(HOST = oradb1-vip.sumsky.net)(PORT = 1521))
 (ADDRESS=(PROTOCOL = TCP)(HOST = oradb2-vip.sumsky.net)(PORT = 1521))
 (ADDRESS=(PROTOCOL = TCP)(HOST = oradb3-vip.sumsky.net)(PORT = 1521))
 (ADDRESS=(PROTOCOL = TCP)(HOST = oradb4-vip.sumsky.net)(PORT = 1521))
 (CONNECT_DATA =(SERVER = DEDICATED)
 (SERVICE_NAME = SRV10)))
```

Table 6.3   *FCF API Parameters*

Parameter	Description
MinLimit	Specifies the minimum number of connection (default value is zero) instances the cache holds at all times. This value will *not* initialize the cache with the specified number of connections. The **InitialLimit** is used for the initial number of connection instances for the cache to hold.
MaxLimit	Specifies the maximum number (default 0) of connection instances the cache can hold. Default Integer. **MAX_VALUE** when the cache is created or reinitialized.
MaxStatementsLimit	Specifies the maximum number of statements that a connection keeps open.

Table 6.3 *FCF API Parameters (continued)*

`InactivityTimeout`	Specifies the maximum time that a physical connection can be idle in connection cache. Value specified is in seconds. Default 0.
`TimeToLiveTimeout`	Specifies the maximum time in seconds that a logical connection can remain open. When `TimeToLiveTimeout` expires, the logical connection is unconditionally closed, the relevant statement handles are canceled, and the underlying physical connection is returned to the cache for reuse.
`AbadnonedConnectionTimeout`	Specifies the maximum time (default 0) that a connection can remain unused before the connection is closed and returned to the cache.
`PropertyCheckInterval`	Specifies the time interval (default value of 900 seconds) at which the cache manager inspects and enforces all specified cache properties.
`ConnectionWaitTimeout`	Specifies cache behavior when a connection is requested and there are already `MaxLimit` connections active. If `ConnectionWaitTimeout` is greater than zero, each connection request waits for the specified number of seconds, or until a connection is returned to the cache. If no connection is returned to the cache before the timeout elapses, the connection request returns null. This parameter has a default value of zero and basically no timeout occurs.
`ValidateConnection`	Set to true, causes the connection cache to test every connection it retrieves against the underlying database. Default is false.
`ClosestConnectionMatch`	Set to true, causes the connection cache to retrieve the connection with the closest approximation to the specified connection attributes. This can be used in combination with `AttributeWeights` to specify what is considered a "closest match." Default is false.

Table 6.3 *FCF API Parameters (continued)*

AttributeWeights	Sets the weights for each connection attribute used when **ClosestConnectionMatch** is set to true to determine which attributes are given highest priority when searching for matches. An attribute with a high weight is given more importance in determining a match than an attribute with a low weight. **AttributeWeights** contains a set of key/value pairs that set the weights for each connection attribute for which the user intends to request a connection.
	The key is a connection attribute, and the value is the weight. A weight must be an integer value greater than 0. The default weight is 1.

In order for the application to be ONS aware, the application using FAN should specify the system property -oracle.ons.oraclehome = < location-of-ons-home> and ensure that the ons.jar file is located on the application CLASSPATH. The ons-home must be the $ORACLE_HOME where ONS is installed on the client machine.

For example, in the following performance and load-testing utility called DBUtil, the command line on a Windows machine will be

```
set ORACLE_HOME=c:\oracle\product\10.1.0\Db_1
set DBUTIL_HOME=C:\DBUtil\DBUtil1.0\DBUtil1.0
set OPMN_LIB=c:\oracle\product\10.1.0\Companion\opmn\lib
set DBUTIL_CLASSPATH=%DBUTIL_HOME%\lib\dbutil.jar; %DBUTIL_HOME%\lib\
commons-collections-3.0.jar; %DBUTIL_HOME%\lib\commons-dbcp-
1.2.1.jar; %DBUTIL_HOME%\lib\commons-pool-1.2.jar; %DBUTIL_HOME%\lib\
log4j.jar; %DBUTIL_HOME%\lib\ojdbc14.jar; %DBUTIL_HOME%\lib\jcommon-
1.0.0-pre2.jar; %DBUTIL_HOME%\lib\jfreechart-1.0.0-
pre2.jar;%OPMN_LIB%\ons.jar;

java -DDBUTIL_HOME=%DBUTIL_HOME% -
Doracle.ons.oraclehome=%ORACLE_HOME% -Xmx150M -Xms150M -cp
%DBUTIL_CLASSPATH% components.db.DBUtilContainer
```

Note: Please refer to Appendix D for an example of using FCF for DML operations in Java.

Using FAN with ODP.NET

■ The user must be using connection pool.

■ After a DOWN event, it

  ■ Cleans up sessions in the connection pool that go to the instance that stops, and ODP.NET proactively disposes of connections that are no longer valid.

  ■ Establishes connections to existing RAC instances if the removal of severed connections brings the total number of connections below the value that is set for the MIN POOL SIZE parameter.

6.2   Load-balancing

Apart from providing system availability and failover functions, a clustered solution should also be able to balance the available resources on all instances against the various user sessions and their workloads. That is, based on the intensity of the process at hand on the various nodes and the availability of resources, a clustered configuration should be able to distribute load across all nodes in the cluster.

In a clustered database environment such as RAC, load-balancing can be based on several criteria or goals, for example, the number of physical connections to each instance in the cluster, the throughput of the various instances in the cluster, the throughput (CPU) of the database servers on the cluster, the user traffic on a database a listener to accept more connections, and so on. While all of these are potential methods in which the nodes and/ or instances in a cluster can be load-balanced, the most common and desired option is to load-balance based on response time of the instances. Under this method the load is not balanced based on the number of sessions but on the number of resources available on the respective instances.

RAC provides several types of load-balancing that are broadly classified based on the type of user connections to the database server.

6.2.1 Applications not using connection pooling

Client load-balancing

When a user makes a connection (illustrated in Figure 6.3) to the database using the definitions provided in the `tnsnames.ora` file on the client machine, the connection is routed to one of the available nodes. This routing is based on the listeners on the respective nodes to accept the connection request from the user or application.

Figure 6.3
*Client Load
Balancing*

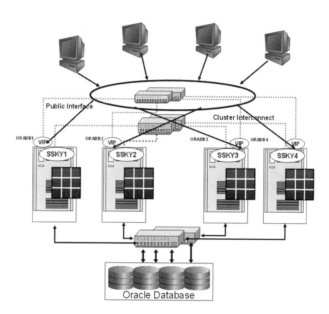

```
SSKYDB =
  (DESCRIPTION=
    (ADDRESS_LIST=
      (FAILOVER=ON)
      (LOAD_BALANCE=ON)
      (ADDRESS=(PROTOCOL=TCP)(HOST=ORADB1-VIP.SUMSKY.NET)(PORT=1521))
      (ADDRESS=(PROTOCOL=TCP)(HOST=ORADB2-VIP.SUMSKY.NET)(PORT=1521))
      (ADDRESS=(PROTOCOL=TCP)(HOST=ORADB3-VIP.SUMSKY.NET)(PORT=1521))
      (ADDRESS=(PROTOCOL=TCP)(HOST=ORADB4-VIP.SUMSKY.NET)(PORT=1521))
    )
  (CONNECT_DATA=
    (SERVER=DEDICATED)
      (SERVICE_NAME=SSKYDB)
      (FAILOVER_MODE=(TYPE=SELECT)
```

```
                    (METHOD=BASIC)
                    (RETRIES=20)
                    (DELAY=15))
       )
       )
```

When several users connect to the database, the listener on any of these nodes can be busy accepting requests from some other user on the network, at which point the client machine is notified. When a callback is received, the SQL*Net will attempt to connect to another address defined in the address list. If the listener on this node is also busy, another address in the list is attempted, and so on, until a connection is established.

Client load-balancing is not based on the availability of resources on the database servers but on the availability of the listener to accept the users' connection requests. To overcome this constraint, Oracle introduced another level of load-balancing called connection load-balancing or server-side load-balancing.

Connection load-balancing

Client load-balancing is between the user session on the client machine and the listener and does not provide any resource-level load-balancing. When several users connect close to one another under client load-balancing, users are distributed across the various listeners, picking an address from the list available. If the clients connect at various intervals, there is the potential that all users will end on the same node or instance. To help resolve this issue, Oracle introduced server-side or connection load-balancing.

Under this method, connections are routed to different instances (least loaded) in the cluster based on load information available to the listener. The PMON process on the respective nodes updates load information to the listener. The frequency, or update interval, is based on the load on the respective nodes; for example, if the load is very low, the update may take up to 10 minutes; on the other hand, on heavily loaded nodes, updates may occur as often as 1-minute intervals.

To implement this load-balancing feature, the parameters listed in Table 6.4 have to be defined.

PMON will register with the listeners identified by the above two parameters defined in the server parameter file. Once registered, PMON will update the listener with profile statistics that allow the listener to route incoming connections to the least loaded instance.

Table 6.4   *Instance Parameters*

LOCAL_LISTENER	This parameter informs the instance regarding the local listener name defined for the node. This parameter is only required to be defined if the listener on the local node is registered on a nondefault port (1521).
REMOTE_LISTENER	The parameter, when defined, informs the instance regarding all other listeners defined on other nodes participating in the cluster.

When an instance starts, PMON registers itself with the listener. This can be verified by checking the listener log file located at $ORACLE_HOME/network/log directory for the service_register string.

When PMON updates the listener with the profile statistics, it also makes an entry in the listener log file. This can be tracked by the service_update string. The frequency of update can also be tracked using the timestamp found against the service_update entries. For example, the following output indicates that the PMON has been updating the listener approximately every five minutes:

```
27-MAY-2005 13:00:39 * service_update * SSKY2 * 0
27-MAY-2005 13:05:22 * service_update * SSKY2 * 0
27-MAY-2005 13:05:22 * service_update * SSKY2 * 0
27-MAY-2005 13:13:02 * service_update * SSKY2 * 0
27-MAY-2005 13:13:02 * service_update * SSKY2 * 0
```

The load statistics available on the listener on the respective nodes are used to reroute any connection to the node that has the least load.

As illustrated in Figure 6.4, the following steps are performed to reroute connection requests based on user workload:

1. A user connection is established to a listener using the client load-balancing options discussed earlier.

2. The listener where the connection was originally established will, based on the load statistics available, reroute the connection to another listener on another node. (The listener information is obtained from the REMOTE_LISTENER parameter.)

Figure 6.4
*Connection or
Server-Side Load
Balancing*

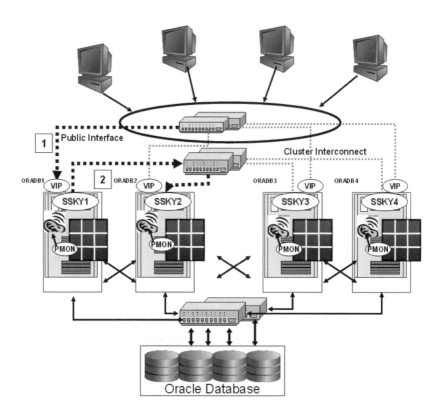

With the introduction and distribution of services across various instances and based on user business requirements, load-balancing criteria will vary. This will depend on having a symmetric or asymmetric distribution of services and on the capacity of the nodes participating in the cluster. For symmetric services and nodes with similar capacity, the absolute session count by instance evenly distributes the sessions across the nodes, and if the service distribution is asymmetric or the nodes do not have a similar capacity, then the run queue length of the respective nodes is used to determine the least loaded node.

```
30-MAY-2005 10:38:07 *
(CONNECT_DATA=(SERVER=DEDICATED)(SERVICE_NAME=SRV7)(FAILOVER_MODE=(BA
CKUP=SRV7_PRECONNECT)(TYPE=SELECT)(METHOD=PRECONNECT)(RETRIES=180)(DE
LAY=5))(CID=(PROGRAM=C:\oracle\product\10.1.0\db_1\bin\
sqlplus.exe)(HOST=REM202231)(USER=Mvallath))) *
(ADDRESS=(PROTOCOL=tcp)(HOST=192.168.2.103)(PORT=3259)) * establish *
SRV7 * 0
30-MAY-2005 10:38:07 *
(CONNECT_DATA=(SERVER=DEDICATED)(SERVICE_NAME=SRV7_PRECONNECT)(FAILOV
```

```
ER_MODE=(BACKUP=SRV7)(TYPE=SELECT)(METHOD=BASIC)(RETRIES=180)(DELAY=5
))(CID=(PROGRAM=C:\oracle\product\10.1.0\db_1\bin\
sqlplus.exe)(HOST=REM202231)(USER=Mvallath))) *
(ADDRESS=(PROTOCOL=tcp)(HOST=192.168.2.103)(PORT=3260)) * establish *
SRV7_PRECONNECT * 12514
```

Oracle provides DBAs with the option of defining goals and determining load-balancing criteria. Load-balancing goals can be

1. *Based on elapsed time.* Under this method, a new ranking referred to as goodness of service is used in the load-balancing algorithm. The load-balancing is driven by the actual service time that would be experienced by the session on a given instance. Ranking compares service time, referred to within the database as the `Elapsed Time Per User Call` metric.

2. *Based on the number of sessions.* Under this method, the load across the various nodes is balanced based on the number of Oracle sessions connected to the database. In this case, the actual resource load or response time or service time is not considered. However, basic count on the number of sessions is considered to determine the least loaded node and where the next session should be connected.

6.2.2 Applications using connection pooling

For applications using connection pooling, Oracle provides a more robust, cleaner, and proactive method of load-balancing called *runtime connection load balancing* (RCLB). Instead of a reactive method used in applications (i.e., the application or session having to connect and then determine the actual load on the system), under the new method, events are used to notify the application regarding the load. Based on this information, connections are established to the least loaded machine.

RCLB relies on the ONS event mechanism, and FCF in applications using Java and OCI or `ODP.NET` subscribe via Oracle's advanced queuing feature. The RCLB feature provides assignment of connections based on feedback from the instances in the RAC cluster. The connection cache assigns connections to clients based on a relative number indicating what percentage of requested connections each instance's service should handle. It is enabled automatically when RAC starts to post service metrics. Service metrics provide service levels and percentage distributions for each instance of a service. Connections to specific instances in the cluster are based on the service metrics available.

Oracle uses the service metric values calculated and stored in the automatic workload repository (AWR) to determine current load characteristics on the various instances. The service metrics are thus forwarded to the master MMON background process. The MMON in turn builds the required load advisory and posts the required advice to AQ, PMON, and the ONS.

Notification mechanisms are based on one of two definitions:

1. *Service time measures the elapsed time versus the demand.* When this option is selected, Oracle examines all of the time consumed in the service from an efficiency and delay perspective and rates this data against the service-level goals set for the service. Using service time or response time for load-balancing recognizes machine power differences, sessions that are blocked in wait, failures that block processing, competing services of different importance. Using the proactive propagation method ensures that work is not sent to overworked, hung, or failed nodes.

2. *Throughput measures the efficiency of the system rather than the delay.* Throughput measures the percentage of the goal response time that the CPU consumes for the service. Basically, throughput is the number of user calls completed in a unit of time.

 Note: RCLB of work requests is enabled by default when FCF is enabled (discussed in Chapter 6). No additional setup or configuration of ONS is required to benefit from RCLB.

To support both connection pooling and non–connection pooling environments, both connection load-balancing and RCLB can coexist with the same service name. However, if they need to coexist, the connection load-balancing goal should be set to SHORT.

Load-balancing definition

Oracle has introduced several methods by which the new load-balancing features can be implemented, either by using Oracle-provided PL/SQL procedures or the EM console.

Connection load-balancing is enabled by setting the CLB_GOAL parameter to appropriate values using the DBMS_SERVICE.CREATE_SERVICE or DBMS_SERVICE.MODIFY_SERVICE packages.

For example:

```
SQL>exec DBMS_SERVICE.MODIFY_SERVICE (SERVICE_NAME=>'SSKYDB',
                                      CLB_GOAL=>1);
```

Valid values for CLB_GOAL are listed in Table 6.5.

Table 6.5   *Connection Load-Balancing Parameters*

Goal Type	Value	Description
CLB_GOAL_SHORT	1	Connection load-balancing based on elapsed time
CLB_GOAL_LONG	2	Connection load-balancing based on number of sessions

Runtime load-balancing is enabled by setting the GOAL parameter in the DBMS_SERVICE.CREATE_SERVICE or DBMS_SERVICE.MODIFY_SERVICE packages.

For example:

```
SQL>exec DBMS_SERVICE.MODIFY_SERVICE(SERVICE_NAME=>'SSKYDB',
                                     GOAL=>1);
```

Valid goal types are listed in Table 6.6.

Table 6.6   *Load-Balancing Goal Types*

Goal Type	Value	Description
GOAL_NONE	0	No load-balancing goal defined
GOAL_SERVICE_TIME	1	Load-balancing based on the service or response time
GOAL_THROUGHPUT	2	Load-balancing based on throughput

Using EM, the load-balancing thresholds can be defined by selecting the appropriate service for edit. Figure 6.5 illustrates the load-balancing definition screen available in EM.

Figure 6.5
EM Load-Balancing Definition

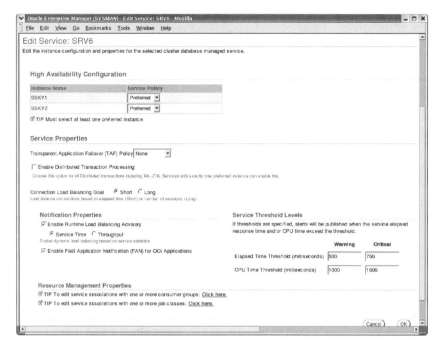

Defining thresholds

Apart from defining goals for load-balancing the cluster, users can define thresholds that will verify activity in the notification service and inform DBAs when such thresholds are reached. Thresholds can be defined either using the EM interface illustrated in Figure 6.5 or using the PL/SQL procedures below:

```
SQL> exec DBMS_SERVER_ALERT.SET_THRESHOLD( -
> METRICS_ID => dbms_server_alert.elapsed_time_per_call,-
> WARNING_OPERATOR=> dbms_server_alert.operator_ge,-
> WARNING_VALUE=>'500',-
> CRITICAL_OPERATOR=>dbms_server_alert.operator_ge,-
> CRITICAL_VALUE=> '750',-
> OBSERVATION_PERIOD=> 15,-
> CONSECUTIVE_OCCURRENCES =>3,-
> OBJECT_TYPE=>dbms_server_alert.object_type_service,-
> OBJECT_NAME => 'SRV6');

PL/SQL procedure successfully completed.
```

The above procedure defines a threshold by elapsed time, with a warning level of 500 seconds, indicated by the variable WARNING_VALUE, and a critical value of 750 seconds, indicated by the variable CRITICAL_VALUE. The procedure further stipulates that a notification should be sent only if the threshold is reached three consecutive times (indicated by CONSECUTIVE_OCCURRENCES) at 15 second intervals (indicated by OBSERVATION_PERIOD).

Verification

Load-balance definitions can be verified using the following query:

```
COL NAME FORMAT A20
SQL> SELECT INST_ID,
            NAME,
            GOAL,
            CLB_GOAL,
            AQ_HA_NOTIFICATION
     FROM GV$SERVICES;


    INST_ID NAME                     GOAL          CLB_G AQ_
---------- -------------------- ------------- ----- ---
          2 SRV6                     NONE          SHORT NO
          2 SSKYXDB                  NONE          SHORT NO
          2 SSKYDB                   NONE          SHORT NO
          2 SYS$BACKGROUND           NONE          SHORT NO
          2 SYS$USERS                NONE          SHORT NO
```

In the above output, service SRV6 has not been configured for runtime load-balancing, and the connection time load-balancing option defined is SHORT. Using the following procedure, the runtime load-balancing goal is changed to THROUGHPUT.

```
SQL> exec
DBMS_SERVICE.MODIFY_SERVICE(SERVICE_NAME=>'SRV6',GOAL=>2);


PL/SQL procedure successfully completed.
```

The new output below from the GV$SERVICES view illustrates this change:

```
SQL> SELECT INST_ID INST,
            NAME,
            NETWORK_NAME,
            GOAL,
            BLOCKED,
            AQ_HA_NOTIFICATION AQ,
            CLB_GOAL
            FROM GV$ACTIVE_SERVICES;


   INST NAME                NETWORK_NAME    GOAL          BLO AQ  CLB_G
   ------ ----------------  -------------   ------------  --- --- -----
      2 SRV6                SRV6            THROUGHPUT    NO  NO  SHORT
      2 SSKYXDB             SSKYXDB         NONE          NO  NO  SHORT
      2 SSKYDB              SSKYDB          NONE          NO  NO  SHORT
      2 SYS$BACKGROUND                      NONE          NO  NO  SHORT
      2 SYS$USERS                           NONE          NO  NO  SHORT
      1 SRV6                SRV6            THROUGHPUT    NO  NO  SHORT
      1 SSKYXDB             SSKYXDB         NONE          NO  NO  SHORT
      1 SSKYDB              SSKYDB          NONE          NO  NO  SHORT
      1 SYS$BACKGROUND                      NONE          NO  NO  SHORT
      1 SYS$USERS                           NONE          NO  NO  SHORT


10 rows selected.
```

6.3   Conclusion

In this chapter, we discussed the high-availability features in RAC. Apart from the basic failover option provided by the clustered solution, RAC provides some additional advanced features like TAF, where the user sessions are migrated to another available instance and data is continuously provided. We also discussed FCF, where the database server sends a notification to the participating servers regarding state changes of the various Oracle services and applications. We discussed how this feature can be implemented using the TNS names-based configuration and how programmatically such a feature can be implemented using the OCI APIs. Further, we discussed the new failover options using ONS and FCF. The chapter also discussed the functional behavior of both of these technologies. The differences between the two failover options are outlined in Table 6.7.

When using FAN with TAF, if a TAF callback has been registered, then the failover retries, and failover delays are ignored. If an error occurs, TAF will continue to attempt to connect and authenticate as long as the callback

Table 6.7 *TAF versus FCF*

TAF	FCF
Relies on retries at the OCI/Net layer. It is the definition in the TNS names file or the OCI definition.	Allows retries at the application level; retries are thus configurable.
Does not work with connection cache.	Works in conjunction with connection cache.
Relies on network calls.	RAC event-based notification and more efficient than detecting failures of network calls.
Reactive failover. Failover is only after the connection has been attempted to the database server.	Proactive failover. Failover is before any attempt to make any server connection. Notification is sent to the application server.
No support for runtime load-balancing. Load-balancing is on a random basis (client load-balancing) or based on updates by the PMON made to the listeners (connection load-balancing).	FCF supports runtime load-balancing across active RAC instances. Connections are made to the various services based on load information received from the database servers using ONS.

returns a value of `OCI_FO_RETRY`. Any delay should be coded into the callback logic.

Also discussed at length were the various load-balancing options supported by RAC, including how they are set up, configured, and monitored. The new RCLB feature available in Oracle Database 10*g* Release 2 gives a truer dynamic load-balancing option, both for connection load-balancing and runtime load-balancing.

Oracle Clusterware Administration Quick Reference

System administration, which includes hardware and operating system administration, has been the domain of system administrators from the very beginning. This distinguishes the kind of work they do from the work done by a DBA. This gap, or the line of differentiation, is probably on the verge of disappearance and will bring unity among these teams, providing a synergy in their knowledge bases. Oracle's Clusterware and ASM (discussed in Chapter 3) and the underlying administrative functionality are probably stepping stones in this direction. Oracle Clusterware provides a new set of commands and utilities that help manage the cluster, including the cluster stack, the registry, and ONS. In this chapter, we list, with examples, a few of the important utilities, commands, and functions that can be helpful in the day-to-day administration of the clusterware and its subcomponents.

 Note: The utilities mentioned in this chapter are available under the ORACLE_HOME/bin and/or the ORA_CRS_HOME/bin directories. Readers are advised to set the environment variables and path definitions discussed in Chapter 4 to invoke these utilities automatically without having to locate these utilities.

Oracle Clusterware is an application stack (discussed in detail in Chapter 2) that resides on top of the basic operating system. Apart from the primary function of managing the nodes participating in the cluster, Oracle's Clusterware adds services that provide a more comprehensive solution compared to third-party cluster managers. The clusterware component is responsible for restarting RAC instances and listeners on process failures and relocating the VIPs on node failure. Oracle provides various utilities and commands to manage the various tiers of the clusterware.

7.1   **Node verification using** olsnodes

The olsnodes command provides the list of nodes and other information for all nodes participating in the cluster. For example:

```
[oracle@oradb4 oracle]$ olsnodes
oradb4
oradb3
oradb2
oradb1
```

Additional cluster-related information can be obtained by adding one or more of the following parameters to the olsnodes command:

1. To list all nodes participating in the cluster with their assigned node numbers, use the following:

    ```
    [oracle@oradb4 tmp]$ olsnodes -n
    oradb4   1
    oradb3   2
    oradb2   3
    oradb1   4
    ```

2. To list all nodes participating in the cluster with the private inter-connect assigned to each node, use the following:

    ```
    [oracle@oradb4 tmp]$ olsnodes -p
    oradb4   oradb4-priv
    oradb3   oradb3-priv
    oradb2   oradb2-priv
    oradb1   oradb1-priv
    ```

3. To list all nodes participating in the cluster with the VIP assigned to each node, use the following:

    ```
    [oracle@oradb4 tmp]$ olsnodes -i
    oradb4   192.168.2.45
    oradb3   192.168.2.35
    oradb2   192.168.2.25
    oradb1   192.168.2.15
    ```

4. To log cluster verification information with more details, options –g (log), –v (verbose), can be used:

```
[oracle@oradb4 oracle]$ olsnodes -v -g
prlslms: Initializing LXL global
prlsndmain: Initializing CLSS context
prlsmemberlist: No of cluster members configured = 256
prlsmemberlist: Getting information for nodenum = 1
prlsmemberlist: node_name = oradb4
prlsmemberlist: ctx->lsdata->node_num = 1
prls_printdata: Printing the node data
oradb4
prlsmemberlist: Getting information for nodenum = 2
prlsmemberlist: node_name = oradb3
prlsmemberlist: ctx->lsdata->node_num = 2
prls_printdata: Printing the node data
oradb3
. . .
. . .
prlsndmain: olsnodes executed successfully
prlsndterm: Terminating LSF
```

It should be noted that the olsnodes utility can be executed with a combination of the above options. For example, for a summarized view of all the information, it could be executed as shown below:

```
[oracle@oradb4 oracle]$ olsnodes -n -p -i -g -v
prlslms: Initializing LXL global
prlsndmain: Initializing CLSS context
prlsmemberlist: No of cluster members configured = 256
prlsmemberlist: Getting information for nodenum = 1
prlsmemberlist: node_name = oradb4
prlsmemberlist: ctx->lsdata->node_num = 1
prls_getnodeprivname: Retrieving the node private name for node =
oradb4
prls_getnodeprivname: Private node name = oradb4-priv
prls_getnodevip: Retrieving the virtual IP for node = oradb4
prls_getnodevip: prsr_vpip_key_len = 281
prls_getnodevip: Opening the OCR key DATABASE.NODEAPPS.oradb4.VIP.IP
prls_getnodevip: OCR key value length = 13
prls_getnodevip: Virtual IP = 192.168.2.45
```

```
prls_printdata: Printing the node data
oradb4  1        oradb4-priv      192.168.2.45
prlsmemberlist: Getting information for nodenum = 2
prlsmemberlist: node_name = oradb3
prlsmemberlist: ctx->lsdata->node_num = 2
prls_getnodeprivname: Retrieving the node private name for node =
oradb3
prls_getnodeprivname: Private node name = oradb3-priv
prls_getnodevip: Retrieving the virtual IP for node = oradb3
prls_getnodevip: prsr_vpip_key_len = 281
prls_getnodevip: Opening the OCR key DATABASE.NODEAPPS.oradb3.VIP.IP
prls_getnodevip: OCR key value length = 13
prls_getnodevip: Virtual IP = 192.168.2.35
prls_printdata: Printing the node data
oradb3  2        oradb3-priv      192.168.2.35
. . .
. . .
prlsndmain: olsnodes executed successfully
prlsndterm: Terminating LSF
```

7.2　Oracle Control Registry

7.2.1　Server control (`srvctl`) utility

Oracle Database 10g replaces the server configuration process that was present in Oracle Database 9i. With this change, the `srvconfig.loc` that identified the location of the server configuration file is replaced with the `ocr.loc` file and is located in the `/etc/oracle` directory on Linux and most UNIX systems, except Sun Solaris, where it is located in `/var/opt/oracle`. On Windows-based systems, it is located in the Windows registry. The server configuration file is now called the OCR.

The resources available within the Oracle cluster are grouped based on the type of information contained in the OCR and the level of its usage. These resources are grouped into two categories as discussed below:

1.　*Resources that apply to the entire node/cluster.* Certain services and components of the Oracle software are configured for each node irrespective of the number of instances and databases on the node. Such applications are grouped under the `nodapps` category. Oracle creates the majority of these applications or services and updates the OCR as part of the Oracle Clusterware installation and configuration process. The remaining resources are added during the database configuration process. To name a few, VIP, ONS, and GSD are some of the applications configured during the Oracle Clusterware installation. The status of these applications can be verified using the following command:

```
[oracle@oradb3 oracle]$ srvctl status nodeapps -n oradb3
VIP is running on node: oradb3
GSD is running on node: oradb3
Listener is running on node: oradb3
ONS daemon is running on node: oradb3
```

Since most of the required applications and their respective entries are already created by the OUI during the installation process, they seldom need to be updated or modified. However, if such an operation is required, Oracle has provided commands and options that are listed with examples in Appendix B.

2. *Resources that apply to each database and instance in the cluster.* As in Oracle Database 9i, the registry can be maintained using the srvctl utility. For example, to add a database, its instances, and services, the following steps can be taken:

    a. Add the database that supports this clustered environment using the following command:

```
oracle$ srvctl add database -d <database name> -o <oracle home
directory>
```

```
[oracle@oradb4 oracle]$ srvctl add database -d SSKYDB -o
/usr/app/oracle/product/10.2.0/db_1
Successful addition of cluster database:SSKYDB
```

This command adds the database SSKYDB to the configuration file with the ORACLE_HOME information.

    b. To add the instances that will share the database defined in the previous step, the following command could be used:

```
oracle$ srvctl add instance -d <database name> -i <instance
name> -n <node name>
```

```
[oracle@oradb4 oracle]$ srvctl add instance —d SSKYDB —i
SSKY1 —n ORADB3
Instance successfully added to node: ORADB3
```

> This command adds the instance named SSKY1 that
> uses the common shared database SSKYDB and will run on
> node ORADB3.

c. Add any database-related services using the following
    syntax:

```
oracle$ srvctl add service -d <name> -s <service_name> -r
<preferred_list> [-a "<available_list>"]

[oracle@oradb4 oracle]$ srvctl add service -d SSKYDB -s SRV6
-r SSKY1 -a SSKY2
```

> Other services, instance, and node information can be
> added to the OCR from any node participating in the
> cluster. The srvctl utility can also be used to check the
> configuration or the status of the clustered databases and
> their respective instances.

d. By checking the status using the srvctl utility, the
    instance-level detail and the corresponding node infor-
    mation can be obtained:

```
srvctl status database -d <database name>
```

> For example, to check the status of a database, use the
> following syntax:

```
[oracle@oradb4 oracle]$ srvctl status database -d SSKYDB -f -v
Instance SSKY1 is running on node oradb4 with online services SRV2
SRV6
Instance SSKY2 is not running on node oradb3
```

> This command displays the names of all instances, the
> list of services configured on those instances, and their
> current states. For example, in the above listing, instance
> SSKY2 and the services configured on it are not running.

However, instance SSKY1 has two online services, SRV2 and SRV6.

 Note: A list of srvctl options with examples can be found in Appendix B.

7.2.2   Cluster services control (crsctl) utility

Oracle has provided a new utility called crsctl for dynamic debugging, tracing, checking, and administration of various subcomponents of the clusterware.

1.   Check the health of the Oracle Clusterware daemon processes with the following:

```
[oracle@oradb4 oracle]$ crsctl check crs
CSS appears healthy
CRS appears healthy
EVM appears healthy
[oracle@oradb4 oracle]$
```

This output shows the health of the three Clusterware processes. The health of each individual process could also be checked using crsctl check css, evm.

2.   Query and administer css vote disks with the following:

```
[root@oradb4 root]# crsctl add css votedisk /u03/oradata/
CssVoteDisk.dbf
Now formatting voting disk: /u03/oradata/CssVoteDisk.dbf
Read -1 bytes of 512 at offset 0 in voting device
(CssVoteDisk.dbf)
successful addition of votedisk /u03/oradata/CssVoteDisk.dbf.
```

In situations where fewer than three vote disks are available or when the vote disk location needs to be moved, then the above command will become useful. This command adds a new vote disk, copying the contents from the existing vote disk at the location specified.

```
[root@oradb4 root]# crsctl query css votedisk
  0.    0    /u02/oradata/CSSVoteDisk.dbf
  1.    0    /u03/oradata/CssVoteDisk.dbf
  2.    0    /u04/oradata/CssVoteDisk.dbf

located 3 votedisk(s).
```

This output lists all vote disks currently configured and in use by the CSS.

3. For dynamic state dump of the CRS, use the following:

```
[root@oradb4 root]# crsctl debug statedump crs
dumping State for crs objects
```

Dynamic state dump information is appended to the crsd log file located in the $ORA_CRS_HOME/log/oradb4/crsd directory.

```
2005-06-02 21:34:04.156:[CRSD][393984944]0State Dump for RTILock
 [CRSD][393984944]0LockName:RES ora.ASMDB.ASMDB1.inst::ThreadId:NULL-
thread
 [CRSD][393984944]0LockName:RES
ora.ASMDB.SRV2.ASMDB1.srv::ThreadId:NULL-thread
 [CRSD][393984944]0LockName:RES ora.ASMDB.SRV2.cs::ThreadId:NULL-
thread
 [CRSD][393984944]0LockName:RES
ora.ASMDB.SRV6.ASMDB1.srv::ThreadId:NULL-thread
 [CRSD][393984944]0LockName:RES ora.ASMDB.SRV6.cs::ThreadId:NULL-
thread
 [CRSD][393984944]0LockName:RES ora.ASMDB.db::ThreadId:NULL-thread
 [CRSD][393984944]0LockName:RES ora.oradb4.ASM1.asm::ThreadId:NULL-
thread
 [CRSD][393984944]0LockName:RES
ora.oradb4.LISTENER_ORADB4.lsnr::ThreadId:NULL-thread
 [CRSD][393984944]0LockName:RES ora.oradb4.gsd::ThreadId:NULL-thread
 [CRSD][393984944]0LockName:RES ora.oradb4.ons::ThreadId:NULL-thread
 [CRSD][393984944]0LockName:RES ora.oradb4.vip::ThreadId:NULL-thread
 [CRSD][393984944]0LockName:_CRS_RDB::ThreadId:NULL-thread
 [CRSD][393984944]0LockName:_ORA_CRS_BOOT::ThreadId:NULL-thread
 [CRSD][393984944]0LockName:_ORA_CRS_FAILOVER::ThreadId:NULL-thread
2005-06-02 21:34:04.161:[CRSD]
[393984944]0LockName:_ORA_CRS_MEMBER_oradb4::ThreadId:3076434496
```

This output is the state dump of the CRS activity. The output will list all the current resident resources and their current thread IDs. For example, the only thread ID assigned at the moment is for the CRS member on node ORADB4.

1.   Verify the Oracle Clusterware version:

```
[oracle@oradb4 log]$ crsctl query crs softwareversion
CRS software version on node [oradb4] is [10.2.0.0.0]
```

This output shows the current version of the Oracle Clusterware.

2.   Verify the current version of Oracle Clusterware being used:

```
[oracle@oradb4 log]$ crsctl query crs activeversion
CRS active version on the cluster is [10.2.0.0.0]
[oracle@oradb4 log]$
```

This output lists the active Oracle Clusterware version being used.

3.   Debug the activites of Oracle Clusterware's several subcomponents, which are modules and perform specific actions on behalf of the cluster services. The crsctl utility provides several options for doing this.

   a.   CRS modules and the functionalities performed are listed in Table 7.1.

Table 7.1   *CRS Modules*

Modules	Description
CRSUI	User interface module
CRSCOMM	Communication module
CRSRTI	Resource management module
CRSMAIN	Main module/driver
CRSPLACE	CRS placement module
CRSAPP	CRS application
CRSRES	CRS resources

Table 7.1 *CRS Modules (continued)*

Modules	Description
CRSOCR	OCR interface/engine
CRSTIMER	Various CRS-related timers
CRSEVT	CRS-EVM/event interface module
CRSD	CRS Daemon

Depending on the module and its functionality, the debug operation can be performed at different levels. Based on the usefulness of the output provided, setting the operation to level two will provide the most useful information. Outputs of several of these modules are illustrated as follows.

    b. Debug all CRS application-level activity. The debug output is generated using the following:

```
[orcrsctl debug log crs "CRSAPP:2"
2005-06-01 22:43:56.798:[CRSAPP][572242864]0Using check
timeout of 600 seconds
2005-06-01 22:43:56.799:[CRSAPP][572242864]0In RunContext
Constructor
2005-06-01 22:43:56.799:[CRSAPP][572242864]0In runScript of
runContext
2005-06-01 22:43:57.652:[CRSAPP][572242864]0RunContext
destructor
2005-06-01 22:44:01.104:[CRSAPP][572242864]0Using check
timeout of 60 seconds
2005-06-01 22:44:01.105:[CRSAPP][572242864]0In RunContext
Constructor
2005-06-01 22:44:01.105:[CRSAPP][572242864]0In runScript of
runContext
2005-06-01 22:44:01.641:[CRSAPP][572242864]0RunContext
destructor
```

This output is the debug information of the CRS applications activity. The output provides the frequency of the context construction and destruction.

    c. Debug all CRS timer activity. The debug output is generated using the following:

```
[root@oradb4 crsd]# crsctl debug log crs "CRSTIMER:2"
```

```
Set CRSD Debug Module: CRSTIMER  Level: 2
[root@oradb4 crsd]#
```

The output from this module generates scheduler-related information for all the resources executed by the CRS on the cluster.

 Note: The following output has been formatted for readability.

```
[CRSTIMER][414956464]0In the loop ..
[414956464]0Firing event Poller ora.oradb4.vip
[414956464]0In the loop ..
[414956464]0Sleeping for (ms) 25940
[561757104]0Scheduling event ScriptTimeoutora.oradb4.vip Delay=63000
Interval=0 Expiration=36550860
[561757104]0Scheduling event got lock ScriptTimeoutora.oradb4.vip
[561757104]0Cancelling event ScriptTimeoutora.oradb4.vip
[414956464]0In the loop ..
[414956464]0Sleeping for (ms) 25240
[561757104]0Scheduling event Poller ora.oradb4.vip Delay=60000
Interval=60000 Expiration=36548500
[561757104]0Scheduling event got lock Poller ora.oradb4.vip
[414956464]0In the loop ..
[414956464]0Firing event Poller ora.oradb4.LISTENER_ORADB4.lsnr
[414956464]0In the loop ..
[414956464]0Sleeping for (ms) 17360
[561757104]0Scheduling event
ScriptTimeoutora.oradb4.LISTENER_ORADB4.lsnr Delay=630000 Interval=0
Expiration=37149000
[561757104]0Scheduling event got lock
ScriptTimeoutora.oradb4.LISTENER_ORADB4.lsnr
[561757104]0Cancelling event
ScriptTimeoutora.oradb4.LISTENER_ORADB4.lsnr
[414956464]0In the loop ..
[414956464]0Sleeping for (ms) 16670
[561757104]0Scheduling event Poller ora.oradb4.LISTENER_ORADB4.lsnr
Delay=600000 Interval=600000 Expiration=37119640
[561757104]0Scheduling event got lock Poller
ora.oradb4.LISTENER_ORADB4.lsnr
[414956464]0In the loop ..
[414956464]0Firing event Poller ora.ASMDB.ASMDB1.inst
[414956464]0In the loop ..
```

```
[414956464]0Sleeping for (ms) 12180
[561757104]0Scheduling event ScriptTimeoutora.ASMDB.ASMDB1.inst
Delay=630000 Interval=0 Expiration=37166370
[561757104]0Scheduling event got lock
ScriptTimeoutora.ASMDB.ASMDB1.inst
[561757104]0Cancelling event ScriptTimeoutora.ASMDB.ASMDB1.inst
[414956464]0In the loop ..
[414956464]0Sleeping for (ms) 11080
[561757104]0Scheduling event Poller ora.ASMDB.ASMDB1.inst
Delay=600000 Interval=600000 Expiration=37137420
[561757104]0Scheduling event got lock Poller ora.ASMDB.ASMDB1.inst
[414956464]0In the loop ..
[414956464]0Firing event Poller ora.oradb4.vip
[414956464]0In the loop ..
[414956464]0Sleeping for (ms) 25720
[561757104]0Scheduling event ScriptTimeoutora.oradb4.vip Delay=63000
Interval=0 Expiration=36611600
[561757104]0Scheduling event got lock ScriptTimeoutora.oradb4.vip
2005-06-01 23:06:17.050:[CRSTIMER][561757104]0Cancelling event
ScriptTimeoutora.oradb4.vip
```

This output lists the scheduling details of the various resources monitored by the CRS subcomponent.

d. Debug all CRS event activity. The debug output is generated using the following:

```
[root@oradb4 crsd]# crsctl debug log crs "CRSEVT:1"
Set CRSD Debug Module: CRSEVT   Level: 1
```

The output from this module generates resource checks to ascertain its execution.

 Note: The following output has been formatted for better readability and only displays data pertaining to one node.

```
2005-06-01 23:15:23.408:[CRSEVT][561757104]0Running check for
resource ora.oradb4.vip
[CRSEVT][561757104]0ora.oradb4.vip[ACTION_SCRIPT] = /usr/app/oracle/
product/10.2.0/crs/bin/racgwrap
[CRSEVT][561757104]0ora.oradb4.vip[SCRIPT_TIMEOUT]=60
```

```
[CRSEVT][561757104]0Resource Poller ora.oradb4.vip returned status 1
[CRSEVT][561757104]0Running check for resource
ora.oradb4.LISTENER_ORADB4.lsnr
[CRSEVT][561757104]0ora.oradb4.LISTENER_ORADB4.lsnr[ACTION_SCRIPT]= /
usr/app/oracle/product/10.2.0/db_1/bin/racgwrap
[CRSEVT][561757104]0ora.oradb4.LISTENER_ORADB4.lsnr[SCRIPT_TIMEOUT]=6
00
[CRSEVT][572242864]0Running check for resource ora.oradb3.vip
[CRSEVT][572242864]0ora.oradb3.vip[ACTION_SCRIPT] = /usr/app/oracle/
product/10.2.0/crs/bin/racgwrap
[CRSEVT][572242864]0ora.oradb3.vip[SCRIPT_TIMEOUT] = 60
[CRSEVT][561757104]0Resource Poller ora.oradb4.LISTENER_ORADB4.lsnr
returned status 1
[CRSEVT][572242864]0Resource Poller ora.oradb3.vip returned status 1
[CRSEVT][572242864]0Running check for resource ora.ASMDB.ASMDB1.inst
[CRSEVT][572242864]0ora.ASMDB.ASMDB1.inst[ACTION_SCRIPT] = /usr/app/
oracle/product/10.2.0/db_1/bin/racgwrap
[CRSEVT][572242864]0ora.ASMDB.ASMDB1.inst[SCRIPT_TIMEOUT] = 600
[CRSEVT][572242864]0Resource Poller ora.ASMDB.ASMDB1.inst returned
status 1
[CRSEVT][572242864]0Running check for resource ora.oradb4.vip
[CRSEVT][572242864]0ora.oradb4.vip[ACTION_SCRIPT] = /usr/app/oracle/
product/10.2.0/crs/bin/racgwrap
[CRSEVT][572242864]0ora.oradb4.vip[SCRIPT_TIMEOUT] = 60
[CRSEVT][572242864]0Resource Poller ora.oradb4.vip returned status 1
[CRSEVT][572242864]0Running check for resource ora.oradb3.vip
[CRSEVT][572242864]0ora.oradb3.vip[ACTION_SCRIPT] = /usr/app/oracle/
product/10.2.0/crs/bin/racgwrap
[CRSEVT][572242864]0ora.oradb3.vip[SCRIPT_TIMEOUT] = 60
[CRSEVT][572242864]0Resource Poller ora.oradb3.vip returned status 1
```

e. Debug all CRS log activity. The debug output is generated using the following:

```
crsctl debug log crs "CRSD:2"

2005-06-01 22:43:00.196:[CRSD][572242864]0entries=
2005-06-01 22:43:00.197:[CRSD][572242864]0entry=owner:root:rwx |
2005-06-01 22:43:00.199:[CRSD][572242864]0entry=pgrp:dba:r-x |
2005-06-01 22:43:00.200:[CRSD][572242864]0entry=other::r-- |
2005-06-01 22:43:00.200:[CRSD][572242864]0entry=user:oracle:r-x |
```

EVM-related modules and the functionalities performed are listed in Table 7.2. Debug data for these modules can be generated similarly to the CRS modules discussed earlier.

Table 7.2   *EVM Modules and Descriptions*

Module Name	Function
EVMD	EVM Daemon
EVMDMAIN	EVM main module
EVMCOMM	EVM communication module
EVMEVT	EVM event module
EVMAPP	EVM application module
EVMAGENT	EVM agent module
CRSOCR	OCR interface/engine
CLUCLS	EVM cluster/CSS information

7.2.3   OCR administration utilities

OCR verification (ocrcheck) utility

This utility checks the health of the OCR. Apart from generating information regarding the OCR, the ocrcheck utility generates a log file in the directory from which this utility is executed.

```
[oracle@oradb3 oracle]$ ocrcheck
Status of Oracle Cluster Registry is as follows :
        Version                 :          2
        Total space (kbytes)    :     262144
        Used space (kbytes)     :       1980
        Available space (kbytes) :     260164
        ID                      :  650714508
        Device/File Name        : /u01/oradata/OCRConfig.dbf
                             Device/File integrity check succeeded
        Device/File Name        : /u03/oradata/OCRConfig.dbf
                             Device/File integrity check succeeded

        Cluster registry integrity check succeeded
```

OCR configuration (`ocrconfig`) utility

This utility provides various options for configuration and administration of the OCR. Functions such as export, import, restore, and so on, are provided by this utility.

a.   Export of the OCR can be performed while the registry is online or offline. To perform an export, the following syntax is used:

```
ocrconfig -export <filename > [-s online]

      [root@oradb4 SskyClst]# ocrconfig -export
OCRExpPostSRV.dmp -s online
```

In this output, using `ocrconfig`, an export of the OCR is taken while the OCR is online.

b.   An OCR can be restored from either an export dump file or a backup file. To import from an OCR file, the following syntax is used:

```
ocrconfig -import <filename>
```

Since the OCR is restored to a previous state by the import operation (from a previously exported file), it is advised that the Oracle Clusterware stack be bounced or restarted.

c.   Oracle performs an automatic backup of the OCR once every four hours while the system is up. While performing automatic backups, Oracle maintains three previous versions of the backup, a backup copy taken at the beginning of the day, and another taken at the beginning of the week before purging the rest.

Oracle performs these automatic backups to the cluster directory (e.g., `$ORA_CRS_HOME/cdata/Sskyclst` as illustrated in the following example) on one of the nodes. Backup is only performed on one node of the cluster, and the backup operation is performed by the `MASTER` node. To check the previous backups, the following syntax is used:

```
[root@oradb4 SskyClst]# ocrconfig -showbackup
```

```
    oradb4 2005/06/03 18:00:29 /usr/app/oracle/product/
10.2.0/crs/cdata/SskyClst
    oradb4 2005/06/03 14:00:29 /usr/app/oracle/product/
10.2.0/crs/cdata/SskyClst
    oradb4 2005/06/03 10:00:28 /usr/app/oracle/product/
10.2.0/crs/cdata/SskyClst
    oradb4 2005/06/02 02:00:20 /usr/app/oracle/product/
10.2.0/crs/cdata/SskyClst
    oradb4 2005/06/01 18:00:18 /usr/app/oracle/product/
10.2.0/crs/cdata/SskyClst
```

The list of backup files at this location can be checked using the following:

```
[root@oradb4 SskyClst]# ls -ltr $ORA_CRS_HOME/cdata/SskyClst
total 30908
-rw-r--r--    1 root      root        4804608 Jun  1 18:00 week.ocr
-rw-r--r--    1 root      root        4833280 Jun  2 02:00 day.ocr
-rw-r--r--    1 root      root        5390336 Jun  3 02:00 day_.ocr
-rw-r--r--    1 root      root        5390336 Jun  3 10:00 backup02.ocr
-rw-r--r--    1 root      root        5398528 Jun  3 14:00 backup01.ocr
-rw-r--r--    1 root      root        5398528 Jun  3 18:00 backup00.ocr
```

In this output, a listing of all backups taken by the CRS is listed. It should be noted that three backups are taken during the day (listed as `backup00.ocr`, `backup01.ocr`, and `backup02.ocr`). The listing also contains a backup maintained for the beginning of the day (`day.ocr`) and another for the week (`week.ocr`).

 Note: Backups performed to individual nodes become a single point of failure when the nodes are not down but are not reachable. It is advised that the backups be moved to the shared storage to provide access to this file from any node in the cluster.

a.   The automatic backup (default) location can be changed using the following syntax:

```
ocrconfig -backuploc <new location of backup>
```

```
[root@oradb4 root]# ocrconfig -backuploc
/u13/oradata/Sskyclst
```

b.   OCR can be restored from a previous backup using the following syntax and option:

```
ocrconfig —restore <backup filename>
```

```
[root@oradb4 root]#ocrconfig -restore backup01.ocr
```

c.   Other options supported by the `ocrconfig` utility include the following:

    i.   To downgrade to a previous version of OCR:

```
ocrconfig -downgrade
```

    ii.   To upgrade to the next version of the clusterware:

```
ocrconfig -upgrade [<user> [<group>]]
```

    iii.   To replace the current OCR and create a new one in another location:

```
ocrconfig -replace ocrmirror <new location>
```

    iv.   To repair the current OCR and automatically fix issues with the registry:

```
ocrconfig -repair ocr <ocr location>
```

```
[root@oradb4 root]# ocrconfig -repair ocr /u01/oradata/
OCRConfig.dbf
```

Note: Clusterware should be shut down before is performed a repair operation.

OCR dump (`ocrdump`) utility

The primary function of this utility is to dump the contents of the OCR into an ASCII-readable format file. The output file is created in the directory where the utility is executed. If no filename is specified, the dump is created in OCRDUMPFILE in the same directory. The utility also generates a log file in the directory from which the ocrdump was executed.

```
[oracle@oradb4 oracle]$ ocrdump [<filename>]
```

Partial dump outputs can also be generated by specifying -keyname <keyword> with the ocrdump command. For example, to generate a dump of all system-level definitions, the following syntax should be followed:

```
[oracle@oradb4 oracle]$ ocrdump –keyname SYSTEM OCRsystemDUMP
```

Note: A list of all keynames for use in the above operation is provided in Table 2.1

7.3   ONS control (`onsctl`) utility

ONS uses a publish/subscribe method to produce and deliver event messages for both local and remote consumers and applications. To the predefined list of nodes in the cluster, the ONS daemon process running locally on respective nodes sends messages to and receives messages from a configured list of nodes identified in the ons.config file.

a.   Verify if ONS is running on the node using the srvctl command:

```
[oracle@oradb4 oracle]$ srvctl status nodeapps –n
oradb4
```

```
VIP is running on node: oradb4
GSD is running on node: oradb4
Listener is running on node: oradb4
ONS daemon is running on node: oradb4
[oracle@oradb4 oracle]$
```

This output lists all the applications running at the node level.

b. Once ONS is verified on the node, ensure that the ONS Daemon is running. This is done using the `onsctl` command:

```
[oracle@oradb4 oracle]$ onsctl ping
Number of onsconfiguration retrieved, numcfg = 3
onscfg[0]
    {node = oradb4, port = 4948}
Adding remote host oradb4:4948
onscfg[1]
    {node = oradb3, port = 4948}
Adding remote host oradb3:4948
ons is running ...
```

This output verifies the communication link between various nodes configured for ONS.

c. If ONS is not running as shown by the above command, ONS needs to be configured with the server and node information. The ONS configuration file is located in `$ORACLE_HOME/opmn/conf/ons.config`:

```
[oracle@oradb4 oracle]$ more $ORACLE_HOME/opmn/conf/
ons.config
localport=6101
remoteport=6201
loglevel=3
useocr=on
nodes=oradb3.sumsky.net:6101,oradb4.sumsky.net:6201,
onsclient1.sumsky.net:6200,onsclient2.sumsky.net:6200
```

The `localport` is the port that ONS binds to on the local-host interface to talk to the local clients. The `remoteport` is the port that ONS binds to on all interfaces for talking to other ONS daemons. The nodes listed in the `nodes` line are all nodes in the network that will need to receive or send event notifications. This includes client machines where ONS is also running to receive FAN events for applications.

d. To configure ONS on the client machines, Oracle client software and the Oracle companion CD should be installed.

Once the software has been installed, the `ons.config` file should also be set up similarly to what is done on the server side. Remember the `localport` and `remoteport` for the client configuration will be different from that defined on the server.

After configuration is complete, ONS is started using the following command:

```
onsctl start.

C:\ onsctl start

ONS started . . .
```

 Note: ONS installation and configuration on the client machines are not required when Oracle Database 10g Release 2 client software is used.

e. Starting ONS on the server side, use the following:

```
[oracle@oradb4 oracle]$ onsctl start
Number of onsconfiguration retrieved, numcfg = 2
onscfg[0]
    {node = oradb4, port = 4948}
Adding remote host oradb4:4948
onscfg[1]
    {node = oradb3, port = 4948}
Adding remote host oradb3:4948
Number of onsconfiguration retrieved, numcfg = 2
onscfg[0]
    {node = oradb4, port = 4948}
Adding remote host oradb4:4948
onscfg[1]
    {node = oradb3, port = 4948}
Adding remote host oradb3:4948
onsctl: ons started
```

Once the server machines have been configured, and the client machines have been set up for ONS, an `onsctl start` will start the communication links between all nodes participating in the ONS framework.

f.   Verifying if ONS is configured and that connections between all servers and client ONS daemon processes are established can be done using the following command:

```
[oracle@oradb4 oracle]$ onsctl ping
Number of onsconfiguration retrieved, numcfg = 3
onscfg[0]
   {node = oradb4, port = 4948}                    --- RAC Node 1
Adding remote host oradb4:4948
onscfg[1]
   {node = oradb3, port = 4948}                    --- RAC Node 2
Adding remote host oradb3:4948
onscfg[2]
   {node = oraclient1.sumsky.net, port = 6200}    --- Client Node
Adding remote host oraclient1.sumsky.net:6200
ons is running ...
```

In this output, `oraclient1.sumsky.net` is a client machine that is part of the ONS communications.

More detailed ONS configuration information can be obtained using the `debug` option with the `onsctl` utility.

```
[oracle@oradb4 oracle]$ onsctl debug
Number of onsconfiguration retrieved, numcfg = 2
onscfg[0]
   {node = oradb4, port = 4948}
Adding remote host oradb4:4948
onscfg[1]
   {node = oradb3, port = 4948}
Adding remote host oradb3:4948
HTTP/1.1 200 OK
Content-Length: 1357
Content-Type: text/html
Response:
======== ONS ========
```

```
Listeners:
NAME     BIND ADDRESS     PORT    FLAGS      SOCKET
-------  --------------   -----   --------   ------
Local    127.000.000.001  6101    00000142      9
Remote   192.168.002.040  6201    00000101     10
Request     No listener
```

```
Server connections:
ID          IP        PORT    FLAGS      SENDQ     WORKER    BUSY  SUBS
------  --------------  -----  --------  ----------  --------  ------  -----
    1  192.168.002.035  6101  00104205        0                 1      0
    3  192.168.002.103  6200  00010005        0                 1      0
    4  192.168.002.101  6200  00104205        0                 1      0
    5  192.168.002.040  4948  00104205        0                 1      0
    6  192.168.002.030  4948  00104205        0                 1      0
```

```
Client connections:
ID          IP        PORT    FLAGS      SENDQ     WORKER    BUSY  SUBS
-------  --------------  -----  --------  ----------  --------  ------  -----
    3  127.000.000.001  6101  0001001a        0                 1      1
```

```
Pending connections:
 ID          IP        PORT    FLAGS      SENDQ     WORKER    BUSY  SUBS
-------  --------------  -----  --------  ----------  --------  ------  -----
    0  127.000.000.001  6101  00020812        0                 1      0
```

```
Worker Ticket: 1/1, Idle: 360
    THREAD    FLAGS
    --------  --------
      4002  00000012
      8003  00000012
      c004  00000012
```

```
Resources:
Notifications:
    Received: 2638, in Receive Q: 0, Processed: 2638, in Process Q: 0
  Pools:
    Message: 24/25 (1), Link: 25/25 (1), Subscription: 24/25 (1)
```

This output provides a comprehensive picture of the ONS details. The different sections show the various tiers and subcomponents that the ONS establishes connection and/or communication with:

- *Listeners.* This section shows the IP address and the port information for the local and the remote addresses.
- *Server connections.* This section shows the servers and ports that this daemon is aware of. Initially, this will correspond to the nodes entry in `ons.config`, but as other daemons are contacted, any hosts they are in contact with will appear in this section.

The other sections in the debug output give information relating to current and previous activity (e.g., messages sent and received, threads currently active).

Note: This output lists the client and server machines that are registered with ONS.

7.4 EVMD verification

EVMD plays a very important function in the RAC architecture: it sends and receives actions regarding resource state changes to and from all other nodes in the cluster. To determine whether the EVMD for a node can send and receive messages from other nodes, the following set of tests should help.

Using the `evmwatch` monitor, utility activities of the EVMD can be verified. The `evmwatch` monitor is a background process that constantly watches for actions; such actions are then parsed to the `evmshow` utility for formatting and display.

For example, `evmwatch -A -t "@timestamp @@"` will monitor for actions sent and received, and such information will be displayed on standard output. The display in this example is from `evmshow;` however, it is automatically started when the `-A` switch is specified. The command `@timestamp` will list the date and time when actions are sent and received by the node:

```
"01-Jul-2005 20:02:26 @@"
```

```
"01-Jul-2005 20:02:27 @@"
"01-Jul-2005 20:02:27 @@"
"01-Jul-2005 20:02:29 @@"
```

Additional details regarding the actions received or sent can also be obtained using additional switches. For example, evmwatch -A -t "@timestamp @priority @" will give the priority of the event received, and the third @name will display the name (shown in the output below) of the service, resource, or application.

```
[root@oradb3 oracle]# evmwatch -A -t "@timestamp @priority @name"
"01-Jul-2005 19:42:36 200 ora.ha.oradb3.ASM2.asm.imcheck"
"01-Jul-2005 19:42:36 200 ora.ha.oradb3.ASM2.asm.imup"
"01-Jul-2005 19:46:58 200 ora.ha.oradb4.ASM1.asm.imcheck"
"01-Jul-2005 19:46:58 200 ora.ha.oradb4.ASM1.asm.imup"
"01-Jul-2005 19:47:48 200 ora.ha.SSKYDB.SSKY1.inst.imcheck"
"01-Jul-2005 19:47:48 200 ora.ha.SSKYDB.SSKY1.inst.imup"
"01-Jul-2005 19:52:38 200 ora.ha.oradb3.ASM2.asm.imcheck"
"01-Jul-2005 19:52:38 200 ora.ha.oradb3.ASM2.asm.imup"
"01-Jul-2005 19:57:00 200 ora.ha.oradb4.ASM1.asm.imcheck"
"01-Jul-2005 19:57:00 200 ora.ha.oradb4.ASM1.asm.imup"
"01-Jul-2005 19:57:50 200 ora.ha.SSKYDB.SSKY1.inst.imcheck"
"01-Jul-2005 19:57:50 200 ora.ha.SSKYDB.SSKY1.inst.imup"
```

The output above illustrates two types of actions sent and received. An imcheck action is sent to determine the state of the resources defined in the OCR, and a subsequent response is received that provides the current state (imup) of the resource (similar to a reply message for the initial verification request). All actions and responses are user-defined (identified by ora) HA services (identified by ha), and all communications are performed at priority 200. The output also illustrates that such verification happens continuously; for example, first at 19:42:36 hours an action is sent to verify the state of instance ASM2 on node oradb3; the action is repeated again at 19:52:38 hours.

Other types of actions sent and received by the EVMD are listed in Table 7.3.

Table 7.3 *EVMD Actions*

Action	Priority	Function
Error	500	No response is received for the action sent.
transition	300	The event is in a state-change process. Normally, the action is received when a resource or service is initially started, stopped, or failing over.
DOWN	200	The resource or service is currently down.
running	300	The service or resource is currently in an execution state. This state is normally seen in cluster services or applications managed by the Oracle Clusterware (e.g., crs).
UP	200	The service or resource specified is up.
imstop	200	This indicates an HA service stop action.
relocatefailed	300	There has been an attempt to relocate a service or resource from one node to another; however, this relocation attempt failed. This action normally follows other actions, such as imstop or stopped.
stopped	300	The application has completely stopped execution.

7.5 Oracle Clusterware interface

In Oracle Database 10g Release 2, Oracle provides a new framework to protect third-party applications in a clustered configuration from failures, by starting, stopping, and relocating them to other nodes in the cluster. This means that Oracle Clusterware can be installed independently of having a RAC license and requires, at a minimum, the following:

1. Cluster of two or more nodes

2. Dedicated private network/interconnect for cluster-related communication

3. Quorum/shared storage location to locate the OCR and vote disks

4. Minimum Oracle license of either an SE or EE version

The Oracle Clusterware consists of two components: (1) the scripting interface, and (2) the Oracle Clusterware API.

7.5.1 Scripting interface framework

The framework calls a control application using a script-based agent. The agent is invoked by the Oracle Clusterware using one of three commands:

Start   Informs the agent to start the application.
Check   Informs the agent to check the application at predefined intervals set when the resource was first registered in the OCR. When this command is executed, it returns a Boolean value of one or zero. Zero indicates that the application is running.
Stop   Informs the agent that it should stop the application.

The details relating to the interaction and management of the application are stored in the OCR.

To add a script to be managed by the clusterware framework, the following steps are to be performed:

1.   *Create an application VIP.* This is required if the application is accessed via network clients. The application VIP allows network address migration when the node fails, and it allows the application to continue using the same address to access the database, avoiding any name resolution issues.

     a.   An application VIP is created by first defining the profile of the application. For example, the following will create an application called `appsvip` using the `crs_profile` utility:

```
[oracle@oradb3 oracle]$ $ORA_CRS_HOME/bin/crs_profile -
create appsvip -t application -a / $ORA_CRS_HOME/bin/
usrvip -o oi=eth0,ov=192.168.2.75,on=255.255.255.0
```

 Note: This syntax does not allow spaces between values for the –o parameter.

This command will create the `appsvip.cap` file in the `$ORA_CRS_HOME/crs/crs/public` directory. The `appsvip.cap` file contains the translation of the parameters used in the `crs_profile` command above, as listed in Table 7.4.

b. Once the profile is created, it needs to be registered with the Clusterware using the `crs_register` utility:

```
[oracle@oradb3 oracle]$ crs_register appsvip
```

This command will register the application `appsvip` with the Oracle Clusterware and make an entry in the OCR. The definition in the OCR can be verified using the `crs_stat` utility:

```
[oracle@oradb3 oracle]$ crs_stat appsvip
NAME=appsvip
TYPE=application
TARGET=OFFLINE
STATE=OFFLINE
```

As noted in the output above, while `appsvip` is registered with the OCR, it currently remains in an offline state.

c. Similar to the database VIP used by the database, the application VIP also needs to be executed as a `root` user. The ownership of the application can be changed using the `crs_setperm` utility as follows:

```
[root@oradb3 root]# crs_setperm appsvip -o root
```

 Note: On UNIX-based systems, the application VIP should run as the root user, and on Windows systems, this should be run as the administrator.

d. While user "root" is the owner of the VIP, the "oracle" user needs to execute this application, hence the privileges will need to be changed, giving `oracle` the `execute` rights:

```
[root@oradb3 root]# crs_setperm appsvip -u
user:oracle:r-x
```

e. Now the new application `appsvip` is ready to be started
    and accessed by another application. This command can
    now be executed as user "oracle":

```
[oracle@oradb3 oracle]$ crs_start appsvip
Attempting to start `appsvip` on member `oradb3`
Start of `appsvip` on member `oradb3` succeeded.
```

 Note: The application `appsvip` will also start automatically on node
reboot.

2. *Create an action program.* This program is used by Oracle Cluster-
    ware to start, stop, and query the status of the protected applica-
    tion. This program can be written in C, Java, or almost any
    scripting language.

3. *Create an application profile.* Similar to the application VIP profile
    created above, an application profile will also need to be created
    using the script defined in the previous step. For example, define
    the `oas_cluster` application:

```
[oracle@oradb3 oracle]$crs_profile -create oas_cluster
-t application -r appsvip -a $CRS_HOME/crs/public/
oas_cluster.scr -o ci=5,ra=60
```

In this output, notice that the additional parameter `-r apps-
vip` indicates a required resource that should be available prior to
starting the application `oas_cluster`. Similarly, `ci=5` indicates
the check interval between verification of the application's health
and availability, and `ra=60` indicates the number of restart
attempts before sending an alert message.

4. *Register the application script with the clusterware.* Register the
    application script with Oracle Clusterware. The `crs_register`
    utility reads the `*.cap` file and updates the OCR. These resources
    can have dependencies on other resources. For example, for
    `oas_cluster` to start, `appsvip` should be started.

At this point, the application is registered with Oracle Clusterware and entries are made in the OCR. Oracle Clusterware can now control the availability of this service, restarting on process failure and relocating on node failure. Once registered, the profile stored in the OCR can be changed dynamically using the `crs_register -update` command.

A simple example for implementing an application to use the clusterware without the VIP would be to script the startup of the EM `dbconsole` and register the script with Oracle Clusterware to start `dbconsole` automatically on reboot of the node.

Table 7.4 *Clusterware Application Configuration Parameters*

Parameter	Description
`NAME`	Name of the application/resource. Identified by the `crs_profile —create` **`resource_name`**
`TYPE`	Type of resource; the two values currently available are application and generic. Identified by `crs_profile - create` `resource_name` **`-t`** < >
`ACTION_SCRIPT`	The script that will manage the HA solution. Identified by `crs_profile — create` `resource_name` **`—a`** < **`action script`** **`location and name>`**
`ACTIVE_PLACEMENT`	The placement or node(s) where this application will reside. Identified by `crs_profile —create` `resource_name` **`—o ap=<active place-`** **`ment policy>`**
`AUTO_START`	Indicator of whether the application/resource will start automatically during system startup. Identified by `crs_profile` **`-o`** **`as=auto_start`** parameter
`CHECK_INTERVAL`	Time (in seconds) between repeated executions of a resource's action program. Identified by `crs_profile` **`—o`** **`ci=<check_interval>`** parameter

Table 7.4   *Clusterware Application Configuration Parameters (continued)*

Parameter	Description
FAILOVER_DELAY	Time delay (in seconds) to wait before attempting to failover a resource. Identified by `crs_profile –o fd=<failover_delay>` parameter
FAILURE_INTERVAL	Time period (in seconds) within which the threshold defined by FAILURE_THRESHOLD count is applied. Identified by `crs_profile –o ci=check_interval` parameter
FAILURE_THRESHOLD	Number of failures allowed within the FAILURE_INTERVAL. The number of failures reaches the threshold value; the resource is set moved to an OFFLINE state. The maximum value allowed for this parameter is 20. Identified by `crs_profile –o ft=<failover_threshold>` parameter
HOSTING_MEMBERS	List of nodes to use in order of preference when the Oracle Clusterware starts or fails over an application on which the resource can run. The list of hosts in this parameter is used if the placement policy defined by the PLACMENT parameter is `favored` or `restricted`. The value is a NULL when PLACMENT is balanced across all nodes in the cluster. Identified by `crs_profile – create resource_name –h < list of hosting members>`
OPTIONAL_RESOURCES	List of resources that, if found running will determine where the resource will run. Used as an optimization to determine the start or failover order. Parameter supports 58 optional resources. Identified by `crs_profile – create resource_name –l < list of optional resources>`

Table 7.4   *Clusterware Application Configuration Parameters (continued)*

Parameter	Description
PLACEMENT	Definition of the rules for choosing the node on which to start or restart an application. This is a restricted parameter. It is balanced and favored when applied to `HOSTING_MEMBERS` parameter, and the current activity determines where a resource will or may run. Valid values are `balanced` (default), `favored`, and `restricted`. The application must be accessible by the nodes that are nominated for placement. Identified by `crs_profile` − `create resource_name` **−p < placement policy>**
REQUIRED_RESOURCES	Resources required by an application that must be running for the application to start. All required resources should have registered with Oracle Clusterware for the application to start. The Oracle Clusterware relocates or stops an application if a required resource becomes unavailable. Required resources should be defined for each node. Identified by `crs_profile` − `create resource_name` **−r <list of one or more required resources>**
RESTART_ATTEMPTS	Number of times Oracle Clusterware attempts to restart a resource on a node before attempting to relocate the resource to another node (if specified). Identified by `crs_profile` **−o ra=<number of restart attempts>** parameter
SCRIPT_TIMEOUT	Seconds (default 60) to wait for a return from the action script. Identified by `crs_profile` **−o st=<script timeout interval specified in seconds>** parameter
UPTIME_THRESHOLD	The time (seconds) that the resource should be up before the clusterware considers it a stable resource. Identified by `crs_profile` **−o ut=uptime threshold** parameter
USR_ORA_ALERT_NAME	An Oracle-generated alert message when conditions such as threshold values are met.
USR_ORA_CHECK_TIMEOUT	The timeout period for the check interval.

Table 7.4   *Clusterware Application Configuration Parameters (continued)*

Parameter	Description
USR_ORA_CONNECT_STR	A connect string used by the application to establish a connection to the database (e.g., `/as sysdba`)
USR_ORA_DEBUG	Values of 0, 1, or 2, which, when set, will produce debug output for the resource.
USR_ORA_DISCONNECT	Indicator of whether to disconnect sessions prior to stopping or relocating a service.
USR_ORA_FLAGS	UNKNOWN
USR_ORA_IF	Parameter used only when the resource is a VIP. It specifies the network.
USR_ORA_INST_NOT_SHUT DOWN	UNKNOWN
USR_ORA_LANG	UNKNOWN
USR_ORA_NETMASK	Parameter used only when the resource is a VIP. It specifies the netmask.
USR_ORA_OPEN_MODE	The default instance start mode. Valid values are `NOMOUNT`, `MOUNT`, and `OPEN`.
USR_ORA_OPI	UNKNOWN
USR_ORA_PFILE	Specification of an alternate parameter file for the resource, or used for other databases managed by the CRS. For example, it's used by `racg` process to start or stop a database instance.
USR_ORA_PRECONNECT	Parameter used for services configured with TAF
USR_ORA_SRV	UNKNOWN
USR_ORA_START_TIMEOUT	UNKNOWN
USR_ORA_STOP_MODE	UNKNOWN
USR_ORA_STOP_TIMEOUT	UNKNOWN
USR_ORA_VIP	Parameter used by the VIP service to store the VIP for the node

Best Practice: For consistency and keeping the definitions error free, the parameters in Table 7.4 are to be defined using the `crs_profile` and not by editing the `*.cap` files directly.

7.5.2 Oracle Clusterware API

The API is used to register user applications to the Oracle Clusterware system so that they can be managed by Oracle Clusterware and made highly available. When an application is registered, the application can be started and its state queried. If the application is no longer to be run, it can be stopped and unregistered from Oracle Clusterware. One of the great flexibilities of using the API is that it can be used to modify, at runtime, how an application is managed by Oracle Clusterware. These APIs communicate with the `crsd` process using an IPC mechanism. The clusterware API

- Is a C API that provides a programmatic interface to the clusterware.

- Provides operational control of resources managed by the clusterware.

- Communicates with the CRS Daemon, which is a clusterware process running outside the database server. The communication occurs through an IPC mechanism.

- Is used to register, start, query, stop, and unregister resources with the clusterware.

7.6 Conclusion

In this chapter, we viewed with illustrations the various configuration and administration utilities for Oracle Clusterware. These utilities provide a helping hand to DBAs, providing insight into several functional aspects of Oracle Clusterware. With the exposure of certain API and programming interfaces, Oracle has provided opportunities to implement third-party and homegrown applications in a high-availability environment.

8

Backup and Recovery

Every single system is prone to failures, be they natural, mechanical, or electronic; they can involve computer hardware, application servers, applications, databases, and network connectivity. Based on the critical nature of the application system, its data, and its everyday use, in the event of these types of failures, an alternative way to provide the required service and/or a method to keep all the systems functioning is needed. Electronic devices such as computer hardware come in many forms to make up the entire enterprise configuration. Normally, protection against hardware failures is achieved by providing redundancy at all tiers of the configuration. This helps because when one component fails, its backup component will take up the slack and help the system continue to function.

On the database side, the storage system that physically stores the data needs to be protected. Mirroring the disk, where the data is copied to another disk to provide safety and failover when a disk in the array fails, provides the required redundancy against disk failures. The disk-redundant configuration is achieved by choosing an appropriate storage solution, as discussed in Chapter 3.

What happens when a privileged user deletes rows from a table in a production database? What happens when this damage is only noticed a few days after the accident occurred? What happens when lightning hits the production center and the electric grid, causing a short circuit that damages the entire storage subsystem? In all of these situations, an alternative method above and beyond the redundant hardware architecture is required. The most practical solution is to have a process in place that will retrieve and recover the lost data.

The solution will be based on the criticality and the business uptime or continuity requirements. If the application and users need access to the database immediately with almost no downtime, then a remote database (disaster recovery site) needs to be maintained, with data feeds using products such as Oracle Data Guard or Oracle Streams keeping the remote location in sync with the primary location. Also, irrespective of the basic business requirements of uptime, data needs to be saved regularly to another media and stored in a remote location. Such a method of data storage will protect the enterprise from losing its valuable data. The method of copying data from a live system for storage in a remote location is called a *backup process.*

Note: Configurations using Oracle Data Guard and Streams are discussed in Chapter 10. Backup and recovery methods for a database under RAC are similar to the procedures used in a single-instance database configuration. RAC supports all the backup features of an Oracle database running in a single-instance mode.

While defining database configuration specifications, the following should be considered:

- If loss of data is unacceptable, the `ARCHIVELOG` mode should be enabled.
- All instances in a RAC configuration should be set to automatic archiving.
- The archive destination for each instance needs to be available to each specific instance only during normal operation, but they have to be made available to the other instances performing recovery following a media failure.
- Raw partitions should not be used for archive log files because each archive will overwrite the previous one.

Based on the type of storage methods selected for the database files, there are several ways to perform a database backup. However, as a best practice when using RAC, Oracle Recovery Manager (RMAN) should be the preferred tool for backup and recovery. When database files are stored on devices configured using ASM, RMAN is the only method supported to back them up.

Note: Considering these requirements, this chapter will only focus on RMAN and other supported backup methods.

8.1   **Recovery Manager**

RMAN is a component of the Oracle database that provides a tightly integrated method for creating, managing, restoring, and recovering Oracle database backups. This tool supports hot, cold, and incremental backups. RMAN provides an option for maintaining a repository called the recovery catalog that contains information about backup files and archived log files. RMAN uses the recovery catalog to automate the restore operation and the media recovery.

RMAN determines the most efficient method of executing the requested backup, restore, or recovery operation and then executes these operations in conjunction with the Oracle database server. The RMAN process and the server can automatically identify modifications to the database and dynamically adjust the required operation to adapt to the changes. For example, if a database restore is done from a two-week-old backup set, the restore operation using RMAN understands all metadata changes until date and applies them from the appropriate backup/archive log files.

RMAN offers a wide variety of new features over the traditional full and hot backup options. Some of the key features are

- Recovery at the block level
- Backup retention policy
- Persistent configuration
- Automatic channel allocation
- Multiplex archived log backups
- Space management during archive logs restoration
- Archive log failover
- Backup of the server parameter file
- Control file auto backup
- Enterprise Manager support

8.2   **RMAN components**

Figure 8.1 illustrates the various components that make up the RMAN process and how these various components interact with each other. It also illustrates how the certified external media process (MML) that backs up

Figure 8.1
RMAN
Components

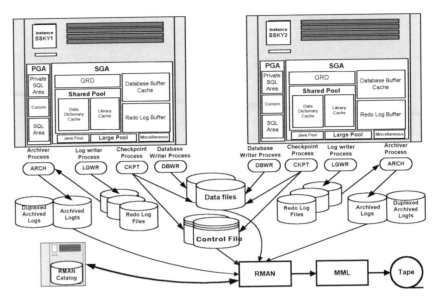

the data to an external medium, such as a tape device, interacts with the RMAN process. Let us briefly look at some of the RMAN components and how they interact with each other:

8.2.1 RMAN process

In order to use RMAN, the RMAN executable has to be invoked. All functions of the backup and recovery process are handled through this executable. This implies that the RMAN process is the central component of the entire backup and recovery operation.

RMAN writes its backup to an exclusive backup format called the *backup set*. A backup set can have many backup pieces. One backup task which can be the backup of a tablespace or database or archived logs can have more than one backup set, but only RMAN can read from these backup sets while performing recovery. The backups of datafiles and archived logs cannot be in the same backup set. By default, any backup set will contain 4 or fewer datafiles or 16 or fewer archived log files. The size of any backup set can be configured by MAXSETSIZE. RMAN inherently backs up only the used blocks and will never attempt to copy never-used blocks, which reduces the overall size of the backups. Starting with Oracle Database 10*g*, one can use binary compression to compress further the backups of datafiles and archived redo log files by merely adding AS COMPRESSED BACKUPSET to the backup commands. No special commands are required to restore this compressed backup set because RMAN is aware of this compression.

RMAN backups can be incremental or full. Incremental backups can only be done for datafiles and capture the changes made to each of the blocks when compared to a base-level backup (level 0). This results in a smaller backup set unless every block has seen a change. The only limitation here is that RMAN has to read all the blocks to select the blocks to be copied to the incremental backup by comparing the System Change Number (SCN) in the block header with the SCN of the parent backup (i.e., level 0). This can be an issue for large databases. To overcome this, Oracle Database 10*g* has introduced a new background process called change tracking, which will keep track of all the changed blocks in a file, and the incremental backup feature, will backup only the blocks recorded in this file. The change tracking feature is discussed later in the chapter.

8.2.2 Channels

In order to communicate with the I/O device, such as a tape or a disk system, RMAN processes need to open a communication link between these devices. There can be multiple such links, called channels. Based on the number of I/O devices to be backed up, several channels can be opened at the same time; these channels can be invoked for parallel or asynchronous access to these devices or configured to backup in sequential order.

8.2.3 Target database

The database that is being backed up by the RMAN process is called the target database. In Figure 8.1, RMAN interacts with one target database called SSKYDB. Since this is a RAC implementation, this database can have two or more instances, for example, SSKY1, SSKY2, SSKY3, and SSKY4. The main difference in the implementation of RMAN in a RAC environment compared to a stand-alone environment is that each instance has a copy of the redo log files, and these redo log files may be archived to an instance-specific archive log destination. These archive log destination disks should be visible from all instances in the clustered configuration. This has two purposes:

1.   For RMAN to backup these archive log files

2.   To provide visibility for recovery purposes during media recovery when the instance to which the archive log files belongs to has crashed

As an alternative, the archive logs can also be located on the shared storage. This is more convenient and a commonly practiced approach for several reasons. Apart from convenience during administration, it also provides easy accessibility when one node in the cluster fails and the database needs to be restored, in which case the RMAN can access the archive logs of the failed node and apply them.

8.2.4 Recovery catalog database

The recovery catalog, as illustrated in Figure 8.1, is optional and is a separate, independent database isolated from the target or primary database. It acts as a repository used by RMAN to store backup and recovery activities performed on the target database. The catalog database does not contain the actual physical backup files from the target database the recovery catalog is an optional component. If the recovery catalog is not used, RMAN information is stored in the control file of the target database.

8.2.5 Media Management Layer

The Media Management Layer (MML) is a media management software layer that has traditionally been used for managing data stored on external storage such as tape. For example, the VERITAS NetBackup and Legato backup utilities are MML products.

8.3   Recovery features

8.3.1 Flash recovery

In Oracle Database 9i, Oracle introduced the concept of the flashback query. When using this feature, Oracle used information from the undo segments to recover quickly all data that was accidentally changed or deleted. An initialization parameter, UNDO_RETENTION, specified the duration to preserve data to be used by the flashback query.

In Oracle Database 10g, this feature has been enhanced. Based on the space allocated for this area, the entire database can be recovered. The flashback retention target specifies how far back into the past the database is restorable. While the FLASHBACK DATABASE command would require RMAN to restore the database, the FLASHBACK TABLE command can be executed from any SQL Plus session. The flashback feature is useful especially to recover from logical corruptions and user-related errors.

In Oracle Database 10*g*, the flash recovery area (FRA), a file system, directory, or ASM disk group can be set up to manage all recovery-related files, including archive logs and backups, and to automate the deletion of files that fall outside the retention policy. Flash recovery is configured using two parameters:

1. *DB_RECOVERY_FILE_DEST.* This is the physical location where the data required to perform the flashback recovery will be retained. In a RAC environment, this should be on shared storage. The physical location can be on either an ASM disk group or a clustered file system such as OCFS; however, it should not be on raw devices because raw devices do not have the ability to store multiple files in these partitions, and when archive logs are stored on a raw device partition, each new archive will overwrite the previous one.

2. *DB_RECOVERY_FILE_DEST_SIZE.* This parameter defines the size of the FRA determines the amount of data that will be stored, and affects the flashback retention target value.

Sizing the flashback area

The recovery area requires a space quota, and because it is bound by a predefined limit, all necessary files that will be managed in this area must be considered when sizing it. If only archive logs and control file backups are needed, then estimate how many archive logs are generated between backups on the busiest day, and multiply their size by two to leave a margin of error.

If archive logs and flashback database logs should be kept, then multiply the archive log sizes on each instance in a RAC cluster between backups by four. If the backup strategy is to have RMAN incremental backups stored in this area, then the typical size of the incremental backup should be determined and that value added. The size of an incremental backup is very dependent on the database workload.

Finally, if archive logs, flashback logs, incremental backups and an on-disk backup must be kept, then add the size of the database minus the size of the temp files. A rough rule of thumb for this final case is two times the database size (minus temp files).

When a flash recovery area is configured and no specific archive destination target is available, parameters have to be defined. FRA will store the archive log files in subdirectories grouped by date. Oracle creates a new

directory every day at midnight, meaning, a new directory is created by date
to store all the archive log files generated that day. The directory names have
the format YYYY_MM_DD. For example, the following directory structure contains the archive logs for dates October 3, 4, and 5, 2005.

```
[oracle@oradb3 oracle]$ ls -ltr /u14/oradata/SSKYDB/archivelog/
total 128
drwxr-x---    1 oracle    dba           131072 Oct  3 00:20 2005_10_03
drwxr-x---    1 oracle    dba           131072 Oct  4 11:40 2005_10_04
drwxr-x---    1 oracle    dba           131072 Oct  5 11:20 2005_10_05
```

The amount of information retained in this area is determined by the
parameter DB_FLASHBACK_RETENTION_TARGET expressed in seconds. This
retention time should also be considered when sizing this area.

Data is purged from this area based on the retention policy and the total
size of the FRA. Besides this parameter, purging from this area is also determined by the amount of space available. Oracle starts removing files from
this area only when the flash recovery area is 90% full and the retention
policy defined by the parameter DB_FLASHBACK_RETENTION_TARGET is
reached; otherwise, it will write information until it is 100% full.

Depending upon the retention policy, RMAN will declare a backup
obsolete. Oracle will automatically handle this task. If the FRA is not used,
this has to be handled manually. Once the files in the FRA have been copied to tape, then they are internally placed on a "Files to Be Deleted" list
(V$RECOVERY_FILE_DEST.RECLAIMABLE). Now, Oracle will automatically
remove files from the FRA whenever space is required in the FRA. Once
you copy the FRA (backup recovery area) to tape, all the space is now
reclaimable by the backup and will be consumed by RMAN whenever
required. RMAN will not remove files from the FRA until the space is
required by future backups. The primary objective here is to keep the backups on disks so that time lost is minimal during recovery. The following
query shows that the FRA area has been backed up to tape using the
RMAN command BACKUP RECOVERY AREA, and now all the space can be
used if required.

```
COL NAME FORMAT A20
SELECT * FROM V$RECOVERY_FILE_DEST
NAME                 SPACE_LIMIT SPACE_USED SPACE_RECLAIMABLE NUMBER_OF_FILES
-------------------- ----------- ---------- ----------------- ---------------
```

```
/usr06/FRA          10737418240 4091265024        4091265024              16
1 row selected


SELECT * FROM V$FLASH_RECOVERY_AREA_USAGE;

FILE_TYPE    PERCENT_SPACE_USED PERCENT_SPACE_RECLAIMABLE NUMBER_OF_FILES
-----------  ------------------ ------------------------- ---------------
CONTROLFILE                   0                         0               0
ONLINELOG                     0                         0               0
ARCHIVELOG                  .94                        .2               8
BACKUPPIECE               12.26                     12.26              12
IMAGECOPY                 50.39                     50.39              13
FLASHBACKLOG                  0                         0               0
```

The FRA cannot be stored on a raw file system. In a RAC environment, the FRA should be on a CFS or ASM. The location and quota must be the same on all the instances. If the LOG_ARCHIVE_DEST_n is not set, then LOG_ARCHIVE_DEST_10 is automatically set to FRA, and archived logs are sent to the location specified by this parameter, as shown below:

```
SQL> archive log list;
Database log mode              Archive Mode
Automatic archival             Enabled
Archive destination            USE_DB_RECOVERY_FILE_DEST
Oldest online log sequence     11
Next log sequence to archive   13
Current log sequence           13
```

8.3.2 Change tracking

Prior to Oracle Database 10g, when RMAN performed incremental backups, the RMAN process would scan through each block in the database, read the block, inspect it, and see if it needed to be backed up. Each time a change block was found, it was written to the backup set. Besides the time taken to perform an incremental backup, scanning through all datafiles to determine changed blocks consumed a large number of resources, causing contention with regular database activity.

In Oracle Database 10g, a new feature called change tracking is introduced to help resolve these issues. Under this feature, all blocks that are changed are written to a predefined and predetermined area by the Change

Tracking Writer (CTWR) background process. The change tracking area is defined for the entire database using the following command:

```
SQL> ALTER DATABASE ENABLE BLOCK CHANGE TRACKING USING FILE
     '/u05/oradata/ChngTrack.dbf';
```

The RMAN incremental backup process will read through this area to determine changed blocks. Once the changed blocks are identified, RMAN will only scan through changed blocks in the respective datafiles and back them up. This improves the overall performance of the database and significantly reduces time consumed for the incremental backup operations. In a RAC configuration, the change tracking area should be on shared storage to allow the CTWR process from each instance to write block changes to a different location (identified by the thread number) on the same file, eliminating any kind of locking or internode block-swapping activity.

By default, Oracle allocates 10 MB of space, when the file is first created, and increases it in 10-MB increments if required. Since the file contains data representing every datafile block in the database, the total size of the database and the number of instances (threads) should be considered when sizing this file.

A rule of thumb used by Oracle for sizing this file is 1/250,000th, or 0.0004%, of the total database size, plus twice the number of threads, plus the number of RMAN backups retained (maximum of eight backups), with a minimum size of 10 MB.

 Note: The block change tracking file records all changes between previous backups for a maximum of eight backups.

The change tracking definition can be verified using the following query:

```
SELECT STATUS,
       FILENAME
FROM   V$BLOCK_CHANGE_TRACKING;

STATUS     FILENAME
---------- ------------------------------
ENABLED    /u05/oradata/ChngTrack.dbf
```

The change tracking area can also be defined on an ASM disk group using the following command:

```
SQL > ALTER DATABASE ENABLE BLOCK CHANGE TRACKING USING FILE '+ASMGRP1';

SELECT STATUS,
       FILENAME,
       BYTES
FROM   V$BLOCK_CHANGE_TRACKING;

STATUS     FILENAME                                                     BYTES
---------- ------------------------------------------------------ ----------
ENABLED    +ASMGRP1/rac10gdb/changetracking/ctf.274.572095019       11599872
```

8.3.3 Backup encryption

Encryption provides maximum security, making contents unreadable without first decrypting the information. Leveraging the Oracle Advanced Security Option (ASO) technology, all RMAN backups are encrypted. This protects users from eavesdropping, tampering, or message forgery and replay attacks. The RMAN backup encryption to disk feature is available with ASO.

The RMAN encryption offers three configurable modes of operation:

1. *Transparent mode* (default) is best suited for day-to-day backup operations, where backups will be restored on the same database they were backed up from. This requires the Oracle Encryption Wallet (OEW).

2. *Password mode* is useful for backups that will be restored at remote locations but must remain secure in transit. Under this mode, the DBA is required to provide a password when creating and restoring encrypted backups. Under this mode, OEW is not required.

3. *Dual mode* is useful when most restorations are made on-site using the OEW, but occasionally off-site restoration is required without access to the wallet. Either a wallet or password may be used to restore dual-mode-encrypted RMAN backups.

To use RMAN encryption, the COMPATIBLE initialization parameter at the target database must be set to at least 10.2.0. RMAN encrypted backups are decrypted automatically during restore and recover operations, as long as the required decryption keys are available, by means of either a user-supplied password or the OEW.

Encryption is enabled by setting a configuration parameter using RMAN:

```
RMAN> CONFIGURE ENCRYPTION FOR DATABASE ON;
```

By enabling encryption using the above command, all RMAN backup sets created by the database will be encrypted.

The V$RMAN_ENCRYPTION_ALGORITHMS view contains a list of encryption algorithms supported by RMAN. If no encryption algorithm is specified, the default encryption algorithm is 128-bit Advanced Encryption Standard (AES).

```
SELECT ALGORITHM_NAME,
       ALGORITHM_DESCRIPTION,
       IS_DEFAULT
FROM   V$RMAN_ENCRYPTION_ALGORITHMS;


ALGORITHM_NAME          ALGORITHM_DESCRIPTION          IS_DEFAULT
--------------------    -------------------------      ----------
AES128                  AES 128-bit key                YES
AES192                  AES 192-bit key                NO
AES256                  AES 256-bit key                NO
```

8.4   Configuring RMAN for RAC

The configuration procedure differs depending on if the flash recovery option is used. Basically, this is the difference between autoarchiving or manual archiving. If no flash recovery feature is used, then a separate archive log destination area should be defined (manual archiving). The archive log files being stored on ASM volumes can be stored in storage media that are only visible to the instance or node that is connected to the device. This is possible only if these devices are visible to the instance or node that is performing the recovery operation.

Step 1 has two separate sets of configuration details concerning the flashback option or archive log option. The remainder of the steps apply in both scenarios.

1. When defining the archive log destination, the following parameters should be set:

```
log_archive_dest          = /u14/oradata/arch/

SSKY1.log_archive_format = 'SSKY1_%T_%S_%r.arc'
SSKY2.log_archive_format = 'SSKY2_%T_%S_%r.arc'
```

The archive log-naming format specified by the LOG_ARCHIVE_FORMAT parameter above includes the resetlogs ID represented by %r as part of the format string. This allows RMAN for easy recovery of a database from a previous backup. When defining the FRA, the following parameters should be set:

```
db_recovery_file_dest      = /u14/oradata/
db_recovery_file_dest_size = 200G
```

Note: No archive log destination parameter is required when using the FRA. Archiving is automatic and will use the same destination as defined by the DB_RECOVERY_FILE_DEST parameter.

If the database is configured to use SPFILE, the parameters can be set dynamically using the following syntax:

```
ALTER SYSTEM SET PARAMETER <parameter name> = <value>
SCOPE=SPFILE;
```

Note: Flash recovery changes can also be made using the EM dbconsole or GC interface, as illustrated in Figure 8.2.

2. The database is shutdown and started in MOUNT mode. The database needs to be in MOUNT mode to enable archiving. At this time, all other instances in the RAC cluster should be shut down.

```
SQL>
SQL> SHUTDOWN IMMEDIATE
Database closed.
Database dismounted.
ORACLE instance shut down.

SQL>
SQL> STARTUP MOUNT
ORACLE instance started.

Total System Global Area  205520896 bytes
Fixed Size                  1218012 bytes
Variable Size              90794532 bytes
Database Buffers          113246208 bytes
Redo Buffers                 262144 bytes
Database mounted.
```

3. Verify this, and if the instance is not in ARCHIVELOG mode, set it to ARCHIVELOG mode.

```
SELECT NAME,
       LOG_MODE
FROM V$DATABASE
/

NAME       LOG_MODE
---------  ------------
SSKYDB     NOARCHIVELOG
```

4. Enable archive log mode using the following command:

```
SQL>
SQL> ALTER DATABASE ARCHIVELOG;

Database altered.
```

5. Verify if the changes have taken effect:

```
SELECT NAME,
       LOG_MODE
```

```
FROM V$DATABASE
/

NAME       LOG_MODE
---------  ------------
SSKYDB     ARCHIVELOG
```

6.   Open the database and start the instances:

```
SQL> ALTER DATABASE OPEN;

Database altered.
```

7.   Verify if archiving is enabled:

```
SQL> ARCHIVE LOG LIST
Database log mode                Archive Mode
Automatic archival               Enabled
Archive destination              USE_DB_RECOVERY_FILE_DEST
Oldest online log sequence       54
Next log sequence to archive     55
Current log sequence             55
```

 Note: In the above output, the archive destination value USE_DB_RECOVERY_FILE_DEST indicates that autoarchiving with flashback recovery is configured.

8.   The next step is to verify if the archive log files are created in the appropriate destinations. To complete this test, perform a redo log file switch using the following command:

```
SQL>ALTER SYSTEM SWITCH LOGFILE
```

9.   Verify if the archive log files are created in the appropriate directory:

```
[oracle@oradb3 archivelog]$ ls —ltr /u14/oradata/SSKYDB/archivelog
total 0
drwxr-x---   1 oracle   dba          131072 Oct  5 00:20 2005_10_05
[oracle@oradb3 oracle]$
```

10.   If using automatic FRA, the next step is to enable this feature:

```
SQL> ALTER DATABASE FLASHBACK ON;
```

11.   Verify if the flashback feature is enabled:

```
SELECT NAME,
        DATABASE_ROLE,
        FLASHBACK_ON
 FROM V$DATABASE;


NAME       DATABASE_ROLE      FLASHBACK_ON
---------  ----------------   ------------------
SSKYDB     PRIMARY            YES
```

Figure 8.2
EM Recovery
Settings

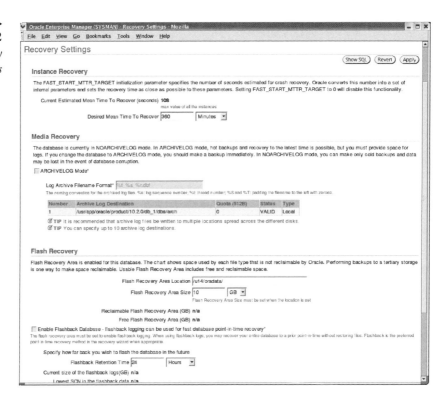

Files backed up using RMAN can be written to disk or tape directly. Many organizations, based on their backup strategies, may decide to keep a few days' worth of backup on disk for easy access if needed, in which case, the backup is stored on disk and then copied from disk to tape through another backup operation. When disks are used for backup, these devices should also be visible from all instances participating in the cluster. In other words, these devices should also be mounted as shareable.

Note: Irrespective of the number of nodes in the cluster, in a RAC environment, the RMAN backup operations are performed by attaching to only one instance.

8.5 **Backup and recovery strategy**

Every organization will require a backup and recovery strategy and, more importantly, routine testing of recovery operations. Regular testing of the backup and recovery strategy will ensure that the business, as it changes its operations and processes, will continue to function and have little to no downtime. The actual strategy depends on organizational needs based on the criticality of data and its availability.

While backups are taken on a predefined schedule, the recovery strategy should be taken into account when defining the frequency and type of backup to be taken. This will help in restoring the database in a timely manner as defined by the business requirements. In other words, are the backups taken at intervals that will help restore a database in case of necessity, and is the time frame acceptable to the business?

8.5.1 **Types of RMAN backups**

Oracle provides two modes of incremental backup:

- *Full or level 0.* A level 0, or full, backup is a full backup of every block in the database. When defining a backup strategy, the full backup acts as a baseline every single time.

- *Incremental or level 1.* This level is simpler and has a shorter operation compared to the full, or level 0, backup. In this situation, only blocks changed since the previous incremental level 0 or level 1 backup will be backed up. Starting with Oracle Database 10*g*, if a block change tracking area is defined, the incremental level 1 backup will scan through this area instead of the entire database.

 Note: The cumulative backup mode (level 2), which existed prior to Oracle Database 10*g*, has been depreciated.

RMAN-based backup strategies are implemented using these backup types. For example, Tables 8.1 and 8.2 illustrate two different backup schedules that support two different business needs. Table 8.2 illustrates a closer backup operation to support a smaller recovery window, limiting itself to using only two or three backup sets in case a complete restore of the database is required. On the other hand, the backup schedule listed in Table 8.1 is dispersed, and the recovery time would be much longer.

Table 8.1   *Backup Schedule One*

Day of Week	Type of Backup
Sunday	Full
Monday	Incremental
Tuesday	Incremental
Wednesday	Incremental
Thursday	Incremental
Friday	Incremental
Saturday	Incremental

Table 8.2 has two backup schedules per day; these backups will be taken approximately 12 hours apart after working around other critical processes running on the system.

Table 8.2   *Backup Schedule Two*

Day of Week	Type of Backup 11:00 AM	Type of Backup 11:00 PM
Sunday	Incremental	Full
Monday	Incremental	Incremental
Tuesday	Incremental	Incremental

Table 8.2 *Backup Schedule Two (continued)*

Day of Week	Type of Backup 11:00 AM	Type of Backup 11:00 PM
Wednesday	Incremental	Incremental
Thursday	Incremental	Incremental
Friday	Incremental	Incremental
Saturday	Incremental	Incremental

8.6 Configuring RMAN

As with similar to installing and configuring a database, Oracle provides options for configuring RMAN. RMAN can be configured using the command line or using the GUI interface available from the EM dbconsole or EM GC.

There are two modes in which RMAN can work:

1. *A catalog mode where all backup-related information is stored.* The catalog is used by RMAN during a recovery operation to determine what files are to be restored and which backup set it contains. As illustrated in Figure 8.1, the catalog is normally a separate database located on a remote node. When the catalog mode is used, the DBA can optionally store the RMAN backup scripts in the catalog for easy execution. In this case, the catalog also acts as a code management repository because, once checked in, any modification will require that the code be checked out, modified, and checked back in.

2. *A noncatalog mode where the control file of the target database is used to store all RMAN-related information.*

For our discussion in this chapter, we will look at the noncatalog mode (i.e., using a control file to store all RMAN-related information).

Based on the backup and recovery strategy defined for the organization, regular backups can be scheduled in one of two ways: by setting up command-level processes to run at scheduled intervals or by using the GUI-based interface provided by EM and its job scheduling interface.

Note: Using the DBMS_SCHEDULER package, command-line tasks can be scheduled to run on the database server.

Select the "Maintenance" tab from the EM database console home page. On this page, all backup and recovery-related tasks are listed under the "High Availability" section illustrated in Figure 8.3. Select the "Backup Settings" option. There are three tabs under this option:

1. *Device.* On this page, define the device where the backups will be stored (i.e., disk or tape), whether the backup will be in compressed format, and where the location of the backup sets will be on the disk.

2. *Backup set.* On this page, determine the size of each backup set, and other definitions will be defined.

3. *Policy.* On this page, the backup policies, such as block change tracking, are defined.

In this section, the disk-based backup option is discussed; later in this chapter, backing up to tape will be discussed.

Depending on the recovery interval and the availability of resources such as storage space, it would be advantageous if a set of backups were maintained on local storage for easy retrieval and copies of them were stored on external media, protecting it from local storage media failures. The local storage option, reduces the time required to retrieve the media from external off-site safety vaults. Considering the performance implications, when a restore of the database objects is required, due to the sequential nature in which the tape media is scanned, obtaining files from a tape device takes comparatively longer than reading directly off disk.

Once the definitions are complete, return to the "Maintenance" tab by using the back arrow on the browser window and select the "Schedule Backup" option. This displays the "Schedule Backup" screen illustrated in Figure 8.4.

As shown in the figure, the Oracle-suggested backup is based on certain predefined rules such as recovery time. Such a strategy may be useful for small to medium-sized organizations where everything has predefined standards and does not require any flexibility.

Figure 8.3
EM Maintenance
Backup/Recovery
Options

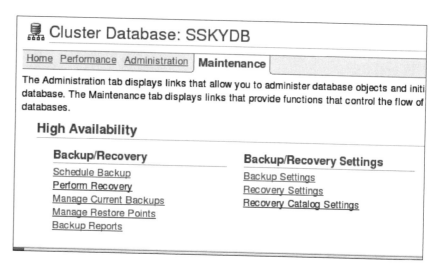

Figure 8.4
EM Schedule
Backup

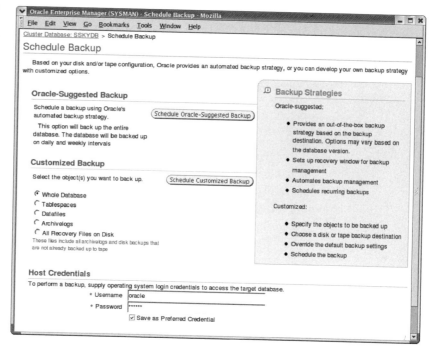

In this screen, select the type of backup to be performed: customized or the Oracle-suggested backup. Choosing the "Customized Backup" option displays the screen illustrated in Figure 8.5.

This screen provides options to configure the type and mode of backup (e.g., will this be a full or incremental backup) and subsequently to define

Figure 8.5
*EM Schedule
Customized
Backup: Options*

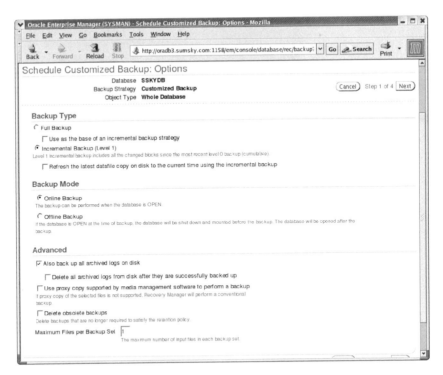

whether it will be an online or off-line backup. For our discussion, let's follow the strategy shown in Table 8.1.

As the name suggests, a full backup will perform a complete backup of the database. This backup is similar to performing an incremental backup at level 0, when the "Use as the base of an incremental backup strategy" option is selected. Following the backup strategy defined in Table 8.1, this option is selected as the primary backup to be executed on Sunday.

The incremental backup will only back up all the changed blocks since the most recent level 0 backup. The incremental backup at level 1 will be selected for a separate backup schedule for Monday, Wednesday, and Friday.

The next step is selecting the backup mode. Based on whether the database can be taken down to complete the backup operation, the appropriate mode can be selected. The online backup will ensure that the database is up and running when the backup is performed. An off-line backup will take the database off-line to perform a backup operation, at which time the database is not usable.

In our backup strategy, since the application and users will be accessing the database around the clock, the online method is selected. Click "Next" for the next screen illustrated in Figure 8.6.

Figure 8.6
EM Scheduled Customized Backup: Settings

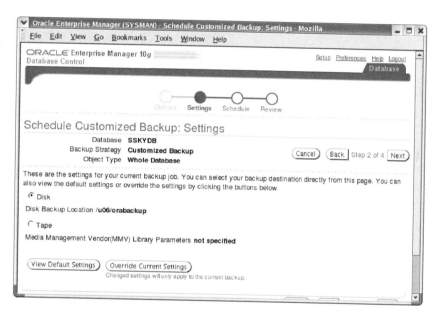

This screen is used to change the default backup settings defined earlier. The backup destination in this case is /u06/orabackup/. Backup definitions can be verified by querying the V$RMAN_CONFIGURATION view.

```
SELECT * FROM V$RMAN_CONFIGURATION


CONF# NAME                                                  VALUE
---- ------------------------------------------------  ----------------------
   1 CONTROLFILE AUTOBACKUP                               ON
   2 CONTROLFILE AUTOBACKUP FORMAT FOR DEVICE TYPE DISK TO '/u06/orabackup/%F'
   3 BACKUP OPTIMIZATION                                  ON
   4 CHANNEL                                              DEVICE TYPE DISK FORMAT    '/
u06/orabackup/%U'
```

Select option "Disk," and select "Next." This will display the screen illustrated in Figure 8.7.

Figure 8.7 provides options to schedule the backup operation. There are options to schedule backups at a regular frequency in a specific time zone,

Figure 8.7
EM Schedule
Customized
Backup: Schedule

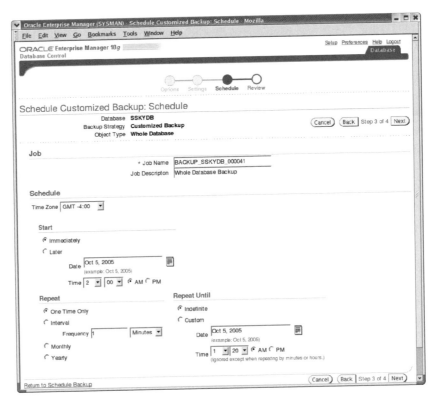

and so on. Following the backup strategy in Table 8.1, the full backup will be scheduled to run on a weekly basis.

Oracle automatically assigns a job name and description to the scheduled backup operation. When all the parameters and times are defined, click "Next." The next screen (not shown) is the review screen. Here EM lists the RMAN script for DBA verification. Once verified, click "Submit Job." Otherwise, modify the definition by selecting the "Back" icon.

The "Submit Job" option will submit the job to run in the interval and time frame specified in Figure 8.7. The backup operation summary can be viewed as illustrated in Figure 8.8.

Progress of the backup operation can be monitored using the GV$SESSION_LONGOPS view:

```
SQL> SELECT INST_ID IID,
        SID,
        OPNAME,
        SOFAR,
```

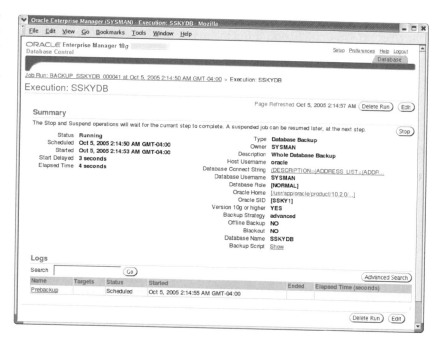

Figure 8.8

*EM Backup
Execution
Summary*

```
        TOTALWORK TOTAL,
        UNITS,
        START_TIME,
        TIME_REMAINING TR,
        ELAPSED_SECONDS ES
FROM GV$SESSION_LONGOPS
WHERE TIME_REMAINING;
```

IID	SID	OPNAME	SOFAR	TOTAL	UNITS	START_TIM	TR	ES
1	119	RMAN: incremental data file backup	20479	62720	Blocks	05-OCT-05	66	32

Note: If scripts are preferred over using the GUI, sample RMAN scripts for setting up RMAN jobs are provided in Appendix B. For a more detailed description of installation and configuration procedures for RMAN, please refer to Oracle-provided documentation.

Once the level 0 backup job has been defined and scheduled, a similar operation should be set up for incremental and cumulative backups.

A strategy does not end with just the type of backup and how frequently these backups are executed. As mentioned earlier, it only ends when it is tested during a simulated failure, and the database is recovered and made available within the time frame stipulated by the business requirements.

8.7   **Reporting in RMAN**

RMAN provides a good reporting mechanism. The RMAN utility provides various details of the backup and several other options. In this section, we will discuss how the reports are generated using the command-line interface by connecting to the target database using RMAN; for example,

```
[oracle@oradb3 oracle]$ rman target rman/<password> nocatalog
```

In the command line above using RMAN, a connection is made to the target database SSKYDB (default) as user rman in nocatalog mode.

Best Practice: For security reasons, with these kinds of operations, it is always good to maintain a separate user account with minimal privileges required for RMAN related operations.

The show all command will list the current configuration definitions used by RMAN:

```
RMAN> show all;

RMAN configuration parameters are:
CONFIGURE RETENTION POLICY TO REDUNDANCY 1; # default
CONFIGURE BACKUP OPTIMIZATION ON;
CONFIGURE DEFAULT DEVICE TYPE TO DISK; # default
CONFIGURE CONTROLFILE AUTOBACKUP ON;
CONFIGURE CONTROLFILE AUTOBACKUP FORMAT FOR DEVICE TYPE DISK TO '/u06/
orabackup/%F';
CONFIGURE DEVICE TYPE DISK BACKUP TYPE TO COMPRESSED BACKUPSET
PARALLELISM 1;
CONFIGURE DATAFILE BACKUP COPIES FOR DEVICE TYPE 'SBT_TAPE' TO 3;
CONFIGURE DATAFILE BACKUP COPIES FOR DEVICE TYPE DISK TO 1; # default
```

```
CONFIGURE ARCHIVELOG BACKUP COPIES FOR DEVICE TYPE 'SBT_TAPE' TO 3;
CONFIGURE ARCHIVELOG BACKUP COPIES FOR DEVICE TYPE DISK TO 1; #
default
CONFIGURE CHANNEL DEVICE TYPE DISK FORMAT    '/u06/orabackup/%U';
CONFIGURE MAXSETSIZE TO UNLIMITED; # default
CONFIGURE ENCRYPTION FOR DATABASE OFF; # default
CONFIGURE ENCRYPTION ALGORITHM 'AES128'; # default
CONFIGURE ARCHIVELOG DELETION POLICY TO NONE; # default
CONFIGURE SNAPSHOT CONTROLFILE NAME TO '/usr/app/oracle/product/
10.2.0/db_1/dbs/snapcf_SSKY1.f'; # default
```

The two definitions in the default configuration worth mentioning are the COMPRESSED BACKUPSET definition and the SNAPSHOT CONTROLFILE definition:

- *COMPRESSED BACKUPSET.* This option makes a compressed version of the backup sets created by the RMAN process.

- *SNAPSHOT CONTROLFILE.* To maintain a read-consistent copy of the control file during its backup operations, RMAN takes a snapshot of the file prior to starting this operation.

The report schema command provides a list of the various tablespaces and datafiles configured for the target database.

```
RMAN> report schema;


Report of database schema


List of Permanent Datafiles
===========================
File Size(MB) Tablespace   RB segs Datafile Name
---- -------- -----------  ------- ------------------------
1    490      SYSTEM       ***     +ASMGRP1/sskydb/datafile/system.256.570232691
2    30       UNDOTBS1     ***     +ASMGRP1/sskydb/datafile/undotbs1.258.570232695
3    370      SYSAUX       ***     +ASMGRP1/sskydb/datafile/sysaux.257.570232693
4    5        USERS        ***     +ASMGRP1/sskydb/datafile/users.259.570232697
5    290      EXAMPLE      ***     +ASMGRP1/sskydb/datafile/example.264.570233083
6    25       UNDOTBS2     ***     +ASMGRP1/sskydb/datafile/undotbs2.265.570233631
```

```
List of Temporary Files
========================
File Size(MB) Tablespace   Maxsize(MB) Tempfile Name
---- -------- -----------  ----------- --------------------
1    25       TEMP         32767       +ASMGRP1/sskydb/tempfile/temp.263.570233053
```

The `list backup summary` command provides a list of backup summary data. It reports when the last backup was taken and at what level (e.g.,
full, incremental), including if the backup was in compressed or noncom-
pressed mode.

```
RMAN> list backup summary;


List of Backups
===============

Key    TY LV S Device Type Completion Time #Pieces #Copies Compressed Tag
------ -- -- - ----------- --------------- ------- ------- ---------- ---
1      B  F  A DISK        05-OCT-05       1       1       NO         TAG20051005T020514
2      B  1  A DISK        05-OCT-05       1       1       NO         BACKUP_SSKYDB_0000_100505021455
3      B  1  A DISK        05-OCT-05       1       1       NO         BACKUP_SSKYDB_0000_100505021455
4      B  1  A DISK        05-OCT-05       1       1       NO         BACKUP_SSKYDB_0000_100505021455
5      B  1  A DISK        05-OCT-05       1       1       NO         BACKUP_SSKYDB_0000_100505021455
6      B  1  A DISK        05-OCT-05       1       1       NO         BACKUP_SSKYDB_0000_100505021455
7      B  1  A DISK        05-OCT-05       1       1       NO         BACKUP_SSKYDB_0000_100505021455
8      B  F  A DISK        05-OCT-05       1       1       NO         TAG20051005T021559
9      B  A  A DISK        05-OCT-05       1       1       NO         BACKUP_SSKYDB_0000_100505021455
10     B  A  A DISK        05-OCT-05       1       1       NO         BACKUP_SSKYDB_0000_100505021455
11     B  A  A DISK        05-OCT-05       1       1       NO         BACKUP_SSKYDB_0000_100505021455
12     B  A  A DISK        05-OCT-05       1       1       NO         BACKUP_SSKYDB_0000_100505021455
13     B  A  A DISK        05-OCT-05       1       1       NO         BACKUP_SSKYDB_0000_100505021455
14     B  A  A DISK        05-OCT-05       1       1       NO         BACKUP_SSKYDB_0000_100505021455
15     B  A  A DISK        05-OCT-05       1       1       NO         BACKUP_SSKYDB_0000_100505021455
16     B  A  A DISK        05-OCT-05       1       1       NO         BACKUP_SSKYDB_0000_100505021455
17     B  A  A DISK        05-OCT-05       1       1       NO         TAG20051005T021750
18     B  F  A DISK        05-OCT-05       1       1       NO
```

The `list incarnation` command lists the current database incarnation numbers:

```
RMAN> list incarnation;



List of Database Incarnations
DB Key  Inc Key DB Name DB ID             STATUS   Reset SCN  Reset Time
------- ------- -------- ----------------- ---      ---------- ----------
1       1       SSKYDB  4275027223        PARENT   1          30-JUN-05
2       2       SSKYDB  4275027223        CURRENT  446075     28-SEP-05
```

Backup operation run status can also be obtained from EM under the
"Maintenance" tab by selecting the "Backup Reports" option. When this

option is selected, a screen similar to the one illustrated in Figure 8.9 is displayed.

Figure 8.9
EM Backup
Reports

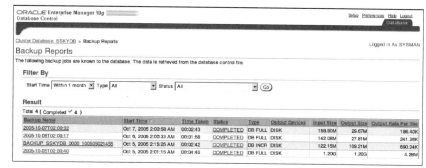

8.8 **Recovery**

Commonly, there are two types of recovery scenarios: instance recovery and database recovery.

8.8.1 **Instance recovery**

Instance recovery recovers the database when an instance crashes midstream during user activity. Unlike in a traditional single-instance database scenario, recovery of an instance in a RAC environment is dynamic and happens while the database is up and active.

As discussed in Chapter 2, one of the primary requirements of a RAC configuration is to have the redo logs of all instances participating in the cluster on the shared storage. The primary reason for such a requirement is to provide visibility of the redo logs of any instance in the cluster to all other instances. This allows any instance in the cluster to perform an instance recovery operation during an instance failure.

Instance failure can happen in several ways; the common reason for an instance failure is node failure. The node failure could be due to power surge, operator error, and so on. Other reasons for an instance failure can be failure of certain background processes fail or a kernel-level exception encountered by the instance, causing an ORA-0600 or ORA-07445 error. By issuing a SHUTDOWN ABORT command, a DBA also cause an instance failure.

Instance failures can be of different kinds:

- The instance is totally down, and the users do not have any access to the instance.

- The instance is up, but when connecting to it, there is a hang situation or a user gets no response.

In the case where the instance is not available, users can continue to access to the database in an active-active configuration, provided that the failover option has been enabled in the application. The failover option, as discussed in Chapter 6, can be enabled either by using the FAN or OCI feature inside the application or by using the SQL client, where the failover options are configured in the tnsnames.ora file.

Recovery from an instance failure happens from another instance that is up and running, that is part of the cluster configuration and whose heartbeat mechanism detected the failure first and informed the LMON process on the node. The LMON process on each cluster node communicates with the CM on the respective node and exposes that information to the respective instances.

LMON provides the monitoring function by continually sending messages from the node on which it runs and often by writing to the shared disk. When the node fails to perform these functions, the other nodes consider that node no longer to be a member of the cluster. Such a failure causes a change in a node's membership status within the cluster.

The LMON process controls the recovery of the failed instance by taking over its redo log files and performing instance recovery.

Instance recovery is complete when Oracle has performed the following steps:

1. *Transaction recovery.* It rolls back all uncommitted transactions of the failed instance

2. *Cache recovery.* It replays the online redo log files of the failed instance.

How does Oracle know that recovery is required for a given datafile?

The SCN is a logical clock inside the database kernel that increments with every change made to the database. The SCN describes a version or a committed version of the database. When a database check-points, an SCN (called the checkpoint SCN) is written to the datafile headers. This is called the start SCN. There is also an SCN value in the control file for every datafile, which is called the stop SCN. The stop SCN is set to infinity while the database is open and running. There is another data structure called the checkpoint counter in each datafile header and also in the control file for each datafile entry. The checkpoint counter increments every time a checkpoint happens on a datafile and the start SCN value is updated. When a datafile is in hot backup mode, the checkpoint information in the file header is frozen, but the checkpoint counter still gets updated.

When the database is shut down gracefully with the SHUTDOWN NORMAL or SHUTDOWN IMMEDIATE command, Oracle performs a checkpoint and copies the start SCN value of each datafile to its corresponding stop SCN value in the control file before the actual shutdown of the database.

When the database is started, Oracle performs two checks (among other consistency checks):

1.   To see if the start SCN value in every datafile header matches its corresponding stop SCN value in the control file

2.   To see if the checkpoint counter values match

If both of these checks are successful, then Oracle determines that no recovery is required for that datafile. These two checks are done for all datafiles that are online.

If the start SCN of a specific datafile doesn't match the stop SCN value in the control file, then at least a recovery is required. This can happen when the database is shut down with the SHUTDOWN ABORT statement or if the instance crashes. Oracle performs a check on the datafiles by checking the checkpoint counters. If the checkpoint counter check fails, then Oracle knows that the datafile has been replaced with a backup copy (while the instance was down), and therefore, media recovery is required.

Note: Instance recovery is performed by applying the redo records in the online log files to the datafiles. However, media recovery may require applying the archived redo log files as well.

8.8.2 **Database recovery**

What happens when multiple instances or instances in a RAC configuration crash? In a RAC configuration Oracle assigns a thread to redo logs that is assigned to an Instance. For example a thread (usually thread 1) is assigned to redo logs of instance 1 and another thread (thread #2) is assigned to redo logs of instance 2 and so on. What is a thread? A thread is a stream of redo and in this case a stream of redo logs assigned to an instance.

When all instances in a RAC configuration fails, the recovery associated with this is called crash recovery, redo is applied one thread at a time because only one instance at a time can dirty a block in cache; in between block modifications the block is written to disk. Therefore a block in a current online file can read redo for at most one thread. This assumption can not be made in media recovery as more than one instance may have made changes to a block so changes must be applied to blocks in ascending SCN order, switching between threads where necessary.

In a RAC environment, where instances could be added or taken off the cluster dynamically, when an instance is added to the cluster a thread enable record is written when a new thread of redo is created, similarly a thread is disabled when an instance is taken offline through a shutdown operation. The shutdown operation places an end of thread (EOT) flag on the log header.

Figure 8.10 illustrates the crash recovery scenario. In this scenario there are three instances SSKY1, SSKY2 and SSKY3 that form the RAC configura-

Figure 8.10
Crash Recovery

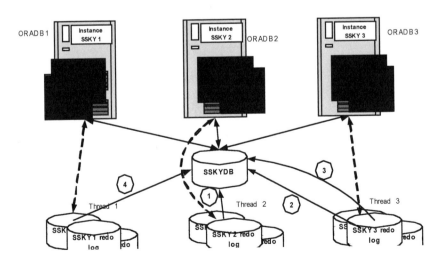

tion. Each instance has set of redo log file and is assigned thread 1, thread 2 and thread 3 respectively.

As discussed above, if multiple instances fail or during a crash recovery, all instances have to synchronize the redo log files by the SCN number during the recovery operation. For example in figure 8.10 above, the first SCN #1 was applied to the database from thread 2 that belongs to instance SSKY2, followed by SCN #2 from thread 3 which belongs to instance SSKY3 and SCN #3 also from thread 3 before applying SCN #4 from thread 1 which is assigned to instance SSKY1.

Any database is prone to failures, and during such failures, there can be loss of data either due to data corruption, human error, or act of nature. In the case of the initial two situations, the database is normally restored either completely, for example, when a disk goes bad, or partially (point in time), when a specific object needs to be restored. In the third situation, an act of nature, a new database will need to be configured and the data restored to it (if the external media is available), or a disaster recovery strategy will need to be implemented. This strategy will require using tools such as Oracle Data Guard or Streams, which will allow users to connect to this disaster recovery location when the primary database is down.

When restoring to the primary database, options available under the backup operation are also available to configure recovery (i.e., using a command-line interface such as SQL Plus /RMAN or the EM GUI interface).

In order to perform a recovery using the GUI, select "Perform Recovery" option from the "Maintenance" screen. The next screen displays the type of recovery to be performed:

- *Whole database recovery.* The entire database is restored from a backup.
- *Object-level recovery.* Only the objects based on the object type selected are restored. Object types supported are datafiles, tablespaces, archived logs, and tables.

Once the type of recovery (e.g., object-level recovery) to be performed is selected, click on "Next." The next screen displays options to perform a point-in-time (PIT) recovery. This screen is displayed because the Object type of restore was selected in the previous screen (Figure 8.11).

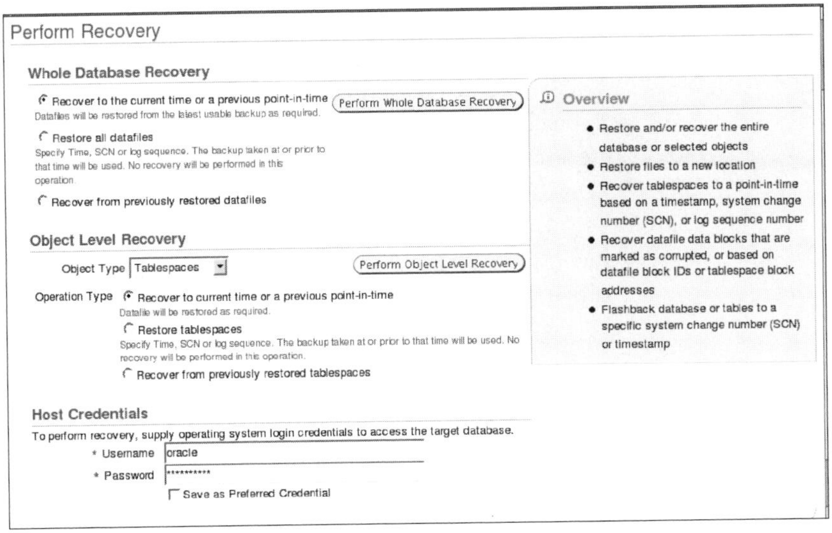

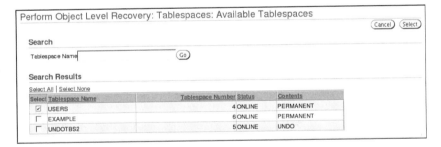

Figure 8.11 *EM Perform Recovery*

Once the type of recovery to be performed is selected, click on "Next." The next screen illustrated in Figure 8.12, is the tablespaces selection screen; select the tablespaces to be recovered. Once the tablespace is selected, click on "Next."

Figure 8.12 *EM Tablespace Recovery: Available Tablespaces*

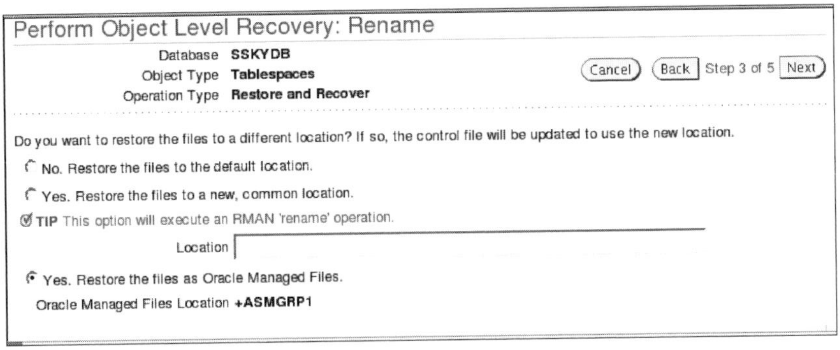

Figure 8.13 *EM Object-Level Recovery Rename Tablespaces*

The next screen, illustrated in Figure 8.13, is the tablespace rename option screen. The tablespace can be renamed to a different location, including an ASM disk group. After making the appropriate selection, click on "Next." This will generate the RMAN script. Verify the script and click on "Submit" to complete the operation. This completes the recovery operation.

PIT recovery can be performed for the entire database or to specific objects or tablespaces, as discussed above. PIT recovery involves the following steps:

1. The PIT to which the database should be recovered is identified.

2. Oracle will take the database objects offline while the recovery process restores the objects from the backup.

3. If the recovery is to a PIT later than the time the backup was taken, Oracle will have to roll forward through the archive logs, applying the changes to the database objects beyond the copy of the backup.

4. When recovery is complete, the database objects can be brought back online.

In a RAC environment, since multiple instances can perform DML operations to the same object, it is quite possible that archive logs from multiple instances may be required to complete the PIT recovery. This is one of the primary reasons why redo logs and archive logs generated by the various instances should be visible to other instances in the cluster.

Best Practice: To avoid single points of failure and to avoid inaccessibility to archive logs stored on local storage when the node is unreachable, archive logs should be stored on shared storage in a RAC configuration.

Applying archive logs from multiple instances

Each instance in the cluster generates its own copy of redo log information and is identified by a thread. In other words, a thread is a stream of redo information. The thread applicable to a specific instance is defined in the server parameter file using the parameter THREAD = <thread number>. When operating the database in ARCHIVELOG mode, each redo log switch will generate an archive log file. The archive log file contains the characteristics including the thread details.

In a RAC environment, more than one instance may make changes to a block, and Oracle may have to read multiple archive log files to complete the recovery. Recovery is performed by applying block changes in ascending SCN order, switching between threads where necessary.

In a RAC environment, when an instance is added to the cluster, a thread-enable record is written when a new thread of redo is created; similarly, a thread is disabled when an instance is taken off-line through a shutdown operation. The shutdown operation places an end of thread (EOT) flag on the redo log header. This indicates to Oracle to stop reading through the log files when performing recovery because, beyond this point, there will be no data pertaining to the instance.

It is a good practice to test all recovery operations either in a test environment or in a development environment to ensure expected behavior. While only a simple case of recovery has been discussed, there are several other types of recovery, such as control file recovery, datafile recovery, and parameter file recovery, which should also be tested and verified.

8.9   Conclusion

In this chapter, we discussed the backup and recovery strategy for an Oracle database. The backup and recovery procedures using the EM interface were discussed by stepping through a backup-to-disk scenario using RMAN. In a RAC environment, it is the a practice to use RMAN for database backups.

9

Performance Tuning

Performance tuning of any application, including the database, is an iterative process. This means that to maintain a healthy database, one must constantly monitor and fine-tune it. During certain periods, an aggressive performance tuning of both the application and database may be required. At other times, only routine continuous monitoring and maintenance may be needed. During this time, system hiccups may be discovered and solutions tried and tested.

The goal of a DBA or the application developer is to provide efficient, well-performing applications with good response time. In order for the application to provide a good response, the system, database, and SQL queries should be well tuned. Systems are tuned based on data collected during periods of poor performance; the evidence and the data collected may provide an indication of where the actual problem resides. For continuous monitoring and tuning of systems, a process or method should be adopted that helps streamline the activity. As in most repeatable situations, a methodology should be adopted, and once it has been validated and approved, it needs to be practiced. This methodology should be iterated every time there is a need to tune the system.

In this chapter, we will look into a scientific approach to troubleshooting, performance tuning, and maintaining a healthy database system. Tuning a RAC implementation has many aspects, and the techniques will vary depending on whether the RAC cluster is preproduction or live. Since a RAC configuration comprises one or more instances connected to a shared database, tuning a RAC configuration ideally starts with tuning the individual instances prior to the deployment of the production cluster. Individual instances in the cluster should be tuned using the same techniques used for single-instance databases. Once the individual instances are tuned, the other tiers, network, interconnect, cluster manager, and so on, should be incorporated into the tuning process.

9.1   Methodology

Problem-solving tasks of any nature need to be approached in a systematic and controlled manner. There needs to be a defined procedure or an action plan, and this procedure needs to be followed step by step from start to finish. During every step of the process, data is collected and analyzed, and the results are fed into the next step, which in turn is performed using a similar systematic approach. Hence, methodology is the procedure or process followed from start to finish, from identification of the problem to problem solving and documentation. A methodology is a procedure or process that is repeatable as a whole or in increments through iterations. During all of this analysis, the cause or reasons for a behavior or problem should be based on quantitative analysis and not on guesswork.

The performance tuning methodology can be broadly categorized into seven steps:

1.   *Problem statement.* Identify or state the specific problem in hand (e.g., poor response time or poorly performing SQL statement).

2.   *Information gathering.* Gather all information relating to the problem identified in step one. For example, when a user complains of poor performance, it may be a good idea to interview him or her to identify what kind of function the user was performing and at what time of the day (there may have been another contending application at that time, which may have caused the slow performance).

3.   *Area identification.* Once the information concerning the performance issue is gathered, the next step is to identify the area of the performance issue. For example, the module in the application that belongs to a specific service type may be causing the performance issue.

4.   *Area drilldown.* Drill down further to identify the cause or area of the performance issue. For example, identify the SQL statement or the batch application running at the wrong time of day.

5.   *Problem resolution.* Work to resolve the performance issue (e.g., tune the SQL query).

6.   *Testing against baseline.* Test to see if the performance issue has been resolved. For example, request that the user who complained test the performance.

7. *Repeating the process.* Now that the identified problem has been resolved, attempt to use the same process with the next problem.

While each of these steps is very broad, a methodical approach will help identify and solve the problem in question, namely, performance. Which area of the system is having a performance problem? Where do we start? Should the tuning process start with the operating system, network, database, instance, or application? Often the users of the application tier complain that the system has a poor response time. Users access an application, and the application in turn communicates with the database to store and retrieve information. When the user who made the request does not get the response in a sufficiently small amount of time, he or she complains that the system is slow.

Starting with poor end user response time may assist in tuning a system in production, but in other scenarios, we may need to tune bottom up (e.g., starting with the hardware platform, tuning the storage subsystem, tuning the database configuration, tuning the instance). Addressing the performance issues using this approach can bring some amount of change or performance improvement to the system with less or no impact on the actual application code. However, if the application is poorly written (e.g., a bad SQL query), tuning the underlying layers will have only a marginal effect.

As a general rule, it is more effective to take a "top-down" approach to database tuning since improvements in the upper layers (e.g., the application) will change the demand experienced by the lower layers (such as the storage system). When an application SQL is poorly tuned, it may cause excessive physical I/O demand, which in turn leads to poor disk service times. Tuning the SQL will both reduce the demand and eliminate the problems at all layers of the application. On the other hand, improving the performance of poorly tuned SQL by optimizing the storage subsystem, perhaps by buying more spindles, is a relatively expensive and ultimately ineffective measure. You also risk the embarrassing situation of having requested expensive hardware upgrades, which are later rendered unnecessary by the creation of an index or the addition of a hint to a problematic SQL.

Therefore, it is usually wise to perform tuning activities in the following order:

1. Tune the application, focusing on reducing its demand for database services. Primarily, this is done through SQL tuning, addi-

tion of indexes, rewording of SQLs or application-level caching. The observable outcome of this stage is a reduction in the rate of logical I/O demands (consistent reads and db (database) block reads) by the application.

2. Eliminate any contention for shared resources, such as locks, latches, freelists, and so on. Contention for these resources may be preventing the application from exhibiting its full demand for database services.

3. Use memory to minimize the amount of logical demand that turns into physical disk I/Os. This involves tuning the buffer cache to maximize the number of blocks of data that can be found in memory and tuning the `PGA_AGGREGATE_TARGET` to minimize I/O resulting from disk sorts and hash joins.

4. Finally, when the physical I/O demand has been minimized, distribute the load as evenly as possible across your disk spindles, and if there are insufficient spindles for the I/O demand you are now observing, add additional disk devices to improve overall I/O bandwidth.

The top-down or bottom-up methodology discussed previously is good for an already existing production application that needs to be tuned. Typically, we find an application's performance has degraded over time, possibly because (1) applications have degraded in performance due to new functionality that was not sufficiently tuned; (2) the user base has increased and the current application does not support the extended user base; and (3) the volume of data in the underlying database has increased, but the storage has not changed to accept the increased I/O load.

While these are issues with an existing application and database residing on existing hardware, a more detailed testing and tuning methodology should be adopted when migrating from a single instance to a clustered database environment. Before migrating the actual application and production enabling the new hardware, the following basic testing procedure should be adopted.

As mentioned earlier, testing of the RAC environment should start with tuning a single-instance configuration. Only when the performance characteristics of the application are satisfactory should tuning on the clustered configuration begin. To perform these tests, all nodes in the cluster except one should be shut down, and the single-instance node should be tuned. Only after the single instance has been tuned and appropriate performance measurements equal to the current configuration or more are obtained should the next step of tuning be started. Tuning the cluster should be performed by adding one instance at a time to the mix. Performance should be measured in detail to ensure that the expected scalability and availability are obtained. If such performance measurements are not obtained, the application should not be deployed into production, and only after the problem areas are identified and tuned should deployment occur.

Note: RAC cannot magically bring performance improvements to an application that is already performing poorly on a single-instance configuration.

Caution: The rule of thumb is if the application cannot scale on a single-instance configuration when the number of CPUs on the server is increased from two to four to eight, the application will not scale in a RAC environment. Indeed, migrating to RAC can conceivably diminish performance of an application that cannot scale in an SMP (multi-CPU) environment.

While running performance tests on the instances by adding one node at a time to the cluster, the following phases should be included in the testing plan:

1.   *Load Testing Phase I.* During this phase, a standard performance benchmarking software load will test the database environment, not including the application schemas and data. The purpose of this test is to verify the database and operating system performance characteristics. Based on the load tests and the statistics collected, the database and environment should be tuned. Once tuned, the testing should be repeated until a maximum or until such point when no or minimal performance gains are noticed. Load-testing tools such as Benchmark Factory (BMF), illustrated in Figure 9.1, or free-load testing tools such as Swingbench[1] or Hammerora[2] provide standard test categories and can be used to test the environment during this phase.

1.   The latest version of the Swingbench software can be downloaded from www.dominicgiles.com.
2.   The latest version of the Hammerora software can be downloaded from http://hammerora.sourceforge.net.

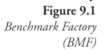

Figure 9.1
*Benchmark Factory
(BMF)*

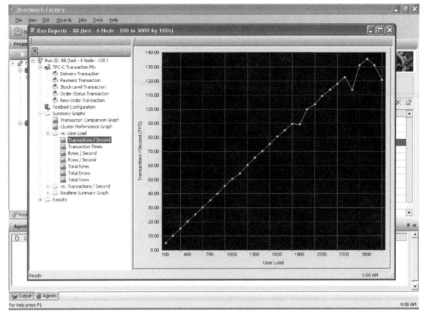

Once a stable environment has been reached, the next step is to test all failure points because, after all, one primary reason to migrate to a clustered environment is availability.

2.   *Availability test.* During this step of testing, the various failure points will have to be tested to ensure that the RAC database will continue to function either as a single instance or as a cluster, depending on where the failure has occurred. For example, from where the node failure occurred, the remaining nodes in the cluster should continue to function. Similarly, when a network switches to the storage array and fails, the redundant switch should continue to operate. Tests should be performed during load, meaning that failures should be simulated, considering that they can happen in live production environments with user activity.

 Note: This is a critical test and should not be compromised. All failure points should be tested until the expected results are achieved.

3.   *Load Testing Phase II.* During this step, a load test should be performed against a production schema (on the new hardware plat-

form) that contains a copy of the actual data from the current live production environment. The purpose of this test is to tune the instance and the database for application workloads not interfacing with the business application. For such a test, an extract of the SQL queries from the application can be used. One method to extract these queries from a live system without user intervention is to extract them using Oracle event 10046 and parsing the trace files generated through an application to extract the queries with their respective bind values. Sample steps to complete phase II are as follows:

a.   In a live production environment, enable Oracle Event Trace 10046 at level 4 after connecting to the server as user sys.

```
ALTER SYSTEM SET EVENTS '10046 TRACE NAME CONTEXT
FOREVER, LEVEL 4';
```

This command generates a trace file in the directory identified by the parameter USER_DUMP_DEST.

Caution: Depending on the activity on the production servers, the number of trace files and their contents could be large and consume a considerable amount of disk space. Please ensure sufficient disk space is available before attempting this step.

b.   Concatenate all the trace files generated by the event in the user dump destination directory into one file.

```
cat *.trc > SQLQueries.trc
```

c.   Using parsing software (sample Perl script provided in Appendix B), replace the bind variables with bind values found in the trace file.

d.   Using the queries extracted from step c, perform a load test simulating the estimated user workload iterating the queries and measuring response times. Remember, this step is also an iterative process, which means that the user load should be gradually increased through iterations, and during each iteration, statistics should be collected. Then, based on the analysis, the instance and database parameters and, most importantly, the SQL queries should be tuned. This test can be performed using either a homegrown tool or third-party software such as BMF or hammerora.

 Note: Performance should be monitored on all the tiers of the database server (i.e., operating system, instance, and database) during both load-testing phases using various performance-monitoring tools, which are discussed later in this chapter along with other performance-tuning methods.

Once the database layer has been tested and tuned simulating user work behavior, the next step is to perform an actual user acceptance test.

4.   *User acceptance testing.* In this step, an organized set of users is requested to perform day-to-day operations using the standard application interface against the new environment. During this test phase, the database environment should be monitored, and data should be collected and analyzed and the environments tuned. With this step, almost all problem areas of the new environment should be identified and fixed.

5.   *Day-in-a life test.* This is the final test where the environment is put through an actual user test by the application users simulating a typical business day.

Through these various stages of testing, all problem areas should be identified and fixed before going live into a production environment. Please note that RAC will not perform any miracles to improve the performance of the application. All applications that do not scale on a single-instance database environment will not scale in a clustered environment. Therefore, it is important to ensure that the application is performing well in the clustered environment during these testing cycles before going live.

 Note: One of the most common failures during preproduction benchmarking is failure to simulate expected table data volumes. Many SQL statements will increase their I/O requirements and elapsed times as table volumes increase. In the case of a full table scan, the relationship will be approximately linear: if you double the size of the table, you double the SQLs' I/O and elapsed time. Indexed-based queries may show better scalability, though many indexed queries will perform range scans that will grow in size with the number of rows in the underlying table. Therefore, a valid benchmark will use a database in which the long-term row counts in key tables have been simulated.

Identification and tuning of the database depends on the type of application, the type of user access patterns, the size of the database, the operating system, and so on. In the next sections of this chapter, the various tuning areas and options are discussed.

9.2   Storage subsystem

Shared storage in a RAC environment is a critical component of the overall architecture. Seldom is importance given to the storage system relative to the size of the database, the number of nodes in the cluster, and so on. Common problems found among customers are as follows:

- *When increasing the number of nodes participating in the cluster, seldom is any thought given to the number of nodes versus the number of interfaces to the storage subsystem and the capacity of the I/O path.* Due to limitations of the hardware, it has been observed on several occasions that the number of slots for the host bus adapter (HBA) and the network interface card (NIC) is insufficient to provide a good I/O capacity, and so is the number of ports on a switch and the number of controllers in a disk array. Care should be taken to ensure that the number of HBAs is equal to the number of disk controllers. Using the disk controller slots to accommodate more disk arrays will have a negative impact on the total throughput.

  For example, on a 16-port fiber channel switch, the ideal configuration is have eight HBAs and eight disk controllers, giving a total throughput of 8 × 200 MB = 1.6 GB/sec.[3] Now, if the number of HBAs is reduced to four to provide room for additional storage, then the total throughput drops by 50% (4 × 200 MB = 800 MB/sec).

  Another area of concern is tuning the operating system to handle the I/O workload. For example, Figure 9.2 is an output from an EM database console that illustrates a high I/O activity against the storage array.

---

3.   Assuming the maximum theoretical payload of 2 Gb/s Fiber Channel is 200 MB/sec.

Figure 9.2
*EM Active Session
Showing High I/O
Activity*

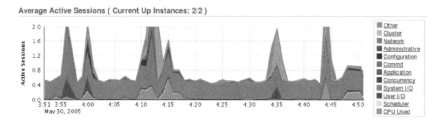

Apart from poorly written SQL queries, high I/O activity against the storage system can occur for a number of reasons:

- Bad configuration of the SAN
- Low disk throughput
- High contention against the storage area
- Bad I/O channel
- High queue lengths

The storage system should be verified beforehand to ensure that all disks in the storage array are of high-performing capacity. While it may be difficult to have the entire storage array contain disks of the same performance characteristics, care should be taken to ensure that disks within a disk group (in the case of ASM) or volume group (in the case of third-party volume managers) are of identical capacity and performance characteristics because a poor-performing disk in a disk group can create inconsistent I/O activity. When using ASM, performance characteristics of the individual disks within a disk group can be monitored using EM, as illustrated in Figure 9.3.

- *Disk I/O can also be improved by configuring Oracle to use asynchronous I/O.* Asynchronous I/O (AIO) can be enabled by installing the following operating system-specific patches:

```
[root@oradb3 root]$ rpm -ivf libaio-0.3.96-3.i386.rpm
[root@oradb3 root]$ rpm -i-f libaio-devel-0.3.96-3.i386.rpm
```

Then, recompile the Oracle kernel using the following commands:

```
make -f ins_rdbms.mk async_on
make -f ins_rdbms.mk oracle
```

Subsequently, the following two parameters have to be set to the appropriate values:

```
DISK_ASYNCH_IO = TRUE  (default)
FILESYSTEMIO_OPTIONS=ASYNCH
```

In a RAC environment, by sharing blocks between instances using the cluster interconnect, Oracle will avoid physical I/O if possible. However, if it must be done to force the data to be saved to disks, then the goal should be to make I/O asynchronous and to eliminate random I/O operations because DBWRn processes often have to write out large batches of "dirty" blocks to disk. If AIO is not available, you may see "free buffer" or "write complete" waits as sessions wait for the DBWRn to catch up with the changes made by user sessions.

Note: Oracle Wait Interface (OWI) is discussed later in this chapter.

AIO allows a process to submit I/O requests without waiting for their completion. Enabling this feature allows Oracle to submit AIO requests, and while the I/O request is being processed, Oracle can pick up another thread and schedule a new I/O operation.

Note: In Oracle Database 10*g* Release 2, during installation Oracle will compile the kernel using the asynch parameters if the appropriate operating system packages are installed. AIO is not supported for NFS servers.

- *Poor performance in Linux environments, particularly with OLAP queries, parallel queries, backup and restore operations, or queries that perform large I/O operations, can be due to inappropriate setting of certain operating system parameters.* For example, by default on Linux environments, large I/O operations are broken into 32K-segment chunks, separating system I/O operations into smaller sizes. To allow Oracle to perform large I/O operations, certain default values at the operating system level should be configured appropriately. The following steps will help users identify the current parameter settings and make appropriate changes:

1. Verify if the following parameters have been configured:

    ```
    # cat /proc/sys/fs/superbh-behavior
    # cat /proc/sys/fs/aio-max-size
    # cat /proc/sys/fs/aio-max-nr
    # cat /proc/sys/fs/aio-nr
    ```

    aio-max-size

    The `aio-max-size` parameter specifies the maximum block size that one single AIO write/read can do. Using the default value of 128K will chunk the AIO done by Oracle.

    aio-nr and aio-max-nr

    aio-nr is the running total of the number of events specified on the io_setup system call for all currently active AIO contexts. If aio-nr reaches aio-max-nr, then io_setup will fail. aio-nr shows the current systemwide number of AIO requests. aio-max-nr allows you to change the maximum value aio-nr can increase to.

    Increasing the value of the `aio-max-size` to 1,048,576 and aio_max_ns parameters to 56K also helps the performance of the ASM disks because ASM performs I/O in 1-MB chunks.

2. Update the parameters by adding the following lines to the /etc/sysctl.conf file:

    ```
    fs.superbh-behavior = 2
    fs.aio-max-size = 1048576
    fs.aio-max-nr = 512
    ```

    This change will set these kernel parameters across reboots. To change them dynamically on a running system, issue the following commands as user root:

    ```
    # echo 2 > /proc/sys/fs/superbh-behavior
    # echo 1048576 > /proc/sys/fs/aio-max-size
    # echo 512 > /proc/sys/fs/aio-max-nr
    ```

- *When configuring disk groups or volume groups, care should be taken in identifying disks of the same performance characteristics.* Such verification can be done using either the simple dd command or any disk calibration tool, such as Orion,[4] for example;

```
dd bs=1048576 count=200 if=/dev/sdc  of=/dev/null
```

This command will copy 200 blocks by reading one block at a time up to a maximum of 1,048,576 bytes from an input device and writing it to an output device. When testing disks for Oracle database, the block size should represent the Oracle block size times the value defined using the parameter MULTI_BLOCK_READ_COUNT to obtain optimal disk performance.

The following is the description of the various options used with the dd command:

- bs=bytes. Reads that many bytes of data at a time.
- count=blocks. Copies the number of blocks specified by the count parameter.
- if=file. Specifies the input file to read data from (e.g., a disk).
- of=file. Specifies the output device of the file where the data will be written.

- *When testing disk performance characteristics, user concurrency should be considered from multiple nodes in a RAC environment.* User concurrency can also be simulated by running multiple dd commands. By using standard operating system commands such as vmstat, the concurrency level can be increased gradually to determine the highest throughput rate and beyond where there is a point of zero increase.

- *Selection of disk volume managers also plays an important part in the overall performance of the database.* This is where the use of ASM comes into play. Deploying databases on ASM will help in automatic distribution of files based on the same methodology, and Oracle will perform the automatic placement of files based on the importance of data.

---

4.   Orion can be downloaded from the Oracle technology network at http://otn.oracle.com.

9.3   **Automatic Storage Management**

Above, we briefly touched on tuning the operating system to help improve the I/O subsystem. ASM performs placement of files across various disks automatically; however, ASM cannot improve the performance of existing poorly performing disks. We discussed earlier that it would be ideal to have all disks in a disk group with the same performance characteristics to

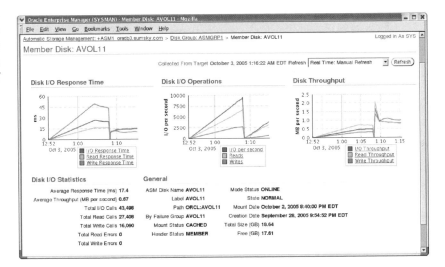

Figure 9.3
I/O Performance at the ASM Disk Level

provide consistent performance. The performance characteristics of individual disks illustrated in Figure 9.3 within a disk group can be monitored using EM.

In Chapter 3, we discussed how an ASM instance and an RDBMS instance will interact for various reasons. During this process of communication and during the various administrative functions performed by ASM on the disk groups, ASM will require resources. Like in a RDBMS instance, despite ASM being a lightweight instance, it also contains an SGA. For example, the default SGA is

```
SQL> show sga

Total System Global Area    92274688 bytes
Fixed Size                   1217884 bytes
Variable Size               65890980 bytes
ASM Cache                   25165824 bytes
```

Note: The ASM cache is defined by the `DB_CACHE_SIZE` parameter.

Note: The SGA is broken into the shared pool, large pool, and shared pool reserved size. Default values for these parameters are:

```
SHARED_POOL_SIZE = 48M
LARGE_POOL_SIZE = 12M
SHARED_POOL_RESERVED_SIZE = 24M
SGA_MAX_SIZE = 88M
```

The SGA for the ASM instance is sized very small. Based on the number of instances or databases communicating with the ASM instance, usually, the default SGA is sufficient. However, when the application performs high I/O activity or when the ASM instance supports more than six Oracle instances, adding resources to the ASM instance is helpful to improve performance (e.g., increasing the `LARGE_POOL_SIZE` to help in the communications between ASM and its clients) [27]. ASM and its functionality are discussed extensively in Chapter 3.

9.4   Cluster interconnect

This is a very important component of the clustered configuration. Oracle depends on the cluster interconnect for movement of data between the instances. Chapter 2 provides a detailed explanation of how global data movement occurs.

Testing the cluster interconnect should start with a test of the hardware configuration. This basic test should ensure that the database is using the correct IP addresses or NICs for the interconnect. The following query provides a list of IP addresses registered with Oracle:

```
COL PICKED_KSXPIA FORMAT A15
COL INDX FORMAT 99999
SELECT * FROM X$KSXPIA;
```

ADDR	INDX	INST_ID	PUB_KSXPIA	PICKED_KSXPIA	NAME_KSXPIA	IP_KSXPIA
3FE47C74	**0**	**1**	**N**	**OCR**	**bond1**	**10.168.2.130**
3FE47C74	1	1	Y	OCR	bond0	192.168.2.30

In the output, bond0 is the public interface (identified by the value Y in column PUB_KSXPIA), and bond1 is the private interface (identified by the value N in column PUB_KSXPIA). If the correct IP addresses are not visible, this indicates incorrect installation and configuration of the RAC environment.

Column PICKED_KSXPIA indicates the type of clusterware implemented on the RAC cluster, where the interconnect configuration is stored, and the cluster communication method that RAC will use. The valid values in this column are

- OCR. Oracle Clusterware is configured.

- OSD. It is operating system dependent, meaning a third-party cluster manager is configured, and Oracle Clusterware is only a bridge between Oracle RDBMS and the third-party cluster manager.

- CI. The interconnect is defined using the CLUSTER_INTERCONNECT parameter in the instance.

Alternatively interconnect information registered by all participating nodes in the cluster can be verified from GV$CLUSTER_INTERCONNECTS view. Cluster interconnect can also be verified by using the ORADEBUG utility (discussed later) and verifying the trace file for the appropriate IP address.

Note: Failure to keep the interconnect interfaces private will result in the instances' competing with other network processes when requesting blocks from other cluster members. The network between the instances needs to be dedicated to cluster coordination and not used for any other purpose.

CLUSTER_INTERCONNECTS

This parameter provides Oracle with information on the availability of additional cluster interconnects that can be used for cache fusion activity. The parameter overrides the default interconnect settings at the operating system level with a preferred cluster traffic network. While this parameter does provide certain advantages over systems where high interconnect latency is noticed by helping reduce such latency, configuring this parameter can affect the interconnect high-availability feature. In other words, an interconnect failure that is normally unnoticeable will instead cause an Oracle cluster failure as Oracle still attempts to access the network interface.

Best Practice: NIC pairing/bonding should be a preferred method to using the CLUSTER_INTERCONNECTS parameter to provide load-balancing and failover of the interconnects.

9.5   Interconnect transfer rate

The next important verification is to determine the transfer rate versus the actual implemented packet size to ensure the installation has been carried out per specification.

The speed of the cluster interconnect depends solely on the hardware vendor and the layered operating system. Oracle depends on the operating system and the hardware for sending packets of information across the cluster interconnect. For example, one type of cluster interconnect supported in Sun 4800s is the UDP protocol. However, Solaris in this specific version has an operating system limitation of a 64-KB packet size for data transfer. To transfer 256 KB worth of data across this interconnect protocol would take more than four round trips. Comparing this to another operating system (e.g., Linux), the maximum supported packet size is 256K. On a high-transaction system where there is a large amount of interconnect traffic, because of user activity on the various instances participating in the clustered configuration, limitations on the packet size can cause serious performance issues.

Tools such as IPtraf on Linux environments (Figure 9.4) or glance on HP-UX environments or utilities such as netstat should help monitor network traffic and transfer rates between instance and client configurations.

Figure 9.4
IPTraf General Network Traffic

```
oracle@oradb3:/home/oracle

IPTraf
 Iface ———————— Total ———— IP —— NonIP —— BadIP —— Activity ————
 lo                916        916         0         0      0.40 kbits/sec
 eth0              6051       6051        0         0    407.60 kbits/sec
 eth1              6048       6048        0         0    411.40 kbits/sec
 eth2              1026       1026        0         0      2.60 kbits/sec
```

IPTraf also helps to look into a specific network and monitor its performance in detail by the type of protocol used for network traffic. For example, in Figure 9.5, network traffic by protocol (TCP and UDP) is displayed, giving outgoing and incoming rates.

Figure 9.5
*IPTraf Statistics
for eth0*

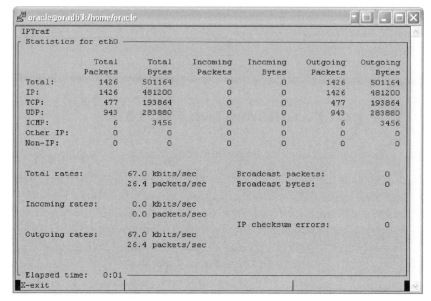

After the initial hardware and operating-system-level tests to confirm the packet size across the interconnect, subsequent tests could be done from the Oracle database to ensure that there is not any significant added latency from using cache-to-cache data transfer or the cache fusion technology. The query below provides the average time to receive a consistent read (CR) block on the system:

```
set numwidth 20
column "AVG CR BLOCK RECEIVE TIME (ms)" format 9999999.9
select
      b1.inst_id,
      b2.value "GCS CR BLOCKS RECEIVED",
      b1.value "GCS CR BLOCK RECEIVE TIME",
      ((b1.value / b2.value) * 10) "AVG CR BLOCK RECEIVE TIME (ms)"
from     gv$sysstat b1,
gv$sysstat b2
where b1.name = 'gc cr block receive time'
and      b2.name = 'gc cr blocks received'
and      b1.inst_id = b2.inst_id ;


INST_ID GCS CR BLOCKS RECEIVED GCS CR BLOCK RECEIVE TIME AVG CR BLOCK RECEIVE TIME (ms)
------- --------------------- ------------------------- ------------------------------
      1                  2758                    112394                         443.78
      2                  1346                      1457                           10.8
```

Note: The data in the GV$SYSSTAT view is cumulative since the last time the Oracle instance was bounced. This does not reflect the true performance of the interconnect or give a true picture of the latency in transferring data. To get a more realistic picture of the performance, it would be good to bounce all of the Oracle instances and test again.

In the output above, it can be noticed that the AVG CR BLOCK RECEIVE TIME for instance 1 is 443.78 ms; this is significantly high when the expected average latency as recommended by Oracle should not exceed 15 ms. A high value is possible if the CPU has limited idle time, and the system typically processes long-running queries. However, it is possible to have an average latency of less than 1 ms with user-mode IPC. Latency can also be influenced by a high value for the DB_MULTI_BLOCK_READ_COUNT parameter. This is because this parameter determines the size of the block that each instance would request from the other during read transfers. and a requesting process can issue more than one request for a block depending on the setting of this parameter and may have to wait longer. This kind of high latency requires further investigation of the cluster interconnect configuration, and tests should be performed at the operating system level to ensure this is not something from Oracle or the parameter.

Note: Sizing of the DB_MULTI_BLOCK_READ_COUNT parameter should be based on the interconnect latency and the packet sizes as defined by the hardware vendor, and after considering the operating system limitations.

If the network interconnect is correctly configured as outlined earlier, then it is unlikely that the interconnect itself will be responsible for high receive times as revealed by GV$SYSSTAT. The actual time taken to transfer a block across the interconnect hardware will normally be only a small fraction of the total time taken to request the block on the first instance, convert any locks that may exist on the block, prepare the block for transfer, verify the receipt of the block, and update the relevant global cache structures. So, while it is important to ensure that the interconnect hardware is correctly configured, it should not be concluded that the interconnect is misconfigured if it is determined that block transfers are slow.

The EM Cluster Cache Coherency screen (Figure 9.6) is also a tool to monitor cluster interconnect performance. The figure displays three important matrixes:

1. *Global cache block access latency.* This represents the elapsed time from when the block request was initiated until it finishes. However, when a database block of any class is unable to locate a buffered copy in the local cache, a global cache operation is initiated by checking if the block is present in another instance. If it is found, it is shipped to the requestor.

2. *Global cache block transfer rate.* If a logical read fails to find a copy of the buffer in the local cache, it attempts to find the buffer in the database cache of a remote instance. If the block is found, it is shipped to the requestor. The global cache block transfer rate indicates the number of blocks received.

3. *Block Access Statistics.* This indicates the number of blocks read and the number of blocks transferred between instances in a RAC cluster.

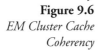

Figure 9.6
EM Cluster Cache Coherency

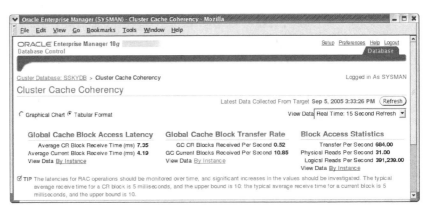

Latencies on the cluster interconnect can be caused by the following:

■ No dedicated interconnect for cache fusion activity has been configured.

■ A large number of processes in the run queues are waiting for CPU or as a result of processor scheduling delays.

■ Incorrect platform-specific operating system parameter settings affect IPC buffering or process scheduling.

■ Slow, busy, or faulty interconnects create slow performance.

One primary advantage of the clustered solution is to save on physical I/O against a storage system, which is expensive. This means that the latency of retrieving data across the interconnect should be significantly lower compared to getting the data from disk. For the overall performance of the cluster, the interconnect latency should be maintained at 6 to 8 ms. *The average latency of a consistent block request is the average latency of a consistent-read request round-trip from the requesting instance to the holding instance and back to the requesting instance.*

When such high latencies are experienced over the interconnect, another good test is to perform a test at the operating system level by checking the actual ping time. This will help to determine if there are any issues at the operating system level. After all, the performance issue may not be from data transfers within the RAC environment. Figure 9.7 (taken from Quest Software's Spotlight on RAC product) provides a comparison of the cluster latency versus the actual ping time monitored at the operating system level. This helps determine the latency encountered at the database level versus any overheads at the operating system level.

Figure 9.7
Cluster Latency versus Average Ping Time

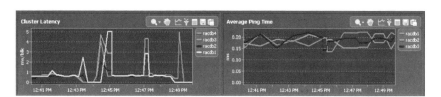

Apart from the basic packet transfer tests that can be performed at the operating system level, other checks and tests can be done to ensure that the cluster interconnect has been configured correctly.

- There are redundant, private, high-speed interconnects between the nodes participating in the cluster. Implementing NIC bonding or pairing will help interconnect load-balancing and failover when one of the interconnects fails. The configuring of bonding or pairing of NICs is discussed in Chapter 4.

- The user network connection does not interfere with the cluster interconnect traffic (i.e., they are isolated from each other).

At the operating system level, the `netstat` and `ifconfig` commands display network-related data structures. The output below for `netstat -i` indicates that there are four network adapters configured, and NIC pairing is implemented:

```
[oracle@oradb3 oracle]$ netstat -i
Kernel Interface table
Iface      MTU Met    RX-OK RX-ERR RX-DRP RX-OVR    TX-OK TX-ERR TX-DRP TX-OVR Flg
bond0     1500 0       3209      0      0      0     4028      0      0      0 BMmRU
bond0:1   1500 0       4390      0      0      0     6437      0      0      0 BMmRU
bond1     1500 0       7880      0      0      0    10874      0      0      0 BMmRU
eth0      1500 0       1662      0      0      0     2006      0      0      0 BMsRU
eth1      1500 0       1547      0      0      0     2022      0      0      0 BMsRU
eth2      1500 0       4390      0      0      0     6437      0      0      0 BMRU
eth3      1500 0       3490      0      0      0     4437      0      0      0 BMRU
lo       16436 0       7491      0      0      0     7491      0      0      0 LRU
```

- bond0 is the public interconnect created using the bonding functionality (bonds eth0 and eth1).

- bond0:1 is the VIP assigned to bond0.

- bond1 is the private interconnect alias created using the bonding functionality (bonds eth2 and eth3).

- eth0 and eth1 are the physical public interfaces; however, they are bonded/paired together (bond0).

- eth2 and eth3 are the physical private interfaces; however, they are bonded/paired together (bond1).

- lo0 indicates that there is a loopback option configured. Verification of whether Oracle is using the loopback option should be made using the ORADEBUG command and is discussed later in this section. The use of the loopback IP depends on the integrity of the routing table defined on each of the nodes. Modification of the routing table can result in the inoperability of the interconnect.

In the netstat output above, MTU is set at 1,500 bytes. MTU definitions do not include the data-link header. However, packet size computations include data-link headers. Maximum packet size displayed by the various tools is MTU plus the data-link header length. To get the maximum benefit from the interconnect, MTU should be configured to the highest possible value supported. For example, a setting as high as 9K using jumbo frames will help improve interconnect bandwidth and data transmission. Jumbo frame configuration is covered in Chapter 4.

Checks can also be done from the Oracle instance to ensure proper configuration of the interconnect protocol. If the following commands are executed as user `sys`, a trace file is generated in the user dump destination directory that contains certain diagnostic information concerning the UDP /IPC configurations:

```
SQL> ORADEBUG SETMYPID
        ORADEBUG IPC
        EXIT
```

The following is an extract from the trace file concerning IPC. The output confirms that the cluster interconnect is being used for instance-to-instance message transfer.

```
admno 0x4768d5f0 admport:
SSKGXPT 0xe453ec4 flags SSKGXPT_READPENDING     info for network 0
        socket no 7      IP 10.168.2.130         UDP 31938
        sflags SSKGXPT_UP
        info for network 1
        socket no 0      IP 0.0.0.0      UDP 0
        sflags SSKGXPT_DOWN
        active 0          actcnt 1
context timestamp 0
        no ports
```

 Note:

- The above output protocol used is UDP. On certain operating systems, such as Tru64, the trace output does not reveal the cluster interconnect information.

- ASM in a cluster environment will also use the interconnect for its interinstance cache transfer activity. The same verification step can also be performed from the ASM instance to ensure that both are correct.

Both the RDBMS and ASM alert logs are another source for this information.

```
Cluster communication is configured to use the following interface(s) for this
instance
  10.168.2.130
Sun Oct  2 21:34:13 2005
cluster interconnect IPC version: Oracle UDP/IP
IPC Vendor 1 proto 2
```

Best Practice: Set the interconnect network parameters to the maximum allowed by the operating system.

9.6   **SQL*Net tuning**

Similar to the network buffer settings for the cluster interconnects, buffer sizes and network parameters for the public interface should also be considered during the performance optimization process.

Network delays in receiving user requests and sending data back to users affect the overall performance of the application and environment. Such delays translate into SQL*Net-related wait events (OWI is discussed later).

Like the MTU settings for the interconnects, the MTU settings for the public interface can also be set to jumbo frame sizes, provided the entire network stack starting with the origin of the user request to the database tier all support this configuration. If any one tier does not support jumbo frames, this means the entire network stepping down to the default configuration of 1,500 bytes.

Like the MTU settings, the Session Data Unit (SDU) settings for the SQL*Net connect descriptor can also be tuned. Optimal SDU settings can be determined by repeated data/buffer requests by enabling SQL*Net and listener trace at both the client and server levels.

SQL*Net tracing can be enabled by adding the following parameters to the SQLNET.ora file on the client machines located in the $ORACLE_HOME/network/admin directory:

```
trace_level_client=16
trace_file_client=client
trace_unique_client=true
trace_timestamp_client=ON
```

Listener tracing on the servers can be enabled by adding the following parameters to the listener.ora file located in the $ORACLE_HOME/network/admin directory:

```
trace_level_server=16
trace_file_server=server
trace_timestamp_server=ON
```

Trace files are generated in `$ORACLE_HOME/network/log` directories on the respective systems. The appropriate parameters should then be added to the connection descriptor on the client system. For example, the following SDU settings in the TNS connection descriptor will set the value of the SDU to 8K:

```
SSKYDB =
  (DESCRIPTION =
      (SDU = 8192)
      (FAILOVER = ON)
    (ADDRESS = (PROTOCOL = TCP)(HOST = oradb1-vip.sumsky.net)(PORT = 1521))
    (ADDRESS = (PROTOCOL = TCP)(HOST = oradb2-vip.sumsky.net)(PORT = 1521))
    (ADDRESS = (PROTOCOL = TCP)(HOST = oradb3-vip.sumsky.net)(PORT = 1521))
    (ADDRESS = (PROTOCOL = TCP)(HOST = oradb4-vip.sumsky.net)(PORT = 1521))
    (LOAD_BALANCE = YES)
  (CONNECT_DATA =
    (SERVER = DEDICATED)
    (SERVICE_NAME = SSKYDB)
    (FAILOVER_MODE =
       (TYPE = SELECT)(METHOD = BASIC)(RETRIES = 10)(DELAY = 3)
  )
 )
 )
```

Similar settings should also be applied to the listener to ensure that the bytes received by the server are also of a similar size. For example, the following SDU settings on the listener will set the receive value to 8K:

```
SID_LIST_LISTENER =
(SID_DESC =
     (SDU=8192)
     (SID_NAME = SSKY1)
   ))
```

9.6.1 Tuning network buffer sizes

As a basic installation and configuration requirement, network buffer size requirements were discussed in Chapter 4. These parameter values are the bare minimum required for RAC functioning. Continuous monitoring and measuring of network latencies can help increase these buffer sizes even further, provided the operating system supports such an increase.

TCP uses a congestion window scheme to determine how many packets can be transmitted at any one time. The maximum congestion window size is determined by how much buffer space the kernel has allocated for each socket. If the buffers are too small, the TCP congestion window will never completely open; on the other hand, if the buffers are too large, the sender can overrun the receiver, causing the TCP window to shut down.

Apart from the wmem_max and rmem_max parameters discussed in Chapter 4, certain TCP parameters should also be tuned to improve TCP network performance.

tcp_wmem

This variable takes three different values, which hold information on how much TCP send buffer memory space each TCP socket has to use. Every TCP socket has this much buffer space to use before the buffer is filled up. Each of the three values is used under different conditions.

The first value in this variable sets the minimum TCP send buffer space available for a single TCP socket; the second value sets the default buffer space allowed for a single TCP socket to use; and the third value sets the kernel's maximum TCP send buffer space. The /proc/sys/net/core/wmem_max value overrides this value; hence, this value should always be smaller than that value.

tcp_rmem

The tcp_rmem variable is pretty much the same as tcp_wmem except in one large area: tells the kernel the TCP receive memory buffers instead of the transmit buffer, which is defined in tcp_wmem. This variable takes three different values, like the tcp_wmem variable.

tcp_mem

The tcp_mem variable defines how the TCP stack should behave when it comes to memory usage. It consists of three values, just like the tcp_wmem and tcp_rmem variables. The values are measured in memory pages (in short, pages). The size of each memory page differs depending on hardware and configuration options in the kernel, but on standard i386 computers, this is 4 KB, or 4,096 bytes. On some newer hardware, this is set to 16, 32, or even 64 KB. All of these values have no real default since they are calculated at boot time by the kernel and should, in most cases, be good for you and most usages you may encounter.

9.6.2 Device queue sizes

As with tuning the network buffer sizes, it is important to look into the size of the queue between the kernel network subsystems and the driver for the NIC. Inappropriate sizing can cause loss of data due to buffer overflows, which in turn causes retransmission, consumes resources, and delays performance.

There are two queues to consider in this area, the txqueuelen, which is related to the transmit queue size, and the netdev_backlog, which determines the receive queue size. These values can be manually defined using the ifconfig command on Linux and Unix systems. For example, the following command will reset the txqueuelen to 2,000:

```
/sbin/ifconfig eth0 txqueuelen 2000
```

Similarly, the receive queue size can be increased by setting the following parameter:

/proc/sys/net/core/netdev_max_backlog = 2000 in the /etc/sysctl.conf file.

Note: Tuning the network should also be considered when implementing Standby or Streams solutions that involve movement of large volumes of data across the network to the remote location.

9.7 SQL tuning

Irrespective of having high-performing hardware, a high-performing storage subsystem, or an abundance of resources available on each of the nodes in the cluster, RAC cannot perform magic to help with poorly-performing queries. Actually, poorly-performing queries can be a serious issue when you move from a single-instance configuration to a clustered configuration. In certain cases, a negative impact on the overall performance of the system will be noticed. When tuning queries, be it in a single-instance configuration or a clustered configuration, the following should be verified and fixed.

9.7.1 **Hard parses**

Hard parses are very costly for the Oracle's optimizer. The amount of validation that has to be performed during a parse consumes a significant number of resources. The primary reason for a hard parse is the uniqueness of the queries present in the library cache or SGA. When a user or session executes a query, the query is parsed and loaded in the library cache after Oracle has generated a hash value for the query. Subsequently, when another session or user executes the same query, depending on the extent of its similarity to the query already present in the library cache, it is reused, and there is no parse operation involved. However, if it is a new query, it has to go through the Oracle parsing algorithm; this is considered a hard parse and is very costly. The total number of hard parses can be determined using the following query:

```
SELECT PA.INST_ID,
       PA.SID,
       PA.VALUE "Hard Parses",
       EX.VALUE "Execute Count"
FROM   GV$SESSTAT PA,
       GV$SESSTAT EX
WHERE  PA.SID=EX.SID
AND    PA.INST_ID=EX.INST_ID
AND    PA.STATISTIC#=(SELECT STATISTIC#
                      FROM   V$STATNAME
                      WHERE  NAME ='parse count (hard)')
AND    EX.STATISTIC#=(SELECT STATISTIC#
                      FROM   V$STATNAME
                      WHERE  NAME ='execute count')
AND    PA.VALUE > 0;
```

Besides when a query is executed for the first time, other reasons for hard parse operations are as follows:

1. *There is insufficient allocation of the SGA.* When numerous queries are executed, they have to be flushed out to give space for new ones. This repeated loading and unloading can create high hard parse operations. The number of reloads can be determined using the following query:

    ```
    SELECT INST_ID,
    ```

```
SQL_TEXT,
LOADS
    FROM    GV$SQLSTATS
    WHERE   LOADS > 100;
```

The solution to this problem is to increase the size of the shared pool using the parameter SHARED_POOL_SIZE. The ideal configuration of the shared pool can be determined by querying the V$SHARED_POOL_ADVICE view.

2.   *Queries that use literals in the* WHERE *clause, making every query executed unique to Oracle's optimizer, cause it to perform hard parse operations.* The solution to these issues is to use bind variables instead of hard-coded values in the queries. If the application code cannot be modified, the hard parse rate can be reduced by setting the parameter CURSOR_SHARING to FORCE (or SIMILAR). Furthermore, soft parse rates can be reduced by setting SESSION_CACHED_CURSORS to a nonzero value.

Hard parsing should be minimized, largely to save on resources and make those resources available for other purposes.

V$/GV$SQLSTATS

This view provides the same information available in V$SQL and V$SQLAREA. However, accessing this view is much more cost-effective compared to the others. Accessing data from GV$SQLSTATS will not require the process to obtain any operating system latches and gives improved response times.

9.7.2   Logical reads

When data is read from physical storage (disk), it is placed into the buffer cache before filtering through the rows that match the criteria specified in the WHERE clause. Rows thus read are retained in the buffer, assuming other sessions executing similar queries may require the same data, reducing physical I/O. Queries not tuned to perform minimal I/O operations will retrieve a significantly larger number of rows, causing Oracle to traverse through the various rows, filtering what is not required instead of directly accessing rows that match. Such operations cause a significant amount of overhead and consume a large number of resources in the system.

Reading from buffer, or logical reads or logical I/O operations (LIO), is cheaper compared to reading data from disk. However, in Oracle's architecture, high LIOs are not cheap enough that they can be ignored because when Oracle needs to read a row from buffer, it needs to place a lock on the row in buffer. To obtain a lock, Oracle has to request a latch from the operating system. Latches are not available in abundance. Often when a latch is requested, one is not immediately available because other processes are using them. When a latch is requested, the requesting process will go into a sleep mode and after a few nanoseconds, will wake up and request the latch again. This time it may or may not obtain the latch and may have to sleep again. These attempts to obtain a latch generally lead to high CPU consumption on the host and cache buffer chains latch contention as sessions fight for access to the same blocks. When Oracle has to scan a large number of rows in the buffer to retrieve only a few rows that meet the search criteria, this can prove costly.

SQLs that issue high logical read rates in comparison to the actual number of database rows processed are possible candidates for SQL tuning efforts. Often the introduction of a new index or the creation of a more selective index will reduce the number of blocks that must be examined in order to find the rows required. For example, let's examine the performance of the following query:

```
SELECT eusr_id,
  us.usec_total_logins,
  eu.eusr_role_cd,
  c.comp_scac_code,
  eu.eusr_login_name,
  ul.usrli_id
FROM el_user eu, company c, user_login ul, user_security us
WHERE ul.USRLI_ACTIVE_STATUS_CD = 'Active'
  AND ul.USRLI_LOGGED_IN_EUSR_ID = eu.EUSR_ID
  AND eu.eusr_comp_id = c.comp_id
  AND eu.eusr_id = us.USEC_EUSR_ID
  ORDER BY c.comp_comp_type_cd, c.comp_name, eu.eusr_last_name
```

call	count	cpu	elapsed	disk	query	current	rows
Parse	1	0.28	0.29	0	51	0	0
Execute	1	0.00	0.00	0	0	0	0
Fetch	1	26.31	40.35	12866	6556373	0	87
total	3	26.59	40.64	12866	6556373	0	87

```
Misses in library cache during parse: 1
```

```
Optimizer goal: CHOOSE
Parsing user id: 33   (MVALLATH)


Rows       Row Source Operation
-------    -----------------------------------------------------
     87    SORT ORDER BY (cr=3176 r=66 w=66 time=346886 us)
     87     TABLE ACCESS BY GLOBAL INDEX ROWID USER_SECURITY PARTITION: 1 1 (cr=3176 r=66 w=66
time=338109 us)
     78      NESTED LOOPS  (cr=3088 r=66 w=66 time=334551 us)
     90       NESTED LOOPS  (cr=2596 r=66 w=66 time=322337 us)
     90        NESTED LOOPS  (cr=1614 r=66 w=66 time=309393 us)
     90         VIEW  (cr=632 r=66 w=66 time=293827 us)
  48390          HASH JOIN  (cr=632 r=66 w=66 time=292465 us)
6556373           TABLE ACCESS FULL USER_LOGIN (cr=190 r=0 w=0 time=138776 us)(object id
24891)
    970           TABLE ACCESS FULL EL_USER (cr=442 r=0 w=0 time=56947 us)(object id 24706)
     90         INDEX UNIQUE SCAN PK_EUSR PARTITION: 1 1 (cr=492 r=0 w=0 time=6055 us)(object
id 24741)
     90        TABLE ACCESS BY LOCAL INDEX ROWID COMPANY PARTITION: 1 1 (cr=982 r=0 w=0
time=10135 us)
     90         INDEX UNIQUE SCAN PK_COMP PARTITION: 1 1 (cr=492 r=0 w=0 time=4905 us)(object
id 24813)
     87       INDEX RANGE SCAN USEC_INDX1 (cr=492 r=0 w=0 time=9115 us)(object id 24694)
```

In the `tkprof` output from a 10046 event trace, which, it should be noted, retrieves just 87 rows from the database, the SQL is processing a large number (6556373) rows from the USER_LOGIN table, and no index is being used to retrieve the data. Now, if an index is created on the USER_LOGIN table, the query performance improves several fold:

```
SQL> create index USRLI_INDX1 on USER_LOGIN(USRLI_ACTIVE_STATUS_CD);

Index created.


Rows       Row Source Operation
-------    -----------------------------------------------------
    487    SORT ORDER BY (cr=3176 r=66 w=66 time=346886 us)
    487     TABLE ACCESS BY GLOBAL INDEX ROWID USER_SECURITY PARTITION: 1 1 (cr=3176 r=66
w=66 time=338109 us)
    978      NESTED LOOPS  (cr=3088 r=66 w=66 time=334551 us)
    490       NESTED LOOPS  (cr=2596 r=66 w=66 time=322337 us)
    490        NESTED LOOPS  (cr=1614 r=66 w=66 time=309393 us)
    490         VIEW  (cr=632 r=66 w=66 time=293827 us)
    490          HASH JOIN  (cr=632 r=66 w=66 time=292465 us)
  56373           INDEX FAST FULL SCAN USRLI_INDX1 (cr=190 r=0 w=0 time=947 us)(object id 28491)
    970           TABLE ACCESS FULL EL_USER (cr=442 r=0 w=0 time=947 us)(object id 24706)
    490         TABLE ACCESS BY LOCAL INDEX ROWID ELOGEX_USER PARTITION: 1 1 (cr=982 r=0 w=0
time=12238 us)
    490          INDEX UNIQUE SCAN PK_EUSR PARTITION: 1 1 (cr=492 r=0 w=0 time=6055 us)(object
id 24741)
```

```
   490      TABLE ACCESS BY LOCAL INDEX ROWID COMPANY PARTITION: 1 1 (cr=982 r=0 w=0
time=10135 us)
   490        INDEX UNIQUE SCAN PK_COMP PARTITION: 1 1 (cr=492 r=0 w=0 time=4905 us)(object
id 24813)
   487      INDEX RANGE SCAN USEC_INDX1 (cr=492 r=0 w=0 time=9115 us)(object id 24694)
```

The optimizer decides to use the new index USRL_INDX1 and reduces the number of rows retrieved. Now, if another index is added to the EL_USER table, further improvement in the query can be obtained.

Indexes that are not selective do not improve query performance but can degrade DML performance. In RAC, unselective index blocks may be subject to interinstance contention, increasing the frequency of cache transfers for indexes belonging to INSERT-intensive tables.

9.7.3   SQL Advisory

Oracle's new SQL Advisory feature in EM is a good option for tuning SQL queries. Oracle analysis data gathered from real-time performance statistics uses this data to optimize the query performance. To use the SQL tuning advisory, select the "Advisory Central" option from the performance page from the db console or EM GC, then select the "SQL Tuning Advisory" option. This option provides the "Top Activity" page (Figure 9.8). Highlighting a specific time frame of the top activity will yield the "Top SQL" page ordered by highest activity (Figure 9.9).

Figure 9.8
EM Top Activity

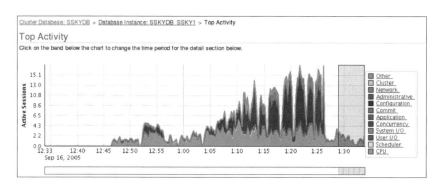

Poor query performance can occur for several reasons, such as

1.   *Stale optimizer statistics.* The Oracle Cost-based Optimizer (CBO) uses the statistics collected to determine the best execution plan. Stale optimizer statistics that do not accurately represent the current status of the data in objects can easily mislead

the optimizer to generate suboptimal plans. Since there is no easy method to determine whether optimizer statistics are up-to-date or stale, this can cause poor execution plans. Starting with Oracle Database 10*g*, optimizer statistics collection has been automated. A new job, GATHER_STATS_JOB, runs the DBMS_STATS.GATHER_DATABASE_STATS_JOB_PROC procedure. The job is automatically scheduled to run every night.

2. *Missing access structures.* The absence of appropriate access structures like indexes and materialized views is a common source of poor SQL performance.

3. *Suboptimal execution plan.* The CBO can sometimes choose a suboptimal execution plan for a SQL statement. This is primarily because of incorrect estimates of some attributes of a SQL statement, such as its cost, cardinality, or predicate selectivity.

4. *Bad SQL.* Queries using Cartesian joins or UNION ALL clauses in SQL queries make the execution plan really expensive and retrieval of the required rows time-consuming.

Figure 9.9
Top SQL

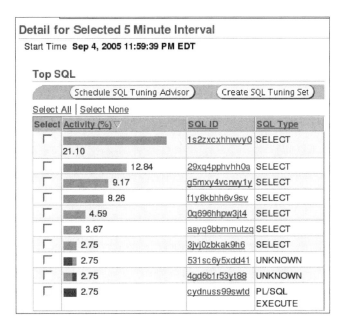

As illustrated in Figure 9.9, the SELECT statement with SQL_ID 1s2zxcxhhwvy0 has the highest activity. Once the queries to be tuned have been identified, click "Schedule SQL Tuning Advisor" and allow Oracle to tune the queries. The tuning process will perform statistics analysis, access path analysis, SQL profiling, and structure analysis before tuning the query. Oracle provides the modified query with a comparison of the execution plan before and after tuning. The changes can then be implemented.

Another option available under the SQL Advisory section is the SQL Access Advisor. This complements the SQL Tuning Advisor functionality, focusing on the identification of indexes, materialized views, and indexes on the materialized views to improve the performance of the entire SQL workload.

9.7.4   Queries with high cluster overhead

Queries not tuned can also be an overhead to performance across the cluster, causing high delays. In Oracle Database 10*g*, four new columns have been introduced to help identify queries that are performing poorly in general and specifically in a RAC environment.

Using the CLUSTER_WAIT_TIME column in the GV$SQLSTATS view, queries that are experiencing cluster-related waits can be identified and tuned. For example, the following lists the SQL queries, giving the wait times experienced at various stages of the operation:

```
SELECT INST_ID INST,
       SQL_ID,
       APPLICATION_WAIT_TIME AWT,
       CONCURRENCY_WAIT_TIME CONWT,
       CLUSTER_WAIT_TIME CLWT,
       USER_IO_WAIT_TIME UIWT
FROM   GV$SQLSTATS
WHERE  USER_IO_WAIT_TIME > 0
ORDER BY USER_IO_WAIT_TIME;
```

INST	SQL_ID	AWT	CONWT	CLWT	UIWT
2	10utkgdw43zmn	0	23007	62106878	263443
2	1h50ks4ncswfn	8874	1628544	76655404	6194443
2	8p23kcbgfqnk4	0	0	151877550	349272
2	gfjvxb25b773h	0	5803	179456437	932921
2	**19v5guvsgcd1v**	0	44526	**184945511**	355544

Once the queries with high cluster wait time have been identified, a specific query can be retrieved using the SQL_ID.

```
SQL> SELECT SQL_FULLTXT FROM GV$SQLSTATS WHERE SQL_ID='19v5guvsgcd1v';

SQL_FULLTEXT
--------------------------------------------------------------------------------
SELECT C.TARGET_GUID, C.METRIC_GUID, C.STORE_METRIC, C.SCHEDULE, C.COLL_NAME, M.
. . .

. . .
```

SQL_FULLTEXT is of data type BLOB. To retrieve the complete information from this column, PL/SQL packages such as DBMS_LOB.READ should be used.

9.8   Sequences and index contention

Indexes, with key values generated using sequences tend to be subject to leaf block contention when the insert rate is high. This is because the index leaf block holding the highest key value is changed for every row inserted as the values are monotonically ascending. This may lead to a high transfer rate of current and CR blocks between nodes. Techniques that can reduce such situations include the following:

- Increase sequence cache size. The difference between sequence values generated by different instances increases successive index block splits and tends to create instance affinity to index leaf blocks. This also improves instance affinity to index keys deriving their values from sequences. This technique may result in significant performance gains for multi-instance INSERT-intensive applications.

- Implement the database partitioning option to physically distribute the data.

- Use locally managed tablespaces (LMTs) over dictionary-managed tablespaces.

- Use automatic segment space management (ASSM), which can provide instance affinity to table blocks and is the default in Oracle Database 10*g* Release 2.

Oracle's sequence mechanism is highly efficient and works well in a RAC environment, except when an attempt is made to "fix" it! A common mistake is to add the ORDER clause to the CREATE SEQUENCE definition. This guarantees that sequence numbers will be issued in ascending order across the cluster, which means that for every sequence number issued, Oracle has to read the last value from the data dictionary to work out the next number (which might have been issued on another instance) and update the data dictionary with the new number. This can have a disastrous impact on applications that need high sequence-generation rates.

9.9   Undo block considerations

Excessive undo block shipment and contention for undo buffers usually happens when index blocks containing active transactions from multiple instances are read frequently. When a SELECT statement needs to read a block with active transactions, it has to undo the changes to create a CR version. If the active transaction in the block belongs to more than one instance, the local and remote undo information needs to be combined for the CR operation. Depending on the number of index blocks changed by multiple instances and the duration of transactions, undo block shipment may become a bottleneck.

Usually this happens in applications that read recently inserted data very frequently and commit frequently. Techniques that can reduce such situations include the following:

- Shorter transactions reduce the likelihood that an index block in the cache contains uncommitted data, thereby reducing the need to access undo information for a consistent read.

- As explained earlier, increasing sequence cache sizes can reduce inter-instance concurrent access to index leaf blocks. The CR version of index blocks modified by only one instance can be fabricated without the need for remote undo information.

9.10   Load-balancing

One primary feature of a clustered environment is the distribution of the workload across the various nodes and instances in the cluster. To achieve this distribution, it is advantageous to place new connections on systems that have a higher number of resources in the cluster. As discussed in

Chapter 6, load-balancing can be configured using EM or Oracle-provided PL/SQL packages. Load-balancing is based on the number of sessions or resources available on the various instances.

Figure 9.10, the "Balance" drilldown from Spotlight on RAC, illustrates the current load across the various nodes in the cluster. While the load is balanced from the CPU and physical writes perspectives, it seems out of balance with respect to the number of LIO operations. As indicated earlier, LIO operations consume significant resources and can be reduced by tuning the SQL queries.

Figure 9.10
Cluster Balance

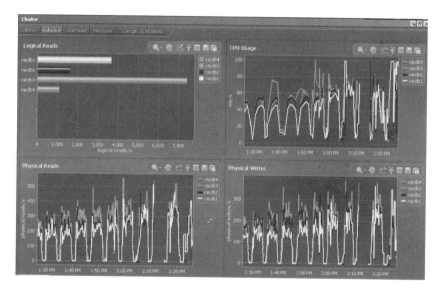

Besides tuning poorly-performing queries, the next step in obtaining a true load-balanced environment is to use the connection pooling feature on the application side and implement the RCLB feature discussed in Chapter 6. Connection pooling is supported by all application servers, such as Oracle 10*g* AS, Weblogic, and Jboss. How do you verify that the RCLB feature is working?

When MMON generates load advices, it is stored in the GV$SERVICEMET-RIC view and is used to communicate with the client of the current load. For example, the following query displays the load characteristics as updated by MMON in the GV$SERVICEMETRIC view. The view is joined with GV$INSTANCE and GV$ACTIVE_SERVICES to obtain additional information.

```
set pagesize 60 space 2 numwidth 8 linesize 132 verify off feedback off
column SERVICE_NAME format a20 truncated heading 'Service'
column INSTANCE_NAME heading 'Instance'  format a10
column SERVICE_TIME heading 'Service Time|mSec/Call' format 999999999
column CPU_TIME heading 'CPU Time |mSec/Call' 99999999
column DB_TIME heading 'DB Time |mSec/Call' 99999999
column THROUGHPUT heading 'Calls/sec' format 99.99 break on SERVICE_NAME skip 1
SELECT  SERVICE_NAME,
        INSTANCE_NAME,
        ELAPSEDPERCALL SERVICE_TIME,
        CPUPERCALL     CPU_TIME,
        DBTIMEPERCALL  DB_TIME,
        CALLSPERSEC    THROUGHPUT
FROM   GV$INSTANCE       GVI,
       GV$ACTIVE_SERVICES GVAS,
       GV$SERVICEMETRIC   GVSM
WHERE GVAS.INST_ID   = GVSM.INST_ID
AND   GVAS.NAME_HASH = GVSM.SERVICE_NAME_HASH
AND   GVI.INST_ID    = GVSM.INST_ID
AND   GVSM.GROUP_ID  = 10
ORDER BY
   SERVICE_NAME,
   GVI.INST_ID;
```

| | | Service Time | | | |
Service	Instance	mSec/Call	CPU_TIME	DB_TIME	THROUGHPUT
SRV1	**SSKY1**	22981	4525.497	22980.72	202.5948
SRV1	**SSKY2**	124837	6111.93	124837.4	141.3127
SSKYDB	SSKY1	0	0	0	0
SSKYDB	SSKY2	1750	1750	1750	1.158301
SYS$BACKGROUND	SSKY1	0	0	0	0
SYS$BACKGROUND	SSKY2	0	0	0	0
SYS$USERS	SSKY1	3608	3608	3608	.3992016
SYS$USERS	SSKY2	0	0	0	0

In this output, service SRV1 on both instances does not seem balanced. The service time on SSKY2 is high, and the overall throughput is low; however, the DB time and CPU time values seem lower. When a message is received by the application server using the FAN technology regarding the current state of the instance, new sessions will be directed by FAN to instance SSKY2.

GV$SERVICEMETRIC

This view contains metric values measured for all the services defined in the database. These values are updated by the MMON process as it captures load and other service-related information from the SGA. Updates to this view happen in five-second and one-minute intervals.

Apart from making updates to the GV$SERVICEMETRIC view, MMON also updates the operating system statistics and uses this information to determine the load characteristics on the various nodes in the cluster. The following query output from GV$OSSTAT provides the operating system statistics.

```
SQL> SELECT * FROM GV$OSSTAT WHERE INST_ID=1;

    INST_ID STAT_NAME                            VALUE   OSSTAT_ID
---------- ------------------------------ ----------  ----------
         1 NUM_CPUS                                 2           0
         1 IDLE_TIME                           134867           1
         1 BUSY_TIME                            82151           2
         1 USER_TIME                            66198           3
         1 SYS_TIME                             15953           4
         1 NICE_TIME                                0           6
         1 RSRC_MGR_CPU_WAIT_TIME                   0          14
         1 LOAD                            6.65917969          15
         1 PHYSICAL_MEMORY_BYTES            433270784        1008
```

GV$OSSTAT

This view contains operating system statistics updated by the MMON process and is used to determine the load on the nodes and servers. The values are in hundredths of a second, as a processor has been busy executing code and is averaged over all processors.

9.10.1 Tracing the load metric capture

RCLB can also be verified by enabling tracing at the database level using event 10735 at level 3. Tracing can be enabled using the following statement:

```
SQL> ALTER SYSTEM SET EVENTS '10735 TRACE NAME CONTEXT
FOREVER, LEVEL 3';
```

The output is generated and stored in the user dump destination directory of the instance, which can be determined after connecting to the database and verifying the parameter USER_DUMP_DEST.

```
SQL> SHOW PARAMETER USER_DUMP_DEST

NAME                 TYPE         VALUE
----------------     ----------   ------------------------------
user_dump_dest       string       /usr/app/oracle/admin/SSKYDB/udump
```

The trace file contains the activities involving the cluster or services that are being monitored. This provides insight into how the client machines using this metric will react. The output of the trace file resembles the following:

```
/usr/app/oracle/admin/SSKYDB/udump/ssky1_ora_23316.trc
Oracle Database 10g Enterprise Edition Release 10.2.0.1.0 - Production
With the Partitioning, Real Application Clusters, OLAP and Data Mining options
ORACLE_HOME = /usr/app/oracle/product/10.2.0/db_1
. . .
Instance name: SSKY1
Redo thread mounted by this instance: 1
Oracle process number: 70
Unix process pid: 23316, image: oracleSSKY1@oradb3.sumsky.net


kswsgsnp : length of KSWS_SYSTEM_SVC is 14
kswsgsnp : length of KSWS_DATABASE_SVC is 9
          Both should be less than 64 to avoid overrun
*** SERVICE NAME:(SRV1) 2005-09-24 23:58:31.636
*** SESSION ID:(91.1) 2005-09-24 23:58:31.635
###session count for SRV1=33
###session count for SRV1=34
*** 2005-09-24 23:59:32.626
SKGXPSEGRCV: MESSAGE TRUNCATED user data 40 bytes payload 200 bytes
SKGXPSEGRCV: trucated message buffer data skgxpmsg meta data header 0x0xbfff54e0
len 40 bytes
SKGXPLOSTACK: message truncation expected
SKGXPLOSTACK: data sent to port with no buffers queued from
SSKGXPID 0xbfff559c network 0   Internet address 10.168.2.140   UDP port number
54589
```

```
SSKGXPID 0xbfff559c network 1    Internet address 220.255.187.12        UDP port
number 3260
SKGXPLOSTACK: sent seq 32763 expecting 32764
SKGXPLOSTACK: lost ack detected retransmit ack
*** 2005-09-25 00:02:38.927
###session count for SRV1=31
###session count for SRV1=30
```

This output illustrates that the MMON's statistics collection is working and configured for the default type and that the load-balance on session is counted. In this case, SRV1 is the service, and Oracle updates the MMON process, which in turn builds the advisory and posts the required advice to the advanced queue (AQ), PMON, and the ONS. The trace output also shows that there were several retransmissions, indicating potential issues with the interconnect.

9.11 Resource availability

Resources available on any machine or node or to an Oracle instance are limited, meaning they are not available in abundance and, if a process on the system needs them, they may not be immediately available. There is a physical limit to the number of resources available on any system. For example, are processor resources limited by the number of CPUs available on the system, and the amount of memory or cache area is limited by the amount of physical memory available on the system. For an Oracle process, this is further limited by the actual amount of memory allocated to the SGA. Within the SGA, the shared pool, the buffer cache, and so on, are again preallocated from the total SGA (defined by the SGA_TARGET_SIZE parameter). These are memory allocations used by a regular single-instance configuration.

In a RAC environment, there are no parameters to allocate any global-specific resources (e.g., global cache size or global shared pool area). Oracle allocates a certain portion of the available resources from the SGA for global activity. The availability of global resources can be monitored using the GV$RESOURCE_LIMIT view. For example, the following query displays the current number of resources available for global activity. In the output below, the availability of resources is limited by the column LIMIT_VALUE, and when these resources are low, the method to increase the limit is to increase the SGA_TARGET and SGA_MAX_SIZE parameters.

The following query generates the output containing the current utilization of resources:

```
SELECT
        RESOURCE_NAME,
        CURRENT_UTILIZATION CU,
        MAX_UTILIZATION MU,
        INITIAL_ALLOCATION IA,
        LIMIT_VALUE LV
FROM    GV$RESOURCE_LIMIT
WHERE MAX_UTILIZATION > 0
ORDER BY INST_ID,
        RESOURCE_NAME
```

RESOURCE_NAME	CU	MU	IA	LV
cmtcallbk	0	1	187	UNLIMITED
dml_locks	2	59	748	UNLIMITED
enqueue_locks	19	27	2261	2261
enqueue_resources	22	45	968	UNLIMITED
gcs_resources	**3447**	**3447**	**18245**	**18245**
gcs_shadows	**2259**	**2579**	**18245**	**18245**
ges_big_msgs	**27**	**28**	**964**	**UNLIMITED**
ges_cache_ress	**338**	**1240**	**0**	**UNLIMITED**
ges_procs	**35**	**36**	**320**	**320**
ges_reg_msgs	**44**	**81**	**1050**	**UNLIMITED**
max_rollback_segments	11	11	187	65535
max_shared_servers	1	1	UNLIMITED	UNLIMITED
processes	31	34	150	150
sessions	37	40	170	170
sort_segment_locks	0	1	UNLIMITED	UNLIMITED
transactions	2	4	187	UNLIMITED

When the SGA_TARGET size was increased by 10M, the global resource allocation also changed to the following new values:

gcs_resources	**2553**	**2553**	**19351**	**19351**
gcs_shadows	**1279**	**1279**	**19351**	**19351**

The rule should be that when the `MAX_UTILIZATION` (`MU`) gets close to the `LIMIT_VALUE` (`LV`) and remains constant at this value for a considerable time, consider increasing the SGA.

9.12 Response time

However large the clustered environment might be or however impressive the hardware that supports it, the primary success factor for any application environment is to provide good user response time (i.e., how quickly are the users getting a response for their operations?). Response time is the time used for the query to perform the actual service, plus any additional overhead time spent by the process waiting for resources. In other words, **response time = service time + wait time**.

Service time is the time used to make database-related calls and is improved by tuning the queries and optimizing the various Oracle parameters. The trick is to determine which part of the application is consuming high service times. A number of commercial tools exist to help measure elapsed time in either benchmarking or production environments.

In the absence of such a tool, the alternative is to try to instrument the application itself. This can be done by inserting timing calls into the application using language-specific syntax or using timing routines. Such embedded routines will log the activity into files, which can then be analyzed to determine poorly performing areas of the application code.

Wait time is the overhead experienced by the processes while performing an operation. Wait time can be due to several reasons. The Oracle Wait Interface (OWI) provides a great instrumentation on the various wait states encountered by database operations. In this section, the common waits encountered in a RAC environment are discussed

9.13 Oracle Wait Interface

OWI, or wait event, in Oracle is a situation when a session puts itself to sleep to wait for some external event to happen. Wait events are classified as system, service, or idle conditions. Idle waits occur when a session is waiting for a work request to be issued. Service wait events are waits for the system to perform asynchronous operations such as I/O or process creation.

Before Oracle Database 10*g*, OWI was driven by the three primary views: `GV$SYSTEM_EVENT`, `GV$SESSION_EVENT`, and `GV$SESSION_WAIT`. These views provided wait times at the system level or at the individual session level.

However, there was no method to isolate waits to a specific set of modules within an application. In Oracle Database 10*g*, with the introduction of a new abstraction class to support SOA, a new view is introduced, GV$SERVICE_EVENT, which provides the intermediate level of instrumentation for performance diagnostics and tuning.

To further streamline the wait events, in Oracle Database 10*g*, wait events have been classified into wait classes. This helps in grouping wait events and directing tuning efforts to the various areas of the environment. The following query illustrates the number of wait events grouped under the various wait classes:

```
SELECT WAIT_CLASS,
       COUNT(*)
FROM   V$SYSTEM_EVENT
GROUP BY WAIT_CLASS;


WAIT_CLASS                COUNT(*)
-------------------- ----------
Concurrency                 8
System I/O                  9
User I/O                    7
Configuration               2
Other                      57
Cluster                    11
Application                 3
Idle                       24
Commit                      1
Network                     3
```

While wait events pertaining to all classes have some direct or indirect impact on a RAC environment, for our discussions, only wait events[5] that belong to the Cluster class will be discussed. In Oracle Database 10*g* Release 2, there are 47 wait events in this class.

 Note: In a clustered environment, all the V$ views, when prefixed with a "G" (meaning global), will provide statistics from all instances in the cluster.

---

5.   For a thorough understanding of wait events, please refer to Oracle Wait Interface: Practical Guide to Performance Diagnostics & Tuning (2004) by Richmond Shee, Kirtikumar Deshpande, and K. Gopalakrishnan.

Wait categorization has changed and taken a strategic direction in Oracle Database 10*g*. Table 9.1 provides a mapping between the Oracle 9*i* wait events and the Oracle 10*g* wait events concerning RAC.

In Table 9.1, the Oracle Database 10*g* wait events are grouped as current or CR-type wait events. Current and CR waits are based on current and CR blocks in the buffer of various instances. What is the difference between CR and current waits?

9.13.1   Consistent read versus current

The first time a block is read into a buffer of any participating instance, it is termed a current block, no matter what the purpose of the user accessing

Table 9.1   *Oracle Database 9i Event to Oracle Database 10g Event Mapping*

Oracle 9i Wait Event	Oracle 10g Wait Event
global cache null to x global cache null to s	gc current block 2-way gc current block 3-way gc current block busy gc current block congested
global cache open x	gc current block 2-way gc current block 3-way gc current block busy gc current block congested gc current grant 2-way gc current multiblock request
global cache s to x	gc current grant 2-way
global cache cr request	gc cr block 2-way gc cr block 3-way gc cr block busy gc cr block congested gc cr grant 2-way gc cr multi block request

the block may be, meaning it can be a `SELECT` operation or a DML operation. The first access is always termed a current operation. Subsequently, when the block is transferred from one instance to another instance because a session on that instance requested the block, it is termed as a CR block.

As discussed in Chapter 2, when a block is required by a process for read purposes, it accesses the block in shared mode. When the block is to be modified, the processes requires a grant from the GCS to access this block in exclusive mode. The frequency of state/grant changes to the block can be obtained by querying the STATE column from the GV$BH view. The following are RAC-related state changes [9]:

- XCUR   exclusive current
- SCUR   shared current
- CR   consistent read
- READ   reading from disk
- WRITE   write clone mode
- PI   past image

When blocks are required by more than one process on the same instance, Oracle will clone the block. The number of times a block can be cloned is defined by the parameter _DB_BLOCK_MAX_CR_DBA[6] and defaults to six, meaning only six cloned copies of the same block of the same data block address (DBA) can exist in the local buffer of an instance (SSKY1 in Figure 9.10) at any given time. In Oracle Database 10g Release 1, Oracle placed the CR blocks in the cold end of the buffer cache. Now the CR blocks are treated like any other data block, and the Touch Count Algorithm (TCA) is used. Under TCA the block read is placed at midpoint (insertion point) in the buffer cache and will have to gain creditability when session access or touch the block, to climb up the stack to reach the hot buffer area. If the block is not touched by other sessions, it will move down the stack and finally get flushed out when the buffer is needed by new blocks.

Similarly, when blocks are required by more than one other instance, Oracle will ship an image of the CR block (if it has not already done so) to the requesting instance. As discussed in Chapter 2, blocks are shipped from one instance to another (Figure 9.11), and the details about which instance contains the block are maintained in the GRD. The number of

---

6.   Underscore parameters should be modified only after consulting with Oracle support.

instances a block can exist on is determined by the parameter _FAIRNESS_THRESHOLD[7] and defaults to four, meaning only four images of the same block of a particular DBA can exist in a RAC cluster (irrespective of the number of instances) at any given time.

Once the holder reaches the threshold defined by the parameter _FAIRNESS_THRESHOLD, it stops making more copies, flushes the redo to the disk, and downgrades the locks [9].

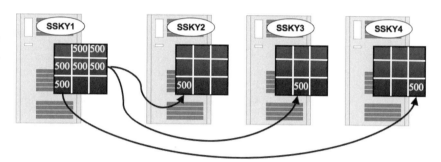

Figure 9.11
Block Cloning and Imaging

Note: While data movement in a RAC environment is at the block level, data modifications are all at the row level (as in a single-instance configuration).

9.13.2 gc cr/current block 2-way/3-way

One primary function of a cluster environment is to share blocks between instances, minimizing access to the physical storage. It is common that blocks will be transferred from one instance to another. The wait events listed in Table 9.1 all relate to the block transfers between the various instances in the cluster. For example, a 2-way event indicates that there was a 2-way shipment to transfer the block in which the requester sends a message to the master, and the master ships the block back to the requester. Similarly, a 3-way event indicates that there were three hops before the block was received by the requestor. A three-hop scenario is illustrated in Figure 9.12.

---

7. Underscore parameters should be modified only after consulting with Oracle support.

Figure 9.12
3-Way Block
Transfer

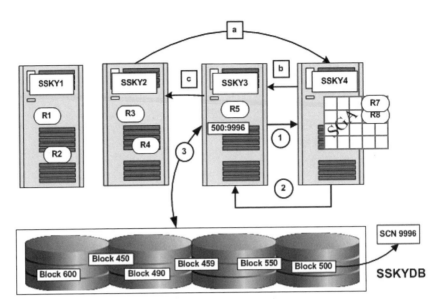

As illustrated in Figure 9.12, in a RAC cluster there are two possibilities when the GCS process has to perform three hops before the requestor receives the block.

1.   Read the block from the disk.

  ▪ Instance SSKY1 requests block 500 from the GCS located on instance SSKY4.

  ▪ Instance SSKY4, after checking against the GRD, determines that neither instance SSKY4 nor any other instance in the cluster has a copy of the block requested. Hence, it sends a message to the requesting instance to read the block from disk.

  ▪ Instance SSKY3 reads the block from disk.

2.   Request another instance to transfer the block.

  ▪ Instance SSKY2 requests block 500 from the GCS located on instance SSKY4.

  ▪ Instance SSKY4 verifies against its GRD and determines that the block is currently held by instance SSKY3. It sends a message to instance SSKY3 requesting that it send a copy of the block to instance SSKY2.

  ▪ Instance SSKY3 accepts the request and sends the block to instance SSKY2.

In the RAC architecture, in order to get a block, the GCS may have to perform two hops if the block requested cannot be found on the local instance because, if the master is located on the instance where the demand for the blocks concerning a specific object is the highest, hence, most likely, the block is going to be present where the master is located. In Oracle Database 10g Release 2, when the demand for the blocks concerning the object increases on another instance, the master will dynamically move or relocate to this new instance. Only when blocks are not found on the master does the GCS need to direct the transfer from another instance or from disk (three hops). Irrespective of the number of instances in the cluster, the GCS process will have to make a maximum of three hops. That is why the RAC architecture scales irrespective of the number of instances in the cluster: no matter how many instances might be associated with the cluster, the number of hops will never exceed three. The 3-way wait values that are significantly high could indicate that the block was never found on the master or the master did not relocate to another instance where the demand is high.

9.13.3 *gc cr/current block congested*

This wait indicates that the request was made to the Distributed Lock Manager (DLM) but ended up waiting, and the foreground process have to retry the request. Under these circumstances, the gc cr/current block congested wait counter is incremented.

Normally, this indicates that the GCS process (LMSn background) is not able to keep up with the requests. LMSn is a single-threaded synchronous process and follows the first in first out (FIFO) algorithm to complete block requests. This means that when multiple requests are received, the GES will place the requests in a queue and send the request to the LMSn process when it has completed a previous operation. In such situations, consideration should be given to increase the number of LMSn processes using the parameter GCS_SERVER_PROCESSES. A good rule of thumb is to set the value of this parameter to one LMSn processes for every two CPUs on the node. Setting it to high values will consume resources and can affect the overall performance of the cluster. LMSn processing delays can also be the result of scheduling delays and high queue lengths experienced by the node at the operating system level.

RAC has several other types of wait events. For a better understanding, the global cache–related wait events have been grouped in Figure 9.13 by the areas they affect.

9.13.4 gc remaster

This wait indicates the delay encountered when remastering the resource master from one instance to another instance in the cluster. In Oracle Database 10*g* Release 2, RAC architecture allows for dynamic remastering from a less busy instance to an instance where the demand for the object is the highest. This movement is called *resource affinity.*

Apart from remastering based on demand, remastering also happens when an instance leaves (fails) or joins the clustered configuration. During instance failure, remastering may happen more than once, first to place the master dynamically on one of the surviving nodes and, second, once the cluster has reached a stable state to reassess the situation and remaster again based on demand. Monitoring the remastering activity is discussed later in the chapter.

Figure 9.13
Wait Events
Grouped

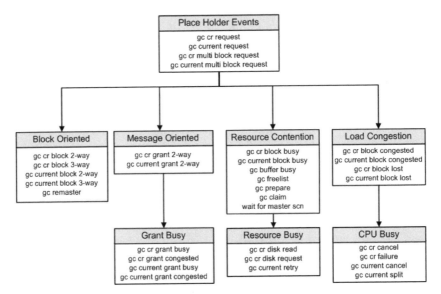

9.13.5 wait for master SCN

Each instance in the cluster will generate its own SCN and, subsequently, using the propagation method, will resynchronize to the highest SCN in the cluster. This wait indicates the number of times the foreground processes waited for SCNs to be acknowledged from other instances in the cluster.

Before Oracle Database 10*g* Release 2, the method of SCN propagation was driven by the parameter MAX_COMMIT_PROPAGATION_DELAY. Setting this value to higher than zero uses the Lamport algorithm. In Oracle Database 10*g* Release 2, this parameter is deprecated and is maintained for backward compatibility only and defaults to zero. This functionality is now driven by the underscore (hidden) parameter _IMMEDIATE_COMMIT_PROPAGATION[8] and has a Boolean value of TRUE or FALSE.

When this parameter is set to TRUE (default), Oracle uses the Block on Commit (BOC) algorithm for messaging. While the method of propagation remains similar to the Lamport algorithm, in the case of BOC, the global high water mark for the SCNs sent and received is maintained, reducing messaging traffic for global SCN synchronization and, in turn, improving overall performance.

9.13.6 gc cr/current request

This event indicates the time spent waiting when a session is looking for a CR version of a block (indicated by the lock element number or class of the buffer in P3 (Table 9.2), and the block number in column P2; it belongs to the file indicated in column P1 in the V$SESSION_WAIT view cannot find it in its local cache, and so has made a request to a remote instance for the block. However, the transferred block has not yet arrived at the requesting instance. The event ends when the requesting session gets the block or permission to read the block from disk.

This event may not always indicate a problem with the GCS requests. Circumstances under which this wait time value is high can be due to the following:

1.   Data blocks are being modified frequently on all instances.

2.   Requests for block have resulted in a cache miss.

3.   LMSn cannot keep up with the high number of CR requests.

4.   There are latency issues with the interconnect.

5.   Several full table scans are being performed.

High waits on this event can be reduced by looking at the system and scheduling delays at the operating system level (e.g., ensuring that the LMSn process gets enough CPU cycles to complete its operation). As explained earlier, increasing the number of LMSn processes may be

---

8.   Underscore parameters should be modified only after consulting with Oracle support.

required. Ensuring that a high-speed interconnect is used will also help reduce waits in this category.

Table 9.2   *Common Block Classes [9]*

Block Class	Description
0	System rollback segment
1	Data blocks
2	Sort blocks
3	Deferred rollback segment blocks (save undo)
4	Segment header blocks
5	Deferred rollback segment header blocks
6	Freelist blocks
7	Extent map blocks
8	Bitmapped space management blocks
9	Space management index blocks
10	Unused

9.13.7   gc current/CR block busy

This wait indicates that a current or CR block was requested and received but was not sent immediately by LMSn because some special condition that delayed the sending was found.

9.13.8   gc current grant busy

This wait indicates that a current block was requested, and a grant message was received. The busy hint implies that the request was blocked because others were ahead of it, or it could not be handled immediately.

9.14   Server/database statistics

Oracle gathers performance-related statistics from various categories that are subsequently analyzed. These statistics help in diagnosing performance-related issues in the database. Several statistics are collected for the RAC environment. Monitoring and tuning the related areas will help improve performance.

Server statistics are stored at the system level or at the session level. As with the OWI, system-level statistics stored in GV$SYSSTAT are a cumulative value of all sessions since the instance was started. On the other hand, GV$SESSTAT contains values for individual sessions that are active at a given point. With the introduction of services in Oracle Database 10*g*, a new view at the service level is also available: GV$SERVICE_STATS.

The RAC-related statistics maintained at the system level can be obtained using the following query:

```
SELECT NAME,
       VALUE
FROM V$SYSSTAT
WHERE NAME LIKE 'g%';
```

NAME	VALUE
global enqueue gets sync	104853
global enqueue gets async	15529
global enqueue get time	3203
global enqueue releases	111512
gcs messages sent	8286
ges messages sent	7656
global enqueue CPU used by this session	816
gc cr blocks served	3461
gc cr block build time	30
gc cr block flush time	18
gc cr block send time	54
gc current blocks served	4458
gc current block pin time	13
gc current block flush time	0
gc current block send time	112
gc cr blocks received	76
gc cr block receive time	67
gc current blocks received	280
gc current block receive time	126
gc blocks lost	89
gc claim blocks lost	0
gc blocks corrupt	0

```
gc CPU used by this session                807
global undo segment hints helped             0
global undo segment hints were stale         0
```

9.14.1 Time model statistics

In Oracle Database 10*g*, a new method of monitoring statistics is introduced called the time model. While the wait event shows where the system is spending time waiting, the time model shows where the system is wasting time doing activities such as reloading the SQL cache or performing a parse operation.

Under the time model method, the time spent at various stages of the process is collected, providing a more detailed level of data for problem diagnosis. Like the database statistics discussed earlier, the time model statistics can also be obtained at the system level from the GV$SYS_TIME_MODEL or at the session level from the GV$SES_TIME_MODEL views. The following query lists the time model statistics at the system level:

```
COL STAT_NAME FORMAT A45
SELECT STAT_NAME,
       VALUE
FROM   V$SYS_TIME_MODEL;


STAT_NAME                                           VALUE
----------------------------------------------- ----------
DB time                                         139911756
DB CPU                                           30228434
background elapsed time                         171121413
background cpu time                              38843962
sequence load elapsed time                         527830
parse time elapsed                               47249379
hard parse elapsed time                          45738124
sql execute elapsed time                        137995412
connection management call elapsed time            402551
failed parse elapsed time                               0
failed parse (out of shared memory) elapsed time        0
hard parse (sharing criteria) elapsed time          14348
hard parse (bind mismatch) elapsed time             12671
PL/SQL execution elapsed time                     6104754
inbound PL/SQL rpc elapsed time                         0
PL/SQL compilation elapsed time                   5856205
```

```
Java execution elapsed time                            0
repeated bind elapsed time                        163961
RMAN cpu time (backup/restore)                         0
```

Of all the statistics available under the time model, the two statistics that are important for diagnosing performance-related issues are DB time (database time) and DB CPU. DB time is the key statistic for the time model and represents the total elapsed time spent servicing user requests on database-related calls. The value includes CPU time spent, plus any non-idle wait time to complete the database operation and waiting on the run queue for CPU. In other words,

```
DB time = Sum of time spent processing all user requests = Sum
of time (Running on CPU + Waiting for Resources + Waiting for
CPU) [10]
```

```
DB time/sec = Total DB time / Elapsed time or Wall clock time
```

DB time is used as a mechanism to measure other time statistic values. Typically, the ratio of the time statistic collected from a wait event to DB time will help determine the total system impact of that wait event. The goal of the DBA is to reduce the DB time to improve the overall performance of the database.

9.15 Service-level metrics

With the support for SOA and Oracle's implementation of a layer of abstraction to the application as services, Oracle has also introduced in Oracle Database 10*g* a new dimension for performance tuning. With services, workloads are visible and measurable, and statistics gathered can be attributed to specific applications or modules within applications. Services provide another level of performance optimization by connecting a specific poorly performing SQL operation to a service instead of the traditional approach where a SQL was always related to a session. Apart from wait events at the service level (discussed earlier) available through the GV$SERVICE_EVENTS view, the following statistics are also collected at the service level:

User calls	Workarea executions – optimal
DB time – response time	Workarea executions – onepass
DB CPU – CPU/service	Workarea executions – multipass
Parse count (total)	Session cursor cache hits
Parse time elapsed	User rollbacks
Parse time CPU	DB block changes
Execute count	gc cr blocks received
SQL execute elapsed time	gc cr block receive time
Opened cursors cumulative	gc current blocks received
Session logical reads	gc current block receive time
Physical reads	Cluster wait time
Physical writes	Concurrency wait time
Redo size	Application wait time
User commits	User I/O wait time

Optionally, Oracle provides additional levels of data collection by defining modules within applications or actions within modules. This helps in easy identification of performance areas within the application. Module and action-level monitoring can be enabled using the following PL/SQL definition:

```
DBMS_MONITOR.SERV_MOD_ACT_STAT_ENABLE (<SERVICE_NAME>,
<MODULE NAME>)
```

For example, to enable statistics collection for module ORDERS in service SRV1, the following should be executed on the database server on any of the available instances:

```
EXEC DBMS_MONITOR.SERV_MOD_ACT_STAT_ENABLE ('SR1','ORDERS');
```

Once monitoring has been enabled, it remains active until it is disabled using the following procedure:

```
EXEC DBMS_MONITOR.SERV_MOD_ACT_STAT_DISABLE (null,null);
```

These definitions can be verified by querying the DBA_ENABLED_AGGREGATIONS table:

```
SELECT AGGREGATION_TYPE,
       QUALIFIER_ID1 MODULE,
       QUALIFIER_ID2 ACTION
FROM DBA_ENABLED_AGGREGATIONS;


AGGREGATION_TYPE         MODULE       ACTION
--------------------     ----------   ---------
SERVICE_MODULE_ACTION    ORDERS       Mixed
SERVICE_MODULE_ACTION    ORDERS       Multiple
SERVICE_MODULE_ACTION    ORDERS       Read
SERVICE_MODULE_ACTION    ORDERS       Update
```

Before monitoring the performance statistics, the application connecting to the database should connect to the SERVICE_NAME being monitored, and the application should have the module identified in the code. The module name can be set in the application using the following procedure:

```
DBMS_APPLICATION_INFO.SET_MODULE (<MODULE NAME>, <ACTION TYPE>);
```

For example, to let the database know which module is being monitored, the following procedure should be executed from inside the application module:

```
EXEC DBMS_APPLICATION_INFO.SET_MODULE ('ORDERS');
```

Apart from monitoring individual modules, performance-related statistics can also be collected for any specific action. For example, the performance of various users executing update statements can also be monitored with the following procedure:

```
EXEC DBMS_MONITOR.SERV_MOD_ACT_STAT_ENABLE
('SRV1','ORDERS','UPDATE');
```

Similarly, inside the application, the ORDERS module, the specific action (UPDATE) being modified should also be identified using the following procedure:

```
EXEC DBMS_APPLICATION_INFO.SET_MODULE ('ORDERS','UPDATE');
```

This feature of collecting a performance matrix for an action type within a module was not available until Oracle Database 10*g* and is a great feature that can easily be taken advantage of. In a RAC environment with DWM implementation, this helps track a module's performance across the cluster.

Once the statistics collection has been enabled on the database server and on the client side, the performance metrics can be collected or monitored. For example, the output from the following script against the GV$SERVICE_STATS view provides a high-level indication that DB time for SRV1 on instance 2 is significantly high.

```
COL STAT_NAME FORMAT A35
COL MODULE FORMAT A10
COL SERVICE FORMAT A15
COL INST FORMAT 999
SELECT INST_ID INST,
       SERVICE_NAME SERVICE,
       STAT_NAME,
       VALUE
FROM   GV$SERVICE_STATS
WHERE  VALUE > 0
AND    SERVICE_NAME ='SRV1'
ORDER  BY VALUE;


INST SERVICE          STAT_NAME                                VALUE
---- ---------------  ----------------------------------- ----------
   2 SRV1             parse count (total)                     114332
   2 SRV1             opened cursors cumulative               114574
   2 SRV1             execute count                           252873
   2 SRV1             session logical reads                  5254843
   2 SRV1             redo size                            21199172
   2 SRV1             cluster wait time                    27815562
   2 SRV1             application wait time                 87809921
   2 SRV1             user I/O wait time                   98546228
```

2 SRV1	concurrency wait time	2055384221
2 SRV1	DB CPU	2156249531
2 SRV1	sql execute elapsed time	6912286900
2 SRV1	parse time elapsed	8681424580
2 SRV1	**DB time**	**9845032706**

To identify the module and action type that caused the high DB time values, use the following script against the view GV$SERV_MOD_ACT_STATS:

```
COL STAT_NAME FORMAT A35
COL MODULE FORMAT A10
COL SERVICE FORMAT A10
COL INST FORMAT 999
COL ACTION FORMAT A8
SELECT INST_ID INST,
       AGGREGATION_TYPE,
       SERVICE_NAME SERVICE,
       MODULE,
       ACTION,
       STAT_NAME,
       VALUE
FROM  GV$SERV_MOD_ACT_STATS;
```

The benefits provided for monitoring activity at the service level do not stop here. Tracing user operations is also available at the module and action level. Oracle generates one trace file per session, connecting to the database using the SERVICE_NAME. Users connecting to the database may get attached to any of the available instances supporting the service. The advantage of tracing at this level is that, when multiple trace files are generated from the current instance or across instances in the cluster, data related to a specific action type can be grouped together. For example, the following procedure will enable tracing of a service at the module and action levels:

```
DBMS_MONITOR.SERV_MOD_ACT_TRACE_ENABLE
(<SERVICE_NAME>,<MODULE NAME>,<ACTION TYPE>);

EXEC DBMS_MONITOR.SERV_MOD_ACT_TRACE_ENABLE
('SRV1','ORDERS','MIXED');
```

Apart from the basic SQL-level trace information, additional information such as wait events encountered (collected by default), bind variables, and values used can also be collected. For example:

```
EXEC DBMS_MONITOR.SERV_MOD_ACT_TRACE_ENABLE (
    SERVICE_NAME  => 'SRV1',
    MODULE_NAME   => 'ORDERS',
    ACTION_NAME   => DBMS_MONITOR.ALL_ACTIONS,
    WAITS         => TRUE,
    BINDS         => TRUE);
```

 Note: The SERV_MOD_ACT_TRACE_ENABLE utility generates trace files similar to the trace files generated using event 10406 at level 1. Enabling wait events and binds will be similar to generating tracing using 10406 at level 12.

Once these procedures are executed on the database server, the trace files are generated in the USER_DUMP_DEST directory on the respective instances. Oracle generates one trace file for every session, connecting to the database using the service SRV1. The trace files can then be consolidated based on different criteria. Based on the example, the trace file will contain information such as SQL statements, wait events encountered, bind variables, and bind values. This trace information can be

1. Analyzed directly using the Transient Kernel Profiler (tkprof) utility.

    ```
    tkprof ssky1.ora.*.trc trcSRV1.prf explain=bmf/bmf
    table=bmf.temp sys=no
    ```

2. Scanned through and extracted by action type using the trcsess utility. Once extracted into a single file, it can be analyzed using the tkprof utility.

    ```
    trcsess output=trcMixed.trc service=SRV1
    module='ORDERS' action=Mixed  ssky1_ora_*.trc

    trcsess [output=<output file name >]
    [session=<session ID>] [clientid=<clientid>]
    [service=<service name>] [action=<action name>]
    ```

```
[module=<module name>] <trace file names>
```

- `<output file name>` is the output destination, default being standard output.
- `<sessionID>` is the session to be traced. `SessionID` is a combination of session index and session serial number.
- `<clientid>` is the client to be traced.
- `<service name>` is the service to be traced.
- `<action name>` is the action to be traced.
- `<module name>` is the module to be traced.
- `<trace file names>` is a space-separated list of trace files with wild card '*' supported.

The following `trcsess` command will extract trace information from the trace file that pertains to service SRV1 but contains all modules and actions:

```
trcsess output=trcSRV1.trc service=SRV1 ssky1_ora_*.trc
```

Similarly, the following `trcsess` command will extract trace information from the trace files that pertain to service SRV1 and module ORDERS, but will contain all actions:

```
trcsess output=trcRead.trc service=SRV1 action=Mixed
module=ORDERS ssky1_ora_*.trc
```

9.16 Identifying blockers across instances

When two users request access to the same row of data for update purposes, all users except the first will remain in wait mode until the first user has committed or rolled back the change. This is true irrespective of whether it is a single-instance configuration or a clustered RAC configuration, with an additional possibility. Apart from users on the same instance, users from other instances can also request the same row at the same time. The following query helps identify a blocking session in a RAC environment:

```
SELECT DECODE(G.INST_ID,1,'SSKY1',2,'SSKY2') INSTANCE,
       S.SID,
       G.TYPE,
       S.USERNAME,
       S.SERIAL#,
       S.PROCESS,
       DECODE(LMODE,0,'None',1,'Null',2,'Row-S',3,'Row-X',4,'Share',5,'S/ROW',
6,'Exclusive') LMODE,
       DECODE(REQUEST,0,'None',1,'Null',2,'Row-S',3,'Row-X',4,'Share', 5,'S/
ROW',6,'Exclusive')REQUEST,
       DECODE(REQUEST,0,'BLOCKER','WAITER') STATE
FROM   GV$GLOBAL_BLOCKED_LOCKS G,
       GV$SESSION S
WHERE  G.SID = S.SID
AND    G.INST_ID = S.INST_ID
ORDER BY STATE
```

INSTANCE	SID	TY	USERN	SERIAL#	PROCESS	LMODE	REQUEST	STATE
SSKY2	132	TX	OE	519	2576:820	**Exclusive**	None	**BLOCKER**
SSKY2	148	TX	OE	78	980:3388	None	Exclusive	**WAITER**
SSKY1	139	TX	OE	114	3192:2972	None	Exclusive	**WAITER**

In this output, the session with SID 132 on instance SSKY2 is the BLOCKER because this session accessed this row first in an exclusive mode and has either committed or rolled back the transaction. Subsequently, the session with SID 148 also on instance SSKY2 requested this same row for update, followed by SID 139 from instance SSKY1. Both of these SIDs will remain as WAITER until the row is available to the session to complete its update operation. Blockers can also be determined from the EM by selecting the "Blocking Sessions" option from the database performance page or by querying BLOCKING_SESSION_STATUS, BLOCKING_INSTANCE, BLOCKING_SESSION columns from V$SESSION view.

9.17 Identifying hot blocks

One primary feature of RAC is to provide scalability by allowing transfer of blocks on user request from one instance to the other, thus avoiding any disk I/O. When the same sets of blocks is requested back and forth between the various instances in the cluster, the sessions requesting the block may have to wait until the holding instance has released it. This back-and-forth movement of the same blocks may indicate or create contention over the interconnect. Identifying such blocks and then analyzing ways in which they can be minimized will help in the overall performance of the cluster. Hot blocks can be identified by querying the V$SEGSTAT view.

9.18 **Monitoring remastering**

One of the primary scalability factors for Oracle is balancing resource demands on each instance by satisfying requests on local nodes where demand for the resource is high. For example, if there are 1,000 users on instance SSKY1 and only 100 users on instance SSKY2 for the EMP table object, it would be more efficient to place the master for the EMP object on instance SSKY1. However, when demand for the object changes, and SSKY2 has more users for the object, then the master should move from instance SSKY1 to SSKY2. This is called *resource remastering*. The following query against the V$DYNAMIC_REMASTER_STATS view gives the current remaster activity for an instance:

```
SELECT REMASTER_OPS,
       REMASTER_TIME,
       REMASTERED_OBJECTS,
       CURRENT_OBJECTS,
       SYNC_TIME
FROM   V$DYNAMIC_REMASTER_STATS;
```

REMASTER_OPS	REMASTER_TIME	REMASTERED_OBJECTS	CURRENT_OBJECTS	SYNC_TIME
2	608	10	10	360

In this output, REMASTER_OPS indicates the number of remaster operations completed this far, REMASTER_TIME indicates the time spent on remaster activities, REMASTERED_OBJECTS indicates the number of objects remastered, the CURRENT_OBJECTS column indicates the number of objects mastered on the current instance that have not been remastered, and SYNC_TIME indicates the amount of time spent in cache synchronization activities during the remaster operation.

Note: All values in this view are cumulative, meaning they reflect the remastering activity since the instance started.

On a clustered configuration with more than two nodes, if the 3-way wait event indicate a significantly high number (numbers greater than 2-way wait events), this would be an indication that remastering was not working or that remaster activity had been disabled. While remastering is based on the number of times the object is touched in a particular instance, the requirement is that it be touched 60 times more than the other instance in a period of approximately 10 minutes. The touch count logic for remastering and the maximum period before remastering occurs are tunable using the underscore parameters _GC_AFFINITY_LIMIT and _GC_AFFINITY_TIME.[9]

In Oracle Database 10*g* Release 2, this feature is enabled by default at the object level. In prior releases, though mastering was maintained at the datafile level, no dynamic remastering occurred.

9.19   **Operating system tuning**

Once the database has been tuned to high performance standards, it is also a good idea to look at the overall performance from the operating system level. Areas of the operating system that influence the performance are CPU utilization and memory utilization.

9.19.1   **CPU utilization**

CPU utilization is the amount of time that the active CPUs on the system are running processes. CPU utilization statistics presented by the sar -u command are displayed as a composite of the %system, %user, and %idle times, where the addition of all three parameters will equate to 100%. A lower %idle time indicates a higher workload.

```
[root@oradb4 oracle]# sar -u 5 6
Linux 2.4.21-e.41smp (oradb4.sumsky.net)          10/03/2005
```

11:06:57 PM	CPU	%user	%nice	%system	%idle
11:07:02 PM	all	89.07	0.00	9.72	1.21
11:07:07 PM	all	55.74	0.00	11.06	33.19
11:07:12 PM	all	73.35	0.00	7.23	19.42
11:07:17 PM	all	90.82	0.00	8.16	1.02
11:07:22 PM	all	90.43	0.00	9.16	0.41
11:07:27 PM	all	91.80	0.00	8.20	0.00
Average:	**all**	**70.06**	**0.00**	**8.92**	**21.02**

9.   Underscore parameters should be modified only after consulting with Oracle support.

System and user statistics represent the proportion of time the CPUs are working on system-related activities or user-based programs, respectively. Characterization of a system's performance in terms of CPU utilization is a widely used approach. In a normal workload, %system should not consume more than 20% of CPU. CPU utilization information is made more significant when combined with the run queue length and run queue occupancy statistics. For example, if the server is running close to the 95% utilization level for most of the day, does this indicate an immediate CPU deficiency on the server? The answer is, it depends. If this is a single-CPU system, and the run queue is consistently at a value of 1, then the answer is, it is difficult to arrive at any definite conclusion. If the run queue length consistently exceeds the number of CPUs on the system, and the run queue occupancy is consistently high, together with a high CPU utilization rate, then this would indicate a CPU deficiency. CPU information can be verified using `cat /proc/cpuinfo` on Linux-based systems and from the Task Manager in Windows-based environments.

An ideal situation for the server is to run consistently under the 80% utilization level with a stable workload. In this situation, the investment in CPU power is justified since the utilization rate is high, yet not at its maximum. The reality of most servers is that workload fluctuates throughout an entire day and rarely shows as stable. The measurement of CPU utilization can help in identifying shortfalls in CPU processing power, especially during peak periods where the demand on CPU resources can exceed availability and cause systemwide performance degradation. The `sar -u` command will generate the CPU utilization statistics.

9.19.2 Memory utilization

Like the processing power provided by the CPUs on a system, the amount of data stored in Oracle's buffer is based on the memory available at the operating system level, meaning a portion of the total memory available is allocated to the Oracle instance on the server in its SGA.

meminfo

Memory information can be obtained using `cat /proc/meminfo` on a Linux-based system and using the Task Manager in a Windows environment.

```
[root@oradb4 oracle]# cat /proc/meminfo
        total:    used:    free:  shared: buffers:  cached:
Mem:  2636144640 2518822912 117321728 699658240 182558720 1304363008
```

```
Swap: 2146787328          0 2146787328
MemTotal:        2574360 kB
MemFree:          114572 kB
MemShared:        683260 kB
Buffers:          178280 kB
Cached:          1273792 kB
SwapCached:            0 kB
Active:          1164964 kB
Inact_dirty:      970368 kB
Inact_clean:           0 kB
Inact_target:     643492 kB
HighTotal:       1703860 kB
HighFree:           2036 kB
LowTotal:         870500 kB
LowFree:          112536 kB
SwapTotal:       2096472 kB
SwapFree:        2096472 kB
BigPagesFree:          0 kB
Committed_AS:    2153424 kB
HugePages_Total:       0
HugePages_Free:        0
Hugepagesize:       4096 kB
[root@oradb4 oracle]#
```

slabInfo

Another statistic collected by the operating system is slabinfo, which provides information about internal kernel caches. Slabs are small allocations of memory, less than a page or not a multiple of page size. The statistics can be useful in determining where the kernel is using too much memory.

```
[root@oradb4 oracle]# cat /proc/slabinfo
slabinfo - version: 1.1 (SMP)
kmem_cache           96     96    244     6     6    1 :   252   126
asm_request         116    118     64     2     2    1 :   252   126
nfs_read_data         0      0    384     0     0    1 :   124    62
nfs_inode_cache       2     17    224     1     1    1 :   252   126
nfs_write_data        0      0    384     0     0    1 :   124    62
nfs_page              0      0     96     0     0    1 :   252   126
ocfs_fileentry       64     64    512     8     8    1 :   124    62
ocfs_lockres        384    384    160    16    16    1 :   252   126
ocfs_ofile          382    444    320    37    37    1 :   124    62
```

```
ocfs_oin              214    340    192   15   17    1 :  252  126

                 active-objects

                     |      allocated-objects

                     |       |       object-size

                     |       |        |   active-slab-allocations

                     |       |        |   |    total-slab-allocations

                     |       |        |   |      |     alloc-size

                     |       |        |   |      |      |

asm_request      116    118     64    2    2      1 :  252  126

                                                   |     |

                                                 limit    |

                                                 batch-count
```

- *active-objects*. After creating a slab cache, you allocate your objects out of that slab cache. This is the count of objects currently allocated out of the cache.

- *allocated-objects*. This is the current total number of objects in the cache.

- *object-size*. This is the size of each allocated object. There is overhead to maintaining the cache, so with a 512-byte object and a 4,096-byte page size, it can fit seven objects in a single page and will waste 512-slab overhead bytes per allocation. Slab overhead varies with object size (smaller objects have more objects per allocation and require more overhead to track used versus unused objects).

- *active-slab-allocs*. This is the number of allocations that have at least one of the allocations objects in use.

- *total-slab-allocs*. This is the total number of allocations in the current slab cache.

- *alloc-size*. This is the size of each allocation in units of memory pages. Page size is architecture specific, but the most common size is 4K.

- The last two items are SMP specific. On SMP machines, the slab cache will keep a per-CPU cache of objects so that an object freed on CPU0 will be reused on CPU0 instead of CPU1 if possible. This improves cache performance on SMP systems greatly.

- *limit*. This is the limit of free objects stored in the per-CPU free list for this slab cache.

- *batch-count*. On SMP systems, when the available object list is refilled, instead of doing them one at a time, a batch of objects are taken at a time.

As illustrated in Figure 9.14, the EM also provides operating system information such as CPU utilization, memory utilization, and disk I/O utilization.

Figure 9.14
EM operating system Monitoring

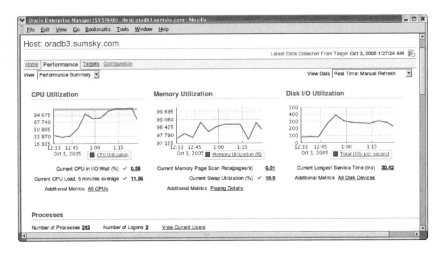

9.20   **Automatic workload repository**

In Oracle Database 10*g*, Oracle introduced a new process to capture and performance statistics called the Automatic Workload Repository (AWR). For those of us who have used STATSPACK in the past, AWR is an enhanced rewrite of this utility with a more user-friendly interface. Statistics and the entire workload information are collected (snapshot) automatically by the MMON background process every 60 minutes (default) and stored in the wrh$

and wri$ tables in the SYSAUX tablespace. Data collected is retained in the AWR for seven days (default) and then automatically purged. During this period, database performance and workload statistics can be generated into a report by comparing two snapshot periods. Unlike a STATSPACK report, AWR collects data on only two levels: TYPICAL (default) and ALL. These levels are driven by the parameter STATISTICS_LEVEL.

AWR snapshots can also be captured manually using the DBMS_WORKLOAD_REPOSITORY.CREATE_SNAPSHOT() procedure and at the ALL level DBMS_WORKLOAD_REPOSITORY.CREATE_SNAPSHOT(flush_level=>ALL);

The number of top SQL queries reported by the AWR is also controlled by the STATISTICS_LEVEL parameter. When the value is TYPICAL the top 30 queries are listed, and when the value is ALL the top 100 queries are listed. This can be overridden in Oracle Database 10*g* Release 2 using the following procedure:

```
DBMS_WORKLOAD_REPOSITORY.modify_snapshot_settings(topnsql =>
200);
```

During typical benchmarking cycles, when a set of performance metrics needs to be saved as a baseline for comparisons, the traditional method used by DBAs has been to export performance data. AWR makes this more convenient using the following procedure:

```
DBMS_WORKLOAD_REPOSITORY.CREATE_BASELINE(<START SNAP ID>,<END
SNAP ID>,<BASLINE NAME><DB ID>);
```

For example, the following procedure will create a baseline QAR1BLINE of the current database instance (default) represented by DB ID in the syntax above.

```
execute DBMS_WORKLOAD_REPOSITORY.CREATE_BASELINE
(459,476,'QAR1BLINE');
```

The baseline definition can be validated by querying the DB_HIST_BASELINE table.

```
COL BASELINE_NAME FORMAT A25
SELECT DBID,
       BASELINE_NAME,
```

```
        START_SNAP_ID,
        END_SNAP_ID
FROM    DBA_HIST_BASELINE;


        DBID BASELINE_NAME               START_SNAP_ID END_SNAP_ID
---------- -------------------------- ------------- -----------
4275027223 QAR1BLINE                            459         476
```

 Note: Creation of a baseline will override AWR automatic purging for the baseline snapshot range.

While AWR does provide information concerning RAC, statistics are collected from all instances and stored by instance number under a common `SNAP_ID` (`SNAP_ID` is the primary key for the AWR and is generated for every snapshot collection); that is, statistics are collected by instance and not at the global level.

AWR reports or snapshot comparisons can be done either by using a command-line interface by executing an Oracle-provided SQL script (`$ORACLE_HOME/rdbms/admin/awrrpt.sql`) or by using the EM interfaces. An HTML file can be generated and viewed using a browser by either method.

The script provides an option to pick a range of snapshots to compare. Once the range is selected, the report is generated in the default directory. In an RAC environment, a report is generated for one instance at a time.

Tuning using the AWR starts with identifying the top five wait events reported in the first page of the report, illustrated in Table 9.3.

Table 9.3 *AWR Top Five Timed Events*

Top 5 Timed Events

Event	Waits	Time(s)	Percent Total DB Time	Wait Class
db file sequential read	228,989	1,767	57.28	User I/O
CPU time		552	17.89	
log file sync	24,925	208	6.74	Commit
log file parallel write	26,983	201	6.53	System I/O
gc buffer busy	12,071	166	5.37	Cluster

Table 9.3 provides the wait events at the instance level and can contain RAC-related wait events as shown for "`gc buffer busy`." AWR also provides a global-level cache load profile illustrating the global cache activity between the various instances in the cluster.

Table 9.4   *AWR RAC Global Cache Load Profile*

Global Cache Load Profile

	Per Second	Per Transaction
Global Cache blocks received:	99.08	14.50
Global Cache blocks served:	101.06	14.79
GCS/GES messages received:	510.95	74.77
GCS/GES messages sent:	494.37	72.34
DBWR Fusion writes:	8.46	1.24
Estd Interconnect traffic (KB)	22.92	

Like STATSPACK, AWR is also organized by sections. When the AWR report is generated in a RAC environment, the second page of this report relates to RAC. Apart from the performance data illustrated in Tables 9.3 and 9.4, other important data is discussed later in this section.

Table 9.5   *AWR RAC Global Cache Load Profile Formula*

Profile	Formula
Global cache blocks received	(gc current blocks received + gc cr blocks received) / elapsed time
Global cache blocks served	(gc current blocks served + gc cr blocks served) / elapsed time
GCS/GES messages received	(gcs messages received + ges messages received) / elapsed time
GCS/GES messages sent	(gcs messages sent + ges messages sent) / elapsed time
DBWR fusion writes	DBWR fusion writes / elapsed time

Table 9.5   *AWR RAC Global Cache Load Profile Formula*

Estimated interconnect traffic	(((gc cr blocks received +
	gc current blocks received +
	gc cr blocks served +
	gc current blocks served) * db_block_size) +
	((gcs messages sent +
	ges messages sent + gcs msgs received +
	ges msgs received) * 200) /1024 / elapsed time)

In Table 9.4, the various profiles are calculated using the formula described in Table 9.5.

The formula in Table 9.5 is based on statistic values obtained from GV$SYSSTAT or GV$DLM_MISC views. Elapsed time is the time between the start and end of the collection period. In the case of an AWR report, the elapsed time is the time between two snapshots being compared. The load profile can be grouped by services using the GV$SERVICE_STATS view to obtain a more focused performance metric.

Table 9.6 provides the overall performance of the instance with respect to global cache movement between instances.

Table 9.6   *AWR RAC Global Cache and Enqueue Services*

Global Cache and Enqueue Services - Workload Characteristics

Avg global enqueue get time (ms):	0.3
Avg global cache cr block receive time (ms):	0.9
Avg global cache current block receive time (ms):	1.0
Avg global cache cr block build time (ms):	0.0
Avg global cache cr block send time (ms):	0.1
Global cache log flushes for cr blocks served %:	2.4
Avg global cache cr block flush time (ms):	8.5
Avg global cache current block pin time (ms):	0.1
Avg global cache current block send time (ms):	0.1
Global cache log flushes for current blocks served %:	0.6
Avg global cache current block flush time (ms):	10.8

The average values in Table 9.6 are also based on statistic values from the GV$SYSSTAT and GV$DLM_MISC views. Once the actual values are computed, the average is determined to provide the overall health of the cluster during the snapshot interval. Table 9.7 illustrates the statistic values used in some of the average values included in Table 9.6.

Table 9.7 *AWR RAC Global Cache Load Profile Formula*

Statistic	Formula	Typical Value (ms)	Upper Limit (ms)
Average global cache cr block receive time	10 × gc cr block receive time / gc cr blocks received	4	12
Average global cache current block receive time	10 × gc current block receive time / gc current blocks received	8	30

AWR provides other RAC-related performance statistics in the AWR report, including the following, to name a few:

- RAC report summary
- Global enqueue statistics
- Global CR served stats
- Global Current served statistics
- Global cache transfer stats
- Global cache transfer statistics aggregated per class

Among these, the Global Cache Transfer Stats is an informative section providing details of block transfers between various instances participating in the cluster. As illustrated in Table 9.8, the transfer is broken down between CR and current requests.

Table 9.8, in conjunction with the section on hot blocks, should determine what database-level tuning is required to reduce this movement and reduce block-request contention.

Table 9.9 lists the differences between a STATSPACK and AWR report.

Table 9.8   *Global Cache Transfer Stats*

Global Cache Transfer Stats

- Immediate (Immed) - Block Transfer NOT impacted by Remote Processing Delays
- Busy (Busy) - Block Transfer impacted by Remote Contention
- Congested (Congst) - Block Transfer impacted by Remote System Load
- ordered by CR + Current Blocks Received desc

		CR				Current			
Inst No	Block Class	Blocks Received	% Immed	% Busy	% Congst	Blocks Received	% Immed	% Busy	% Congst
2	data block	290	100.00	0.00	0.00	2,135	97.29	0.00	2.71
2	Others	10	100.00	0.00	0.00	3	100.00	0.00	0.00
2	undo header	5	100.00	0.00	0.00	1	100.00	0	0
3	data block	390	100.00	3.07	1.70	4,505	165.29	0.00	13.43
3	Others	19	100.00	0.00	0.00	3	100.00	0.00	0.00
3	undo header	12	100.00	0.00	0.00	1	100.00	0	0

Table 9.9   *AWR versus STATSPACK*

AWR	STATSPACK
It automatically configured by the DBCA.	Manual installation and configuration are required using scripts.
It automatically purges data older than seven days (can be changed).	A manual purge routine is required.
A reporting option is available via both EM and scripts. Output can be in either HTML or ASCII text format.	Reports are generated only via scripts, and the output is always in ASCII text format.
It contains Oracle provided PL/SQL packages to create baselines.	Baselines can be maintained by exporting data or by not purging the existing data.
Statistics are collected by the **MMON** process every 60 minutes (default) and stored in the AWR.	Data is actually collected by the script during execution. The script can be configured to run automatically by scheduling it at regular intervals using **DBMS_JOB** or **DBMS_SCHEDULER**.
Data from the AWR is used by other performance diagnostic tools, such as ADDM and ASH (discussed later in this chapter).	Data collected is only used by the STATSPACK reporter.
It requires an additional Oracle license.	No additional license is required.

9.21　**Automatic Database Diagnostic Monitor**

The Automatic Database Diagnostic Monitor (ADDM, pronounced "Adam") is a self-diagnostic analysis and reporting tool that is part of Oracle Database 10*g*. Earlier, we discussed the hourly capture (snapshot) of performance statistics by the AWR process. As illustrated in Figure 9.15, ADDM uses these snapshots and provides advice about what and where the problem is, what areas of the system are affected, what has caused performance issues if any, and what can be done to improve the overall performance of the database.

Figure 9.15
AWR and ADDM Process Flow

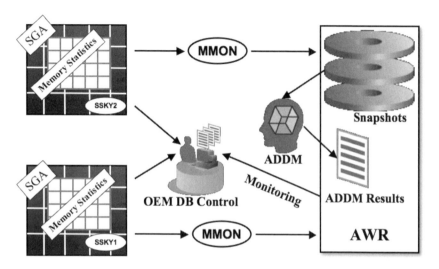

Like AWR, ADDM can also be generated using the EM or the `addmrpt.sql` script available in the `$ORACLE_HOME/rdbms/admin/` directory. These reports are stored by default for 30 days in the database before being purged. These reports are generated on thresholds predefined (but which can be modified) for a predetermined set of areas. For example, the user I/O is defined by the parameter `DBIO_EXPECTED` and defaults to 1,000 ms. Another parameter that is used to calculate the amount of database time spent is the `DB_ELAPSED_TIME` parameter, which defaults to 0 ms. Both of these parameters can be modified using the `DBMS_ADVISOR.SET_DEFAULT_TASK_PARAMETER` PL/SQL procedure.

ADDM functionality can be accessed by selecting the "Advisor Central" page from two levels: (1) clustered database performance page and (2) database instance performance page. As illustrated in Figure 9.16, once ADDM is selected, the EM automatically generates an analysis report on the latest

Figure 9.16
*EM ADDM RAC
Database Activity*

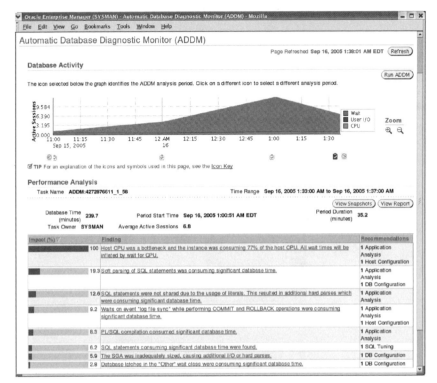

AWR snapshot available and allows for regeneration of analysis based on another snapshot period.

In Figure 9.16, ADDM provides an overall performance of the database and a list of findings based on the analysis of the snapshots selected. Apart from providing the findings, the analysis also reports on the percentage of impact. In this case, the impact for "Host CPU was a bottleneck" is 100%. To understand the areas of impact and the recommendations for fixing this issue, click on the specific finding. Once this is selected, the EM provides the recommendations (Figure 9.17).

As illustrated in Figure 9.17, the recommendations or actions required are both valid. The system is low on CPU because at the time of testing only one CPU was present. The other recommendation of using ODRM is also valid and helps in implementing a DWM environment.

Note: ODRM and DWM are discussed in Chapter 5.

Figure 9.17
*EM ADDM RAC
Performance
Finding Details*

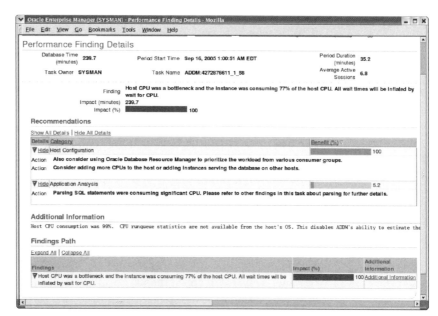

Similarly, as illustrated in Figure 9.18, ADDM has identified that the LMSn background processes are not able to keep up with the workload. Currently, only one LMSn background process is present. A good rule of thumb is to configure one LMSn process for every two CPUs on the server.

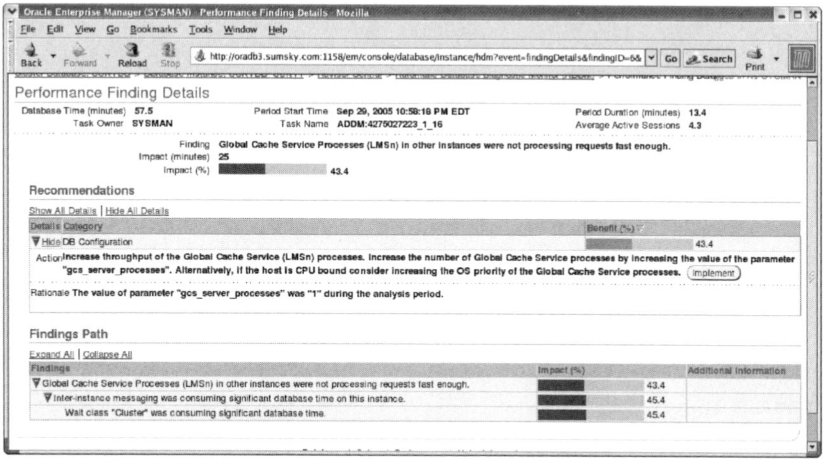

Figure 9.18
*EM ADDM RAC
Performance
Finding Details*

ADDM is also a good source for identifing high-load SQL statements. Every run of ADDM produces a report containing its analysis and recommendations. These reports are stored by default for 30 days in the database before being purged. Apart from identifying high-load SQL statements, ADDM will also recommend running SQL advisors on them to obtain optimal performance benefits.

9.22 Active session history

AWR provides snapshots containing performance characteristics of the database; ADDM analyzes this information and provides guidelines and suggestions on how to fix it. However, a one-time occurrence of any issue is not a good indication of any specific performance problem. For instance, when a user reports a bug in his or her application, the developer is interested to find out if this bug is repeatable or reproducible. Only then will the developer spend time investigating it; otherwise, he or she will consider it a minor issue because a one-time occurrence of an issue does not really provide sufficient data to fix the problem. After repeated occurrences data becomes consistent and tunable. Similarly, in a database environment, problems do arise, systems do slow down, and occasional high spikes do occur. However, unless this happens consistently over a length of time (past, present, and future), there is no real concern.

Active session history (ASH, pronounced "ash") tries to bridge this gap. ASH helps perform analysis of transient problems lasting for a few minutes or over various dimensions, such as time, SQL_ID, module, action, and so on. As mentioned earlier, unlike the other reactive reporting issues, ASH is based on a sampled history of all events happening in the database. ASH data captured for all active sessions and stored is essentially a fact table (GV$ACTIVE_SESSION_HISTORY) in a data warehouse environment, with the columns representing the dimensions of the fact table. In this view, there are about 13 important dimensions of data. However, in the case of ASH, all contents are in memory and are accessing very quickly.

```
SQL> desc gv$active_session_history;
 Name                                     Null?    Type
 ---------------------------------------- -------- ------------
 INST_ID                                           NUMBER
 SAMPLE_ID                                         NUMBER
 SAMPLE_TIME                                       TIMESTAMP(3)
 SESSION_ID                                        NUMBER
 SESSION_SERIAL#                                   NUMBER
 USER_ID                                           NUMBER
 SQL_ID                                            VARCHAR2(13)
```

SQL_CHILD_NUMBER	NUMBER
SQL_PLAN_HASH_VALUE	NUMBER
FORCE_MATCHING_SIGNATURE	NUMBER
SQL_OPCODE	NUMBER
SERVICE_HASH	NUMBER
SESSION_TYPE	VARCHAR2(10)
SESSION_STATE	VARCHAR2(7)
QC_SESSION_ID	NUMBER
QC_INSTANCE_ID	NUMBER
BLOCKING_SESSION	NUMBER
BLOCKING_SESSION_STATUS	VARCHAR2(11)
BLOCKING_SESSION_SERIAL#	NUMBER
EVENT	**VARCHAR2(64)**
EVENT_ID	NUMBER
EVENT#	NUMBER
SEQ#	NUMBER
P1TEXT	VARCHAR2(64)
P1	**NUMBER**
P2TEXT	VARCHAR2(64)
P2	**NUMBER**
P3TEXT	VARCHAR2(64)
P3	**NUMBER**
WAIT_CLASS	**VARCHAR2(64)**
WAIT_CLASS_ID	NUMBER
WAIT_TIME	NUMBER
TIME_WAITED	NUMBER
XID	RAW(8)
CURRENT_OBJ#	NUMBER
CURRENT_FILE#	**NUMBER**
CURRENT_BLOCK#	**NUMBER**
PROGRAM	**VARCHAR2(48)**
MODULE	**VARCHAR2(48)**
ACTION	**VARCHAR2(32)**
CLIENT_ID	VARCHAR2(64)

Like to the AWR and ADDM features, ASH reports can also be generated from the EM console or using the `ashrpt.sql` script located in the `$ORACLE_HOME/rdbms/admin` directory on the database server.

9.23 EM Grid Control

All of the EM-related reports and functionality discussed previously are part of the default dbconsole configuration that is defined by DBCA while creating the database. In a RAC environment, the console is defined on the node where the DBCA was executed.

Apart from the dbconsole, the DBCA provides current database-related information. Another version that captures a performance-related matrix and saves it in a repository is the EM Grid Control (GC). While in this chapter we have been looking at optimization features for the RAC database, the GC supports all tiers of the application:

- Database tier
- Web tier
- Application tier

At the database tier, apart from the traditional functionalities provided by the dbconsole, the GC provides a holistic view of the RAC cluster.

9.23.1 Cluster latency/activity

GC monitors the internode data transfer between the various instances in the cluster. The cluster Interconnects page displays all the interconnects that are configured across the cluster. Both public and private interfaces are identified and shown with their statistics, such as transfer rate and related errors. This screen helps identify configuration problems with the interface setup and performance problems with the interconnect latency.

9.23.2 Topology view

In the Oracle Database 10*g* Release 2 version of GC, Oracle has added a new cluster database home page called the Topology page that displays a graphical view of the entire cluster, including the database instances, listeners, ASM instances, and interfaces. From the Topology page, the administrator can also launch various administrative and configuration functions, like startup and shutdown, monitoring of configurations, and so on.

Figure 9.19
Spotlight on RAC

9.23.3 Spotlight® on RAC

When there are configurations with a large number of nodes, it is convenient to view the cluster as a whole, identify specific issues with any one instance in the cluster, and receive immediate notification by an alarm. In other words, instead of navigating through each instance to find out exactly where the problem is, a console or dashboard kind of tool that provides one view, such as in Figure 9.19, is beneficial. Figure 9.19 is a dashboard screen from Spotlight on RAC. It provides one dashboard view of the cluster and highlights issues with any instance in the cluster. For example, in Figure 9.19, nodes "Venus" and "Earth" are currently high on CPU usage, and an alarm is being raised. Hovering over the alarm will provide details of the alarm, and by drilling down, the specific individual metric relating to the CPU can be identified.

Figure 9.19 also illustrates one view of the three tiers of the database server, the interconnect or global data movement at the top, the specific instances, and the storage or I/O subsystem at the bottom.

9.24 **Conclusion**

RAC performance depends on how well the application and SQL queries are tuned to access the database. A poorly performing query in a single-instance database will also perform poorly in a RAC environment. Usage of best practices plays an important role.

In this chapter, we looked at the various areas of application and the database, considering the areas that can be improved. In addition, the various ways of identifing specific issues, like blockers, frequency of remastering, and so on, were covered.

The primary goal of the chapter was to identify and help in the diagnostic process of a RAC database. It does not cover all the areas of troubleshooting; several more areas of the database affect the cluster performance directly or indirectly. Please note that an issue discussed in this chapter may not be relevant in other environments and should be tested before implementation.

10

MAA and More

In Chapter 6 we discussed the various features of Oracle Database 10*g* RAC, that provide high availability within the boundaries of the configured cluster. We discussed how this cluster shares one single copy of the physical database, allowing users connected to any instance participating in the cluster to access the data from this one common database. While RAC does provide availability between the various instances participating in the cluster, Oracle Corporation can never guarantee that this one cluster will not be a single point of failure as some disasters and errors are beyond Oracle's control. For example, earthquakes, floods, and power outages can destroy a data center, rendering the cluster inaccessible. Due to the infrequent occurrence of such disasters, several organizations do not always consider planning for such natural calamities to be critical to their business. However, considering the vital importance of data and survival of the business, it is imperative for businesses to have a working plan to protect data using available technologies.

To address some of the failures in a clustered environment, one or more other products can be combined with the RAC environment, providing a more robust solution. These products include Data Guard, Oracle Streams, extended clusters, and other third-party tools.

 Note: At this time, all of these options are only available with the EE and cannot be used with the Standard Edition RAC. However, the Streams apply process is an exception and is available in all editions of Oracle Database 10*g*.

10.1 **Data Guard**

Oracle Data Guard functionality was initially introduced in Oracle Database 8*i* as the standby database and was subsequently enhanced in Oracle Database 9*i* and 10*g*. The main purpose of this product is to provide data protection for the primary database environment by copying data from one location (primary) to another (secondary), protecting it from natural disasters and human error. Thus, when the primary environment is not available, data can still be accessed from the secondary environment, until the primary environment is accessible, at which time the application can be connected back to the primary environment.

Because of its simplicity of implementation and fullness of protection against site disasters, database corruptions, and user errors, Data Guard combined with RAC makes up Oracle's Maximum Available Architecture (MAA) blueprint. This blueprint is the most widely investigated and documented by Oracle.

Oracle provides two methods of implementing the Data Guard feature:

1.   Physical standby

2.   Logical standby

To understand the two different methods of standby, let's look at the differences between them. The two methods differ in the following aspects:

- Physical standby has a block-by-block database structure identical to the primary database. A logical standby is an independent database and, if desired, can contain only a subset of the primary database.

- Both physical and logical standbys are created and maintained by shipping the redo log files from the primary to the standby location and applying them. The physical standby (Redo Apply) technology applies redo data on the physical standby database using the Oracle server's standard recovery techniques. The logical standby (SQL apply) on the other hand keeps the logical standby database synchronized with the primary database by transforming the data in the redo logs received from the primary database into SQL statements and then executing the SQL statements on the standby database. Since physical standby has to be identical (block-by-block) to the primary database, this feature does not allow any creation of additional tables in the standby database, whereas the logical standby database can contain tables or objects not present on the primary database.

- Since physical standby is an identical copy of the primary database, it supports all data types, and there are no restrictions on what it can contain. However, logical standby does not support all data types and objects. While the list keeps getting shorter with each release, as of Oracle Database 10*g* Release 2, the unsupported objects can be obtained using the following query:

```
COL OWNER FORMAT A5
COL TABLE_NAME FORMAT A18
COL COLUMN_NAME FORMAT A23
COL DATA_TYPE FORMAT A22
SELECT DISTINCT OWNER,
       TABLE_NAME,
       COLUMN_NAME,
       DATA_TYPE
FROM   DBA_LOGSTDBY_UNSUPPORTED
ORDER BY OWNER, TABLE_NAME;
```

OWNER	TABLE_NAME	COLUMN_NAME	DATA_TYPE
OE	CATEGORIES_TAB	CATEGORY_DESCRIPTION	VARCHAR2
OE	CATEGORIES_TAB	CATEGORY_ID	NUMBER
OE	CATEGORIES_TAB	CATEGORY_NAME	VARCHAR2
OE	CATEGORIES_TAB	PARENT_CATEGORY_ID	NUMBER
OE	CUSTOMERS	CUST_ADDRESS	CUST_ADDRESS_TYP
OE	CUSTOMERS	CUST_GEO_LOCATION	SDO_GEOMETRY
OE	CUSTOMERS	PHONE_NUMBERS	PHONE_LIST_TYP
OE	WAREHOUSES	WAREHOUSE_SPEC	XMLTYPE
OE	WAREHOUSES	WH_GEO_LOCATION	SDO_GEOMETRY

While both types of standby databases can be implemented in either a single-instance or RAC configuration, for our discussion in this chapter, we will focus only on a RAC implementation. As discussed earlier, RAC is a high-availability solution, but such a solution can also fail due to situations beyond our control. Under these circumstances, as a precautionary measure, it is advisable to keep a copy of the primary database at a remote location far enough away to avoid any same-site failures (e.g., acts of nature) and to keep it automatically synchronized. This way when the primary database fails and is inaccessible, the application will have some support.

10.1.1   Data Guard architecture

The basic architecture (illustrated in Figure 10.1) of a standby solution consists of a primary database and one standby database. The standby database can be either physical or logical. Standby architecture also supports multiple standby locations or cascaded standby configuration. Cascaded configuration involves a standby database configured from another standby. Typically, this type of configuration involves one physical standby as the primary standby, with other cascaded targets being either a physical or a logical standby database. In either case, Oracle supports configuration of up to nine standby destinations.

The process of migrating data from the primary to the standby location is performed by the LGWR process or the ARCH process, depending on the level of protection desired for the primary database.

Figure 10.1
Basic Standby Architecture

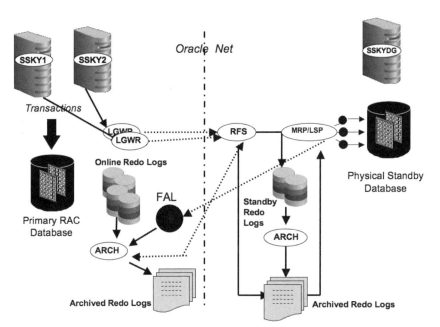

As shown in Figure 10.1, the primary component or service of the Data Guard configuration is to get the database changes from the primary to the standby site. This function is performed by the redo transport service, where either all the archive redo log files are shipped, using the ARCH process, to the standby site after the redo log switch operation on the primary database or net changes written to the redo logs are shipped by the LGWR on a real-time basis to the standby site. When an asynchronous type (ASYNCH) of configuration is enabled or before writing to the redo logs, the LGWR will ship a copy to the standby site when a synchronous type (SYNC) of configuration is enabled. The primary site determines the standby locations from the LOG_ARCHIVE_DEST_n parameter. For example, the following LOG_ARCHIVE_DEST_2 parameter defines the target site where redo data should be transmitted as instance SSKYDG:

```
LOG_ARCHIVE_DEST_2='SERVICE=SSKYDG LGWR SYNC AFFIRM
VALID_FOR=(ONLINE_LOGFILES,PRIMARY_ROLE)
DB_UNIQUE_NAME=SSKYDG'
```

Redo data transmitted from the primary database is received by the remote file server (RFS) process on the standby system, where the RFS process writes the redo data to archived log files or standby redo log files. Redo data can be applied either after the redo is written to the archived log file or standby redo log file or, if real-time apply is enabled, directly from the standby redo log files.

Once the data has been transferred to the standby location, the log apply service will perform the tasks of applying the changes to the standby database. The data written to the archive log files or the standby redo log files of the standby server are then applied by the redo apply (MRP)/SQL apply (LSP) process to the standby location.

Under certain circumstances, either because of network failures or a busy source environment, a gap builds up between the target sending the information and the destination receiving the changes and applying them. Since the MRP/LSP process has no direct communication link with the primary database to obtain a copy of the missing archive files, such gaps or archive gaps are resolved by the fetch archive log (FAL) client and server, identified by the initialization parameters FAL_CLIENT and FAL_SERVER.

Data Guard Broker

Oracle provides an optional layer of management called the Data Guard Broker (DGB). It is optional when the basic level of Data Guard functionality is being implemented. With added features such as fast-start failover (discussed later), DGB is required. The function of the broker is to logically group, manage, and monitor the primary and standby environments. Once the various locations of the configuration are registered with the broker, it will manage the availability and failover functionality of the environments.

DGB is identified by the Data Guard Monitor (DMON) background process, and once configured, it runs on both the primary and standby sites and provides these basic functionalities:

- It manages the entire Data Guard configuration, including all databases, redo transport services, and log apply services.

- It manages the protection mode for the broker configuration.

- It helps manage the manual switchover and failover by controlling the entire operation from one single location.

- It configures the failover to occur automatically upon loss of the primary database, increasing availability without manual intervention.

- In a RAC environment, it helps integrate all instances participating in the cluster into the configuration and only performs failover when all instances in the cluster have failed.

Fast-start failover

In Oracle Database 10*g* Release 2, a new feature has been introduced called fast-start failover (FSFO). This feature provides the ability to automatically fail over to a designated, synchronized standby database in the event of the loss of the primary database without requiring manual intervention. In addition, following an FSFO, the primary database is automatically reconfigured as a new standby database when the issues with the primary database are fixed, and it has been brought back into the configuration. This enables Data Guard to restore disaster protection in the configuration easily, without complex manual steps, improving the robustness of the disaster-recovery features of Data Guard.

Implementing the FSFO feature requires that the environment be managed by the DGB, which is the broker agent that actually performs the failover. However, unlike the failover options available in the previous version of Data Guard, the failover is automatic and is controlled through another new process called the Observer.

The Observer is a separate (watchdog) process incorporated into the Data Guard command-line interface (DGMGRL) client. It is a lightweight thin client and can be located on any system that contains the Oracle client with the DGMGRL. The Observer continuously monitors the primary database and the target standby database for possible failure conditions.

The underlying rule of FSFO is that out of these three participants, whichever two can communicate with each other will determine the outcome of FSFO. For example, if the primary database becomes unavailable, the Observer confirms with the target standby database that the primary database is unavailable, and if the target standby database is in a synchronized state with the primary database, it initiates an FSFO to the target standby database.

Best Practice: The Observer should run on a separate computer at a separate location from that of the primary and target standby databases so that it will not be subject to any failures that affect the primary or standby hosts.

FSFO configuration requires the following compliance:

- The primary database and at least one of the standby databases (configured for fast failover) should be set to maximum availability protection mode (i.e., the redo transport service for the designated standby target defined using the `LOG_ARCHIVE_DEST_n` parameter should be set with `LGWR SYNC`).

- The designated Observer node should have the DGMGRL utility installed and have Oracle Net connectivity to both primary and standby environments.

- The environment should be set up for real-time apply to minimize failover time.

- All databases participating in the configuration should have `FLASH-BACK` enabled. This can be done using the `ALTER DATABASE FLASH-BACK ON` statement after the appropriate parameters and flashback area have been defined.

Note: Configuration of DGB and FSFO functionality is discussed later in this chapter.

Failover situations include the following:

- The primary site has failed.

- All instances participating in the primary RAC configuration have failed.

- The network between the primary and Observer, as well as the primary and the standby locations, have failed, stopping the movement of redo log files. Under this scenario, the connection between the Observer and the standby should be present to enable the Observer to confirm that the configuration is synchronized.

- A SHUTDOWN ABORT has been issued on the primary location, and all instances participating in the cluster have failed.

- I/O errors have been caused by one or more datafiles that have been taken offline in the primary environment. In this situation, FSFO will not wait until the threshold is met but will failover immediately.

10.1.2 Workshops

The following workshops will help in understanding the implementation of the Data Guard environment.

Basic physical standby

As stated earlier, a physical standby database is a block-for-block copy of the primary instance, which means all changes, including metadata changes to the system tablespace or Oracle's data dictionary, will be copied to the standby location and applied. This operation keeps the entire primary database in sync with the standby database. In this section of the workshop, a basic physical standby is discussed step by step. The primary database is in a RAC environment using ASM for storing database files, and the standby location is a single-instance Oracle database.

Note: Although Oracle supports having primary and standby databases of nonidentical configuration (e.g., RAC and non-RAC), when the primary (RAC) database fails, the business is to continue by using the standby database, so consideration should be given to ensure that the standby database is identical in configuration to the primary environment.

1.   The databases are required to be in ARCHIVE LOG mode with the FLASHBACK option enabled.

Note: The steps required to enable the ARCHIVE LOG and/or FLASHBACK option are discussed in Chapter 8.

2.   Enable force logging of the primary database, which will ensure that all database changes are logged, even when certain operations were run using the NOLOGGING option:

```
SQL> ALTER DATABASE FORCE LOGGING;
```

3.   Verify if the password file exists for the primary database:

```
[oracle@oradb3 oracle]ls -ltr $ORACLE_HOME/dbs
  -rw-r-----   1 oracle   dba        40 Dec 12 15:14 initSSKY1.ora
  -rw-r-----   1 oracle   dba      1536 Dec 12 15:17 orapwSSKY1
```

4.   Verify if the remote password parameter is set to EXCLUSIVE:

```
SQL> show parameter password

NAME                           TYPE        VALUE
------------------------------ ----------- ----------------------
remote_login_passwordfile      string      EXCLUSIVE
SQL>
```

5.   Create standby redo log file groups. The number of standby redo log files should match the number of regular redo log files on the primary instance. The number of redo log files required is calculated using the following formula:

(maximum number of log files for each thread + 1) × maximum number of threads

For a four-instance cluster with three redo log groups each, the number of standby redo log files would be 16 ([three log files for each thread + 1] × four instances). The size of each of the standby log files should be the same as the regular redo log files for the instance.

```
SQL>ALTER DATABASE ADD STANDBY LOGFILE GROUP 5
('+ASMGRP1') SIZE 51200K;
SQL>ALTER DATABASE ADD STANDBY LOGFILE GROUP 6
```

```
('+ASMGRP1') SIZE 51200K;
    SQL>ALTER DATABASE ADD STANDBY LOGFILE GROUP 7
('+ASMGRP1') SIZE 51200K;
    SQL>ALTER DATABASE ADD STANDBY LOGFILE GROUP 8
('+ASMGRP1') SIZE 51200K;
    SQL>ALTER DATABASE ADD STANDBY LOGFILE GROUP 9
('+ASMGRP1') SIZE 51200K;
    SQL>ALTER DATABASE ADD STANDBY LOGFILE GROUP 10
('+ASMGRP1') SIZE 51200K;
```

6. Verify the creation of the standby redo log file groups:

```
SELECT GROUP#,
       THREAD#,
       SEQUENCE#,
       ARCHIVED,
       STATUS
FROM V$STANDBY_LOG;
```

```
GROUP#      THREAD#   SEQUENCE# ARC STATUS
---------- ---------- ---------- --- ----------
        5          1        105 YES ACTIVE
        6          1          0 NO  UNASSIGNED
        7          0          0 YES UNASSIGNED
        8          0          0 YES UNASSIGNED
        9          0          0 YES UNASSIGNED
```

7. Add a similar set of standby redo log files to the physical standby database. Since the physical standby in our discussion is a non-RAC configuration, the number of standby redo logs is four ([3 redo log files + 1] × one instance).

```
ALTER DATABASE ADD STANDBY LOGFILE GROUP 5 ('/usr/app/
oracle/oracle/oradata/SSKYDG/onlinelog/
group_5.283.dbf') SIZE 51200K;
ALTER DATABASE ADD STANDBY LOGFILE GROUP 6 ('/usr/app/
oracle/oracle/oradata/SSKYDG/onlinelog/
group_6.283.dbf') SIZE 51200K;
ALTER DATABASE ADD STANDBY LOGFILE GROUP 7 ('/usr/app/
oracle/oracle/oradata/SSKYDG/onlinelog/
group_7.283.dbf') SIZE 51200K;
ALTER DATABASE ADD STANDBY LOGFILE GROUP 8 ('/usr/app/
```

```
oracle/oracle/oradata/SSKYDG/onlinelog/
group_8.283.dbf') SIZE 51200K;
```

8. Modify and add the following required standby parameters on the primary database:

```
DB_NAME=SSKYDB
DB_UNIQUE_NAME=SSKYDB
LOG_ARCHIVE_CONFIG='DG_CONFIG=(SSKYDB,SSKYDG)'
LOG_ARCHIVE_DEST_1='LOCATION=+ASMGRP1/SSKYDB/
VALID_FOR=(ALL_LOGFILES,ALL_ROLES)
DB_UNIQUE_NAME=SSKYDB'
LOG_ARCHIVE_DEST_2='SERVICE=SSKYDG LGWR ASYNC
VALID_FOR=(ONLINE_LOGFILES,PRIMARY_ROLE)
DB_UNIQUE_NAME=SSKYDG'
LOG_ARCHIVE_DEST_STATE_1=ENABLE
LOG_ARCHIVE_DEST_STATE_2=ENABLE
REMOTE_LOGIN_PASSWORDFILE=EXCLUSIVE
LOG_ARCHIVE_FORMAT=%t_%s_%r.arc
LOG_ARCHIVE_MAX_PROCESSES=30
LOCAL_LISTENER=LISTENER_SSKYDB
```

9. Copy the modified parameter file from the primary instance to the physical standby location and further modify the following parameters required on the physical standby database, at the same time disabling all cluster-related parameters:

```
DB_NAME=SSKYDB
DB_UNIQUE_NAME=SSKYDG
FAL_SERVER=SSKYDG
FAL_CLIENT=SSKYDB
DB_FILE_NAME_CONVERT='SSKYDG','SSKYDB'
LOG_FILE_NAME_CONVERT='+ASMGRP1/SSKYDB/','-   /usr/app/
    oracle/oracle/oradata/SSKYDG/'
STANDBY_FILE_MANAGEMENT =AUTO
db_create_file_dest=/usr/app/oracle/oracle/oradata/
    SSKYDG
db_recovery_file_dest=/usr/app/oracle/oracle/oradata/
    SSKYDG
db_recovery_file_dest_size=4294967296
LOCAL_LISTENER = LISTENER_SSKYDG
```

```
undo_tablespace=UNDOTBS1

background_dump_dest=/usr/app/oracle/oracle/admin/
    SSKYDG/bdump
core_dump_dest=/usr/app/oracle/oracle/admin/SSKYDG/
    cdump
user_dump_dest=/usr/app/oracle/oracle/admin/SSKYDG/
    udump
audit_file_dest=/usr/app/oracle/oracle/admin/SSKYDG/
    adump

#cluster_database_instances=2
#cluster_database=true
#SSKY1.instance_number=1
#SSKY2.instance_number=2
#SSKY2.thread=2
#SSKY2.undo_tablespace=UNDOTBS2
#SSKY1.thread=1
```

 Note: At this stage, it is important to verify and cross-check all parameters to be sure that they are configured and defined correctly. The parameters of utmost importance are DB_UNIQUE_NAME and LOG_ARCHIVE_DEST_1. While the DB_NAME on both the primary and standby databases remains the same, the DB_UNIQUE_NAME is different.

10.   Restart both the primary and the physical standby databases to enable the modified parameters.

 Note: If the instances (both the primary and physical standby databases) do not have SPFILE enabled, create an SPFILE from the PFILE using the following syntax:

```
SQL> CREATE SPFILE=< file location> from PFILE ='/usr/
app/..../initSSKY.ora'
```

11.   Add TNS name entries on the primary database for the physical standby database and on the physical standby environment for the primary database.

12. With the primary database in an OPEN state, perform a full backup of the primary database using RMAN.

 Note: Backing up the database in an OPEN state will update the control file (if the RMAN catalog is not being used) with the backupset information.

13. Once backup is complete, shut down the database and restart it in a MOUNT state. Create the standby control file using RMAN as follows:

```
RMAN > BACKUP CURRENT CONTROLFILE FOR STANDBY;
```

14. Copy the control file and the backup sets to the physical standby database environment; place the control file in a location as defined in the local parameter file and the backup sets in a similar directory location defined during the backup operation.

15. Verify if the password file is present and, if it is not found, create a password file for the physical standby database:

```
[oracle@oradb2 dbs]$ orapwd file=orapwSSKYDG entries=32
password=oracle
```

16. Using the PFILE created in step 8, start the standby database (SSKYDG) in a NOMOUNT state:

```
SQL> startup nomount pfile=initSSKYDG.ora;
ORACLE instance started.

Total System Global Area   167772160 bytes
Fixed Size                   1218292 bytes
Variable Size               62916876 bytes
Database Buffers            96468992 bytes
Redo Buffers                 7168000 bytes
```

17. Using RMAN, connect to the primary database as TARGET and the physical standby database as AUXILIARY:

```
[oracle@oradb2 oracle]rman target sys/oracle@sskydb
nocatalog auxiliary / trace restore_stndby_db.log
```

Note: The `trace` switch will create a log file for the RMAN session activity.

18.   Execute the following RMAN backup script:

```
[oracle@oradb2 scripts]$ more rman_10_recover_phydb.sql
RUN
{
# The DUPLICATE command uses an automatic sbt channel.
# Because the target datafiles are spread across
multiple directories,
# run SET NEWNAME rather than DB_FILE_NAME_CONVERT
SET NEWNAME FOR DATAFILE 1 TO '/usr/app/oracle/oracle/
oradata/SSKYDG/datafile/o1_mf_system_1ssgdndr_.dbf';
SET NEWNAME FOR DATAFILE 2 TO '/usr/app/oracle/oracle/
oradata/SSKYDG/datafile/o1_mf_undotbs1_1ssgdnn4_.dbf';
SET NEWNAME FOR DATAFILE 3 TO '/usr/app/oracle/oracle/
oradata/SSKYDG/datafile/o1_mf_sysaux_1ssgdng2_.dbf';
SET NEWNAME FOR DATAFILE 4 TO '/usr/app/oracle/oracle/
oradata/SSKYDG/datafile/o1_mf_users_1ssgdnpp_.dbf';
SET NEWNAME FOR DATAFILE 5 TO '/usr/app/oracle/oracle/
oradata/SSKYDG/datafile/o1_mf_example_1ssgh559_.dbf';
DUPLICATE TARGET DATABASE FOR STANDBY
DORECOVER;
}
```

Note: The script uses the `SET NEWNAME` command to rename the datafile to a new location. This step is required if the datafiles restored are to a different directory structure compared to the primary environment. In this example, the primary environment uses ASM.

19.   Now, change the database from a `NOMOUNT` state to a `MOUNT` state:

```
SQL> ALTER DATABASE MOUNT
```

20.   Since the standby database has been brought to the same level as the primary database, it is ready to receive data changes from the primary database on a regular basis. The redo apply can be performed either in a batch mode or on a real-time basis.

a. To apply redo in a batch basis, the following command should be executed:

```
SQL> ALTER DATABASE RECOVER MANAGED STANDBY
DATABASE DISCONNECT FROM SESSION;
```

b. To apply redo on a real-time basis, the following command should be executed:

```
SQL> ALTER DATABASE RECOVER MANAGED STANDBY DATABASE
USING CURRENT LOGFILE;
```

21. Verify/test if the configuration is working by performing a log switch on the primary. This will cause a data transfer to the physical standby and the data will be applied. To verify this, perform a manual log file switch operation on the primary database environment:

```
SQL> ALTER SYSTEM SWITCH LOGFILE;
```

22. The following query verifies if the physical standby database was recovered after the RMAN RESTORE operation:

```
SELECT INCARNATION#,
       RESETLOGS_ID,
       STATUS
FROM  V$DATABASE_INCARNATION;


INCARNATION# RESETLOGS_ID STATUS
------------ ------------ -------
           1    562360180 PARENT
           2    576860186 CURRENT
```

23. On the physical standby instance, verify if the archive log files are being applied using the following query:

```
SELECT SEQUENCE#,
       FIRST_TIME,
       NEXT_TIME,
       APPLIED
FROM  V$ARCHIVED_LOG
ORDER BY SEQUENCE#;
```

```
SEQUENCE# FIRST_TIME            NEXT_TIME            APP
---------- -------------------- -------------------- ---
       129 28-DEC-2005 06:01:49 28-DEC-2005 22:02:31 YES
       130 28-DEC-2005 22:02:31 28-DEC-2005 23:37:02 YES
       131 28-DEC-2005 23:37:02 28-DEC-2005 23:37:56 YES
       132 28-DEC-2005 23:37:56 28-DEC-2005 23:39:22 YES
```

This completes a basic physical standby configuration. In this configuration, the data is moved from the primary to the physical standby site and applied on a regular basis. No DGB is involved. When using the DGB, all of these steps will have to be performed, except that the primary physical standby configuration will be managed and monitored using the DGB.

Data Guard Broker

In the earlier section on basic physical standby, the steps required to configure a physical standby database were discussed. As indicated earlier, the entire standby configuration can be maintained and monitored using a DGB. While this tool is optional, it is being discussed as a step toward implementing a new feature in Oracle Database 10*g* Release 2, namely, fast-start failover.

 Note: This section assumes that a physical standby database has been configured using the steps discussed in the previous section.

1.   The first step in the configuration of the DGB is to ensure that all databases (both primary and standby) participating in the Data Guard configuration have two copies of the DGB configuration file identified by the parameters `DG_BROKER_CONFIG_FILE1` and `DG_BROKER_CONFIG_FILE2`. By default, these files are created in the `$ORACLE_HOME/dbs` directory. If the environment is a RAC database, the configuration files should be located on shared storage.

     These configuration files contain entries that describe the state and properties of the configuration (such as the sites and databases that are part of the configuration, the roles and properties of each of the databases, and the state of each of the elements of the configuration). A two-file concept is used to maintain the current and the previous good states of the configuration.

     a.   Since, in this example, the physical standby database is a single-instance configuration, the file is maintained in its default `$ORACLE_HOME/dbs` directory:

```
SQL> show parameter dg_broker_config

NAME                        TYPE          VALUE
----------------------      ----------    ------------------------------
dg_broker_config_file1      string        /usr/app/oracle/oracle/product
                                          /10.2.0/db_1/dbs/dr1SSKYDG.dat
dg_broker_config_file2      string        /usr/app/oracle/oracle/product
                                          /10.2.0/db_1/dbs/dr2SSKYDG.dat
```

b. In the RAC environment (primary database), the configuration file should be located on shared storage, and since
in this example, the RAC environment uses ASM as its
primary data storage solution, these files are also located
on ASM:

```
SQL> ALTER SYSTEM SET DG_BROKER_CONFIG_FILE1='+ASMGRP1' SCOPE=BOTH;
SQL> ALTER SYSTEM SET DG_BROKER_CONFIG_FILE2='+ASMGRP1' SCOPE=BOTH;
```

This will create two configuration files in the ASMGRP1/
SSKYDB/DATAGUARDCONFIG directory and create an alias for these
individual files in the ASMGRP1/SSKYDB/DATAFILE directory.

```
SQL> show parameter dg_broker_config

NAME                      TYPE      VALUE
----------------------    -------   ------------------------------
dg_broker_config_file1    string    +ASMGRP1/sskydb/datafile/dr1sskydb.dat
dg_broker_config_file2    string    +ASMGRP1/sskydb/datafile/dr2sskydb.dat
```

 Note: The physical location of the configuration files can be verified using
the ASM command-line utility discussed in Chapter 2. For example, the
following illustrates its primary location in the DATAGUARDCONFIG directory
and the alias definition in the DATAFILE directory:

```
ASMCMD> ls -ltr DATAGUARDCONFIG/
Type              Redund   Striped   Time            Sys   Name
DATAGUARDCONFIG   MIRROR   COARSE    DEC 28 23:00:00  Y    SSKYDB.350.577196987
DATAGUARDCONFIG   MIRROR   COARSE    DEC 28 23:00:00  Y    SSKYDB.351.577196993

ASMCMD> ls -ltr DATAFILE/dr*
Type Redund Striped Time Sys   Name
                    N     drlsskydb.dat => +ASMGRP1/SSKYDB/DATAGUARDCONFIG/
SSKYDB.350.577196987
```

```
                         N    dr2sskydb.dat => +ASMGRP1/SSKYDB/DATAGUARDCONFIG/
SSKYDB.351.577196993
ASMCMD>
```

2. The next step is to set the parameter that will enable the DGB to monitor this configuration. This parameter should also be enabled on both the primary and the physical standby environments. The primary function of this parameter is to indicate that the database is part of the DGB configuration.

```
SQL> ALTER SYSTEM SET DG_BROKER_START = TRUE
SCOPE=BOTH;
```

This parameter will also start the Data Guard Monitor (DMON) background process, and as illustrated below, the information is recorded in the alert logs of the respective instances:

```
Thu Dec 15 16:29:48 2005
ALTER SYSTEM SET dg_broker_start=TRUE SCOPE=MEMORY;
DMON started with pid=59, OS id=21751
Starting Data Guard Broker (DMON)
```

Once these parameters are defined, the DGB should be enabled to start monitoring the environment. This could be done in one of two ways, from the EM GC interface (Figure 10.2) or using the command-line utility called DGMGRL.

 Note: Since the EM GC has additional licensing requirements and in order to make the configuration and monitoring simple for readers, the focus of this section is to use the DGB command-line utility (DGMGRL).

3. Using DGMGRL, connect to the primary database as illustrated:

```
[oracle@oradb2 ~]$ dgmgrl
    DGMGRL for Linux: Version 10.2.0.1.0 - Production

    Copyright (c) 2000, 2005, Oracle. All rights reserved.

    Welcome to DGMGRL, type "help" for information.
```

```
DGMGRL> connect sys/<password>@SSKYDB
Connected.
DGMGRL>
```

4. Using a SQL*Plus session, verify if the DB_UNIQUE_NAME parameters match the database names on the respective servers. Based on our example/workshop, this should be SSKYDB on the primary database and SSKYDG on the standby database.

5. Create configuration information for the primary database. Every set of configurations managed by the DGB is assigned a unique name; for our example/workshop, the name is SSKYDR_OPTION.

```
DGMGRL> CREATE CONFIGURATION 'SSKYDR_OPTION' AS PRIMARY
DATABASE IS 'SSKYDB' CONNECT IDENTIFIER IS SSKYDB;
Configuration "SSKYDR_OPTION" created with primary
database "SSKYDB"
```

6. Verify if the configuration has been created using the SHOW CONFIGURATION command:

```
DGMGRL> show configuration

Configuration
  Name:                 SSKYDR_OPTION
  Enabled:              NO
  Protection Mode:      MaxPerformance
  Fast-Start Failover:  DISABLED
  Databases:
  SSKYDB - Primary database

Current status for "SSKYDR_OPTION":
DISABLED
```

7. Now, add the physical standby database to the Data Guard configuration using the DGB:

```
DGMGRL> ADD DATABASE 'SSKYDG' AS CONNECT IDENTIFIER IS
SSKYDG MAINTAINED AS      PHYSICAL;
Database "SSKYDG" added
DGMGRL> show configuration
```

```
Configuration
   Name:                          SSKYDR_OPTION
   Enabled:                       NO
   Protection Mode:               MaxPerformance
   Fast-Start Failover: DISABLED
   Databases:
     SSKYDB - Primary database
     SSKYDG - Physical standby database


Current status for "SSKYDR_OPTION":
DISABLED


DGMGRL>
```

When the standby database is added to the DGB configuration, it registers a special service name db_unique_name_XPT with the standby listeners for redo transport services. On the primary database, the broker extracts the listener address from the LOCAL_LISTENER initialization parameter and uses the service name db_unique_name_XPT and the value of INSTANCE_NAME to construct the connect descriptor so that redo transport services transmit archived redo log files to the standby apply instance. With this definition, the LOG_ARCHIVE_DEST_2 parameter of the primary database is also automatically reset to the following:

```
LOG_ARCHIVE_DEST_2  =
service="(DESCRIPTION=(ADDRESS_LIST=(ADDRESS=(PROTOCOL=TCP)(H
OST=oradb2.summersky.biz)(PORT=1521)))(CONNECT_DATA=(SERVICE_
NAME=SSKYDG_XPT)(INSTANCE_NAME=SSKYDG)(SERVER=dedicated)))",L
GWR SYNC AFFIRM delay=0 OPTIONAL max_failure=0
max_connections=1 reopen=300 db_unique_name="SSKYDG" register
net_timeout=180  valid_for=(online_logfile,primary_role)
```

8. Once both the primary and standby databases have been added to the configuration, the DGB services need to be enabled. It is important to ensure the following:

    a. Both databases are configured and using the SPFILE option.

    b. Both databases are configured with the LOCAL_LISTENER parameter.

c.   The instance name, DB_UNIQUE_NAME, and SERVICE_NAME are identical on both the primary and standby database.

If any of the above parameters/definitions are wrong, this will cause errors when enabling the configuration. For example, if SPFILE is missing, the following errors can be noticed in the alert log file:

```
    DG 2005-12-23-14:29:40   0 2 0 NSV1: NetSlave received
error ORA-16525 from target remote site. See trace file.
    DG 2005-12-23-14:29:40   0 2 0 RSM0: HEALTH CHECK ERROR:
ORA-16797: database is not using a server parameter file
    DG 2005-12-23-14:29:40   0 2 577808635 DMON: Database
SSKYDG returned ORA-16525

DGMGRL> ENABLE CONFIGURATION;
```

This command will enable the DGB configuration named SSKYDR_OPTION.

9.   The configuration can be verified using the SHOW CONFIGURATION command from the DGMGRL command prompt as follows:

```
DGMGRL>SHOW CONFIGURATION

Configuration
  Name:               SSKYDR_OPTION
  Enabled:            YES
  Protection Mode:    MaxPerformance
  Fast-Start Failover: DISABLED
  Databases:
    SSKYDB - Primary database
    SSKYDG - Physical standby database

Current status for "SSKYDR_OPTION":
SUCCESS
```

This completes the DGB configuration; at this point, all Data Guard functionality is monitored and managed via the DGB utility either using DGMGRL or the EM GC tools. As illustrated in the previous output, the Data Guard configuration has been set up for MaxPerformance (default) protection mode, and the FSFO either is disabled or has not yet been enabled.

The next step in the process is to take advantage of the new Oracle Database 10*g* Release 2 feature by enabling FSFO. This will protect the environment by providing higher availability and making the switch over from standby to primary environments and back again simpler, further reducing downtime.

Fast-start failover

The DGB will be used in the configuration of the FSFO feature. Similar to configuration of the standby database, FSFO can also be configured using EM GC (as illustrated in Figure 10.2) or interactively using the DGMGRL utility. The various steps to enable FSFO using DGMGRL are as follows:

1. The first step in this process is to ensure/verify that the LogXpt-Mode property of the DGB is configured to send and receive the log files in a SYNC mode. This is performed from the DGMGRL command prompt as follows:

    ```
    DGMGRL> show database 'SSKYDG' 'LogXptMode';
       LogXptMode = 'SYNC'
    DGMGRL> show database 'SSKYDB' 'LogXptMode';
       LogXptMode = 'SYNC'
    DGMGRL>
    ```

    If this is not set to the value of SYNC, set the property value using the following command:

    ```
    DGMGRL> EDIT DATABASE 'SSKYDB' SET PROPERTY
    'LogXptMode' = 'SYNC';
    ```

2. Change the current protection mode of the DGB configuration from MaxPerformance to MaxAvailability:

    ```
    DGMGRL> EDIT CONFIGURATION SET PROTECTION MODE AS
    MAXAVAILABILITY;
    Operation requires shutdown of instance "SSKY1" on
    database "SSKYDB"
    Shutting down instance "SSKY1"...

    Database closed.
    Database dismounted.
    ORACLE instance shut down.
    ```

Figure 10.2
*EM GC FSFO
Configuration*

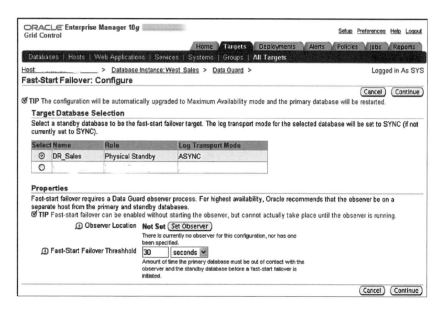

```
Operation requires startup of instance "SSKY1" on
database "SSKYDB"
Starting instance "SSKY1"...

DGMGRL> SHOW CONFIGURATION
Configuration
     Name:                  SSKYDR_OPTION
     Enabled:               YES
     Protection Mode:       MaxAvailability
     Fast-Start Failover: DISABLED
     Databases:
          SSKYDB - Primary database
          SSKYDG - Physical standby database

Current status for "SSKYDR_OPTION":
SUCCESS
```

3.   Now set the failover target database by setting the DGB property
     FastStartFailoverTarget. In this case, the failover target envi-
     ronment is SSKYDG. Configuring this property informs the DGB
     as to which database environment should be activated if the pri-
     mary database fails or which database environment should be
     activated when subsequently the physical standby database envi-
     ronment fails or a manual switchover is to be performed.

```
DGMGRL> EDIT DATABASE 'SSKYDB' SET PROPERTY
FastStartFailoverTarget ='SSKYDG';
Property "faststartfailovertarget" updated

DGMGRL> EDIT DATABASE 'SSKYDG' SET PROPERTY
FastStartFailoverTarget ='SSKYDB';
Property "faststartfailovertarget" updated
```

4. The next step is to configure the failover threshold value. This property tells the DGB, once the Observer does not receive a response from the current primary database for how long (in seconds) the Observer should attempt reconnecting to the primary database before initiating FSFO.

```
DGMGRL> EDIT CONFIGURATION SET PROPERTY
FastStartFailoverThreshold = 60;
Property "faststartfailoverthreshold" updated
```

5. The next step is to enable the FSFO feature. In order to enable FSFO, the standby database configuration should be in an observation mode. In other words, the third component Observer should be started. To start the observer with DGMGRL, issue the following command on the Observer computer:

```
DGMGRL> START OBSERVER;
```

Note: The Observer is a continuous foreground process; thus, the command-line prompt on the Observer computer does not return until you issue the STOP OBSERVER command from another DGMGRL session. To issue commands and interact with the broker configuration, you must connect through another DGMGRL client session.

6. Now enable the FSFO feature using the following command, and verify the configuration using the SHOW   CONFIGURATION command:

```
DGMGRL> ENABLE FAST_START FAILOVER;
Enabled.
```

```
DGMGRL> SHOW CONFIGURATION VERBOSE;

Configuration
  Name:                  SSKYDR_OPTION
  Enabled:               YES
  Protection Mode:       MaxAvailability
  Fast-Start Failover: ENABLED
Databases:
  SSKYDB - Primary database
  SSKYDG - Physical standby database
         - Fast-Start Failover target

Fast-Start Failover
 Threshold: 60 seconds
 Observer:  oradb2.sumsky.net


Current status for "SSKYDR_OPTION":
SUCCESS
```

7.   Synchronization status between all instances of the primary data-
      base and physical standby environment can be obtained by query-
      ing certain columns from GV$DATABASE:

```
COL INST FORMAT 999
COL NAME FORMAT A8
COL FFS FORMAT A18
COL FFCT FORMAT A8
COL FFT FORMAT 9999
COL FFOP FORMAT A6
COL FFOH FORMAT A20
SELECT INST_ID INST,NAME,
       FS_FAILOVER_STATUS FFS,
       FS_FAILOVER_CURRENT_TARGET FFCT,
       FS_FAILOVER_THRESHOLD FFT,
       FS_FAILOVER_OBSERVER_PRESENT FFOP,
       FS_FAILOVER_OBSERVER_HOST FFOH
FROM   GV$DATABASE;


INST NAME     FFS             FFCT       FFT FFOP   FFOH
---- -------- --------------- -------- ----- ------ --------------------
   2 SSKYDB   UNSYNCHRONIZED  SSKYDG      60 YES    oradb2.sumsky.net
```

```
     1 SSKYDB    UNSYNCHRONIZED SSKYDG        60 NO        oradb2.sumsky.net


SQL> /


INST NAME     FFS            FFCT      FFT FFOP   FFOH
---- -------- -------------- -------- ----- ------ --------------------
     2 SSKYDB    SYNCHRONIZED   SSKYDG        60 YES       oradb2.sumsky.net
     1 SSKYDB    SYNCHRONIZED   SSKYDG        60 YES       oradb2.sumsky.net
```

10.1.3   Failover

One primary reason for setting up a standby configuration is to protect the data in the primary environment and make it available to the application if the primary database becomes unavailable. Until Oracle Database 10*g* Release 2, when such failures happened and the standby database needed to be invoked for use, apart from the nightmares that DBAs faced with getting the standby site functional in a smooth and easy manner, they faced an even bigger nightmare when it came to getting the original primary database up to date with changes (i.e., failing over and swapping the functionality from the original standby back to the original primary databases). In this release with the FSFO feature, failover can be transparent; in addition, standby roles can also be switched. A failover using the Data Guard option can be of two types: (1) planned failover or (2) unplanned failover.

Planned failover

Planned failover is where the primary database is required to be brought down for hardware and/or software maintenance. Here the DBA will perform a manual switchover of the environment from primary to standby. Such an operation is performed with the DGB using the SWITCHOVER TO <database> command. In our example, since the primary database is in a RAC configuration, all instances except one should be shut down using the SHUTDOWN IMMEDIATE option. The last instance should be kept available until both the primary and standby have SYNCHRONIZED the activities. The failover status can be determined using the following query:

```
COL INST FORMAT 999
COL INSTN FORMAT A6
COL FFS FORMAT A16
COL FFCT FORMAT A7
COL FFT FORMAT 999
```

```
COL FOP FORMAT A4
COL FFOH FORMAT A20
COL DUN FORMAT A6
COL DBR FORMAT A10
COL DGB FORMAT A10
SELECT GVD.INST_ID INST,
       GVI.INSTANCE_NAME INSTN,
       GVD.FS_FAILOVER_STATUS FFS,
       GVD.FS_FAILOVER_CURRENT_TARGET FFCT,
       GVD.FS_FAILOVER_THRESHOLD FFT,
       GVD.FS_FAILOVER_OBSERVER_PRESENT FFOP,
       GVD.OPEN_MODE OM,
       GVD.DB_UNIQUE_NAME DUN,
       GVD.DATABASE_ROLE DBR
FROM   GV$DATABASE GVD, GV$INSTANCE GVI
WHERE  GVD.INST_ID=GVI.INST_ID;

INST INSTN  FFS             FFCT    FFT FFOP  OM         DUN    DBR
---- ------ --------------- ------- --- ----- ---------- ------ ---------
   1 SSKY1  SYNCHRONIZED    SSKYDG   60 YES   READ WRITE SSKYDB PRIMARY
   2 SSKY2  SYNCHRONIZED    SSKYDG   60 YES   READ WRITE SSKYDB PRIMARY
```

Shut down all instances except one instance, and verify the status:

```
INST INSTN  FFS             FFCT    FFT FFOP  OM         DUN    DBR
---- ------ --------------- ------- --- ----- ---------- ------ ---------
   1 SSKY1  SYNCHRONIZED    SSKYDG   60 YES   READ WRITE SSKYDB PRIMARY
```

Using the same query, verify that the standby database has the SYNCHRO-NIZED status also, and once this is confirmed, start the SWITCHOVER operation using the DGMGRL utility:

```
INST INSTN  FFS             FFCT    FFT FFOP  OM        DUN    DBR
---- ------ --------------- ------- --- ------ -------- ------ ----------------
   1 SSKYDG SYNCHRONIZED    SSKYDG   60 YES   MOUNTED  SSKYDG PHYSICAL STANDBY

DGMGRL> connect sys/oracle
Connected.
DGMGRL> switchover to 'SSKYDG';
Performing switchover NOW, please wait...
```

This operation will start the shutdown of the only remaining RAC instance:

```
Operation requires shutdown of instance "SSKY1" on database "SSKYDB"
Shutting down instance "SSKY1"...
ORA-01109: database not open

Database dismounted.
ORACLE instance shut down.
```

The next step in the SWITCHOVER operation is for the DGB to shut down the standby database and change the state from STANDBY to PRIMARY:

```
Operation requires shutdown of instance "SSKYDG" on database "SSKYDG"
Shutting down instance "SSKYDG"...
ORA-01109: database not open

Database dismounted.
ORACLE instance shut down.
```

The DGB attempts to start the new primary and new standby instances, but unfortunately since the listeners are not aware of these shutdown instances, Oracle returns an ORA-12514 error. At this time, a manual intervention is required to start up the databases:

```
Operation requires startup of instance "SSKY1" on database "SSKYDB"
Starting instance "SSKY1"...
Unable to connect to database
ORA-12514: TNS:listener does not currently know of service requested in
connect descri

Failed.
You are no longer connected to ORACLE
Please connect again.
Unable to start instance "SSKY1"
You must start instance "SSKY1" manually
Operation requires startup of instance "SSKYDG" on database "SSKYDG"
You must start instance "SSKYDG" manually
Switchover succeeded, new primary is "SSKYDG"
```

Once failover is complete, the query should be executed to verify the current state of both databases. Using the same query as before, the new values are as follows:

New primary database: SSKYDG

INST	INSTN	FFS	FFCT	FFT	FFOP	OM	DUN	DBR
1	**SSKYDG**	SYNCHRONIZED	SSKYDB	60	YES	READ WRITE	SSKYDG	**PRIMARY**

New standby database SSKYDB *and instances* SSKY1 *and* SSKY2:

INST	INSTN	FFS	FFCT	FFT	FFOP	OM	DUN	DBR
1	**SSKY1**	SYNCHRONIZED	SSKYDB	60	YES	MOUNTED	SSKYDB	**PHYSICAL STANDBY**
2	**SSKY2**	SYNCHRONIZED	SSKYDB	60	YES	MOUNTED	SSKYDB	**PHYSICAL STANDBY**

This completes the SWITCHOVER operation; a similar operation is performed to change the databases back to their original states. While the entire switchover activity is transparent, Oracle, behind the scenes, will make the required parameter modifications to change the states of the respective databases before requesting a STARTUP operation.

Unplanned failover

Unplanned failover occurs when the primary database environment is having problems due to either natural disasters or human errors and a temporary environment is required so that the application can access the data, and business can continue. When configured correctly, when all instances in a RAC configuration (primary database) fail, the Observer will automatically perform the required operations to make the standby database usable. The failover steps are as follows:

1.   The Data Guard is in a steady state transmitting the redo log from the primary to the standby locations.

2.   The Observer is in a monitoring state of the configuration. During this period, the Observer tracks both the standby and the primary databases.

3.   Let us assume an act of nature has occurred, causing the primary database, including all instances in the cluster, to crash.

4.   The Observer detects that the primary database is not responding. The Observer repeatedly tries to connect, and after the number of seconds defined by the `FastStartFailoverThreshold`, the DGB property declares that the primary environment is not available.

5.   The Observer at this point needs to verify with the standby database if it is ready to fail over and begins the failover process. The Observer initiates conversion of the standby database/instance from a Standby state to a Primary state. While the Observer initiates this process, the `RFS` background process on the standby instance performs the conversion. During this conversion process, depending on how active the primary database has been, it may take several minutes for the migration to complete.

   a.   The standby database is taken into a `NOMOUNT` state after performing a dismount of the already mounted instance.

   b.   A new control file is created with the required default parameters.

   c.   Database recovery is performed.

   d.   The database is handed back over to the Observer and placed in a `GUARD ALL` status.

   e.   The database is opened.

   f.   All of the required standby redo log files are added back to the configuration.

The following output shows the entries reported on the Observer console while the unplanned failover is in progress:

```
Copyright (c) 2000, 2005, Oracle. All rights reserved.

Welcome to DGMGRL, type "help" for information.
DGMGRL> connect sys/< >@sskydb
Connected.
DGMGRL> start observer
Observer started
```

This output is the initiation of the failover process from primary to the standby database:

```
21:09:38.47  Thursday, December 29, 2005
Initiating fast-start failover to database "SSKYDG"...
Performing failover NOW, please wait...
Failover succeeded, new primary is "SSKYDG"
21:13:09.14  Thursday, December 29, 2005
```

This output is the initiation of the failover process from standby (new primary) to the primary database when the standby (new primary) fails:

```
21:27:05.22  Thursday, December 29, 2005
Initiating reinstatement for database "SSKYDB"...
Reinstating database "SSKYDB", please wait...
```

6. The target standby database becomes the new primary database. Users can start accessing data just as they would with any normal database. At this point, it is very important to consider the configuration differences between the original primary and the new primary. If the configurations are not identical, the servers cannot process the same workload.

7. At this stage, depending on how long it takes to repair the old primary, there can be a period where only one database is available. Once the old primary database is repaired, the Observer reestablishes the connection.

8. The Observer automatically reinstates the old primary database to be the new standby database. At this stage, the redo transmission starts from the new primary database to the new standby database. The environment is back in a maximum availability mode.

In this specific scenario, since the primary and the standby are not of an identical configuration, it is important to switch the states back to their original states (i.e., the new standby should be switched back as a primary database). This can be accomplished using the switchover operations discussed in the "Planned Failover" section.

10.1.4   FAN and TAF

In the case where the failover target is a physical standby database, TAF-enabled applications will receive notification, causing them to disconnect from the primary and reconnect to the new primary database (standby). This allows applications to connect to the new primary soon after getting the notification instead of having to wait for the TCP timeout period, as would be the case for a site failure.

The RAC database will send a FAN/ONS DB_DOWN event notification to the client machines. The client applications can use the appropriate OCI calls, translate these events, and perform the appropriate action by connecting to the standby database. If the standby environment is also a RAC configuration, a similar event can be received, monitored, and reacted upon, making it a complete transparent failover solution.

 Note: FAN and TAF features are discussed in Chapters 5 and 6, respectively.

10.1.5   Adding instances

When a node or instance is added to the cluster (primary or standby) databases, the DGB will automatically register them and add the instance to the current Data Guard configuration, provided the following parameters are defined:

```
SSKY4.DG_BROKER_CONFIG_FILE1='+ASMGRP1/sskydb/datafile/dr1SSKYDB.dat'
SSKY4.DG_BROKER_CONFIG_FILE2='+ASMGRP1/sskydb/datafile/dr2SSKYDB.dat'
```

 Note: While RAC supports the use of '*' notation while defining database initialization parameters that apply to all instances in the cluster, the DG_BROKER_CONFIG_FILEn parameter remains an exception. This parameter needs to be qualified with the instance name, for example:

```
SSKY1.DG_BROKER_CONFIG_FILE1
```

Once the parameter file is defined and all other basic instance configurations are complete, the first time a new instance is started, the DGB will perform the required operation and add it to the configuration. The following output shows the activities performed by the DGB:

```
[oracle@oradb4 bdump]$ tail -100 drcSSKY4.log
DG 2005-12-30-19:40:57  0 2 0 DMON: >> Starting Data Guard Broker
bootstrap <<
DG 2005-12-30-19:40:57  0 2 0 DMON: Attach state object
DG 2005-12-30-19:40:59  0 2 0 DMON: chief lock convert for bootstrap
DG 2005-12-30-19:40:59  0 2 0 DMON Registering service
SSKYDB_SSKY4_harvest with listener(s)
DG 2005-12-30-19:40:59  0 2 0 Executing SQL [ALTER SYSTEM REGISTER]
DG 2005-12-30-19:40:59  0 2 0 SQL [ALTER SYSTEM REGISTER] Executed
successfully
DG 2005-12-30-19:41:00  1010000 4 578432460 DMON: Dynamically adding
instance SSKY4 to database SSKYDB
DG 2005-12-30-19:41:00  1010000 4 578432460 Added one instance for
resource 16842752.
DG 2005-12-30-19:41:00  1010000 4 578432460 DMON: ADD_INSTANCE: success
DG 2005-12-30-19:41:00  1010000 4 578432460 DMON: Evaluating critical
status of standbys in configuration
DG 2005-12-30-19:41:01  0 2 0 DMON Registering service SSKYDB_DGB with
listener(s)
DG 2005-12-30-19:41:01  0 2 0 Executing SQL [ALTER SYSTEM REGISTER]
DG 2005-12-30-19:41:01  0 2 0 SQL [ALTER SYSTEM REGISTER] Executed
successfully
DG 2005-12-30-19:41:01  1010000 4 578432460 DMON: metadata updated, I am
site 01001000 instance 2
DG 2005-12-30-19:41:01  0 2 0 #### NSV network timeout value set to 0
seconds by INSV
DG 2005-12-30-19:41:05  0 2 0 INSV: Received message for inter-instance
publication
DG 2005-12-30-19:41:05  0 2 0 req_id 1.0.578432460, opcode ADD_INSTANCE,
phase RESYNCH, flags 8005
DG 2005-12-30-19:41:06  0 2 0 INSV: All instances have replied for message
DG 2005-12-30-19:41:06  0 2 0 req_id 1.0.578432460, opcode ADD_INSTANCE,
phase RESYNCH
DG 2005-12-30-19:41:06  1010000 4 578432460 DMON: Data Guard Broker
initiated operation complete
DG 2005-12-30-19:41:06  1010000 4 578432460 DMON: ADD_INSTANCE operation
completed
DG 2005-12-30-19:41:06  1010000 4 578432460 DMON: Entered
rfm_release_chief_lock for ADD_INSTANCE
```

10.2 Oracle Streams

Oracle Streams is a solution for the propagation and management of data, transactions, and events either within a database or from one database to another. It is particularly strong when the need is to distribute subsets of data to one or more databases continuously. Databases participating in Streams can differ in hardware platform, database release, database structure and character set. Streams can be configured to replicate to another database (one-way) or to replicate between two databases (bi-directional). While the former method can be easy to implement and manage, the latter can be complex because it requires configuration of conflict resolution rules at the table or column level.

While a larger effort is required when implementing the read/write option, it does offer the most flexible environment for rolling upgrades across releases as the different systems can use different versions of Oracle.

Oracle provides a set of elements that allow users to control what information is put into a stream, how the stream flows or is routed from one node to another, what happens to events in the stream as they flow into each destination, and how the stream process ends. By specifying the configuration of the elements acting on the stream, a user can address specific requirements.

Like the logical standby limitations discussed earlier, not all datatypes are supported by Oracle Streams. Querying the DBA_STREAMS_UNSUPPORTED view will provide a list of unsupported objects. For example, the following query will help determine the unsupported objects in the CRM schema.

```
SELECT TABLE_NAME,
       REASON
FROM DBA_STREAMS_UNSUPPORTED
WHERE OWNER='CRM';
```

10.2.1 Architecture

The movement of streams of data or events from one node or database (source) to another (target) is performed in three basic stages:

- Retrieval (capture)
- Staging (propagation)

■ Consumption (apply)

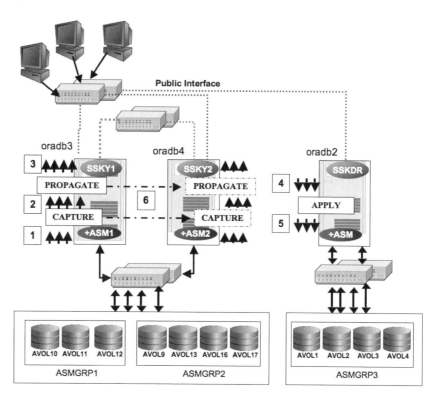

Figure 10.3
*Streams
Architecture and
Process Flow*

10.2.2 Capture

The capture step (indicated by step 1 in Figure 10.3) of the streams process is to collect events, which include database changes and data changes, and to place them into a staging area.

The capture process retrieves data extracted from the redo log, either by hot mining the online redo logs (normal operation) or, if the current redo log is not available (due to a delayed processing of the capture event), by mining archived redo log files. The names of the log files processed are recorded by the Oracle kernel process in the alert log files of the instance where the capture process is executing.

```
Sat Dec  3 13:38:27 2005
LOGMINER: Begin mining logfile:/u14/oradata/archivedata/SSKYDB/1_9_576039966.dbf
Sat Dec  3 13:39:38 2005
LOGMINER: Begin mining logfile: +ASMGRP1/sskydb/onlinelog/group_6.276.576048861
```

```
Sat Dec  3 13:39:38 2005
LOGMINER: End mining logfile: /u14/oradata/archivedata/SSKYDB/1_9_576039966.dbf
Sat Dec  3 13:39:38 2005
LOGMINER: Begin mining logfile: +ASMGRP1/sskydb/onlinelog/group_3.266.576040043
Sat Dec  3 13:39:39 2005
LOGMINER: End mining logfile: +ASMGRP1/sskydb/onlinelog/group_6.276.576048861
```

Data is retrieved from these log files based on a set of rules. *Rules are a predefined set of conditions based on business requirements to determine what type of change events should be captured.* These rules can be generic (e.g., capturing all changes for the entire database or schema), or they can be very specific, where only changes pertaining to a table or subset of a table are captured. After retrieving the data, the capture process formats it into a Logical Change Record (LCR) and queues it into a queue table (staging) for further processing. During this process, Streams can transforma this captured data by changing its format, data type, column name, or table name. *Transformation can be performed on events entering the staging area, leaving the staging area, or between staging areas.*

A single capture process can provide LCRs for multiple destination databases. As a result, the capture process may need to get information related to an LCR, which is stored in an archive log until that LCR has been applied on every target database and the capture dictionary has been updated. Therefore, it is possible that the capture process may need an old archive log to restart the capture process. Hence, it is important that archived logs remain available until the capture process has finished with them.

User applications can explicitly enqueue user messages representing events into the staging area. These messages can be formatted as LCRs, which will allow them to be consumed by the apply engine, or they can be formatted for consumption by another user application.

10.2.3　Types of capture

The Streams capture process can be configured to run locally on the source database or remotely on a downstream (destination) database as follows:

- *Local capture.* This is the traditional type of capture that existed with Streams since its initial release. Under this type of capture, the database changes are mined from the log files/archive log files at the source database, and only the changes that meet the rules defined are placed in the queue for propagation to the destination database(s).

- *Downstream capture.* In this type of capture, the capture process runs on a database other than the source database., The redo/archive log files from the source database are copied using the log transport services to the downstream database. The process captures changes in these files at the downstream database. This is a primary differentiator from a logical standby, where the standby must perform both the capture and apply in the same database. Streams can distribute to other databases using downstream capture which would be the same as with a local capture. As of Oracle Database 10*g* Release 2, redo logs from the source database can perform near real-time mining of the standby redo logs, reducing the latency of capture from the source database.

 Note: While both types of captures have their own advantages and disadvantages, in this chapter the local capture type is discussed.

10.2.4 Activation of the capture process

The capture process is performed through the background process Cnnn, where nnn is the capture process number. Oracle starts one background process for every capture process, and supports up to 999 such processes (c001 through c999 background processes) per database. Typically a single capture process is defined per database. In a RAC environment, the Streams background process resides on only one of the instances in the cluster. The capture process runs on the instance that owns the queue, in other words on the instance where the queue was originally created from. The owning instance of the queue can be determined by querying the OWNER_INSTANCE column for the queue table from DBA_QUEUE_TABLES view. DBAs can determine which instance is currently performing the capture process in one of two ways: (1) by checking the background processes at the operating system level, or (2) by using the entries in the alert log files (i.e., if the primary and secondary queue ownerships have not been established).

The instance on which you create the queue is the initial owning instance. If that instance goes down, the ownership switches automatically. You can control which instances are considered primary and secondary by setting the ownership with the DBMS_AQADM.ALTER_QUEUE_TABLE procedure. If the primary ownership is defined, then, if that instance is available, the Streams processes and services will run on that instance. If it is unavailable, the ownership will move to the secondary ownership. If both primary and secondary are unavailable, the ownership will migrate to a surviving instance. When the primary instance becomes available, the queue and its associated processes and services will automatically move back to the primary instance. `DBA_QUEUE_TABLES` is the view that identifies the primary and secondary ownership as well as the current owner instance for the queues in the queue table.

Capture process is started using the following command

```
SQL> EXEC DBMS_CAPTURE_ADM.START_CAPTURE( -
          capture_name=>'STRMADMIN_CAPTURE');


Sat Dec  3 16:44:49 2005
ALTER SYSTEM SET
service_names='SYS$STRMADMIN.STREAMS_QUEUE.SSKYDB.REGRESS.RDB
MS.DEV.US.ORACLE.COM' SCOPE=MEMORY SID='SSKY2';
Sat Dec  3 16:44:50 2005
Streams CAPTURE C001 started with pid=37, OS id=8590
Sat Dec  3 16:45:14 2005
```

In the previous output, the first entry adds the service name to the instance where the Streams capture process will execute and then starts the background process `C001` automatically during database restart.

Streams uses Oracle LogMiner to mine the log files and extract data based on the rules.

Once the capture process has started, additional processes are automatically started. As the capture process starts, the capture starts three additional processes performing tasks related to LogMiner: reader, builder, and preparer. These LogMiner processes are identified by `P001`, `P002`, and `P003`, respectively.

```
Sat Dec  3 16:45:14 2005
LOGMINER: Parameters summary for session# = 1
LOGMINER: Number of processes = 3, Transaction Chunk Size = 1
LOGMINER: Memory Size = 10M, Checkpoint interval = 10M
LOGMINER: session# = 1, reader process P000 started with pid=39 OS id=9700
LOGMINER: session# = 1, builder process P001 started with pid=41 OS
id=9727
```

```
LOGMINER: session# = 1, preparer process P002 started with pid=42 OS
id=9729
```

The function of the reader process is to read the redo log or archive log and divide it into regions or sections. The function of the preparer process is to scan the regions defined by the reader process and perform prefiltering of changes found in the redo log. During this phase, partial evaluation of the selection based on the rules defined is performed. Records of interest (matching the rules) are converted into LCRs. The builder process will merge the LCRs generated by the preparer into the queue. While building the rows, the builder ensures that the SCN order of these redos is preserved.

The primary goal of the Streams capture process is to continuously mine the redo log files for changes. On occasion, for example, on database restart or heavy load conditions, a redo log switch might occur, causing the current redo log file to be unavailable. At this time, the archive log files (as illustrated below) for the corresponding redo log files are mined for the information.

```
Fri Dec  2 13:08:17 2005
LOGMINER: Begin mining logfile: /u14/oradata/SSKYDB/
archivelog/2005_12_02/o1_mf_1_116_1s105o2n_.arc
Fri Dec  2 13:09:15 2005
LOGMINER: End mining logfile: /u14/oradata/SSKYDB/archivelog/
2005_12_02/o1_mf_1_116_1s105o2n_.arc
Fri Dec  2 13:09:17 2005
```

When a capture process, is initially created, a copy of the data dictionary is placed in the redo logs. When capture is started, it processes this information to populate the LogMiner and Streams multiversion data dictionary (separate from the primary data dictionary of the source database) for the source database. This data dictionary is also placed into the queue for delivery to the target database. Propagations and apply processes use this data dictionary to track the database objects from a particular source database.

The capture process performs its functions through various stages. These stages, listed in Table 10.1, can be obtained by querying the STATE column in the V$STREAMS_CAPTURE view.

Table 10.1 *Streams Capture States*

State	Description
INITIALIZING	The capture process is getting started and initialized.
WAITING FOR DICTIONARY REDO	The capture process is currently in a wait state. It is waiting for the redo log files containing the dictionary build related to the first SCN to be captured to be completed.
DICTIONARY INITIALIZATION	It is processing a dictionary build.
MINING	It is mining the redo log files.
LOADING	It is processing information in stages. This also indicates the progress of the loading activity.
CAPTURING_CHANGES	It is scanning the redo log for changes satisfying the rules.
WAITING FOR REDO	It is waiting for new redo log files to be mined.
EVALUATING RULE	It is evaluating a change against a capture process rule set.
CREATING LCR	It is converting a change into an LCR.
SHUTTING DOWN	It is stopping the capture process.
PAUSED FOR FLOW CONTROL	The capture of new events is paused due to slow propagation or slow consumption rate. This state is performed to avoid LCR spillage to disk queues.

In a RAC environment, the capture process will mine the log files of all instances participating in the cluster from the instance where the capture process is activated. This raises a primary question as to what happens when this instance fails?

Failover. Like any process or session failover in a RAC environment (failover is discussed in Chapter 6), when the instance or node executing the Streams capture process fails, the capture process and the buffer queue will fail over to one of the other surviving instances in the cluster (illustrated by step 6 in Figure 10.3). During this period of failure, there is a pause in activity while Oracle performs instance recovery. Once instance recovery is complete, the service definition is automatically added to the new instance using the **ALTER SYSTEM** command, and then the capture background process is started, followed by the LogMiner processes.

10.2.5 Staging (propagation)

The next step is to stage the mined events. The staging area is a queue that provides a service to store and manage captured events (illustrated by step 2 in Figure 10.3). As discussed earlier, the events captured from the redo logs and/or the archive log files are stored in memory in the buffer queue. This is considered the staging area because, from this queue, the data can be dequeued by the desired processes (illustrated by step 3 in Figure 10.3) and applied to the destination environment. The destination can be local to the same database or remote. If the destination is a remote environment, the dequeued data is propagated to another queue (apply queue) in the target database (illustrated by step 4 in Figure 10.3). The queue from which the events are propagated is called the *source queue*, and the queue that receives the events is called the *destination queue*. There can be a one-to-many, many-to-one, or many-to-many relationship between source and destination queues. Propagation is always between a source queue and a destination queue via a database link. In Oracle Database 10g Release 2 it is strongly recommended that the additional parameter queue_to_queue be set to TRUE. The propagation between the source queue and the destination queue is also performed by the job queue configured with DBMS_JOB. There is a coordinator process to ensure this propagation is completed and various job processes (J00*) spin up to perform the work.

Best Practice: For easy administration and maintenance reasons, it is recommended that separate queues for each capture and apply process be configured.

10.2.6 Consumption (apply)

This step of the Streams process is to retrieve committed transactions from the staging areas and apply them to the database. Since the destination where the data should be stored can be local to the source database or remote (via a Transport Gateway to a non-Oracle database), the function of the apply process is to retrieve these rows and apply them to the destination database (illustrated by step 5 in Figure 10.3). Like the capture process, the apply process can also be based on rules or simply apply all that is received. The propagation process on the source database will push the data to the remote database, where this is stored in the apply queues and subsequently applied to the database.

The default apply engine applies DML changes and DDL changes represented by implicitly (streams capture process) or explicitly captured (application Enqueue to disk) LCRs. The default apply engine will detect conflicts where the destination row has been changed and does not contain the expected values. If a conflict is detected, then a resolution routine may be invoked.

The apply engine can also be customized to pass the LCR or a user message to a user-defined procedure known as a DML or DDL handler. This provides the greatest amount of flexibility in processing an event. A typical application of a user-defined procedure might be to reformat the data represented in the LCR before applying it to a local table (e.g., field format, object name, and column name mapping transformations). A user-defined procedure can also be used to perform column subsetting or to update other objects at the target database that may not be present in the source database.

User applications can explicitly dequeue LCRs or user messages from the receiving staging area. This allows a user application to efficiently access the data in a Streams staging area. Streams can send notifications to registered PL/SQL or OCI functions, giving the applications an alternative to polling for new messages. Of course, applications can still poll, or even wait, for new subscribed messages in the staging area to become available.

10.2.7 Activation of the apply process

As with the capture process, Oracle performs the apply actions through a background process identified by Annn, where nnn is the apply process number. Oracle starts one background process for every apply definition and supports up to 999 such processes (a001 through a999 background processes) per database.

The apply process is started using the following command

```
SQL> EXEC DBMS_APPLY_ADM.START_APPLY( -
                    apply_name => 'STRMADMIN_APPLY);
Fri Dec  2 11:54:31 2005
Streams APPLY A001 started with pid=18, OS id=25036
Streams Apply Reader started P000 with pid=19 OS id=25038
Streams Apply Server started P001 with pid=23 OS id=25040
```

Information regarding the apply process start and stop activity is recorded in the alert log file of the destination database. As illustrated in the previous output, the apply process consists of the following additional components:

- A *reader server* (identified by P000) that dequeues events. The reader server computes dependencies between LCRs and assembles events into transactions. These dependencies are used to schedule the execution order of the transactions when multiple apply servers are configured.

- A *coordinator process* (identified by A001) that gets the transactions from the reader server and passes them to the apply servers in the appropriate order. The coordinator function is performed by the apply process identified by Annn.

- The *apply server* (identified by P001) that applies the LCRs to database objects as DML or DDL statements. Multiple apply servers can be configured to apply transactions in parallel by setting the parallelism parameter of apply.

Note: If the destination database is also a RAC environment, the apply process resides on one of the instances in the cluster. When the owner instance became unavailable, then the apply process is restarted automatically on one of the other available instances.

10.2.8 Streams configuration workshop

Two levels of configuration steps have to be completed. While Oracle provides a GUI-based configuration option via the EM console, for the purposes of our discussions, a step-by-step approach using the command-line interface is covered for easier understanding.

As discussed earlier, like the standby database configuration, the target databases can have either a clustered or a single-instance configuration. While the steps required for these configurations are not different, the processing can be.

Source database

The configuration procedure differs depending on if the flash recovery option is used or not. This means the difference between auto archiving and manual archiving. If no flash recovery feature is used, then a separate archive log destination area should be defined (manual archiving). The archive log files stored on ASM volumes only visible to the instance or node that is connected to the device.

1.   The databases are required to be in archive log mode with the flashback option enabled.

Note: The steps required to the enable archive log and/or the flashback option are discussed in Chapter 8 and have been omitted here to avoid repetition.

2.   Verify and set up the parameters required for the capture and propagation processes:

```
SQL> ALTER SYSTEM SET GLOBAL_NAMES = TRUE SCOPE=BOTH;
```

The values of the following parameters should be increased by the minimum values indicated to support the Streams configuration:

```
SQL> ALTER SYSTEM SET JOB_QUEUE_PROCESSES = 4
SCOPE=BOTH;
SQL> ALTER SYSTEM SET SHARED_POOL_SIZE = 100M
SCOPE=BOTH;
SQL> ALTER SYSTEM SET STREAMS_POOL_SIZE = 500M
SCOPE=BOTH;
SQL> ALTER SYSTEM SET PROCESSES = 100 SCOPE=BOTH
```

Caution: The values specified for these parameters are only for illustration purposes. The actual values for these parameters may vary based on the type of configuration and extent of database activities in the implementation environment.

Note: If automatic memory management is enabled by setting the SGA_TARGET parameter, then the SHARED_POOL_SIZE and STREAMS_POOL_SIZE parameter definitions are not required. However, the value of the SGA_TARGET parameter should be increased appropriately for streams.

3.   Change the cluster database parameter and open the database:

```
SQL>ALTER SYSTEM SET CLUSTER_DATABASE=TRUE
SCOPE=SPFILE;
SQL>ALTER DATABASE OPEN;
```

4.   Define a tablespace to store all of the Streams administrator–related objects and data:

```
SQL>CREATE TABLESPACE STREAMS_TBS DATAFILE '+ASMGRP1';
```

5.   Create the Streams administrative user:

```
SQL>CREATE USER STRMADMIN IDENTIFIED BY <PASSWORD>
SQL>DEFAULT TABLESPACE STREAMS_TBS TEMPORARY TABLESPACE
TEMP;
```

6.   Grant the administrator all of the required privileges to manage the queuing process:

```
SQL> EXEC DBMS_STREAMS_AUTH.GRANT_ADMIN_PRIVILEGE
('STRMADMIN');
```

 Note: The `DBMS_STREAMS_AUTH.GRANT_ADMIN_PRIVILEGE` procedure, which is new in Oracle Database 10*g*, replaces the lengthy process of granting individual privileges in the prior versions of Oracle.

To verify if all of the privileges are granted, the following procedure with the additional parameters will provide the list in the file `streams_admin_privs.sql` created in the directory identified by the `DIRECTORY_NAME` parameter [25]:

```
SQL> CREATE DIRECTORY dumpdir AS '/home/oracle/scripts/';
SQL> BEGIN
   DBMS_STREAMS_AUTH.GRANT_ADMIN_PRIVILEGE(
                    GRANTEE        => 'STRMADMIN',
                    FILE_NAME      =>
'streams_admin_privs.sql',
                    DIRECTORY_NAME => 'dumpdir');
      END;
```

7.   Add remote database information into the local TNSNAMES file of all nodes in the cluster:

```
cd $ORACLE_HOME/network/admin
vi tnsnames.ora

SSKYDR =
  (DESCRIPTION =
    (ADDRESS = (PROTOCOL = TCP)(HOST = oradb2.sumsky.net)(PORT =
1521))
    (CONNECT_DATA =
    (SERVER = DEDICATED)
    (SERVICE_NAME = SSKYDR.REGRESS.RDBMS.DEV.US.ORACLE.COM)
    )
  )
```

8.   Connect to the database as the Streams administrator (STRMADMIN), create a database link, and verify by executing a remote query. The database link is used by the source database to propagate changes to the destination database.

```
SQL> CREATE DATABASE LINK SSKYDR CONNECT TO STRMADMIN IDENTIFIED BY
STRMADMIN USING 'SSKYDR.REGRESS.RDBMS.DEV.US.ORACLE.COM';

SQL> SELECT * FROM GLOBAL_NAME@SSKYDR;

GLOBAL_NAME
----------------------------------------------------------------
SSKYDR.REGRESS.RDBMS.DEV.US.ORACLE.COM

SQL> SELECT TABLE_NAME FROM USER_TABLES@SSKYDR;

TABLE_NAME
------------------------------
STREAMS_QUEUE_TABLE
AQ$_STREAMS_QUEUE_TABLE_S
SYS_IOT_OVER_50630
AQ$_STREAMS_QUEUE_TABLE_T
AQ$_STREAMS_QUEUE_TABLE_H
AQ$_STREAMS_QUEUE_TABLE_G
AQ$_STREAMS_QUEUE_TABLE_I
```

9.   As the Streams administrator, create the Streams capture queue. The capture process stores all LCRs in these queues. The LCRs are then picked up by the propagator.

```
SQL> BEGIN
        DBMS_STREAMS_ADM.SET_UP_QUEUE( -
            QUEUE_NAME=>'STREAMS_QUEUE', -
            QUEUE_TABLE=>'STREAMS_QUEUE_TABLE', -
            QUEUE_USER=>'STREAMSADMIN', -
            STORAGE_CLAUSE=>'TABLESPACE STREAMS_TBS'); -
     END;


SQL> SELECT TABLE_NAME FROM USER_TABLES;

TABLE_NAME
----------------------------
STREAMS_QUEUE_TABLE
AQ$_STREAMS_QUEUE_TABLE_S
SYS_IOT_OVER_52309
AQ$_STREAMS_QUEUE_TABLE_T
AQ$_STREAMS_QUEUE_TABLE_H
AQ$_STREAMS_QUEUE_TABLE_G
AQ$_STREAMS_QUEUE_TABLE_I
```

10.   Connect as `sys` or `system` and enable forced logging at the tablespace or database level as appropriate. This step is important to ensure that all changes made to the source database are also available for capture and propagation to the destination. The command will force logging of tables that have been configured with the `NO LOGGING` option:

```
SQL> ALTER DATABASE FORCE LOGGING;
```

11.   The next step in the process is to add the rules for data capture and propagation. All data including any DDL changes will be transferred from the source database to the target database for the schema named `CRM`. To add these rules, the Streams administrator requires DBA privileges. To grant the DBA privileges, connect as `SYS` or `SYSTEM` to the database and perform the grant operation:

```
SQL> CONNECT SYSTEM/<password>;

SQL> GRANT DBA TO STRMADMIN;
```

12.   Connect as the Streams administrator (STRMADMIN) and add cap-
       ture rules for the CRM schema:

```
SQL> CONNECT STRMADMIN/<password>;

SQL> BEGIN
        DBMS_STREAMS_ADM.ADD_SCHEMA_RULES ( -
            SCHEMA_NAME =>'CRM', -
            STREAMS_TYPE =>'CAPTURE', -
            STREAMS_NAME=>'STRMADMIN_CAPTURE', -
            QUEUE_NAME=>'STREAMS_ADMIN.STREAMS_QUEUE', -
            INCLUDE_DML=>TRUE, -
            INCLUDE_DDL=>TRUE);
     END;
```

       In this procedure definition, the rules are captured at the data-
       base schema level. All changes made to the CRM schema will be
       captured by the capture process.

 Note: Similar to schema level capture, Streams also supports capturing at
the individual table level or at the database level

13.   Add propagation rules using the Oracle-provided PL/SQL proce-
       dure DBMS_STREAMS_ADM.ADD_SCHEMA_PROPAGATION_RULES:

```
SQL> BEGIN
        DBMS_STREAMS_ADM.ADD_SCHEMA_PROPAGATION_RULES ( -
        SCHEMA_NAME=>'CRM', -
        STREAMS_NAME=>'STRMADMIN_PROPAGATE', -
        SOURCE_QUEUE_NAME=>'STRMADMIN.STREAMS_QUEUE', -
        DESTINATION_QUEUE_NAME=> 'STRMADMIN.STREAMS_QUEUE@SSKYDR', -
     SOURCE_DATABASE_NAME=>'SSKYDB',
        INCLUDE_DML=>TRUE, -
        INCLUDE_DDL=>TRUE,
        QUEUE_TO_QUEUE=>TRUE);
     END;
```

This procedure collects the events captured and stored in the STRMADMIN.STREAMS_QUEUE and moves them to the destination queue STRMADMIN_STREAMS_QUEUE in the destination database identified by SSKYDR. The procedure further qualifies that both DDL and DML changes will be included in the propagation.

At this stage, all of the basic-level configuration steps for the source database are complete. The target database (SSKYDR) should be configured and made ready before other steps are completed.

Note: The destination database should be installed and started before proceeding to the next step.

Target database

1.   Verify and set all of the parameters required for the apply process:

```
SQL> ALTER SYSTEM SET GLOBAL_NAMES = TRUE SCOPE=BOTH;
```

The values of the following parameters should be increased by the minimum values indicated to support the Streams configuration:

```
SQL> ALTER SYSTEM SET JOB_QUEUE_PROCESSES = 4
SCOPE=BOTH;
SQL> ALTER SYSTEM SET SHARED_POOL_SIZE = 100M
SCOPE=BOTH;
SQL> ALTER SYSTEM SET STREAMS_POOL_SIZE = 500M
SCOPE=BOTH;
SQL> ALTER SYSTEM SET PROCESSES = 100 SCOPE=BOTH
```

Caution: The values specified for these parameters are only for illustration purposes. The actual values for these parameters may vary based on the type of configuration and extent of database activities in the implementation environment.

Note: If automatic memory management is enabled by setting the SGA_TARGET parameter, then the SHARED_POOL_SIZE and STREAMS_POOL_SIZE parameter definitions are not required. However, the value of the SGA_TARGET parameter should be increased appropriately for Streams.

2.   Define a tablespace to store all of the Streams administrator-related objects and data:

```
SQL> CREATE TABLESPACE STREAMS_TBS DATAFILE
'+ASMGRP1';
```

 Note: In this case, ASM is used for data storage on the target database as well. This is not a requirement. The target database can be of any file system type (e.g., ext3, OCFS, RAW) in the Linux operating system or other operating system-specific file systems for their respective platforms.

3.   Create the streams administrative user:

```
SQL>CREATE USER STRMADMIN IDENTIFIED BY <password> DEFAULT —
TABLESPACE STREAMS_TBS TEMPORARY TABLESPACE TEMP;
```

4.   Grant the administrator all of the required privileges to manage the queuing process:

```
SQL> EXEC DBMS_STREAMS_AUTH.GRANT_ADMIN_PRIVILEGE
('STRMADMIN');
```

 Note: The `DBMS_STREAMS_AUTH.GRANT_ADMIN_PRIVILEGE` procedure, which is new in Oracle Database 10*g*, replaces the lengthy process of granting individual privileges in the prior versions of Oracle.

To verify if all of the privileges are granted, the following procedure with the additional parameters will provide the list in the file `streams_admin_privs.sql` created in the directory identified by the `DIRECTORY_NAME` parameter [25]:

```
SQL> CREATE DIRECTORY dumpdir AS '/home/oracle/scripts/';

SQL> BEGIN
    DBMS_STREAMS_AUTH.GRANT_ADMIN_PRIVILEGE(
```

```
                              GRANTEE        => 'STRMADMIN',
                              FILE_NAME      =>
      'streams_admin_privs.sql',
                              DIRECTORY_NAME => 'dumpdir');
            END;
```

5.   As the Streams administrator, create the Streams capture queue:

```
      SQL> BEGIN
              DBMS_STREAMS_ADM.SET_UP_QUEUE( -
                QUEUE_NAME=>'STREAMS_QUEUE', -
                QUEUE_TABLE=>'STREAMS_QUEUE_TABLE', -
              QUEUE_USER=>'STRMADMIN', -
              STORAGE_CLAUSE=>'TABLESPACE STREAMS_TBS'); -
              END;


      SQL> SELECT TABLE_NAME FROM USER_TABLES;

      TABLE_NAME
      ------------------------------
      STREAMS_QUEUE_TABLE
      AQ$_STREAMS_QUEUE_TABLE_S
      SYS_IOT_OVER_52309
      AQ$_STREAMS_QUEUE_TABLE_T
      AQ$_STREAMS_QUEUE_TABLE_H
      AQ$_STREAMS_QUEUE_TABLE_G
      AQ$_STREAMS_QUEUE_TABLE_I
```

6.   Connect as the Streams administrator, and add the schema apply
      rules:

```
      SQL >EXEC DBMS_STREAMS_ADM.ADD_SCHEMA_RULES( -
              schema_name => 'CRM',-
              streams_type => 'APPLY',-
              streams_name=>'STRMADMIN_APPLY',-
              queue_name=>'STRMADMIN.STREAMS_QUEUE',-
              include_dml=> TRUE,-
              include_ddl=> TRUE,-
              source_database=>'SSKYDB');
```

This procedure will define the schema rules for the apply process for schema CRM received from the source database SSKYDB.

7.   Determine and obtain the current SCN from the source database. To ensure that no data is lost, this step is to be performed before the target copy is made. This SCN will be used as a starting point for the capture process to begin the streaming activity. The current SCN can be obtained from the GV$DATABASE.CURRENT_SCN column:

```
SET NUMWIDTH 18
SQL> SELECT INST_ID, CURRENT_SCN FROM GV$DATABASE;
```

INST_ID	CURRENT_SCN
1	655066
4	655067
3	655067
2	655067

```
SQL> /
```

INST_ID	CURRENT_SCN
1	655081
2	655081
4	655081
3	655081

This query lists the latest SCN of the source database. This SCN marks the beginning of the capture and apply process.

 Note: Notice in the previous query output that the SCNs are out of sync in the first output; this is because of the delay in the SCN synchronization process between the various instances. Under these circumstances, take the highest SCN in such situations or repeat the query until the SCNs are in sync. Also note that setting the NUMWIDTH to a value higher than 18 displays the SCN in exponential notation.

8. After the data has been propagated, it needs to be applied to the appropriate schema. Identify the user in the database that will apply the changes. In this case, the Streams administrator will also apply changes to the CRM schema in the target environment:

```
SQL> EXEC DBMS_APPLY_ADM.ALTER_APPLY(-
            apply_name=>'STRMADMIN_APPLY',-
            apply_user=>'STRMADMIN');
```

This completes the basic configuration at the target database. The next step is to configure the instantiation process.

If the schema being streamed to the destination database is new and is being configured on the source and target databases for the first time, no data migration or initial schema setup is required. The Streams process will automatically create the tables and data as it gets populated on the source database. However, if the CRM schema has been in use for some time (as in this case), then the schema with the tables and data should be created as a baseline on the target database. This process can be accomplished either by an export/import process using datapump, transportable tablespace option, or restoration of an RMAN backup.

Once the schema has been imported to the target environment, the next steps are to enable streaming of data on a real-time basis.

If the data instantiation is performed using datapump of if the data instantiation was performed with the Oracle Import utility with the STREAMS_INSTANTIATION parameter set to "Y" skip step 8.

9. Set the SCN on the target database to allow the apply process to start the schema instantiation at this SCN. This is performed using the following PL/SQL package:

```
SQL> EXEC DBMS_APPLY_ADM.SET_SCHEMA_INSTANTIATION_SCN (-
            source_schema_name=> 'CRM',-
            source_database_name=>'SSKYDB',-
            instantiation_scn=> 655081);
```

The SCN captured from the source database is set at the destination database. The apply process will ignore all SCNs lower than 655081.

10.   Start the apply process, using the following PL/SQL package:

```
SQL> EXEC DBMS_APPLY_ADM.START_APPLY
        ( -apply_name => 'STRMADMIN_APPLY');
```

11.   Enable propagation schedule at the source database. Connect as the Streams administrator and execute the following PL/SQL procedure:

```
SQL>  EXEC DBMS_PROPAGATION_ADM.START_PROPAGATION
('STRMADMIN_PROPAGATE') ;
```

12.   The following procedure starts the capture process, mines redo logs, and enqueues the mined redo information into the associated queue:

```
SQL> EXEC DBMS_CAPTURE_ADM.START_CAPTURE( -
        capture_name=>'STRMADMIN_CAPTURE');
```

This procedure prepares the source database to begin the capture process.

Once step 12 is completed successfully, all changes made to the CRM schema on the source database (SSKYDB) will be propagated and applied to the destination database (SSKYDR).

This completes the basic configuration of the Streams process.

10.3 Extended clusters

Traditionally, computer systems that provide a primary processing source have been centrally located in one data center of an organization. This is also true with a RAC environment, where two or more nodes that make up the cluster are located in one data center. The primary reason for such a configuration has been administration; however, limitations in networking technology and security have also played a significant role in location deci-

Table 10.2 *Networking Distance Limitations [14]*

Type of Network	Maximum Distance
Fast/Wide SCSI	25 m
Gigabit Ethernet Twisted Pair	50 m
Short-Wave FibreChannel	500 m
FDDI Networking	100 km[*]
Long-Wave FibreChannel	10 km
Finisar Gigabit Interface Converters (GBICs)	80 km
Dense Wave Division Multiplexing (DWDM)	100 km

* FDDI Networking is a ring topology therefore; the maximum effective distance supported between data centers is 50 kilometers [14].

sions. Table 10.2 shows some of the distances possible with a few of the available technologies.

A typical failure of this centralized data center would mean loss of data or loss of access to the computers located there. To solve these issues, organizations have usually implemented one or two of the solutions discussed earlier, namely, Data Guard or Oracle Streams, to move data to a remote location and allow access to this remote location. Several hardware vendors support another type of clustered configuration called extended clusters.

Under this option, one or more nodes are located in one data center while another set of one or more nodes is located at a second and/or third data center. These nodes across data centers are configured to behave as one unit, meaning that accessing any of these individual nodes will access the same dataset. While the behavior in this type of configuration is similar to that of any RAC cluster, its configuration differs primarily due to the distance between the various nodes in the cluster.

10.3.1 Architecture

While the components that make up the extended cluster may differ, they are very similar to a traditional RAC cluster with respect to the Oracle software functioning. All components present in a RAC architecture are available in this configuration; however, the basic hardware components and the network transport mechanism differ.

Figure 10.4
*Extended Cluster
Architecture*

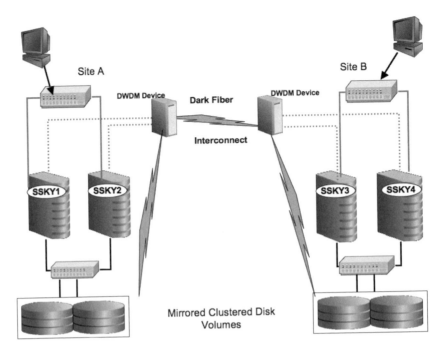

An extended cluster is a disaster recovery option where, instead of locating the entire cluster at one central location, the computers are distributed across the campus. As illustrated in Figure 10.4, the two sites each make up two nodes located at Site A and two other nodes located at Site B. They are connected through a high-speed network normally using a DWDM technology and dark fiber.

Wavelength Division Multiplexing (WDM) is an optoelectronic technology that uses multiple lasers and transmits several wavelengths of light (lamdas) simultaneously over a single optical fiber. Each signal travels within its unique color band, which is modulated by the data (e.g., text, voice, video). WDM enables the existing fiber infrastructure of the telephone companies and other carriers to be dramatically increased. DWDM enables a single optical fiber to simultaneously carry multiple traffic-bearing signals, thereby increasing the capacity of a fiber many times over. DWDM systems can support more than 150 wavelengths, each carrying up to 10 Gbps. Such systems provide more than a terabit per second of data transmission on one optical strand, which is thinner than a human hair.

While high-speed dark fiber is used for data communication, data is co-located at all of the sites using disk mirroring technology, such as host-based mirroring (CLVM), or remote array-based mirroring. Both types of mirroring have their advantages and disadvantages; for example, with host-based mirroring, disks across all sites participating in the configuration appear as one set, and data gets sent to all locations simultaneously. For remote array-based mirroring, data is written to only one location (primary) and then gets mirrored to the other locations. Because of this, the remote array-based mirrored configuration takes longer for failover when the primary site fails.

When using extended clusters, both sites should have copies (via Oracle redundancy) of the voting disk and OCR. A third site should also be selected to host a copy of the quorum/voting disk. This will serve the same exact functionality as Data Guard's FSFO Observer and will allow either site to continue if the other fails. This third site does not have the same network connectivity requirements as the two nodes, but can be accessed simply via a WAN.

10.3.2   Drawbacks

While providing failover benefits when one of the sites fail, this configuration has several disadvantages:

- Distance limitations restrict usage to a small proximity within a campus or metro area. Such low distances usually do not provide full coverage because many natural disasters that affect any one site normally affect the other location also.

- Distance limitations cause some performance concerns, directly affecting the I/O and cache fusion timing. For example, when using host-based mirroring, since data is written to all locations simultaneously, network delays can affect overall system performance. Such impacts can be minimized with DWDM using SAN buffer credits.

Note: When distances beyond 20 km are required, it is important that the configuration be validated for performance through a proof of concept. Distances above 100 km are not recommended.

- Mirroring issues can cause both copies to be out of sync, leading to discrepancy of data.

- Array-based mirroring can cause a system outage if the site with the active copy fails.

- Compared to the GigE solution used in a traditional RAC, DWDM solutions are very expensive if they are not already present between the two sites.

- Unlike the Streams and RAC or Data Guard and RAC solutions discussed earlier, an extended RAC environment is still a single database and thus is more susceptible to corruption.

10.4 Conclusion

In this chapter, high-availability solutions from Oracle were discussed. RAC can become a single point of failure, not because of its technology but because of disasters beyond our control, such as acts of nature. Under these circumstances, to protect the data and to provide continued access to it so business can continue, it is a good practice to colocate the data using some of the technologies discussed such as Data Guard or Oracle Streams. If there are issues with all hardware being located at one central location, solutions such as extended clusters can be considered, but only after conducting a careful analysis of the pros and cons of such a configuration.

Best Practices

by Kirk McGowan, Oracle Corporation

Oracle Database 10*g* RAC enables the Oracle database to run real applications on clusters. By real applications, we mean that RAC supports mainstream business applications of all kinds. This includes popular packaged products such as SAP, PeopleSoft, and Oracle E*Business Suite, as well as in-house developed applications. It includes both OLTP and DSS. It also includes Oracle's unique ability to effectively support mixed OLTP/DSS environments.

RAC is also a key component in Oracle's grid strategy. Commodity hardware, such as blade servers, and commodity operating systems, such as Linux (but not limited to Linux), offer the most compelling cost benefits for grids. Grids leverage these commodity components to achieve maximum utilization. Oracle RAC provides an essential mechanism for cost-effective and incremental provisioning of DB servers. Applications running on RAC can dynamically leverage more systems provisioned to them. Similarly, these applications can easily relinquish these servers when they no longer need them.

Oracle Database 10*g* introduces many new features specifically for the grid and is designed to simplify and reduce the cost of managing the Oracle environment. A by-product of this is the blurring of traditional lines of responsibility between system administrators (SAs) and database administrators (DBAs). For example, volume management has historically been an SA religion; ASM includes a volume manager. Although Oracle's grid story extends far beyond RAC itself, RAC remains a cornerstone of Oracle's grid strategy. The focus of this chapter is on strategies and best practices for deploying applications on RAC, specifically leveraging the Oracle "Full Stack," which includes Oracle Database 10*g*, RAC, Oracle Clusterware, and ASM.

11.1   Planning

A successful RAC implementation is not all about the mechanics of installing the software, building the database, and tweaking the knobs to make it perform the way you want it to. Many of the challenges encountered at customer sites have been related to unreasonable expectations, misunderstandings about what RAC is and what it isn't, and inadequately defined objectives for the RAC implementation. Having these important issues addressed up front allows the administrator to put together a structured implementation plan that gives the best opportunity to realize the desired business benefits.

11.1.1   Understand RAC architecture

Understanding the architecture is an obvious initial step prior to implementing any technology. Yet there is a great deal of confusion and misunderstanding in the marketplace around clustering in general. This alone easily creates some fundamental misconceptions about what RAC is and how it should be implemented. It is beyond the scope of this chapter to provide a complete primer on clustering architectures—or the detailed hardware and software components that make up those architectures—but some things to consider in reviewing cluster-related literature include

- Distinctions between hardware clustering and software/database clustering
- Shared nothing versus shared data versus shared cache DB architectures
- Active-passive versus active-active
- Hot standby versus mutual takeover versus distributed load clustering

Terminology aside, it is important to note that all clustering architectures provide some degree of high availability through redundancy of components. However, only RAC and the hardware cluster architecture on which it is based provide scalability benefits that allow adding capacity incrementally as demand dictates, in addition to the HA benefits, for any type of application.

Getting past the terminology is the first step. The next step is understanding the hardware and software components that makeup the architecture. The primary difference between stand-alone systems and clustered environments is the interconnect and shared storage. The distinction between RAC and more traditional HA clusters takes this one step further, where the interconnect needs to be high bandwidth and low latency, and the shared storage must be configured for shared *concurrent* access. Network attached storage (NAS), Small Computer System Interface (SCSI, pronounced "skuzzy"), and fiber storage are all compatible. GigE is currently the best choice for the private interconnect across all platforms. Each cluster configuration can be a little bit different, so it is important to work closely with the hardware vendor to identify specific driver and/or patch requirements for the cluster being implemented. The hardware vendors should also be made aware of the fact that the cluster is for a RAC system.

The cluster software is the key enabling technology for RAC and also the key differentiator with respect to various cluster architectures and platform-specific implementations of those architectures. At a minimum, RAC requires a cluster software framework that can provide concurrent access to the same storage and the same set of datafiles from all nodes in the cluster, a communications protocol for enabling IPC across the nodes in the cluster, and a mechanism for monitoring and communicating the status and membership of the nodes in the cluster. With Oracle Database 10*g* RAC, Oracle provides a fully integrated, fully functional cluster manager (called Oracle Clusterware) across all platforms. Oracle Clusterware negates the requirement that existed in Oracle Database 9*i* (on most platforms) for a third-party cluster manager. In fact, it is recommended to use Oracle Clusterware rather than 3rd party cluster managers as way of further simplifying the technology stack by reducing the number of moving parts.

The shared storage environment can be a bit confusing at first glance. Several different types of files must be accommodated, including Clusterware files, database files, recovery files, configuration files, and the binary files that are part of the software tree(s). The Clusterware files and the database files, as noted above, must reside on shared *concurrent* access storage, whereas this is not a strict requirement for the other types of files. In Oracle Database 10*g*, ASM provides a very simple and consistent interface for managing shared database storage, as well as recovery files, across all platforms. This solves the problem of having different, often expensive, third-party volume managers that differ across platforms in multivendor information technology (IT) environments.

11.1.2 Set your expectations appropriately

It is not hard to understand how such marketing messages as "RAC enables your application to scale with no code changes" and "RAC makes your system unbreakable" can easily get watered down to something like "RAC makes any application scalable" or even "RAC is all you need for high availability." In terms of practical expectations, the following much more accurately represent reality:

- *If your application will scale transparently on SMP, then it is realistic to expect it to scale well on RAC, without having to make any code changes to the application.* The corollary to this is that if you have significant points of contention on a single instance, RAC will not resolve the contention and, in fact, may even expose the problem more dramatically.

- *RAC eliminates the database instance and the node itself as a single point of failure and ensures database integrity in the case of such failures.*

When it comes to implementations, expectations need to come from an understanding of the technology, not from an interpretation of the marketing buzz. Many challenges with deployments originate from a misunderstanding of exactly what RAC can and cannot do.

The two statements above represent the two key aspects of RAC. The first is scalability. RAC is not magic. It cannot make a nonscalable application scalable. Scalability is a direct function of the degree of contention introduced by the application for system resources and data. RAC does provide a very low overhead and a scalable protocol to do database cache synchronization. The protocol involves at most a 3-way communication, regardless of the number of nodes. So, if the application behaves in a way that does not involve a lot of contention for shared resources, the protocol will get invoked relatively infrequently, and the application will scale very well. Alternatively, if there are many points of serialization or contention, the application *will not* scale well. So, if the application won't scale in moving from a four-processor to an eight-processor SMP configuration, then it almost certainly won't scale going from a single four-processor box to a cluster of two four-CPU boxes.

In terms of application changes, while it may be true that logic in the application need not be changed in order to deploy successfully on RAC, this does not mean that you do not have to do anything in terms of configuring the database connection mechanisms or turning on facilities in the database that are designed specifically in the current release to improve performance, scalability, availability, or manageability. Additionally, there is no substitute for good design. If there are known points of contention or serialization in the application code, and these can be changed reasonably easily, then you can expect the scalability realized in both the SMP and the clustered environments to be that much better.

From a high availability perspective, RAC is primarily a database failover technology. It ensures that in the event of node or instance failure, the failed instance will be recovered, the database will be returned to a transactionally consistent state automatically, and there is an alternate access path (via a surviving node in the cluster) for the application to access the data. RAC provides a highly available database service. The integration of Oracle Clusterware with Oracle Database 10*g* RAC extends this HA capability further in a couple of ways:

- *The clusterware framework introduces a consistent, cross-platform VIP.* This eliminates the exposure applications have to TCP/IP timeout delays on failure of the network stack.
- *Workload Management framework* allows implementers to virtualize the database service in a way that eliminates the need to "hard-wire" applications to specific nodes or database instances.

What often isn't understood is that RAC by itself currently does nothing to preserve application connections, login context, and session state. It provides no protection from network failures, storage failures, human errors, data errors, or site disasters. When a node or instance goes away, it is up to the application to react to that event and take some action. As such, RAC is not an end-to-end high-availability solution. RAC is a critical piece of the technology stack when you are trying to achieve high-availability service-level objectives, but much more is required if those service levels are to be fully realized.

11.1.3   Define your objectives

Without clear objectives in mind, you have no way of determining whether or not you have actually achieved what you set out to do. Objectives need to be categorized, quantified, and measured in some way. High availability, incremental scalability, server consolidation, database consolidation, reduced total cost of ownership (TCO), improved capacity utilization, and so on, are all possible categories of objectives.

- High-availability objectives may be defined in terms of a Service Level Agreement (SLA) with specific tolerances for downtime associated with various types of outages. For example, target recovery time after node, storage, or network failure or recovery point objective in the case of database or site failure. SLA's must be defined to a sufficiently granular level (i.e., if loads must complete in a maximum amount of time, if response times for specific workloads must not exceed a certain threshold, if maintenance windows cannot exceed a certain duration, and soon, then these need to be well defined in advance). There must be a clear understanding by all involved of the tolerance for failures, outages, brownouts, data loss, and so forth, for the various components of the application.

- Scalability objectives typically vary depending on workload type: online versus batch, DSS versus OLTP, and the like. Scalability represents the relationship between workload, system capacity, and response/processing time. "Scale-up" involves increasing system capacity for a proportional increase in workload, while keeping response/processing/throughput time constant. "Speed-up" involves reducing or improving response/processing time by increasing system capacity, while maintaining a constant workload. Scalability objectives need to be defined clearly in terms of scale-up or speed-up.

- Server or database consolidation objectives are conceptually much easier to achieve and are often tied to TCO objectives, but they are typically dependent on more subjective measures like ease of use or ease of management, making it more difficult to actually measure success. For example, reducing the number of databases or servers by 50% may well be a reasonable objective, but it is unlikely that those consolidation efforts on their own will be sufficient to lower operating costs by 50%, although the motivation for doing such a consolidation will certainly be based on some projected cost savings.

Different organizations and even different applications within an organization have different primary business drivers. Whatever the business drivers are, the objectives need to be clearly defined with the drivers in mind. These objectives then help define the project plan, and the testing plan, and they help maintain a focus throughout the implementation. Far too often we have seen implementations without well-defined objectives run into problems that consume large amounts of resources to resolve, when there is neither value to the business to have them resolved, nor exposure a consequence for not having it resolved. No technology is perfect; it only needs to be good enough to realize the objectives.

11.1.4   Build a project plan

This is perhaps the most obvious component of the planning phase. However, there are several issues worth noting that may easily be missed in a project plan and are particularly important in a RAC environment:

- *Partner with your vendors.* This is important for two reasons:

    1. You have the best opportunity of acquiring and staging a cluster configuration that has been well tested and proven.

    2. You have a stakeholder in the problem diagnosis and resolution process.

    In a best-case scenario, you have a single systems vendor, Oracle as your software infrastructure vendor, and your custom or third-party application. Integration is the single most difficult task for IT professionals. With only three vendors, you minimize the points of integration, and you have relatively few places to turn in trying to diagnose and resolve a problem.

    In a more typical scenario, particularly in the Linux on Intel environments, you will have different vendors for the machines themselves, for the I/O subsystem, for the network, for the operating system, possibly for the clusterware, plus Oracle, and one or more application providers. This has the potential to be a diagnostic nightmare if and when a problem arises.

    Fortunately, many of the technology vendors have worked very closely to provide a well-integrated and tested technology infrastructure. By effectively partnering with your chosen vendors, you will quickly learn what technology components have been tested and are known to work well together. Additionally, preinstalled, preintegrated, and fully regression tested clusters may be available from some vendors; these can be a real fast track to a successful RAC implementation and can significantly improve mean time to resolution of any problems.

- *Use proven strategies for building mission-critical systems.* Minimizing the number of integration points, eliminating single points of failure, maximizing Mean Time Between Failures (MTBF), minimizing Mean Time to Recovery (MTTR), using proven technology components, avoiding $x.0$ releases, and so on, are all pertinent to achieving the objectives. Many of the strategies in successfully deploying mission-critical systems boil down to minimizing risk. It is also worth noting that inherent risk exists in being too cautious. New technology allows you to do things that you couldn't do before. Technology changes rapidly. By being too cautious, you risk not only failing to achieve the objectives you set, but also becoming obsolete in a very short time with no opportunity to realize a return on the investment. The strategy cannot be risk avoidance but rather must be risk mitigation and management.

- *Address knowledge gaps and training requirements.* Clusters and clustered databases are new to most organizations. High availability is nontrivial to implement. Scalability is not often well understood. These issues can easily work against you. Formal training on specific technologies like the storage subsystem, the volume manager, the clusterware, or RAC is always useful. There is, however, no substitute for experience. Leveraging the skills of people with experience can help you in your own environment and has proven to be immensely beneficial. There is no shame in not knowing something. There is only shame in not identifying what you don't know in the planning phase. Hiring someone simply to do a cluster install and configuration or a RAC install/config is a low-value proposition, but when you combine that effort with well-defined technology and knowledge transfer objectives, you have a truly worthwhile investment. The technology components are not the only areas where knowledge gaps tend to exist. For example, high availability is actually a discipline. HA cannot be achieved by technology alone. It requires sound policies, procedures, and disciplined operational behaviour in order to achieve. Many organizations ignore the criticality of basic HA disciplines, like proactive systems monitoring, strict change control, thorough testing, and continuous process improvement, and their role in achieving target service levels. Much of this knowledge could be considered IT 101, but revisiting such basics with all project team members is an invaluable knowledge transfer exercise.

- *Establish support mechanisms and escalation procedures.* Although a great deal of the design effort that goes into building a clustered environment is an attempt to mitigate problems in the technology stack when they occur, it is inevitable that some kind of problem will occur that will require vendor assistance to resolve. As a result, it is critical to understand how to maximize the effectiveness of vendor support organizations to your advantage. Understanding the organizational structure, the diagnostic mechanisms, processes, and tools, the routing mechanisms, the escalation procedures, and expected turnaround times for various types of issues are all critical to minimizing mean time to resolution. It is also appropriate to note that cluster-related problems are fundamentally different; they are more complex to diagnose and resolve because they involve a complex interaction of multiple distinct systems. Fundamental systems problems may manifest differently in a cluster, so it is critical that these be experienced and understood in advance. Again, partnering and joint ownership of issue resolution, with an expectation that some back-and-forth work may be required to get to root causes, are critical to overall success.

11.2 Implementation

Assuming the planning has been done with the aforementioned considerations in mind, implementation can be reasonably straightforward. Conceptually, implementation involves acquiring and configuring the necessary hardware and operating system, implementing the cluster software and RDBMS software, building a RAC database, deploying your applications to the RAC environment, doing some structured testing and tuning, and finally migrating into production.

It is worth noting that RAC is a technology that is really only possible as a result of the convergence of several disparate technology advancements:

- Intelligent I/O subsystems (SANs)
- Sophisticated high-bandwidth hardware interconnects
- Efficient low-latency communication protocols

It turns out you can actually run RAC on two laptops with a dual-ported shared SCSI drive and a 10 Mbps Ethernet network between them. This is instructive in terms of understanding the absolute minimum requirement to allow RAC to function, but is of use for little more than demonstration purposes. This points out the need to design and build your

RAC cluster environment from the ground up with your objectives clearly in mind:

- The I/O subsystem needs to be able to handle the required throughput and scale to handle anticipated growth. SAN technology can virtually assure that the I/O subsystem is not a scalability bottleneck, but if the I/O subsystem doesn't scale, the rest of the system won't scale either.

- The interconnect technology should be scalable to handle the amount of traffic generated by the cache synchronization mechanism (which is directly related to the amount of contention created by the application). It is advisable to implement the highest bandwidth interconnect that is available for a given platform. The volume of synchronization traffic directly impacts the bandwidth requirement, and messaging delays are highly dependent on the IPC protocol. The interconnect is not something you should risk having underconfigured, assuming scalability is a key objective. The current recommendation for all platforms is gigabit Ethernet and UDP (TCP on Win2K). For some larger-scale systems, it is possible that the interconnect bandwidth requirement will exceed a single 1-Gb Ethernet. The highest volume of traffic that has been observed in production customer implementations is on the order of 2.5 Gbps, in which case 3 × 1Gb interconnects were used. The Oracle Database 10*g* life cycle should see the introduction of support for emerging technologies like InfiniBand, which have the potential to improve interconnect scalability (and standardization) for large numbers of nodes, but these technologies will require extended test cycles to ensure both scalability and stability for any given target application.

- The cluster infrastructure needs to scale to handle the number of nodes required to provide sufficient processing capacity for anticipated growth in workload. Most cluster frameworks today differ in terms of the maximum number of nodes they can handle. Most can support a minimum of four nodes today, and some can support hundreds. The Oracle Clusterware in Oracle Database 10*g* Release 2 currently supports up to 100 nodes. This will also be driven by your scalability objectives and capacity requirements.

- The nodes may or may not need to be scalable to provide additional capacity in terms of CPU or memory. The ability to scale both within a machine as well as across machines is often desirable. Linux machines claim to be able to scale up to eight CPUs, but most systems are still two or four CPU nodes. SMP scalability in Linux beyond four CPUs is not well proven, so the current recommendation is to stick with four CPU machines.

Note: Systems with a minimum of two CPUs are recommended, primarily due to processor scheduling latencies. RAC is a messaging protocol that requires CPU cycles to do its work and maintain a clear view of node and instance membership in the cluster. Node evictions can be seen in any cluster where critical processes are deprived of the CPU they need to do their work. Having multiple CPUs eliminates the need for the operating system to have to schedule all work on a single CPU.

- Single Points of Failure (SPOFs) need to be eliminated in the hardware and software stack. Power supplies, HBAs, NICs, switches, interconnects, operating system images, software trees, and so, on all represent potential SPOFs. The degree to which you attempt to eliminate these will be a function of your high-availability SLAs. Remember that if you have only a single interconnect or a single path from each node to the storage, a NIC or HBA failure will render that node unusable, with a proportional decrease in systemwide processing capacity. An interconnect switch failure could render all but a single node unusable, and a SAN switch failure could render the entire cluster unusable. Redundancy needs to be built into these components as dictated by the SLAs.

- Sufficient processing capacity should be provided such that the loss of a node in the cluster does not impact the ability to achieve service-level objectives.

- The workload management strategy must be determined so it is clear how the application is actually going to connect to the various nodes and instances, how it is going to choose what connection to use to execute a particular unit of work, and how it is going to react to failed connections. Workload distribution can be on a per-connection basis or, based on server CPU load, perhaps on an application basis. Different strategies may be more appropriate than others depending on the implementation

- A management infrastructure must be set up and configured to monitor the system, control management costs, and manage to the targeted service levels.

11.2.1 Cluster installation/configuration

Validating the cluster infrastructure using the Oracle-provided cluster verification utility, prior to installing the Oracle software, will save you considerable time and potential headaches. The OUI is cluster aware and, in fact,
depends on the cluster's being operational to install RAC and build a cluster
database. Ensuring full read/write access to the shared storage (either raw
devices or cluster file system) and ensuring that the cluster communication
is occurring over the correct private interconnect should be the minimal
validation checks. Specific patch levels for both the operating system and
clusterware are generally documented in the Oracle installation/configura-
tion guide for your specific platform.

In addition to validating the cluster, there are several additional best
practices related to the physical configuration and operating system configuration of the system in preparation for RAC:

- Use asynchronous I/O where possible (use `trace` or `strace` to confirm it is in use).

- Use S.A.M.E. methodology[1] for storage configuration when using
traditional storage methods. ASM essentially implements S.A.M.E.
"under the covers."

- Set UDP packet send and receive parameters to max (usually 256K).

- Exercise caution in the use of jumbo frames on the interconnect. It
can be tricky to set up, it must be fully supported all the way through
the NIC/switch interconnect infrastructure, and performance gain is
not substantial unless there are a large number of blocks transferred.

- Ensure `ssh` is properly configured. Oracle Database 10*g* installer uses
`ssh` (although it will revert to `rsh` if `ssh` is not available) to complete
the install across all nodes in the cluster.

- Confirm that the Oracle user has been created with the identical
group number and UID on all nodes.

- Confirm that hostname matches `/etc/hosts` on all nodes.

- Configure NTP on all nodes to help sync the clocks and facilitate
problem diagnosis based on timestamps.

---

1.   See Optimal Storage Configuration Made Easy, by Juan Loaiza, Oracle Corporation, at
http://otn.oracle.com/deploy/availability/pdf/oow2000_same.pdf.

- Ensure interconnect redundancy. Use multiple physical interconnects and use NIC teaming/bonding software to present Oracle Clusterware and Oracle RDBMS with a single logical network interface for the interconnect. The implementation is platform specific, but technologies like Etherchannel, or HP's auto-port aggregation (APA) can be used to accomplish this task. Note that some of these technologies are for HA/failover purposes only, whereas others are capable of doing load-balancing across multiple physical interconnects. Be aware of the differences. In general, if there is a choice, it is simpler (and safer) to start with an active-passive configuration on the interconnect, unless there is a clear understanding in advance that the capacity of a single GigE is insufficient for the application needs.

11.2.2 Shared storage configuration

Several different types of files must be considered when designing the storage configuration: database files, recovery files, CRS files, configuration files, and binary files (software trees).

- Use storage-level mirroring and Oracle's multiplexing to protect the voting disk and OCR disk.

- Use a large number of similarly sized "disks."

- Confirm shared access to storage "disks" from all nodes.

- Include space for flash recovery area.

- Configure I/O multipathing software to mask HBA or SAN switch failures:

  - ASM must only see a single (virtual) path to the storage.
  - Multipathing configuration is platform specific (e.g., Powerpath, SecurePath).
  - It is important to note that the software used in providing interconnect redundancy and I/O multipathing is not provided by Oracle and, as a result, is not part of the standard regression tests conducted by Oracle prior to releasing new versions. It is incumbent on the customer to test these components fully, both in isolation and as part of the overall software/technology stack being implemented.

- Establish a file system or location for ORACLE_HOME (and CRS and ASM HOME).

11.2.3 Oracle Clusterware (CRS) installation/configuration

CRS provides all the functionality required to manage your cluster database, including node membership, group services, global resource management, and high-availability functions. CRS is essentially the high-availability framework. It manages resources and is controlled by command-line programs. The HA framework function is essentially to know what resources are supposed to be running, determine if they are running, get them running if they are not, and report any changes in state.

Default, out-of-the-box failover times should be on the order of 90 to 120 seconds. This includes detection/determination that a failure (or hang) has occurred, application notification, cluster reconfiguration time, Oracle reconfiguration time, cache recovery, and transaction recovery. Default parameters have been tested and should not be altered without a clear business need to reduce failover times. Altering the default parameter settings can significantly increase the likelihood of false failover scenarios, so any changes must be fully tested with production workloads prior to actually implementing them on a production system.

CRS installation and configuration is reasonably straightforward. The following are some specific points to note about the CRS installation:

- CRS is *required* to be installed and running prior to installing 10*g* RAC.

- CRS must be installed in a different location from the ORACLE_HOME (e.g., ORA_CRS_HOME).

- Shared location(s) or devices for the voting file and OCR file must be available *prior* to installing CRS.

  - Use raw devices, unless you are using a CFS for the binaries.
  - Reinstallation of CRS requires reinitialization of devices, including permissions.

- CRS and RAC require that the private and public network interfaces be configured prior to installing CRS or RAC.

- Specify a virtual interconnect for CRS communication.

- The supported method to stop/start CRS in 10*g* Release 2 is crsctl start/stop crs.

A couple of useful Metalink notes have been written related to CRS install and configuration:

- Note: 279793.1   How to Restore a Lost Voting Disk in 10*g*

- Note: 268937.1   Repairing or Restoring an Inconsistent OCR in RAC

- Note: 239998.1   10*g* RAC How to Clean Up After a Failed CRS Install

11.2.4   Oracle RAC installation/configuration

If the cluster has been installed and configured correctly, then Oracle RDBMS and RAC install will go smoothly. It is a good practice to return to the platform-specific *Oracle Installation and Configuration Guide* and confirm that all documented prerequisites have been met, including disk space for the software, memory requirements, /tmp and /swap space, and operating system and clusterware patch levels. It is also useful to check Metalink for "Step-by-Step Installation of RAC" technical notes and/or OTN for additional RAC quickstart guides for your specific platform.

The current version recommendation is 10.2.0.1 and contains many important fixes. As with previous releases, it has proven advantageous to use a staging area on disk both to avoid having to swap CDs during the install and to improve the speed of the install. The OUI will automatically detect the cluster and install the Oracle software, including RAC, on the selected nodes of the cluster. Using NFS mounts for ORACLE_HOME is not recommended due to the single point of failure this introduces, as well as the fact that some node-specific configuration information is still stored in ORACLE_HOME.

- Ensure only the public interfaces(s) are selected, not the private interconnect.

- Ensure the VIP is registered in DNS since this will be the primary address applications (tnsnames) will connect to and that listeners will be configured to listen on.

- Confirm (ifconfig on most platforms) that the new VIP interface is visible (e.g., eth0:1).

Note: If a cluster is moving to a new data center (or subnet), it is necessary to change IPs. The VIP is stored within the OCR, and any modification or change to the IP requires additional administrative steps. (Please see Metalink Note: 276434.1 for details.)

Note.264847.1 How to Configure Virtual IPs for 10*g* RAC

11.3 Database creation

The DBCA is the recommended way to create and initially configure RAC databases. DBCA simplifies database creation, automatically configures some important features, and is fully cluster aware. At a minimum, it is recommended to use it to build the database creation scripts, which can subsequently be executed manually. DBCA performs several functions in the creation process that would otherwise have to be dealt with manually:

- It properly sets MAXINSTANCES, MAXLOGFILES/MAXLOGMEMBERS, MAXLOGHISTORY, and MAXDATAFILES to avoid downtime in having to re-create the control file.

- It creates all tablespaces as locally managed (LMTs: EXTENT MANAGEMENT LOCAL).

- It creates all tablespaces with Automatic Segment Space Management (ASSM: SEGMENT SPACE MANAGEMENT AUTO).

- It configures automatic UNDO management.

- It uses SPFILE instead of multiple init.ora file.

Note: LMTs, ASSM, and automatic UNDO are also single-instance recommendations and so are not specific to RAC. DBCA will configure these important features in the creation of noncluster databases as well as they greatly simplify space management and reduce contention on the data dictionary. ASSM is particularly useful in RAC databases because it eliminates the need to set freelists and freelist groups and allows for dynamic affinity of space to instances.

The ASM configuration is also performed initially as part of DBCA. Further configuration can be accomplished via the well-documented SQL interface to the ASM instance. Best practices are well documented in another source[2] and have also been discussed in Chapter 3; however, it is worth noting a number of these best practices here:

- Create a minimum of two disk groups (e.g., database area and flash recovery area).

- Physically separate the database and flashback areas, making sure the two areas do not share the same physical spindles.

- Use disk groups with a large number of similarly sized disks.

- Make sure disks span several back-end disk adapters.

- If mirroring is done in the storage array, set REDUNDANCY=EXTERNAL.

- Where possible, use the pseudo-devices (multipath I/O) as the disk string for ASM.

- Use Oracle Managed Files (OMFs) with ASM.

- Use system or user templates to simplify and ensure attribute consistency in file creation.

After running DBCA, you should have a fully configured RAC database up and running on all nodes of the cluster and an ASM instance running on each node. At this stage, a series of validation checks should be performed.

Validate the cluster (CRS) configuration as follows:

1. Query the OCR to confirm the status of all defined services:
   `crs_stat -t`

HA Resource	Target	State
`ora.BCRK.BCRK1.inst`	`ONLINE`	`ONLINE on sunblade-25`
`ora.BCRK.BCRK2.inst`	`ONLINE`	`ONLINE on sunblade-26`
`ora.BCRK.db`	`ONLINE`	`ONLINE on sunblade-25`
`ora.sunblade-25.ASM1.asm`	`ONLINE`	`ONLINE on sunblade-25`

2. See Oracle Database 10g Automatic Storage Management Technical Best Practices, By Nitin Vengurlekar, Oracle Corporation, at www.oracle.com/technology/products/database/asm/pdf/asm_best_practices.pdf.

HA Resource	Target	State
ora.sunblade-25.LISTENER_SUNBLADE-25.lsnr	ONLINE	ONLINE on sunblade-25
ora.sunblade-25.gsd	ONLINE	ONLINE on sunblade-25
ora.sunblade-25.ons	ONLINE	ONLINE on sunblade-25
ora.sunblade-25.vip	ONLINE	ONLINE on sunblade-25
ora.sunblade-26.ASM2.asm	ONLINE	ONLINE on sunblade-26
ora.sunblade-26.LISTENER_SUNBLADE-26.lsnr	ONLINE	ONLINE on sunblade-26
ora.sunblade-26.gsd	ONLINE	ONLINE on sunblade-26
ora.sunblade-26.ons	ONLINE	ONLINE on sunblade-26
ora.sunblade-26.vip	ONLINE	ONLINE on sunblade-26

The actual interconnect (and protocol) RAC is using in the database instance (and ASM is using in the ASM instance) can be validated as follows:

```
SQL> oradebug setmypid
SQL> oradebug ipc
```

The information written to a trace file in the user_dump_dest will indicate the IP address:

```
SSKGXPT 0x2ab25bc flags          info for network 0
          socket no 10    IP 204.152.65.33        UDP 49197
          sflags SSKGXPT_UP
          info for network 1
          socket no 0     IP 0.0.0.0      UDP 0
          sflags SSKGXPT_DOWN
```

Additionally, the following query can be used to check which interconnect is used: (or preferably select * from gv$cluster_interconnects;)

```
SQL> SELECT * FROM GV$CLUSTER_INTERCONNECTS;
```

```
INST_ID NAME            IP_ADDRESS       IS_ SOURCE
------- --------------- ---------------- --- ------------------------------
      1 eth1            10.16.0.1        NO  Oracle Cluster Repository
      2 eth1            10.16.0.2        NO  Oracle Cluster Repository
```

Valid values for the column SOURCE are: Oracle Cluster Repository (OCR), Operating System Dependent, Cluster Interconnects

11.4 Application deployment

In general, deploying your application to a RAC environment follows the same guidelines as for a single instance. As such, single-instance tuning recommendations still very much apply:

- SQL tuning more often than not yields the greatest benefits. Ensuring an optimal execution plan, using shared SQL and bind variables, minimizing parse failures, and minimizing full table scans all contribute greatly to scalability in a single-instance environment.

- Sequence caching yields benefits in a single-instance environment. Since sequence number generation is a point of serialization, sequence caching benefits are magnified in a RAC environment.

- Partitioning large objects has an obvious benefit in terms of manageability and potentially with performance as well. This will have magnified benefits in a RAC environment for DML-intensive objects.

- Tune instance recovery (FAST_START_MTTR_TARGET) to balance performance versus availability.

- Avoid DDL because this can create contention issues in the data dictionary that get magnified in a RAC environment.

There are no special application design or coding considerations required for RAC. All applications that run well in a single-instance Oracle Database 10*g* environment should run well on RAC, and as mentioned earlier, all applications that scale well on SMP should scale well on RAC. This actually highlights two of the biggest challenges that have been encountered in deploying applications on RAC:

1. The application has never before been run or thoroughly tested in a single-instance environment, so performance problems observed in the RAC environment are automatically attributed to RAC.

2. The application doesn't scale well on SMP, so scalability observed in RAC is very poor.

Experience has shown that it actually makes sense to deploy applications first to a single-instance environment, and then to RAC. There are several optimizer changes in each major release, as well as numerous feature enhancements and performance improvements that can change application behavior from previous releases. If you take the time to determine how your application behaves first in Oracle Database 10*g*, and take steps to optimize it there first, you will save yourself a great deal of time and aggravation. Likewise, making an effort to determine how your application will scale on SMP, where scalability bottlenecks occur, and where contention or hot spots are in a single instance, will go a long way toward helping you understand how it should behave when deployed on RAC. In a few cases, we have seen some performance and scalability improvements by implementing some kind of workload partitioning, since arbitrarily balancing workload creates artificial or self-induced contention that is easily avoided. In a couple of cases, primarily in configurations involving a large number of CPUs, we have seen RAC actually scale better than SMP.

Services are a new RDBMS feature in Oracle Database 10*g* for workload management that divide the universe of work executing in the database to achieve higher utilization of the IT capacity. Each workload represents a logical business function based on workload attributes, such as application function, quality of service, application priority, preferred topology, and job class. Services enable the workloads to be measured and managed to efficiently deliver the capacity on demand. The services are tightly integrated with the Oracle database and are maintained in the Oracle Database 10*g* Data Dictionary. The Database Resource Manager allocates resources to these services depending on their priority. The ability to deploy and redeploy different services based on business requirements delivers efficient and cost-effective utilization of resources. This is fundamental to grid computing for businesses.

- Instrument your applications using service, module, and action and enable statistics aggregation for important modules and actions. The AWR maintains a variety of performance statistics for services based on the work being done in the RDBMS. Instrumenting with module and action allows more granular monitoring and management of the application.

■ Set response time and CPU thresholds for services based on your AWR history. This allows you to manage to SLAs.

■ Retain AWR history to provide service-level history, root-cause analysis, and capacity data.

■ Use session-based balancing for long-lived connections, such as connection pools. Use service quality for runtime load-balancing.

■ Use the Oracle Database 10*g* JDBC Implicit Connect Cache for load-balancing and high availability.

 Note: Services and distributed workload management is discussed in detail in Chapter 5

11.5   Operations

Operationally, managing a RAC database is essentially the same as managing a single instance, with a few, mostly mechanical differences. Starting and stopping instances using the `srvctl` and `crs` management infrastructure provided with RAC, managing multiple threads of redo, and monitoring RAC traffic across the interconnect are really the only differences. We still see people raise some initial concerns around the manageability of the RAC environment, but once they understand the few differences from the single-instance environment, which most users are already familiar with, RAC is simply an incremental step in the Oracle knowledge base.

The real challenges users tend to encounter operationally are not directly related to the technology stack, but are by-products of the stack. Clustered databases (and RAC in particular) blur traditional IT job roles and responsibilities because they involve not just DBA skills, but also an understanding of storage administration, network administration, and cluster/systems administration. Problems that arise in the storage or I/O subsytem or at the operating system or network levels can manifest in various undesirable cluster behaviours that can be difficult for a traditional DBA to diagnose. Close teamwork between those involved in these job roles is the only means of ensuring business SLAs can be met.

The second area of operational challenge tends to evolve out of the nature of the applications being deployed on RAC. Scalability and particularly high availability are characteristics and requirements of business-critical systems. So many of the critical aspects noted in the "Planning" section, if insufficiently addressed, will directly (and negatively) impact operations and the ability ultimately to achieve SLAs.

11.5.1 Production migration

Planning and successfully executing the final deployment of the application and the transition into an operational phase transcends the technology itself. Most successful deployments are a direct result of adherence to strong systems development and deployment disciplines, and most problems at production rollout and postproduction are a result of lapses in these processes and procedures. Structured test plans, detailed and rehearsed production migration plans, tight system and application change control procedures, standards and systems integrity disciplines, detailed and rehearsed backup and recovery procedures, comprehensive security and auditing plans, and so on, are all key components in a successful final production rollout.

These disciplines have been around for years and in most cases form the operational backbone in larger IT shops, particularly those that have legacy mainframe environments. Large UNIX shops now generally have reasonably well-established processes, largely adapted from mainframe environments, although, historically, virtually anything that was UNIX-based was, by definition, undisciplined. Smaller shops have not had the benefit of the same experience and tend to have fewer resources to establish the same level of structure and discipline.

Due to the nature of RAC deployments, largely into mission critical–type environments, adherence to these systems disciplines is truly a critical success factor. Recognizing that not all organizations have the resources necessary to address all of these issues in a comprehensive manner, three items have proven to be the most critical in customer environments to date:

- *Separate environments for development, test, QA/UAT, and production.* It is critical that test systems closely mirror production systems in that they maintain a consistent set of patches to match what is deployed in production. Test/QA environments also need to be RAC clusters.

- *System-level change control.* Changes should only be applied to one system element at a time. This allows for speedy problem identification and reversal in case problems occur. Changes should always be applied first to test systems, and their impact should be well understood prior to implementing them in production.

- *Application change control.* This is particularly important for e-commerce companies whose business is essentially their websites. To be competitive, frequent changes to the website application must be made. Nevertheless, it is critical that these changes be tracked. An untracked change should never be introduced. If failures occur, it is critical to be able to quickly and accurately identify the most recent series of changes that were made and to back them out if necessary. In addition, the impact of these application changes on underlying system components must be monitored.

Without these key issues's being addressed, even simple configuration changes or patch applications to any of the technology stack run the risk of creating a clusterwide outage and virtually eliminating the benefit of having a fully redundant processing environment.

11.5.2   Backup and recovery

The only real complexity associated with backup and recovery that is specific to RAC versus a single-instance environment is the fact that there are multiple threads of redo and that the redo logs and archive logs from all instances must be backed up to ensure full recoverability. RMAN is the easiest mechanism for performing this task. It has been designed to be RAC aware and to understand these minor differences. The configuration of RMAN to manage a RAC environment is discussed in Chapter 8. The process is further simplified under Linux if you are using OCFS.

11.5.3   Database monitoring and tuning

Database monitoring and tuning is covered in Chapter 9. The most important observation is that there is very little to monitor and tune that is specific to RAC. Never ignore the basics of system monitoring. Long periods of not monitoring will inevitably lead to potentially serious problems.

- Monitor CPU utilization. It should never be 100%.

- Monitor disk I/O service times. They should never be over acceptable thresholds.

- Monitor the run queue to ensure that it is at the optimal level.

The following Linux operating system monitoring tools will inevitably prove useful:

■ Overall tools	`sar, vmstat`
■ CPU	`/proc/cpuinfo, mpstat, top`
■ Memory	`/proc/meminfo,   /proc/slabinfo, free`
■ Disk I/O	`iostat`
■ Network	`/proc/net/dev, netstat, mii-tool`
■ Kernel version and release	`cat /proc/version`
■ Types of I/O cards	`lspci -vv`
■ Kernel modules loaded	`lsmod, cat /proc/modules`
■ List all PCI devices (HW)	`lspci -v`
■ Startup changes	`/etc/sysctl.conf, /etc/rc.local`
■ Kernel messages	`/var/log/messages,    /var/log/ dmesg`
■ Operating system error codes	`/usr/src/linux/include/asm/ errno.h`
■ Operating system calls	`/usr/sbin/strace-p`

Additionally, familiarity with single-instance performance monitoring and tuning is essential:

- Identify and tune contention using `V$SEGMENT_STATISTICS` to identify objects involved.

- Concentrate on bad SQL if CPU bound.

- Tune I/O. If the storage subsystem is saturated, adding more nodes or instances won't help.

A few key techniques are worth noting in the context of successfully deploying an application on RAC:

- Maintain a balanced load on underlying systems (e.g., database, operating system, storage system). This is not only important for optimal performance, but it can become critical for reliability.
  - Avoid excessive load on individual components (e.g., a single node in a cluster or an individual I/O subsystem) which, can invoke aberrant behavior and failures that would not normally be experienced.
  - Avoid any load that goes beyond the red line.
  - Periodically, address imbalances through constant monitoring.
  - Use ADDM reports and the AWR. There is a wealth of information in them and they are essential tools in establishing a clear system performance baseline for normal operations, and allowing the determination of critical thresholds for alerting mechanisms.
- Use scripts and tracing:
  - STATSPACK does not currently provide the exact details of which blocks or segments are incurring contention.
  - A simple way to check which blocks are involved in wait events is to monitor V$SESSION_WAIT and use that information to trace to the corresponding segments.
  - Trace events, like 10046 at level 8, can provide additional details about wait events.
  - Alert logs and trace files should be monitored for events, as on a single instance.
- Supplement database monitoring with system-level monitoring.
  - Tools like OSWatcher provide invaluable system-level data that can be correlated to cluster and/or database events
  - Network statistics and/or storage or I/O statistics can also be useful in helping quickly get to the root cause of problems that manifest at the cluster or database levels.

11.6 Conclusion

This discussion has encompassed observations and best practices that have been derived from the experiences of hundreds of customers currently running their applications in production on RAC. They are intended as guidelines (as opposed to a cookbook) and are based on the best available knowledge at the time of writing. Although no piece of software is perfect, the promise of Real Application Clusters is *real* and allows you to take an important step toward grid computing. Following these best practices will enable you to run your applications successfully on Oracle Real Application Clusters.

References

1. Vallath, Murali. *Real Application Clusters.* Burlington, MA: Digital Press, 2003.

2. Vaidyanatha, Gaja Krishna. "Implementing RAID on Oracle Systems." *Proceedings of Oracle Open World 2000*. Accessed at: www.oracle.com.

3. Loaiza, Juan. "Optimal Storage Configuration Made Easy." Accessed at: www.oracle.com

4. "Linux Ethernet Bonding Driver Mini How-To Page." The Linux Kernel Archives. Accessed at: www.kernel.org.

5. Postel, J. "Internet Protocol," RFC 760, USC/Information Sciences Institute, January 1980.

6. Postel, J. "Transmission Control Protocol," RFC 761, USC/Information Sciences Institute, January 1980.

7. Fink, Daniel. "Rollback Segment and Undo Internals," UKOUG 2002 conference.

8. Vaidyanatha, Gaja Krishna, Kirtikumar Deshpande, and John A. Kostelac, Jr. *101 Oracle Performance Tuning.* Berkeley, CA: Oracle Press, 2001.

9. Shee, Richmond, Kirtikumar Deshpande, and K. Gopalakrishnan. *Oracle Wait Interface: A Practical Guide to Performance Diagnostics and Tuning.* Emeryville, CA: Oracle Press, 2004.

10. Gongloor, Prabhaker, Graham Wood, and Karl Dias. "Performance Diagnosis Demystified: Best Practices for Oracle 10g." Oracle Open World 2005, Oracle Corporation.

11. Millsap, Cary. *Optimizing Oracle Performance.* Sebastopol, CA: O'Reilly, 2003.

12. Foster, Ian, and Carl Kesselman. *The Grid: Blueprint for a New Computing Infrastructure*. San Francisco: Morgan Kaufmann, 1999.

13. The Globus Alliance. Accessed at www.globus.org.

14. "Designing Disaster Tolerant High Availability Clusters," *HP Invent*, March 2004.

15. Shee, Richmond. "Got Waits? A Wait Approach to Performance Tuning and Optimization," IOUG Live 2001. Accessed at: www.ioug.org.

16. Vallath, Murali. "High Availability Using Transparent Application Failover on Real Application Clusters," Oracle Open World 2000. Accessed at: www.oracle.com.

17. Vallath, Murali. "High Availability Using Transparent Application Failover on Real Application Clusters." Technical Feature, Oracle Scene, *UKOUG Journal*, Issue 12, Winter 2002. Accessed at: www.ukoug.org.

18. Adams, Steve. "IXORA." Accessed at: www.ixora.com.au.

19. Multiple articles and papers from Metalink and Tech Net, Oracle Corporation. Accessed at: http://metalink.oracle.com.

20. Oracle Documentation (Version 8.1.7, Version 9.1.0, Version 9.2.0, Version 10.1.0, Version 10.2.0). Oracle Technology Network, Oracle Corporation. Accessed at: http://technet.oracle.com.

21. Harrison, Gary. *Oracle SQL High Performance Tuning*. Upper Saddle River, NJ: Prentice Hall, 2000. Accessed at: www.phptr.com.

22. Morle, James. *Scaling Oracle 8i*. New York: Addison Wesley, 2000. Accessed at: www.aw.com/cseng.

23. Haisley, Stephen. "Transaction Management in Oracle 9*i*," UKOUG Presentation, 2002. Accessed at: www.ukoug2002.org.

24. Millsap, Cary. "Why 99% Cache Hit Ratio Is Not OK." Hotsos.com, 2001. Accessed at: www.hotsos.com.

25. Deshpande, Kritikumar. "Oracle 10g: Data Replication Made Easy." RMOUG Training Days 2006. Accessed at www.rmoug.org.

26. Vengurlekar, Nitin. "ASM Technical Best Practices" Metalink Note: 265633.1.

27. Mahmood Zafar, Fernandez Anthony, Scalzo Bert and Vallath Murali Testing Oracle 10*g* RAC Scalability. DELL PowerSolutions, March 2005.

B

Utilities and Scripts

B.1 SRVCTL – Server Control

In this section let's look at the Server Control (SRVCTL) commands provided by Oracle to manage the clustered databases from the command line. The SRVCTL command-line utility has been enhanced from its previous releases to support additional functionality offered by Oracle Database 10*g*.

The command is divided into three parts: part 1 is the actual operation to be performed, part 2 is the object that is being operated on, and part 3 is a set of optional parameters that help streamline the operation.

Usage: `srvctl <command> <object> [<options>]`

The supported object types are

`database`	This indicates that the operation is primarily targeted to the entire database.
`instance`	This indicates that the operation is primarily targeted to the database instance.
`service`	This references a application service that belongs to a database and or instance running on a specific node.
`nodapps`	This references an application that is applicable to the entire node in the cluster. Normally, all applications/ervices running on the node depend on its existence.
`asm`	The object commands relate to the ASM instance.
`listener`	The object commands related to the LISTENER on the node.

START command

srvctl start object -d <db_name>	Start specified RAC database
-i <instance_name,>	Start named instances if specified; otherwise, entire RAC
-n <node,…>	Start instances on named nodes
-s <stage,…>	List of stages to start (`stage= inst, lsnr`)
-x <stage,…>	Except these stages
-c <connect string>	Connect string (default: `/as sysdba`)
-o <options>	Options to startup command (for example force or nomount)
-S <status level>	Intermediate status level for console
-h	Print usage

Usages

This starts the instances that are configured for a database (for example, SSKYDB) and listeners in a RAC:

```
srvctl start database -d  SSKYDB
```

To start the instance SSKY1 and its listeners:

```
srvctl start instance -d SSKYDB -i SSKY1
```

To start only instance SSKY1:

```
srvctl start instance -d SSKYDB -i SSKY1 -s inst
```

To start only listeners for node ORADB1:

```
srvctl start listener -n oradb1
```

STOP command

Usages

Stop instances in database SSKYDB:

srvctl stop	\<object\>	Stop specified RAC database
	–d \<db_name\>	
	-i \<instance_name,\>	Stop named instances if specified, otherwise entire RAC
	-n \<node,…\>	Stop instances on named nodes
	-c \<connect string\>	Connect string (default: /as sysdba)
	-o \<options\>	Options to shutdown command (for example force or nomount)
	-S \<status level\>	Intermediate status level for console
	-h	Print usage

```
srvctl stop database -d SSKYDB
```

Stop instance SSKY1 with an option and with debug output:

```
srvctl stop instance -d SSKYDB -i SSKY1 -s inst -o immediate -D 3
```

Stop the instance on node oradb1:

```
srvctl stop instance –d SSKYDB –n oradb1 –x lsnr
```

Stop database SSKYDB with connection string system/manager:

```
srvctl stop database -d SSKYDB -c 'system/manager'
```

STATUS command

`srvctl status <object> -d <db_name>`	Check specified RAC database
`-i <instance_name,>`	Check named instances if specified; otherwise entire RAC
`-c <connect string>`	Connect string (default: `/as sysdba`)
`-S <status level>`	Intermediate status level for EM console
`-D <debug level>`	Debug level
`-h`	Print usage

Usages

Get status of database SSKYDB:

```
srvctl status database –d SSKYDB
```

For example:

```
[oracle@oradb1 oracle]$ srvctl status database -d SSKYDB
Instance SSKY1 is running on node oradb1
Instance SSKY2 is running on node oradb2
Instance SSKY3 is running on node oradb3
Instance SSKY4 is running on node oradb4
```

Get status of instance SSKYDB:

```
srvctl status instance –d SSKYDB –i SSKY1
```

Get status of the node applications on node ORADB1:

```
[oracle@oradb1 oracle]$ srvctl status nodeapps -n oradb1
VIP is running on node: oradb1
GSD is running on node: oradb1
Listener is running on node: oradb1
ONS daemon is running on node: oradb1
```

CONFIG command

srvctl status <object> –d <db_name>	Show configuration for specified RAC database
-n <node,…>	Only show services on named nodes
-D <debug level>	Debug level
-V	Show version
-h	Print usage

Usages

Get configuration of database SSKYDB:

```
srvctl config database –d SSKYDB
```

For example:

```
[oracle@oradb1 oracle]$ srvctl config database -d SSKYDB
oradb1 SSKY1 /usr/app/oracle/product/10.2.0/db_1
oradb2 SSKY2 /usr/app/oracle/product/10.2.0/db_1
oradb3 SSKY3 /usr/app/oracle/product/10.2.0/db_1
```

ADD and REMOVE commands

srvctl add <object> -d <db_name>	Name of database to add
-i <instance_name,>	Name of instance to add
-n <node,…>	Name of node on which to add an instance
-D <debug level>	Debug level
-h	Print usage

srvctl remove object -d <db_name>	Name of the object to be removed from the OCR
-i <instance_name,>	Name of instance to delete
-D <debug level>	Debug level
-h	Print usage

Usages

Add database SSKYDB:

```
srvctl add database –d <database name>  -o <oracle home>
```

For example:

```
srvctl add database –d SSKYDB –o /usr/app/oracle/product/
10.2.0/db_1/
```

Add an instance to SSKYDB:

```
srvctl add instance –d <database name>  -i <instance name>  -
n <node name>
```

For example:

```
srvctl add instance –d SSKYDB –i SSKY1 –n oradb1
```

Delete/remove instance SSKY2 from SSKYDB:

```
srvctl remove instance –d <database name>  -i <instance name>
```

For example:

```
srvctl remove instance –d SSKYDB –i SSKY2
```

Delete database SSKYDB:

```
srvctl remove database –d <database name>
```

E.g.,

```
srvctl remove database –d SSKYDB
```

B.2 Cluster ready service (CRS) utility

Status command

crs_stat	List all resources registered with the Oracle Clusterware
crs_stat -t	List all resources registered with the Oracle Clusterware in a tabular form
crs_stat -v	List all resources registered with the Oracle Clusterware with resource startup information such as failover threshold, restart count, and so on.
crs_stat -ls	List all resources registered with the Oracle Clusterware in a tabular form giving the execution permission details

```
crs_stat -ls

[oracle@irvadb101 oracle]$ crs_stat -ls
Name              Owner        Primary PrivGrp          Permission
-----------------------------------------------------------------
ora....G11.srv oracle         dba                      rwxrwxr--
ora....10G1.cs oracle         dba                      rwxrwxr--
ora....11.inst oracle         dba                      rwxrwxr--
ora....12.inst oracle         dba                      rwxrwxr–
...................
ora....101.vip root           dba                      rwxr-xr--
ora....SM2.asm oracle         dba                      rwxrwxr--
ora....02.lsnr oracle         dba                      rwxrwxr--
ora....102.gsd oracle         dba                      rwxr-xr--
ora....102.ons oracle         dba                      rwxr-xr--
ora....102.vip root           dba                      rwxr-xr--
...............
```

Register command

`crs_register resource_name`	Register the specified resource with the Oracle Clusterware
`crs_register resource_name -update`	Update information to an already registered resource

Start command

`crs_start resource_name`	Start the specified resource registered with the Oracle Clusterware
`crs_start -all`	Start with startup status all resources registered with the Oracle Clusterware
`crs_start –all –q`	Start all resources registered with the Oracle Clusterware in quite /silent mode
`crs_start resource_name –c cluster_member`	Start the specified resource on a specific member in the cluster

Stop command

`crs_stop resource_name`	Stop the specified resource registered with the Oracle Clusterware
`crs_stop -all`	Stop all resources registered with the Oracle Clusterware and provide stop status
`crs_stop –all –q`	Stop all resources registered with the Oracle Clusterware in quite /silent mode
`crs_stop resource_name –c cluster_member`	Stop the specified resource on a specific member in the cluster.

Relocate command

`crs_relocate resource_name`	Relocate the specified resource from the current instance to another instance registered for the resource with the Oracle Clusterware
`crs_relocate resource_name -c cluster_member`	Relocate the specified resource to a specific member in the cluster

Setup command

crssetup config	Configure and startup the cluster on all registered member nodes
crssetup add	Add specified nodes to the cluster
crssetup del	Delete specified node(s) from the cluster
crssetup shutdown	Shutdown the selected nodes in the cluster

B.3   ORADEBUG - Oracle Debugger

```
[oracle@oradb1 oracle]sqlplus '/as sysdba'

Oracle Database 10g Enterprise Edition Release 10.2.0.1.0 - Production
With the Partitioning, Real Application Clusters, OLAP and Data Mining
options

SQL> oradebug help
HELP            [command]               Describe one or all commands
SETMYPID                                Debug current process
SETOSPID        <ospid>                 Set OS pid of process to debug
SETORAPID       <orapid> ['force']      Set Oracle pid of process to debug
SHORT_STACK                             Dump abridged OS stack
DUMP            <dump_name> <lvl> [addr] Invoke named dump
DUMPSGA         [bytes]                 Dump fixed SGA
DUMPLIST                                Print a list of available dumps
EVENT           <text>                  Set trace event in process
SESSION_EVENT   <text>                  Set trace event in session
DUMPVAR         <p|s|uga> <name> [level] Print/dump a fixed PGA/SGA/UGA
variable
DUMPTYPE        <address> <type> <count> Print/dump an address with type info
SETVAR          <p|s|uga> <name> <value> Modify a fixed PGA/SGA/UGA variable
PEEK            <addr> <len> [level]    Print/Dump memory
POKE            <addr> <len> <value>    Modify memory
WAKEUP          <orapid>                Wake up Oracle process
SUSPEND                                 Suspend execution
RESUME                                  Resume execution
FLUSH                                   Flush pending writes to trace file
CLOSE_TRACE                             Close trace file
TRACEFILE_NAME                          Get name of trace file
LKDEBUG                         Invoke global enqueue service debugger
NSDBX                           Invoke CGS name-service debugger
-G              <Inst-List | def | all> Parallel oradebug command prefix
-R              <Inst-List | def | all> Parallel oradebug prefix (return
output
```

```
SETINST        <instance# .. | all>      Set instance list in double quotes
SGATOFILE      <SGA dump dir>           Dump SGA to file; dirname in double
quotes
DMPCOWSGA      <SGA dump dir> Dump & map SGA as COW; dirname in double quotes
MAPCOWSGA      <SGA dump dir>           Map SGA as COW; dirname in double
quotes
HANGANALYZE    [level] [syslevel]        Analyze system hang
FFBEGIN                                  Flash Freeze the Instance
FFDEREGISTER                             FF deregister instance from cluster
FFTERMINST                               Call exit and terminate instance
FFRESUMEINST                             Resume the flash frozen instance
FFSTATUS                                 Flash freeze status of instance
SKDSTTPCS      <ifname>  <ofname>        Helps translate PCs to names
WATCH          <address> <len> <self|exist|all|target>  Watch a region of
memory
DELETE         <local|global|target> watchpoint <id>    Delete a watchpoint
SHOW           <local|global|target> watchpoints        Show  watchpoints
CORE                                     Dump core without crashing process
IPC                                      Dump ipc information
UNLIMIT                                  Unlimit the size of the trace file
PROCSTAT                                 Dump process statistics
CALL           <func> [arg1] ... [argn]  Invoke function with arguments
```

B.4   Perl Script

 Note: This script is referenced in Chapter 9.

The below mentioned script will use the trace file generated using event 10046 at level 4 or 8 and extract the queries by placing the appropriate bind variables and values into the actual query.

```
#!/usr/bin/perl -w
# parsetrace.pl - read Oracle trace log and print queries
# author: Murali Vallath
# Copyright 2003-2006 Summersky Enterprises LLC
# usage: parsetrace.pl infile outfile

use strict;

my $dirname = ".";
my $log_file = "ParseTracesql.log";
```

```
my $query = "";
my @bind_variables = ();
my $query_count = 0;

unlink($log_file) unless !(-e $log_file);

opendir(DIR, $dirname) or die "can't opendir $dirname: $!";
open(LOG_FILE, ">> $log_file") or die "can't open file for writing: $!\n";

while (defined(my $file = readdir(DIR))) {

    # process all files in "$dirname/$file" that end in .trc
    if ($file =~ /.*\.trc$/) {
        open(TRACE_FILE, "$file") or die "no trace files found! $!\n";
        print "\nprocessing $file";

        # process all of this trace file
        while(<TRACE_FILE>) {

            # get the query from between "PARSING IN CURSOR" and "END OF
STMT"
            if ($_ =~ /PARSING IN CURSOR/) {

                # get the next line
                chomp($_ = <TRACE_FILE>);

                # build query - append lines until "END OF STMT" is hit or EOF
                while ($_ !~ /END OF STMT/) {
                    $query .= $_;
                    if ($_ = <TRACE_FILE>) {
                        chomp;
                    } else {
                        last;
                    }
                }
                if (($query =~ /SELECT/i) && ($query =~ /:\d/) &&
                    ($query !~ /privilege#/) &&
                    ($query !~ /eusr.*/) &&
                    ($query !~ /obj#/)) {

                    # trim whitespace and remove extra whitespace between
atoms
                    $query =~ s/^\s+//;
                    $query =~ s/\s+$//;
                    $query =~ s/\s+/ /g;
```

```
                        # get bind variables - append lines until "EXEC" is hit
or EOF

                        while (($_ !~ /EXEC/) && ($_ !~ /=====/)) {
                            if ($_ =~ /value=/) {
                                push(@bind_variables, $_);
                            }
                            if ($_ = <TRACE_FILE>) {
                                chomp;
                            } else {
                                last;
                            }
                        }

                        # show 'em what we got with the bind variables
                        if (scalar @bind_variables > 0) {
                        } else {
                            last;
                        }

                        # show 'em what we got with it all put together
                        my $position = 1;
                        foreach my $item(@bind_variables) {
                            # clean up
                            $item =~ s/^\s+//;
                            $item =~ s/\s+$//;
                            $item =~ s/value=//;
                            $item =~ s/"//g;
                            $item =~ s/0:0:0//g;
                            $query =~ s/:$position/$item/g;
                            $position++;
                        }

                        # last check - make sure there are no bind varibles with
                        # no values in them - e.g. APPT_ID != NVL(:4, -1)
                        if ($query !~ /\D:\d/) {
                            print ".";
                            print LOG_FILE "$query\n/\n\n";
                            $query_count++;
                        }


                }   # end of SELECT query/bind varibale display

            }   # end of getting the query from between "PARSING IN CURSOR"
and "END OF STMT" and bind variables
```

```
            # clear out the query scalar and bind variable array for the next
query
                $query = "";
                @bind_variables = ();

        }   # don't want this line, get the next line

    }   # end of this trace file, get the next file
}

# facts and figures
print "\n\nFound $query_count valid SELECT queries\n";


# shut it down
closedir(DIR);
close(LOG_FILE);
```

B.5   RMAN Scripts

Backup using RMAN at level 0:

```
#rman_level0_backup.sql
#
# Incremental backup script at level 0 (full backup)
# The script will backup all the datafiles, control file and archive log files
#
# Author: Murali Vallath
# Company: Summersky Enterprises LLC
# e-mail: murali.vallath@summersky.biz
#
change archivelog all validate;
run
{
allocate channel SSKYLIMS1 type disk;
allocate channel SSKYLIMS2 type disk;
backup
    incremental level 0
    tag Inc_db_level0
    format '/u02/oradata/rman_backup/BCK_%d_%s_%p_%t'
    ( database  filesperset 5
      include current controlfile );
    sql 'alter system archive log current';
```

```
backup
    filesperset 14
    tag Inc_db_level0
    format '/u02/oradata/rman_backup/ARC_%d_%s_%p_%t'
    ( archivelog all not backed up 2 times );
release channel SSKYLIMS1;
release channel SSKYLIMS2;
}
allocate channel for maintenance device type disk;
delete archivelog until time 'sysdate-7' backed up 2 times to disk;
delete obsolete device type disk;
crosscheck backup;
delete noprompt expired backup;
```

The script above performs the following operations:

1. It allocates two channels for the operation.

2. It performs an incremental backup at level 0 of the database files allocating five files per set. While backing up the datafiles, it will also backup the control file.

3. It performs a backup of the archive log files, allocating 14 files per set. While backing up the archive log files, only files that have not been backed up at least twice will be included in the file set.

4. Allocated channels are released.

5. A few maintenance operations are performed, for example, deleting all archive log files that have been backed up at least two times, after which all old RMAN backup files are purged.

Note: A similar set of scripts could be written for level 1.

All scripts used in this book can be downloaded from
www.summersky.biz. Use code SSKY10GRAC.

C

Oracle Clustered File System

The Oracle Clustered File System (OCFS) was developed by Oracle Corporation to simplify the management of RAC database datafiles on Linux and Windows operating systems. OCFS allows administrators to take advantage of a file system for Oracle database files (datafiles, control files, and archive logs) and configuration files.

C.1   OCFS 1.0

OCFS 1.0 is the first version of the clustered software that was released by Oracle and supports Linux kernel version 2.4. While this specific version has several limitations compared to competitive products in the market, for an open-source version and from an ease of handling perspective, it has provided several benefits to the DBA, primarily having to deal with RAW devices. Installation of the OCFS requires that a private network be configured and consists of these general steps:

1.   OCFS is developed by Oracle Corporation as open-source software and is available with source code under a general public license (GPL) agreement. The latest version of the OCFS packages can be obtained from either of the following websites:

- http://otn.oracle.com/tech/linux/content.html

- http://www.ocfs.org/ocfs

The package comprises three files:

- Support file that contains all of the generic packages required for OCFS. The file is identified with a version of the release (e.g., `ocfs-support-1.0.10-1.i686.rpm`).

- Tools file that contains all packages to install the various tools required for the configuration and management of OCFS. This file is also identified with a version number of the release (e.g., `ocfs-tools-1.0.10-4.i686.rpm`).
- Linux kernel module, which is specific to the release of the Linux kernel. For example, if the kernel release of the Linux operating system is 21.-27.smp, then the file that needs to be downloaded is `ocfs-2.4.9-e-smp-1.0.14-1.i686.rpm`.

Note: The Linux kernel release can be determined using the `uname -a` command; for example,

```
# uname -a
Linux oradb3.sumsky.net 2.4.21-32.ELsmp #1 SMP #1 SMP Mon
Mar 7 23:20:16 PST 2005 i686 i686 i386 GNU/Linux
```

2. The OCFS packages (RPM files) must to be installed in the appropriate `/lib/modules` tree in use by the operating system kernel as the `root` user in a specific order. The packages are installed using the following syntax:

```
rpm –Uvh <ocfs_rpm_package>
```

Install the support RPM file:

```
rpm –Uvh ocfs-support-1.0.10-1.i686.rpm
```

Install the correct kernel module RPM file for the system:

```
rpm –Uvh ocfs-2.4.9-e-smp-1.0.14-1.i686.rpm
```

Install the tools RPM file:

```
rpm –Uvh ocfs-tools-1.0.10-1.i686.rpm
```

Note: It is important to install the kernel module RPM file before installing the tools file. If this order is not followed, the install processes will generate an error with the following message: `ocfs = 1.0.9 is needed by ofcs-tools-1.0.10-1`.

3.   The next step is to configure the `ocfs.conf` located in the `/etc` directory. This can be performed using the Oracle-provided configuration tool `ocfstool` from an X-windows interface as user `root` (Figure C.1). The tool is invoked using the following command: `/usr/bin/ocfstool`.

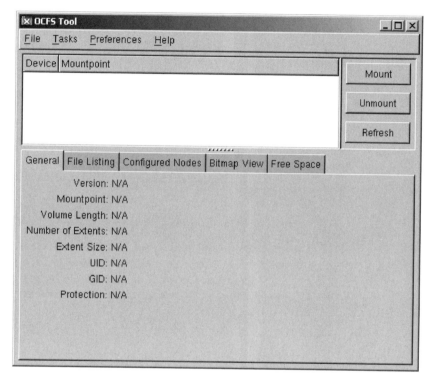

Figure C.1
OCFS Tool
Interface

Use the "Generate Config" option under the "Tasks" menu to generate an OCFS configuration file. Once generated, the `/etc/ocfs.conf` file will contain the following entries:

```
[root@oradb3 root]# more /etc/ocfs.conf
#
# ocfs config
# Ensure this file exists in /etc
#

        node_name = oradb3-priv.sumsky.com
        ip_address = 10.168.2.130
        ip_port = 7000
```

```
comm_voting = 1
guid = 18036DC188D0F530D2CC000FB54549EA
```

Where: node_name is the private node name.

ip_address is the IP address of the private interconnect

ip_port is the port number that will be used for communication purposes

guid is a group user ID that is generated from the Ethernet adapter hardware address and is unique across all nodes in the cluster

 Note: The group user ID can also be generated using the ocfs_uid_gen –c command, which updates the guid in the /etc/ocfs.conf file. The remainder of the file can also be created manually.

4.   OCFS needs to be started every time the system is started. This is done by adding the following lines to the /etc/rc.d/rc.local file:

```
/sbin/load_ocfs
```

5.   To check if OCFS is loaded, the following command should be executed:

```
[root@oradb3 root]# lsmod | grep ocfs
ocfs                    299072  15
```

6.   Once OCFS has been loaded and verified, the next step in the configuration process is to create the raw partitions, or LUNs, in accordance with OFA standards. This is done using the Linux fdisk utility:

```
fdisk /dev/sdb
```

The size of partitions should take into consideration the block size used during the format operation. Oracle supports a block size in the 2K to 1MB range. The max partition size is derived using the following formula:

```
block_size * 1M * 8 (Bitmap size is fixed to 1M)
```

If the block size is 2K, the partition size would be

```
(2 * 1024) * (1M * 1024 * 1024) *8 = 16GB
```

Note: Like all file systems, OCFS has an operational overhead; the overhead will be approximately 10 MB, which is used for the files, metadata (i.e., the "system files" that are stored at the end of the disk and the partition headers). This operational overhead should be taken into consideration when creating smaller partitions.

7.　Once the partitions are created using the `fdisk` utility, they have to be formatted under OCFS. This step can be performed using the `ocfstool` utility or manually from the command line. This step should also be performed as user `root`. This process also defines the block size for the partition. For optimal performance benefits, it is recommended that the block size be set at 128K.

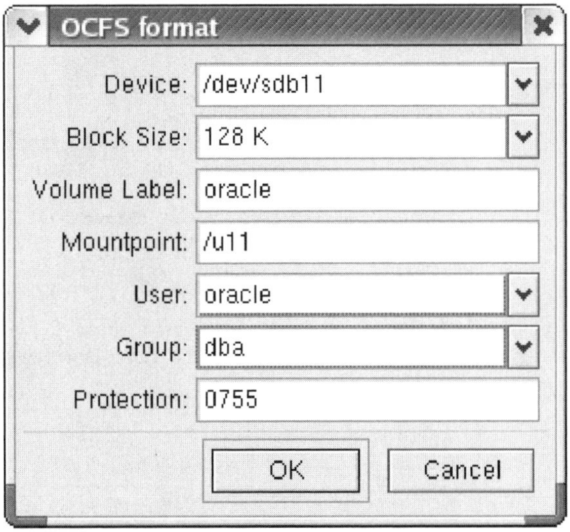

Figure C.2
OCFS Tool Format Option

```
┌─────────────────────────────────────────┐
│ ⌄  OCFS format                        ✕ │
├─────────────────────────────────────────┤
│      Device: │/dev/sdb11          │ ⌄  │
│  Block Size: │128 K               │ ⌄  │
│ Volume Label:│oracle              │    │
│   Mountpoint:│/u11                │    │
│        User: │oracle              │ ⌄  │
│       Group: │dba                 │ ⌄  │
│  Protection: │0755                │    │
│                                         │
│          │   OK   │   │ Cancel │        │
└─────────────────────────────────────────┘
```

After invoking the `ocfstool` (`/usr/bin/ocfstool`), the format option (Figure C.2) under the Tasks tab is used to format the partitions with OCFS.

Formatting can also be performed interactively from the command line using the Oracle-provided format executable /sbin/ mkfs.ocfs.

```
[root@oradb3 oracle]#mkfs.ocfs -F -b 128 -L ora01 -m /
u01 -u 500 -g 500 -p 0775 /dev/sdb1
Cleared volume header sectors
Cleared node config sectors
Cleared publish sectors
Cleared vote sectors
Cleared bitmap sectors
Cleared data block
Wrote volume header
```

In the above command, -u 500 is the user ID of the Oracle user, -g 500 is the Group ID that the Oracle user belongs to, -p 0775 is the privilege on the directory, and /dev/sdb1 is the physical disk being formatted.

As discussed in Chapter 4, the Oracle credentials can be obtained using the following command:

```
[oracle@oradb3 oracle]# id oracle
uid=500(oracle) gid=500(dba)
groups=500(dba),501(oinstall),502(oper)
```

The syntax for the mkfs.ocfs executable and its options are as follows:

```
usage: mkfs.ocfs -b block-size [-C] [-F] [-g gid] [-h] -L
volume-label -m mount-path [-n] [-p permissions] [-q] [-u
uid] [-V] device
```

```
        -b Block size in kilobytes
        -C Clear all data blocks
        -F Force format existing OCFS volume
        -g GID for the root directory
        -h Help
        -L Volume label
        -m Path where this device will be mounted
        -n Query only
```

> –p Permissions for the root directory
> –q Quiet execution
> –u UID for the root directory
> –V Print version and exit

8.   The next step is to mount the formatted OCFS partitions. Prior to mounting these partitions, the appropriate mount points (directories) need to be created. This can be performed using the following command:

```
mkdir -p /u01 /u02 /u03
```

9.   Once the mount points are created, they can be mounted using the ocfstool utility or from the command line using the mount command:

```
mount -t ocfs /dev/sdb1 /u01
```

 Note: The mount points must be the same for all nodes in the cluster.

10.   The last step is to configure OCFS to mount the devices automatically each time the machine is booted. This is done by adding the devices to the /etc/fstab file using the following syntax:

```
<partition device name> <mount point name> <file system> _netdev 0 0
```

For example:

```
/dev/sdb1          /u01              ocfs    _netdev 0 0
/dev/sdb2          /u02              ocfs    _netdev 0 0
/dev/sdb3          /u03              ocfs    _netdev 0 0
/dev/sdb4          /u04              ocfs    _netdev 0 0
/dev/sdb5          /u05              ocfs    _netdev 0 0
```

C.2   **OCFS2**

OCFS2 is the next generation of the Oracle Cluster File System, which supports Linux kernel 2.6 and higher. It is an extent-based POSIX-compliant file system. Unlike the previous release (OCFS), OCFS2 is a general-purpose file system that can store not only database-related files on a shared disk, but also Oracle binaries and configuration files (shared Oracle home), making management of RAC easier. In this section we will discuss the steps involved in installing and configuring OCFS2 in a Linux environment.

1.   Download the OCFS-related packages from the OCFS website at www.ocfs.org.

The packages consist of two sets of RPMs and are contained in the following three files:

■ Linux kernel module, which is specific to the release of the operating system kernel. For example, if the kernel release of the Linux operating system is 2.6.9-22.EL, the file that needs to be downloaded is `ocfs2-2.6.9-11.0.0.10.3.EL-1.0.1-1.i686.rpm`.

■ Unlike OCFS version 1.0, OCFS2 does not require any support files; instead, the tools RPMs are split into two ocfs-tools packages that include the command-line tools and the ocfs2console, which includes the GUI front end for the tools.

Note: The Linux kernel release can be determined using the `uname -a` command. For example:

```
[oracle@oradb3 oracle]$ uname -a
Linux oradb3.sumsky.net 2.6.9-22.EL #1 Mon Sep 19
18:20:28 EDT 2005 i686 i686 i386 GNU/Linux
[oracle@oradb3 oracle]$
```

2.   The OCFS2 packages must to be installed as the root user. The RPMs are installed using

`rpm -install`, which will create a fresh install

`rpm -upgrade`, which will upgrade the existing version if one is present or will make a fresh install

```
# [root@oradb3 root]rpm -Uvh ocfs2-2.6.9-22.EL-1.0.7-
1.i686.rpm \
            ocfs2console-1.0.3-1.i386.rpm \
            ocfs2-tools-1.0.3-1.i386.rpm
```

```
Preparing...
######################################### [100%]
   1:ocfs2-tools
######################################### [ 33%]
   2:ocfs2-2.6.9-22.EL
######################################### [ 67%]
   3:ocfs2console
######################################### [100%]
```

3.   The next step is to configure OCFS. OCFS2 has a configuration file located in /etc/ocfs2 called cluster.conf. This file contains basic cluster-related information, such as the nodes participating in the cluster. While Oracle allows dynamic changes to this file, changes to the name or IP address will require that the cluster be restarted for the changes to take effect. It is important that the contents of the file be identical on all nodes in the cluster.

     a.   The configuration can be performed either manually or using the Oracle-provided GUI console. Using the OUI requires that the terminal from which this installer is run be X-windows compatible. If it is not, an appropriate X-windows emulator should be installed and the emulator invoked using the DISPLAY command using the following syntax:

```
export DISPLAY=<client IP address>:0.0
```

For example:

```
[oracle@oradb3 oracle]$export DISPLAY=192.168.2.101:0.0
```

Next, from the command line, execute the following command, which will display the main console screen (Figure C.3):

```
/usr/sbin/ocfs2console
```

Select the "Configure Nodes" option under the "Cluster" menu (Figure C.2). This will start the OCFS cluster stack (Figure C.4) and generate the configuration file, if it is not already

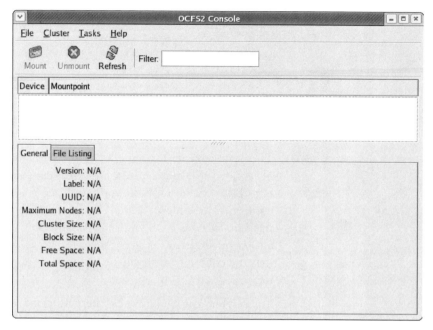

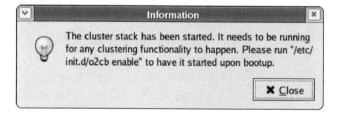

present. Once this is complete, the file is located in `/etc/ocfs2/`
`cluster.conf`.

b. In the next screen "Node Configuration" (not shown),
click the "Add" button to add nodes to the cluster. Enter
the node name (same as the hostname), the IP address,
and port. The console assigns node numbers sequentially
from 0 to 254.

Once all the nodes are added, propagate the configuration to all
the nodes by clicking the "Propagate Configuration" option under
the item "Cluster" menu. As the console uses `ssh` to propagate the
file, it is important that the user equivalence be defined. The steps
to configure user equivalence are discussed in Chapter 4.

Once all the nodes are added as active to OCFS, select the "Quit" option from the "File" menu to complete the configuration.

The output from a four-node cluster configuration would be

```
[oracle@oradb1 oracle]more /etc/ocfs2/ocfs2.conf

cluster:
node_count = 4
name = SskyOCFS

node:
ip_port = 7777
ip_address = 192.168.2.10
number = 0
name = oradb1
cluster = SskyOCFS

node:
ip_port = 7777
ip_address = 192.168.2.20
number = 1
name = oradb2
cluster = SskyOCFS

node:
      . . . . .
```

Please note that the structure of the configuration file has two sections: (1) the header, called the *cluster stanza*, which contains the cluster-level information (basically, the number of nodes in the OCFS cluster and the name assigned to the cluster), and (2) the body called the *node stanza*, which contains the individual node details.

4. As mentioned earlier, OCFS2 comes bundled with its own cluster stack, O2CB. The stack includes the following cluster services:

    ■ NM: Node Manager that keeps track of all the nodes in the `cluster.conf`

- HB: Heartbeat service that issues up/down notifications when nodes join or leave the cluster
- TCP: Service that handles communication between the nodes
- DLM: Distributed lock manager that keeps track of all locks, its owners, and status
- CONFIGFS: User space-driven configuration file system mounted at /config
- DLMFS: User space interface to the kernel space DLM

All the cluster services have been packaged in the o2cb system service. Because all the operations (e.g., format, mount) require that the cluster be online, start it before continuing to format.

The status of a service can be verified using the following command:

```
[root@oradb3 ~]# /etc/init.d/o2cb status
Module "configfs": Not loaded
Filesystem "configfs": Not mounted
Module "ocfs2_nodemanager": Not loaded
Module "ocfs2_dlm": Not loaded
Module "ocfs2_dlmfs": Not loaded
Filesystem "ocfs2_dlmfs": Not mounted
[root@oradb3 ~]#
```

   a. It's important that the stack be started before you proceed with the disk configuration. O2cb can be started using the start command; for example;

```
[root@oradb3 ~]# /etc/init.d/o2cb load
Module "configfs": OK
Filesystem "configfs": OK
Module "ocfs2_nodemanager": OK
Module "ocfs2_dlm": OK
Module "ocfs2_dlmfs": OK
Filesystem "ocfs2_dlmfs": OK
```

b. Once all the modules required for the cluster stack are loaded, the next step is to start the OCFS cluster Ssky-OCFS:

```
[root@oradb3 ~]# /etc/init.d/o2cb online SskyOCFS
Starting cluster ocfs2 : OK
```

c. The next step is to add and configure o2cb to start on reboot on the respective nodes in the cluster:

```
[root@oradb3 ~]# /etc/init.d/o2cb configure
Configuring the O2CB driver.
This will configure the on-boot properties of the O2CB
driver.
The following questions will determine whether the
driver is loaded on boot. The current values will be
shown in brackets ('[]'). Hitting
<ENTER> without typing an answer will keep that current
value. Ctrl-C
will abort.
Load O2CB driver on boot (y/n) [n]: y
Cluster to start on boot (Enter "none" to clear) []:
SskyOCFS
Writing O2CB configuration: OK
```

This completes the basic OCFS2 installation and configuration process. o2cb has several commands to stop, start, and so on, which can be obtained using the help option:

```
[root@oradb3 ~]# /etc/init.d/o2cb help
Usage: /etc/init.d/o2cb {start|stop|restart|force-
reload|enable|disable|configure|load|unload|online|offl
ine|status}
[root@oradb3 ~]#
```

5. Once OCFS has been loaded and verified, the next step in the configuration process is to create the raw partitions or LUNs in accordance with OFA standards. This is done using the Linux fdisk utility:

```
[root@oradb3 root]fdisk /dev/sdb
```

6. Once the partitions are created using the `fdisk` utility, they have to be formatted under OCFS. This step can be performed using the `ocfs2console` utility or manually from the command line. After invoking the `ocfs2console` (`/usr/sbin/ocfs2console`), the format option (Figure C.5) under the tasks tab is used to format the partitions with OCFS.

Figure C.5
*Format Disks
Using OCFS2
Console*

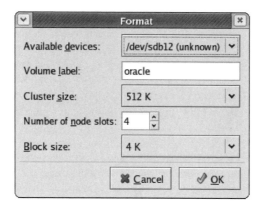

Formatting can also be performed interactively from the command line using the Oracle-provided format executable `mkfs.ocfs2`. 4k block size, 512K cluster size to support four nodes in the cluster.

```
[root@oradb3 root]mkfs.ocfs2 -b 4K -C 512K -N 4 -L
ora01 /dev/sdb2
mkfs.ocfs2 0.99.15-BETA16
Overwriting existing ocfs2 partition.
Proceed (y/N): y
Filesystem label=ora01
Block size=4096 (bits=12)
Cluster size=524288 (bits=15)
Volume size=31474820096 (655359 clusters) (5242872
blocks)
21 cluster groups (tail covers 10239 clusters, rest
cover 524288 clusters)
Journal size=37554432
Initial number of node slots: 4
Creating bitmaps: done
Initializing superblock: done
Writing system files: done
```

```
Writing superblock: done
Writing lost+found: done
mkfs.ocfs2 successful
```

The syntax for the `mkfs.ocfs2` executable and its options are
as follows:

```
[root@oradb3 ocfs2ss]# mkfs.ocfs2
Usage: mkfs.ocfs2 [-b block-size] [-C cluster-size] [-N
number-of-node-slots [-L volume-label] [-J journal-
options] [-HFqvV] device [blocks-count]
```

7.   The next step is to mount the formatted OCFS partitions. Prior
     to mounting these partitions, the appropriate mount points
     (directories) need to be created. This can be performed using the
     following command:

```
[root@oradb3 root]mkdir -p /u01 /u02 /u03
```

8.   Once the mount points are created, they can be mounted using
     the `ocfs2console` utility or from the command line using the
     mount command:

```
[root@oradb3 root]mount -t ocfs2 /dev/sdb2 /u01
```

9.   The last step is to configure OCFS to mount the devices auto-
     matically each time the machine is booted. This is done by add-
     ing the devices to the `/etc/fstab` file using the following syntax:

```
<partition device name> <mount point name> <file system> _netdev 0 0
```

```
For example:
/dev/sdb1                /u01                        ocfs2     netdev 0 0
/dev/sdb2                /u02                        ocfs2     netdev 0 0
/dev/sdb3                /u03                        ocfs2     netdev 0 0
/dev/sdb4                /u04                        ocfs2     netdev 0 0
/dev/sdb5                /u05                        ocfs2     netdev 0 0
```

Note: Oracle database users must mount the volumes containing the voting disk, OCR, datafiles, redo logs, archive logs, and control files with the `datavolume` mount option to ensure that the Oracle processes open the files with the `o_direct` flag. All other volumes, including Oracle home, should not be mounted with this mount option.

To mount the volume containing Oracle datafiles, voting disk, and so forth, use the following syntax:

```
[root@oradb3 root]mount -t ocfs2 -o datavolume /dev/sdb5 /u05
[root@oradb3 root]mount /dev/sdb5 on /u05 type ocfs2 (rw,datavolume)
```

10. Oracle also provides several command-line utilities to verify the functioning and details of the OCFS drives.

   a. *File system check.* This is performed by the `fsck` utility using one of the following formats:

```
[root@oradb3 ocfs2ss]# fsck.ocfs2 -h
fsck.ocfs2: invalid option -- h
Usage: fsck.ocfs2 [ -fGnuvVy ] [ -b superblock block ]
                    [ -B block size ] device

Critical flags for emergency repair:
  -n            Check but don't change the file system
  -y            Answer 'yes' to all repair questions
  -f            Force checking even if file system is clean
  -F            Ignore cluster locking (dangerous!)

Less critical flags:
  -b superblock Treat given block as the super block
  -B blocksize  Force the given block size
  -G            Ask to fix mismatched inode generations
  -u            Access the device with buffering
  -V            Output fsck.ocfs2's version
  -v            Provide verbose debugging output
```

   b. *Listing existing OCFS2 volumes on the storage.* This utility lists all of the OCFS2 mounted volumes:

```
# mounted.ocfs2 -f
Device    FS      Nodes
/dev/sdb1 SskyOCFS oradb1, oradb2, oradb3, oradb4
/dev/sdb2 SskyOCFS oradb1, oradb2, oradb3, oradb4
/dev/sdb3 SskyOCFS oradb1, oradb2, oradb3, oradb4
/dev/sdb5 SskyOCFS oradb1, oradb2, oradb3, oradb4
/dev/sdb6 SskyOCFS oradb1, node90
/dev/sdb7 SskyOCFS Not mounted
/dev/sdb8 SskyOCFS Not mounted
/dev/sdb9 SskyOCFS Not mounted
```

C.3   Conclusion

In this appendix section, we discussed the installation procedures for both OCFS Release 1.0 and OCFS Release 2.0. Both releases support two specifically different versions of Linux kernels. OCFS Release 1.0 will only work with Linux kernel 2.4, and OCFS Release 2.0 (OCFS2) will only work with Linux kernel 2.6.

TAF and FCF using Java

D.1 TAF example using Java

```
public interface OracleOCIFailover{

// Possible Failover Types
public static final int FO_SESSION = 1;
public static final int FO_SELECT  = 2;
public static final int FO_NONE    = 3;
public static final int;

// Possible Failover events registered with callback
public static final int FO_BEGIN  = 1;
public static final int FO_END    = 2;
public static final int FO_ABORT  = 3;
public static final int FO_REAUTH = 4;
public static final int FO_ERROR  = 5;
public static final int FO_RETRY  = 6;
public static final int FO_EVENT_UNKNOWN = 7;

public int callbackFn (Connection conn,
                Object ctxt, //any thing the user wants to save
        int type, //one of the above possible Failover Types
        int event ); //One of the above possible Failover Events
```

In case of a failure on one of the instances, Oracle tries to restore the connections from the failed instance to an active instance. This failover process from the failed instance to the active instance could, depending on the number of sessions being failed over, cause a small delay, in which case it is a good practice to notify the user.

The following code illustrates the usage and implementation of TAF from a java application. The sections are explained in detail later in this appendix.

```java
//java imports
import java.sql.Connection;
import java.sql.Statement;
import java.sql.ResultSet;
import java.sql.SQLException;
import java.sql.DriverManager;

//Oracle imports
import oracle.jdbc.OracleConnection;
//log4j imports.
import org.apache.log4j.Category;

public class TAFDetailsExample {

  /* Connection object to handle the database connection*/
  private Connection con = null;
  /**
  *   TAFCallbackFn class implements the interface provided
  *   by Oracle in case of FailOver
  */
  private TAFCallbackFn clbFn = null;
  /* Failover string */
  private String strFailover = null;
  /* Statement object to execute query */
  private Statement stmt = null;
  /* Result set object to hold the results of the query*/
  private ResultSet rs = null;
  /* used for getting an instance of log4j for this class. */
  protected static Category cat =
        Category.getInstance(TAFDetailsExample.class.getName());

  /**
   * Constructor.
   */
  public TAFDetailsExample() {
  }
  public static void main(String[] args) {
```

```
            TAFDetailsExample tafDE = new TAFDetailsExample();
            // This method handles database connections.
            tafDE.handleDBConnections();
            try {
                // This method is used to execute query
                tafDE.runQuery();
                cat.debug(tafDE.toString());
                // This method is used to free the resources allocated
                tafDE.closeConnections();
            } catch (SQLException e) {
                e.printStackTrace();
            }
        }
        /**
         *  This method is used to clear all the resources allocated.
         * @throws SQLException
         */
        void closeConnections() throws SQLException {
            rs.close();
            stmt.close();
            con.close();
            cat.debug("Allocated Resources are free now.");
        }


    /**
     * This method is used to handle the database connection with specific
     * connection strings.
     */
     void handleDBConnections() {
```

Section 1

```
        try {
            // Register the Oracle driver
            DriverManager.registerDriver(
                    new oracle.jdbc.driver.OracleDriver());
// Create a Connetion to the database with specific connection string
            con = (OracleConnection) DriverManager.getConnection(
                    "jdbc:oracle:oci:@PRODDB ",
                    "user",
                    "pwd");
            if (con != null)
```

```
            this.RegisterFailOver(); //register failover
        } catch (SQLException e) {
            cat.debug("Error Occurred while registering Failover.");
            e.printStackTrace();
        }
    }
```

Section 2

```
/**
 * This Function registers the class that implements the
 * Oracle OCIFailover Interface. This is done to notify Oracle
 * that in case of a failure the callback function in the
 * registered class is to be invoked.
 */
void RegisterFailOver() throws SQLException {
    clbFn = new TAFCallbackFn();
    strFailover = new String("Register Failover");
    // Registers the callback Function.
    ((OracleConnection) con).registerTAFCallback(clbFn, strFailover);
    cat.debug(" Failover Registered Successfully. ");
}
/**
 * This method is used to execute query.
 */
void runQuery() {
  try {
      stmt = con.createStatement();
  } catch (SQLException e) {
    e.printStackTrace();
  }
  long startTime = 0;
  long endTime = 0;
  /**
   * This loop is used for testing purposes only.
   */
  for (int i = 0; i < 20000; i++) {
      startTime = System.currentTimeMillis();
      try {
      /**
       *  This query is just used for testing purposes. In a real life
       *  scenario the query is dynamically passed and can be any valid
```

```
        *   SQL statement.
        */
          String query =
              "SELECT USP.USPRL_ID," +
                     "USP.USPRL_FIRST_NAME, USP.USPRL_LAST_NAME, " +
                     "USP.USPRL_CITY, USP.USPRL_STATE_ID," +
                     "COMP.COMP_NAME, COMP.COMP_TYPE_CD, " +
                     "USP.USPRL_EMAIL, USP.USPRL_PHONE,  " +
                     "COMP.COMP_SCAC_CODE, USP.USPRL_LOGIN_NAME, " +
              "FROM USER_PROFILE USP, COMPANY COMP," +
             "WHERE   UL.USRLI_ACTIVE_STATUS_CD='ACTIVE'" +
             "AND   USP.USPRL_COMP_ID = COMP.COMP_ID" +
          "ORDER BY COMP.COMP_COMP_TYPE_CD,COMP.COMP_NAME, " +
                  " USP.USPRL_LAST_NAME";


              rs = stmt.executeQuery(query);
          } catch (SQLException e) {
```

Section 3

```
/**
 * The limitations for failover prevent INSERT, DELETE, UPDATE
 * and transactional statements from failing over.
 * The possible errors that Oracle could throw in such a
 * situation can be handled and we can get a new connection
 * and execute the statements keeping the failure transparent
 * to the user. The possible errors for handling are.
 */
if ((e.getErrorCode() == 1012) ||(e.getErrorCode() == 1033) ||
    (e.getErrorCode() == 1034) ||(e.getErrorCode() == 1089) ||
    (e.getErrorCode() == 3113) ||(e.getErrorCode() == 3114) ||
    (e.getErrorCode() == 12203)||(e.getErrorCode() == 12500) ||
    (e.getErrorCode() == 12571)) {


cat.debug("Node failed while executing" +
        "INSERT/DELETE/UPDATE/TRANSACTIONAL Statements");
// Get another connection
handleDBConnections();
// re execute the query.
runQuery();
} else
// The failure is not due to a node failure.
```

```java
            e.printStackTrace();
        }
        endTime = System.currentTimeMillis();
        if (cat.isDebugEnabled())
            cat.debug("Execution Time for the query is  " +
                        (endTime - startTime) + "  ms.");
            }
        }
    public String toString() {
        StringBuffer sb = new StringBuffer();
        try {
            sb.append("\nResultset values are " + "\n" + rs.getType());
        } catch (SQLException e) {
            e.printStackTrace();
        }
        return sb.toString();
    }
}
//Java imports
import java.sql.Connection;
import java.sql.SQLException;
//log4j imports
import org.apache.log4j.Category;
//Oracle imports
import oracle.jdbc.OracleOCIFailover;
public class TAFCallbackFn implements OracleOCIFailover {

    private static Category cat =
Category.getInstance(TAFCallbackFn.class.getName());

    public TAFCallbackFn() {
        }
    /**
     * This callback function will be invoked on failure of a node
     * or lost connections
     * @param connection – The failed connection which will be restored
     * @param o – Used to hold the user Context object
     * @param type – failover type
     * @param event – failover event
     * @return – In case of an error return FO_RETRY else return 0
     */
```

```
public int callbackFn(Connection connection, Object o, int type, int
event) {

    String foType[] = { "SESSION", "SELECT", "NONE" };
    String foEvent[] = { "BEGIN", "END", "ABORT", "REAUTHORISE",
                         "ERROR", "RETRY", "UNKNOWN" };
    try {
      cat.debug("The connection for which the failover occurred is :"
                 + connection.getMetaData().toString());
        } catch (SQLException e) {
            e.printStackTrace();
        }
        cat.debug("FAILOVER TYPE is :   " + foType[type-1]);
        cat.debug("FAILOVER EVENT is : " + foEvent[event-1]);

        switch (event) {
            case FO_BEGIN:
                cat.info("Failover event is begin ");
                break;
            case FO_END:
                cat.info("Failover event is end");
                return 0;
            case FO_ABORT:
                cat.info("Failover is aborted");
                break;
            case FO_REAUTH:
                cat.info("Failover needs reauthorization");
```

Section 4

```
                break;

            case FO_ERROR:
            cat.info("Error occurred while failing over. Retrying " +
                     "to restore connection. ");
    try {
    Thread.sleep(2000);//sleep for 2 seconds
    } catch (InterruptedException e) {  // Trap errors
        cat.error("Error while causing the currently
executing thread to sleep");
    }
    return FO_RETRY;
    default:
```

```
            cat.info("Default is returned");
        }
        cat.debug("Before returning from the Callback Function.");
        return 0;
    }
}
```

Section 1 illustrates how the Oracle JDBC driver is registered and the connection obtained from the DriverManager. Implementation of TAF requires the usage of an Oracle JDBC thick driver. Only when a thick driver is used will the client-side Oracle NET files be used to obtain connectivity to the database.

Section 2 illustrates how once a connection is established, the class that is implementing the Oracle interface should be registered with Oracle.

This notifies Oracle that, in the case of a failure, the callback function, which is implemented in the class TAFCallbackFn, is to be called. Oracle also provides the failover type (SESSION, SELECT, or NONE) and the present failover event. (The failover types are implemented using the tnsnames.ora file and are illustrated in the TAF implementation section of this appendix)

All of the above-mentioned limitations for failover need to be handled so that the failure is transparent to the user. The possible errors that can be thrown by Oracle in such a case are handled, the connection is reestablished, and the query is reexecuted as specified in Section 3 of the code. Oracle exception code ORA-01012 maps to SQL exception error code 1012.

When the connection is established and the failover has ended, the FO_END event is sent back to the application saying that the failover has completed.

Transitions may not always be smooth; if an error is encountered during the restoration of a connection to the failed-over instance, the FO_ERROR event is sent to the application indicating the error and requesting the application to handle this error appropriately. Under these circumstances, the application can provide a retry functionality where the application will rest or sleep for a predefined interval and send back an FO_RETRY event. If during a subsequent attempt a similar error occurs, the application will retry again for the number of retry attempts specified. Section 4 of the code deals with the FO_ERROR event.

FCF example using Java

```java
import oracle.jdbc.pool.OracleDataSource;

import java.sql.SQLException;
import java.sql.Connection;

public class FANEnabledConnectionManagerExample {

    public static Connection getConnection() {
        if (ods == null) {
            initializeDataSource();
        }
        Connection conn = null;
        try {
            conn = ods.getConnection();
        } catch (SQLException e) {
            e.printStackTrace();
        } finally {
        }
        return conn;
    }

        public static void main(String[] args) {
        initializeDataSource();
        Connection conn = getConnection();
        /**
         * use the connection.
         */
        try {
            if(conn != null)
            conn.close();//This returns the connection to the cache.
        } catch (SQLException e) {
            e.printStackTrace();
        }
    }

    public static void initializeDataSource() {
        if (ods == null) {
            try {
                ods = new OracleDataSource();
                ods.setUser("user");
```

```
                        ods.setPassword("password");


/**
* FCF Supports both thin driver and OCI driver.
* For OCI driver, just mention the service name in the tnsnames.ora file
* For thin driver specify the connection string.
*/
                        ods.setURL("ConnectionURL");
                        java.util.Properties cacheProperties = new
java.util.Properties();

                        cacheProperties.setProperty("MinLimit", "5");
                        cacheProperties.setProperty("MaxLimit", "20");
                        cacheProperties.setProperty("InitialLimit", "3");
                        cacheProperties.setProperty("InactivityTimeout", "1800");
                        cacheProperties.setProperty("AbandonedConnectionTimeout",
"900");

                        cacheProperties.setProperty("MaxStatementsLimit", "10");
                        cacheProperties.setProperty("PropertyCheckInterval", "60");


                        ods.setConnectionCacheName("FanConnectionCache01");//Name of
the connection Cache. This has to be unique
                        ods.setConnectionCachingEnabled(true);
                        ods.setConnectionCacheProperties(cacheProperties); //set the
cache properties.
                        /**
                         *
                         */
                        ods.setFastConnectionFailoverEnabled(true);//Enable the Fast
connection Failover.
            } catch (SQLException e) {
                e.printStackTrace();
            } finally {
            }
        }
    }


    /**
     * The DataSource which is used to get connections.
     */
    private static OracleDataSource ods = null;
}
```

Sequence of events:

1.   Create the data source with the implicit connection cache enabled.

2.   Set the connection cache properties (e.g., `MinLimit`, `MaxLimit`). This is not required.

3.   Two types of connections are lying beneath: logical connections and physical connections.

4.   When the cache is created, physical connections are created, which hold the connection information and wrap themselves with logical connections and return the logical connection when the user asks for one.

5.   Use `setFastConnectFailover(true)` to enable FCF. How easy is it?

6.   When the FCF is enabled, a daemon is started in the JVM, which listens to the ONS event.

7.   When the node goes down, an ONS event is thrown, and the JVM receives the notification and passes it onto the subscriber.

8.   When a node-down event notification is received, a worker thread closes all of the physical connections in the cache to the failed node.

9.   If this happens when the connection is being used by the application, the transaction is rolled back, and a connection closed exception is thrown (`ORA-17008`). The application is now responsible for handling the error.

10. The cache now refreshes itself to accommodate the initial properties.

E

Migration(s)

E.1   Oracle 9*i*R2 to 10*g*R2 RAC

 Note: This is an extract of an article by Murali Vallath that appeared on Oracle Technology Network at www.oracle.com/technology/pub/articles/vallath_rac_upgrade.html. It is included here with permission.

In this two-part section, the various steps to be taken when upgrading an Oracle 9i Release 2 (9*i* R2) RAC environment configured on OCFS to an Oracle 10g Release 2 (10*g* R2) RAC configured on ASM are detailed. In the first part, we discuss a basic upgrade to Oracle Database 10*g* Release 2 and, subsequently in the second part, we discuss how the data can be migrated from OCFS to Oracle ASM.

E.1.1   Current environment

The environment selected for the upgrade is a four-node Red Hat Linux AS 2.1 Cluster (illustrated in Table E.1).

Figure E.1   *Oracle Database 9i Release 2 RAC Environment*

Database Name	Number of Nodes	Database Version	Number of Instances	O/S Kernel Version	Clustered File System	Cluster Manager
SSKYDB	Four Nodes – oradb1, oradb2, oradb3 and oradb4	9.2.0.4	Four Instances – SSKY1, SSKY2, SSKY3 and SSKY4	Red Hat Advanced Server 2.1 Kernel - 2.4.9-e.41smp	OCFS 1.0	Oracle Cluster Manager (ORACM)

The upgrade process can be broken down into the following steps:

1. Dependencies and prerequisites
2. Configuration of network components
3. Installation of Oracle Clusterware
4. Installation of Oracle software
5. Database upgrade
6. Housekeeping

1. Dependencies and prerequisites

The first primary step in any software installation is to verify the system requirements and certification matrix for the operating system and the hardware platform; in the case of an upgrade, you will also need to verify all application patch levels.

For example, one primary requirement for Oracle Database 10g Release 2 is that it requires Red Hat Enterprise Linux (RHEL) 3 update 4 or RHEL 4. Apart from the basic operating system version, verify the following additional packages. But first, ensure that a valid, complete backup of the system is available before making any changes to the existing configuration, including operating system and Oracle data files.

1.1   Upgrade the operating system from Red Hat AS 2.1 to Red Hat Enterprise Release (RHEL) 3.0 update 4 i.e. Kernel version 2.4.9-e.41smp to 2.4.21-27.

1.2   Install and verify the required additional operating system packages:

```
[root@oradb3 oracle]# rpm -qa | grep -i gcc
compat-gcc-c++-7.3-2.96.128
compat-gcc-7.3-2.96.128
libgcc-3.2.3-42
gcc-3.2.3-42
[root@oradb3 oracle]# rpm -qa | grep -i openmotif
openmotif-2.2.3-3.RHEL3
openmotif21-2.1.30-8
```

```
[root@oradb3 oracle]# rpm -qa | grep -i glibc
glibc-2.3.3-74
glibc-utils-2.3.3-74
glibc-kernheaders-2.4-8.34.1
glibc-common-2.3.3-74
glibc-headers-2.3.3-74
glibc-devel-2.3.3-74
[root@oradb3 oracle]# rpm -qa | grep -i compat
compat-libstdc++-7.3-2.96.128
compat-gcc-c++-7.3-2.96.128
compat-gcc-7.3-2.96.128
compat-db-4.0.14-5
compat-libstdc++-devel-7.3-2.96.128
[root@oradb3 oracle]#
```

1.3   Update the kernel parameters with the following values:

```
kernel.core_uses_pid = 1
kernel.hostname = oradb3.sumsky.net
kernel.domainname = sumsky.net
kernel.shmall = 2097152
#kernel.shmmax = 536870912
kernel.shmmax = 2147483648
kernel.shmmni = 4096
kernel.shmseg = 4096
kernel.sem = 250 32000 100 150
kernel.msgmnl = 2878
kernel.msgmnb = 65535
fs.file-max = 65536
net.ipv4.ip_local_port_range = 1024 65000
net.core.rmem_default = 262144
net.core.wmem_default = 262144
net.core.rmem_max = 262144
net.core.wmem_max = 262144
```

1.4   Add the following parameters to /etc/security/limits.conf:

```
oracle          soft    nproc       2047
oracle          hard    nproc       16384
oracle          soft    nofile      1024
oracle          hard    nofile      65536
```

1.5   Establish user equivalence with SSH:

Depending on the node from which the Oracle installation will be performed using the Oracle Universal Installer (OUI), Oracle copies files from the node where the installation is performed to all the other remaining nodes in the cluster. Such a copy process is performed either by using the Secured Shell (ssh) Protocol where available or by using the remote copy (rcp). In order for the copy operation to be successful, the oracle user on all the RAC nodes must be able to log in to other RAC nodes without having to provide a password or passphrase.

For security reasons, most organizations prefer ssh based operations to remote copy (rcp). Take the following steps to configure the oracle account to use ssh logins without using any passwords:

1.   Create the authentication key for user oracle. To create this key, change the current directory to the default login directory of the oracle user and perform the following operation:

```
[oracle@oradb4 oracle]$ ssh-keygen -t dsa -b 1024
Generating public/private dsa key pair.
Enter file in which to save the key (/home/oracle/.ssh/id_dsa):
Created directory '/home/oracle/.ssh'.
Enter passphrase (empty for no passphrase):
Enter same passphrase again:
Your identification has been saved in /home/oracle/.ssh/id_dsa.
Your public key has been saved in /home/oracle/.ssh/id_dsa.pub.
The key fingerprint is:
b6:07:42:ae:47:56:0a:a3:a5:bf:75:3e:21:85:8d:30
oracle@oradb4.sumsky.net
[oracle@oradb4 oracle]$
```

Perform this step on all nodes in the cluster. Keys generated from each of the nodes in the cluster should be appended to the authorized_keys file on all nodes, meaning that each node should contain the keys from all other nodes in the cluster.

```
[oracle@oradb4 oracle]$ cd .ssh
[oracle@oradb3 .ssh]$ cat id_dsa.pub > authorized_keys
```

After the keys have been created and copied to all nodes, `ora-cle` user accounts can connect from one node to another `oracle` account on another node without using a password. This allows for the OUI to copy files from the installing node to the other nodes in the cluster. The following output is the verification showing that the `ssh` command from node `ORADB3` to other nodes in the cluster worked:

```
[oracle@oradb3 oracle]$ ssh oradb3 hostname
oradb3.sumsky.net
[oracle@oradb3 oracle]$ ssh oradb4 hostname
oradb4.sumsky.net
[oracle@oradb3 oracle]$ ssh oradb3-priv hostname
oradb3.sumsky.net
[oracle@oradb3 oracle]$ ssh oradb4-priv hostname
oradb4.sumsky.net
```

Note: When performing these tests for the first time, the operating system will display a key and prompt the user to accept or decline. Enter `Yes` to accept and register the key. Tests should be performed on all other nodes across all interfaces (with the exception of the virtual IP [VIP]) in the cluster.

2. Configuration of network components

In addition to the public and private network already configured in Oracle 9i Release 2, Oracle Database 10*g* requires additional IP addresses that will be mapped to the public address as VIPs. The VIPs should be added to the `/etc/hosts` file on all nodes in the cluster, as well as all nodes accessing the database. Oracle recommends that the VIP be added to DNS.

```
root@oradb3 oracle]# more /etc/hosts
127.0.0.1       localhost.localdomain localhost
192.168.2.10    oradb1.sumsky.net oradb1
192.168.2.20    oradb2.sumsky.net oradb2
192.168.2.30    oradb3.sumsky.net oradb3
192.168.2.40    oradb4.sumsky.net oradb4
#Private Network/interconnect
10.168.2.110    oradb1-priv.sumsky.net oradb1-priv
```

```
10.168.2.120    oradb2-priv.sumsky.net oradb2-priv
10.168.2.130    oradb3-priv.sumsky.net oradb3-priv
10.168.2.140    oradb4-priv.sumsky.net oradb4-priv
# VIP
192.168.2.15    oradb1-vip.sumsky.net oradb1-vip
192.168.2.25    oradb2-vip.sumsky.net oradb2-vip
192.168.2.35    oradb3-vip.sumsky.net oradb3-vip
192.168.2.45    oradb4-vip.sumsky.net oradb4-vip
```

3. Installation of Oracle Clusterware

Oracle Database 10*g* introduced a new version of the cluster manager software called Oracle Clusterware (called Cluster Ready Services [CRS] in Oracle Database 10*g* Release 1). Oracle Clusterware differs from the Oracle Cluster Manager that exists in the Oracle 9i environment; it will have to be installed into a separate home.

Oracle Clusterware creates two different files: The Oracle Cluster Repository (OCR) and the Oracle Cluster Synchronization Service (CSS) voting disk. The Oracle 9i server manager file identified in /var/opt/oracle/srvConfig.loc that exists on the shared storage will become the new OCR file required in Oracle Database 10*g*. The voting disk (similar to the quorum disk in Oracle 9*i*) requires three isolated locations on the shared storage, and each should be 20 MB in size. Create three identical locations of 20 MB on the shared storage.

 Note: In Oracle Database 10*g* Release 2, Oracle also provides options to create and maintain redundant OCR files. Creation of redundant OCR files is covered in the "Housekeeping" section.

3.1   Three locations are on mount point /u02, /u03, and /u04. As they will be stored on OCFS, the devices need to be formatted and mounted on all nodes in the cluster.

```
[root@oradb3 root]# mkfs.ocfs -F -b 128 -L ora02 -m /u02 -u
200 -g 200 -p 0775 /dev/sdb6
Cleared volume header sectors
Cleared node config sectors
Cleared publish sectors
```

```
Cleared vote sectors
Cleared bitmap sectors
Cleared data block
Wrote volume header
```

Similarly, format the other two partitions using OCFS:

```
[root@oradb3 root]# mkfs.ocfs -F -b 128 -L ora03 -m /u03 -u 200 -g 200 -p
0775 /dev/sdb7
[root@oradb3 root]# mkfs.ocfs -F -b 128 -L ora04 -m /u04 -u 200 -g 200 -p
0775 /dev/sdb8
```

3.2   Mount these devices on all nodes using the following command:

```
mount -t ocfs /dev/sdb6 /u02
mount -t ocfs /dev/sdb7 /u03
mount -t ocfs /dev/sdb8 /u04
```

3.3   To allow the operating system to mount these devices every time the node is restarted, add devices to the /etc/fstab file:

```
[oracle@oradb3 oracle]$ more /etc/fstab
LABEL=/            /                    ext3    defaults        1 1
none               /dev/pts             devpts  gid=5,mode=620  0 0
none               /proc                proc    defaults        0 0
none               /dev/shm             tmpfs   defaults        0 0
/dev/sda2          swap                 swap    defaults        0 0
/dev/cdrom         /mnt/cdrom           udf,iso9660 noauto,owner,kudzu,r 0 0 0
/dev/fd0           /mnt/floppy          auto    noauto,owner,kudzu 0 0
/dev/sdb5          /u01                 ocfs    _netdev 0 0
/dev/sdb6          /u02                 ocfs    _netdev 0 0
/dev/sdb7          /u03                 ocfs    _netdev 0 0
/dev/sdb8          /u04                 ocfs    _netdev 0 0
/dev/sdb9          /u05                 ocfs    _netdev 0 0
/dev/sdb10         /u06                 ocfs    _netdev 0 0
/dev/sdb14         /u14                 ocfs    _netdev 0 0
```

3.4   Oracle has introduced a new utility called Oracle cluster verification utility (CVU). CVU is part of the clusterware software and can be located on the DVD media under the "Clusterware" directory. Using the various parameters, this utility can deter-

mine the status of the cluster during the various stages of installation and configuration as well as verify individual components
of the cluster.

The OUI automatically runs CVU at the end of the installation of Oracle Clusterware to verify its status. At this stage,
before beginning installation of the Oracle Clusterware, the following two verifications should be performed.

 Note: Read the instructions in the `clusterware/cluvfy` directory on the
DVD about how to install the CVU before installing Oracle Clusterware.

  a. If the hardware and operating system configuration is
     complete, then do the following:

```
[oracle@oradb3 bin]$ cluvfy stage -post hwos -n oradb1,oradb2,oradb3,oradb4
Performing post-checks for hardware and operating system setup
Checking node reachability...
Node reachability check passed from node "oradb3".
Checking user equivalence...
User equivalence check passed for user "oracle".
Checking node connectivity...
Node connectivity check passed for subnet "192.168.2.0" with node(s)
oradb4,oradb3,oradb2,oradb1.
Node connectivity check passed for subnet "10.168.2.0" with node(s)
oradb4,oradb3,oradb2,oradb1.
Suitable interfaces for the private interconnect on subnet "192.168.2.0":
Suitable interfaces for the private interconnect on subnet "192.168.2.0":
oradb4 eth0:192.168.2.40 eth0:192.168.2.45
oradb3 eth0:192.168.2.30 eth0:192.168.2.35
oradb2 eth0:192.168.2.20 eth0:192.168.2.25
oradb1 eth0:192.168.2.10 eth0:192.168.2.15
Suitable interfaces for the private interconnect on subnet "10.168.2.0":
oradb4 eth1:10.168.2.140
oradb3 eth1:10.168.2.130
oradb2 eth1:10.168.2.120
oradb1 eth1:10.168.2.110
Checking shared storage accessibility...
Shared storage check passed on nodes "oradb4,oradb3,oradb2,oradb1".
Post-check for hardware and operating system setup was successful on all the
nodes.
```

b. Perform appropriate checks on all the nodes in the node list before setting up OCFS:

```
[oracle@oradb3 oracle]$ cluvfy stage -pre cfs -n
oradb1,oradb2,oradb3,oradb4 -s /dev/sdb
```

c. Perform appropriate checks on all the nodes in the node list before setting up Oracle Clusterware:

```
[oracle@oradb3 cluvfy]$ cluvfy stage -pre crsinst -n
oradb1,oradb2,oradb3,oradb4
Performing pre-checks for cluster services setup
Checking node reachability...
Node reachability check passed from node "oradb1".
Checking user equivalence...
User equivalence check passed for user "oracle".
Checking administrative privileges...
User existence check passed for "oracle".
Group existence check passed for "oinstall".
Membership check for user "oracle" in group "oinstall" [as Primary]
failed.
Check failed on nodes:
        oradb4,oradb3,oradb2,oradb1
Administrative privileges check passed.
Checking node connectivity...
Node connectivity check passed for subnet "192.168.2.0" with node(s)
oradb4,oradb3,oradb2,oradb1.
Node connectivity check passed for subnet "10.168.2.0" with node(s)
oradb4,oradb3,oradb2,oradb1.
Suitable interfaces for the private interconnect on subnet
"192.168.2.0":
oradb4 eth0:192.168.2.40 eth0:192.168.2.45
oradb3 eth0:192.168.2.30 eth0:192.168.2.35
oradb2 eth0:192.168.2.20 eth0:192.168.2.25
oradb1 eth0:192.168.2.10 eth0:192.168.2.15
Suitable interfaces for the private interconnect on subnet
"10.168.2.0":
oradb4 eth1:10.168.2.140
oradb3 eth1:10.168.2.130
oradb2 eth1:10.168.2.120
oradb1 eth1:10.168.2.110
```

```
Checking system requirements for 'crs'...
Total memory check passed.
Check failed on nodes:
        oradb4,oradb3,oradb2,oradb1
Free disk space check passed.
Swap space check passed.
System architecture check passed.
Kernel version check passed.
Package existence check passed for "make-3.79".
Package existence check passed for "binutils-2.14".
Package existence check passed for "gcc-3.2".
Package existence check passed for "glibc-2.3.2-95.27".
Package existence check passed for "compat-db-4.0.14-5".
Package existence check passed for "compat-gcc-7.3-2.96.128".
Package existence check passed for "compat-gcc-c++-7.3-2.96.128".
Package existence check passed for "compat-libstdc++-7.3-2.96.128".
Package existence check passed for "compat-libstdc++-devel-7.3-
2.96.128".
Package existence check passed for "openmotif-2.2.3".
Package existence check passed for "setarch-1.3-1".
Group existence check passed for "dba".
Group existence check passed for "oinstall".
User existence check passed for "nobody".
System requirement failed for 'crs'
```
Pre-check for cluster services setup was successful on all the nodes.

3.5   Install Oracle Clusterware

Before installing the clusterware, shut down the Oracle database and the Oracle Database 9*i* listener. Ensure that the Oracle Database 9*i* Cluster Manager (oracm) and GSD are currently up and running on all nodes in the cluster.

Running the OUI requires that the terminal from where this installer is run be X-windows compatible. Otherwise, an appropriate X-windows emulator should be installed and the emulator invoked using the DISPLAY command using the following syntax:

```
export DISPLAY=<client IP address>:0.0
```

For example:

```
[oracle@oradb3 oracle]$export
DISPLAY=192.168.2.101:0.0
```

The OUI can be run from the DVD directly, or you can execute the installer after copying the contents from the DVD onto the hard disk. If executing from the DVD, change the directory to `cd /media/dvd/clusterware`. Execute the `runInstaller` file.

1. Unset `ORACLE_HOME`.

2. After the welcome, click the "Next" button.

3. Specify the CRS file locations, following the OFA standards and providing a separate home for CRS; an appropriate file location would be `/usr/app/oracle/product/10.2.0/crs`:

   ```
   Name: OraCr10g_home1
   Path: /usr/app/oracle/product/10.2.0/crs
   ```

4. Specify the cluster configuration:

   ```
   Cluster Name: SskyClst (Default 'crs')
   Cluster Nodes:
   ```

Public Node Name	Private Node Name	Virtual Host Name
oradb1	oradb1-priv	oradb1-vip
oradb2	oradb2-priv	oradb2-vip
oradb3	oradb3-priv	oradb3-vip
oradb4	oradb4-priv	oradb4-vip

5. Specify network interface usage:

Interface Name	Subnet	Interface Type
eth0	192.168.2.0	Public
eth1	192.168.2.0	Private

6. Specify the voting disk location: *Voting disk configuration.* Select "Normal Redundancy." (If Oracle Clusterware is to maintain redundant copies of the voting disk, and if external mirroring is available, select "External Redundancy.")

Voting Disk Location	/u02/oradata/CSSVoteDisk.dbf
Additional Voting Disk 1 Location	/u03/oradata/CSSVoteDisk.dbf
Additional Voting Disk 2 Location	/u04/oradata/CSSVoteDisk.dbf

7.   After the summary, click on "Install."

8.   Once installation is complete, OUI prompts to execute the /usr/
      app/oracle/product/10.2.0/crs/root.sh script on all nodes
      in the cluster, starting with the node where OUI is running. The
      root.sh file will create the CSS voting disk with the cluster
      information and start the required cluster service daemon pro-
      cesses. When the script is executed on the last node, apart from
      the cluster service daemon processes, the script will also configure
      the VIP and other cluster application services.

```
[root@oradb4 crs]# ./root.sh
WARNING: directory '/usr/app/oracle/product/10.2.0' is not
owned by root
WARNING: directory '/usr/app/oracle/product' is not owned by
root
WARNING: directory '/usr/app/oracle' is not owned by root
Checking to see if Oracle CRS stack is already configured
/etc/oracle does not exist. Creating it now.
Setting the permissions on OCR backup directory
Oracle Cluster Registry configuration upgraded successfully
WARNING: directory '/usr/app/oracle/product/10.2.0' is not
owned by root
WARNING: directory '/usr/app/oracle/product' is not owned by
root
WARNING: directory '/usr/app/oracle' is not owned by root
clscfg: EXISTING configuration version 3 detected.
clscfg: version 3 is 10G Release 2.
assigning default hostname oradb3 for node 1.
assigning default hostname oradb2 for node 2.
assigning default hostname oradb1 for node 3.
assigning default hostname oradb4 for node 4.
Successfully accumulated necessary OCR keys.
Using ports: CSS=49895 CRS=49896 EVMC=49898 and EVMR=49897.
node <nodenumber>: <nodename> <private interconnect name>
<hostname>
node 1: oradb3 oradb3-priv oradb3
node 2: oradb2 oradb2-priv oradb2
node 3: oradb1 oradb1-priv oradb1
node 4: oradb4 oradb4-priv oradb4
clscfg: Arguments check out successfully.
```

NO KEYS WERE WRITTEN. Supply -force parameter to override. -force is destructive and will destroy any previous cluster configuration.
Oracle Cluster Registry for cluster has already been initialized
Startup will be queued to init within 30+60 seconds.
Adding daemons to inittab
Expecting the CRS daemons to be up within 600 seconds.
CSS is active on these nodes.
       oradb3
       oradb2
       oradb1
       oradb4
CSS is active on all nodes.
Waiting for the Oracle CRSD and EVMD to start
Waiting for the Oracle CRSD and EVMD to start
Waiting for the Oracle CRSD and EVMD to start
Waiting for the Oracle CRSD and EVMD to start
Oracle CRS stack installed and running under init(1M)
Running vipca(silent) for configuring nodeapps

Creating VIP application resource on (4) nodes...
Creating GSD application resource on (4) nodes...
Creating ONS application resource on (4) nodes...
Starting VIP application resource on (4) nodes...
Starting GSD application resource on (4) nodes...
Starting ONS application resource on (4) nodes...
Done

On completion of the Oracle Clusterware installation, the following files are created in their respective directories:

    a.   Clusterware files are provided:

```
[root@oradb3 root]# ls -ltr /etc/init.d/init.*
-r-xr-xr-x   1 root      root        3197 Aug 13 23:32 /etc/init.d/init.evmd
-r-xr-xr-x   1 root      root       35401 Aug 13 23:32 /etc/init.d/init.cssd
-r-xr-xr-x   1 root      root        4721 Aug 13 23:32 /etc/init.d/init.crsd
-r-xr-xr-x   1 root      root        1951 Aug 13 23:32 /etc/init.d/init.crs
[root@oradb3 root]#
```

b. The operating system–provided `inittab` file is updated with the following entries:

```
[root@oradb3 root]# tail -5 /etc/inittab
# Run xdm in runlevel 5
x:5:respawn:/etc/X11/prefdm -nodaemon
h1:35:respawn:/etc/init.d/init.evmd run >/dev/null 2>&1 </dev/null
h2:35:respawn:/etc/init.d/init.cssd fatal >/dev/null 2>&1 </dev/null
h3:35:respawn:/etc/init.d/init.crsd run >/dev/null 2>&1 </dev/null
```

c. The server configuration file locater present in the `/var/opt/Oracle` directory is nulled with the following value:

```
[root@oradb3 root]# more /var/opt/oracle/srvConfig.loc
srvconfig_loc=/dev/null
```

d. The installer updates a new locater file, identified by `ocr.loc` present in the `/etc/oracle` directory, with the repository location information:

```
[root@oradb3 root]# more /etc/oracle/ocr.loc
ocrconfig_loc=/u01/oradata/SrvConfig.dbf
local_only=FALSE
```

9. Click "OK" after the `root.sh` script has run on all nodes.

10. Ensure completion of all configuration assistants: (Oracle Notification Server Configuration Assistant, Oracle Private Interconnect Configuration Assistant and Oracle Cluster Verification Utility).

11. At the end of installation, click "Exit."

12. Verify if the clusterware has all the nodes registered using the `olsnodes` command:

```
[oracle@oradb1 oracle]$ olsnodes
oradb1
oradb2
oradb3
oradb4
[oracle@oradb1 oracle]$
```

13.   Verify if the cluster service is started, using the `crs_stat` command:

```
[oracle@oradb1 oracle]$ crs_stat -t
Name                Type          Target    State     Host
------------------------------------------------------------
ora.oradb1.gsd application    ONLINE    ONLINE    oradb1
ora.oradb1.ons application    ONLINE    ONLINE    oradb1
ora.oradb1.vip application    ONLINE    ONLINE    oradb1
ora.oradb2.gsd application    ONLINE    ONLINE    oradb2
ora.oradb2.ons application    ONLINE    ONLINE    oradb2
ora.oradb2.vip application    ONLINE    ONLINE    oradb2
ora.oradb3.gsd application    ONLINE    ONLINE    oradb3
ora.oradb3.ons application    ONLINE    ONLINE    oradb3
ora.oradb3.vip application    ONLINE    ONLINE    oradb3
ora.oradb4.gsd application    ONLINE    ONLINE    oradb4
ora.oradb4.ons application    ONLINE    ONLINE    oradb4
ora.oradb4.vip application    ONLINE    ONLINE    oradb4
```

14.   Verify if the VIP services are configured at the operating system level:

The VIP address is configured and added to the operating system network configuration, and the network services are started. The VIP configuration can be verified using the `ifconfig` command at the operating system level:

```
[oracle@oradb3 oracle]$ ifconfig -a
eth0     Link encap:Ethernet  HWaddr 00:D0:B7:6A:39:85
         inet addr:192.168.2.30  Bcast:192.168.2.255
Mask:255.255.255.0
         UP BROADCAST RUNNING MASTER MULTICAST  MTU:1500  Metric:1
         RX packets:123 errors:0 dropped:0 overruns:0 frame:0
         TX packets:67 errors:0 dropped:0 overruns:0 carrier:0
         collisions:0 txqueuelen:0
         RX bytes:11935 (11.6 Kb)  TX bytes:5051 (4.9 Kb)

eth0:1   Link encap:Ethernet  HWaddr 00:D0:B7:6A:39:85
         inet addr:192.168.2.35  Bcast:192.168.3.255
Mask:255.255.252.0
         UP BROADCAST RUNNING MASTER MULTICAST  MTU:1500  Metric:1
```

```
RX packets:14631 errors:0 dropped:0 overruns:0 frame:0
TX packets:21377 errors:0 dropped:0 overruns:0 carrier:0
collisions:0 txqueuelen:0
RX bytes:6950046 (6.6 Mb)  TX bytes:19706526 (18.7 Mb)
```

 Note: The ":1" in "eth0:1" indicates that the VIP address for the basic host is eth0. When the node fails, eth0:1 will be moved to one of the surviving nodes in the cluster. The new identifier for the VIP on the failed-over server will be indicated by eth0:2 or higher, depending on what other nodes have failed in the cluster and had their VIPs migrated.

4. Installation of Oracle software

    a.   At the welcome screen, click "Next."

    b.   Select installation type "Enterprise Edition."

    c.   Specify home details:

```
Name: OraDb10g_home1
Path: /usr/app/oracle/product/10.2.0/db_1
```

    d.   Specify the hardware cluster installation mode:

```
Select "Cluster Installation"
Click on "Select All"
```

    e.   Verify that all product-specific prerequisite checks are successful before proceeding.

The following checks are performed:

- Checking physical memory requirements (expected 922 MB)
- Checking swap space (expected 824 MB)
- Checking network configuration requirements
- Oracle supports installation on systems with DHCP-assigned public IP. However, the primary network interface should be configured with a static IP address.
- Validating ORACLE_BASE location
- Checking ORACLE_HOME path for space
- Checking for system clean-up
- Checking for Oracle home incompatibilities
- Checking Oracle Clusterware version

     f.   Select the configuration option.

        ■ Select "Install database Software only"

     g. After the summary, click on "Install."

     h. When installation is complete, OUI will prompt you to execute the `/usr/app/oracle/product/10.2.0/db_1/root.sh` script from another window as the `root` user on all nodes in the cluster.

     i.   Click on "OK" after `root.sh` has run on all nodes.

     j.   At the end of installation, click on "Exit."

15.   Database upgrade

Oracle provides three methods by which the database can be upgraded from Oracle Database 9*i* Release 2 to Oracle Database 10*g* Release 2:

     a. Using the database upgrade assistant (DBUA) through the OUI

     b. Using the DBUA in silent mode

     c. Manually using Oracle-provided upgrade scripts.

5.1   Using the DBUA through the OUI

This is the most convenient and a more completely automated method for the upgrade. The DBUA, when invoked, will perform all of the tasks required from conversion to migration to adding all additional features present in Oracle Database 10*g* Release 2.

Requirements:

1.   Make a full cold backup of the database before commencing the upgrade process.

2.   The `/etc/oratab` file should have the 9i database listed.

3.   Oracle 9i Cluster Manager (`oracm`) should be up and running on all nodes.

4.   Oracle 9i Listener should be running on all nodes, and the database services should be registered.

5.   The Oracle 9i database and all instances should be up and running on all respective nodes in the cluster.

1.   At the welcome screen read instructions and click on "Next."

2.   *Step 1 of 9: Databases.* A list of all available databases (SSKYDB) on the node is displayed. Select the database to upgrade, enter the password for username (sys), and click on "Next."

3.   *Step 2 of 9: SYSAUX Tablespace.* Oracle Database 10g requires the SYSAUX tablespace be created. If the definition and characteristics of the tablespace are satisfactory, click on "Next."

4.   *Step 3 of 9: Recompile Invalid Objects.* Select "Recompile invalid objects at the end of upgrade", click on "Next."

5.   *Step 4 of 9: Server Parameter File.* Select "Use Server Parameter File (SPFILE)," click on "Next."

6.   *Step 5 of 9: Backup.* Select "I have already backed up my database," if a valid backup of the database is available; otherwise, select "I would like this tool to back up the database" and specify the backup directory. Click on "Next."

7.   *Step 6 of 9: Management Options.* Select the appropriate management option.

8.   *Step 7 of 9: Database Credentials.* Select "Use Different Passwords" and enter the passwords for the DBSNMP and SYSMAN users.

9.   *Step 8 of 9: Database Services.* Add all the desired services and their details.

10.   *Step 9 of 9: Summary.* After verifying the "Database Upgrade Summary," click on "Finish" to begin the upgrade operation.

11.   *Progress.* The DBUA performs the various steps to complete the upgrade process.

12.   *Summary.* Displays the upgrade summary. Click on "Exit."

13.   At this stage, the following is the status of the upgrade:

      a.   The database has been upgraded from Oracle Database 9i Release 2 to Oracle Database 10g Release 2.

      b.   The datafiles reside on OCFS 1.0.

      c.   Like all other datafiles, the spfile resides on a shared file system.

      d.   A new OEM DB console has been configured on port 1158.

14.   Verify if the database upgrade and all required components have been upgraded.

a.   Verify if all the required modules have been upgraded using the following Oracle-provided script:

```
SQL> @$ORACLE_HOME/rdbms/admin/utlu102s.sql
```

b.   Verify if all instances in the cluster are started.

c.   The DBUA has configured the OEM DB console at the following address location:

```
http://oradb3.sumsky.com:1158/em
```

■ Verify if the DB console is up and running using the enterprise Manager control utility (emctl):

```
[oracle@oradb3 oracle]$ emctl status dbconsole
TZ set to US/Eastern
Oracle Enterprise Manager 10g Database Control Release 10.2.0.1.0
Copyright (c) 1996, 2005 Oracle Corporation.  All rights reserved.
http://oradb3.sumsky.com:1158/em/console/aboutApplication
Oracle Enterprise Manager 10g is running.
------------------------------------------------------------------
Logs are generated in directory /usr/app/oracle/product/10.2.0/db_1/
oradb3_SSKY1/sysman/log
[oracle@oradb3 oracle]$
```

5. Housekeeping

1.   Set up redundancy for OCR files.

Unlike in Oracle Database 9*i*, the importance of OCR in Oracle Database 10*g* has increased dramatically. OCR is used by the Oracle Clusterware to determine what services and applications need to be started during the startup of the instance, what services have been configured for the HA solution and have been defined for failover when the current holding instance fails, and so on.

With the information contained in the OCR, Oracle Database 10*g* Release 2 supports duplexing of the OCR file.

While the DBCA prompts the DBA with the OCR duplexing screen during a fresh install of Oracle Database 10*g* Release 2, it does not provide the option during an upgrade. The upgrade simply converts the OCR repository from Oracle 9*i* to Oracle 10*g*, but does not duplex.

If external hardware mirroring is not available for the disk containing the OCR file, a redundant copy of the OCR file will have to be generated manually using the Oracle-provided OCR configuration utility (`ocrconfig`):

Syntax:

```
ocrconfig —replace  ocrmirror <new location>


[root@oradb4 root]# ocrconfig -replace ocr /u03/
oradata/SrvConfig.dbf
```

 Note: The OCR configuration utility generates a log file for all operations in the directory:

```
$ORACLE_HOME/log/<hostname>/client/ocrconfig_<pid>.log
```

---

2.   Backup the OCR files.

During the clusterware installation, an automatic backup feature is also configured to back up the OCR files from the clusterware master node that has been up continuously for a duration of four hours. The backup operation and file destinations could be verified using the OCR configuration utility.

```
[oracle@oradb3 oracle]$ ocrconfig –showbackup
oradb4     2005/08/18 18:14:59      /usr/app/oracle/product/
10.2.0/crs/cdata/SskyClst
oradb4     2005/08/18 14:14:59      /usr/app/oracle/product/
10.2.0/crs/cdata/SskyClst
oradb4     2005/08/18 10:14:58      /usr/app/oracle/product/
10.2.0/crs/cdata/SskyClst
oradb4     2005/08/18 02:14:57      /usr/app/oracle/product/
10.2.0/crs/cdata/SskyClst
```

This command indicates that the backup for the OCR file has been running from node `oradb4` on its locale storage; however, it does not indicate the actual backups. The backup files can be listed using the following:

```
[oracle@oradb4 oracle]$ cd /usr/app/oracle/product/10.2.0/crs/cdata/
SskyClst/

[oracle@oradb4 SskyClst]$ ls -ltr
total 19620
-rw-r--r--    1 root      root          4014080 Aug 18 02:14 week.ocr
-rw-r--r--    1 root      root          4014080 Aug 18 02:14 day.ocr
-rw-r--r--    1 root      root          4014080 Aug 18 10:14 backup02.ocr
-rw-r--r--    1 root      root          4014080 Aug 18 14:14 backup01.ocr
-rw-r--r--    1 root      root          4014080 Aug 18 18:14 backup00.ocr
[oracle@oradb4 SskyClst]$
```

The above indicates three outputs, backup00.ocr, backup01.ocr, and backup02.ocr, that are four hours apart. Apart from the backup maintained for the last 12 hours (three backups 4 hours apart), Oracle also maintains one backup file for the day (day.ocr) and another for the week (week.ocr).

Storing OCR backups on the local storage of any single node limits access to the file when that node fails, creating a single point of failure. For example, if node oradb4 has failed, the OCR backup files cannot be accessed from other files in the cluster. The backup destination has to be moved to shared storage, providing access to all nodes in the cluster using the backuploc parameter.

```
ocrconfig -backuploc < new location of backup>
```

The following command will change the OCR backup destination to shared storage located at /u13/oradata/Sskyclst:

```
[root@oradb4 root]# ocrconfig -backuploc /u13/oradata/
Sskyclst
```

3.   Set up environment variables.

For easy administration and navigation between the various disk locations, several different environment variables should be defined in the login profile, for example,

```
[oracle@oradb3 oracle]$ more .bash_profile
# .bash_profile
```

```
# Get the aliases and functions
if [ -f ~/.bashrc ]; then
        . ~/.bashrc
fi
# User specific environment and startup programs
export ORACLE_BASE=/usr/app/oracle
export ORACLE_HOME=$ORACLE_BASE/product/10.2.0/db_1
export ORA_CRS_HOME=$ORACLE_BASE/product/10.2.0/crs
export ASM_HOME=$ORACLE_BASE/product/10.2.0/asm
export AGENT_HOME=/usr/app/oracle/product/10.2.0/EMAgent

export PATH=.:${PATH}:$HOME/bin:$ORACLE_HOME/bin
export PATH=${PATH}:$ORA_CRS_HOME/bin
export PATH=${PATH}:/usr/bin:/bin:/usr/bin/X11:/usr/local/bin:/sbin
export ORACLE_ADMIN=$ORACLE_BASE/admin
export TNS_ADMIN=$ORACLE_HOME/network/admin

export LD_ASSUME_KERNEL=2.4.19
export LD_LIBRARY=$ORACLE_HOME/lib
export LD_LIBRARY=${LD_LIBRARY}:/lib:/usr/lib:/usr/local/bin
export LD_LIBRARY=${LD_LIBRARY}:$ORA_CRS_HOME/lib

export CLASSPATH=$ORACLE_HOME/JRE
export CLASSPATH=${CLASSPATH}:$ORACLE_HOME/jlib
export CLASSPATH=${CLASSPATH}:$ORACLE_HOME/rdbms/jlib
export CLASSPATH=${CLASSPATH}:$ORACLE_HOME/network/jlib
export THREADS_FLAG=native
export ORACLE_SID=SSKY1
```

4.   Remove Oracle 9i Release 2 home.

If this is the only database that was present in the cluster and there are no more Oracle 9i Release 2 databases, the Oracle 9i Release 2 home and other related components can be uninstalled and removed from the servers.

E.2   **Data migration from OCFS to ASM**

In the first part of this section, an Oracle Database 9i Release 2 database was upgraded to Oracle Database 10*g* Release 2. In this section the steps required to migrate the data from OCFS to ASM are discussed.

OCFS 1.0 was introduced in Oracle Database 9i to make management of database files in a clustered environment such as RAC easier on environments such as Linux and Windows. Prior to this, management of files depended on creating raw partitions to enable sharing of files between multiple instances in the cluster. OCFS 1.0, although written for a clustered environments, had several limitations (e.g., it did not permit storing of non-Oracle files, and it did not follow any true standards).

OCFS 2.0 released recently for Linux kernel 2.6 and Windows 2003 server removes these barriers present in its predecessor version by allowing non-Oracle files to be stored, providing opportunities for having a single Oracle home for the entire cluster. While several of the limitations that existed in version 1.0 have been removed, OCFS continues to carry limitations present in any traditional volume management software, such as Veritas File System, Tru64, or raw devices, meaning functions such as adding or removing of disks from an already existing volume are not possible without bouncing through heaps and loops. Such limitations have been totally eliminated when using ASM.

Oracle ASM, introduced in Oracle Database 10*g* Release 1, alleviates the need for clustered file systems and third-party volume managers to store Oracle database files. ASM is also limited, however, to storing Oracle database files and isn't suitable for storing Oracle Clusterware–specific files or a shared Oracle home. (A shared Oracle home is supported starting with OCFS 2.0.)

Apart from being built into the Oracle kernel, this new technology provides great benefits to a DBA in the areas of volume management, dynamic rebalancing of file extents, and performance benefits. The full description of Oracle ASM is beyond our scope here, but technical information is available at OTN's Oracle ASM homepage //www.oracle.com/technology/products/database/asm/index.html.

1. Set dependencies and prerequisites.

Disks for ASM can be set up as pure raw disks, or raw logical units (LUNs) or using Oracle-provided library files. In this section, we will discuss the usage of setting up disks for ASM using the library files.

1.1   Download and install the following (optional) ASM library packages for your Linux distribution from OTN:

 a.   oracleasm-support-2.4.0-1.i386.rpm

       b.   oracleasm-2.4.21-27.EL-1.0.4-2.i686.rpm (driver for UP kernel) or oracleasm-2.4.21-27.ELsmp-1.0.4-1.i686.rpm (driver for SMP kernel)

       c.   oracleasmlib-2.0.0-1.i386.rpm

1.2   Install the ASM library packages.

Connect to the node as the user root to install the packages as follows:

```
# su root
# rpm -Uvh oracleasm-support-1.0.2-1.i386.rpm \
                    oracleasmlib-1.0.0-1.i386.rpm\
                    oracleasm-2.4.21-EL-1.0.0-1.i686.rpm
Preparing... #####################################
[100%]
```

This output shows the installation of the ASM library packages on Red Hat Enterprise Linux (RHEL) 3 update 4 or RHEL 4. Install these packages on all nodes in the cluster.

1.3   Set up disks using the ASM Library (ASMlib)

The installation of the ASM library packages places a utility in the /etc/init.d/ directory called oracleasm. This utility is used to configure and initialize the various disks for ASM. The next step is to configure ASM:

```
# /etc/init.d/oracleasm configure
Configuring the Oracle ASM library driver.

This will configure the on-boot properties of the Oracle ASM library
driver.  The following questions will determine whether the driver is
loaded on boot and what permissions it will have.  The current values
will be shown in brackets ('[]').  Hitting without typing an answer
will keep that current value.  Ctrl-C will abort.

Default user to own the driver interface []: oracle
Default group to own the driver interface []: dba
Start Oracle ASM library driver on boot (y/n) [n]: y
Fix permissions of Oracle ASM disks on boot (y/n) [y]: y
Writing Oracle ASM library driver configuration          [  OK  ]
Creating /dev/oracleasm mount point                      [  OK  ]
```

```
Loading module "oracleasm"                                    [  OK  ]
Mounting ASMlib driver filesystem                            [  OK  ]
Scanning system for ASM disks                                [  OK  ]
```

Note: ASM should be configured similarly on all nodes participating in the cluster.

Once the ASMlib configuration is complete, the ASMlib modules for Linux are loaded, and scripts are configured to load them again at system boot time. The loading of the modules after system reboot may be verified using the lsmod command, as follows:

```
# lsmod
Module                 Size  Used by      Tainted: GF
parport_pc            18724  2  (autoclean)
lp                     8932  0  (autoclean)
parport               36800  2  (autoclean) [parport_pc lp]
autofs                13204  0  (autoclean) (unused)
oracleasm             14224  1
ocfs                 297856  7
audit                 89592  1
```

1.4   Create ASM disk volumes.

This step is performed to initialize the disk volumes using the ASM library. Performing this step will make the disks available to ASM to configure into disk groups. This step is also performed using the oracleasm script:

```
/etc/init.d/oracleasm createdisk <volume name> <physical disk name>

# /etc/init.d/oracleasm createdisk AVOL11 /dev/sdg
  Creating Oracle ASM disk "AVOL11"                          [  OK  ]
# /etc/init.d/oracleasm createdisk AVOL12 /dev/sdg
  Creating Oracle ASM disk "AVOL12"                          [  OK  ]
# /etc/init.d/oracleasm createdisk AVOL13 /dev/sdg
  Creating Oracle ASM disk "AVOL13"                          [  OK  ]
```

1.5　Verify disk creation.

The `listdisks` parameter can be used with the `oracleasm` utility to verify that all of the disks configured are visible to ASM:

```
$ /etc/init.d/oracleasm listdisks
AVOL11
AVOL12
AVOL13
[oracle@oradb3 oracle]$
```

2.　Install ASM and create the ASM instances.

Once the disk volumes have been created using the Oracle-provided ASM utilities, the next step is to create an ASM instance.

In Oracle Database 10*g* Release 2, Oracle provides an option to install ASM in a separate home, which provides advantages in configuration management. In particular, it allows for upgrading the version of ASM while maintaining multiple versions of RDBMS.

If ASM is to be configured in a separate home, installation steps to install Oracle discussed in the first part of this section will have to be repeated, now to a new home (`ASM_HOME`) location (e.g., `/usr/app/oracle/product/10.2.0/asm`). However, if no separate home is configured, ASM instances can be created using the Database Configuration Assistant (DBCA) available under the original `ORACLE_HOME` as described below.

An ASM instance is created using the DBCA.

2.1　Start `dbca`:

```
$ dbca
```

2.2　At the welcome screen select Oracle Real Application Clusters database and click on "Next."

2.3　*Step 1 of 15: Options.* Select "Configure Automatic Storage Management."

2.4　*Step 2 of 4: Node Selection.* Click on "Select All" to select all nodes in the list of nodes.

2.5   *Step 3 of 4: Create ASM Instance.*

■ Add password for user SYS.

■ Select "Create server parameter file (SPFILE)." Specify a destination on the shared storage. Once these parameters are
entered, DBCA will start creating the ASM instances on all
nodes in the cluster.

■ Click on "OK" to confirm creation of ASM instances.

2.6   *Step 3 of 3: ASM Disk Groups.* List any available ASM disk
groups. If a new group needs to be created, click on "Create
New."

2.7   *Step 5 of 5: Create Disk Group.* A list of ASM-ready volumes is
listed. Enter a valid ASM disk group name (ASMGRP1) and select
the volumes to be part of this group (ORCL:AVOL11 and
ORCL:AVOL12). Click on "OK" when selection is complete. This
will create the disk group ASMGRP1 and mount the disk group on
all ASM instances.

Note: Depending on the number of datafiles to be migrated, multiple ASM
disk groups may be required.

2.8   Click on "Finish" when all required disk groups are created.

2.9   Verify if the ASM instances are up and running using the following operating system command:

```
$ ps -ef | grep asm_
oracle     7450     1  0 22:45 ?        00:00:00 asm_pmon_+ASM1
oracle     7452     1  0 22:45 ?        00:00:00 asm_diag_+ASM1
oracle     7455     1  0 22:45 ?        00:00:00 asm_psp0_+ASM1
oracle     7464     1  0 22:45 ?        00:00:01 asm_lmon_+ASM1
oracle     7475     1  0 22:45 ?        00:00:00 asm_lmd0_+ASM1
oracle     7479     1  0 22:45 ?        00:00:00 asm_lms0_+ASM1
oracle     7491     1  0 22:45 ?        00:00:00 asm_mman_+ASM1
oracle     7493     1  0 22:45 ?        00:00:00 asm_dbw0_+ASM1
oracle     7495     1  0 22:45 ?        00:00:00 asm_lgwr_+ASM1
oracle     7497     1  0 22:45 ?        00:00:00 asm_ckpt_+ASM1
oracle     7499     1  0 22:45 ?        00:00:00 asm_smon_+ASM1
oracle     7501     1  0 22:45 ?        00:00:00 asm_rbal_+ASM1
oracle     7503     1  0 22:45 ?        00:00:00 asm_gmon_+ASM1
```

```
oracle     7554   1   0 22:45 ?        00:00:00 asm_lck0 +ASM1
oracle     8504   1   0 22:46 ?        00:00:00 asm_pz99 +ASM1
oracle    12959   1   0 22:49 ?        00:00:00 asm_pz98 +ASM1
```

2.10   Verify if the ASM disk group is created and mounted successfully:

```
$ export ORACLE_SID=+ASM1
$ sqlplus '/as sysdba'
SQL*Plus: Release 10.2.0.1.0 - Production on Wed Aug 17 22:52:09 2005
Copyright (c) 1982, 2005, Oracle.  All rights reserved.
Connected to:
Oracle Database 10g Enterprise Edition Release 10.2.0.1.0 -
Production
With the Partitioning, Real Application Clusters, OLAP and Data Mining
options
```

```
SQL> SELECT INST_ID,NAME,STATE,TYPE FROM GV$ASM_DISKGROUP;
```

INST_ID	NAME	STATE	TYPE
1	ASMGRP1	MOUNTED	NORMAL
2	ASMGRP1	MOUNTED	NORMAL
3	ASMGRP1	MOUNTED	NORMAL
4	ASMGRP1	MOUNTED	NORMAL

3. Migrate datafiles to ASM

Oracle supports conversion of the entire database or a subset of datafiles to ASM via two methods: Recovery Manager (RMAN) and Enterprise Manager (EM) 10*g*. In this section, we describe this process using EM.

3.11   First, verify the current datafiles in the database using SQL Plus:

```
SQL> select name from v$datafile;

NAME
------------------------------------------------------
/u14/oradata/SSKYDB/system01.dbf
/u14/oradata/SSKYDB/undotbs01.dbf
```

```
/u14/oradata/SSKYDB/tools01.dbf
/u14/oradata/SSKYDB/users01.dbf
/u14/oradata/SSKYDB/cwmlite01.dbf
/u14/oradata/SSKYDB/drysys01.dbf
/u14/oradata/SSKYDB/indx01.dbf
/u14/oradata/SSKYDB/xdb01.dbf
/u14/oradata/SSKYDB/undotbs02.dbf
. . .
. . .
```

3.12   Verify if the EM console is started using the `emctl` utility:

```
$ emctl status dbconsole
TZ set to US/Eastern
Oracle Enterprise Manager 10g Database Control Release 10.2.0.1.0
Copyright (c) 1996, 2005 Oracle Corporation.  All rights reserved.
http://oradb3.sumsky.com:1158/em/console/aboutApplication
Oracle Enterprise Manager 10g is running.
----------------------------------------------------------------
Logs are generated in directory /usr/app/oracle/product/10.2.0/db_1/
oradb3_SSKY1/sysman/log
```

If the DB console is not started, it can be started using the following command:

```
$ emctl start dbconsole
TZ set to US/Eastern
Oracle Enterprise Manager 10g Database Control Release 10.2.0.1.0
Copyright (c) 1996, 2005 Oracle Corporation.  All rights reserved.
http://oradb3.sumsky.com:1158/em/console/aboutApplication
Starting Oracle Enterprise Manager 10g Database Control........
started.
----------------------------------------------------------------
Logs are generated in directory /usr/app/oracle/product/10.2.0/db_1/
oradb3_SSKY1/sysman/log
```

3.13   Invoke the EM DB console by connecting a browser to the following address:

```
http://oradb3.sumsky.net:1158/em
```

3.14   Select the "Administrator" tab on this main page.

3.15   Under the "Change Database" section, select the "Migrate to ASM" option.

3.16   Enter the SYS password and the "Host Credentials" where the ASM instance will be created.

3.17   Map the existing datafiles to the appropriate ASM diskgroups. Once this is complete, EM will create a job to perform the task. OEM uses DBMS_SCHEDULER to create and schedule the job.

3.18   Next is the review screen, highlighting the files that will be migrated to ASM.

3.19   After verifying if the datafiles have been mapped to the appropriate disk groups, click on "Submit" to submit the job and start the migration process. Once the job has been submitted successfully, a verification screen is displayed.

3.20   At this stage, the job will perform the following actions automatically:

- Shut down all instances in the cluster

- Mount the database on one instance, normally the instance from which the DB console is invoked

- Copy the files to the ASM disk group and rename them in the control file

- Drop the temp files

- Open the database

- Add the temp files in the ASM disk group

- Drop the log files and create them in the ASM disk group with two members

 Note: The alert log of the instance where the DB console is executed provides a step-by-step set of actions performed by Oracle to complete the migration.

3.21   Verify against the alert log file to confirm status of the migration process.

3.22   Once this is complete, verify the confirmation using the following query:

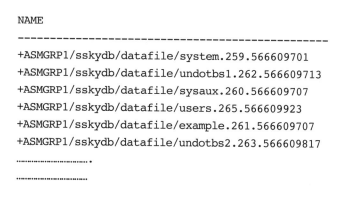

```
SQL> SELECT NAME FROM V$DATAFILE;

NAME
----------------------------------------------------
+ASMGRP1/sskydb/datafile/system.259.566609701
+ASMGRP1/sskydb/datafile/undotbs1.262.566609713
+ASMGRP1/sskydb/datafile/sysaux.260.566609707
+ASMGRP1/sskydb/datafile/users.265.566609923
+ASMGRP1/sskydb/datafile/example.261.566609707
+ASMGRP1/sskydb/datafile/undotbs2.263.566609817
..............................·
..............................
```

```
SQL> SHOW PARAMETER PFILE

NAME                  TYPE         VALUE
--------------------  -----------  ------------------------------
spfile                string       +ASMGRP1/sskydb/spfilessky2.ora_22
```

```
SQL> SHOW PARAMETER RECOVERY_FILE

NAME                                  TYPE         VALUE
------------------------------------  -----------  ----------------
db_recovery_file_dest                 string       +ASMGRP1
db_recovery_file_dest_size            big integer  2280M
```

Congratulations! You have successfully migrated your datafiles from OCFS to Oracle ASM.

Command-line utility

A command-line interface introduced in Oracle Database 10*g* Release 2 provides visibility into the disk layout and file layout structure that ASM has implemented when creating the disk groups and files stored on these disk groups. The command-line interface utility is called asmcmd.

The environment variables ORACLE_HOME and ORACLE_SID determine the instance to which the program connects, and asmcmd establishes a connection to it, in the same manner as a sqlplus / as sysdba. The user must be a member of the SYSDBA group.

```
$ export ORACLE_SID=+ASM1
$ asmcmd
ASMCMD>
```

The commands supported by asmcmd are similar to Linux and Unix commands. For example, to look at the contents of the storage disks, use ls from the asmcmd command prompt:

```
ASMCMD> ls -ltr
State    Type    Rebal  Unbal  Name
MOUNTED  NORMAL  N      N      ASMGRP2/
MOUNTED  NORMAL  N      N      ASMGRP1/
```

Similarly, you can change the directory to any of the groups using the cd command from the asmcmd command prompt. For example:

```
ASMCMD [+] > cd ASMGRP1
ASMCMD [+ASMGRP1] > ls -ltr
Type  Redund  Striped  Time       Sys  Name
                                  Y    SSKYDB/
```

E.3   Conclusion

In this two-part appendix, we discussed the steps required to migrate an Oracle Database 9*i* Release 2 RAC configuration to an Oracle Database 10*g* Release 2 environment; subsequently we also discussed how the data can be migrated from OCFS to Oracle ASM using the Enterprise Manager 10*g* dbcontrol.

F

Adding Additional Nodes to an Existing Oracle 10g R2 Cluster on Linux

 Note: This is an extract of an article by Murali Vallath that appeared on the Oracle Technology Network (www.oracle.com/technology/index.html); it is included here with permission.

One of the primary business requirements of a RAC configuration is scalability of the database tier in the entire system. This means that when the number of users increases as the business grows, additional instances can be added to the cluster, thus distributing the load. In Oracle Database 10g, this specific feature of adding nodes has become much easier compared to previous releases. Oracle incorporates the plug-and-play feature with a few minimum steps of setup, after the node /instance is brought to a usable state.

In this section, we will discuss the steps required to add a node to an existing RAC cluster.

F.1   Current environment

The environment selected for the upgrade is a four-node Red Hat Linux cluster, as illustrated in Figure F.1. The task is to add an additional node, making it a five-node cluster.

To make the discussion process easier, we will group the process into the following steps:

1.   Dependencies and prerequisites

2.   Configuration of network components

3.   Establishing user equivalence with ssh.

Database Name	Number of Nodes	Database Version	Number of Instances	O/S Kernel Version	File System	Cluster Manager
SSKYDB	Four nodes: oradb1, oradb2, oradb3, and oradb4	10.2.0.1	Four instances: SSKY1, SSKY2, SSKY3, and SSKY4	Red Hat Advanced Server 3.0 Linux sum-sky.net 2.4.21-32.ELsmp	OCFS 1.0 and ASM	Oracle Clusterware

Figure F.1
Oracle 10g Release 2 RAC Environment

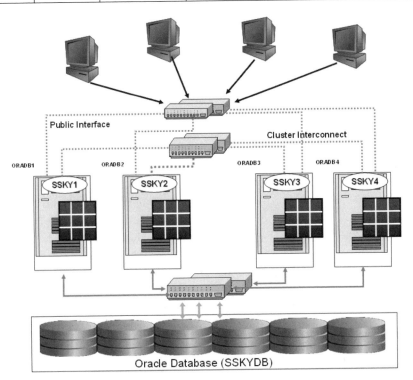

4. Installation of Oracle Clusterware

5. Installation of Oracle software

6. Addition of New Instance(s)

7. Housekeeping

1. **Dependencies and prerequisites**

The first primary step in any software installation or upgrade is to ensure that a complete backup of the system is available. This includes the operating system and data files. Then, the next step is to verify the system requirements, operating system versions, and all application patch levels. The new node should have the identical version of the operating system, including all patches required for Oracle. In this scenario, since the operating system residing on nodes 1 through 4 is Red Hat Linux 3.0 the new node should have the same version. To keep the naming conventions identical to the previous nodes, the new node is named oradb5. Apart from the basic operating system, the following packages required by Oracle should also be installed:

1.1   Install and verify the required additional operating system packages:

Log in to the system as user root and install the following rpm files:

```
[root@oradb5 root]# rpm -qa | grep -i gcc
compat-gcc-c++-7.3-2.96.128
compat-gcc-7.3-2.96.128
libgcc-3.2.3-42
gcc-3.2.3-42
[root@oradb5 root]# rpm -qa | grep -i openmotif
openmotif-2.2.3-3.RHEL3
openmotif21-2.1.30-8
[root@oradb5 root]# rpm -qa | grep -i glibc
glibc-2.3.3-74
glibc-utils-2.3.3-74
glibc-kernheaders-2.4-8.34.1
glibc-common-2.3.3-74
glibc-headers-2.3.3-74
glibc-devel-2.3.3-74
[root@oradb5 root]# rpm -qa | grep -i compat
compat-libstdc++-7.3-2.96.128
compat-gcc-c++-7.3-2.96.128
compat-gcc-7.3-2.96.128
compat-db-4.0.14-5
compat-libstdc++-devel-7.3-2.96.128
[root@oradb5 root]#
```

1.2   Update the kernel parameters with the following values:

```
kernel.core_uses_pid = 1
kernel.hostname = oradb5.sumsky.net
kernel.domainname = sumsky.net
kernel.shmall = 2097152
#kernel.shmmax = 536870912
kernel.shmmax = 2147483648
kernel.shmmni = 4096
kernel.shmseg = 4096
kernel.sem = 250 32000 100 150
kernel.msgmnl = 2878
kernel.msgmnb = 65535
fs.file-max = 65536
net.ipv4.ip_local_port_range = 1024 65000
net.core.rmem_default = 262144
net.core.wmem_default = 262144
net.core.rmem_max = 262144
net.core.wmem_max = 262144
```

1.3   Add the following parameters to /etc/security/limits.conf:

oracle	soft	nproc	2047
oracle	hard	nproc	16384
oracle	soft	nofile	1024
oracle	hard	nofile	65536

1.4   Add devices to /etc/fstab:

Copy the device definitions from one of the existing nodes to oradb5.

```
[root@oradb5 root]$ more /etc/fstab
LABEL=/                     /              ext3    defaults        1 1
none               /dev/pts        devpts  gid=5,mode=620  0 0
none               /proc           proc    defaults        0 0
none               /dev/shm        tmpfs   defaults        0 0
/dev/sda2          swap            swap    defaults        0 0
/dev/cdrom         /mnt/cdrom      udf,iso9660 noauto,owner,kudzu,ro
0 0
/dev/fd0           /mnt/floppy     auto    noauto,owner,kudzu 0 0
/dev/sdb5          /u01            ocfs    _netdev 0 0
```

```
/dev/sdb6          /u02          ocfs    _netdev 0 0
/dev/sdb7          /u03          ocfs    _netdev 0 0
/dev/sdb8          /u04          ocfs    _netdev 0 0
/dev/sdb9          /u05          ocfs    _netdev 0 0
/dev/sdb10         /u06          ocfs    _netdev 0 0
/dev/sdb14         /u14          ocfs    _netdev 0 0
```

1.5   Create the administrative user.

Every installation of Oracle software requires an administrative user account on each node. In all nodes 1 through 4, the administrative owner is `oracle`. The next step is to create an administrative user account on node oradb5. While creating this user account, it is important that the UID and the GID of user `oracle` be identical to those of the other RAC nodes. This information can be obtained using the following command:

```
[oracle@oradb1 oracle]$ id oracle
uid=500(oracle) gid=500(dba)
groups=500(dba),501(oinstall), 502(oper)
```

Connect to oradb5 (a Linux- or Unix-based environment) as user `root` and create the following operating system groups:

```
groupadd -g 500 dba
groupadd -g 501 oinstall
groupadd -g 502 oper
```

Once the groups have been created, create the `oracle` user account as a member of the `dba` group using the following command, and subsequently reset the user password using the `passwd` (password) command:

```
useradd -u 500 -g dba -G dba, oper oracle

passwd oracle
Changing password for user oracle.
New password:
Retype new password:
passwd: all authentication tokens updated successfully.
```

Once the groups and the user have been created, they should be verified to ensure that the output from the following command is identical across all nodes in the cluster:

```
[root@oradb5 root]$ id oracle
uid=500(oracle) gid=500(dba)
groups=500(dba),501(oinstall), 502(oper)
```

2.   **Configuration of network components**

Add all network addresses to the /etc/hosts file on node oradb5. Also, cross-register node oradb5 information the on other four nodes in the cluster.

```
root@oradb5 root]# more /etc/hosts
127.0.0.1       localhost.localdomain localhost
192.168.2.10    oradb1.sumsky.net oradb1
192.168.2.20    oradb2.sumsky.net oradb2
192.168.2.30    oradb3.sumsky.net oradb3
192.168.2.40    oradb4.sumsky.net oradb4
192.168.2.50    oradb5.sumsky.net oradb5

#Private Network/interconnect
10.168.2.110    oradb1-priv.sumsky.net oradb1-priv
10.168.2.120    oradb2-priv.sumsky.net oradb2-priv
10.168.2.130    oradb3-priv.sumsky.net oradb3-priv
10.168.2.140    oradb4-priv.sumsky.net oradb4-priv
10.168.2.150    oradb5-priv.sumsky.net oradb5-priv

# VIP
192.168.2.15    oradb1-vip.sumsky.net oradb1-vip
192.168.2.25    oradb2-vip.sumsky.net oradb2-vip
192.168.2.35    oradb3-vip.sumsky.net oradb3-vip
192.168.2.45    oradb4-vip.sumsky.net oradb4-vip
192.168.2.55    oradb5-vip.sumsky.net oradb5-vip
```

3.   **Establishing user equivalence with SSH**

When adding nodes to the cluster, Oracle copies files from the node where the installation was originally performed to the new node in the cluster. Such a copy process is performed either by using `ssh` protocol where available or by using remote copy (`rcp`). In order for the copy operation to be successful, the `oracle` user on the RAC node must be able to log in to the new RAC node without having to provide a password or passphrase.

Currently, the existing four nodes are configured to use `ssh`. To configure the `oracle` account on the new node to use `ssh` without using any passwords, the following tasks should be performed:

1. Create the authentication key for user `oracle`. In order to create this key, change the current directory to the default login directory of the `oracle` user and perform the following operation:

```
[oracle@oradb5 oracle]$ ssh-keygen -t dsa -b 1024
Generating public/private dsa key pair.
Enter file in which to save the key (/home/oracle/.ssh/
id_dsa):
Created directory '/home/oracle/.ssh'.
Enter passphrase (empty for no passphrase):
Enter same passphrase again:
Your identification has been saved in /home/oracle/
.ssh/id_dsa.
Your public key has been saved in /home/oracle/.ssh/
id_dsa.pub.
The key fingerprint is:
b6:07:42:ae:47:56:0a:a3:a5:bf:75:3e:21:85:8d:30
oracle@oradb5.sumsky.net
[oracle@oradb5 oracle]$
```

2. Keys generated from the new node should be appended to the `/home/oracle/.ssh/id_dsa/authorized_keys` file on all nodes, meaning each node should contain the keys from all other nodes in the cluster.

```
[oracle@oradb5 oracle]$ cd .ssh
[oracle@oradb5 .ssh]$ cat id_dsa.pub > authorized_keys
```

Once the keys have been created and copied to all nodes, `oracle` user accounts can connect from one node to an `oracle` user account on another node without using a password. This allows for the OUI to copy files from the installing node to the other nodes in the cluster. The following output is the verification showing the ssh command from node oradb1 to node oradb5 in the cluster:

```
[oracle@oradb1 oracle]$ ssh oradb1 hostname
oradb1.sumsky.net
[oracle@oradb1 oracle]$ ssh oradb5 hostname
Oradb5.sumsky.net
[oracle@oradb1 oracle]$ ssh oradb1-priv hostname
oradb1.sumsky.net
[oracle@oradb1 oracle]$ ssh oradb5-priv hostname
Oradb5.sumsky.net
```

 Note: When performing these tests for the first time, the operating system will display a key and request that the user accept or decline. Enter Yes to accept and register the key. Tests should be performed on all other nodes across all interfaces in the cluster except for the VIP.

3.   **Installation of Oracle Clusterware**

Oracle 10g Release 2 Clusterware is already installed on the cluster. The task here is to add the new node to the clustered configuration. This task is performed by executing the Oracle-provided utility called addnode located in the $ORA_CRS_HOME/bin directory. Oracle Clusterware has two files—the Oracle cluster registry (OCR) and the Oracle Cluster Synchronization Service (CSS) voting disk—that contain information concerning the cluster and the applications managed by the Oracle Clusterware. These files need to be updated with the information concerning the new node. The first step in the clusterware installation process is to verify if the new node is ready for the install.

3.1   Verify the cluster.

Oracle has introduced a new utility called the Oracle cluster verification utility (OCVU). The OCVU is part of the clusterware software and can be located on the DVD media under the clusterware directory or in the $ORA_CRS_HOME/bin directory on one of the existing nodes in the cluster. Using the appropriate parameters, this utility determines the status of the cluster. At this stage, before beginning installation of the Oracle Cluster-ware, two verifications should be performed:

a. If the hardware and operating system configuration is complete, execute the following commnd:

```
[oracle@oradb1 oracle]$ $ORA_CRS_HOME/bin/cluvfy stage -post
hwos -n oradb1,oradb5
Performing post-checks for hardware and operating system
setup
Checking node reachability...
Node reachability check passed from node "oradb1".
Checking user equivalence...
User equivalence check passed for user "oracle".
Checking node connectivity...
Node connectivity check passed for subnet "192.168.2.0" with
node(s) oradb5,oradb1.
Node connectivity check passed for subnet "10.168.2.0" with
node(s) oradb5,oradb1.
Suitable interfaces for the private interconnect on subnet
"192.168.2.0":
oradb5 eth0:192.168.2.50 eth0:192.168.2.55
oradb1 eth0:192.168.2.10 eth0:192.168.2.15
Suitable interfaces for the private interconnect on subnet
"10.168.2.0":
oradb5 eth1:10.168.2.150
oradb1 eth1:10.168.2.110
Checking shared storage accessibility...
Shared storage check failed on nodes "oradb5".
Post-check for hardware and operating system setup was
unsuccessful on all the nodes.
```

As highlighted, the above verification failed with the storage check verification. Node oradb5 was unable to see the storage devices. When this was investigated, it was determined that the disks did not have sufficient permissions. If the installation were continued, ignoring this error, the Oracle Clusterware installation would have failed.

Once the issue was resolved and the verification step executed again, it succeeded as follows:

```
Checking shared storage accessibility...
Shared storage check passed on nodes "oradb5,oradb1".
```

**Post-check for hardware and operating system setup was
successful on all the nodes.**

b. Perform appropriate checks on all of the nodes in the
node list before setting up Oracle Clusterware:

[oracle@oradb1 cluvfy]$ cluvfy stage -pre crsinst -n oradb1,oradb5

Performing pre-checks for cluster services setup

Checking node reachability...

Node reachability check passed from node "oradb1".

Checking user equivalence...

User equivalence check passed for user "oracle".

Checking administrative privileges...

User existence check passed for "oracle".

Group existence check passed for "oinstall".

Membership check for user "oracle" in group "oinstall" [as Primary]
failed.

Check failed on nodes:

      Oradb5,oradb1

Administrative privileges check passed.

Checking node connectivity...

Node connectivity check passed for subnet "192.168.2.0" with node(s)
oradb5,oradb1.

Node connectivity check passed for subnet "10.168.2.0" with node(s)
oradb5,oradb1.

Suitable interfaces for the private interconnect on subnet
"192.168.2.0":

oradb5 eth0:192.168.2.50 eth0:192.168.2.55

oradb1 eth0:192.168.2.10 eth0:192.168.2.15

Suitable interfaces for the private interconnect on subnet
"10.168.2.0":

oradb5 eth1:10.168.2.150

oradb1 eth1:10.168.2.110

Checking system requirements for 'crs'...

Total memory check passed.

Check failed on nodes:

      oradb5,oradb1

Free disk space check passed.

Swap space check passed.

System architecture check passed.

Kernel version check passed.

Package existence check passed for "make-3.79".

Package existence check passed for "binutils-2.14".

```
Package existence check passed for "gcc-3.2".
Package existence check passed for "glibc-2.3.2-95.27".
Package existence check passed for "compat-db-4.0.14-5".
Package existence check passed for "compat-gcc-7.3-2.96.128".
Package existence check passed for "compat-gcc-c++-7.3-2.96.128".
Package existence check passed for "compat-libstdc++-7.3-2.96.128".
Package existence check passed for "compat-libstdc++-devel-7.3-
2.96.128".
Package existence check passed for "openmotif-2.2.3".
Package existence check passed for "setarch-1.3-1".
Group existence check passed for "dba".
Group existence check passed for "oinstall".
User existence check passed for "nobody".
System requirement failed for 'crs'
Pre-check for cluster services setup was successful on all the nodes.
```

3.2   Install Oracle Clusterware.

Using the OUI requires that the terminal from which this installer is run should be X-windows compatible. If it is not, an appropriate X-windows emulator should be installed and the emulator invoked with the DISPLAY command using the following syntax:

```
export DISPLAY=<client IP address>:0.0
```

For example:

```
[oracle@oradb1 oracle]$export DISPLAY=192.168.2.101:0.0
```

The next step is to configure the clusterware on the new node oradb5. For this step, as mentioned earlier, Oracle has provided a new executable called addNode.sh which is located in the $ORA_CRS_HOME/oui/bin directory.

1.   Execute the script $ORA_CRS_HOME/oui/bin/addNode.sh.

2.   At the welcome screen, click the "Next" button.

3.   At the Specify Cluster Nodes to Add to Installation screen. OUI lists existing nodes in the cluster, and on the bottom half of the screen, it lists the new node(s) information to be added in the appropriate columns. Once the information is entered, click the "Next" button.

Public Node Name	Private Node Name	Virtual Host Name
oradb5	oradb5-priv	oradb5-vip

4.   A the Cluster Node Addition Summary, verify if the new node is listed under the "New Nodes" drilldown, and click the "Install" Button.

5.   Once all required Clusterware components are copied from oradb1 to oradb5, OUI prompts to execute three files:

   a.   /usr/app/oracle/oraInventory/orainstRoot.sh on node **oradb5**

```
[root@oradb5 oraInventory]# ./orainstRoot.sh
Changing permissions of /usr/app/oracle/oraInventory to 770.
Changing groupname of /usr/app/oracle/oraInventory to dba.
The execution of the script is complete
[root@oradb5 oraInventory]#
```

   b.   /usr/app/oracle/product/10.2.0/crs/install/rootaddnode.sh on node **oradb1**. The addnoderoot.sh file will add the new node information to the OCR using the srvctl utility. Note the srvctl command with the nodeapps parameter at the end of the script output.

```
[root@oradb1 install]# ./rootaddnode.sh
clscfg: EXISTING configuration version 3 detected.
clscfg: version 3 is 10G Release 2.
Attempting to add 1 new nodes to the configuration
Using ports: CSS=49895 CRS=49896 EVMC=49898 and EVMR=49897.
node <nodenumber>: <nodename> <private interconnect name> <hostname>
node 5: oradb5 oradb5-priv oradb5
Creating OCR keys for user 'root', privgrp 'root'..
Operation successful.
/usr/app/oracle/product/10.2.0/crs/bin/srvctl add nodeapps -n oradb5
-A oradb5-v ip/255.255.255.0/bond0 -o /usr/app/oracle/product/10.2.0/
crs
[root@oradb1 install]#
```

    c. /usr/app/oracle/product/10.2.0/crs/root.sh on
    node **oradb5**.

```
[root@oradb5 crs]# ./root.sh
WARNING: directory '/usr/app/oracle/product/10.2.0' is not owned by
root
WARNING: directory '/usr/app/oracle/product' is not owned by root
WARNING: directory '/usr/app/oracle' is not owned by root
Checking to see if Oracle CRS stack is already configured
/etc/oracle does not exist. Creating it now.

OCR backup directory '/usr/app/oracle/product/10.2.0/crs/cdata/
SskyClst' does not exist. Creating now
Setting the permissions on OCR backup directory
Setting up NS directories
Oracle Cluster Registry configuration upgraded successfully
WARNING: directory '/usr/app/oracle/product/10.2.0' is not owned by
root
WARNING: directory '/usr/app/oracle/product' is not owned by root
WARNING: directory '/usr/app/oracle' is not owned by root
clscfg: EXISTING configuration version 3 detected.
clscfg: version 3 is 10G Release 2.
assigning default hostname oradb1 for node 1.
Successfully accumulated necessary OCR keys.
Using ports: CSS=49895 CRS=49896 EVMC=49898 and EVMR=49897.
node <nodenumber>: <nodename> <private interconnect name> <hostname>
node 1: oradb1 oradb1-priv oradb1
node 2: oradb2 oradb2-priv oradb2
node 3: oradb3 oradb3-priv oradb3
node 4: oradb4 oradb4-priv oradb4
clscfg: Arguments check out successfully.

NO KEYS WERE WRITTEN. Supply -force parameter to override.
-force is destructive and will destroy any previous cluster
configuration.
Oracle Cluster Registry for cluster has already been initialized
Startup will be queued to init within 90 seconds.
Adding daemons to inittab
Expecting the CRS daemons to be up within 600 seconds.
CSS is active on these nodes.
```

```
    oradb1
    oradb2
    oradb3
    oradb4
    oradb5
CSS is active on all nodes.
Waiting for the Oracle CRSD and EVMD to start
Oracle CRS stack installed and running under init(1M)
Running vipca(silent) for configuring nodeapps
IP address "oradb-vip" has already been used. Enter an unused IP
address.
```

The error above, "oradb-vip has already been used," was because the VIP was already configured on all nodes except oradb5. Once the root.sh has completed execution, the installation can be verified using the following command:

```
[root@oradb5 oraInventory]# crs_stat -t -c oradb5
Name            Type        Target    State     Host
-------------------------------------------------------------
ora.oradb5.gsd application   ONLINE    ONLINE    oradb5
ora.oradb5.ons application   ONLINE    ONLINE    oradb5
ora.oradb5.vip application   ONLINE    ONLINE    oradb5
```

In this specific installation, NIC bonding has been configured for the interconnect. Hence, the silent VIPCA configuration was unable to recognize the correct VIP addresses. It is important to execute VIPCA manually before proceeding.

What is NIC bonding?

NIC bonding, or NIC pairing, is a method of pairing multiple physical network connections into a single logical interface. This logical interface will be used to establish a connection with the database server. By allowing all network connections that are part of the logical interface to be used during communication, this provides load-balancing capabilities, which would not otherwise be available. In addition, when one of the network connections fails, the other connection will continue to receive and transmit data, making it fault tolerant.

Note: For additional information on NIC bonding and its configuration, please refer to Chapter 4.

    d.   Manually configuring VIP using VIPCA

         i.   Immediately after executing `root.sh` from the command prompt on node `oradb1` (or the node from which the add node procedure is being executed), invoke `vipca` also as user `root`.

Note: VIPCA will also configure GSD and ONS resources on the new node.

        ii.   At the Welcome screen, click the "Next" button.

       iii.   *Step 1 of 2: Network Interfaces.* A list of network interfaces is displayed. Select the network public network interface to which the VIP will be assigned / mapped. Normally, it is the first interface in the list (`eth0`), but in this specific situation, since bonding is enabled for the private interconnect, and the list is displayed in alphabetical order, the `bond0` interface will be at the top of the list. Click "Next" when done.

       iv.   *Step 2 of 2: Virtual IPs for cluster nodes.* For each node name in the list, provide the VIP alias name and the VirtualIP address in the appropriate columns. Click "Next" when done.

        v.   Summary. A summary of the current selected configuration is listed. Click "Finish" when all settings are correct.

       vi.   *Configuration Assistant Progress Dialog.* This screen displays the progress of the VIP, GSD, and ONS configuration process. Click "OK" when prompted by VIPCA.

      vii.   Configuration Results. This screen displays the configuration results. Click "Exit" to end VIPCA.

On completion of the Oracle Clusterware installation, the following files are created or updated in their respective directories:

a. Clusterware files are created:

```
[root@oradb5 root]# ls -ltr /etc/init.d/init.*
-r-xr-xr-x  1 root     root         3197 Aug 13 23:32 /etc/init.d/init.evmd
-r-xr-xr-x  1 root     root        35401 Aug 13 23:32 /etc/init.d/init.cssd
-r-xr-xr-x  1 root     root         4721 Aug 13 23:32 /etc/init.d/init.crsd
-r-xr-xr-x  1 root     root         1951 Aug 13 23:32 /etc/init.d/init.crs
[root@oradb5 root]#
```

b. The operating system provided `inittab` file is updated with the following entries:

```
[root@oradb5 root]# tail -5 /etc/inittab
# Run xdm in runlevel 5
x:5:respawn:/etc/X11/prefdm -nodaemon
h1:35:respawn:/etc/init.d/init.evmd run >/dev/null 2>&1 </dev/null
h2:35:respawn:/etc/init.d/init.cssd fatal >/dev/null 2>&1 </dev/null
h3:35:respawn:/etc/init.d/init.crsd run >/dev/null 2>&1 </dev/null
```

6. Click "OK" after all of the listed scripts have run on all nodes.

7. At the end of installation, click "Exit."

8. Verify if the clusterware has all the nodes registered using the `olsnodes` command:

```
[oracle@oradb1 oracle]$ olsnodes
oradb1
oradb2
oradb3
oradb4
oradb5
[oracle@oradb1 oracle]$
```

9. Verify if the cluster service is started using the `crs_stat` command:

```
[oracle@oradb1 oracle]$ crs_stat -t
Name            Type            Target    State      Host
-----------------------------------------------------------------
```

```
ora.oradb1.gsd application    ONLINE    ONLINE    oradb1
ora.oradb1.ons application    ONLINE    ONLINE    oradb1
ora.oradb1.vip application    ONLINE    ONLINE    oradb1
ora.oradb2.gsd application    ONLINE    ONLINE    oradb2
.......  ....
ora.oradb3.vip application    ONLINE    ONLINE    oradb3
ora.oradb4.gsd application    ONLINE    ONLINE    oradb4
ora.oradb4.ons application    ONLINE    ONLINE    oradb4
ora.oradb4.vip application    ONLINE    ONLINE    oradb4
ora.oradb5.gsd application    ONLINE    ONLINE    oradb5
ora.oradb5.ons application    ONLINE    ONLINE    oradb5
ora.oradb5.vip application    ONLINE    ONLINE    oradb5
```

10. Verify if the VIP services are configured at the operating system level.

The VIP address is configured and added to the operating system network configuration, and the network services are started. The VIP configuration can be verified using the `ifconfig` command at the operating system level.

```
[oracle@oradb5 oracle]$ ifconfig -a
eth0      Link encap:Ethernet  HWaddr 00:90:27:B8:58:10
          inet addr:192.168.2.50  Bcast:192.168.2.255
Mask:255.255.255.0
          UP BROADCAST RUNNING MASTER MULTICAST  MTU:1500  Metric:1
          RX packets:123 errors:0 dropped:0 overruns:0 frame:0
          TX packets:67 errors:0 dropped:0 overruns:0 carrier:0
          collisions:0 txqueuelen:1000
          RX bytes:583308844 (556.2 Mb)  TX bytes:4676477 (4.4 Mb)


eth0:1    Link encap:Ethernet  HWaddr 00:90:27:B8:58:10
          inet addr:192.168.2.55  Bcast:192.168.3.255
Mask:255.255.252.0
          UP BROADCAST RUNNING MASTER MULTICAST  MTU:1500  Metric:1
          RX packets:14631 errors:0 dropped:0 overruns:0 frame:0
          TX packets:21377 errors:0 dropped:0 overruns:0 carrier:0
        collisions:0 txqueuelen:1000
        RX bytes:8025681 (7.6 Mb)  TX bytes:600 (600.0 b)
        Interrupt:11 Base address:0x2400 Memory:41300000-41300038
```

Note: eth0:1 indicates that it is a VIP address for the basic host eth0. When the node fails, eth0:1 will be moved to one of the other surviving nodes in the cluster. The new identifier for the VIP on the failed-over server will be indicated by eth0:2 or higher, depending on what other nodes have failed in the cluster and been migrated by the VIP.

4.   **Installation of Oracle software**

The next step is to install the Oracle software on the new node oradb5. For this, as mentioned earlier, Oracle has provided a new executable called addNode.sh which is located in the $ORACLE_HOME/oui/bin directory.

1.   Execute the script $ORACLE_HOME/oui/bin/addNode.sh.

2.   At the Welcome screen, click "Next."

3.   *Specify Cluster Nodes to Add to Installation.* In this screen, OUI lists existing nodes in the cluster, and on the bottom half of the screen, it lists the new node(s). Select the node oradb5. Once the information is entered, click the "Next" button.

4.   *Cluster Node Addition Summary.* Verify if the new node is listed under the "New Nodes" drilldown and click the "Install" Button.

5.   When the copy of Oracle software to node oradb5 is complete, OUI will prompt you to execute the /usr/app/oracle/product/10.2.0/db_1/root.sh script from another window as the root user on the new node(s) in the cluster.

```
[root@oradb5 db_1]# ./root.sh
Running Oracle10 root.sh script...

The following environment variables are set as:
    ORACLE_OWNER= oracle
    ORACLE_HOME=  /usr/app/oracle/product/10.2.0/db_1

Enter the full pathname of the local bin directory: [/usr/local/bin]:
The file "dbhome" already exists in /usr/local/bin.  Overwrite it? (y/
n)
[n]: y
    Copying dbhome to /usr/local/bin ...
```

```
The file "oraenv" already exists in /usr/local/bin.  Overwrite it? (y/
n)
[n]: y
   Copying oraenv to /usr/local/bin ...
The file "coraenv" already exists in /usr/local/bin.  Overwrite it?
(y/n)
[n]: y
   Copying coraenv to /usr/local/bin ...


Creating /etc/oratab file...
Entries will be added to the /etc/oratab file as needed by
Database Configuration Assistant when a database is created
Finished running generic part of root.sh script.
Now product-specific root actions will be performed.
```

6. Click on "OK" after the root.sh has run on node oradb5.

7. At the end of installation, click on "Exit."

6. Addition of new instance(s)

DBCA has all the required options to add additional instances to the cluster.

Requirements:

a. Make a full cold backup of the database before commencing the upgrade process.

b. Oracle 10gR2 Clusterware should be running on all nodes.

1. At the Welcome Screen, select the "Oracle Real Application Cluster database," and click "Next."

2. *Step 1 of 8: Operations.* All operations that can be performed using the DBCA are listed. The operation of interest to us is "Instance Management." Select this option, and click "Next."

3. *Step 2 of 8: Instance Management.* Instance management operations that can be performed are listed. Select "Add an Instance," and click "Next."

4. *Step 3 of 8: List of cluster databases.* Clustered databases running on the node are listed. In this case, the database running on node

oradb1 is SSKYDB. Select this database. On the bottom part of the screen, DBCA requests, "Specify a user with SYSDBA system privileges."

Username: sys

Password: <   >, and click "Next."

5.   *Step 4 of 8: List of cluster database instances.* The DBCA lists all of the instances currently available on the cluster. Verify if all instances are listed and click "Next."

6.   *Step 5 of 7: Instance naming and node selection.* The DBCA lists the next instance name in the series and requests the node on which to add the instance. In our example, the next instance name is SSKY5, and the node name is oradb5. Click "Next" after making the appropriate selection. At this stage, there is a small pause before the next screen appears as the DBCA determines the current state of the new node and what services are configured on the existing nodes.

7.   *Step 6 of 7: Database Services.* If the current configuration has any database services configured, this screen will appear (otherwise, it is skipped). In our example, the current configuration has two services, CRM and PAYROLL, defined. This screen prompts the user to configure them across the new instance. Make the appropriate selections, and click "Next" when ready.

8.   *Step 7 of 7: Instance Storage.* In this screen, the DBCA will list the instance-specific files, such as undo tablespaces and redo log groups. Verify if all required files are listed and click "Finish."

9.   *Database Configuration Assistant: Summary.* After verifying the Summary, click "OK" to begin the software installation.

10.   DBCA verifies the new node oradb5, and since the database is configured to use ASM, prompts with the following message: "ASM is present on the cluster but needs to be extended to the following nodes: [oradb5]. Do you want ASM to be extended?" Click "Yes" to add ASM to the new instance.

11.   In order to create and start the ASM instances on the new node, Oracle requires the listener to be present and started. The DBCA prompts with requesting permission to configure the listener using port 1521 and listener name LISTENER_ORADB5. Click "Yes" if the

default port is good, or else click "No" and manually execute NetCA on oradb5 to create the listener using a different port.

12. At the Database Configuration Assistant" progress screen, once instance management is complete, the user is prompted with the following message: "Do you want to perform another operation?" Click "No" to end.

13. At this stage, the following is the status:

   a. The clusterware has been installed on node oradb5 and is now part of the cluster.

   b. The Oracle software has been installed on node oradb5.

   c. The ASM5 and new Oracle instance SSKY5 have been created and configured on oradb5.

14. Verify if the upgrade is successful.

   a. Verify if all instances in the cluster are started. Verify this using the V$ACTIVE_INSTANCES view from any of the participating instances, for example:

```
SQL> select * from v$active_instances;

INST_NUMBER INST_NAME
----------- ----------------------------------
          1 oradb1.sumsky.net:SSKY1
          2 oradb2.sumsky.net:SSKY2
          3 oradb3.sumsky.net:SSKY3
          4 oradb4.sumsky.net:SSKY4
          5 oradb5.sumsky.net:SSKY5
```

   b. Verify if all ASM disk groups are mounted and the datafiles are visible to the new instance.

```
SQL> SELECT NAME,STATE,TYPE FROM V$ASM_DISKGROUP;

NAME                             STATE        TYPE
-------------------------------- ------------ ------
ASMGRP1                          CONNECTED    NORMAL
ASMGRP2                          CONNECTED    NORMAL

SQL> SELECT NAME FROM V$DATAFILE;
```

```
NAME
-----------------------------------------------------------------
+ASMGRP1/sskydb/datafile/system.256.581006553
+ASMGRP1/sskydb/datafile/undotbs1.258.581006555
+ASMGRP1/sskydb/datafile/sysaux.257.581006553
+ASMGRP1/sskydb/datafile/users.259.581006555
+ASMGRP1/sskydb/datafile/example.269.581007007
+ASMGRP1/sskydb/datafile/undotbs2.271.581029215
```

    c. Verify if OCR is aware of the following:

       i. The new instance in the cluster

```
[oracle@oradb1 oracle]$ srvctl status database -d
SSKYDB
Instance SSKY1 is running on node oradb1
Instance SSKY2 is running on node oradb2
Instance SSKY3 is running on node oradb3
Instance SSKY4 is running on node oradb4
Instance SSKY5 is running on node oradb5
```

       ii. The database services

```
[oracle@oradb1 oracle]$ srvctl status service -d SSKYDB
Service CRM is running on instance(s) SSKY1
Service CRM is running on instance(s) SSKY2
Service CRM is running on instance(s) SSKY3
Service CRM is running on instance(s) SSKY4
Service CRM is running on instance(s) SSKY5
Service PAYROLL is running on instance(s) SSKY1
Service PAYROLL is running on instance(s) SSKY5
```

7.   **Housekeeping**

For easy administration and navigation, several different environment variables should be defined in the login profile, for example:

```
[oracle@oradb5 oracle]$ more .bash_profile
# .bash_profile
```

```
# Get the aliases and functions
if [ -f ~/.bashrc ]; then
        . ~/.bashrc
fi
# User specific environment and startup programs
export ORACLE_BASE=/usr/app/oracle
export ORACLE_HOME=$ORACLE_BASE/product/10.2.0/db_1
export ORA_CRS_HOME=$ORACLE_BASE/product/10.2.0/crs

export PATH=.:${PATH}:$HOME/bin:$ORACLE_HOME/bin
export PATH=${PATH}:$ORA_CRS_HOME/bin
export PATH=${PATH}:/usr/bin:/bin:/usr/bin/X11:/usr/
local/bin:/sbin
export ORACLE_ADMIN=$ORACLE_BASE/admin
export TNS_ADMIN=$ORACLE_HOME/network/admin

export LD_ASSUME_KERNEL=2.4.19
export LD_LIBRARY=$ORACLE_HOME/lib
export LD_LIBRARY=${LD_LIBRARY}:/lib:/usr/lib:/usr/
local/bin
export LD_LIBRARY=${LD_LIBRARY}:$ORA_CRS_HOME/lib

export CLASSPATH=$ORACLE_HOME/JRE
export CLASSPATH=${CLASSPATH}:$ORACLE_HOME/jlib
export CLASSPATH=${CLASSPATH}:$ORACLE_HOME/rdbms/jlib
export CLASSPATH=${CLASSPATH}:$ORACLE_HOME/network/jlib
export THREADS_FLAG=native
export ORACLE_SID=SSKY5
```

F.2   Conclusion

In this section, we discussed how to add nodes and instances to an existing Oracle 10gR2 RAC cluster. RAC enables plugging in an instance with no downtime. This feature provides easy scalability by helping distribute the workload by seamlessly bringing a new instance into an existing cluster. In this appendix section, we added a new node to an existing configuration of four nodes. The following table shows the new configuration:

Database Name	Number of Nodes	Database Version	Number of Instances	O/S Kernel Version	File System	Cluster Manager
SSKYDB	Five Nodes – oradb1, oradb2, oradb3, oradb4, and **oradb5**	10.2.0.1	Five instances: SSKY1, SSKY2, SSKY3, SSKY4, and **SSKY5**	Red Hat Advanced Server 3.0 Linux sum-sky.net 2.4.21-32.ELsmp	OCFS 1.0 and ASM	Oracle Clus-terware

Index

The RAC SIG organizes at least one live web seminar every month. Admission is free, all you need is some time to join the webcast and learn from the experts!

The RAC SIG also hosts a discussion forum on our website. Have a question? Post it and you will find an answer from another RAC SIG member or directly from Oracle ...

Share your knowledge and learn from your peers, that's what the RAC SIG is all about!

Join the
Oracle RAC SIG...

at

www.oracleracsig.org